UNITED AND INDEPENDENT

UNITED AND INDEPENDENT

John Quincy Adams

on American Foreign Policy

EDITED BY

PATRICK J. GARRITY

& BEN JUDGE

CLAREMONT
BOOKS

BOOKS

NEW YORK · LONDON

First American edition published in 2022 by Encounter Books, an activity of Encounter for Culture and Education, Inc., a nonprofit, tax-exempt corporation.
Encounter Books website address: www.encounterbooks.com

Manufactured in the United States and printed on acid-free paper. The paper used in this publication meets the minimum requirements of ANSI/NISO Z39.48–1992 (R 1997) (*Permanence of Paper*).

FIRST EDITION

LIBRARY OF CONGRESS CATALOGING-IN-PUBLICATION DATA

Names: Adams, John Quincy, 1767–1848, author. | Garrity, Patrick J., editor. | Judge, Ben, 1986– editor.
Title: United and independent : John Quincy Adams on American foreign policy / edited by Patrick J. Garrity & Ben Judge.
Other titles: John Quincy Adams on American foreign policy
Description: [New York, New York] : Encounter Books, [2022] | Includes bibliographical references and index. |
Identifiers: LCCN 2022005896 (print) | LCCN 2022005897 (ebook) | ISBN 9781641772396 (hardcover) | ISBN 9781641772402 (ebook)
Subjects: LCSH: Adams, John Quincy, 1767–1848. | United States—Foreign relations—1783–1865—Sources. | United States—Politics and government—1783–1865—Sources.
Classification: LCC E337.8 .A2 2022 (print) | LCC E337.8 (ebook) | DDC 327.730092--dc23/eng/20220429
LC record available at https://lccn.loc.gov/2022005896
LC ebook record available at https://lccn.loc.gov/2022005897

1 2 3 4 5 6 7 8 9   20 22

| CONTENTS |

Two men are responsible for this work. The first is John Quincy Adams. The second is Patrick Garrity. They each contributed careers dedicated to American politics and strategy. And while their upbringings and paths could not be more different, the two are bound together by two loves: first, for their native land and its unique character; second, for the written word.

Of course, both men had help. Adams may be America's most prolific public official, but it took effort to make his writings accessible. Fortunately, much is available through the superb publications (in print and online) of the Massachusetts Historical Society, Founders Online, and older collections – notably, those produced by his son Charles Francis Adams, and Worthington C. Ford.

Then there is Dr. Garrity. Research assistance came from Jeremiah Regan, whose depth of thought and attention to detail will make the soon-to-be Dr. Regan a great scholar in his own right. As for the copyediting, Gabriel Bartlett set the gold standard. Their efforts made what you have in hand the second-best version of this volume. Unfortunately, we will never have the best. Dr. Garrity passed away before this work could reach completion.

Dr. Garrity was, however, alive long enough to learn the volume would be published. That would not have happened without the support of Larry Arnn and Matthew Spalding at Hillsdale College, Ryan Williams at the Claremont Institute, and, of course, Roger Kimball, Sam Schneider, and Amanda DeMatto at Encounter Books.

So what is this volume? It is not a biography; it does not address family events or relationships. Nor is it a comprehensive analysis of the thought of John Quincy Adams; it ends after his presidency and only addresses his thoughts on slavery insofar as they relate to his analysis of foreign affairs.

This volume is a guide, an education in how to consider America's conduct on the world stage. It is for current and future participants in America's foreign affairs, whose decisions will judge the ultimate success of this work.

BEN JUDGE
Irvine, CA

Scholarship about John Quincy Adams has ebbed and flowed over the years. The biographical work of the Yale historian Samuel Flagg Bemis (*John Quincy Adams and the Foundations of American Foreign Policy* in 1949 and *John Quincy Adams and the Union* in 1956) is among the best. Of late, there has been renewed interest in Adams focused on his diplomatic and foreign policy career, which is a welcome turn and unsurprising, as Adams shaped and personified the Founders' views of America and its relationship to the world at several key points during the early republic. Whenever Americans are thinking about (or rethinking) their country's relationship to the world, it is good to look to John Quincy Adams.

Unfortunately, foreign policy choices today are often presented as various alternatives between two abstract categories: "idealism," meaning that nations should be motivated by ideals to the exclusion of practical concerns and self-interest; and "realism," meaning that nations are motivated primarily by the desire for more military and economic power or security rather than by principles. These two approaches share the wrong assumption that principle and power are opposites and contradictory: that principle can only be altruistic and must be shielded from interest and power, and that a nation pursuing its interests is by definition selfish and immoral.

Likewise, following these abstract distinctions, we tend to look at actors and decisions in light of doctrines that become policy straightjackets – one-size-fits-all strategies to be maintained despite a varied and changing world. If policymakers deviate, they are pilloried for inconsistency rather than praised for applying the doctrine's guidance in particular circumstances. This misunderstands both the statesman as well as the doctrine. Doctrines, as Patrick Garrity has pointed out elsewhere, should serve as "a strategic compass," for "even if they do not always point to a true north, they provide the basic orientation with which to navigate through the dark forests of international relations."

The better approach, understood by the Founders as well as by John Quincy Adams, reflecting the classical understanding of politics that formed their worldview, relates principles and practice through the great virtue of practical wisdom or prudence. Foreign affairs – dealing with friends and enemies in a dynamic and often unstable world, where an allegiance to principle and a clear recognition of the requirements and limits of international politics are not only complementary but also, rightly understood, inseparable – is especially the realm of prudence. For one thing, it is impossible to predetermine the extent, priority, and immediacy of the nation's security requirements, which shift with the balance of world forces over which one nation often has little control. Likewise, it is impossible to foresee the challenges and opportunities for advancing principles and long-term objectives in a world often hostile to those principles. It is difficult to know beforehand what to do at any particular time and place. Nevertheless, as the Declaration of Independence explains, prudence will dictate when it is the right and duty of a people to provide new guards for their future safety and happiness.

To call John Quincy Adams an idealist or a realist, or an isolationist or a noninterventionist, fails to distinguish between a particular policy conditioned by the times and the permanent principles that underlie the policy and inform changing circumstances. Adams is neither so categorical nor so doctrinaire. The particulars – offense or defense, aggression or restraint, war or peace – were matters of deliberation, judgment, and prudence. But those decisions, to partake in the virtue of prudence, must also be related to a true conception of the human good, as Aristotle teaches. For John Quincy Adams, those truths – human liberty, equal rights, and the consent of the governed – were expressed best in the Declaration of Independence.

A thoughtful and scrupulous scholar, Patrick J. Garrity dedicated his best work to understanding and explaining the principles of the American regime and America's greatest statesmen, especially in their thoughts and actions concerning national security and international relations. He was a student of the two unique and remarkable teachers who defined the Claremont Graduate School at its height: Harry V. Jaffa, the eminent Lincoln scholar who was himself a student of Leo Strauss, and the less well-known but equally compelling Harold W. Rood, the great teacher of international politics and national security who had been an infantryman in General Patton's Third Army during World War II. The academic mind of Claremont is properly associated with political thought, but it was at its best when high political philosophy was joined with the rough and tumble of geopolitics and strategy. "The distinction between politics and strategy diminishes as the point of view is raised," Winston Churchill reminds us in *The World Crisis*. "At the summit true politics and strategy are one." The archetypal Claremont student studied with both Professor Jaffa and Dr. Rood, and spent as much time with Aristotle, Aquinas, Machiavelli, or Locke as with Washington, Lincoln, and Churchill – or perhaps John Quincy Adams. Dr. Garrity had long focused on and written extensively about the statesmanship of John Quincy Adams, and he was in the process of writing a scholarly biography of Adams and pursing several unique lines of study at the time of his death. Much of his work, and the work of similar minds, can be found at Classics of Strategy and Diplomacy, which is now a project of Hillsdale College.

Statesmanship is best understood not by reading history backward to justify an academic approach or to solidify a popular doctrine but by coming to understand the statesman as he understood himself. This is best done not by selective quoting or overemphasizing exceptions but through a comprehensive knowledge of the statesman's own writings, public documents, and speeches; not with the luxury of hindsight but in the context of the circumstances under which they deliberated, made decisions, and explained their thoughts and actions. This selection of writings, collected and introduced by Dr. Garrity and Dr. Benjamin Judge, is intended to do that concerning John Quincy Adams's statesmanship in service to the young but growing American nation.

MATTHEW SPALDING

July 4, 2021

| INTRODUCTION |

JOHN QUINCY ADAMS is arguably America's most distinguished diplomat, taking into account the length and breadth of his public service and his influence on American foreign policy. He was the son of John Adams, a Founding Father and the author of the Model Treaty of 1776 and negotiator of the Treaty of Paris. As a teenager he served as secretary to his diplomat-father and his colleagues in Europe. He penned nationally prominent essays that anticipated and defended the Washington administration's approach to the conflict among European powers during the French Revolution. He served as minister to the Dutch Republic, Prussia, Russia, and Britain. He headed the American delegation that negotiated the end of the War of 1812. His tenure as secretary of state under President James Monroe was highlighted by a treaty that extended the nation's boundaries to the Pacific and by the enunciation of a doctrine that guided American foreign policy for decades to come. As president, he supported cooperative hemispheric relations based on a liberalized law of nations and the freedom of religion.

In the course of this remarkable journey, John Quincy documented his ideas and actions through his writings, speeches, letters, diary entries, and state papers. The sheer volume of this matter is staggering, even leaving out the personal, religious, philosophical, literary, and political elements that are woven into the corpus. For instance, he sent over 150 dispatches to the secretaries of state and the treasury during his three-year tenure in the Netherlands; to say nothing of the dozens of letters to family and friends.

To aid those interested specifically in learning more about the man and his views on foreign policy, the editors have compiled a collection of the most important and often-cited works, such as his famous oration of July 4, 1821. We divide the volume into ten sections, corresponding chronologically to the phases of his career. Each section has a short introduction specific to that period. Framing each document is a header that briefly provides context and highlights a particular point or argument of interest.

We have annotated lightly – sufficiently, we hope, to allow the nonspecialist reader to follow the action and the argument, but without being bogged down in the details provided by complete scholarly collections. Wherever possible we have included the full text but, given the immensity of the available material and John Quincy's style of writing, we have used discretion to abridge certain documents. In most cases, we include the full text in the electronic supplement. We have based our transcripts on the best available primary sources.

To be sure, we may have left out items that others might deem essential. John Quincy sometimes offered variants of his policy position to different audiences; these arguments were generally consistent, but some contain interesting nuances. In such cases we have selected those documents that seem to offer the best and most concise picture of his position. We provide references to other documents produced by John Quincy that relate to the matter at hand. In some instances, we have found it difficult to distinguish between foreign and domestic policy issues, and probably have erred on the side of exclusion of the former.

Treating his years as secretary of state was particularly difficult. He sent out numerous detailed instructions to American officials abroad, constantly adjusting policy as events warranted. These changes are sometimes explained in his diary, but sometimes not. This makes it difficult to single out particular documents or diary entries as particularly revealing. We necessarily avoid the day-to-day back-and-forth, except concerning the formulation of what became known as the Monroe Doctrine. In addition, although Adams was now making rather than executing policy, he did so under the direction of Monroe, who had the final say and who was often closely involved in the process. Adams mainly had his way, and the two were in general agreement, but it was not always so, especially on wording, where the president was inclined to tone down the secretary's blunt language. As a result, there are cases where a document may not precisely reflect Adams's own views.

In general terms, we have attempted to identify key points of decision and items that indicate John Quincy's general approach to foreign policy. We can only say that we have exercised our best judgment, given that it would be impossible to include everything.

To us, certain consistent themes clearly emerge. Diplomacy, it is often said, is the art of the possible. John Quincy Adams undoubtedly would have agreed. But he would have added that the possible must be guided by a set of political principles that define the national interest. In 1809, John Quincy wrote: "There are two political principles that form the basis of the system of policy best suited to the interests and the duties of this country. One in relation to its internal concerns, UNION, the other in respect to its intercourse with foreign nations, INDEPENDENCE. These principles are the keys to my political creed."[1]

These two guiding principles – union and independence – were in fact closely interrelated. Throughout his career he fought separatist movements in the North and the South. A foreign policy of independence was a necessary complement to that of a strong Union. To retain its independence, he was emphatic that the United States must remain aloof from the quarrels and wars of Europe, and particularly avoid "entangling alliances." Strict neutrality was the default position. America would add its moral support to the cause of true freedom in the world and would aid that cause indirectly through diplomacy if it could, but it would not go abroad in search of monsters to destroy. This posture would prevent foreign influence from distorting American politics or involving it in unnecessary wars that threatened the Union.

By national greatnesses, John Quincy clearly meant more than the sheer power that the Union could wield in international affairs; he also meant its signal contributions to the improvement of the condition of mankind. Adams believed that self-improvement was the God-given duty of individuals and communities. America's contributions would, first, be the vindication of republican (constitutional) government, which rested in turn on the principles enunciated in the Declaration of Independence. Second, the Union would expand, by peaceful means, the realm of political freedom across the entire North American continent. Third, the United States would, in a manner consistent with its national interest and circumstances, support a liberalized law of nations that supported international peace and commercial prosperity. Finally, America would play a leading role in promoting the higher dimensions of civilization – the arts and sciences, literature, and the like, at a time when John Quincy believed those lights were being extinguished throughout Europe. None of this was remotely possible with a divided Union.

A Union pursuing a foreign policy of independence must have a national security structure adequate to the task, beginning with the principle of executive primacy in international affairs. The United States must have an ocean-going navy capable of breaking a blockade of its coasts, and securing its hemispheric and oceanic commerce against piracy and privateering. It did not need a large standing army but forces would have to be proficient in all forms of combat, including combined arms. The security structure depended on sound government finances, which included a sufficient level of taxation. The president and his cabinet must have the most current intelligence of the goals and actions of the powers of Europe, especially when it came to the possible outbreak of war. This required posting experienced diplomats and consular officials in critical locations.

We do not intend to present John Quincy as an infallible oracle or unchallenged guide to American foreign policy. His understanding of the national honor and interest at various times in his career are worthy of debate. His strategic assessment of the international situation, and the motivations of other nations and their leaders, was not always accurate. Despite his protestations that morality must guide foreign policy, he did not always assume the unquestioned high ground – there was enough of the practicing lawyer in him to take on the dubious case of a client and make it his own. The justifications of his own actions could be self-serving, arguably intended to advance his political career. He struggled, largely unsuccessfully, to separate the interests of his slave-holding country from his personal opposition to the peculiar institution. He unapologetically believed that Indian culture was retrograde and destined to be extinguished, although he believed that process should take place without force or fraud – something that he discovered was well-nigh impossible. His diplomatic style, reflecting his personality, was often abrasive and even condescending – for better or worse. He had his critics, then and now. We attempt to provide readers with sufficient context to make their own judgment. But we do not hide our view that if he was not infallible, there have been none his superior.

We end our collection in 1829, as John Quincy was shown out of the highest office in the land. Never again would he exercise the same kind of direct influence on American diplomacy. But as things turned out, his public career was hardly at an end. Most notably, he became the most prominent antagonist of what he termed the slavocracy. At times this ardent patriot and religious man questioned the cause of his country and even the existence of his God. Did he also question whether his own past policies and apparent diplomatic triumphs had contributed to the morass in which the nation now found itself? That is a subject for another time and another volume.

CHAPTER ONE

EARLY LIFE, 1767–1794

INTRODUCTION

JOHN QUINCY ADAMS was born into politics and war. As a small child in Boston, John Quincy lived in a town under British occupation. From the heights near the family farm in Braintree, he and his mother Abigail witnessed the distant fire and smoke of the Battle of Bunker Hill. From the Continental Congress in Philadelphia, his father, John Adams, sent home detailed reports of the military resistance and diplomatic steps needed to sustain the revolution. Beginning in February 1778, John Quincy accompanied his father on two wartime diplomatic assignments in Europe, as his father's personal secretary. He served in a similar capacity for Francis Dana during Dana's assignment as American envoy to Russia from 1781 to 1783. He became fluent in French, the universal diplomatic language of the day, and at The Hague and in Paris he studied classical texts with his father.

Most importantly, John Quincy imbibed the substance and style of his diplomat-father. In addition to being on the congressional committee that drafted the Declaration of Independence, John Adams was chiefly responsible for the development of the Model Treaty. Although intended to guide negotiations with the French, the treaty was a template for what Adams thought America's foreign policy should be. Its guiding principle was to make only commercial connections with other states, while avoiding military and political ties, so as to avoid foreign entanglements. The new nation needed time to consolidate its economic position, develop a true sense of national sovereignty, and strengthen the government. War, even a defensive one, distracted from those goals. The times and experiences devoted to those goals exposed John Quincy Adams to the early foundations of American foreign policy.

The teenaged John Quincy could have stayed in Europe as long as he liked. He could have studied at a great university like Leyden or Oxford; or he could have served as an aide to his father, who had been appointed in 1785 as the first American minister to the Court of St. James's. But John Quincy was determined to return to the country of his birth. To remain any longer abroad, he believed, was to forfeit his character as an American and the opportunity to serve his country, both of which were at the center of the Adams family creed of duty. So, after seven years abroad, he returned to Massachusetts to attend Harvard College.

John Quincy's first public appearance came when he joined a heated debate over the French Revolution, which more broadly addressed the proper form of republican government and political change. The most famous and influential of these arguments were Edmund Burke's *Reflections on the Revolution in France* and Thomas Paine's riposte, *The Rights of Man*. Most Americans – notably, John Adams's old friend, Thomas Jefferson – were delighted with developments in France, which they regarded as the natural extension of their own revolution. One prominent public figure differed – John Adams. Now vice president, Adams wrote a series of newspaper essays, under the title Discourses on Davila, which warned that the French Revolution was ill-conceived and bound to end in violence and anarchy.

When the American edition of Paine's tract was published in Philadelphia in April 1791, it included a preface written by Thomas Jefferson: "I am extremely pleased to find it will be reprinted here, and that something is at length to be publicly said against the political heresies which have sprung up among us. I have no doubt our citizens will rally a second time round the standard of Common Sense." John Adams – and everyone else –

immediately assumed that Jefferson's allusion to "political here-sies" referred to him. His early performance in office as vice president, as well as the Davila essays, had given him the wide-spread reputation that he hankered after monarchy, especially given his prominent criticism of the French Revolution.

John Adams did not reply to Jefferson's apparent public insult. But his son, writing a series of essays under the pseudonym Publicola, did. Jefferson and many others assumed that Publicola was the vice president. These public arguments cemented the rift between the elder Adams and Jefferson and formed a decisive event in the creation of the opposing political parties, known to history as the Federalists and Democratic Republicans.

In the spring of 1793, the Washington administration faced a critical choice: How to react to news of the outbreak of war between revolutionary France and England without first know-ing how the belligerents would treat American maritime com-merce and its vulnerable frontiers. What to do, for example, if the new French minister to the United States, Edmund Charles Genet (Citizen Genet), demanded that the United States enter the war on its behalf to defend its property in the West Indies? The French cause was highly popular in America, but the United States had strategic commitments to France stemming from the two countries' alliance of 1778. Furthermore, some American supporters of the French Revolution wanted to be drawn into the war as part of a global crusade for democracy.

The Washington administration responded with a proclama-tion of neutrality in April 1793. Thomas Jefferson, the secretary of state, thought that the proclamation was premature and failed to show the proper gratitude to France. The United States, at the very least, should have first required Britain to pay a diplomatic price for the United States to remain neutral. But others, such as Secretary of the Treasury Alexander Hamilton, preferred a neu-tral posture that inclined the United States toward Britain. It was widely rumored that, in retaliation, Genet had threatened to appeal to the people at Washington's expense.

These events enticed John Quincy, who was struggling to establish his law practice in Boston, to reenter the national arena by writing a series of newspaper essays and public addresses. Writing as Publicola and Marcellus, John Quincy immediately took to the public prints to offer his approach to American foreign policy. Then, on July 4, 1793, John Quincy delivered an address to the town of Boston in which he reflected on how the principles of the American Revolution were bound eventually to undermine monarchical absolutism everywhere. John Quincy concluded his prolific year in 1793 with another set of newspaper essays. Writing as Columbus, he outlined the various ways in which foreign agents, such as Genet, could destroy the American character. These writings, together, articulated themes that would inform John Quincy's whole public life. They also put on display his deep command of foreign affairs – a command that the Washington administration acknowledged and would soon enlist on its behalf.

CORRESPONDENCE AND DIARY ENTRIES, APRIL 1778–APRIL 1785

During his time abroad as a child and young man, John Quincy saw much of Europe – he was the greatest traveler of his age, according to his father – and he developed distinctive impressions of the peoples and governments with which he would later deal in an official capacity. He and his sister Abigail (Nabby) frequently compared thoughts on the "National Characters" they had observed in Europe. For instance, when the Adams party traveled through Spain en route to Paris during the winter of 1780, John Quincy was struck by the poverty, and the prevalence of fat priests and thin peasants, in an absolutist Catholic regime; this left him with an impression that undoubtedly affected his later views of Spanish America. He saw first-hand the effects of serfdom in Prussia, Poland, and Russia. In 1785, he and John Adams were given a close preview of French revolutionary ideas by the Marquis de Lafayette – ideas that appalled both of them.

DIARY ENTRY (ASTORGA, SPAIN), JANUARY 3, 1780

In the first volume of this journal I promised to give a description of several things.[1] I will now give one of the Roads, Houses, men, &c from Corunna as far as this place. The roads in General are very bad. The Lodgings I will not attempt to describe for it is impossible. However I will say something about them. We did not once lodge with the mules but not much better. They shew us chambers in which anybody would think a half a dozen hogs had lived there six months. I have in my first volume said something about Castellano. We have not met with any place quite so bad as that but we have come very near it. Sometimes we might see a chimney but it is very seldom. They have a large flat stone in the middle of the room and they punch two or three holes in the roof of the house out of which some of the Smoke goes and the rest must be borne with. They never wash nor sweep their floors from the time the houses are made to the time they are pull'd down. The roofs of the houses are generally a parcel of boards cover'd with straw.[2] As for the People they are Lazy, dirty, Nasty and in short I can compare them to nothing but a parcel of hogs. Their cloaths are commonly of a dirt colour and their Breeches are big enough for to put a bushel of Corn in besides themselves. I do not wonder at it. Poor Creatures they are eat up by their preists. Near three quarters of what they earn goes to the Preists and with the other Quarter they must live as they can. Thus is the whole of this Kingdom deceived and deluded by their Religion. I thank Almighty God that I was born in a Country where anybody may get a good living if they Please. Thus have I given a description of several things. At another opportunity I will give one of several others.

JOHN QUINCY ADAMS (ST PETERSBURG) TO JOHN ADAMS, AUGUST 21, 1781 (O.S.)

HONOUR'D SIR

O.S. St Petersburg August 21st 1781

N.S. 1 September 1781

We arrived here on Monday the 16/27 instant having left Amsterdam the N.S. 7th of July And rode the greatest part of the way day and night. The distance is about 2400 English Miles.[3]

The first place of any consequence we stopp'd at was Berlin the capital of the king of Prussia's Dominions; this is a very pretty town, much more so than Paris, or London as Mr. Dana says; but it will be still more so if the present King's plan is adopted by his successor, for wherever there is a row of low, small houses he sends the owners out of them, pulls them down and has large, elegant houses built in the same place and then sends the owners in again. But notwithstanding this, he is not beloved in Berlin, and everybody says publicly what he pleases against the king; but as long as they do not go any farther than words, he don't take any notice of it but says that as long as they give him all he asks, they may say what they will.[4]

But they have a great reason to complain of him, for he certainly treats them like Slaves; Among other things, if a farmer has two or more sons the eldest inherits all the land and all the others (when of age) are soldiers for life at a gros and a half which is about two pence sterling per day, and they must with that find their own provisions; if a farmer has but one Son He inherits his land; whenever a Vacation happens in any regiment, he chuses one of his subjects to fill the place and this subject from that time becomes a soldier for life; everybody that is tall enough is subject to this law. In peace time the Native troops are disbanded Nine months in a year, and in all that time their pay ceases and they must get their living as they can.

There is nothing very remarkable in Dantzic, Konigsberg, or

Riga; in coming to this last we pass'd thro' Courland, a province which does strictly speaking belong to Poland but Russia has much more influence there than Poland itself in that Province. All the Farmers are in the most abject slavery, they are bought and sold like so many beasts, and are sometimes even chang'd for dogs or horses. Their masters have even the right of life and death over them, and if they kill one of them they are only obliged to pay a trifling fine; they may buy themselves but their masters in general take care not to let them grow rich enough for that; if anybody buys land there he must buy all the slaves that are upon it.

Narva is the last place which we stopp'd at before our arrival here, it is a small, insignificant town but will be always famous for the battle fought there. As to this place, I have not been here long enough to know much about it, but by what we have seen of it I think it to be still handsomer than Berlin. The streets are large and the houses very well built but it is not yet half finish'd and will require another century to be render'd compleat.[5]

Just before we got to Berlin, by the carelessness of a postillion our carriage overset and broke so that Mr. Dana was obliged to buy another there but luckily nobody was hurt by the fall.

Nothing else Extraordinary befel us on our journey.

I am your dutiful Son, John Q. Adams

JOHN QUINCY ADAMS (THE HAGUE) TO ABIGAIL ADAMS, JULY 23, 1783[6]

HONOURED MAMMA
    Hague July 23d. 1783

It is indeed a long time since I have receiv'd any Letters from my friends in America, and I must own I have been a little behind hand within these two years; in writing to them. However, I hope they will consider that I have been all that time, almost at the world's end, or to make the best of it, in such an *out of the-way* place, as made it very inconvenient for me to write: But I should think myself deficient in my duty, if I should let pass the present opportunity; without giving you some account of my travels, since I left Mr. Dana.

I Set off, from Petersbourg the 19/30 of last October, in company With Count Greco an Italian gentleman with whom I was acquainted, at that place: and on account of the badness of the roads and weather; and of our having a great number of considerable water passages, which had began to freeze over, did not arrive in Stockholm, the capital of Sweeden untill the 25th. of November. The distance is about 800 English Miles. I stay'd at Stockholm about 6 weeks and was much pleas'd with the polite manner in which the people of the Country treat strangers. Sweeden is the country in Europe which pleases me the most. That is; of those I have seen. Because their manners resemble more those of my own Country, than any I have seen. The King is a Man of great Abilities. In the Space of one day from being ~~one of~~ the most dependent, he rendered himself one of the most absolute Monarchs of Europe. But he is extremely popular, and has persuaded his people that they are free; and that he has only restor'd them their ancient constitution. They think they are free, and are therefore happy.

However in the interior parts of the Kingdom he has lost a little of his Popularity because he has laid some heavy taxes upon Brandy, and some other articles.[7]

I Left Stockholm the 31st. of December and was obliged to stop at a small town call[ed] Norrkiöping at about 120 miles from Stockholm, for a fortnight, because of a very heavy fall of Snow which happen'd just at that time; I stopp'd also about 3. weeks at Gottenburg, and arriv'd at Copenhagen, the Capital of Denmark (it is about 600. miles from Stockholm) the 15th. of February of the present year. I found there Count Greco who had taken a different road from Stockholm. He had taken a place in a vessel which was to sail three days after my arrival, for Kiel a town in

Germany near Hamborough: not to lose the opportunity I took a place in the same vessel, but after having waited three weeks for a Good wind The harbour froze up and we were obliged after all to go to Hamborough by Land. The people in Denmark treat strangers with a great deal of Politeness and Civility, but not with the same open-heartedness, which they do in Sweeden. The government is entirely Monarchical. But it astonishes me, that mankind a whole people can place at the Head of their goverment such a Man as the king of Denmark because his father was a king. The hereditary prince it seems is at least possess'd of common sense, and is regarded in the Country as a prodigy, as he indeed is, if he is compared to his father.[8]

I arrived at Hamborough (which is about 300 English Miles from Copenhagen) on the 11th. of March. I stay'd there near a Month: it is a large city; quite commercial, and will I dare say, carry on hereafter a great deal of Trade with America. But its commerce is somewhat restrain'd because it is surrounded by the Dominions of the King of Denmark, and of the Elector of Hanover. The Danes have built a town, at about a quarter of a Mile from Hamborough, which is become now its rival in commerce, the Hamburgers have named this Place Al-te-na, which signifies, *much too near* as indeed it is for their commercial interests.

The [last] city where I made any stay before I arriv'd at Amsterdam was *Bremen* which is another commercial Republic but the city is much smaller than Hamborough. It was anciently one of the Hanseatic league; and has been in a much more flourishing condition than it is at present. There are at Bremen some publick cellars, which are famous. I drank there some Rhenish wine about 160. Years old. I stay'd only four days at Bremen and arriv'd at Amsterdam the 15th. and at this Place the 21st. of April, and here I have been ever since. Hamborough is about 450 English Miles from this Place.

Last night, at about 11. o'clock, Pappa arrived here from Paris all alone, only accompanied by a Servant; he intends to return to Paris in about three weeks.[9]

I hope, Charles, and Tommy are both well, and my dear Sister, who has been very obliging within these three years. I have receiv'd already from her two letters. I should take it as a great favour if she would favour me with some more; I have quite left off criticizing, especially upon faults in Language at least untill I shall be myself less faulty in this respect.

I am your most dutiful, and affectionate Son.
J. Q. Adams

JOHN QUINCY ADAMS (PARIS) TO ABIGAIL ADAMS, SEPTEMBER 10, 1783

HONOURED MAMMA
Paris September 10th: 1783

As you have ordered me in a Letter which I have Lately receiv'd to give you my own Observations on the Countries thro' which I have travelled, the following are some upon Russia; but I must previously beg you will remember, that you Say in your Letter that you expect neither the precision of a Robertson, nor the Elegance of a Voltaire, therefore you must take them as they are.[10]

The government of Russia is entirely despotical. The Sovereign is absolute, in all the extent of the word. The persons, the Estates, the fortunes of the Nobility depend entirely upon his Caprice. And the nobility have the same power over the people, that the Sovereign has over them. The Nation is wholly composed of Nobles and Serfs, or in other words, of Masters and Slaves. The Countryman is attached to the Land in which he is born; if the Land is sold he is sold with it; and he is obliged to give to his Landlord the portion of his time, which he chuses to demand. It is commonly two days in the week, I think. Others make them pay a sort of tax, of two or three Roubles a year (N.B. that a Rouble is 4 shillings sterling or thereabouts). This makes a large

Revenue for the Landlords if they have a great Number of Serfs. And there are some of the Nobles who have an amazing Quantity of them: out of each five hundred they are obliged to furnish one to the Empress every year, and this forms her Army. I have been assured from good Authority that there is one Nobleman who furnishes 1300 men a year to the Empress, according to that the number of his Slaves would be 650,000. Supposing each of these Slaves pay him a Rouble a year his revenue will be more than 100,000 £ Sterling per annum.

This form of Government is disadvantageous to the Sovereign to the Nobles and to the People; for first, it Exposes the Sovereign every Moment to Revolutions of which there have been *already* four in the Course of this Century vizt: when Anne, Dutchess of Courland was set upon the throne, which was the right of Elizabeth, daughter of Peter the first. This was done by some Noblemen who wanted to limit the prerogatives of the Sovereign, and be more powerful themselves. And they thought, they would find Anne more ready to agree to their Stipulations than Elizabeth because she had no right to the Crown. But she soon overturned all their Schemes; for as soon as she found herself well seated upon the throne, she rendered herself Absolute, by reinstating the Ancient form of Government; and banished all those who had made those restrictions, this was the second Revolution. The third was when Elizabeth dethroned *Iwan* an infant of 6 months old, and had him shut up in a Tower where he lived 20 years and was then murdered in it. And the 4th. when Peter the third was dethroned by the present Empress: this I think is sufficient proof that the Government is disadvantageous for the Sovereign. *Secondly*, As the Nobles all depend wholly upon the Sovereign they are always in danger, of their estates being confiscated, and themselves sent into Siberia. It is commonly the fate of the favourites. Menzicoff, the Dolgoroucki's, Biron, Bestucheff, Osterman, L'Estocg, all these have been the sport of Fortune. For some time the favourites of the Emperors and then sent to Siberia into exile, there to live in Misery. The History of Menzicoff is the most extraordinary, and he did not deserve his fate. He was born at Moscow, he was of low extraction, and used to Carry about the Streets, while a Child, pies, and sing ballads. Peter the first, saw him several times, and asked him several Questions; his answers pleased him so much that he took him to the Palace, and by degrees he became the favourite of the Emperor, who gave him the title of Prince and made him general of his Army &ca. At the battle of Pultowa, he saved the Empire, because [by] a manoeuvre of his he was the means of the battle's being decided in favour of the Emperor. During the whole Reign of Peter the 1st. and that of Catharine he was high in favour, but under that of Peter the 2d. he was stripped of all his dignities, his fortune which was immense, was confiscated, and himself sent in exile, where he died in misery. This is very nearly the history of all the others. An author who has written upon Russia (Manstein's Memoirs of Russia) says he has seen Lands change masters three or four times in the Course of a year. This is certainly not advantageous for the Nobility. And Thirdly, as to the People, Nobody I believe will assert that a People can be happy who are subjected to personal Slavery. Some of these Serfs are immensely rich: but they are not free and therefore they are despised, besides they depend still upon the Nobles, who make them contribute the more for their riches. A Nobleman wants money, if he has any rich Serfs, he sends and lets one of them know that he must have at such a time a thousand Roubles (more or less according to Circumstances). This the Serf has a right to refuse: but in that Case his Landlord orders him to go and work upon such a piece of Ground: so he is obliged either to give the money or to go and work. The richer they are the more the nobles prize them: thus a Common man costs but 80 or 100 Roubles at most: but I have seen a Man who gave to his Landlord for his Liberty and that of his descendents 450,000 Roubles. This proves the esteem they have for Liberty: even where one would think they should not know that such a thing exists.

As I am a little pressed for time, and as my Letter has already run to a considerable Length, I must for the present subscribe myself your most dutiful Son.

J Q Adams

JOHN QUINCY ADAMS (THE HAGUE) TO ELIZABETH CRANCH, APRIL 18, 1784

MY DEAR COUSIN
The Hague April 18th. 1784

While I was at St. Petersbourg, I had, the Pleasure, of receiving a Letter from you; I answered it, but since that time I have shamefully neglected writing to you. I own my fault, and promise to repair it for the future; and I hope, that you will pardon me, upon that Condition. The only reason I had for it, was a bad one. I feared that if I wrote, you would perceive that the improvements I had made, were by no means equal to the expectations, you had conceived, of the improvements, which, (from the advantages I enjoyed) I ought to have made: and this false shame continually withheld my Pen. But I have now got over it, and will for the future, confide entirely, in the indulgence of my Friends.

It is now going on upon the fifth year since I left last my Native Country. I have in that space of time, visited almost all the Nations of Europe; and the further I go, the more I love and cherish the place of my Birth. I know of no punishment, that would give me more Pain, than to be condemned to pass my Life in Europe. But of all the European Nations, I think I should prefer England.[11] Because I think it has preserved its Liberty the best, and because, in many things, the manners and Customs there, are the least unlike, those of our Country, of any Part of Europe. Last Fall my honoured Parent, having had a violent Fever at Paris, was advised for the benefit of his Health, to pass some time in England: we arrived in London the 26th. of October. It is the largest City I have seen; and both for convenience, and beauty is far superior to Paris. A few days after our arrival we went to see the Monuments in Westminster Abbey, which is surely one of the greatest curiosities in the Place. I own I was struck with Awe and Veneration, at finding myself on the spot, where lay the Remains of the greatest part of the Sages, and Heroes, which Great-Britain has produced, but I felt a painfull Sensation, at seeing a superb monument, erected to Major André, to reflect how much degenerated that Nation must be, which can find no fitter Objects for so great an honour, than a Spy, than a man whose sad Catastrophe, was owing to his unbounded Ambition, and whose only excuse for his conduct, was his Youth; as if youth, gave a Man the right to commit wicked and Contemptible Actions.[12] The Monuments in the Abbey are for the most part simple, and are not remarkable, for their Sculpture. There is only one monument extraordinarily beautiful. It is of one Mr. Robert Gascoyne, and his Lady. It represents a Lady lying sick, in the arms of her Husband, Death from beneath the tomb holds the dart, which the Husband wards off: the terror and anguish, which appear in the countenance of the Husband are most admirably expressed, and it is looked upon as one of the finest Pieces of Sculpture extant. St. Paul's Church, which is so much talk'd of, did not answer my expectations. Its steeple is very high, and you might have a very fine view of all the City from it, if the smoke was not too thick, to be able to see far: but the Church itself appears to be rather a heavy building, and looks more to advantage on the outside than within. The British Museum Contains a great Number of very curious things. Besides, numbers of ancient medals, Statues, Urns, etc. there is a collection of Letters written by the hands of all the Kings and Queens of England since Henry the 8th. Little or no instruction can be acquired from such a thing; yet I felt a certain Pleasure, which I could not well account for, at seeing the original productions of Persons so illustrious, especially of Queen Elizabeth, of whom there are several Letters in the Collection; another thing, much more ancient, an original of the *Magna Charta*, is also there, and several other very curious Manuscripts.

Sir Ashton Lever's Museum, contains the completest collection of natural history, (such as stuff'd birds and beasts, insects, minerals &c) of any in Europe; but what is still more curious, he has a whole Room ornamented with instruments and articles of dress, of the Inhabitants of those Countries alone, which were discovered in the last voyage of the unfortunate Captain Cook. The dress is entirely made of birds feathers, and their warlike instruments, of stone, besides some necklaces, and a kind of Coat of mail, of dogs teeth. The Tower is remarkable for the admirable disposition of the small arms, which are all placed in a most beautiful order: there are also some wild beasts there, but no great number. They show still many old things, and among others, the axe with which the famous Earl of Essex (they say,) was beheaded. The royal treasure, or Regalia, is also kept there. It consists of a number of crowns, scepters, &c. The crown which the Kings wear at their coronation is said to be worth a million. The money might I think have been better employed. By particular favour we got sight of the Queen's Palace, called Buckingham House, because it was built by, Villers duke of Buckingham, favourite of Charles the first. There we saw the Apartments, of the King, of the Queen, and, of the rest of the family, as also a great number of beautiful paintings, by the greatest Masters, at the Head of which are the Cartoons of Raphael, looked upon as the Master Pieces of the Art. But besides this we also saw there the models in miniature of every fortress, and of every Man of War in the service of the Government.

There my dear Cousin, is as exact an account as my memory is capable of giving, of the most remarkable things I saw in London; while we were in the Kingdom we took a jaunt to Oxford and Bath. At Oxford in somme of the Colleges of the University, there are things worth notice, but which would give you little or no entertainment to hear. On that Journey, as well as in the one from

Dover to London, and the one from London to Harwich, when we entered, and departed from the Kingdom, we had Occasion to remark, that it might be a most happy Country, for Nature seems to have been really partial in their favour; but the general corruption and Vice, which possesses them all, high and low, effectually prevents them from being happy, as it is impossible, as well for whole Nations, as for particular persons to be Vicious and happy.

But I fear of becoming tedious, and ~~must~~ will therefore after desiring you to present, my dutiful Respects to your honoured Parents, and my best compliments to my Cousins, conclude in subscribing myself invariably Your affectionate friend and Cousin.

J. Q. Adams

ESSAYS OF PUBLICOLA

John Quincy's Publicola essays, written to criticize Thomas Paine's Rights of Man, brought out several important themes that later marked his diplomatic career. First, Publicola was the beginning of a life-long effort by John Quincy to distinguish in the public mind between the American and French revolutions. Second, he argued that the standard for justifying the resort to revolution was very high, and that outsiders should not encourage or support foreign revolutions, as Paine was attempting to do in England. Third, and most controversially, Publicola defended the principles underlying the English constitution, the best of which he claimed had been adopted in republicanized fashion by the United States. Publicola suggested that these principles, adapted prudently to the particular character of their peoples, should guide political change in other nations – a course he did not believe the French revolutionaries were following. Fourth, in Publicola X, he emphasized the importance of vesting the powers of conducting foreign relations in the executive rather than the legislative branch, with due allowance for the role of the legislature in preventing the abuse of those powers.

PUBLICOLA I (COLUMBIAN CENTINEL, *JUNE 8, 1791*)

MR. RUSSELL,

SIR, The late Revolution in France, has opened an extensive field of speculation to the philosopher and to the politician. An event so astonishing and unexpected in its nature, and so important in its consequences, naturally arrested the peculiar attention of the whole civilized world. The friends of liberty and of man, have seen with pleasure, the temples of despotism, levelled with the ground, and the genius of freedom rising suddenly in his collected and irresistible strength, and snapping in an instant all the cords with which, for centuries, he had been bound. Upon the downfall of the arbitrary system of government in France, there appears to have been but one sentiment, and that sentiment of exultation; but while the friends of humanity have rejoiced at the emancipation of so many millions of their fellow creatures, they have waited with anxious expectation to see upon what foundations they would attempt to establish their newly-acquired liberty. The proceedings of their Representative Assembly have been contemplated in very different points of view, by men of names equally illustrious, and of characters equally favourable to the cause of liberty. Among the publications which have appeared upon the subject, two pamphlets, founded upon very different principles, appear to have been received with the greatest avidity, and seem calculated to leave the deepest impression.[13] The one written by Mr. Burke, which is one continued invective upon almost all the proceedings of the National Assembly since the Revolution, and which passes a severe and indiscriminating censure upon almost all their transactions: The other the production of Mr. Paine, containing a defence of the Assembly, and approving everything they have done, with applause as undistinguishing as is the censure of Mr. Burke. We are told, that the copy from which an edition of this work was reprinted at Philadelphia, was furnished by the Secretary of State, and was accompanied by a letter, from which the following extract has been published in most of our newspapers. "I am extremely pleased to find that it is to be re-printed here, and that something is at length to be publicly said, against the *political heresies* which have sprung up among us. I have no doubt our citizens will rally a second time round the standard of *Common Sense*."[14]

I confess, Sir, I am somewhat at a loss to determine, what this very respectable gentleman means by *political heresies*. Does he consider this pamphlet of Mr. Paine's as the canonical book of political scripture? As containing the true doctrine of popular infallibility, from which it would be heretical to depart in one single point? The expressions, indeed, imply more; they seem, like the Arabian prophet, to call upon all true believers in the *Islam* of democracy, to draw their swords, and, in the fervour of their devotion, to compel all their countrymen to cry out, "There is but one Goddess of Liberty, and Common Sense is her prophet."

I have always understood, Sir, that the citizens of these States were possessed of a full and entire freedom of opinion upon all subjects, civil as well as religious; they have not yet established any infallible criterion of orthodoxy, either in church or state: their principles in theory, and their habits in practice, are equally averse to that slavery of the mind, which adopts, without examination, any sentiment that has the sanction of a venerable name. *Nullius in verba jurare magistri* is their favorite maxime; and the only political tenet which they would stigmatize with the name of heresy, would be that which should attempt to impose an opinion upon their understandings upon the single principle of authority.

I believe, also, Sir, that the citizens of America are not at present disposed to rally round the standard of any man. In the full possession and enjoyment of all the freedom, for which they have gone through so arduous a conflict, they will not, for the poor purpose of extinguishing a few supposed political heresies, return to the horrors of a civil contest, from which they could reap no possible benefit, and which would probably terminate in the loss of that liberty for which they have been so liberal of their treasure and of their blood.

If, however, Mr. Paine is to be adopted as the holy father of our political faith, and this pamphlet is to be considered as his Papal Bull of infallible virtue, let us at least examine what it contains. Before we determine to join the standard, let us inquire what are the articles of war to which our General requires our submission. It is the glorious characteristic of truth, at once to invite and bid defiance to investigation. If any opinions which have sprung up among us have really led us astray from the standard of truth, let us return to it, at the call of Mr. Paine, or of any other man who can show us our errors. But, Sir, if upon examination, even this testament of orthodoxy shall be found to contain many spurious texts, false in their principles and delusive in their inferences, we may be permitted, notwithstanding our reverence for the author, at least to expunge the apocryphal doctrine, and to confine our faith to the genuine tenets of real political inspiration. It is my intention to submit to the public a few observations, which have occurred to me upon the perusal of this pamphlet, which has so clear and valid a title to the public attention. But I must here observe, that I wish to avoid every appearance of disrespect, either to the real parent of this production, or to the gentleman who has stood its sponsor in this country. Both these gentlemen are entitled to the gratitude of their countrymen; the latter still renders important services in a very dignified station. He is a friend to free inquiry upon every subject, and he will not be displeased to see the sentiments which he has made his own by a public adoption, canvassed with as much freedom as is consistent with the reverence due to his character.

PUBLICOLA II (COLUMBIAN CENTINEL, JUNE 11, 1791)

SIR, In that part of Mr. Paine's pamphlet which he has chosen to call the miscellaneous chapter, he observes that, "when a man in a long course attempts to steer his course by anything else than some *polar truth* or *principle*, he is sure to be lost." I have sought for the polar principle to which his exertions were directed in this publication, and I must acknowledge I have sought in vain. His production is historical, political, miscellaneous, satirical, and panegyrical. It is an encomium upon the National Assembly of France. It is a commentary upon the rights of man, inferring questionable deductions from unquestionable principles. It is a severe satire upon Mr. Burke and his pamphlet upon the English Government, upon Kings, upon Nobility, and Aristocracy; it is a narrative of several occurrences, connected with the French Revolution, and it concludes with a kind of prophetical impulse, in the expectation of an *"European Congress to patronize the progress of free government, and promote the civilization of nations with each other."* The object which he promised to himself, in this publication, is not so dubious as the principle on which he wrote. His intention appears evidently to be, to convince the people of Great Britain that they have neither Liberty nor a Constitution – that their only possible means to produce these blessings to themselves, is to "topple down headlong" their present government, and follow implicitly the example of the French. As to the right, he scruples not to say, "that which a whole nation chuses to do, it has a right to do." This proposition is a part of what Mr. Paine calls a system of principles in opposition to those of Mr. Burke, and it is laid down without any sort of qualification. It is not my intention to defend the principles of Mr. Burke; truth is the only object of my pursuit, and I shall without hesitation refuse my assent to every principle inconsistent with that, whether it proceeds from Mr. Burke, Mr. Paine, or even from the illustrious National Assembly of France. This principle, that a whole nation has a right to do whatever it pleases, cannot in any sense whatever be admitted as true. The eternal and immutable laws of justice and of morality are paramount to all human legislation. The violation of those laws is certainly within the power, but it is not among the rights of nations. The power of a nation is the collected power of all the individuals which compose it. The rights of a nation are in like manner the collected rights of its individuals; and it must *follow* from thence, that the powers of a nation are more extensive than its rights, in the very same proportion with those of individuals. It is somewhat remarkable that, in speaking of the exercise of the particular right of forming a Constitution, Mr. Paine himself denies to a nation that omnipotence which he had before so liberally bestowed. For this same nation, which has a right to do whatever it pleases, has no right to establish a Government in *hereditary succession*. It is of infinite consequence, that the distinction between *power* and *right* should be fully acknowledged, and admitted as one of the fundamental principles of Legislators. A whole nation, such as France, England, or America, can act only by representation; and the acts of the representative body must be considered as the acts of the nation. We must go farther, and say, that the acts of the majority in the Representative Assembly are the acts of the whole body, and consequently of the whole nation. If, therefore, a majority thus constituted are bound by no law human or divine, and have no other rule but their sovereign will and pleasure to direct them, what possible security can any citizen of the nation have for the protection of his unalienable rights? The principles of liberty must still be the sport of arbitrary power, and the hideous form of despotism must lay aside the diadem and the scepter, only to assume the party-colored garments of democracy.

The system of principles upon which Mr. Paine advances this assertion is intended to prove, that the English nation have a right to destroy their present form of Government, and to erect another. I am not disposed to deny this right, nor is it at present necessary to examine whether Mr. Burke's opinions upon this subject are not directed rather against the expediency than the abstracted rights of such a measure. It may, however, not be improper to trace the origin of Mr. Paine's arguments against the principles maintained by Mr. Burke. Doctor Price has asserted, that by "the principles of the Revolution in 1688[15] the people of England had acquired the right, 1. To choose their own Governors. 2. To cashier them for misconduct; and, 3. To frame a Government for themselves." Mr. Burke endeavors to prove that the principles of the Revolution[16] in 1688, so far from warranting any right of this kind, support a doctrine almost diametrically opposite. Mr. Paine, in reply, cuts the Gordian knot at once, declares the Parliament of 1688 to have been downright usurpers, censures them for having unwisely sent to Holland for a King, denies the existence of a British Constitution, and invites the people of England to overturn their present Government, and to erect another upon the broad basis of national sovereignty, and government by representation. As Mr. Paine has departed altogether from the principles of the Revolution, and has torn up by the roots all reasoning from the British Constitution, by the denial of its existence, it becomes necessary to examine his works upon the grounds which he has chosen to assume. If we judge of the production from its apparent tendency, we may call it an address to the English nation, attempting to prove that they have a right to form a new Constitution, that it is expedient for them immediately to exercise that right, and that, in the formation of this Constitution, they can do no better than to imitate the model set before them by the French National Assembly. However immethodical his production is, I believe the whole of its argumentative part may be referred to these three points. If the subject were to affect only the British nation, we might leave them to reason and act for themselves; but, Sir, these are concerns equally important to all mankind; and the citizens of America are called upon from high authority to *rally* round the *standard* of this champion of Revolutions. I shall therefore now proceed to examine the reasons upon which he founds his opinions relative to each of these points.

The people of England have, in common with other nations, a natural and unalienable right to form a Constitution of Government, not because a whole nation has a right to do whatever it chooses to do, but because Government being instituted for the common security of the natural rights of every individual, it must be liable to alterations whenever it becomes incompetent for that purpose. The right of a people to legislate for succeeding generations derives all its authority from the consent of that posterity who are bound by their laws; and therefore the expressions of perpetuity used by the Parliament of 1688, contain no absurdity; and expressions of a similar nature may be found in all the Constitutions of the United States.

But, Sir, when this right is thus admitted in its fullest latitude, it must also be admitted, that it ought never to be exercised but in cases of extreme urgency: Every nation has a right as unquestionable to dissolve the bands of civil society, by which they are united, and to return to that state of individual imbecility in which man is supposed to have existed, previous to the formation of the social compact. The people of America have been compelled, by an unaccountable necessity, distressing in its operation, but glorious in its consequences, to exercise this right; and whenever a nation has no other alternative but the degradation of slavery, or the formidable conflict of a Revolution, the generous spirit of freedom will not hesitate a moment in the choice. Whether the people of France were, at the period of their Revolution, reduced to that unhappy situation, which rendered it absolutely necessary to overthrow their whole system to its foundation, is a question upon which the ablest patriots among themselves have differed, and upon which we are inadequate to decide. Whether the people of England are now in that calamitous predicament, is a question more proper for our discussion, and upon which I shall take the liberty to examine the reasoning of Mr. Paine.

PUBLICOLA X (COLUMBIAN CENTINEL, JULY 20, 1791)

The next article upon which Mr. Paine has pronounced the superiority of the French Constitution, is upon the subject of making war and peace. The right, he says, is placed where the expense is, that is, in the nation: Whereas "in England, the right is said to reside in a metaphor, shown at the Tower for six pence or a shilling a piece." He answers himself again in this passage, and shows the folly of placing such a formidable right in a metaphor; but in this instance as in the former, there is much wit and no truth; and I must take the liberty to affirm in contradiction to Mr. Paine, that the French Constitution has not, nor could not place the right of declaring war, where the expense must fall; and that the English Constitution has not placed this right in a metaphor.

The expense of supporting wars must in all countries be defrayed by the nation, and every individual must bear his proportion of the burthen. In free countries that proportion must always be determined by the representatives of the people; but the right of deciding when it may be expedient to engage in a war, cannot possibly be retained by the people of a populous and extensive territory, it must be a delegated power; and the French Constitution has vested it in the National Assembly. By the English Constitution it is vested in the supreme executive officer; but to guard against the abuse of this formidable power, it has given to the representatives of the people, the exclusive right of providing for the support of the war, and of withholding the supplies, "the sinews of war," if it should ever be declared contrary to the sense of the people themselves. Mr. Paine supposes a perplexity, which is warranted neither by theory nor by the experience of history. "If the one rashly declares war," says he, "as a matter of right; and the other peremptorily withholds the supplies as a matter of right, the remedy becomes as bad or worse than the disease." But every war in England must be the war of the people: The King is in reality no more than the organ of the nation, and must be more than an idiot to declare a war, upon which he must depend altogether upon them for its support, without being certain of that support. Imaginary conclusions drawn by reasoning against the inevitable order of things, are unworthy of a politician, and should be left as a feeble resource for the satirist. To have given his objection even an appearance of plausibility, Mr. Paine should have mentioned an instance, when this clashing of the rights of the King and of the Commons has ever been productive of the ill effects which his fancy has sagaciously drawn from them.

Indeed Mr. Paine himself, upon further reflection, acknowledges the futility of his objection, and says "that in the manner the English nation is represented, it signifies not where this right resides, whether in the Crown or in the Parliament." But I apprehend, if the representation in England were as perfect as human wisdom could devise, their present system with respect to peace and war, would comprise all the advantages of the French system, and at the same time be free from many inconveniences, to which that must be liable.

It must be clear to everyone that the French have not, as Mr. Paine pretends, united the *right* and the *expense*: The impracticability of such an union, must be equally evident; and the only question which can establish a fair ground of comparison, between the two constitutions is, *Whether it is expedient to delegate to the legislative, or whether to the executive authority, the right of declaring war*.

As I am not yet a convert to Mr. Paine's opinion that a nation has a right to do what it pleases, I must be allowed to say that they have a right to make war upon their neighbors, without provocation. The people by their representatives must judge, when the provocation is sufficient to dissolve them from all the obligations of morality and humanity, by which nations are bound to preserve the blessings of peace. But when they have determined that the great law of self-preservation, to which all other laws must give way, or that the laws which they have enacted in consequence of the primitive contract which united all their power for the benefit of every individual, compel them to appeal for justice to the God of battles, then, the declaration of war, the formal act, by which they announce to the world their intention to employ the arm of power in their own defence, seems to be the proper attribute of the executive power. The difference, therefore, between the English and French constitutions, considered in this light, can involve only a question of propriety, and as such the English appears to me to deserve the preference.

If this idea should be considered as heretical, I must beg leave to call to my assistance the authority of Rousseau, a name still more respectable than that of Mr. Paine, because death has given the ultimate sanction to his reputation. "The act of declaring war," says he in his Social Compact, "and that of making peace, have been considered as acts of sovereignty, which is not the case; for either of those acts is not a law, but only an application of the law; a particular act which determines the operation of the law, as will be clearly perceived when the idea annexed to the word law shall be ascertained." The spirit of the English constitution is perfectly agreeable to this idea.

But let us consider this subject a little further. Whenever a difference arises between two nations which may terminate in a war, it is proper and customary, that previous negotiations should be held, in order to use every possible means of settling amicably the dispute. These negotiations, the appointment of the agents by whom they are to be conducted, and the communication of the proposals for accommodation, which are respectively offered by either of the parties, are all appropriated to the executive department. When the restoration of peace becomes expedient in the opinion of the people, agents must again be appointed, and proposals of pacification must again be made. It is obvious to every man, that in the management of these concerns the utmost secrecy and despatch are frequently of essential necessity to the welfare of the people; but what secrecy can ever be expected, when every instruction to an ambassador, every article of a proposed treaty, and every circumstance of information from the minister, in the progress of his operations, must be known to twelve hundred men assembled in the capital of the republic; what probability of despatch, when all these things must be debated in this Assembly of 1200 men; where everything must in the necessary order of events be opposed, by interested individuals and irritated factions, who may protract the discussion for months or years at their pleasure.

By the Constitution of the United States, it is true, the right of declaring war is vested in the Congress, that is, in the legislative power. But it is in the point of form that it agrees with the Constitution of France; it has wisely placed the management of all negotiations and treaties, and the appointment of all agents and ministers in the executive department; and it has so thoroughly adopted in this instance the principles of the English Constitution, that although it has given the Congress the right of declaring war, which is merely a difference of form, it has vested in the President, with the advice of the Senate as his executive council, the right of making peace, which is implied in that of forming treaties. This is not the first instance in which Mr. Paine's principles attack those of the constitutions of his country. Highly as we may revere, however, the principles which we are under every obligation to support, we may without irreverence acknowledge that they partake of the human imperfection from which they originated, and if Mr. Paine's principles in opposition to them, are in any instance founded upon eternal truth, we may indulge the hope, that every necessary improvement will be adopted in a peaceable and amicable manner by the general consent of the people. But if the principles of Mr. Paine, or those of the French National Assembly, would lead us by a vain and delusive pretence of an impracticable union, between the right of declaring, and the expense of supporting a war, to the sacrifice of principles founded in immutable truth, if they could persuade us, by establishing in the legislative body all negotiations with foreign nations relative to war and peace, to open a thousand avenues for base intrigue, for furious faction, for foreign bribery, and domestic treason, let us remain immoveably fixed at the banners of our constitutional freedom, and not desert the impregnable fortress of our liberties, for the unsubstantial fabric of visionary politicians.[17]

ESSAYS OF MARCELLUS

In the spring of 1793, the Washington administration faced a critical choice: how to react to news of the outbreak of war between revolutionary France and England without first knowing how the belligerents would treat American commerce and its vulnerable frontiers. John Quincy (Marcellus) immediately took to the public prints to offer his advice, articulating a principle that would guide his approach to American foreign policy throughout his career – that of maintaining neutrality in all wars among European powers and involving exclusively European interests. Justice, self-interest, and self-preservation were the touchstones of John Quincy's insistence that neutrality was to the nation's fundamental advantage. It was not to be overridden by revolutionary sympathies or the temptation to take advantage of Europe's distresses.

MARCELLUS I (COLUMBIAN CENTINEL, APRIL 24, 1793)

At a period, when all the European powers with whom we have any considerable commercial intercourse, are involved in war, it becomes an interesting question to every American, what line of conduct ought to be pursued by the United States as a nation, and by their citizens as individuals, in relation to the contending parties. The individual must follow the dictates of his own discretion, and the path to be pursued by the nation must be pointed out by the wisdom of the National Legislation: But upon a subject in which all are so deeply interested, it is the right, and in some measure the duty of every citizen, to express his opinions with decency, but with freedom and sincerity.

The solution of the question as it respects the country, involves in itself an answer to that which relates to individuals. There have indeed been certain suggestions in the public papers, and in private circles something similar has been heard, of an intention among some of our fellow citizens to arm privateers, and commit depredations upon the commerce of one of the parties under the authority of another. It is to be hoped that this violation of the laws of nature and nations, this buccaneering plan of piratical plunder, may not in any instance be carried beyond the airy regions of speculation, and may never acquire the consistency of practical execution. If the natural obligations of justice are so feeble among us, that avarice cannot be restrained from robbery, but by the provisions of positive law, if the statute book is to be our only rule of morality to regulate the observance of our duties towards our fellow creatures, let those whose ideas of equality are so very subservient to their private interests, consult the treaties between the United States and the several powers now at war, which by the constitution of the United States, are declared to be "the supreme law of the land," and in the 21st, the 19th and the 20th articles of the several treaties of commerce with France, Holland and Prussia, they will find, that by taking letters of marque or arming privateers with commissions under either of the powers against either of the others, they would subject themselves to the punishment of pirates. There can be no doubt but that a similar act of hostility against any subject of the king of Great Britain, would be a direct violation of the 7th article of the treaty of peace. If we were not bound by any treaty whatever, with either of the nations, the natural obligation of neutrality would operate upon us individually, unless the nation should take a decisive part in favor of one of the parties. Every citizen would be legally responsible for all the property which he might seize with violence under a commission to which he could not be entitled, and if he should preserve himself from the punishment of piracy, he would be liable to make entire satisfaction for all the damage he might occasion, and to restore his ill-acquired plunder.[18]

It is indeed of material importance to the commercial interest of this country, that our merchants should show a peculiar degree of circumspection in their conduct, because the country becomes at a season so critical as this, in some measure responsible for them. In the just and honorable pursuit of their legitimate interest, it is the duty of the nation to support them with all its force and all its authority. In time of war, the subjects of all belligerent powers are frequently disposed to violate the rights of neutral nations. The master and the crew of a privateer, fitted out and cruising for the sole purpose of seizing upon defenceless wealth, and stimulated by the prospect of a valuable spoil, often feel the full force of disappointed rapaciousness, when after a long chase they discover that the ship, upon the plunder of whose cargo they had already feasted their imaginations, is rescued from their violence by the protection of a neutral flag. They are not apt to be nice in their distinctions of morality. Their disappointed passions often seek a vent against the unarmed opulence which eludes their grasps, and they are frequently guilty of insolence, and sometimes of oppression towards those who are not in a condition to resent their injustice. In such case the individuals of the neutral nation, who suffer in consequence of such lawless proceedings, have no remedy but to call upon the sovereign of their own country to support them in their demand for satisfaction: Should any complaints arising from causes like this become a subject of negotiation, between the United States and either of the contending parties, it behoves us all, as we value our interests, or our reputation, that no occasion to retort a complaint that the neutrality was first violated on our part, should be given. In order to obtain justice, for any citizen who may suffer by the iniquity of a foreigner, we must disavow in the most decisive manner, all acts of iniquity committed by our own citizens, and our government can never have an expectation of gaining a compensation for the *injured* individual, unless they can compel the *injuring* individual to make compensation in his turn.

To expatiate upon the natural injustice and wickedness of privateering under a foreign commission against a nation at peace with us, would be as idle as an attempt "to add a perfume to the violet." The practise of privateering, even in its most excusable form, between nations formally at war, has been condemned by the most amiable and virtuous moralists. In the treaty between the United States and the King of Prussia, it is provided that in case war should arise between the contracting parties, "All merchant and trading vessels employed in exchanging the products of different places, and thereby rendering the necessaries, conveniences and comforts of human life more easy to be obtained, and more general, shall be allowed to pass free and unmolested: and neither of the contracting powers shall grant or issue any commission to any private armed vessel, empowering them to take or destroy such trading vessels or interrupt such commerce." This clause in the treaty, which was I believe the first instance in which two great nations have adopted this system of benevolence and humanity, has been justly admired and applauded; it was adopted by the late French National Assembly, when they declared war against the Emperor of Germany, and the real friends of mankind must regret that the policy is abandoned at this time, when the war extends to all the great commercial nations of Europe. For, if as the poet, with more than poetical truth, has said, "War is murder," the plunder of private property, the pillage of all the regular rewards of honest industry and laudable enterprise, upon the mere pretence of a national contest, to the eye of reason and justice, can appear in no other light than that of highway robbery. If, however, some apology for the practice is to be derived from the uncontrollable laws of necessity, or from the iniquitous law of war, certainly there can be no possible excuse for those who incur the guilt without being able to plead the palliation; for those who by violating the rights of nations in order to obtain a licence for rapine, manifestly show, that it is only the lash of the executioner that binds them to the observance of their civil and political duties.[19]

MARCELLUS II (COLUMBIAN CENTINEL, MAY 4, 1793)

Non nostrum, tantas componere lites.[20]

Having attempted in a late paper to show that a rigid adherence to the system of Neutrality between the European nations now at war, is equally the dictate of justice and of policy, to the individual citizens of the United States, while the Nation remains neutral, the question recurs, what is the line of conduct prescribed to the nation itself, at this delicate juncture, by those immutable laws of justice and equity, which are equally obligatory to sovereigns and to subjects, to republics and to kings. I shall not make any consideration of general policy a separate subject of inquiry, because I hold it to be one of the most undeniable principles of government, that the truest policy of a nation consists in the performance of its duties. The rights of nations are nothing more than an extension of the rights of individuals to the great societies, into which the different portions of mankind have been combined; and they are all mediately or immediately derived from the fundamental position which the author of Christianity has taught us as an article of religion, and which the revised declaration of rights of the National Convention in France have declared, to contain the essence of liberty. "Liberty," says the new Declaration of Rights, "consists in the power of doing whatever is not contrary to the rights of others." "Whatsoever," says the Saviour of mankind, "you would that men should do to you, do ye even so to them." Let us therefore be cautious to do nothing contrary to the rights of others, and we shall continue to enjoy and to deserve the blessings of freedom. Let us do as we should choose others might do to us, and we shall deserve the favors of Heaven.

If these are the principles upon which our national conduct is to be grounded, it will follow, that an impartial and unequivocal neutrality between the contending parties is prescribed to us as a duty, unless we are bound by some existing contract or stipulation, to make a common cause with one of them.

I have already said it: The natural state of all nations, with respect to one another, is a state of peace – *damus petimusque vicissim*:[21] It is what we have a right to expect *from* them, and for the same reason it is our duty to observe it *towards* them. In addition to this natural obligation, we are bound by express treaties with France, England, Holland and Prussia, to observe the laws of peace with the subjects of their different governments, and we have no right to interfere in their contentions. Whatever may be the current of our sentiments, or of our opinions; whatever may be the language suggested by our passions, or the wishes inspired by our affections, we are not constituted judges of the respective merits of their cause. From a feeling of gratitude towards a nation which assisted us in the days of our own calamity,[22] we may be disposed to throw a veil over their own errors and crimes, and wish them that success which their frantic enthusiasm has rendered so improbable. As the descendants of Englishmen, we may be willing to lose the memory of all the miseries they inflicted upon us in our just struggle against them, and even the relics of their resentment, which still refuse the complete fulfilment of the treaty of peace,[23] and we may wish them still to retain their reputation for successful courage and conduct in war. As men, we must undoubtedly lament the effusion of human blood, and the mass of misery and distress which is preparing for the great part of the civilized world; but as the citizens of a nation at a vast distance from the continent of Europe; of a nation whose happiness consists in a real independence, disconnected from all European interests and European politics, it is our duty to remain, the peaceable and silent, though sorrowful spectators of the sanguinary scene.

With the reasons for neutrality suggested by these considerations of natural duty and of positive stipulation, a forcible argument concurs, derived from our interest. In the general conduct of all the commercial European nations, the advantages which will be thrown into our hands, and the activity and vigor which will be given to every branch of our commerce, are too obvious to need any discussion. As the natural consequence of war, the necessities of all the belligerent powers must increase in proportion as their means of supply will diminish, and the profits, which must infallibly flow to us from their wants, can have no other limitation than the extent of our capacity to provide for them.

With all these inducements to a decided neutrality, let us look at the other side of the medal, and see what would be the consequence of our making ourselves partizans of the contest. First, we should be engaged in a quarrel, with the laws of nations against us. It would be a violation of our political duties; a departure from the principles of national justice, and an express breach of the positive stipulations of peace and friendship with the several belligerent powers, contained in the treaties which I have already mentioned. An act of partiality in favor of either party would be an act of perfidy to the other.

I have so full a confidence in the equity and virtue of my countrymen, that I should rest the argument on this point, if I had not perceived that a contrary system of policy is avowed by men of some influence among us, and openly recommended in some of the public prints of the day. A system, which professing to arise from an extraordinary attachment to the cause of Liberty and Equality, may in reality be traced to the common sources of private avarice, and private ambition, perhaps at once the cause and effect of an implicit devotion to France, and an antipathy to England, exceeding the limits of a national resentment.

To men of this description, arguments derived from the obligations of natural justice, or of written contract will be perfectly nugatory. "The Rights of Man," will be their answer to the one, and "Liberty and Equality," to the other. I apply, therefore, to a principle of more efficacious operation in their minds, if their own interest is in any degree connected with that of their country, and ask them what would be the inevitable consequence of a war with all Europe, excepting only the present prevailing power of France? The experience of the late war, would perhaps discourage an attempt on the part of Great Britain to conquer this Continent, but we have a sea-coast of twelve hundred miles everywhere open to invasion, and where is the power to protect it? We have a flourishing commerce, expanding to every part of the globe, and where will it turn when excluded from every market of the earth? We depend upon the returns of that commerce for many necessaries of life, and when those returns shall be cut off, where shall we look for the supply? We are in a great measure destitute of the defensive apparatus of war, and who will provide us with the arms and ammunition that will be indispensable? We feel severely at this moment, the burden of our public debt, and where are the funds to support us in the dreadful extremity to which our own madness and iniquity would reduce us? Not to mention the infallible destruction of our finances, and the national bankruptcy, which the friends of the system I am combating, would perhaps welcome as a blessing. Are these, Sir, imaginary apprehensions, or are they objects of trivial moment? Our national existence may depend upon the event of our councils in the present crisis, and to advise us to engage voluntarily in the war, is to aim a dagger at the heart of the country.

UNITED AND INDEPENDENT

AN ORATION, PRONOUNCED JULY 4, 1793, AT THE REQUEST OF THE INHABITANTS OF THE TOWN OF BOSTON, IN COMMEMORATION OF THE ANNIVERSARY OF AMERICAN INDEPENDENCE

John Quincy's defense of the Washington administration's policy of neutrality in the Marcellus essays, and his previous support for the English constitution in Publicola, left him open to the charge of being an antirepublican reactionary at a time when American enthusiasm for the French Revolution was at its height. The oration gave him the opportunity to refute these charges. He also set out one of the major assumptions that guided his understanding of international politics. The American Revolution was a world-historic event, planting the seeds of liberty and heralding the approaching fall of the governments of Europe amid the dissolution of the feudal order. John Quincy expressed optimism that the outcome would be new governments founded on the principles of freedom and political equality. On this score he certainly had near-term doubts, but he did believe that the old order was going, and that the rights of man would, or at least could, eventually win out. But that required the United States to remain true to its revolutionary principles, and probably for a great deal of time to come.

IT has been a custom, sanctioned by the universal practice of civilized Nations, to celebrate with anniversary solemnities, the return of the days which have been distinguished by events the most important to the happiness of the people. In countries where the natural dignity of mankind, has been degraded by the weakness of bigotry, or debased by the miseries of despotism, this customary celebration has degenerated into a servile mockery of festivity upon the birthday of a sceptered tyrant, or has dwindled to an unmeaning revel, in honour of some canonized fanatic, of whom nothing now remains but the name, in the calendar of antiquated superstition. In those more fortunate regions of the earth where Liberty has condescended to reside, the cheerful gratitude of her favoured people has devoted to innocent gaiety and useful relaxation from the toils of virtuous industry the periodical revolution of those days which have been rendered illustrious by the triumphs of freedom.

AMERICANS! Such is the nature of the institution which again calls your attention to celebrate the establishment of your national Independence. And surely since the creation of the heavenly orb which separated the day from the night, amid the unnumbered events which have diversified the history of the human race, none has ever occurred more highly deserving of celebration by every species of ceremonial, that can testify a sense of gratitude to the DEITY, and of happiness, derived from his transcendent favours.

IT is a wise and salutary institution, which forcibly recalls to the memory of freemen, the principles upon which they originally founded their labouring plan of state. It is a sacrifice at the altar of Liberty herself; – a renewal of homage to the Sovereign, who alone is worthy of our veneration; – a profession of political fidelity, expressive of our adherence to those maxims of liberal submission and obedient freedom, which in these favoured climes, have harmonized the long-contending claims of liberty and law. By a frequent recurrence to those sentiments and actions upon which the glory and felicity of the Nation rest supported, we are enabled to renew the moments of bliss which we are not permitted to retain; we secure a permanency to the exaltation which the Constitution of Nature has rendered fleeting, and a perennial existence to enjoyments which the lot of humanity has made transitory.

THE "feelings, manners and principles" which led to the Independence of our Country; such, my friends and fellow-citizens is the theme of our present commemoration. The field is extensive; it is fruitful: but the copious treasures of its fragrance have already been gathered by the hands of genius; and there now remains for the gleaning of mental indigence, nought but the thinly scattered sweets which have escaped the vigilance of their industry.

THEY were the same feelings, manners and principles, which conducted our venerable forefathers from the unhallowed shores of oppression; which inspired them with the sublime purpose of converting the forests of a wilderness into the favourite mansion of Liberty; of unfolding the gates of a new world, as a refuge for the victims of persecution in the old. The feelings of injured freedom, the manners of social equality, and the principles of eternal justice.

HAD the Sovereigns of England pursued the policy prescribed by their interest, had they not provoked the hostilities of their Colonists against the feeble fortress of their authority they might perhaps have retained to this day an Empire which would have been but the more durable, for resting only upon the foundation of immemorial custom, and national affection.

INCUMBERED however with the oppressive glory of a successful war, which had enriched the pride of Britain, with the spoils of her own oppulence, and replenished the arrogance in proportion as it had exhausted the resources of the nation; an adventurous ministry, catching at every desperate expedient to support the ponderous burden of the national dignity, and stimulated by the perfidious instigations of their dependents in America, abandoned the profitable commercial policy of their predecessors, and superadded to the lucrative system of monopoly, which we had always tolerated as the price of their protection, a system of internal taxation from which they hoped to derive a fund for future corruption, and a supply for future extravagance.

THE nation eagerly grasped at the proposal. – The situation, the condition, the sentiments of the colonies, were subjects upon which the people of Britain were divided between ignorance and error. The endearing ties of consanguinity, which had connected their ancestors, with those of the Americans, had been gradually loosened to the verge of dissolution, by the slow but ceaseless hand of time. Instead of returning the sentiments of fraternal affection, which animated the Americans, they indulged their vanity with preposterous opinions of insulting superiority: they considered us, not as fellow-subjects equally entitled with themselves to every privilege of Englishmen; but as wretched outcasts, upon whom they might safely load the burden, while they reserved to themselves the advantages of the national grandeur. It has been observed, that the nations the most highly favoured with freedom, have not always been the most friendly to the liberty of others. The people of Britain, expected to feel none of the oppression which a parliamentary tyranny might impose upon the Americans; on the contrary, they expected an alleviation of their burden, from the accumulation of ours, and vainly hoped that by the stripes inflicted upon us, their wounds would be healed.

THE King – Need it be said, that he adopted as the offspring of his own affections, a plan so favourable to the natural propensity of royalty towards arbitrary power. Depending upon the prostituted valour of his mercenary legions, he was deaf to the complaints, he was inexorable to the remonstrances of violated freedom. Born and educated to the usual prejudices of hereditary dominion, and habitually accustomed to the syren-song of adulation, he was ready to believe what the courtly tribe about his throne did not fail to assure him; that complaint was nothing more than the murmur of sedition, and remonstrance the clamour of rebellion.

BUT they knew not the people with whom they had to contend. A people, sagacious and enlightened to discern, cool and deliberate to discuss, firm and resolute to maintain their rights.

FROM the first appearance of the system of parliamentary oppression under the form of a stamp-act, it was met, by the determined opposition of the whole American Continent. The annals of other nations have produced instances of successful struggles to break a yoke previously imposed; but the records of History did not perhaps furnish an example of a people whose penetration had anticipated the operations of tyranny, and whose spirit had disdained to suffer an experiment upon their liberties. The ministerial partizans had flattered themselves with the expectation that the Act would execute itself; that before the hands of Freedom could be raised to repel the usurpation, they would be loaded with fetters; that the American Samson would be shorn of his locks while asleep; and when thus bereaved of his strength, might be made their sport with impunity. – Vain illusion! – Instantaneous and forceful, as an electric spark, the fervid spirit of resistance pervaded every part of the country; and at the moment, when the operation of the system was intended to commence, it was indignantly rejected, by three millions of men; high-minded men, determined to sacrifice their existence, rather than resign the Liberty, from which, all its enjoyments were derived.

IT is unnecessary to pursue the detail of obstinacy and cruelty on the one part; of perseverance and fortitude on the other, until the period when every chord which had bound the two countries together, was destroyed by the violence of reciprocal hostilities, and the representatives of America, adopted the measure, which was already dictated by the wishes of their constituents; they declared the United Colonies free, sovereign and independent States.

AMERICANS! let us pause for a moment to consider the situation of our country, at that eventful day when our national existence commenced. In the full possession and enjoyment of all those prerogatives for which you then dared to adventure upon "all the varieties of untried being," the calm and settled moderation of the mind, is scarcely competent to conceive the tone of heroism, to which the souls of freemen were exalted in that hour of perilous magnanimity.

SEVENTEEN times has the sun, in the progress of his annual revolutions, diffused his prolific radiance over the plains of Independent America. Millions of hearts which then palpitated with the rapturous glow of patriotism, have already been translated to brighter worlds; to the abodes of more than mortal freedom.

Other millions have arisen to receive from their parents and benefactors, the inestimable recompense of their achievements. A large proportion of the audience, whose benevolence is at this moment listening to the speaker of the day, like him were at that period too little advanced beyond the threshold of life to partake of the divine enthusiasm which inspired the American bosom; which prompted her voice to proclaim defiance to the thunders of Britain; which consecrated the banners of her armies; and finally erected the holy temple of American Liberty, over the tomb of departed tyranny. It is from those who have already passed the meridian of life; it is from you, ye venerable assertors of the rights of mankind, that we are to be informed, what were the feelings which swayed within your breasts and impelled you to action, when, like the stripling of Israel, with scarce a weapon to attack, and without a shield for your defence, you met, and undismayed, engaged with the gigantic greatness of the British power. Untutored in the disgraceful science of human butchery; destitute of the fatal materials which the ingenuity of man has combined, to sharpen the scythe of death; unsupported by the arm of any friendly alliance; and unfortified against the powerful assaults of an unrelenting enemy, you did not hesitate at that moment, when your coasts were infested by a formidable fleet, when your territories were invaded by a numerous and veteran army, to pronounce the sentence of eternal separation from Britain, and to throw the gauntlet at a power the terror of whose recent triumphs was almost co-extensive with the earth – The interested and selfish propensities which in times of prosperous tranquility have such powerful dominion over the heart, were all expelled, and in their stead, the public virtues, the spirit of personal devotion to the common cause, a contempt of every danger in comparison with the subserviency of the country, had assumed an unlimited controul. The passion for the public, had absorbed all the rest; as the glorious luminary of heaven extinguishes in a stood of refulgence the twinkling splendor of every inferior planet. Those of you my countrymen, who were actors in those interesting scenes, will best know, how feeble, and impotent is the language of this description to express the impassioned emotions of the soul, with which you were then agitated: yet it were injustice to conclude from thence, or from the greater prevalence of private and personal motives in these days of calm serenity, that your sons have degenerated from the virtues of their fathers. Let it rather be a subject of pleasing reflection to you, that the generous and disinterested energies, which you were summoned to display, are permitted by the bountiful indulgence of Heaven to remain latent in the bosoms of your children. From the present prosperous appearance of our public affairs, we may admit a rational hope that our country will have no occasion to require of us those extraordinary and heroic exertions which it was your fortune to exhibit. But from the common versatility of all human destiny, should the prospect hereafter darken, and the clouds of public misfortune thicken to a tempest; should the voice of our country's calamity ever call us to her relief, we swear by the precious memory of the sages who toiled, and of the heroes who bled in her defence, that we will prove ourselves not unworthy of the prize, which they so dearly purchased; that we will act as the faithful disciples of those who so magnanimously taught us the instructive lesson of republican virtue.

SEVEN years of ineffectual hostility, an hundred millions of treasure fruitlessly expended, and uncounted thousands of human lives sacrificed to no purpose, at length taught the dreadful lesson of wisdom to the British Government, and compelled them to relinquish a claim which they had long since been unable to maintain. The pride of Britain, which should have been humbled, was only mortified. With sullen impotence, she yielded to the pressure of accumulated calamity, and closed with reluctance an inglorious war, in which she had often been the object, and rarely the actor of a triumph.

THE various occurrences of our national history, since that period, are within the recollection of all my hearers. The relaxation and debility of the political body, which succeeded the violent exertions it had made during the war: the total inefficacy of the recommendatory federal system, which had been formed in the bosom of contention; the peaceable and deliberate adoption of a more effectual national constitution by the people of the union, and the prosperous administration of that government, which has repaired the shattered fabric of public confidence, which has strengthened the salutary bands of national union, and restored the bloom and vigour of impartial justice, to the public countenance, afford a subject of pleasing contemplation to the patriotic mind. The repeated unanimity of the nation has placed at the head of the American councils, the heroic leader, whose prudence and valour conducted to victory the armies of freedom; and the two first offices of this Commonwealth, still exhibit the virtues and employ the talents of the venerable patriots, whose firm and disinterested devotion to the cause of Liberty, was rewarded by the honourable distinction of a British proscription. Americans! the voice of grateful freedom is a stranger to the language of adulation. While we wish these illustrious sages to be assured that the memory of their services is impressed upon all our hearts, in characters, indelible to the latest period of time, we trust that the most acceptable tribute of respect which can be offered to their virtues, is found in the confidence of their countrymen. From the fervent admiration of future ages, when the historians of America, shall trace from their examples the splendid pattern of public virtue, their merits will receive a recompense of much more precious estimation than can be conferred by the most flattering testimonials of contemporaneous applause.

THE magnitude and importance of the great event which we commemorate, derives a vast accession from its influence upon the affairs of the world, and its operation upon the history of mankind. It has already been observed that the origin of the American Revolution bears a character different from that of any other civil contest, that had ever arisen among men. It was not the convulsive struggle of slavery to throw off the burden of accumulated oppression, but the deliberate, tho' energetic effort of freemen, to repel the insidious approaches of tyranny. It was a contest involving the elementary principles of government, a question of right between the sovereign and the subject which in its progress had a tendency to introduce among the civilized nations of Europe, the discussion of a topic the first in magnitude, which can attract the attention of mankind, but which for many centuries, the gloomy shades of despotism had overspread with impenetrable darkness. The French nation cheerfully supported an alliance with the United States, and a war with Britain, during the course of which a large body of troops and considerable fleets were sent by the French government, to act in conjunction with their new allies. The union which had at first been formed by the coalescence of a common enmity, was soon strengthened by the bonds of a friendly intercourse, and the subjects of an arbitrary prince, in fighting the battles of freedom, soon learnt to cherish the cause of Liberty itself. By a natural and easy application to themselves of the principles upon which the Americans asserted the justice of their warfare, they were led to inquire into the nature of the obligation which prescribed their submission to their own sovereign; and when they discovered that the consent of the people is the only legitimate source of authority, they necessarily drew the conclusion that their own obedience was no more than the compulsive acquiescence of servitude, and they waited only for a favourable opportunity to recover the possession of those enjoyments, to which they had never forfeited the right. Sentiments of a similar nature, by a gradual and imperceptible progress, secretly undermined all the foundations of their government; and when the necessities of the sovereign reduced him to the inevitable expedient of appealing to the benevolence of the people, the magic talisman of despotism was broken, the spell of prescriptive tyranny was dissolved, and the pompous pageant of their monarchy, instantaneously crumbled to atoms.

THE subsequent European events which have let slip the dogs of war, to prey upon the vitals of humanity; which have poured the torrent of destruction over the fairest harvests of European fertility; which have unbound the pinions of desolation, and sent her forth to scatter pestilence and death among the nations; the scaffold, smoking with the blood of a fallen monarch; the corpse-covered field, where agonizing nature struggles with the pangs of dissolution; permit me my happy countrymen, to throw a pall over objects like these, which could only spread a gloom upon the face of our festivity. Let us rather indulge the pleasing and rational anticipation of the period, when all the nations of Europe shall partake of the blessings of equal liberty and universal peace. Whatever issue may be destined by the will of Heaven to await the termination of the present European commotions, the system of feudal absurdity has received an irrecoverable wound, and every symptom indicates its approaching dissolution. The seeds of Liberty are plentifully sown. However severe the climate, however barren the soil of the regions in which they have been received, such is the native exuberance of the plant, that it must eventually flourish with luxuriant profusion. The governments of Europe must fall; and the only remaining expedient in their power, is to gather up their garments and fall with decency. The bonds of civil subjection must be loosened by the discretion of civil authority, or they will be shivered by the convulsive efforts of slavery itself. The feelings of benevolence involuntarily make themselves a party to every circumstance that can affect the happiness of mankind; they are ever ready to realize the sanguine hope, that the governments to rise upon the ruins of the present systems will be immutably founded upon the principles of freedom, and administered by the genuine maxims of moral subordination and political equality. We cherish with a fondness which cannot be chilled by the cold unanimated philosophy of scepticism, the delightful expectation that the cancer of arbitrary power will be radically extracted from the human constitution; that the sources of oppression will be drained; that the passions which have hitherto made the misery of mankind, will be disarmed of all their violence, and give place to the soft controul of mild and amiable sentiments, which shall unite in social harmony the innumerable varieties of the human race. Then shall the nerveless arm of superstition no longer interpose an impious barrier between the beneficence of Heaven, and the adoration of its votaries: then shall the most distant regions of the earth be approximated by the gentle attraction of a liberal intercourse: then shall the fair fabric of universal Liberty rise upon the durable foundation of social equality, and the long-expected aera of human felicity, which has been announced by prophetic inspiration, and described in the most enraptured language of the Muses, shall commence its splendid progress – Visions of bliss! with every breath to Heaven we speed an ejaculation that the time may hasten, when your reality shall be no longer the ground of votive supplication, but the theme of grateful acknowledgment: when the choral gratulations of the liberated myriads of the elder world, in symphony, sweeter than the music of the spheres, shall hail your country, Americans! as the youngest daughter of Nature, and the first-born offspring of Freedom.

ESSAYS OF COLUMBUS

For John Quincy, the controversy over Citizen Genet provided the opportunity to warn of the dangers to union and independence created by foreign influence in the American political process. Writing in the Boston newspapers as Columbus, he argued that the critical vulnerability exposed by Genet was the tendency of domestic factions to link themselves with a foreign nation to gain political power that they could not otherwise achieve. This tendency, Columbus said, would create a cycle that would subvert republican government. In response to one faction aligning with a foreign nation, that faction's political opponents, as a matter of political calculation and self-preservation, would seek out their own connection with a foreign power. This cycle would turn American political parties into agents of foreign nations.

COLUMBUS II (COLUMBIAN CENTINEL, DECEMBER 24, 1793)

When the Minister from the French Republic declared his deter-mination to appeal from the decision of the regular and consti-tuted authority, upon the construction of certain treaties, to the people of America, the first sentiments which the declaration excited in the breasts of that people, was the spontaneous emo-tion of the heart. They considered it as an insolent outrage offered to the man, who was deservedly the object of their grateful affec-tion; as an insult upon the character of their common friend and benefactor, and they spurned the attempt to degrade their Hero, with scorn and disdain. "The people," says Junius, "are seldom mistaken in their opinions, in their sentiments they are never wrong." When the Americans were rudely called upon to pro-nounce upon the conduct of the patriot, whose disinterested vir-tues and superior talents had been employed in their service through all the vicissitudes of fortune; whose generous magna-nimity had supported them in the most distressing moments of national depression; whose expanded patriotism had participated with rapture in the most blissful scenes of national exultation; the glory of their war, and the ornament of their peace; when a beardless foreigner, whose name was scarcely enrolled upon the catalogue of Liberty; a petulant stripling, whose commission from a friendly power was his only title to their respect, and whose only merit was his country, presumed to place himself in opposi-tion to the *father of their country*, and to call for their approbation to support his claims, they viewed the application as an indignity offered to themselves, and even before their judgment had delib-erated upon the merits of the case, they rejected the arrogant pretensions of the foreigner, with pointed indignation.

When they came, however, to consider the transaction inde-pendent of any reference to their own prepossessions and feel-ings they immediately perceived, that the earlier decision of their judgment was perfectly conformable to the dictates of their hearts and that the voice of reason and justice was in exact unison with that of their affections. They had delegated to the Congress of the United States the power to regulate their commercial intercourse with foreign nations. They had delegated to the President, the power of negotiating with the ministers of foreign power, and with the concurrence of the Senate, to make treaties with them. They had specially directed their President in the Constitution, which defined his authority and prescribed his duties, to "take care, that the laws be faithfully executed;" and, if, in the course of his administration, a difference of opinion upon the meaning of a national compact should arise between him and the agent of a foreign power, they had not reserved to themselves the right of judging between them. Nor did they imagine, that they had thereby imparted to their Chief Magistrate, a power in the smallest degree arbitrary.

For if the construction, upon which his measures were grounded, should be erroneous, they had provided a judiciary power, competent to correct his mistakes. If he proceeded upon a wilful and treacherous misinterpretation, they had secured the means of removing him from his office by impeachment; but in either case, they had retained no appellate jurisdiction to themselves. It was therefore clearly demonstrated, that the intention of the Minister, was no less hostile to the Constitution, than insulting to the government of the Union. Nor was the measure of the Envoy supported by a shadow of right on his part. A foreign Agent, his official powers were circumscribed within the limits of his commission; and his right to negotiate was only commensurate with his credentials. Where then was the commission; where were the credentials, which authorised him to treat with the people of America, through any other medium than that of their government? He had not, he could not have any at all, and the impotent menace of the Minister could serve no other purpose, than to betray the ignorance and heedless rashness of the man.

The few remaining partizans of the citizen Minister among us were aware of the inauspicious operation, which this declaration would have upon the public mind, and struggled with fruitless endeavor, to extricate him from the net which his own folly had woven; they shuffled and equivocated; they quibbled and denied; but their ingenuity could not keep pace with his impetuosity. No sooner did their toilsome industry raise a feeble rampart in his defence, than his own violence would immediately batter it down. Did they venture to dispute the fact? He was ready to produce "damning proof" against himself, and with many self-admiring commendations upon his own republican frankness and energy, to silence every friendly sceptic, by an avowal of his guilt. Did they strain every nerve to create a distinction in his behalf, and explain his intention of appeal, to be merely an insult upon the person of the Chief Magistrate, and not upon the government of *America*? He was sure to disclaim so frail a discrimination, and to declare that he was incapable of disrespect to the "Hero of Liberty," but that his threat was pointed at the government of the Union. It was in vain to search for precedents of diplomatic impudence, to give a color of authority to his proceedings; worm-eaten records of elder times, the musty prescriptions of superannuated wisdom, could afford no measure for the mighty grasp of his aspiring ambition. The learned sages of national jurisprudence, whose indefatigable labors had compiled a system of rules for the conduct of sovereign powers, founded upon the immutable laws of natural justice, and the immemorial practice of civilized nations, had too long been rewarded for their exertions, by the veneration of ages. They had all written in chains, and could therefore be no guides for him who had been so recently let loose.

The appeal is therefore made. Addresses to the Republicans of New York; Letters to the President of the Union; Letters to Citizen Duplaine, to General Moultrie; Letters to the Secretary of State; Letters to the Lieutenant Governor of *Massachusetts*; Protests against the revocation of Citizen Duplaine's exequatur, "and all the weapons of a wordy war," crowd in rapid succession upon the public prints; as if the judgment of the people, like the kingdom of Heaven, were to be taken by violence. But though the

Minister "can call spirits from the vasty deep," yet it is beyond the reach of his magic, to "make them come when he calls for them." The people hear his ravings, with the same indifference, that they hear the roaring of the ocean on the beach. It is the evidence of a tempest at a distance, which heightens their enjoyment of the serene tranquility of their own hemisphere. The Ambassador finding this attempt lately to fail, though baffled, does not appear to be disconcerted: his original and inventive genius multiplies with amazing facility the American Jurisdictions, and in the fury and whirlwind of his passions for appealing, he appeals not only to the people of *America*, but to the Congress of the Union, and to the Legislature of *Massachusetts* also. Appeal at any rate he must; and as he has already been acknowledged to be the first typographical negotiator, he may with equal propriety be admitted to the claim of the first *Minister of Appeals* upon record.

Waiving for the present any observations upon the two last of these appeals, which are equally unwarrantable with the first; and setting aside the constitutional objection to the first, which has already been the subject of some of the preceding reflections; I must now request your indulgence, Mr. Russell, with a few remarks upon the mode in which the Minister has conducted his appeal to the people, and upon the wisdom of the constitutional policy, which has entrusted the exclusive right of political communication with foreign powers to the government of the Union.

The declaration of the Ambassador, was understood, at the time, as meaning, that he would raise an insurrection of the people against the measures of the government. It could not easily admit of any other construction, because insurrection is the only method whereby the people can reverse the decisions of their government. If however any doubt could be entertained of the meaning conveyed by the expression, the uniform tenor of every measure adopted by the Minister since that period, serves to confirm the opinion which was formed at first. The numerous newspaper publications which have been already mentioned, are so many addresses to the people of *America*; else why is the correspondence of a foreigner intruded upon the American public? All those letters, addressed to particular individuals, that pretended answer to a complimentary address from the republicans of *New York*, that doughty protest against the dismission of citizen Duplaine, crammed like a loaded blunderbuss, with all the future vengeance of the French republic, all must be considered as the mere vehicles of sedition against the government of the Union. Else why are a few citizens of *New York* addressed as constituting the whole American Republic? And why is an official, though very irregular communication to the chief magistrate of this commonwealth, immediately published in the newspapers, by the authority of the protestor, before anything has been transacted upon it? No doubt they are all meant as appeals to the people of *America*; appeals to their generosity, appeals to their gratitude, but above all, appeals to their fears. The people of *America*, however, are not easily terrified or cajoled into measures apparently destructive to their own happiness. The resentment of the whole nation was not easily to be excited without a cause, against a government which was daily gaining upon all their affections by promoting their happiness. Mr. Genet therefore endeavors to support his failing influence by connecting himself and his interests with a particular party of American citizens, separate from the whole body of the people: a party professing republican sanctity beyond the rest of their fellow-citizens, and scarcely endeavoring to disguise sentiments, hostile to the national government of the country. How far this connection has proceeded, and whether any regular plan of operations has been concerted between these new associates, cannot be fully ascertained; but we have known an American jury, compelled by the clamors of a collected multitude, to acquit a prisoner without the unanimity required by our laws. We have heard of printed caricatures circulating through *Philadelphia*, representing the President of the Union, and a Judge of the Supreme Court, with guillotine suspended over their heads. We have seen twenty citizens of *Boston*, all of them inoffensive, many of them personally respectable, held up as objects of detestation, to the crew of a French armed vessel, and posted at the mast; we have known a citizen of *New York*, and a member of their Legislature, threatened by an anonymous assassin with inevitable death, for expressing with the freedom of an American, his opinion upon the proceedings of the Minister; and we now witness the formation of a lengthening chain of democratic societies, assuming to themselves the exercise of privileges, which belong only to the whole people, and under the semblance of a warmer zeal for the cause of liberty, than the rest of the people, tacitly preparing to control the operations of the government and dictate laws to the country. Heretofore, in the most exasperated times of our political dissentions, upon occasions when the public mind had been raised to the highest pitch of irritation, the sacred obligations of a jury, have always been preserved inviolate, and no American ever thought of giving a bias to their decisions, by the menace of external violence; as little would an American villain have thought of the guillotine as an instrument of punishment. The proscription of our citizens under the designation of aristocrats was evidently effected by a combination of foreign habits with domestic malice. Even the expedient of threatening assassination by anonymous letters, was I believe unprecedented among us: And as to the democratic societies, they are so perfectly affiliated to the Parisian Jacobins, that their origin from a common parent cannot possibly be mistaken. These symptoms never originated in the healthy constitution of American freedom; they are all indications of an imported distemper, a distemper in comparison with which, if it should spread over the continent, the pestilence which has so lately depopulated a sister city, and called for the exertions of all our tenderest sympathies, was a public blessing.

To divide in order to govern, has been one of the favorite maxims of political villany, ever since the relative stations of tyrant and slave have been the fashion of the world. Every public measure of the French Minister, since the profession of his resolution to appeal, may be traced to the policy of arming one part of

America against the other. His intended application to Congress to pass his official conduct under their examination militates against all the principles which he has professed as much as against the American constitution; but he expects it will furnish him with an opportunity to "place under the inspection of *every member*, his instructions, his correspondence, his conferences," and if the whole body, in imitation of their constituents should turn their ear from the voice of the charmer, some individuals may perhaps be found among them, who will listen with complacency. If he cannot corrupt the sacred fountain of legislation, he hopes at least to poison some of the streams which flow from it. If he cannot make the Congress itself subservient to his factious purposes, he expects at least to inflame the divisions, which have naturally arisen from the collision of opinions and interests in an assembly of freemen. By dividing the parts, he hopes to control the whole.

The same disposition is discovered in his application to the commander in chief of the Commonwealth, and in his demand that the *Legislature of Massachusetts* should suspend their legislative functions to sit as a court of judication upon the official conduct of Duplaine. He could not imagine that our general court had forgotten the interdiction pronounced by the constitution of the state, against the exercise on their part of any judicial powers, other than those which are necessarily involved in the execution of their legislative duties: – But the nice and delicate interstructure of our general and particular governments had not escaped his penetration. He saw two mighty powers participating in large portions of the American sovereignty. He perceived that although they had been skillfully contrived to co-operate in conducting the affairs of the people, yet that the several proportions of the public authority had not been distributed between them with such perfect accuracy, as to leave their respective rights in every instance unquestionable. Had not his acquaintance with the operations of the human heart informed him of the natural tendency which two separate and concurrent powers must have to mutual hostility, a recent occurrence which has appeared since his arrival in *America*, might have taught him that when *"two authorities are up; neither supreme; confusion may be most easily introduced into the gap, to take the one by the other."* From a comparative view of all these transactions, it appears therefore clear, as the noon-day beam, that the intention of the Ambassador has been to lay hold of every prejudice, to fasten upon every passion, which could be raised in opposition to the government, and to weaken the force of United America, by placing its component parts in hostile array against each other.

And now, Sir, do not the consequences of this foreign usurpation force themselves with irresistible conviction upon the heart of every American, who feels interested in the independence of his country? Among the nations of antiquity, the *Athenians* were equally distinguished for the freedom of their government, the mildness of their laws, the sagaciousness of their understanding, and the urbanity of their manners. Their Constitution was purely democratic, and their penal laws were few; but the bare appearance of a stranger in the assemblies of the people, they made punishable with death, from a deep and well-grounded conviction, that of all the dangers which encompass the liberties of a republican State, the intrusion of a foreign influence into the administration of their affairs, is the most alarming, and requires the opposition of the severest caution. The American Constitution was framed upon the same principles, and provides with equal vigilance, though in a different form, against the same evil. It has entrusted with punctilious nicety all the political intercourse of the country, with other nations, to the several departments of the national government. It does not permit any of the States upon any terms whatever, to enter into a treaty, alliance, or confederation; nor without the consent of Congress so much as to enter into any agreement or compact with a foreign power. And if the wisdom of this provision needed any proof in addition to the whole tenor of human history, the train of events which is the subject of these remarks would support it, with *"confirmation strong as proof of holy writ."*

In a state of civil and political liberty, parties are to the public body, what the passions are to the individual. And as the passions are said to be the elements of life, so the animated and vivifying spirit of party seems to be essential to the existence of genuine freedom. Like the passions, too, it is a prolifick source of misery, as well as of enjoyment: Like them it requires a severe and continual exertion of restraint and regulation, to prevent its breaking out into excesses destructive to the Constitution. It can be no subject of lamentation to a rational mind, to perceive the political differences which arise among our own citizens. Even the degree of warmth which mingles itself in our civil discussions, is an inconvenience necessarily connected with the enjoyment of our most valuable rights; the candidates for popular favor may endeavor to further their personal views, by standing forth as the advocates and champions of the public interest, and diversify their claims in proportion to the diversity of public opinions; the people suffer no detriment from their animosities; and the general welfare is perhaps promoted, by placing the jealousy of one patriot as a guard over the ambition of another. But here let it rest.

The interference of foreigners upon any pretence whatever, in the dissensions of fellow-citizens, must be as inevitably fatal to the liberties of the State, as the admission of strangers to arbitrate upon the domestic differences of man and wife is destructive to the happiness of a private family. If the partizans of any particular faction cease to rely upon their own talents and services to support their influence among their countrymen, and link themselves in union with an external power, the principles of self-defence, the instinct of self-preservation itself, will suggest a similar connection to their opponents; whichever of the party nominally prevails, the whole country is really enslaved; alternately the sport of every caprice, that directs the conduct of two foreign sovereigns, alternately the victim of every base intrigue which foreign hatred and jealousy may disguise under the mask of friendship and benevolence.

Is this a condition tolerable to the imagination of American freemen? Is this a state for which the country has, with such glorious exertions, strained at every nerve, and bled at every vein, in throwing off the shameful fetters of a foreign bondage? Was it worthy of the toils which our sages, and our heroes endured? Was it worthy of the generous and heroic self-devotion, which offered the slaughtered thousands of our friends and brethren, as a willing sacrifice at the holy altar of American Independence, to be made the miserable bubbles of foreign speculation, to be blown like feathers to and fro as the varying breath of foreign influence should be directed: to be bandied about from one nation to another, subservient to the purposes of their mutual resentments, and played with as the passive instruments of their interests and passions? Perish the American! whose soul is capable of submitting to such a degrading servitude! Perish the American, whose prostituted heart could forsake the genuine purity of our national worship, and offer at a foreign shrine the tribute of his slavish adoration!

It was to eradicate, as far as human skill could effect, a weed so noxious to our political soil; it was to deprive the honourable spies from foreign nations of the means of tampering with particular portions of the American people, that the policy of their national Constitution confined their agency to the government of the Union. Without attempting to involve ourselves in the mazes of ancient history, let us attend only to the occurrences which have happened within our own recollection. If we inquire what is the cause which has been within a quarter of a century, fatal to the Liberties of *Sweden*, of *Geneva*, of *Holland*, and of *Poland*, the answer will be one and the same. It was the association of internal faction, and external power; it was the interference of other nations in their domestic divisions; and if, while all these terrible examples of national humiliation and misery are staring us in the face, we behold a foreign Agent among ourselves, violating the spirit and intention of our Constitution, and pursuing every measure which can tend to involve us in the same ruin, and add us to the melancholy catalogue of subjugated free-men; while we drop a tear to the memory of their Liberty, let us remain firm and immoveably faithful to our own; and remember that the eye of the basilisk is less to be dreaded, than the designs of such a man.

CHAPTER TWO

MINISTER TO THE DUTCH REPUBLIC, 1794–1797

INTRODUCTION

On June 3, 1794, after attending a meeting of the proprietors of the Boston theater, John Quincy Adams stopped by the post office and picked up a letter from Philadelphia. The letter, dashed off on the afternoon of May 26, was from his father. "The Secretary of State called upon me this morning to inform me by order of the President that it was determined to nominate you to go to Holland as Resident Minister." John Adams argued that he should accept: "Your Knowledge of Dutch and French, your Education in that Country, your Acquaintance with my old Friends there will give you Advantages beyond many others. It will require all your Prudence and all your other Virtues as well as your Talents.... Go and see with how little Wisdom this World is governed."[1]

After agreeing to the post, John Quincy traveled to Philadelphia for meetings with President Washington, Secretary of State Edmund Randolph, and Secretary of the Treasury Alexander Hamilton. From them he learned that his assignment would be focused on managing America's loans with the Dutch Republic, and to report on developments in Europe. He was ordered to stop first in London to pass on a diplomatic pouch to Chief Justice John Jay. Jay had been dispatched by Washington to negotiate a settlement of outstanding differences between the two countries left over from the Revolutionary War treaty of peace, as well as from the recent British depredations against American commerce.

When John Quincy arrived in London, he was informed by Jay and Thomas Pinckney, the American minister in London, that a treaty was nearing completion. Under the draft treaty, the British agreed to evacuate the western posts they had held since the end of the Revolutionary War by June 1796, and to permit limited trade with the British West Indies during the present war and for two years thereafter. The governments would arbitrate three disputed matters: the eastern boundary of Maine; the claims of Americans to compensation for recent maritime seizures; and the claims of British merchants to debts held against American citizens prior to the Revolution. The American negotiators, however, essentially abandoned the revolutionary era's goal of freedom of the seas. Jay set aside a critical element of John Adams's Model Treaty of 1776 – free ships make free goods – which had become an integral part of the 1778 commercial agreement with France as well as in America's other treaties. Jay's draft treaty moved considerably toward the preferred British definition of neutral rights. The United States also explicitly foreswore the use of coercive economic instruments, such as commercial discrimination against the ships and goods of the other nation, and debt sequestration, which the Republicans in the United States believed were essential tools in dealing with Britain.

On his arrival in the Netherlands in November 1794, John Quincy tried to maintain a low diplomatic and social profile. The country was riven between competing pro-French and pro-English factions. Matters were complicated when a French army occupied the country in January 1795. One of the principal tasks of an American minister abroad was to gather information and to provide analysis of important developments to his superiors in the United States. John Quincy provided a stream of detailed reporting to Philadelphia about the situation in the Netherlands and Europe. He relied on the following: first-hand observations; frequent meetings with Dutch officials, important private citizens,

American businessmen, and travelers; the careful study of documents and local and foreign newspapers; and the comparison of thoughts with others in the diplomatic community. These sources had to be filtered critically, especially when he felt that he might be manipulated by foreign agents and businessmen. Of particular interest was the policy that France adopted toward its new Dutch "sister republic." He analyzed the myriad changes in the French government and its growing hostility to the United States, and the effect of revolution on European politics and civilization.

John Quincy had assumed that dealing with American finances in the Netherlands would be relatively easy. Unfortunately, the consortium of bankers that managed the loans seemed alarmingly indifferent to the importance of making payments on time, especially if it involved any short-term risk of their own capital. For his part, the American minister was determined to uphold the financial standing of his country. Earlier in life, John Quincy had railed against the nation's failure to support public credit overseas. Now he was confronted with the prospect of an American default on his watch. He badgered the bankers constantly. He had to tread carefully, given Secretary of the Treasury Hamilton's initial instructions to defer to them.

In mid-October 1795, John Quincy received an urgent dispatch from Secretary of State Randolph to proceed immediately to London on business related to Jay's treaty. The Senate, in a special session held in secret, approved the treaty by the barest of constitutional majorities (20–10) while rejecting the provision limiting the size of American ships to the British West Indies to seventy tons. When news of the terms of the treaty leaked out, the Republican opposition exploded with anger because of what it regarded as a virtual capitulation to Britain. John Quincy was particularly concerned by reports that the US House of Representatives might refuse to fund the treaty, in which case the British would undoubtedly refuse to evacuate the posts they still held in the American Northwest. War would be the likely result.

Within a few weeks of arriving back at The Hague in May

1796, John Quincy was relieved immensely to learn that the House of Representatives, by the narrowest of margins, had finally approved legislation to implement the Jay Treaty. Now that the British had definitely agreed to surrender the American frontier posts, John Quincy thought that a cold peace with Britain had been achieved. France would again become the most immediate threat to the United States. He observed with alarm the continued deterioration in Franco-American relations caused (so the French insisted) by America's hostile actions – especially Jay's treaty, which they claimed to be a virtual alliance with Britain. John Quincy believed this was an erroneous, misinformed view. The United States was acting well within its legitimate rights as a neutral party, which actually benefited, or at least did not unfairly disadvantage, France. Based particularly on recent conversations in London, he believed that this misapprehension had been fostered by a radical cabal associated with the US diplomatic mission in Paris and the American minister, James Monroe. The cabal supposedly included Fulwar Skipwith, the American consul in Paris, Joel Barlow, the poet of democracy, and Thomas Paine. A number of foreign revolutionaries, including the United Irishman Wolfe Tone, were also said to circulate in Monroe's company.

As John Quincy understood matters, the cabal had convinced members of the newly constituted Directory that American foreign policy was being formulated by a narrow pro-British faction, and that the American people remained solidly behind France and their revolution. The solution, so the French had been told, was to make France's displeasure clear; to use all means to convince the public to refute the Jay Treaty and bring America into the war against Britain; and to elect as president a true friend, Thomas Jefferson, over the pro-British George Washington or his presumptive heir, John Adams. John Quincy assumed that this message was not being countered in Paris by Monroe, whether or not he was a member of the cabal himself.

In his role as minister in the Netherlands, John Quincy had no official standing or authorization to intervene in diplomacy with

France. He felt compelled, however, to try to establish backchannels to offer an accurate picture of American policy to France's more reasonable elements. He made his case to friendly Dutch republican leaders, such as Rutger Jan Schimmelpenninck, who he knew had contacts with their French counterparts. He tried unsuccessfully to arrange a meeting with Talleyrand when the ex-bishop passed through the Netherlands. His most promising channel proved to be Joseph Pitcairn, the American vice consul in Paris. Pitcairn had previously provided John Quincy with a good deal of useful information on the current French political scene, and he had cultivated a number of high-level contacts. Early the following year, he sent his brother Thomas to France, ostensibly on a sightseeing trip, as an unofficial emissary.

In August 1796, John Quincy learned that President Washington had appointed him as the new US representative to Portugal, with the rank of minister plenipotentiary. During the transition, however, there was a complication. In September 1796, Washington confirmed he would not stand for a third term. Federalist John Adams and Republican Thomas Jefferson were the main contenders to succeed him. John Quincy asked his father, if he was elected, not to consider him for any new government post, lest there be charges of nepotism and the establishment of an Adams dynasty. He also warned John Adams that all the art and intrigue of the French government would be hurled against him during and after the election, in favor of Jefferson. The Directory was not the only foreign influence at work in American politics, however: "You will also be prepared, I presume, for an opposition equally malignant though more concealed and perhaps, during the first period altogether inactive, from the rival influence of Great Britain."[2]

Meanwhile, things went from bad to worse in America's relations with France. The French Directory suspended its treaties with the United States and refused to receive Charles Cotesworth Pinckney, Washington's appointee as the new US minister to Paris, replacing Monroe. Reports reached The Hague that American vessels, sailing from British ports, had been seized and carried into French harbors, mainly by privateers who claimed American citizenship. French ships were also said to be attacking American vessels in the West Indies and encouraging the Algerines to resume attacks on US commerce in the Mediterranean. The French minister to the United States, Pierre Charles Adet, openly meddled in the presidential election in favor of the Republicans. Meanwhile, John Quincy heard via the diplomatic rumor mill that France planned to invade Canada and restore its rule there; that the Directory had revived Genet's plans to revolutionize Mexico; and that Paris had obtained from Spain title to Louisiana and the Floridas. After the election, Adet suspended diplomatic relations and sailed for home. The United States seemed as close to war with France as it had been with Britain in 1794. All of this was now John Adams's problem.

In July 1797, John Quincy finally received authorization from Secretary of State Timothy Pickering to proceed to Portugal to assume his new ministerial post. But there was a sudden change of plans: President Adams had decided to nominate him as minister plenipotentiary of the United States to the Kingdom of Prussia. John Adams did so on the grounds that he wanted John Quincy to negotiate treaties of commerce with Prussia and Sweden. Moreover, the president believed that Berlin was a far better place than Lisbon for one of the most respected American diplomats to gather essential intelligence: "I have reason to think that your whole Correspondence public and private has been as much esteemed as that of any former American Minister and more admired for a brilliancy of Style, and a freedom Independence and boldness of Sentiment, as well as a Sagacity equal to any [Conjecture] of material Events. Go on my worthy Son – in your glorious Career and may the Blessing of God crown you with Success."[3]

DIARY ENTRY (LONDON), OCTOBER 22, 1794

John Quincy's first official opportunity to apply his principles of American foreign policy occurred in October 1794, when he arrived in London to convey a pouch of diplomatic material to Chief Justice John Jay. Jay, together with the American minister to Britain, Thomas Pinckney, briefed John Quincy on the contents of a draft agreement with London, which was nearing completion, and asked for John Quincy's opinion. Jay and Pinckney's view was that, with all its defects, the draft agreement was preferable to war. John Quincy, although he thought something better might have been done, agreed. He based this judgment on the standards he believed should determine whether the United States should enter into any war voluntarily or should follow a diplomatic path that had a high probability of leading to war. That is, whether the nation's honor (independence) was fundamentally being challenged; whether there was a reasonable prospect of achieving military success that would materially benefit the nation; and whether the nation was assured it was not fighting for an unjust cause that violated the rights of other nations and their citizens.

22d. We passed this forenoon like the two former, and at length got through the discussion of the Treaty. It is far from being satisfactory to those gentlemen; it is much below the standard which I think would be advantageous to the country; but, with some alterations which are marked down, and to which it seems there is a probability they will consent, it is, in the opinion of the two plenipotentiaries, preferable to a war. And when Mr. Jay asked me my opinion, I answered that I could only acquiesce in that idea.

There are three points of view in which this instrument may be considered. As it respects the satisfaction to be received by the United States; as it relates to the satisfaction to be made; and as a permanent treaty of Commerce.

In the first place, the satisfaction proposed to be made to the United States for the recent depredations upon her commerce, the principal object of Mr. Jay's Mission. It is provided for in as

ample a manner as we could expect. That complete indemnification will be made to every individual sufferer, I fear, is impossible; but as the evil is done and cannot be recalled, I know not well
how we could require more than the stipulations of this treaty
contain. The delivery of the posts is protracted to a more distant
period than would be desirable; but the compensation made for
the past and the future detention of them will, I think, be a sufficient equivalent. The commerce with their West India Islands,
partially opened to us, will be of great importance, and indemnify us for the deprivation of the fur trade since the Treaty of
peace, as well as for the negroes carried away contrary to the
engagement of the Treaty, at least as far as it respects the nation.[4]

As to the satisfaction we are to make, I think it is no more than
in justice is due from us. The indemnity promised to British subjects, for their losses resulting from the non-compliance with the
Treaty on our part, is to be settled in the same manner with that
which our citizens are to receive, and in fact is to depend upon
the fulfilment of their engagement to deliver the posts. The
Article which provides against the future confiscation of debts
and of property in the funds, is useful, because it is honest. If its
operation should turn out more advantageous to them, it will be
more honorable to us; and I never can object to entering formally
into an obligation to do that which, upon every virtuous principle, ought to be done without it.

As a Treaty of Commerce, this Treaty will indeed be of little
use to us – and we never shall obtain anything more favorable, so
long as the principles of the Navigation Act are so obstinately
adhered to in this country. This system is so much a favorite with
the nation, that no Minister would dare depart from it. Indeed I
have no idea that we shall ever obtain, by compact, a better footing for our Commerce with this country than that on which it
now stands. And therefore, the shortness of time limited for the
operation of this part of the compact is, I think, beneficial to us.[5]

The Article proposed by Lord Loughborough, the Chancellor,
is certainly extremely liberal; although Mr. Jay thinks it best to

leave it as a subject for future consideration. It is, that in either country, the subjects or citizens of the other shall be exempted from *all the disabilities of alienage*. Such an Article would certainly tend to promote the friendly intercourse between the Nations, and I do not know that it could produce any material inconvenience to either. But it would be necessary to have an Act of Parliament to confirm the stipulation here, which, his Lordship says, may be obtained without difficulty. A more material obstacle arises from the Constitution of the United States, with one clause of which such an Article would certainly militate.[6]

This nobleman, who, during the American contest, was so conspicuous in his opposition to our principles and pretensions, by the name of Wedderburn, has assured Mr. Jay that at present, that controversy having been once determined and the point of separation settled, his dispositions are perfectly friendly towards America; that he thinks it for the interest of both countries to assimilate and draw together as much as possible; and that his sincere wishes are to facilitate the most liberal and amicable intercourse.[7]

The proposition which I have mentioned, and several others of inferior importance but equal liberality, seem to prove that his assurances are not disingenuous or false. And I think the intention of every man, who aims at levelling the barriers which perpetuate the unnecessary separation of Nations, and widen the distance between man and man, is at least deserving of applause.

We dined with Mr. Pinckney. Mr. Rutledge, and a Mr. Deas of Carolina, were of the company, as were also Mr. and Mrs. C. There was nothing particular observable in the former gentleman, and C. is the same prating coxcomb that he was ten years ago, though not quite so boisterous. He rattled away like a parrot, against the Ministry, who he said had no capacity, and defied the whole world to show one single wise measure they had adopted, since they entered into this foolish war.[8]

The conversation happening to turn upon the success of Lord Cornwallis[9] in India, C. affirmed that the Marquis was not entitled to any credit at all for what he had done there. It was impossible for him not to succeed. He went out with a force infinitely superior to any that had ever been employed in that country before, and the nations he subdued were totally unfit for war, and unable to contend with European forces. Lord Clive had done a thousand times more, with means incomparably smaller. Mr. Jay told him, he undervalued the character of the Indians, and said that he had always had a regard for Tippoo Saib, and his father Hyder Ali. "And for my part," he added, "I always wished them success." I was happy that in this respect my opinion coincided with Mr. Jay, notwithstanding C.'s confident assurance. His anti-ministerial invectives carried an appearance of affectation, as if he thought they gave him a kind of importance. In short, I can safely apply to him the observation which Dr. Johnson[10] made respecting Churchill, upon being told that he had lampooned him under the name of Pomposo – "I always thought him a shallow fellow; and I still think him so."

When I came home, for the first time since my arrival here, I began upon my letters to America.

JOHN QUINCY ADAMS (THE HAGUE) TO JOHN ADAMS, MAY 22, 1795

In May 1795, John Quincy arrived at a strategic conclusion about France's policy toward the United States that he felt merited attention in Philadelphia. The French government, in his view, planned to use its influence in America to defeat Jay's treaty in the US Senate. This would trigger an American war with Britain, without committing the French to come to America's aid. If the United States approved Jay's treaty, he believed that the French would likely accommodate themselves to an independent and neutral America. But if the Treaty were rejected, he fully expected that French influence in America would become much more active, using revolutionary blandishments to incite American republicans into action against the government.

John Quincy also developed one additional insight that later helped guide his approach toward France – the mutability of French revolutionary politics. He believed the political wheel in Paris would turn again, leading to a different government in France that might be more reasonable, although certainly not pro-American. It would be incumbent on the United States to assess such changes properly and to take advantage of them.

The Hague, May 22, 1795.

MY DEAR SIR:

My last letter acknowledged the receipt of your favor of February 11. That of December 2 has since reached me. By the same opportunity I have letters from my brother Charles of March 12. And I have seen Boston papers to the 1st of April. Our information from America is yet generally indirect and our means of conveyance few, difficult and uncertain.

The appointment, which places me here is undoubtedly respectable, much beyond the line of my pretensions, and the advantage of seeing Europe at the present moment, is personally a subject of particular gratification to me. The situation which I was obliged to abandon for this gave me nothing, or very little in *possessions*, but a fair and rational *prospect*, infinitely more pleasing than those now before me. My sacrifice was merely of an expectancy, but a very valuable one in every point of view. It was independence, usefulness and personal consideration; but above all the increasing attachment of friends, which every probability led me to expect would be durable. The benefit of your advice and instructions, the society however interrupted and partial of my mother and the rest of the family, though I feel severely the loss of them, were yet so inevitable and of impossible consistency with an absence beyond the Atlantic, that I do not reckon them in the account.

As it respects my country that has certainly gained nothing by the exchange. To speak the sentiments of my heart without equivocation, an American Minister at the Hague is one of the most useless beings in creation. The whole corps diplomatique here, according to a late French production of considerable merit, *n'est plus qu'une Assemblée de nouvellistes*, and the actor must have not an humble but a degraded idea of himself, who can be satisfied with the part of receiving the pay of a nation for the purpose of penetrating the contents of a newspaper.

As a single private individual I flatter myself that my mite of contribution to the public service in America was more valuable than any that I can render at present. The retribution is equally inconsistent with propriety. At present I am liberally paid for no service at all. There my only reward for considerable labor, and some political courage, was abuse, sometimes upon myself which was of very little consequence to me, but much more frequently upon an object entitled to all the veneration of the whole people, as much as he was possessed of mine, and who was persecuted for my offences with a malignancy and a brutality such as among mankind is experienced only by virtue and integrity; but which real crimes and infamy are too much respected ever to suffer.

At length, after four months of suspense upon the fate of this country, a treaty to acknowledge the independence and sovereignty of the Batavian people without a Stadtholder was signed on the 17th instant, by two members of the French Committee of Public Safety (Rewbell and Sieyes), and four deputies from the States General.[11]

This treaty will undoubtedly be published in the American newspapers before my letter can reach you, and I hope it will be a subject of serious reflection to every American. It shows in the clearest light at what price the friendship and assistance of France as a Republic is estimated by her own government. Let it be remembered that from the commencement of the war they have declared themselves the enemies of the Stadtholder and his government, but the *friends* and *allies* of the Dutch people. These friends and allies, after considering this territory during four months as a conquest, and treating it accordingly, though with all possible civility and some generosity, finally exact as conditions for acknowledging the liberty and independence of their friends and allies, a very considerable dismemberment of territory, a perpetual pledge of political subserviency, and one hundred million of florins in cash. *Non tali auxilio.*[12]

These facts are the more deserving of consideration, because I have several reasons to suppose that the policy of the French government at present is to make *use* of the United States, as they are now making use of these Provinces, that is, as an instrument for the benefit of France, as a passive weapon in her hands against her most formidable enemy. Being at a distance from Paris and having no regular connection with any members of that government, I am unable to trace the causes of my suspicions to a very certain source. I have not the means of ascertaining any considerable variety of facts, from the combination of which a conclusion to warrant any affirmative declaration could be drawn, and the communication with France itself is so liable to accident, that I am unable to correspond with Mr. Monroe so confidentially as would be necessary to determine how far my conjectures are founded.[13]

From the occurrences of the last year, it is certain that a prodigious alteration in the relative position of the European powers towards one another has taken place. The centre of combination has been equally removed by the victories of France and by the misfortunes of Poland. The drunken madness of political fanaticism has subsided surprisingly. The ruin of France remains therefore the only centre of union to the coalesced powers, but this principle is no less repulsive on one side than it is attractive on the other. New interests have arisen to form different combinations from those of the war as it began, and they have already been productive of a considerable revolution of policy, discovered in many public events and distinguishable from other circumstances.

The tendency of these new interests is to unite the efforts of Austria, Russia and Britain, for the present moment, in one common pursuit; but it unites equally all the rest of Europe against them.

This combination is unquestionably formidable, and it has an immense advantage in the pecuniary resources of Great Britain. They remain at least for present occasion in undiminished vigor, while those of France are exhausted in proportion to the violence of those exertions that have acquired her splendid triumphs.

It is not to be doubted but that France intends to unite against her three remaining rivals and enemies as many European powers as possible. The policy has been indeed clearly discovered in speeches made to the National Convention by members of the Executive Committee, in which mention has escaped of nations "which had observed neutrality, wise in its principle, but which has become insufficient," where subsidies to be given for the purpose of causing a diversion have been suggested, and where numerous objections have been made to prove that Spain, Prussia and Holland are all deeply interested in the future success of the French cause.

The intention of employing the United States likewise as an useful enemy to Great Britain has not been so openly avowed. And long since the arrival of the French armies in this country, the Representatives with whom I have had occasion to converse have declared themselves to be entirely satisfied with the neutrality of the United States. They do not at present say expressly the contrary, but they observe, that it is very extraordinary that the treaty signed by Mr. Jay last November should yet be kept secret.

It is impossible that they should imagine there is anything in that treaty with which France can have any pretence to interfere. It is therefore the treaty itself, which does not suit these views, because they consider it as the means of terminating differences, which their own interest leads them to wish may terminate in a rupture.

If these conjectures have as much foundation as I apprehend, the whole French influence in America will exert itself with more than usual activity to prevent the ratification of the treaty, and to produce at all events a war between the United States and Great Britain, not assuredly from regard to our interest, which they respect as much as they do that of their friends and allies the

Hollanders, but because they are sensible of how much importance our commerce is to Great Britain, and suppose that the loss of it would make that nation outrageous for peace, and compel the Minister to make it upon the terms they are disposed to dictate.

It was probably the intention of the Brissotine party, the Executive Council, who sent Genet to America to involve the United States in a war with Britain, but in such a manner as should be imperceptible to ourselves, as should have the appearance of being entirely a war of our own, and should leave France free from all engagements, in full liberty to make her own peace, whenever she might think proper, and leave us to extricate ourselves as we could. This plan was not successful in its execution, and perhaps was abandoned by the Executive Committee, which rose upon the ruins of the Council. To them the neutrality of the United States was at least as beneficial as any assistance they could expect from them in a state of war, or at least by appearing to pursue a different policy, they meant to make it an instrument of odium against the party they had then defeated. That Committee has been sacrificed in its turn. Everything done by them is an object of execration. They are Jacobins, Terrorists, Royalists, drinkers of blood, robbers, scourges of the human race, everything that a victorious party can make of one that is defeated. The truth of the fact seems to be that the Brissotine party have resumed their superiority in the Convention, and have derived among the people some consideration, more from the detestation of their predecessors, than from their own merits. They have resumed the principles and the policy, which the decemviral government had abandoned, and among the rest perhaps the design of fomenting a war between America and Great Britain. They have sent to America a new minister, to take the place of Fauchet; a man, who has been heretofore employed by them in their revolutionary manoeuvres at Geneva, and who, as one of the Representatives lately a member of the Committee of Public Safety told me, was substituted instead of the other, whose "talents and experience are found to be not equal to the importance of the mission."[14]

I have considered it as an indispensable duty that I owe to my country to express to you, Sir, my ideas and suspicions upon a subject of so much importance: in my public correspondence I have scarcely hinted at them, because they are but suspicions, and because there is another source, from which more accurate information is to be expected, and will doubtless be received. At least if my conjectures are groundless they will be harmless, because the state of affairs in America will prove them to be fallacious. If they are well founded, it may not be useless that the symptoms breaking forth in this quarter of the world should be known to you, and combined with those that will discover themselves in America.

If their present views really are to draw the United States into a war with Britain, their only motive for it must be to accelerate their own peace. The general sentiment of the French at the present moment, if I mistake not, is less cordial towards the Americans than it has been. They envy us the immense advantage we have derived from our neutrality; they think we have grown rich upon their impoverishment; that we have drained them of their specie, and they do not scruple to charge our merchants who have supplied their most urgent necessities, with having taken advantage of their wants to extort extravagant profits upon their commerce. Peace has become an object of extreme necessity to them; their finances, their commerce, their manufactures, their agriculture, their population, all by an inseparable chain are connected in a dependence upon the return of peace. Yet the brilliancy of their victories, and especially the security of the prevailing party, make it indispensably necessary to them to insist upon conditions, to which their enemies in the present state of affairs will certainly not submit. It is for their benefit alone, therefore, that they wish to see us engaged, and should they succeed in this intention the principal, perhaps the only use they will make of their success will be to obtain more glorious terms of peace for themselves.

The President of the United States has so decidedly adopted and maintained the policy of neutrality, and it has proved so advantageous to the country, that it is perhaps an idle apprehension that can imagine it will again be endangered. Before this letter reaches you, the question upon the ratification of the treaty signed in November will undoubtedly be decided. The die will be cast; the point of peace or enmity with Britain settled. If by a ratification of the treaty, perhaps a coolness on the part of France will again be discernible, but from which no ill consequences whatever are to be dreaded. If the treaty should be rejected, the French influence and French intrigue, always so active and powerful among us, will become much more busy than they have ever been before.

On the first supposition their disappointment will have no serious consequence, because they have still great need of our supplies, because the policy of their government under every possible variation will always be to conform the style of their pretentions in their political relations with us to the degree of firmness or of acquiescence discovered on our part, and because our friendship and neutrality must be more agreeable and advantageous to them than a state of variance. Failing in their favorite object, they will eventually content themselves with that which they consider as the next best, and very possibly the situation of their internal concerns may once more make it the interest of a prevailing faction to alter the system of external policy, in order by the restoration of cordiality with their neighbors, to cast an odium upon their rivals at home.

If the treaty should not be ratified, the French will exert themselves for the purpose of hurrying us into a war, which may hasten their means of making peace, and in which they may be under no obligation of making a common cause with us. Their partizans, perhaps, in declamations or in newspapers will promise wonders from their co-operation; their official characters possibly may employ a great number of what they call *phrases*, but will have no power to contract any substantial engagements; we shall be friends, brothers, allies, fellow-freemen, loaded with all the tenderness of family affections introduced by a political prosopopeia into national concerns, and the final result of the whole matter will be, that all this tender sympathy, this amiable fraternity, this lovely coalescence of liberty, will leave us the advantage of being sacrificed to their interests, or of purchasing their protection upon the most humiliating and burdensome conditions, and at the same time of being reduced to the condition of glorying in our disgrace, and hailing the instrument of our calamity as the weapon of our deliverance.

I wish that the situation of affairs in America may be such as shall afford a full demonstration, that these are ideas merely visionary, and above all I wish that we may never have occasion for any political connections in Europe. The alarming prospects of famine, which threaten every part of this hemisphere, may perhaps contribute more than any other circumstance to a general pacification, which if it should be effected will in truth be nothing more than a suspension of arms.

The internal state of France is critical, and will probably experience a considerable change in the course of the present year. It is impossible, however, to anticipate at this distance what turn it will take. They are weary of their revolutionary government, and universally convinced that the Constitution which has been accepted can never be carried into execution in its present state. As they do not yet venture to lay it entirely aside, they have contrived to propose a supplementary addition under the name of *organic laws*. A committee of eleven members has been chosen by the Convention to prepare them and the result of their labors will soon be presented to the Assembly. The weakness of their present government is the principal subject of complaint at this time, and the principles of moderation are found incompetent to repress the movements of popular indignation and revenge. The execution of sixteen persons formerly composing part of the revolutionary tribunal under the government of Robespierre, has recently taken place at Paris with the sanction of legal forms, but at Lyons the impatience of the people has anticipated the decision of justice, and on the 4th of this month the sanctuary of the prisons was again violated, and sixty or seventy persons were sacrificed by the people, as an atonement for the cruelties of which they had been heretofore the principal agents.

I am, &c.

JOHN QUINCY ADAMS TO SECRETARY OF STATE TIMOTHY PICKERING, DECEMBER 22, 1795 (PRIVATE)

From November 1795 to May 1796, John Quincy's temporary diplomatic assignment in London allowed him the time and opportunity to systematize his thinking about the second major element in America's strategic triangle – its former colonial master, Britain. In this private letter to Secretary of State Pickering, John Quincy concluded that Britain's immediate strategic purpose was to remove France as a commercial and maritime rival. But London's deeper design was to engross the world's commerce, and to do this it had to contain American trade. Until it became much stronger, the United States could not expect to shake Britain's grandiose maritime pretensions or its formal adherence to the illiberal Navigation Laws. But time, in John Quincy's view, was on America's side. Even in the short run, internal and external difficulties often dictated a relaxation in British practices, if not its principles; and perhaps opportunities to carve out reasonable trading accommodations, if not a comprehensive settlement. Prudence, not passion, dictated peace with England for now. The time for vengeance would come.

SIR:

One of the favorite objects of this government is an increase of the dominions in the East and West Indies. A formidable expedition with 25,000 troops has recently sailed for the latter, but has already met with two gales of wind extremely violent, which have damaged many of the vessels, and reduced considerably the numbers of men that go together. It has also been delayed in its departure at least three months later than was intended. It appears to be the general opinion here that it must inevitably succeed, that its force will be irresistible, and the whole island of St. Domingo is already in possession of this country by anticipation. Yet if it should fail, Englishmen may remember that it will not be the first instance of an invincible armada defeated, and considering the climate to which they are going the loss of three months of the season may be considered as equivalent to the loss of half of their men.[15]

That they may succeed is not I think to be wished by Americans. For, Sir, it appears more and more clear that the real and ultimate object of this government in their present war, is to establish the commercial and maritime supremacy of the nation over the ruins of those of France. They have hitherto been so far successful in this project, that they are encouraged vigorously to pursue it, and if they can terminate the war by obtaining possession of Corsica, of the Cape of Good Hope, and of Martinico, with their own navy greatly increased, and that of France equally reduced, they will have gone very far towards securing their purpose. It is intimated by the ministerial partisans that little hesitation will be made here at giving up the Austrian Netherlands, and even the cause of the Stadtholder in the United Provinces, provided an indemnity shall be given to this country by an accession to its transmarine possessions. I have very little doubt of the fact, because the sacrifice of allies and the abandonment of solemn previous stipulations, would operate only as a removal of the mask, as soon as the purpose for which it was taken has been secured.

It is not merely from views of commercial aggrandizement, however, that the posession of the French islands in the West Indies is held as an object of the first magnitude in this country. It enters into all their calculations relative to the United States. It forms a part of their defensive system, and they believe that their commercial existence depends in some measure upon the event.

This may serve as a clue to the extreme anxiety which they have uniformly discovered since the commencement of this war to exclude the Americans not only from their own, but from all the foreign islands. It explains the orders of the 6th of November, 1793.[16] It accounts for their obstinate adherence to that clause in the 12th article of the late treaty, which has been suspended.[17] It is the key to that singular principle which they are now determined on their single authority to establish as the settled law of nations, that no other than the customary peace trade can be allowed to neutral nations, by a belligerent party in time of war. Anything that shall serve as a barrier between the United States and the West Indies will be attempted by them, and in addition to all their other grounds of alarm, they are now apprehensive that if France should retain her islands at the peace, she will be compelled, by her own want of navigation, to leave the intercourse between them and the United States as free to the latter as it has been since this war, and that she will be unable to resume the exclusive system at least for several years. The genius of the navigation act shudders at the prospect, and will think thousands of mere human lives, and millions of treasure, most profitably spent in preventing the reality.

But, as Mr. Hammond says, it is impossible for them to think of everything, and they sometimes find themselves obliged to yield to an irresistible course of events. I am sensible how dangerous a thing it is to deliver an opinion upon future occurrences, else I would venture to foretell that whatever *commercial* negotiations may at any time be carried on between the United States and Britain, whatever is given by the latter will be extorted by the necessity of the times, and nothing will be conceded to any liberality of system. There is no such thing as commercial liberality in the country. To engross the commerce of the world to themselves is the professed or secret wish of every heart among them, and if there are a very small number who believe that the prosperity of other nations would rather advance than prejudice their own, the effect of this opinion is destroyed by the political consideration that their views would not be secured by their own *positive* advantage, without a correspondent *negative* for all other nations. The character of the former supposition is equality, but all *their* ideas run towards their superiority.[18]

It is, therefore, a circumstance very remarkable that at this time there is before the Privy Council a proposal for admitting into the ports of this country the produce of foreign West India Islands, in neutral vessels – rum, sugar, coffee and cocoa, for re-exportation, and cotton and molasses for consumption here. The merchants appear to be of opinion that this will soon be permitted by proclamation, and if so the present would certainly be a favorable moment to us for negotiation upon this subject. But what has induced them to be prepared for a regulation so different from the spirit of the condition to the 12th article of the treaty? It is because their adherence to their own system has driven the Americans into another course of trade, from which it has not been practicable to exclude them: because that other course of trade not only tends to carry their custom elsewhere, but to give them the means and opportunity of tracing new channels for their commerce: because the merchants of this country are losing their American commissions, and ten per cent of profit upon the whole balance of the trade in the rate of exchange; in short, because their own apparent interest forces them to an indulgence equally adverse to their feelings and their principles. But if they can obtain possession of the French Islands, then the old maxims of exclusion will be revived in all their force, and instead of resigning themselves to a mere participation of our profits, they will boldly resume the purpose of intercepting them from us.

The scarcity of grain has still an appearance so alarming, that the Parliament besides many regulations to reduce the consumption have also encouraged its importation by a bounty upon wheat, and upon Indian corn. It was at first proposed to make a distinction, so as to give a larger bounty on the importations from the Mediterranean, than on those from America; but they were finally put upon the same footing. The wants of Europe during the ensuing year will undoubtedly turn to the benefit of the United States as much as they have ever yet done, but on their part they must not suffer their patience to be yet exhausted. The American will infallibly triumph over the European system eventually, provided it be pursued with as much perseverance. But an hour of haste or resentment indulged in at the present moment would take the advantage which it now possesses from its hand, and throw the scale of probable success on this side of the water.

All my letters to you, Sir, public and private, have delivered my sentiments with a freedom which perhaps needs an apology, and which certainly nothing but an unlimited confidence can reconcile with personal prudence. A sense of duty it is hoped will be admitted at least as my excuse, and if my opinions are in any instance warped by prejudice, I am persuaded that your discernment will distinguish, and hope your candor will overlook them.

I remain, etc.

JOHN QUINCY ADAMS (THE HAGUE) TO JOSEPH PITCAIRN, NOVEMBER 13, 1796

In late 1796 and early 1797, John Quincy sent a series of letters to the American vice consul in Paris, Joseph Pitcairn, which were to be passed on unofficially to moderate political figures in France. He wanted to counteract the erroneous impressions that radical Americans were fomenting in the minds of the French. John Quincy insisted that France's policy of hostility toward the United States and its meddling in American domestic politics were having the opposite effect of the one intended. He stressed the fundamental unity of the American people on essential matters of foreign policy, however divided they might appear to be to outsiders. Their unity was based on the common conviction that neutrality in the wars of Europe was in America's best interest. John Quincy was not as certain privately that such a consensus actually existed – there remained a radical pro-French faction –

but he thought that effective unity would be the case under strong executive leadership, as Washington had shown. But John Quincy wanted to get across something he did believe to be true – that Jefferson, if he was chosen president over John Adams, would not reverse Washington's policy in any basic way merely to accommodate France.

DEAR SIR:

I have successively received at due time your favors of the 20th and 28th ultimo, and of the 3rd instant, and renew my thanks for the interesting information they contain. If the French government have determined upon the capture of enemy property on board of neutral vessels, I do not apprehend that we shall suffer materially from the resolution. It will, however, serve to show the degree of regard in which they hold, not only the rights of neutral nations, but their own engagements. There are people in America who to serve certain purposes are forever harping upon the gratitude which they pretend the United States owe to France, and the French themselves are not unfrequently disposed to make a merit of what was certainly a very interested policy. The present government are perhaps disposed to cancel our supposed obligations by violating the stipulations of their treaties. It is my opinion that there is a strong debt of reciprocal obligations between the United States and France, or rather, to speak the only honest language upon a political concern, the relations between the two nations were formed upon a very important common interest which still exists, and must continue long to exist. That common interest prescribes a cordial harmony and a punctual performance of treaties on both sides. The American government is unquestionably and sincerely disposed to cultivate that harmony and faithfully to adhere to its engagements, but it expects a similar return; and I am persuaded that if the French propose to themselves an influence in America by the assumption of a supercilious tone of negotiation, or by disregarding their stipulations, they will fail of success and lose much of the influence which they actually possess.

The Minister Delacroix means not well to the harmony of the two countries, and there are prejudices and passions of other individuals which will labor to interrupt the good understanding, which the interest of both requires. But I am persuaded it will eventually be restored, because the mutual interest is too strong and must prevail over all the efforts of prejudice, passion, or intrigue.[19]

There is a great ignorance of the character and sentiments of the American people in France among those who imagine that any manoeuvre of *theirs* could turn an election against the President of the United States. Their invectives and their calumnies may add a few more to the number of his detractors, or take away some who admired him from fashion or from personal motives; but among the great mass of the people he stands fixed as the foundations of the world, and France will find it more easy to go through five and twenty revolutions at home, than to root out that man's merits and services from the memory of Americans, or a proper sense of them from their hearts.

It is probable, however, that if the President persists in his intention to retire, the French will soon forget their political resentment against him. As to his system of policy they will do well to acquiesce in that, for they will not overturn it. You think they will endeavor to promote the election of Mr. Jefferson, and you are probably right; but if Jefferson is elected, I speak with confidence in saying that he will inflexibly pursue the same general system of policy which is now established. Perhaps even you may smile and hesitate in believing this prophecy. I may be mistaken, but have no doubt myself upon the subject, and am willing to have my conjectures judged by the test of events.[20]

Our friends, therefore, *must* return upon their steps, unless they are determined to cast off a sincere and faithful and *very useful* friend. As to their being discovered, that is, their motives and their views, I suppose they do not expect to avoid that. They must know that they *have been long* since discovered. Their islands and their marine are strong ties. The weariness of their people at the war which yet burthens them, the total want even of a plausible pretext to quarrel with America, and the very possible chance that they may again be in want of our bread, will prolong our peace, and if the Minister Delacroix is succeeded by an abler or a wiser man, he will feel the advantage of preserving influence by using it with moderation.

I am, &c.

JOHN QUINCY ADAMS TO JOHN ADAMS, JANUARY 14, 1797

In a series of letters to John Adams, designed for the contingency that his father would soon be in charge of foreign policy, John Quincy expressed the view that there remained a narrow diplomatic path that would provide for American security. The new president should not operate on the assumption that war with the French was inevitable; nor should he allow himself to be pushed into one. John Quincy believed that France could be brought around to abandon its design to drive America into the war against Britain, and to resume amicable intercourse with the United States. The key was to convince the Directory that its strategy of remodeling the US Constitution and dividing the people from their government had failed. The United States, to tread this narrow path, must maintain the Washington-Adams policy of strict neutrality, address any legitimate French concerns (for example, by making full, clear, and explicit denial of any commercial advantages or facilities of military provisionment to the British), promote its case publicly to American and European opinion, and persuade or induce the House of Representatives more decidedly to concur in the established system of diplomatic evenhandedness. America should favor neither belligerent; nor should it try to play one off against the other.

MY DEAR SIR:

I received yesterday your favor of October 28, and it is by several weeks the latest letter that I have from America. It tells me that the elections were going on with as little bitterness as could be expected, and this in the present circumstances is grateful intelligence. But all my American correspondents, public and private, as they appear to care nothing about the affairs of Europe, seem alike to think us indifferent to those of America. This inattention will eventually produce consequences very serious to our country and its government. There are others who feel the importance of European intercourse and an incessant vigilance towards it more forcibly, and cultivate it more assiduously. They have at least succeeded to make hard work for the government of the United States. In my letters to you last summer will be found as clear an anticipation as my observations could discover and my reflections combine of the events which are now taking place. I have not been silent on the subject to the Secretary of State. Of nearly thirty letters which I have written him since my return from England, I have an acknowledgment that four have been received. In one of your late letters it is intimated to me that the correspondence has not been on my part sufficiently frequent with the Treasury Department. I shall endeavor to avoid that complaint in future, but I hope it will be considered just that some suggestion should be made to me of the *objects* upon which in formation is desired, some instructions upon which a correspondence can be founded, and some sort of returns to the earnest solicitations which my letters have contained of measures to direct my conduct, and to provide for the punctuality of the United States in this country. To an urgent letter from me to the Secretary of the Treasury, written on the 13th of last June, I am still panting for an answer. The provision which I so long since entreated to be made in season has been now nearly two months defective. I am assaulted by dunning creditors on one side, by impatient bankers on the other, and month after month elapses in profound silence of advices or remittances from America.

While the payments are failing, rumors of troubles and dissensions in the United States spread abroad, the funds depreciate, I am called upon from every quarter to know what the *real* accounts from thence are, and have only to confess that *my* accounts are two or three months in arrear of the current course.[21]

It is not for the pleasure of complaining that I mention these circumstances; but on the one hand, I regret that a want of these reciprocal communications disenables me from so useful a discharge of my duty as my own wishes would dictate; and on the other, that I sometimes take great pains to compare and combine symptoms that occur in Europe to announce what an attentive correspondence from America would inform me to be an old story there, thoroughly understood, and about which all my toils would be perfectly useless. An instance of the last kind, considerably important, is that of the suspicions intimated in my letter to you N.24. When I wrote it I had not heard a syllable of the French project upon our western territory.[22] But the concurrence of several circumstances which I then noticed to you convinced me, that something very pernicious to the United States was in agitation, though I could not precisely divine what it was. Afterwards, from the American newspapers when I received them, and especially from the President's address to the people, I found that I might spare myself the trouble of endeavoring to detect what was already abundantly discovered, and that it would be needless to lose myself in a chase of probabilities, to throw a new mite of conjecture into the settled balance of demonstration.[23]

I have already written you an account of the refusal of the French Directory to receive Mr. Pinckney, and the apparent alliance between them and the internal enemies of the American government.[24] But since my last letter Mr. Monroe has delivered his letters of recall, and upon that occasion made a speech which was answered by the President of the Directory, Barras. Mr. Monroe's address indicates what his language and conduct will be upon his return. The same unqualified devotion to the French will, which made him so confidential with Fauchet[25] upon the parties within the United States before he set out upon his mission, has influenced him in this last transaction; and at the moment when a national indignity, outrageous as it was unprovoked, was offered to his country, he still condescends to flatter them, by an eulogy upon the *generous services*, which they themselves have long since publicly and officially declared to have been *merely the fruit of a vile speculation*; by a declaration as false as it is dishonorable to America, that the principles of their Revolution and of ours were the same; by an exulting reference to his military services in our war; and by an ostentatious avowal of his partiality for the present cause of France, and all this without even hinting the mission of Mr. Pinckney, whose personal and patriotic merits are surely not inferior to his own. The answer of Barras is such that I scarcely know which it inspires most, of indignation at the design which it developes, or of contempt for the mode of its execution. In comparison with it the language of Genet[26] was decency and modesty. The public opinion concerning it in Europe appears unanimous. I have not heard it mentioned by an individual but with disgust at its thrasonical bombast, and ridicule at its bullying menaces. This tone has been instigated by their American partisans, who have suggested to them that the American government and people must be frightened into a violation of their treaty with Britain and of their neutrality. The affectation of parade which was made on this occasion, the display of Ambassadors from Sardinia, from a Duke of Parma, and a Bey of Tunis, the trophies from the battle of Arcola, and the commandant of the national guards, all you may be sure were designed to look and sound very tremendous. They really think the American people not only as ignorant of Europe as they themselves are of America, but moreover idiots and cowards, upon whom tinsel can with the utmost facility be palmed for bullion, and with whom a Bey of Tunis or an Infant Duke of Parma would furnish as potent a proof of the invincible prevalence of the French power, as the Empires of Austria, Russia, or Great Britain. In reality their selection of ambassadors to witness their triumph over Mr. Monroe has in it something burlesque. Tremble, O ye people of America, for at the moment when a French Director announces the fury of France against your government, his Republic, rich by her liberty, surrounded by a retinue of victories, and strong by the esteem of her allies, displays before your eyes her dubious Italian trophies, and her expiatory embassies from the Duke of Parma and the Bey of Tunis! All this in substance is perfectly ridiculous; but coupled with the insolence of Barras's speech, with his professed distinction between the government and the people of the United States, with his compliments to Mr. Monroe, and his recommendation to him to go home and represent the American people there, it fully proves that the design of attack upon the government by a renewal of Genet's *appeal to the people* is prepared and concerted, so as to open upon the commencement of a new administration. They very evidently expect great effects from this manoeuvre; their American partisans in Europe already exult, as if our rupture with Great Britain was completely effected, the friends of our government are alarmed and fearful that they will be intimidated into submission, or abandoned by the people their only support; that this patronage of France will give such weight to the efforts of faction that they will be no longer resistible, and the system of neutrality will necessarily be overturned. To say that I myself am without profound anxiety in this respect would be idle and false. The character, temper and conduct of the two last Houses of Representatives in Congress have made it impossible to discard apprehensions for the future, and the measures which the popular leaders of the antifederal party have adopted, sanctioned and justified, remove every hope that any scruple of independence, patriotism or justice will interfere between the views of France and *their* active exertions to support them.

I presume, however, that there is in the American government a spirit which will not tamely submit to be bullied out of its system, even by the combined insolence of a French Directory, with the utmost malignity of internal faction. I presume also, that a great majority of the American people will see through the object of this transaction, and despise the insidious attempt to separate and discriminate them from their government. I *hope* that to the future President of the United States, whoever he may be, the peace of his country, its honor, and its justice will be as dear as they are to the present, and while every honest voice is uttering admiration, and every humane heart ejaculating blessings to the name of Washington, that his successor, by exhibiting a continuance of the same wisdom, firmness and moderation, will prove to the sceptics in political speculation, that the American soil is fruitful of those virtues, and the American people determined to support them.

A rupture of our treaty with Great Britain is in a manner the professed demand upon which the French Directory have made these recent terrific demonstrations; a suspension of our trade with Britain will perhaps be required, as a condition for a restoration of their good-will.[27] That this is their clear design, I have long since written you. How far they will go to obtain their end, it is impossible to say. It will depend in a great measure upon the support they meet from their party in America. If our government discover a single symptom of a disposition to yield; or if the House of Representatives for the ensuing Congress should from its complexion encourage the hopes of obtaining a majority adverse to the system of the Executive, the Directory will not scruple at any measure of hostility which they may imagine, or be persuaded, will increase their influence by the arguments of fear. It is painful to say it, but I am afraid it is true, that they will be instigated from America to repeat and accumulate hostilities to promote the purpose. But if the executive should maintain that dignified firmness and moderation which has hitherto distinguished it, and the Representatives more decidedly concur in the established system of neutrality than they have done, the French government will inevitably retreat, abandon their design of driving us into the war, and be willing to resume their amicable intercourse with that of the United States.

In forming this opinion, which is perfectly decided in my mind, I draw the conclusion both from their present mode of proceeding, and from their conduct hitherto with *all* the other neutral nations. My letters of last summer have given you a detail of their proceedings to defeat all the neutrality in Europe, and of their various success according as the neutral state was or was not totally in their power. In Florence, Venice, Genoa and Lucca they succeeded; but in Sweden, in Denmark, in Turkey, and even in Prussia, they totally failed. Their experiment upon Sweden has probably thrown that power permanently into the Russian scale, and had they not desisted from their intrigues and menaces against Denmark, they would have met with the same disappointment there.

Notwithstanding their refusal to receive Mr. Pinckney, they have authorized a public denial of the report that they had suspended all intercourse with the government of the United States; at the same time their affectation of courtship to the people of the United States shows that their real object is only to intimidate, and indeed in their present situation, however they may bluster, they have no inclination to increase the number of their enemies.

In order to defeat the views of further hostility which may be urged by the domestic enemies of the government, and to deter the Directory from proceeding any further, it appears to me a very important and very effectual measure would be for the American government, by the means of some official paper, to expose, in a clear and explicit manner, the total want of provocation by them that would palliate the injustice and insolence of the Directory; to show beyond the power of refutation, as might be done with perfect ease, that France has not the smallest pretext for a rupture; to state the unquestionable right of the United States to contract the engagements of the British treaty, and to disclaim in the most explicit manner every idea of violating any of the previous engagements with France; to prove that the British treaty itself protects every former stipulation with other powers, and at the same time decisively to repel every pretence that the United States were ever dependent upon France for anything more than obligations of reciprocal and equal alliance. An official paper of this kind, written with coolness and temper, like the letter demanding the recall of Genet, would have a very favorable effect upon the public opinion of all Europe, and of France in particular, where the people are already heartily sick of war, and where upon the appearance of such a statement, the Directory would not dare take any further violent measures. For even now everybody inquires what the United States have done, or what the occasion is of this conduct of the Directory; nothing is stated to the public, but a vague pretence of a more favorable stipulation for military provisionings to the British than to them, and an intimation of studied obscurity that the American government had condescended to the *suggestions* of their ancient tyrants. In the paper mentioned in my last letter this word *suggestions* is likewise used, when they say, that the "fatal treaty *passed* (in the House of Representatives) only by a majority of two," notwithstanding wretched *suggestions*. Perhaps you may not be aware that they mean by this word to intimate *bribery*. This is undoubtedly its meaning, and the obliquity of the expression is for the sake of eluding the repulse of a just indignation, which a direct assertion of the same thing would naturally rouse. But in another paper from the same source, and published alike in the *Rédacteur*, they have produced the lie in all its naked malignity and deformity. For they charge Great Britain with endeavoring to overthrow the *balance of Europe* by abandoning Poland to its fate, and by enriching herself with the spoils of the French commerce, *by a treaty perfidiously purchased* – "par un traité perfidement acheté."

Indeed, cruel and false as this intimation is, it cannot be surprising not only that they should advance, but even that they should believe it. During several months, if the concurring reports of many different persons may be believed, Mr. Monroe made no scruple or hesitation to say in public and mixed companies, that he had not the smallest doubt but Mr. Jay was bribed to sign the treaty, and to one person he added that *to his certain knowledge*, when Mr. Jay was employed to negotiate for our navigation of the Mississippi, he did in fact negotiate against it. The French, alas! have but too clearly discovered that at least one man high in the American government was not only susceptible of bribery, but capable of begging it; and where they had such satisfactory proof of a readiness for prostitution to them, it cannot be wondered that they should believe the imprudent and iniquitous prejudices of Mr. Monroe's opinions, of a like propensity in others, though towards a different direction.[28]

You will however perceive in the present conduct of the Directory what sort of a disposition they bear towards an administration at the head of which you may be placed. They know perfectly well how inflexibly you maintained the honor and interest of America in former times against the insidious policy of Vergennes, and they know equally the consistency and firmness of character, which will alike maintain the same cause against their more pernicious designs.[29] Whatever, therefore, their artifices, working upon popular passions and concerted with antifederal partisans, can *effect*, you will take it for granted they will endeavor. Should the suffrages of the American people impose upon you the burthen of the chief magistracy, it will be necessary to consider this as a settled point, as a source of embarrassments and obstacles, against which every possible counteracting provision must be made. If the helm of our public affairs should be committed to other hands, they will certainly be more favored by the French Directory, so long as it shall be under the government of Sieyès; but I hope they will not be found more ready to sacrifice the welfare of America to the humble pupil of Favier and Franklin, than yours.[30]

The Directory is composed of discordant materials, but they have divided their functions into several departments, and the transaction of all business relative to each particular department is left to one member. The department of the foreign affairs is thus held by Rewbell, a man of strong nerves and weak brain, altogether under the direction of Sieyès, whose cool head, unfeeling heart, and cowardly disposition, have been noticed to you in former letters. He dared not take himself a seat which was offered him in the Directory, but he knew that the opinions of his old colleague would be at his disposal, and has accordingly always governed him. This circumstance is well known; for Sieyès, having among his other qualities some vanity, takes care to have it understood that he is the manager of Rewbell. It seems to be a sort of association, in which each supplies the qualities denied to the other. One is the soul, and the other the body. One enjoys the profit and parade with the personal dangers of office, and the other has its management and conduct, but without its responsibility. Sieyès bears a personal ill-will to you, a political ill-will to the prosperity and union of the United States, and a speculative ill-will to the principles of our Constitution; and with all these dispositions concurring together, no proof of malevolence that may hereafter be given will be unexpected to you. I have formerly suggested that no scruple of morality will interfere, to prevent the use of any means by which the French government may think a desirable end attainable, and my opinion is founded, not only upon their uniform conduct through all their Revolutions, but upon the professed principles avowed by the publications of those who have been employed in the direction of their public affairs. The memoirs of Dumouriez, of Madame Roland, and of Garat, are full of proofs that this idea is not without foundation.

A resolution not to be moved, a candor and moderation not to be angered, a sincere regard for the welfare and wish for the friendship of France, with a temper not to be intimidated by menaces or forced by hostilities, unfolded clearly to the sense and understanding of all the world, I am convinced, would go far to disarm them of all the weapons upon the efficacy of which they now place their dependence. Something must be done, and I beg leave again to repeat the solicitation, that a more steady and systematic attention to the affairs of Europe in general may be paid by the government. The President, indeed, has told us, and I am profoundly convinced of the justice and importance of the advice, that we ought not to involve ourselves at all in the political

systems of Europe, but to keep ourselves always distinct and separate from it. But even to effect this, constant and early information of the current events and of the political projects in
contemplation is no less necessary than if we were directly concerned in them. It is necessary for the discovery of the efforts
made to draw us into the vortex, in season to make preparations
against them. From one of the quotations in this letter, it is
observable that France very formally considers the United States
as forming a weight in the balance of Europe. France must, therefore, necessarily conduct itself towards us upon this supposition.
Britain will with equal certainty do the same. It behooves us to be
the more cautious and vigilant to counteract all their intrigues
and exertions on either side to make us the instruments or the
victims of their conquering or plundering ambition. The late king
of Prussia always answered with his own hand every dispatch
from every one of his ministers abroad. If he had no instructions
to give, yet he never failed to acknowledge the receipt of the dispatch, and recommend to the minister a continuance of his zeal
and industry. The mere effect of such an *example* spreads in more
than a geometrical ratio. Negligence on one side creates it on the
other, and I know from personal experience how readily indolence and carelessness will creep in upon the steadiest resolutions
of industry, with an apology derived from a reciprocal inattention. Until Mr. Pickering was appointed to the State Department
my letters were scarcely ever answered, and of more than fifty
letters that I wrote the receipt not of five was ever acknowledged.
With regard to me and my mission, it might not be of material
consequence; but the case was the same with all the other ministers of the government in Europe; all were neglected, and it
would have been but natural if many had been tempted thereby
to inattention in return.[31]

If this Letter should find you restored to the character only of
a private Citizen, its contents will not perhaps be very interesting. If otherwise I do not presume that it will be of any other
service than as it may give some little information. The Question

is already or must be very soon decided. I hope that the moment of its decision and its subsequent results will find you still possessed of the same personal indifference, and public concern which has marked every former part of your political career: and I delight myself with the reflection that the chair of the Union or the farm at Quincy will furnish no other difference than that between the Elevation and the retirement of Wisdom and Virtue.

There is not much authentic news current at this time. – It appears that the new Emperor of Russia, has formally acknowledged the French Republic. – The rupture of the negotiations between France and Britain I have mentioned in a former Letter – The great naval expedition from Brest was really destined against Ireland. It appears probable that it will not succeed, and one division of the fleet with four or five thousand Men has already returned to Brest. – No certain material intelligence from Italy, except symptoms of discontent, and indiscipline in that as well as in all the other French armies. Here the Assembly are debating their plan of Constitution, *one* and *indivisible*.

I am with invariable duty and affection, your Son
John Q. Adams

JOHN QUINCY ADAMS (THE HAGUE) TO JOSEPH PITCAIRN, MARCH 9, 1797

In his backchannel communications to the French, John Quincy acknowledged that there was an "English influence" of concern in the United States – but its cause and remedy were different from the ones imagined by France. "There is not one man in the American government that has any partialities towards Great Britain, but there is a great English influence acting among the people of America, an influence, which by wise and prudent measures may be diminished, but which cannot, and will not, be violently rooted out, because deeply involved and indissolubly connected with our own interests.... By

*forcing a rupture upon us, France necessarily assimilates and unites
the interests of America with those of Great Britain ..."*

DEAR SIR:

That there has been a vast deal of error and misrepresentation,
with regard to the opinion of the American people, is beyond a
doubt, and unfortunately the reports and statements to the
French government have all come from biassed sources. All their
ministers, from the time of Genet, have been misled by connecting themselves with a party opposed, either to the Constitution,
or to the administration of our government, and who had interests of their own to answer, by instilling prejudices in the minds
of the French ministers.[32] Listening to leaders of Jacobin clubs,
and catching at every paltry paragraph in a newspaper which
combined abuse upon the government with a parade of enthusiasm for France, they have never sufficiently attended to that cool
and deliberate public opinion, which has never yet failed to determine eventually the American measures, and to defeat which,
every expedient has been repeatedly tried, and as constantly has
failed.[33] Whether the accredited minister of the United States in
France, or other officers, have not been themselves too much
under the influence of a party spirit opposed to their own government, to make their representations in the name and behalf of
that government zealous and active, as it might and should have
been, may at least be a subject of doubt, and if their conduct,
instead of exhibiting the ardent desire to justify their government,
and to maintain its harmony with that to which they were sent,
has on the contrary been a continued series of censure upon the
measures of their own employers, it is not to be supposed that they
have contributed, in any degree, to remove prejudices, which
they so fully participated. Indeed I know not of a single opportunity that the French executive have had to hear the truth stated to
them with candor respecting American affairs. The dispositions
which some of our own countrymen have manifested, to bucca-
neer and plunder upon the property of their fellow citizens, is

indeed a disgrace to the nation. But that such men, despised and detested by their own countrymen as much as they deserve, should be listened to as designating the public opinion of that very country which they have renounced, and which has renounced them, is much to be regretted, though I much fear that it has been and yet is the case.

You mention an opinion that they begin to take into their calculation some of these things in the councils, if not in the Directory. But how is it intended to renew a discussion with our government, which has been so thoroughly cut off by the suspension of their minister's functions at Philadelphia, and their refusal to receive the American minister at Paris. It is impossible for the proceedings of one nation towards another, to be more offensive than those of the French government have been for the last five months towards us; it is impossible that they should mean a continuance of peace, unless they mean also to renew the intercourse, which they have violently stopped, and which I cannot possibly think the American government will first renew. Do you know, therefore, whether they mean to restore the powers of Adet? Or to send any other person in his stead? If you have any indication for an opinion upon this point, I shall be obliged to you to let me know it.[34]

It is true, as you observe, that the Americans, who in case of a rupture between the two countries, would take the French side, would not have the same chance of payment in case of failure as our refugees had from Britain. But it may be a subject of consideration to the French, that there would in such case be many and many a *claim* of indemnity for sacrifices made in their *cause*, and that every *encouragement* now given to such people will be turned into an obligation for supporting such claims. Our Loyalists, as they were called in the contest with Great Britain, were very much like the party which France now countenances and believes. They affected a superior, or rather an exclusive, attachment to the British government; they labored constantly to inspire prejudices against the rest of their countrymen in the minds of their patrons;

flattered and irritated all their resentments, spurred them on to the war, and after it was over, called for compensation as having sacrificed everything in the British cause. The claim was found so equitable that they obtained it: not that the British government thought themselves bound to make good the losses of their subjects in the war; no such principle was ever admitted or pretended. No: but because they had encouraged these people in their opposition to the general interests and measures of their countrymen; because they had allowed and confirmed their pretensions of being their friends, and had thereby led them to make such sacrifices unavoidable. It is far from impossible but that France may conduct in the same way, and the example is worthy of consideration by those who are at the head of affairs.

There is an opinion, which has been very artfully and industriously circulated by our most inveterate antifederalists and Jacobins, that there are persons in our government inclined towards the English interests, an English party. You know with how much perseverance such a partiality was attributed to Mr. Hamilton, and has since been to President Washington himself. To him alone could Barras intend to make the application of his insulting innuendo, about the condescension of the American government to the suggestions of their ancient tyrants. It is, I am thoroughly convinced, all a party manoeuvre, a trick perfectly understood by all French public men; a *tactique*, as they call it, to make their adversaries unpopular by fixing upon them odious imputations. There is not one man in the American government that has any partialities towards Great Britain, but there is a great English influence acting among *the people* of America, an influence, which by wise and prudent measures may be diminished, but which cannot, and will not, be violently rooted out, because deeply involved and indissolubly connected with our own interests. This influence it has doubtless been the policy of the American government to check, to control, and to weaken; it will still be their policy, unless France by her rashness, and insolence, and impetuosity make it absolutely necessary to sacrifice that object, and to encourage the British influence. But indeed if we are compelled to look upon France as an enemy, we shall not find it difficult to obtain a much closer friendship with Britain than we have ever had, much closer than I, or any American friendly to France, desires. By forcing a rupture upon us, France necessarily assimilates and unites the *interests* of America with those of Great Britain; an union of interests inevitably produces intimacy of connection, and after discharging us from all the obligations of our treaty with her, by the formal renunciation of its stipulations on her part, France may finally discover what a difference there is in a treaty between us and Britain, securing all the preferences which we had before stipulated for France, and a treaty in which the same or similar preferences would be secured to her rival.[35]

We are all fully sensible how important it is for us to preserve the friendship of France, but if France, presuming upon the disposition which is universally prevalent among us, should think us ready to give up everything to her good will and pleasure, she will find to her cost, as well as to ours, that we do not *depend* upon her either for our liberty or our independence. The result of her measures will be to cast away a valuable friend, a faithful ally, and to strengthen her own enemy by so powerful an accession.

Your arguments and calculations that we could subsist without any navigation of our own are certainly just, and I hope will be properly weighed. But a war with France would by no means suspend our navigation; it would not even to a considerable degree diminish it. The only consequence would be, that instead of its trading directly with all Europe, it would principally center in the trade with England. French privateers might infest it more or less, and it would be burdened with a heavier load of insurance than it is at present. But Great Britain would be prompted by every possible inducement to protect it, and the result would only be to promote her object of grasping all commerce into her own hands or within her own dominions.

I am, &c.

JOHN QUINCY ADAMS (THE HAGUE) TO JOHN ADAMS, APRIL 3, 1797

As John Quincy prepared to leave for his new diplomatic posting in Portugal, he passed on to the newly inaugurated President Adams a revised assessment about French intentions toward the United States. It appeared the Directory had determined that the United States would never be a proper ally against Britain because of London's influence in the Eastern states. The French solution was now to wage war against the American government and sponsor the creation of a Southern-Western republic that would balance the East. For John Quincy, this confirmed his views about the vital importance of Union and independence. The perception, much less the reality, of domestic divisions, especially those based in geography, encouraged foreign meddling in American affairs. Competing domestic factions in turn would be tempted to seek out foreign allies. The country would be militarized. Under such circumstances, it would be impossible to sustain a policy of neutrality among European powers. One path led America to war, civil and international; the other path to peace and the vindication of republican government.

MY DEAR SIR:

But there appears to prevail at present a design still more pernicious as it strikes directly at our national *Union*. From the present conduct of the Directory it cannot be questioned but that they are determined upon a war with the government of the United States. There are also numerous proofs that in the prosecution of this war they are preparing to derive support from a part of the American people. The policy upon which they proceed appears to be this: that the Atlantic, or at least the eastern states, cannot be governed by the influence of France, and therefore that a southern republic must be formed in alliance with France to serve as a balance against the others. But in order to form this republic France must make war against the present government of the United States, in the progress of which she can send an army to support and assist her allies of the new republic, and hereby they will effect two purposes at once; that of weakening by division a rising power which they behold with suspicion and jealousy; and that of disencumbering themselves from a considerable portion of the army, the return of which into France they already dread. They wish to form a republic in America as they are now forming a republic in Italy, to provide for the subsistence of their troops, or at least to be themselves rid of them; and thus you will observe that they step towards war with America regularly, as they step towards peace with the House of Austria. They are constantly in expectation of this peace, and it will probably be made in the course of this spring or the following summer.

In one of my late letters I wrote that they had no idea of sending an army to America, and I formed my opinion from the state of their marine and the impossibility they are under of restoring it for a long time. But various circumstances now lead me to a different opinion, and with respect to the marine, they are preparing to turn all their exertions towards it, as may be collected clearly from the pamphlet of Theremin which I sent you a few days ago.

You will find in the newspapers which I send at this time, that Thomas Paine has left Paris, and is going to America. Another of the French papers says that he is going with Mr. Monroe *"to repair the mischief done by the administration of Washington."*

The plan of the Western Republic in alliance with France, to oppose against the rising Republic of the United States, must have been formed as early as the time of Genet's instructions. How much earlier it was formed it is perhaps not necessary to conjecture. That Paine was in the secret originally seems very probable. That he is now going to America to promote the design, I firmly believe. I see in some late American papers that he wrote to Bache last summer the necessity which the French government found themselves under to *distinguish between the American government and the people.* His pamphlet against the late President I have not seen, but am told that it is another edition of Adet's appeal to the people. What his conduct will be is easily foreseen. The French government calculate that in the war they intend, the eastern states will side with their government, but that our western country and perhaps the southern states will side with them. Paine therefore is going *"pour semer ses étincelles d'embrasement"* for which Madame Roland judged him so proper.[36] Paine indeed is pursuing his vocation. He has no country; no affections that constitute the pillars of patriotism. But going with Mr. Monroe – where can the imagination stop in reflecting upon these things? Can Monroe? Can – I have done. I remember the late President's advice not to admit hastily suspicions against the designs of citizens in distant parts of the Union, and I will yet hope that a formal purpose to sever the Union into two parts, by the help of a French war against the whole, is at least not extensively intended or known; and that it will never meet with encouragement or support from men, who ought to consider the Union as the principle paramount to all others in the policy of every American.[37]

I am, &c.

CHAPTER THREE

MINISTER TO PRUSSIA, 1797–1801

INTRODUCTION

AFTER A DIFFICULT PASSAGE through the Baltic from London, John Quincy reached Prussia in November 1797. Unfortunately, King Frederick William II was on his deathbed, and John Quincy's credentials as the American minister had been made specifically to that monarch. John Quincy could not transact official business until he presented updated credentials from his government, addressed to the new king. This put on hold the negotiation of a commercial treaty, as well as the possible exploration of American support for a Prussian-backed league of armed neutrality.

For the time being, he focused on the second part of his assignment – gathering intelligence about European affairs. Before leaving for Berlin, and especially in conversations with his successor in The Hague, William Vans Murray, John Quincy developed an understanding of the new administration's policies. In his Inaugural Message of March 4, 1797, his father had offered conciliatory language toward France. It was publicly known that he had reached out to his old friend and now political opponent, Vice President Thomas Jefferson, to try to reach an understanding with moderate Republicans about a joint approach to foreign policy. Jefferson was initially interested, but his Virginia associate, James Madison, persuaded him otherwise.

Federalist Party leaders, including members of the cabinet, feared that the president was planning to appease France, and they made clear their opposition to any understanding with the Republicans. In the meantime, Americans learned that the French had done the following: they had issued a new naval order against commerce – the *arête* of 12 Ventose (March 2, 1797), which authorized the confiscation of British goods from American vessels; they had held that neutral ships must possess a French-approved crew and passenger manifest; and they had decreed that Americans found on board vessels belonging to Great Britain would be considered pirates and treated without mercy.

John Adams called Congress into a special session to deal with the crisis. His message to Congress recommended building a number of naval frigates and creating adequate coastal defenses, enlarging specialized branches of the regular army (artillery and cavalry), and establishing a provisional army. But the message also included a proposal to make a fresh attempt at negotiation. In late May the president nominated a three-man American commission to France: South Carolinian Charles Cotesworth Pinckney, the current American minister-designate to France; John Marshall, a moderate Federalist from Virginia; and Elbridge Gerry, an Adams family friend from Massachusetts.

For many Americans, the president's policies were schizophrenic. The Republicans believed that British naval and economic tyranny was the gravest threat to the nation's security. They argued that military threats against France were bound to scuttle the possibility of a negotiated settlement with Paris and lead to war against America's natural friend. French depredations were regrettable, but they were the natural response to having been betrayed by the United States as the result of Jay's treaty. The Republicans managed to vote down several defensive proposals in the House of Representatives. Key Federalists, especially the faction that became known as the High Federalists – which included Secretary of State Timothy Pickering, Secretary of War James McHenry, Secretary of the Treasury Oliver Walcott, and Alexander Hamilton – contended that Britain ought to be supported as the lone bulwark against the civilization-wrecking

French revolutionaries. (John Quincy termed them "the English Party.") In their view, President Adams's promise of negotiations with the French undermined public support for the necessary steps to prepare the country for war – and, if the talks were consummated, could only confirm America's status as a French satellite.

For John Quincy, the United States was compelled, as a matter of right and national interest, to defend itself against French depredations. But he deduced that his father, despite holding a hard rhetorical line and advocating for military buildup, would continue to pursue a diplomatic solution. These policies were not contradictory but complementary. John Quincy would look for avenues to reinforce that viewpoint, both in Europe and in America. He also speculated on how the United States might use the conflict to facilitate the removal of European colonies from the Western Hemisphere.

The immediate good news for the United States, John Quincy told President Adams, was that contrary to his earlier fears, France was so committed to its European and Egyptian adventures that it was not in a position to dispatch a large invasion force to North America or the West Indies. The most serious threat from France, as John Quincy had long maintained, was not a military attack, but political intrigue – in this case, a campaign to bring down his father's administration, particularly through its supporters in the House of Representatives.

French actions made it increasingly difficult to follow John Quincy's narrow path of national unity, firmness, and diplomacy. New maritime regulations further threatened neutral American commerce. As to the American peace initiative, Foreign Minister Marquis de Talleyrand, while avoiding direct talks with the US delegation, employed unofficial intermediaries – W, X, Y, and Z – to make outrageous demands on the United States. The agents informed the Americans that, before the negotiations proceeded, the Directory must receive an "explanation" – an apology, as the commissioners understood it – for the president's hostile remarks to Congress the previous May. The American government must be willing to assume all the claims of its citizens against the French government, pay an indemnity to American merchantmen for French confiscations, and grant a loan to the Directory to the amount of 32 million Dutch guilders. To grease the skids, it was suggested that the American commissioners provide to Talleyrand a "personal compensation" – a bribe – of some fifty thousand pounds.

When the American commissioners refused to consider these terms, the French intermediaries became even more insistent. Once the impending French invasion of Britain succeeded, they warned, the United States would be completely exposed to French military power. They threatened to instigate a civil war in the United States and warned that the American coast would be ravaged by the French navy.

In March 1798, at the request of Congress, the Adams administration published the dispatches of its commissioners. The XYZ Affair, as it came to be known, created an instant sensation on both sides of the Atlantic. Americans were outraged – a sentiment that Federalist leaders were happy to encourage. Pledges of support poured in for President Adams. Congress – despite a relatively close vote in the House – finally authorized merchantmen to arm, and it permitted naval actions against French privateers along the American coast. Whatever the legal niceties, the United States was now in a naval conflict – what became known as the "Quasi-War" – with France. At the request of President Adams, George Washington agreed to come out of retirement and serve as commander of the American army. Hamilton, at Washington's insistence, was named second in command, much to the president's displeasure. And Congress passed several laws, most famously the Alien and Sedition Acts, aimed at curbing the influence of French operatives and sympathizers. John Adams did not request such legislation but neither did he oppose it.

Despite widespread sentiment among Federalists for a formal declaration of war against France, the president did not make such a request to Congress. He did offer hard-line responses to public petitions offering support, but he felt hamstrung by Republican opposition to more substantial defense buildup. He also wanted to keep open a peaceful solution if and when the French showed a willingness to settle on reasonable terms. Maritime successes by the US Navy strengthened his hand, as did tacit cooperation with the Royal Navy.

The French opened up a diplomatic back channel through Murray, when Louis Andre Pinchon, formerly secretary to the French mission to the United States, arrived in The Hague. At first, Pinchon did not claim to be operating in an official capacity, but his approach to Murray was evidently an attempt to reopen diplomatic relations with America. Or was this merely a ruse to embarrass the United States and further divide the country? Murray responded cautiously and sought John Quincy's advice about how to proceed, because he had no authorization to engage the French. From early July to the end of September 1798, through this stream of detailed correspondence, John Quincy had been made almost completely privy to Murray's doings. Perhaps the most important contribution that he made to the back-channel negotiations was that he did not disapprove of them, even though he suspected the French were up to no good. Had he done so, Murray, already skittish, would have desisted from – or at least limited – his contacts with the French.

The key question was, would the French offer credible "assurances" through Murray, such that there would be no repetition of the XYZ Affair, and that Paris would negotiate seriously? And of what must the assurances consist? Based substantially on reports from Murray and his old friend Gerry, in February 1799 President Adams offered provisionally to send another three-man commission, which included Murray, to France. The president insisted that the French must offer acceptable assurances but, as a precondition for negotiations, he did not demand that France revoke its most egregious naval decrees. He also ordered that the planned expansion of the army be halted. John Adams was also undoubtedly influenced by John Quincy's views, which were conveyed to him directly by John Quincy's secretary Thomas Adams, who had returned to Philadelphia from Berlin in January 1799. The president reached this decision despite strenuous opposition from his Federalist Party and much of the cabinet. The commission eventually convened in Paris in February 1800.

John Quincy, in the meantime, received his revised credentials to Prussia and began negotiating a new commercial agreement with Berlin. But Secretary Pickering ordered him to abandon the liberal maritime principle of "free ships make free goods," and otherwise to follow the lead of Jay's treaty, with its concessions to the British-preferred standards of the rights of neutrals. John Quincy doubted that the Prussians – friendly now with France and strong advocates of neutral trade – would accept these alterations to the original treaty with the United States.

For some time, John Quincy and Count Haugwitz, the principal Prussian negotiator, exchanged notes and commercial treaty drafts. In May 1799, Haugwitz accepted John Quincy's language with the exception of the critical provision concerning "free ships make free goods." John Quincy decided that substitute language provided by Haugwitz suited the same purpose. The final text was agreed to in July 1799 and approved by the US Senate in February 1800.

On October 15, 1800, John Quincy read in the *Leipzig Gazette* a report that France and the United States finally signed an agreement (the Convention of Mortefontaine). Unfortunately, news of the convention reached the United States too late to influence the presidential election. John Adams was narrowly defeated by Thomas Jefferson. The president's loss resulted from the opposition by Jefferson's Republicans – who had long accused the elder Adams of being a closet monarchist – but also from a split among High Federalists, who favored a tougher line toward France and much closer ties with Britain.

When John Adams heard rumors that President-elect Jefferson might ask John Quincy to serve in another diplomatic post, he decided to put an end to the matter. He assumed that John Quincy would not want to be subject to the sort of humiliation he himself had experienced during the Revolution, when he was often left in official limbo while on diplomatic service. "It is my opinion this minister ought to be recalled from Prussia," the president informed the new secretary of state, John Marshall. "Justice would require that he be sent to France or England, if he should be continued in Europe. The mission to St. James is perfectly well filled by Mr. [Rufus] King; that to France is no doubt destined for some other character. Besides, it is my opinion that it is my duty to call him home."[1]

In late April 1801, John Quincy received his official letter of recall from Secretary Marshall. On arriving back in Massachusetts, he initially resisted entering politics, especially given the treatment his father had received. "I feel strong temptation and great provocation to plunge into political controversy," he noted in his journal. "But I hope to preserve myself from it by the considerations which have led me to the resolution of renouncing. A politician in this country must be a man of party. I would fain be the man of my whole country."[2]

His plans to stay out of politics did not last long. He was elected state senator in 1802, and later that year he was narrowly defeated for a congressional seat. In 1803, as part of a bargain with the High Federalists, including Timothy Pickering, he was selected by the Massachusetts legislature to serve in the US Senate.

JOHN QUINCY ADAMS (BERLIN) TO JOHN ADAMS, JANUARY 31, 1798

John Adams was one of the original and strongest advocates of eschewing political ties with any European state in order to keep the United States out of European wars. John Quincy agreed wholeheartedly. But, as the latter pointed out in this private letter to his father, it was impossible to keep out of European affairs entirely while

American commerce – the source of its current national prosperity – was closely tied to the competing economies of Britain and France. The solution was not to abandon overseas commerce altogether and adopt a China-like isolationism, or to align exclusively with either maritime great power, but "to have friends other than either."

MY DEAR SIR:

I have met here several gentlemen in the diplomatic line who claim an acquaintance with you during your residence in Europe. The Baron d'Alvensleben, now one of the ministers in the department of foreign affairs, and the Baron Schultz von Ascherade, now minister from Sweden here, represented their respective courts at the Hague when you were there in 1788 just before your return to America. Upon my arrival here I found the Baron de Rosenkrantz, Minister from Denmark. He was either secretary of the Danish legation or chargé des affaires in Holland at the period of your reception there. All these gentlemen have desired me to present them to your remembrance. The Baron de Rosenkrantz was peculiarly obliging to me upon my first arrival, sought me out and rendered me many of the kind services which are necessary to a total stranger in a novel situation. He has since been appointed by the Danish cabinet to attend the Congress at Rastadt, where he now is, though to return hereafter the Congress. In the meantime there is left here only a chargé des affaires. I met him in company last evening. He inquired of me whether the United States had a minister at Copenhagen. You remember what I wrote you from the Hague of similar intimations given me there. This gentleman, upon my answering, that we had not, repeated the same topics which had been urged by the Danish legation at the Hague, of the commercial relations between the two countries and the similarity of their maritime interests. There have been so many of these advances from Denmark that it seems to me they deserve some attention; considering especially that the pass of the Sound is theirs, and that the whole Baltic trade, that of Russia, Sweden, and most of the *direct* commerce that we can ever have with Prussia, will thus depend much upon their control.[3]

The French minister here, Caillard, remembered me as an old acquaintance and interpreter for Mr. Dana at St. Petersburg, where he was at that time secretary of the French legation. He has been very civil and obliging to me, and I believe wishes for a conciliation between our countries. I have related to the Secretary of State the substance of conversations I have had with him relative to our affairs.[4]

The only ministers of foreign powers with whom I have had no communication, other than an exchange of cards, are the Prince Reuss the Austrian and Count Panin the Russian envoys. The former seldom appears except when the indispensable etiquette requires his attendance at court. The Emperor's Ambassador you can imagine will not readily be a favorite at Berlin. The King is now ill with the measles; when he first was taken and before the nature of his disorder was ascertained, a report was freely circulated that he had caught the scarlet fever by infection carried to him by Prince Reuss at an audience which he had just after visiting a person sick of that distemper.[5] Since the measles have become unequivocal the rumor has dropped, and only leaves evidence of a disposition somewhere to fasten odious imputations upon the Imperial minister. The King is attended by an *English* physician, who first spread the idea tracing the royal illness to Prince Reuss. I believe he was honest in the opinion. I have had in my own family too good reason to be satisfied with his skill and goodness of disposition, to suspect him of designing an unfounded report so necessarily prejudicial to an innocent man. But when conjecture looks round for the origin of an *unpleasant* effect, we may fairly conclude that cause upon which it most readily fixes not to be a remarkably pleasant one. I believe that I have already intimated to you that I have had reason to think the mission from the United States here peculiarly agreeable from the circumstance that they had sent none yet to Vienna. It is a sort of precedency of compliment with which they feel themselves flattered. But the sentiments at Vienna from the same circumstance will naturally be different and opposite. This may perhaps account for the distance which Prince Reuss observes towards me, which I should not perhaps have remarked but for its strong contrast with the apparent earnestness of notice that I have received from all the court here, and from all the foreign ministers excepting him and Count Panin. There may be something of the same kind in his motives, and I must also add that in both cases it may be the mere effect of personal character, or of accident. You know that when Lafayette was liberated the Austrian Cabinet at least endeavored to make merit of it towards the United States, by saying that the Emperor consented to it in consequence of the application from America, and expressing his goodwill towards us; and perhaps you may have noticed that this happened just at the time when the European prints announced the American mission to Berlin.[6] Since the House of Austria has become mistress of the state of Venice, the prospect of its becoming a maritime power of importance has very much increased, and if we get fully into the Mediterranean, we shall certainly have considerable commercial relation with her dominions.

I mention these things to you because I am persuaded you will attribute them to their true and proper motives. It is the interest both of Britain and France to contract and narrow our connections with all the other European powers. No one better than you knows how inflexibly that policy was always pursued by France under her monarchical government; she has not now abandoned it. The writers of the Directory even now exultingly threaten that if we do not appease their wrath, we shall make no more treaties unless with the Indians; and the citizen Caillard the other day told me that if France should succeed in this expedition against England, (of which he was far, he said, from being sure) she would then proclaim the universal and unlimited liberty of the seas, and there should thenceforth be *no more treaties of commerce*.

The partisans of Great Britain in our country have favored the very same system from the same principles, though of opposite application. As England wants to keep all our commerce to herself, she very naturally is averse to the means which are calculated to extend it elsewhere. Both these descriptions of people have known very well how to take advantage of the popular arguments which promote their views. They have told us that we have nothing to do with the affairs and quarrels of Europe, and that a diplomatic intercourse with its governments would tend to involve us unnecessarily in its wars, and they have alarmed us with calculations of the expense to which every additional minister in Europe would subject the people of the United States.

The experience of the last six years has abundantly shown how impossible it is to keep us disconnected with the affairs of Europe, while we have such essential mercantile connections with the great maritime states; and the numerous injuries we have suffered alternately from both parties amply prove how essential it is to our interests to have other friends than either. In every naval war it must be the interest of Britain and of France to drawer to force us into it as parties, while it must always be our unequivocal interest to remain neutral. In the present war I am confident we have suffered more for want of a free intercourse, communication and concert, with the neutral states in Europe, than would discharge five times the expense of maintaining ministers with them, and if we should finally be forced out of the system which the government has had so much at heart and compelled to engage in hostilities for our own defence, it may be in some measure attributed to the neglect of a good understand ing with the nations which have had an interest similar to ours, that is a neutral interest....

Some of the newspapers have intimated that Mr. Morris (Gouverneur) was charged by the British Ministry with such a negotiation here, and Prince Ferdinand (brother of the Great Frederick) assured me that it was so, adding that it was thought a very strange proposal for *an American* to make.[7] Baron Alvensleben the first time that I saw him asked me several questions about Mr. Morris, who he said had given much dissatisfaction here. I told him that Morris had long ceased to be in any sort of employ under the American government, and hinted that I had seen a newspaper paragraph pretending that he was now in the English service, of which however I was altogether ignorant. «Pour vous parler franchement» (said he) «je crois que c'est un volontaire en politique, qui ne tient ses pourvoirs que de lui même.» [8] From the two anecdotes I conclude either that the British government did employ Morris and afterwards disavowed him, or that he pretended to have authority from them, when in truth he had none. This at least is certain, that he has made himself very obnoxious both here and at Vienna, where he received an express order to quit the Austrian territory. The same *intimation* was given him at Berlin, though not in so formal a manner. His conduct has nowhere been such as to do honor or credit to his country, if it may be judged by its effects. He is yet wandering about at some of the small German Courts, and had left Hamburg but a short time before I came through it in October.

I remain, &c.

JOHN QUINCY ADAMS (BERLIN) TO WILLIAM VANS MURRAY, JULY 14, 1798

John Quincy and his colleague in The Hague had been exchanging ideas about the future of the French and English colonies in the Caribbean (most immediately, the French possession of San Domingo). John Quincy had long believed that such colonial relationships were unjust and bound ultimately to fail. Should – and, if so, how should – the United States expedite the process? Here John Quincy contended that these islands were naturally connected with the American continent and not that of Europe. And he speculated that it would be possible for the United States to establish a relationship with them different from that of a metropolitan master and a colonial servant – that is, leaving their governments free and independent and protected by the United States, which would exclusively supply their needs and convey their produce.

DEAR SIR:

The English papers last arrived here announced another measure, as of the 1st or 2nd of June, more decisive and more effectual yet than any of the former; a suspension of commercial intercourse with all French territories until the settlement of the differences. I wish it may be true, but neither my letters nor the papers mention such a measure as contemplated.

I hope that their West India Islands will not be forgotten. We can and must do something there. Our newspapers say, that their generals of color are decidedly with us and in case of war will declare for us. Yes, my dear sir, free and independent, in close alliance and under guarantee of United States. With the navy which our enemies are forcing upon us, we can in my opinion unquestionably maintain such a state of things. Those islands will not be English if they can help it, and we ought not to give them away. The natural connection of the West Indies is with the American and not with the European continent, and such a connection as I have in my mind, a more natural connection than that of metropolis and colony, or in other words master and servant. In close alliance, leaving them as to their government totally to themselves, we can protect their independence, furnish them with necessaries, and stipulate for the exclusive carriage of their produce. Think upon this idea which is yet crude and undigested in my mind, and may be unsolid. I know not whether *France* will declare formal war against the government of United States, very probably she may. But she has been making war this year and a half, and will certainly not cease it until she has completely ruined us, or until we formally resist. Until she can send her Rapinats to plunder all our property at home, public and private, to place, and displace and replace, at pleasure our future directors and legislators, or until we prove to her that the spirit of freedom and independence is not with us totally extinct, as it is in every part of Europe excepting England.[9]

JOHN QUINCY ADAMS (BERLIN) TO WILLIAM VANS MURRAY, SEPTEMBER 25, 1798

John Quincy had been convinced that, despite signals from France it was softening its position toward the United States, the French were merely playing their old game of political intrigue, to divide and conquer the American people. But after reading several months of reports from Murray about his conversations with Louis Pinchon, the unofficial French emissary, he thought there was a possibility that the French really might be open to a settlement, not out of a change of heart but because of military setbacks in the Old World, such as the defeat of Napoleon's fleet at the Battle of the Nile. If that was truly the case, America's best policy was likewise one of peace – but only if France met American terms in advance of a full restoration of diplomatic relations by revoking its illegal maritime decrees and fully restoring the United States' neutral rights.

DEAR SIR:

Under the circumstances, which have recently taken place and the system of conduct now pursued by 3 towards us, my own opinion inclines unequivocally for a *negotiation*. I can really conceive at present a *possibility*, that they may seriously wish a state of peace with us, and if so have not the most distant doubt but that our best policy dictates peace with them. We stand at present upon fair ground. If they will make offers sufficient to cover our complaints and remove the causes of them, I am persuaded they will be accepted and cordially hope they will. But to remove the cause of complaint they must restore to us *unequivocal rights of neutrality*, with which the law of 29 nivose is totally inconsistent.

I perceive that Cauzard (the member who so honourably

attacked that law in the Journal of 500.) declares that the Moniteur did not give a just account of his speech, but gave it in a garbled, mutilated state, suppressing many of the statements "to the publicity of which the speaker attached a particular interest." Yet even as it appeared its arguments were unanswerable to honest men, and others could only say "that the repeal would discourage privateers" – and that "the English could purchase neutral papers." Without the repeal of that law, it is idle for us to think of being at peace with them. Its execution alone constitutes the worst war, that they can carry on against us.

Yet I believe the possibility, that they may now wish peace with us, for they will probably have their hands full from other quarters. The fleet with which Bonaparte *had been*, is beyond all doubt principally if not entirely destroyed. The Directory say that their troops entered Cairo the 23rd of July; other accounts announce them as very near to

> "that Serbonian bog,
> "Between Damietta and mount Casius old
> "Where *armies whole have sunk*.

But even if the statement of the *message* be true – the Porte is certainly provoked to the utmost, at this invasion of Egypt. It is very confidently said here, that it has formally declared war against France. If not, there is every probability that it soon will. Russia is equally determined, and in consequence of the concert of these two late inveterate enemies a Russian fleet is already at the gates of the Thracian Bosphorus and ready to pass the Straits with the *consent* of the Turks, as soon as the wind will permit. This Russian fleet is to join that of England, and must give the complete controul of the Mediterranean to the combined powers, and cout off all communication, or at best all means of reinforcement from France to the Egyptian army. Whether they will be able to maintain themselves there, without help, against the Country and the climate, time must discover. As to their proceeding to India, I have no faith in that yet.

Their Irish plans promise them less than ever. The neck of rebellion in that Country appears to be broken and the whole system, which was so formidably organized, utterly overthrown. The result has been such as no doubt mightily to strengthen the British Ministry in England and to weaken the opposition, whose principal leaders were so foolish as to testify W. O'Connor's loyalty.

On the Continent there is too much probability that they will still domineer. Their peace with the Empire, and I believe with Austria is in their own hands. This little check may persuade them to conclude it. In that case Russia will hang back, the Poarte make its terms, and England again have to stand sole combatant. Then too, I suspect Bona would resume her old system of conduct toward us. But at last we are sure that the more her maritime force gets crippled, the less formidable she will be to us.

Yours always.

JOHN QUINCY ADAMS (BERLIN) TO JOHN ADAMS, SEPTEMBER 25, 1798

In this lengthy report to his father – dated the same day as his letter to Murray – John Quincy offered essentially no grounds for believing that French policy toward the United States might have changed. He offered President Adams standards by which to judge French sincerity – "an offer of indemnity for past depredations and security against the future." Thomas Adams carried this letter and other reports from John Quincy back to America at a critical time when the president was deciding whether to send a new delegation to France.[10]

MY DEAR SIR:

I have not for some weeks, perhaps for some months, written directly to yourself. – The current information in this part of the world, which could prove interesting, I have however communicated from time to time in letters which though not directed to yourself, were intended for your perusal – and amidst the numerous dangers of capture which every letter must be exposed to, on its passage, I could not write with confidence, not having a cypher with you, and doubting the propriety of using that which I have with the Secretary of State, for private correspondence with you – I now enclose however, by my brother, who will be the bearer of this Letter, a cypher, which may be used in future in case of necessity, though I shall willingly spare you the trouble of decyphering, as well as myself that of cyphering, upon every occasion which shall not positively require it.

This Country is at present far from fruitful in materials for a political correspondence. I have heretofore informed you what for some years past has been the system of this Government in its foreign affairs, and that a change of reign has produced no alteration it. A system of neutrality must indeed depend upon a state of War, between other powers, and as Peace has been now made upon the Continent, almost a year and an half between the great powers towards which the Prussian neutrality was applied, it should seem that there could be no further occasion for its continuance. – But that Peace has been hitherto nothing more than an armistice always ready to break out in new hostility, and during which the most strenuous exertions have been made to draw Prussia into a new combination to contend against the all destroying doctrines and all devouring domination of France. – This however has been steadily refused here – The doctrines indeed are detested; but Peace and prosperity are considered as the best security against them – The domination is dreaded; but War, it is apprehended would only render it more inevitable. – And there is a consideration of great weight to be taken into the account when the conduct of this Government is to be estimated; the feelings of the Nation. – The angry passions of this people, are all directed against its two formidable neighbours, the Russians and Austrians: these, they consider as their natural enemies, and it would be easy to animate their resentments against them, to such a degree as prepares men for obstinate and violent struggles. But France they consider as their natural friend and ally – they have no fear of her doctrines, but on the contrary their secret wishes rather favour their progress, and as they feel nothing of her domination, they cannot or will not perceive the danger of it so long as she makes not her direct attack against them. – These sentiments not only pervade the people in general, but they are very prevalent through the army, which did not willingly fight the french five years ago, and which would undoubtedly be still more reluctant now.[11]

Besides this, it is certain that the army itself is no longer what it was under Frederic the second.[12] Even the twenty-three last years of his life, with the exception of a single campaign in 1778, were years of Peace. The military discipline was relaxed by his immediate successor – In his polish and french campaigns this army was found not invincible, and its latest recollections are not crowned with the trophies of victory. – The treasure which Frederic the 2d: and his father, during two long reigns had accumulated, eleven short years were more than sufficient entirely to dissipate, and at the accession of the present king those two great pillars of the Prussian power, were so weakend and dissolved, that with all the new additions of territory and revenue, which the final partition of Poland brought with it, cannot restore without years of constant vigilance, and rigorous œconomy, the vigour and energy, which an extraordinary man had given, and a weak one had lost to the power of Prussia.[13]

The king appears to be fully sensible of what the interest of his Country and his own requires, and turns an unremitted attention to the restoration of a severe discipline, and to the recovery of the pecuniary resources, the sinews of War – For both these purposes, Peace is absolutely necessary, and upon these grounds the pacific system of Prussia, so severely censured, and subject to such great and serious objections rests for its justification.

Peace is likewise an object of the greatest importance to the Emperors both of Germany and of Russia. But they would have sacrificed it again by the formation of a new Coalition, if Prussia had consented to join them. The disposition of Russia has been discovered by the fleats which she has already sent to join those of England in the North Seas, and by other measures which I shall not repeat here, because they have been detailed elsewhere in letters which will undoubtedly be submitted to your perusal. – To the same source I refer for an account of the Events which have produced a state of War between France and the Porte, and for the current news relative to the great french expedition against Egypt, and the fate of the fleat which escorted their army thither.[14]

It is however very doubtful to me whether the war between Austria and France will be seriously renewed. The appearances of such an Event, have been owing altogether to that domineering tone which France has constantly preserved, and to her maintaining extravagant pretensions, upon the construction of the articles in the Peace of Campo Formio, and upon the satisfaction for the insult upon Bernadotte[15] – Her late check will teach her to withdraw some of those pretensions, and the Emperor will be glad to seize the opportunity of preserving Peace sometime longer.[16]

The present situation of the affairs of France, however, combining with the spirit which she at length finds roused in the United States, have produced a great and important change in her conduct towards us. It is no longer an overbearing and insolent minister of external relations, who keeps three ministers waiting five months without reception, and, after attempting to dupe and swindle them by his pimping spies, insults us by a discrimination injurious to the rights of an independent nation, and disgraceful to the objects of his choice.[17] No longer a self-imagined conqueror, dictating apologies and prescribing tribute as the preliminaries to hearing for claims of justice. In proportion as our spirit of resistance has become manifest, theirs of oppression and extortion has shrunk back. Even Mr. Gerry returned home with a full persuasion that the dispositions in France towards us were altogether pacific. That gentleman unfortunately was not qualified for negotiation with such men as now govern France. He was charmed with words; he was duped by professions; he had neither the spirit nor the penetration absolutely necessary for dealing with adversaries at once so bold, so cunning, and so false. Since his departure they have redoubled their pretences of moderation and peaceable dispositions. They have totally changed their system of conduct but their purposes remain the same. The manner in which they received Doctor Logan, who made no scruple to give himself out as the envoy of the French party in America; and the manner in which they wished to blind our government by a pretence of not having received him, will be known to you more directly than from hence.[18] You will judge from what motives such a species of duplicity could proceed. They are at present very industrious in spreading abroad the idea that they wish reconciliation with the United States, and are extremely desirous of a new negotiation. All this for the present is probably nothing more than a design to lull us into security, and especially to divide the people of the United States from their government. They have discovered by their arrogance, and indignities, and pretended contempt of our friendship, they have only weakened their own party in America, and given strength and vigor to the friends of government. But at the same time they have seen our people grasp at every shadow of conciliation, and cling to every transient semblance of peace, with such ardor and anxiety, that they now think it sufficient to damp all that energy which has surprised them by its unexpected appearance, if they affect a desire of returning friendship.

All this, however, will be deemed mere artifice while they continue to violate the rights of neutrality; a mere lullaby to keep us inactive and defenceless, until they shall have more leisure to point their whole force against us. As long as there is no offer of indemnity for past depredations or security against the future, we should be worse than idiots to trust their professions at a time when we know them contradicted by their conduct. The law of 29 Nivôse remains yet in full force. A recent attempt was made in the Council of Five Hundred to obtain its repeal. Its injustice and pernicious tendency were demonstrated in their full extent. But it was answered that the repeal would discourage the privateers, and that the English could purchase neutral papers by the load. The Council passed to the order [of the] day, and refused the common advantage of publication to the speech of the member who moved the repeal (Couzard). The *Moniteur* gave this speech in such a mutilated manner that its author openly declared the misrepresentation, and nothing further was done upon a subject in which Couzard himself proved in his speech France was violating the most sacred laws of nations and making herself enemies of every people.[19]

She has indeed many other modes of producing the same effect – The general system of tyranny which she pursues towards all her neighbours has so often been exposed, that the perpetual repetition of its details in the current events of the time grows tedious even to disgust. – I have therefore in my late correspondence paid little attention to those details – I have left it to the newspapers to inform you how Switzerland, Sardinia, Rome, Malta and Egypt have in turn been treated by the *great* Nation, the Jonathan Wild of Nations – There you will find that conquest and revolution, fire and the sword are carried to every quarter of the Earth, accompanied by the very same professions of friendship and Peace, as are now lavished upon us. – No declaration of War has been made in any one of these instances. – The last is peculiarly remarkable – An army of forty thousand men has invaded Egypt by the orders of the Directory, who never hinted to the Legislative Councils, where it was destined or against whom it was directed. – They now send a message and say – "your armies have landed at Alexandria, and entered Cairo; they are to be the liberators of the Egyptians and the avengers of the wrongs inflicted by the *Beys*; upon Frenchmen. – We declared no War *because there was no one against whom to declare it* – Not the Porte, because we had no enmity to the turkish government, but on the contrary go as its friends and avengers – Not against the Beys, because they are a mere banditti, not worthy the honour of a declaration of War." – Upon such arguments as these a Country is invaded and conquered, and the Council of 500 without a murmur or a scruple pass a resolve that the Army of Egypt has deserved well of the Country – Of a Country where an express article of the Constitution says that the right of declaring War shall be exercised exclusively by the Legislature.[20]

At Rastadt the german empire continues to implore Peace, and France continues to advance burdensome conditions for granting it – the former has now fully consented to demolish Chreubreitstein – the only fortress which has proved impregnable during the present War. The only good security against invasion for the future – They have further consented to cede the island of St: Peter upon the Rhine, with the left banks of which the great Nation is no longer satisfied, from the instant when they are yielded to her.[21]

I am, &c.

P.S. Mr: Bourne our Consul at Amsterdam, would be glad to be employed upon any temporary service, for which the Government may have occasion, as in the present circumstances his situation at Amsterdam is not advantageous to him; all commerce between that place and the United States being suspended. I have heretofore given you my opinion of his merit, and have had no reason to alter it – I believe him to be a deserving man, though I know not what occasion there may be for such an employment as he wishes, nor indeed very precisely what that is.

I have before mentioned to you the desire of the Baron de Thulemeier, to be remembered to you. I frequently meet him and scarcely ever without his renewing the request, and making enquiries after you, and whether I have lately heard from you.[22]

JOHN QUINCY ADAMS (BERLIN) TO ABIGAIL ADAMS, MAY 7, 1799

John Quincy still doubted French sincerity in reopening diplomatic relations. But through Abigail Adams he wanted his father to know that he appreciated the difficult political circumstances in which the president found himself. The United States could not continue in a halfway situation, between peace and war, and Congress would not declare war. The controversial appointment of a new peace condition would soon be seen as wise and necessary.

MY DEAR MOTHER:

The latest accounts we have from America announce three circumstances of no small importance – the appointment of a new commission to treat with France,[23] the capture of the French frigate *l'Insurgente* by our frigate *Constellation*, and the symptoms of a new insurrection against the national government in the western part of Pennsylvania.[24] Though we are informed that the appointment of the new commission was attended with great divisions in the public opinion concerning the expediency of the step, I trust that in the course of a few months it will be generally seen and acknowledged that the measure was proper and wise. The situation in which we stood before, halfway between peace and war, could not continue, and as the legislative body had thought proper not to declare war, I can see no substantial reason why the large advances made towards a new negotiation and the solicitations to that effect of the French government should be rejected. I have not indeed for my own part any opinion of the sincerity of their professions, and expect very little from their justice; nor do I suppose they have ability, if they had the inclination, to restore the property they have plundered from our merchants, or an indemnity for it. But I believe that negotiation at present may put a stop to further depredation, and that a more advantageous arrangement may be obtained than after a longer delay. After the close of ever so long a war we should have still less prospects of compensation for still greater losses, and there is no probability that there will be ever a period, when the desire of accommodation with us will be stronger than at present. This disposition will be confirmed by the capture of their frigate, which will tend to convince them that our naval power is not so contemptible as they have represented to the world and to themselves. Two years ago they published in a pamphlet, written undoubtedly at the command of the Directory, that all our sea captains were ignorant sots, and that since the death of Mr. Gillon we could not call a single good sea officer into our service. I wish that the captains of all our frigates would give them proofs equally substantial, that our marine can furnish very good officers yet with that given by Commodore Truxtun. There is one in whom I have not the same confidence, and I am sorry he commands the *Boston* frigate. I have had occasion to know that he was utterly unfit for the station. I have lately heard that he has been dismissed. They have related the affair between the *Constellation* and *l'Insurgente* in the Paris papers with unusual modesty. They say that the frigate had 44 guns, but the American had 18-pounders and the French only twelves, so that the capture of the French ship was the *necessary result of her inferiority*. This circumstance is much less satisfactory to them, than the prospect of a new rebellion, which has manifested itself in Northumberland County, Pennsylvania. There is in that part of our country a spirit which I believe will never be suppressed but by force. "Though brutal that contest and foul," I very much fear we shall be forced to come to it, and when we do, have no doubt but the good cause will prove itself as superior to its opposers in it, as it always has in that of reason. Such things as these insurrections, however, injure very much the estimation of our country with the rest of the world, and give cause of exultation to our enemies in Europe, who are deficient neither in numbers nor virulence.

The spirit of party has indeed done so much injury among us in various shapes, that it has given our very national character an odious aspect in the eyes of many observing foreigners. The

English newspapers last spring gave an account of the transactions of our national House of Representatives in the affairs between Lyon and Griswold, heading the relation in large characters with "American Manners."[25] Porcupine's pamphlet exposing Judge M'Kean's conduct towards him was republished in England, and commented on under a title altered from the "Democratic" to the "Republican Judge."[26] His charge to the grand jury upon that occasion has been represented as a specimen of our judiciary proceedings, and it has been said with truth, that there is not a country in Europe, unless it be France, where a judge could so act and so speak, without condemning himself not only to universal infamy, but to forfeit his place. It is not however alone in England, where we may expect that everything to our disadvantage will find busy tongues and willing ears, that such things are circulated. Here in Germany a man by the name of Bülow, after travelling twice in the United States has published two volumes entitled, "The Republic of North America in its present Condition."[27] It is one continued libel upon the character and manners of the American people, written with considerable ingenuity. It contains beyond all doubt a vast deal of falsehood, but every American who feels for the honor of his country must confess with shame that it also contains too much of truth. The author's mode of collecting facts appears generally to have been, to gather from the newspapers and from private malignity all the abuse which the most inveterate partisans of opposite political sentiments have imputed reciprocally to each other, and to deal it out all as equally true and equally stigmatizing to the national character. The book has been a good deal read in Germany, and, as it has been two years published, would have been long since translated and published in England, did not the writer show himself as inimical to the English government as to the American people. I think it very probable that the work will someday or other find its way to the English press.

There has also been published within these few months, in English, in French, and in German, the travels of La Rochefoucault-

Liancourt in the United States.[28] He writes with the feelings of a Frenchman, and probably with a wish so far to recommend himself to the governing party in France as to obtain a permission to return. He discovers a proportionate degree of asperity against the English and their government, which appears to be somewhat embittered by an order from Lord Dorchester forbidding him to go into lower Canada.[29] But with respect to Americans he discovers much candor, and speaks well of almost everybody. I inclose a translation of what he says about a person of our acquaintance which will perhaps amuse you.

JOHN QUINCY ADAMS (BERLIN) TO JOHN ADAMS, NOVEMBER 25, 1800

By this time, news reached Europe that President Adams had in all likelihood been defeated by the Republicans for reelection. John Quincy faced the difficult task of offering his condolences to his father. He emphasized the president's extraordinary success in avoiding a disastrous full-scale war with France (which many of the High Federalists demanded) – without resorting to bribes and sacrificing the interests of the United States – yet preventing the country from becoming a tributary of the French (as the Republicans seemed to favor). At the same time, the agreement with France, which was the most favorable thing that America could reasonably hope for, did not lead to renewed conflict with Britain. In John Quincy's view, President Adams's virtuoso political, military, and diplomatic performance merited the highest praise: "you were the man, not of any party, but of the whole nation."

MY DEAR SIR:

Many months have passed since I received a line from you, or from my dear mother. From my brother Thomas I have no letter of a later date than July, and from the Department of State I have but one dated since last February. Perhaps I am to impute the greater part of this seeming oblivion of my American correspondents to my own remissness during the last winter. For six months, however, I have scarcely suffered a week to pass without writing, and unless my letters should have been unfortunate beyond the common proportion of failures, many of them must before this have reached the United States. I have not written, indeed, directly to you since July, but I suppose most of my letters to my brother, written upon my tour into Silesia, have been perused by you, and have given you frequent information of our situation.[30]

I have, therefore, been obliged to depend upon the accounts from America contained in the public newspapers and the private intelligence of some Americans in Europe. All these concur in representing the state of parties and the temper of the public mind in such a state, as to leave scarce a doubt but that a change will take place at the ensuing election, which will leave you at your own disposal, and furnish one more example to the world, how the most important services to the public and a long laborious life, anxiously and *successfully* devoted to their welfare, are rewarded in popular governments.

As I know that from the earliest period of your political life you have always made up your account to meet sooner or later such treatment in return for every sacrifice and every toil, I hope and confidently believe that you will be prepared to bear this event with calmness and composure, if not with indifference; that you will not suffer it to prey upon your mind, or affect your health; nor even to think more hardly of your country than she deserves. Her truest friends I am persuaded will more keenly feel your removal from the head of her administration than yourself. Your long settled and favorite pursuits of literature and of farming will give you full employment, and prevent that craving void of the mind which is so apt to afflict statesmen out of place; which conjures up a spectre to haunt them, or embitters them against their own species in a degree that renders their own lives miserable.[31]

In your retirement you will have not only the consolation of a consciousness that you have discharged all the duties of a virtuous citizen, but the genuine pleasure of reflecting, that by the wisdom and firmness of your administration you left that very country in safe and honorable peace, which at the period of your entrance into office was involved in dangerous and complicated disputes with more than one formidable foreign power. That without the smallest sacrifice of national honor and dignity you have succeeded in settling a quarrel with France which, under any other system of conduct than that which you pursued, would at this moment have burst into a most ruinous and fatal war, or could only be pacified by disgraceful and burthensome humiliations. The merit of this system, too, is so entirely and exclusively your own, that we are told it was disapproved by almost all the principal leaders of the party friendly to the constitution and the union, the great supporters of your last election. Nay, the general opinion is, that to this defection of your friends, originating solely in your adherence to the system you had adopted against their opinions, must be ascribed your removal from the chair at this time. Indeed, my dear sir, if this be the case, it is not your fame or honor that will suffer by the result. The common and vulgar herd of statesmen and warriors are so wont to promote on every occasion their private and personal interest at the expense of their country, that it will be a great and glorious preeminence for you to have exhibited an example of the contrary, of a statesman who made the sacrifice of his own interest and influence the real and unquestionable benefit of his country.

I am fully convinced that the gentlemen who were so much dissatisfied with your determination to send the last mission to France acted from motives of pure patriotism at first, however they may have suffered wounded pride and angry passions to influence their conduct since. But in their aversion to the last embassy they certainly proceeded upon inaccurate information as to the general state of things in Europe, and upon judgments into which there entered more of temper than of consideration. Had the issue of the mission been eventually unsuccessful, it would still have been a measure grounded upon the soundest policy; but if ever the wisdom of a questionable plan was justified to the utmost by the event, it has been so on this occasion. The convention with France has not indeed given us everything we could have wished; but it has secured us more than we ever could have obtained without it, and has entirely removed the danger of a war which must probably have ended in a dissolution of our union. And this arrangement will not even occasion a difference between us and England, since the British government have given a formal assurance that they see nothing in the Convention of which they have reason to complain.

Probably the individual sufferers under the French depredations, and the party who declared themselves so strongly against the late negotiation, will think the want of a stipulation for complete indemnity a sufficient objection against the conclusion of the treaty.[32] But those who know how impossible any stipulation of indemnity is to obtain where it cannot be compelled, or how illusive and nugatory it would be if made, will be convinced, as I think the people of the United States in general will be convinced, that the convention taken altogether is highly advantageous to us.[33] Let then a thinking and impartial man compare the situation of the United States on the 4th of March, 1797, when you assumed the functions of their first Executive magistrate, with their situation on the same day 1801, when I here suppose they will cease. Let him observe them at the first period, at the point of war to every appearance inevitable with France and Spain, yet at the same time having the highest reason to complain against the treatment of Great Britain. At the last period in full and, as far as human foresight can judge, in safe and permanent peace with all these powers. And let him ask himself how much of this favorable change ought justly to be ascribed to you; the answer will flash with the light of demonstration; had you been the man of one great party which divides the people of the United States, you might have purchased peace by tribute under the name of loans and bribes, under that of presents, by sacrificing with pleasure, as one of the leaders of that party formally avowed his disposition to do, the rights of the Union to the pleasure of France by answering her injuries with submission and her insults with crouching. Had you been the man of the other party, you would have lost the only favorable moment for negotiating peace to the best advantage, and at this moment would have seen the United States at open war with an enemy in the highest exultation of victory, without an ally and, in the general opinion of the world if not in real truth, little better than once more a colony of Great Britain.[34] In resisting, therefore, with all the energy which your constitutional power enabled you to exercise and all your personal influence could excite among your countrymen, the violence of France, you saved the honor of the American name from disgrace and prepared the way for obtaining fair terms of reconciliation. By sending the late mission you restored an honorable peace to the nation, without tribute, without bribes, without violating any previous engagement, without the abandonment of any claim of right, and without even exciting the resentment of the great enemy of France. You have, therefore, given the most decisive proof that in your administration you were the man not of any party, but of the whole nation, and if the eyes of faction will shut themselves against the value of such a character, if even the legal and constitutional judgment of your country as expressed by their suffrages at an election will be insensible to it, you can safely and confidently appeal from the voice of heated and unjust passions, to that of cool and equitable reason, from the prejudices of the present to the sober decision of posterity.

Whatever changes may take place in the political system of the new world, they cannot be more extraordinary than those which are happening from day to day in the old – The chain of important events which within these few years have multiplied so far beyond the common course of human affairs, appears to be spreading with accelerated rapidity in proportion as we draw nearer to the commencement of another century. – The spirit of Jacobinism, which has so largely contributed to the calamities which have long afflicted this quarter of the globe, would scarcely have imagined two years ago, to find in the Emperor of Russia its greatest aid and support, and in General Bonaparte its most formidable enemy. For as on the one hand, Paul affords a striking example of the ill consequences of power in hereditary succession, Bonaparte on the other proves as forcibly the tendency of all the absurd and wicked theories of equality and fraternity, and representative democracy, to end in absolute and hereditary sway.[35]

You remember with what impetuous fury Paul began about eighteen months ago, an active War against France; and how he broke off all intercourse with Denmark and Prussia, because they declined joining him and the coalition[36] – You have reason to remember it, as he express'd his willingness at that time to make a commercial Treaty with us, upon condition that we should not negotiate for Peace with France – Britain and Austria were then his dear allies, and the Emperor of Germany, the best friend (according to his own expression) he had in the world – All this tenderness of affection is blown away like the wind of yesterday – Denmark and Prussia have become his dearest friends and allies. He insults the Romish emperor in his court Gazette, and refuses to receive embassies from him – Embargoes all English ships in his ports, sequesters all english property in his dominions, and proclaims the English Nation, to be not a race of human beings, but a vermin that infest the sea. – In the meantime he makes his Peace with France, and by indulging the violence of his resentments against Austria and England forgets entirely that he is throwing all his weight into a scale which already preponderates too much, and the load of which his own Nation will soon feel to its ruin.

France will doubtless derive immense advantages from this temper, and from the vehemence with which he gratifies it – Whatever Austria's sins against Russia were, (and they admit of no excuse, of no palliation) they have at least been dearly expiated – Even a vindictive spirit might be soothed into compassion, by the state to which Austria has been reduced; and to leave her at the mercy of an inexorable and triumphant enemy, is what Russia ought to be the last of European powers to do – Yet, not content with this, Russia, without any apparent motive, proceeds to press upon the only remaining power which can withstand in any degree the overbearing weight of France, and takes the present moment to press as hard upon England, as upon Austria – His proposal to the three other Northern powers, for the revival of the armed neutrality will be known to you before you receive this letter; and such has been in frequent instances of late the insolence and excesses of the british navy towards neutral powers, that if the Russian Emperor had only gone thus far, his conduct might have been justified by the principles of sound policy, and must have had the approbation of other nations – But such is the violence with which he proceeds, that he will probably force England into a war with him before his plan of the armed neutrality can be accomplished, and without his aid and influence the system would hardly be strong enough to support itself

It is so difficult to account for the excessive rancour and inveteracy of Paul, against his late allies, from any rational motive of interest or of policy, that many persons acquainted with the state of the court at St. Petersburg, ascribe them, rather to the peculiar character and temper of the man, and to the influence of certain personages, such as are usually possess'd of the real dominion in almost all despotic governments – His ostensible ministers for foreign affairs the Counts Rostopsin and Panin, are supposed to be very far from suggesting, or approving the present system; but they have little or no influence, and he scarcely sees them from one month's end to another. His great favourite is a man who bears the name of Kutaizow, and sometimes of Ivan Paulowitz, because the Emperor, when Grand-Duke was his god-father at his baptism – He is by birth a Turk; was taken, when quite a child, at the siege of Bender, and given by the Russian general who commanded there, to the Emperor, who had him educated at his own expence, and then took him into his service as his valet de chambre – From this menial office he has raised him to places of the highest rank in the empire, and loaded him with wealth and honours. – This turkish slave, travestied into a Russian nobleman, keeps a french opera-singer by the name of Chevalier, who was sent for, between two and three years ago, and went from Hamburg to St: Petersburg – For this woman it is said the Emperor himself indulged a transient fancy, and she has so well improved the moment of his kindness, and the subsidiary, but more durable attachment of his favourite, that from a very threadbare subsistence, with which she entered Russia, she has already amassed a splendid fortune. Through this channel it is reported the first advances were made towards the negotiation, which is still carried on between France and Russia; the present state of which I have mentioned in so recent a letter which I presume will be submitted to your perusal, that it would be superfluous for me to say anything further about it here.

Such is the government of a country, where arbitrary power is established in one person, by hereditary succession – In France, the scenes of a democratic revolution are approaching towards their catastrophe – The power of the first Consul, is little more limited than that of the Emperor of Russia; but his authority is new, and far from being firmly established[37] – The Jacobins can never forgive his desertion of their cause, and a very recent conspiracy has been detected, the object of which was to assassinate him. One of the principal persons concerned in this plot was an Italian sculptor, by the name of Ceracchi, who is well-known in America, and whose conduct has for many years been that of a fanatic revolutionist – Among the rumours circulating in the european world, of which it is not easy to ascertain the authenticity, it is asserted that Bonaparte in consequence of this intended attempt upon his person became sensible of the necessity of designating his successor, in case any accident should befall him, and sent expressly for General Moreau, whom he thought best entitled to this distinction; that this measure gave extreme dissatisfaction to the Consul's brother Lucian, and produced an altercation between them, the result of which was that Lucian was sent away upon a special mission abroad – This last circumstance at least is true, though it is not yet known where the Minister of the interior is gone – But there are men it seems in France who either desire or pretend to desire that the sovereign power should be given as an inheritance to the family of Bonaparte – Several pamphlets have within these few weeks been gratuitously distributed about Paris and in the departments, arguing from a great variety of considerations the expediency and even the necessity of adopting this system; and it is not positively certain whether the propagation of these sentiments is to be imputed to the real friends, or to the concealed enemies of the first Consul – I am for my own part most inclined to think them the insidious expedients of the royal party, or else of the Jacobites themselves, to excite an odium against the present possessor of the Chief magistracy. Whatever the real fact may be, Bonaparte certainly feels the desire of giving duration and permenency to his authority-There is but one alternative for his ambition: that of settling down peaceably, as a brother to the other European monarchs, or of becoming at the head of his armies the conqueror of them all – It is alike uncertain which of these careers is most suitable to the Consul's inclination; and which of them he would find most difficult in the execution. –

One of his brothers, a young man of two or three and twenty has lately been here, attended by two officers, nearly of his own age – He is a colonel in the army, and travels to acquire military knowledge. He was treated here universally with as much distinction as is shewn to a foreign prince, and is now gone upon a short tour through the Prussian provinces.

It would be of little use to tell you the mere news of the day, which is of little importance, and which would be no longer news when my letter shall reach you. At this season of the year I can scarcely ever expect that you should receive a letter from me within four months of its date, though from England you get the public intelligence usually in the course of two – On the 22d: of this month the hostilities between the French and Austrians were to recommence, and unless Austria should consent to negotiate her peace, separately from England (for that is the point upon which they broke off) the french according to every probability will before the new year be in possession of Vienna. – The necessity of the case will therefore beyond all doubt eventually compel Austria to treat separately, and Great-Britain will of course be obliged to do the same thing. – Her distresses are so rapidly accumulating upon her that the consequences are highly menacing even to her internal tranquility, yet there is a large fund of stubbornness in the English character, which it seems to me will for some time longer prevent the conclusion of her peace with France.

Ever devotedly yours.

JOHN QUINCY ADAMS (BERLIN) TO WILLIAM VANS MURRAY, JANUARY 27, 1801

Alexander Hamilton's public attacks on President Adams led John Quincy to reflect on the dangerous logic behind the High Federalists' determination to maintain a large army when there was little or no chance of a French invasion. To be sure, there was some reasonable argument to having an army at hand to check projects of disunion and rebellion, under the pretext of dealing with a foreign threat. But this could never be the basis of defending the Constitution, which rested on the attachment and good sense of the people – weak as this had appeared at times.

DEAR SIR:

I have not seen the pamphlet of General Hamilton, but am much gratified or rather consoled that it is such as you describe in your favor of the 20th instant. From the title I had heard of it before I supposed it consisted of personalities rather than censures upon public measures.[38] As to objections against your mission, I have long been at perfect ease on that account.[39] Had Hamilton, or any of his friends, even dared to avow publicly the only strong and real argument they had, I considered it as no longer formidable. An external wound must sometimes be kept open to prevent the internal humors from destroying the body. Without a quarrel abroad the government would not have an army at hand to check projects of disunion and rebellion. This is their only solid ground, but I very much doubted whether Hamilton himself would have the courage to confess it. Now although the strength of the antifederal party and their evident designs to dissolve the Union give this argument great plausibility, there seems to be a plausible answer to it. Our Constitution professedly rests upon the *good sense* and *attachment of the people*. This basis, weak as it may appear, has not yet been found to fail. To support it the aid of military force must indeed occasionally be called in, but ought not to be substituted as the permanent foundation in its stead. To make a foreign war the motive for keeping an army on foot, the evidence must be plain and unequivocal that it was inevitable, not only in its origin, but in its continuance. For if the people once discover (and you could not conceal it from them long) that you maintain the war for the army, while you tell them you maintain the army for the war, you lose their attachment forever, and their *good sense* will immediately side against you. Then your army will be the *sole support* you have. You will have effected in substance if not in forms a total revolution in government. Your internal enemies will then have the hearts of the people in their favor, will very soon be able to raise and bring force against your force, and the chaos of civil war will ensue. No, if the attachment of the people must desert us, let it at least be altogether in their own wrong. Let us knit our system of policy so closely with their interests, that they cannot tear one without rending the other. Then, if after all we must come to disunion and civil war, the consciousness of pure unalloyed justice and right will be the highest ornament of our victory, or the most impregnable refuge of our defeat.

So far am I then from having any concern in future about the French negotiation, that I confidently believe it will be considered as one of the President's most distinguished services, and the greater the opposition against it by those who, under the name of his friends, would have been his leaders, the more honorable I am persuaded the result will prove to him. What the true point of my anxiety has in this case been I will candidly tell you, when I shall have seen Hamilton's publication. As for the man, I too have always had a very high opinion of his talents and of his services. His system of finance I did consider as more complicated than was necessary, and the purity of his principles from frailties of *ambition* as not absolutely unquestionable. The rancor and the baseness of the means exerted against him by his enemies and rivals gave his merit an additional value and a stronger claim to support. Perhaps these rivals hurt in a way even unexpected to themselves. Perhaps by using infamous weapons against him they habituated his mind to consider the employment of them as warrantable. This degradation of soul, which you so justly describe in one of your late letters as the too natural result of our newspaper electioneering altercations, is to such a character as Hamilton's a greater injury, than all the charges that envy or malice under the mask of public spirit were ever able to conjure against him.

I am persuaded with you that if the armed neutrality ends in war, Great Britain will at sea be constantly triumphant. Nor do I suppose this is doubted by the Powers forming the league themselves. But there is Constantinople to comfort Russia, and there is Hanover to indemnify Prussia. If the principles of the armed neutrality be to these powers any object at all, it is but a very minor and secondary one indeed. Sweden and Denmark were coaxed and dragged and pushed into the measure, which they will pay for at a tremendous price. Upon them it was what in the old French law used to be called a *rape by seduction*, and you see that no sooner has Paul had his will of the poor frail ones than he casts one of them off with the most ineffable contempt.[40] Though I somewhat scruple whether we can supply England with hemp, and tar, and iron, quite so soon and to such an extent as you anticipate, I have not the smallest doubt but that she will get these articles. She will get them indirectly from her enemies themselves. The sale of the goods is at least as necessary to them as their purchase is to her, and as you say of her manufactures, mutual want will burst through the very strongest barriers of war. When this plan of a new armed neutrality was first in agitation I was inclined to think we might take a part in it as far as could be consistent with our engagements, and so wrote home. The principles are more liberal than those of England and if generally adopted would prove a real benefit to humanity. But from the moment when the drift of the two *great* parties to this league was evident, I have been convinced that our policy is to have nothing to do with it, and all my dispatches have been calculated to impress as much as possible that opinion.

Your recollections as to the first place of our meeting form such a doubly pleasing association of ideas that I am unwilling to believe them not exactly accurate. Mr. W. Vaughan's house has in my remembrance the advantage of being the spot where our acquaintance commenced.[41] We dined there together. Had an interesting conversation upon the merits of the Christian and the Mahometan *Paradise*, and went in the evening to hear a debate at Coachmaker's hall. But whenever our friendship began I hope and trust that no spot on this earth is destined to witness its end, but that I shall ever as at this moment be invariably yours.

JOHN QUINCY ADAMS (BERLIN) TO THOMAS BOYLSTON ADAMS, FEBRUARY 14, 1801[42]

John Quincy argued that the United States should be able to avoid the accumulation of taxes and debts – the inseparable conditions of military government – which plagued Europe. (In Britain, despite its celebrated insular condition, this plague was manifested through the impressment of seamen and the accumulation of massive debts.) But this was true only if it maintained the Union. So long as the United States remained united, a large permanent army would never be necessary, because the natural increase in the nation's population and wealth would make external invasion across the Atlantic increasingly impractical. A divided America, on the other hand, would create opportunities for foreign aggression – and Americans would soon begin to fight among themselves.

The burthens, to which I referred at the close of my last letter, & to which the inhabitants of Silesia are subjected under the Prussian Government are. 1. The compulsory obligation of serving the king as soldiers. 2. The obligation of giving quarters to the troops – and 3. Of performing personal labor, & furnishing horses for the king's use, that of his army, & of his civil officers at prescribed & underated prices. While the province belonged to the house of Austria, the people were in the same manner liable to these duties. But they were apparently far less oppressive, because proportionably speaking there was no army levied, maintained, or stationed in garrison within the province, which required the performance of these services. At present, of the 40,000 men, which formed the Silesian army about one half are natives of the Province, enroll'd as a thing of course, & doomed from their birth to military service. A certain district is allotted to each regiment within which it is to be recruited. The commander has a list of all the inhabitants of the district liable to enrollment, & sends an officer annually round to measure, inspect, and register for service the young men, who have attained the age of service. The exemptions from this duty are, Only sons and eldest sons of farmers, who are considered as necessary for the tillage of the ground – Weavers & persons engaged in some other useful trades – Persons upon whose labor infant families, or an aged mother depend for subsistance – Foreigners settled in the country & their children – The city of Breslau, & the inhabitants of the mountains & mountain towns, for the sake of the linen manufactures. The service of the soldiers in time of peace, is required only during three months in the year, when they are assiduously trained & exercised, & which close with the month of August, when the king reviews them at Neyss & at Breslau – This, Frederic the second never failed to do. His successors have frequently omitted it, & the last summer was the first instance of it under the present reign. During the remainder of the year, the native Silesian soldiers are on furloug[h]. Their pay continues, but is not received by them. It is the perquisite of the Captain's, whose interest is thus engaged not to keep their men longer in service than is absolutely necessary.

The author of an excellent work upon the state of Silesia before & since the year 1740, from which the information in most of my late letters is collected, alledges arguments to prove that the advantages derived from the army to the province are more than sufficient to balance its inconveniences. He says that the garrisons in the towns of course put in circulation a quantity of money, afford subsistance to tradesmen of all descriptions, & furnish a market for the produce of the farmer. He likewise mentions it as the principal means of contributing to the civilization of upper Silesia, where but for this the people would still be deep plunged in barbarism. The military service habituates the peasant youth to principles of order & cleanliness: which they communicate more, or less among their neighbours upon returning to reside among them. Yet there is no question, but that the circulation of money, the civilization of the people, order, cleanliness, & refinement of manners, is far greatest in the capital, & in the mountain towns, which are not favored with the liberal garrisons, & these civilizing soldiers.

The obligation of quartering troops is in time of peace confined to the cities – Not more than two thirds of these have garrisons, but a tax for quartering is assessed alike upon all, & the produce is applied to the payment of the householders, who actually lodge soldiers. The allowance is of eight groshen (about 25 cents) a month for a man, & six groschen for a horse. In the principal fortresses, Barracks have been built at the king's expence, which alleviate in some degree this burthen upon the citizens.

The most oppressive & iniquitous of all these duties is that of furnishing labour, horses, and other articles at regulated &

inadequate prices. The famers are thus obliged to furnish post horses for all persons travelling in the Service of the king at the rate of three groschen a mile for each horse. The post masters make them do the same for all travellers by what is called extra-post, & while they allow the peasants only three groschen they charge the traveller ten for every horse he takes. Thus by the intervention of the Government, the traveller & his conductor are both oppressed, & defrauded, for the benefit of the postmaster. Is it surprizing that the people give their horses in such cases with extreme reluctance, & that travellers are obliged to wait six hours together at a post house for horses? The government, itself as a corrective to its own iniquity is obliged to make regulations, which are meant to relieve the peasant, but which contribute no less to the vexation & delay of the traveller – Thus a limited weight of baggage is allowed, & the postilions are not obliged to drive faster than three of our miles an hour – This wretched administration of the post offices is not peculiar to Silesia – It prevails all over Germany, & every traveller with post horses through this country, witnesses the natural & unavoidable effect of such a cause. When an extraordinary number of horses is required for the service of the army, for work at the fortresses, or the magazines, the requisitions are distributed by the respective Landraths round the number of circles designated by the Domain chambers. The prices are regulated by the government. The same rule prevails with regard to the provisions, & stores necessary for the troops in time of war.

Upon the same principle all day labourers, & poor tenants to work at the building, or repairing the fortresses, for wages prescribed by the Government. When it is considered what an immense expence of labor Frederic the Second bestowed upon the fortifications of Silesia; this will appear no trifling object in his reign – It is said, that he always paid the workmen liberally; often beyond the common market rate of workmen's wages; but still the badge of servitude remains.

It is impossible for an American to contemplate this accumulated load of taxes and services which are the inseparable attendants of a military government without a sigh over the condition of human society in Europe, and an ejaculation of gratitude to Heaven for that in his own country. In imputing these evils to the European *condition of society*, I am sensible the opinion is not conformable to that which faction so delights to prattle, and knowing ignorance to repeat; but I believe it to be the truth. Europe being divided into a number of wholly independent states, it is by their armies alone that they can defend themselves against the encroachments of each other. This spirit of encroachment is so far from being extinguished by the flood of philosophy which poured upon that self-conceited dupe, the eighteenth century, that it never burnt with a more consuming blaze than at the birth of this her daughter. This system of partitions was a contrivance of the greatest of the good old Lady's royal favorites, and she has left it as a precious inheritance to her child. What a number of sovereign states have been swallowed up in the vortex of the last ten years, for the crime of being weak and unable to resist an invading army! What a number more are upon the point of suffering the same fate! The tendency of Europe is so manifestly towards consolidation that, unless it should suddenly and unexpectedly take a different turn, in a few years there will be not more than four or five sovereign states left of the hundreds which covered the surface of this quarter of the globe. An army, therefore, is as necessary to every European power which has any hope of long existence as air to the motion of the lungs, and France through the whole course of the revolution has been so convinced of this, that she has not only kept on foot such armed myriads hitherto, but has settled for her peace establishment one of the largest armies in Europe. Now it is impossible that such armies should be levied, recruited, and maintained, without principles and measures of continual compulsion upon the people. Hence France in her republican state has continued to practice them under the name of conscription, and requisition, and loan, more than the most despotic of enemies.[43] Hence England, a country justly renowned for its liberty, has always been obliged to adopt the system as her insular situation modifies it with regard to her – by the impressment of seamen for her navy. And if she has hitherto avoided the other part of it, requisition or the compulsive raising of stores, provisions, labor, etc., it has only been by draining the pockets of posterity and loading their shoulders with debts which will end in bankruptcy.

It is from the consideration of these things more than from any others that I look to the *Union* of our country as to the sheet anchor of our hopes, and to its dissolution as to the most dreadful of our dangers. So long as we remained united, a large *permanent* army can never be necessary among us. The only occasion which can require a great military force will be to withstand external invasion, a danger to which we shall become daily less exposed as our population and strength increase. If once we divide, our exposure to foreign assault will at once be multiplied in proportion to the number of states into which we shall split, and aggravated in proportion to the weakness of every single part compared with the strength of the whole. The temptations of foreign powers to invade us will increase with the prospect of success which our division will present them, and fortresses and armies will be then the only security upon which the disunited states can rely for defence against enemies from abroad. This is not the worst. Each of the separate states will from the moment of disunion become with regard to the others a foreign power. Quarrels, of which the seeds are too thickly sown, will shoot up like weeds in a rank soil between them. Wars will soon ensue. These must end either in the conquest of one party by the other, or in frail, precarious, jealous compromises and momentary truces under the name of peace, leaving on both sides the burden of its army as the only guarantee for its security. Then must the surface of our country be bristled over with double and treble ranges of rock hewn fortresses for barriers, and our cities turned into gaols by a circumference of impenetrable walls. Then will the great problem of our statesmen, too, be what proportion of the people's sweat and blood can be squeezed from them to maintain an army without producing absolute death. I speak in the sincerity and conviction of my soul in declaring that I look upon standing armies, intolerable taxes, forced levies, contributions, conscriptions, and requisitions, as the unavoidable and fatal chain of which disunion is but the first link.

You will think this train of reflections has led me very far from Silesia; but if in the Roman Senate, whatever the subject in deliberation was, Cato's opinion always concluded with the asserveration that Carthage must be destroyed, surely an American citizen with much more reason may infer from every topic the sentiment that the union must be preserved.

Since the last letter in which I took notice to you, of the current affairs of the present age, the prospect of a coalition against England has drawn considerably to a head, & spread further over the Continent of Europe. England has declared war against Russia, & laid an Embargo upon all the Swedish & Danish vessels in her ports; at the same time she professes her determination to meet the league of armed neutrality with defiance – But the Prussians vessels are excepted from the embargo, through Prussia has acceeded to the convention, & it is doubtful whether she can maintain a state of neutrality were she ever so much disposed to it. Indeed to judge from present probability there is not one state upon the continent of Europe, but will be shortly joined in the combination against Britain, & those of our countrymen, who bear the most rancerous mind against her, may flatter themselves with a seemingly well grounded hope that her profound humiliation, if not her utter ruin are at hand. Meanwhile the sentimental affection between Paul the Emperor, & Buonaparte the Consul grows warmer from day to day – They promise to become the very Nisus & Euryalus of princes – Mr. Kalitchew, who had just been appointed Russian vice Chancellor, & goes as Ambassador to Paris, & the poor french Pretender, Louis. 18. is ordered to remove from his place of refuge at Mittau. The English government have sent about 20,000 men to help the Turks to drive the french out of Egypt, but the Russian Ambassador at Constantinople has protested against this, & plainly told the Turk, that if he suffers the English to assist him, he has nothing less to expect, than the whole weight of Paul's vengeance. This interference may probably save the English army, but will not probably save the turkish empire. When Constantine tran[s]ferr'd the seat of Rome's *external* dominion to Byzantium, he little thought he was only preparing a spot for its final extinction. When Mahomet II. established upon its ruins the capital of his triumphant Turks, as little did he think it the place, which would witness the last gasp of the Ottoman power. With both these examples before him, Paul dreams not that Constantinople may prove alike, the mere mausoleum of Russian greatness, & languished for it with all the fi[e]rceness of his mother's passions.

There are reports, not yet however authenticated that the preliminaries of peace between France & Austria were signed at Luneville the 26th. of last month.[44] The armistice is now general, & the Emperor has provisionally surrendered every place he held in Italy, except Venice. Whether he will keep even that at the peace is a great question. At Paris the Consul's power is consolidating – Ceracchi the sculptor, Arena, & two others have just been executed for a *design* to assassinate him. So you see, it has already got to be treason to *compass* his death. Two others have been shot for being concerned in blowing up the infernal machine, which has so narrowly escaped.[45] These examples will strike terror, & may give some security to a situation, eminently perilous, as that of the first consul must yet be esteemed.

CHAPTER FOUR

UNITED STATES SENATOR, 1803–1808

INTRODUCTION

In October 1803, Jefferson called a special session of Congress to approve his purchase of the Louisiana territory from France.[1] Travel problems delayed John Quincy from taking up his post in the Senate, causing him to miss by one day a vote to accept the treaties with the French that set out the terms of the purchase.

Most Federalists opposed the action as being unconstitutional and as designed to weaken the political interests of New England. John Quincy was sympathetic to much of the Federalist concerns. But he made it abundantly clear that he would have voted in the affirmative for the treaties. He concluded that the federal government had the constitutional authority by treaty to purchase foreign territory. He believed that the acquisition was justified on national security grounds. If Napoleon obtained military control of Louisiana and especially of the Mississippi River, he could aspire to create a North American empire that dominated the Gulf of Mexico and effectively hemmed the United States in on the other side of the Allegheny Mountains. In the coming days, John Quincy supported the House bill that created bonds to finance the purchase and compensated American citizens for spoliation claims against the French government.

But John Quincy subsequently voted with the Federalists

against virtually all other legislation supported by the Jefferson administration that affected the governing of the new territory. He opposed bills or amendments that authorized the president to divide the territory administratively into the Territory of New Orleans and the Territory of Louisiana, to appoint officials to govern the territories, and to apply American laws, especially tax laws, to the Louisianans. His reasoning, however, was unique, and it was accepted by neither party. He argued that Congress lacked the moral and constitutional authority to pass laws that affected the people of Louisiana without a formal vote of approval.

John Quincy brought forward three resolutions of protest against the Louisiana territorial bill, on the principle of no taxation without representation.[2] He even opposed legislation to limit the importation of slaves into the new territory, according to the principle that any limitations on the citizens of Louisiana enacted by Congress were illegitimate, including this one. He unsuccessfully sought a constitutional amendment that would give Congress the power to incorporate and make citizens of the inhabitants of any new territories and to make laws for their governance.

In the meantime, John Quincy came to believe that a small cadre of Federalists had begun privately to discuss steps to advance the establishment of Northern confederacy. During his time abroad, John Quincy thought that the greatest threat to the Union came from the South and radical elements of the Republican Party. As he understood the new conspiracy, Federalist legislative majorities in the Northern states – New England, New York, and perhaps New Jersey and Pennsylvania – would repeal their election laws for federal representatives and recall or refuse to send their senators to Washington. These states would gradually withdraw from the Union, take over their customs houses, and eventually establish a central government of their own.

But that did not make him a Republican. For now, he hewed closely to the Federalist position, opposing especially Jefferson's efforts to remodel the judiciary through impeachments of hostile federal judges. In its own way, he thought, this was nearly as pernicious to the Union and the Constitution as the Northern conspiracy.

During the congressional session of 1805–1806, talk of war dominated the proceedings. Neutral American commerce again seemed to be in serious jeopardy. For the decade following Jay's treaty, the United States and Britain had enjoyed a tense but workable arrangement that allowed American commerce to flow legally or tacitly during wartime. But when the Anglo-French War resumed in 1803, the British decided to crack down in order to close off American carrying trade between France, Spain, and their colonies (the *Essex* Decision). In what seemed to be a grim replay of the events of 1793, hundreds of American merchant ships were seized. British ships hovered off the American coast. The Royal Navy's impressment of suspected British deserters serving on American merchant ships, which had been a persistent if low-grade problem for some time, accelerated.

The French, meanwhile, implemented the so-called Continental System – notably, the Berlin and Milan decrees – which was designed to strangle British commerce but which inevitably impinged on America's neutral trade as well. The United States also faced difficulties with France's ally, Spain. The Spanish refused to recognize the legitimacy of the American purchase of the Louisiana territory from Napoleon, and they resisted Jefferson's pressure to reach a similar deal over the Floridas. In his Annual Message in December 1805, the president warned that Madrid was stirring up trouble with the Indian tribes and abusing American citizens. The Spanish minister, the marquis de Casa Yrujo, publicly objected to the president's language and also circulated letters to the other foreign ministers in Washington, making offensive references to the president and his conduct. John Quincy bristled at Yrujo's presumption and introduced a bill authorizing the president to expel a foreign diplomat. The president and the Republicans rejected the bill because they regarded it as a means of expressing no confidence in the foreign policy of the president, as well as an impingement on his constitutional authority.

Jefferson did in fact demand Yrujo's recall, but John Quincy feared that the president was still captive to a pro-French course and would attempt to appease the Spanish and their French masters by buying them off. He saw evidence of this when the Republican-dominated House passed resolutions calling on the president to make concessions to Spain on the western boundaries of Louisiana in exchange for the Floridas. John Quincy staunchly opposed the so-called Two Million Act when it arrived in the Senate in mid-January 1806. He was convinced that west Florida had been included in the original Louisiana Purchase, that in any case $2 million was extravagant, and that new funds would find themselves in French public and private coffers.

Likewise, John Quincy feared that Jefferson would talk tough about the British but fall back on tactics of economic coercion. That said, he did not see a better solution from the Federalists, who argued that Britain was the last remaining bulwark of civilization against French tyranny. Even if the United States did not formally ally itself with London, it must accept harsh British maritime practices as a necessary price to be paid to the common cause. In addition, the Federalists pointed out, American merchants were still able to work around British restrictions sufficiently to make handsome profits.

John Quincy would have nothing to do with what he regarded as appeasement of the British, whose real agenda was to control US commerce for their own profit and to restore America to a colonial status. The United States, in his view, should pursue an evenhanded rejection of the illegitimate claims of all foreign nations. The national character demanded it.

John Quincy believed that the proper solution against Britain – one that John Adams had pursued successfully during the crisis with France – was to combine tough rhetoric at home with serious defensive measures, especially the buildup of the navy, while leaving the door open for negotiation. In his view, Jefferson should avoid measures of economic retaliation that would damage New England's commerce and give credence to Federalist accusations that the South was determined to destroy the North's economy in order to dominate the Union. John Quincy believed that the old Washington-Adams policy of peace through strength, together with ongoing British diplomatic and strategic setbacks on the Continent against Napoleon, would most likely lead to a success-ful arrangement with London that preserved America's neutral rights. Or, if a war could not be avoided, the nation would be better prepared to meet it, in large part because it would not have alienated New England.[3]

With this in mind, John Quincy tried to provide the administra-tion and the country with some backbone. He was chosen to an ad hoc committee on foreign affairs, which reported three resolu-tions on the British matter. The first two, authored by John Quincy, attacked the *Essex* decision as "unprovoked aggression upon the property of the citizens of these United States, a wanton violation of their neutral rights and a direct encroachment upon their national independence," and requested that the president "demand" reparations for the lost property. The third resolution called for a non-importation policy against Britain. John Quincy – alone among the Federalists – supported subsequent non-importation legisla-tion, even though he personally did not favor it. He thought it a price to be paid to encourage a tougher Republican response, and an experiment to demonstrate whether sanctions, or the threat of sanctions, could be effective. Jefferson, in any case, requested that non-importation be suspended, pending further negotiations with Britain. Its implementation was eventually delayed until December 14, 1807. The hope was that a diplomatic mission to London could reach an agreement that would set aside differences sufficiently to maintain a cold peace, as John Jay had done in 1794.

Toward the end of the congressional session in March 1807, Jefferson told John Quincy that he had just received a copy of a treaty with Britain negotiated by William Pinckney and James Monroe. The president did not hide his unhappiness. He complained that the treaty contained no satisfactory article on the impressment of men from American ships. In addition, the British negotiators delivered a declaration that the king reserved the right to retaliate against Napoleon's own declaration of a blockade against England (the Berlin Decree), unless the United States should resist it. America would effectively have to accept the British doctrine of a paper blockade. Jefferson decided that he would not even submit the treaty to the Senate, although he would continue further negotiations and retain suspension of the Non-Importation Act.

John Quincy agreed with Jefferson's decision. He believed that the terms were "in some respects even less advantageous" than those of Jay's treaty, which John Quincy supported reluctantly in 1794 only because he had concluded that it would keep the United States out of war. He believed that the effect of the Monroe-Pinkney Treaty would be to plunge the country into conflict with England within twelve months. Because the president was, rightly, unwilling to ratify the treaty in its present form, John Quincy believed that he was correct in withholding it from the Senate and thus taking on personal responsibility for its rejection – despite the predictable howls from the Federalists.

On June 22, 1807, the *Chesapeake*, a US Navy frigate en route to the Mediterranean, was stopped off the coast of Norfolk, Virginia, by a British warship, the *Leopard*. The *Leopard* hailed the *Chesapeake* and demanded that her officers be allowed to board and search for British deserters. Her commanding officer, Commodore James Barron, refused. The *Leopard* opened fire, killing three sailors and wounding eighteen.

These events brought John Quincy into legislative activity associated with national defense. He was selected as a member of committees dealing with the naval appropriations bill and the defense of ports and harbors. He supported the request of the secretary of the Navy to add two hundred additional gunboats for harbor defense (although he personally favored building seagoing frigates). He listened with interest at one of Jefferson's dinners to Robert Fulton's proposals for experimenting with naval torpedoes. He sponsored a resolution calling on the administration to provide a report on impressment. He chaired a committee that issued the so-called Aggression Bill, which provided that no British armed vessel enter American waters unless reparation for the *Chesapeake* attack had been made to the president's satisfaction. The bill also forbade entrance to any vessel that had committed trespass or spoliation on any American merchant vessel.

Rumors began circulating that the British had issued a new Order in Council, professedly in retaliation for the Berlin Decree. American ships sailing to the Continent would be seized unless they first stopped in Britain and paid prohibitive duties – which would render them liable to seizure under Napoleon's Continental System. The United States was caught in a vise. The effect of both belligerent policies, if implemented, would effectively shut down neutral trade. The British threat, according to Jefferson, was obviously more immediate and serious. To protect the "essential resources of the country" that were employed in foreign commerce, Jefferson offered only one fundamental recommendation – "an inhibition of the departure of our vessels."

In other words, Jefferson had issued an embargo. All ships, except those capable of local voyages only, would be confined to port. Presumably, this would save American vessels from seizure and deprive the belligerent powers of much-needed raw materials and foodstuffs. The United States had temporarily resorted to such a drastic measure before, in 1794, when war with Britain seemed imminent. The Jefferson administration was officially silent on the details and on underlying policy. That was left for Congress to determine. As soon as the president's message was received, the Senate appointed a committee to recommend appropriate legislation. John Quincy was voted a member. He was initially inclined to oppose an embargo; he doubted it would be effective and he knew that it would disrupt New England's commerce, further dividing the region from the rest of the nation. But he was persuaded by Republican members that it was a necessary part of the president's diplomatic strategy. He viewed it as an experiment to see how willing people were to support their government and defend their rights.

During the debate in the full Senate, John Quincy argued for immediate adoption of the bill. He put forward the administration's case, as best he understood it, that the embargo was the only alternative to war, and that any delay would provide a window for ships to sail into harm's way as their owners risked one last profitable voyage before the embargo took effect. The American merchant fleet now in port or able to return would be safe temporarily, while the executive undertook further diplomacy and, presumably, strengthened the nation's defenses. John Quincy assumed that the embargo would be superseded in a few months, by legislative action or by war.

The Federalists erupted. They accused the president of provoking war with England and of seeking an offensive and defensive alliance with France. The embargo, according to the Federalists, was being pursued as part of a plan of fundamental hostility by the Republican South and West to the commercial and maritime interests of the North. And while the Federalists did not control the White House, they did control both houses of the Massachusetts state legislature, giving John Quincy no prospect of reelection by that body. His term of office, however, extended through the following March. He fully expected to attend the next session of Congress, beginning that fall. According to custom, the election for senator would not be held in the legislature until the following February. John Quincy's political opponents, however, tried to force his hand by choosing the next senator during the current session of the General Court. In June 1808 they elected Federalist James Lloyd Jr. The vote was 248–213 in the House and 21–17 in the Senate. A few days later, the Federalists pushed through several resolutions, drafted by Christopher Gore, which instructed their congressional members to vote to repeal the embargo. When he heard this, John Quincy immediately walked to the residence of Harrison Gray Otis, president of the Senate, and left a letter of resignation.

For some months he had been thinking about a substitute for the current policy. John Quincy's initial position was that, under the circumstances, it had been a choice between war and an embargo; but that the embargo must be a temporary measure. He believed that the embargo had prevented war, saved merchant shipping, and defended American rights. But it was not succeeding as a coercive measure against the belligerents, and Congress was little inclined to declare war. New England was on the verge of revolt, stirred not only by the damage to its commerce but also by the draconian measures the administration had taken to enforce the embargo.

For his part, Quincy sought a middle ground. He agreed with the Republicans that simply taking off the embargo would represent submission, but he urged his contacts in Washington to substitute a non-intercourse act against France and Britain. This would open trade with all other countries, with the promise of opening it to either or both belligerent powers if they relaxed their illegal systems. It would not surrender the defense of American rights, but it would serve to dissipate the popular passions that had built up and fed the revival of Federalist disunionism.

Perhaps influenced in part by John Quincy's argument, Jefferson and his successor, James Madison, followed that route. And rumors circulated that Madison planned to appoint him to a major government position.

NOTES OF A SPEECH TO THE US SENATE ON THE TAXATION OF LOUISIANA, US SENATE, JANUARY 1804

John Quincy was an ardent American expansionist, but only for what he regarded as the right reasons and in the right way. Specifically, he thought, the establishment of governmental power over hitherto foreign peoples must follow the principles of the Declaration of

Independence, which requires the consent of the governed – of both those in the newly acquired territories, and those in the existing union. Ideally, this should occur before the United States laid claim to those lands, but in exceptional circumstances – such as the fleeting strategic opportunity posed by Napoleon's offer to sell Louisiana – the consent could legitimately be obtained retroactively. This particular case involved a people whose speech and manners were truly foreign, making mutual consent even more imperative. In this speech, John Quincy defended his effort, in the form of Senate resolutions, to oppose mandated federal taxation of the citizens of Louisiana.

When the resolution to appoint a committee for the purpose of preparing a form or forms of government for Louisiana was first before the Senate, I objected against it as premature. I did not think it possible that during the present session of Congress we should obtain the knowledge or information absolutely necessary to proceed advisedly in a career of such vast importance. It was my opinion that our first and most urgent care should be to obtain for Congress the powers indispensable for the performance of our own engagements, and that we should have ample leisure for the exertion of our power over the country we have newly acquired. To perform what we had promised was in my view of things the task of most immediate pressure before us, while we could not wield with too prudent and wary hand the rod of empire and dominion which we had assumed over a foreign people. On both these cardinal points of policy I had the misfortune to find myself in a very small minority. The principles adopted by the majority of the Senate were in both instances the reverse of those with which I concurred. It was said that my anxiety for the fulfil- ment of our national engagements was overweaning and prema- ture. That it was better policy to follow the example which the union had exhibited under the old confederacy and break the treaty without scruple, until the power with whom we made it should call us to account for the breach. But on the other hand the ardor for legislating amply compensated for the coolness of punctuality, and, even before we knew whether peaceable possession of the country had been obtained, it was judged not too early to prepare forms of government for a people whose language we do not understand, whose manners opinions and prejudices are totally variant from our own, and of whom we know nothing more than could be collected from a couple of small pamphlets, compiled indeed with laudable industry and care from the little information our Executive government had been able in the course of three or four months to obtain, but sent to us with an express caution not to rely upon them as official.

In both these decisions of the Senate it was my duty to acquiesce. The Committee to prepare a form or forms of Government for Louisiana was appointed and their report is now the subject of consideration.

My first objection against this bill is derived from the principle upon which I opposed the appointment of the Committee. If ever there was an occasion upon which a legislative assembly ought to adopt as the basis of their measures the old and wholesome adage *festina lente*, it must surely be when they are about to undertake the task which the acquisition of Louisiana has imposed upon us. In order to impress our minds with the full conviction of this truth, let us seriously contemplate the extent and nature of that task. It is nothing less than to accomplish a total revolution, not only of government and laws, but of the principles upon which they are founded; over a people consisting of an hundred thousand souls; over a people of whom we may yet be said to know nothing, as they with still less exception know nothing of us; over a people whose subjection to our authority has been established *without their previous consent*, and whose liberty, property and religion, we are bound by solemn obligation to protect.

In order to effect this revolution without violence and oppression, it must be done by slow, gradual and well considered measures; and it is of primary importance to lay the foundations upon proper principles. The first step we should take, therefore, seems to be, that of legitimating our authority of acquiring the right to make laws for that people *at all*. By the treaty with France we have acquired all the rights of sovereignty over the inhabitants of Louisiana which France could impart; but as, to use the language of our declaration of independence, the *just* powers of a government can be derived only from the *consent of the governed*, the French Republic could not give us the right to make laws for the people of Louisiana, without their acquiescence in the transfer. I never considered this as an objection against the ratification of the treaty, because I did not deem it indispensable that this consent of the ceded people should precede the conclusion of the compact. That would indeed have been the most natural and most eligible course of proceeding, had it been practicable, and such was the opinion of our own executive before the negotiation of the treaty. But theoretic principles of government can never be carried into practice to their full extent. They must be modified and accommodated to the situations and circumstances of human events and human concerns. But between those allowances necessary to reconcile the rigor of principle with the resistance of practice, and the total sacrifice of all principle, there is a wide difference. If in the Louisiana negotiation our government had insisted on obtaining the consent of the people before the conclusion of the treaty, in all probability the treaty itself never could have been concluded. A momentary departure from the inflexible rigor of theory was, therefore, perfectly justifiable, and in concluding the treaty we acquired a power over the territory and over the inhabitants which requires, so far as relates to the latter, one thing more to make it a just and lawful power. I mean their own consent. For although the necessity of the case might excuse us for not having obtained this consent beforehand, it could not absolve us from the obligation to acquire it afterwards. And as nothing but necessity can justify even a momentary departure from those principles which we hold as the most sacred laws of nature and of nations, so nothing can justify extending the departure beyond the bounds of the necessity. From the instant when that ceases the principle returns in all its force, and every further violation of it is error and crime.

If any gentleman can controvert the principle that by the laws of nature, of nations and of God, *no people has the right to make laws for another people without their consent* unless it be by right of *conquest*, I shall be glad to hear him; and if he can furnish to my unbiassed reason an *apology* for lending my hand to make a single law for the people of Louisiana without their consent, expressed or implied, I will not only vote for any proper law that may be proposed, but confess myself under deep obligation to the gentleman who shall solve my scruples. As to the right of conquest it must be out of the question. We can have no right of conquest over a people who have never injured us. The law of conquest is a law of slavery, and the people of Louisiana whose liberty we are solemnly bound to protect are not slaves.

In support of this principle I have already quoted the highest possible authority for an American citizen; I mean, the Declaration of Independence. Is that not sufficient? What says the Constitution under which we act? "We the people, &c. for ourselves and our posterity – for the United States of America." Not for the people of Louisiana nor for any other people. The people of the United States knew they had no right to exercise or to delegate the powers of legislation over another nation, and they expressly limited the operations of the Constitution to the United States of America, to themselves and their posterity.

The objections which I have urged hitherto against the passage of this bill have been either to particular details, or to points of expediency and considerations of justice and equity. Powerful as those are to my mind they are, however, of an order inferior to that which I now feel it my duty to make. I cannot prevail upon myself to vote for a law with a clear and undoubting conviction of my own mind that Congress have not the shadow of a right to pass it. Such is my conviction with regard to the act upon which we are now to decide. I long indulged the hope that the discussion of this question would have been avoided, that no alteration in the laws, and more especially no attempt to tax the people of Louisiana, would have been made, until in some shape or other their formal assent to our authority and acquiescence to our jurisdiction should have been obtained. I have been disappointed and we are now called upon at one and the same time to make a Constitution of government for a people who have never recognized our supremacy over them, and to tax *for our own benefit* a people of strangers, without admitting them to representation and without asking their consent.

The act upon which we are now to vote is an act to tax and very heavily to tax the people of Louisiana without their consent. This I apprehend Congress have no *right* to do.

1. Because it violates the natural rights of the people.

2. Because it violates the third Article of the Treaty of cession.

3. Because no such authority was or could be delegated by the Constitution.

4. Because it violates the principle of our national independence.

5. It violates the natural rights of the people of Louisiana.

PUBLIUS VALERIUS, NO 3, THE REPERTORY, *OCTOBER 30, 1804*

On the eve of the presidential election, John Quincy publicly reviewed Jefferson's national security policy. He disparaged an ineffective naval campaign against the Barbary Pirates, and repeated the Federalist complaints about the effects of the Louisiana Purchase, which accelerated the relative decline of New England and the Maritime states.

From the peculiar stress with which Mr. Morton dwelt upon the first article of his intended panegyric upon the general government, it is fair to presume that he considered the others as less important in themselves, or less calculated to produce the impression he intended; and I shall therefore bestow less time in commenting upon them. The reduction of the army to a peace establishment was, indeed, a thing which on the complete restoration of peace, would have followed, of course, under any administration. The work had been chiefly accomplished before Mr. Jefferson's elevation, and in all probability this subject would have slept in peace, but for the opportunity it afforded of hoisting in that ingenious execration against standing armies in time of peace, a *sentiment*, the justice of which I shall not contest, any more than the propriety of its expression in any commendation of Mr. Jefferson.

But when the disposition of our naval force and the Barbary war are held up as objects of glory to our general government, whatever our candor or our desire to approve may be, we struggle to applaud in vain, and however reluctantly, must say that in the sycophant we lose sight, utterly lose sight of the American. What can be meant by the assertion that we have *dictated* terms of peace to *some* of the Barbary powers, and *rendered harmless* the hostility of others? I say, not to what some, but to what one of the Barbary powers have we dictated terms of peace. The treaty between us and the Emperor of Morocco was broken by one of his cruisers, which captured an American vessel. By a fortunate accident, and not by any previous disposition by the government of our naval force, one of our frigates met and captured the Moorish cruiser and her prize. The Emperor of Morocco disavowed the act of hostility committed by his cruiser; we restored to him, without indemnity or satisfaction, two of his ships which we had in our possession, and are taxed to pay the captors of those same ships their prize money, for taking them, amounting to one-half their value.

The statement is not made for the purpose of censuring any part of the proceedings of the general government in relation to the Emperor of Morocco. Our seamen were very justly entitled to the prize money for their captures. But the simple fact is that the people of the United States have paid many thousand dollars, and restored two armed ships; for what? Why, for the Emperor of Morocco to disavow the violation of his treaty with us! Is this dictating terms of peace?

But further: the whole of these transactions, excepting the provision for the payment of the prize money, took place, without a single disposition of the general government concerning it. The violation of the treaty, the capture of the Moorish ships, the disavowal of the Emperor, and the restoration of his cruisers to him, all took place before the government had a suspicion of a rupture with Morocco. Undoubtedly the most honorable credit is due to the Captains Bainbridge and Rodgers and their gallant companions, for the capture of the Moorish ships; and their restoration by the consul, Mr. Simpson, to obtain the recognition of the old treaty, was, as the President justly styles it, "temperate and correct conduct." But it must be a braggart temper, indeed, which can boast of *such* an accommodation, as dictating terms of peace.

If this idle rodomontade is a reflection upon the modesty of the nation, the other part of the assertion, that the general government has *rendered harmless* the hostility of other Barbary powers, is an insult upon the calamities of our countrymen. What! when by the hostilities of the very meanest of those powers we have lost one of the best frigates in the navy. When her brave commander, and four hundred of our fellow citizens are languishing in captivity at Tripoli, are we to be told that their chains are rivetted by harmless hostilities? When nearly a million of dollars a year have just been added to the burdens upon our commerce, for a *Mediterranean fund*, to support the dispositions now first made of an efficient armament against those paltry pirates, is it a time to talk of having rendered their hostilities harmless? We read of the Emperor Caligula, that he made a triumphal entry at Rome, because he had picked up cockle shells on the beach of the German ocean; Mr. Morton improves upon the ideas of Caligula, and goes to the dungeons of Africa to pluck laurels for the brows of Mr. Jefferson.

Of the purchase of Louisiana I shall not now undertake to discuss the policy. That it is a great and important feature of Mr. Jefferson's administration is unquestionably true. Whether it will prove a blessing or a curse to this Union, it is only future time that can determine. This much we know, that the price of the purchase will be paid almost entirely by the Eastern and Atlantic states. Thus much we know, that when admitted as members of the Union, the whole weight and power of the purchased territories will be thrown into the scale of southern and western influence. In the relative situation of the United States, New England and the Maritime States have been constantly declining in power and consequence; they must continue to decline in proportion as the growth of the southern and western parts shall be more rapid than theirs. This vibration of the centre of power, being founded in nature, cannot be resisted, and as good citizens it is our duty to acquiesce in the event; but to this increasing ascendancy of the south and west, the acquisition of Louisiana adds an immense force, never contemplated in the original compact of these states. We are still to learn whether this excessive southern preponderance will be enjoyed with moderation, or used with generosity. Should it prove otherwise, and the present symptoms are by no means favorable, the people of America will have no cause to thank Mr. Jefferson for his Louisiana bargain. New England particularly, the dupe of her own good nature, will find that she has been made to bear the charge of aggrandizing a rival interest, for the degradation of her own. We are willing to hope for better things; but while the cost of the Louisiana purchase hangs like a mill stone upon the neck of our commerce; and while all its advantages are in fallacious hope and precarious conjecture, it is not a time for New England men especially to celebrate as an achievement deserving their gratitude, a measure of so very problematical an issue.

In arriving at the last specific item of Mr. Morton's eulogium, which speaks of our government's "desire to remain in peace with all the belligerent nations of Europe, and their *firmness* to vindicate the rights of our citizens against the aggressions of any," we are at a loss to imagine to what solitary fact his words can possibly bear an allusion. The desire to remain at peace with all the nations of Europe *but one* has, indeed, been conspicuous enough; but their firmness to vindicate our rights! Where has it ever been manifested. There is but one way of accounting for Mr. Morton's inferences from facts, and that may be called, the rule of *inverse* deduction; or the rule of making inferences in direct contradiction to their premises. Or to adopt the words of Hudibas,

As by the way of innuendo
Lucus is made a *non* lucendo.

Thus when Mr. Livingston in a public memorial formally proposes that France and the United States should make a *common cause* against Great Britain, Mr. Morton thinks it an indisputable proof of our government's desire to remain at peace with all the world. Mr. Monroe, as far as any part of his negotiations is known to the public, is constantly giving similar proofs of a pacific disposition. The treatment of the British minister at Washington has been exactly conformable to such indications, and Mr. Livingston, to place this desire of peace beyond all question, has recently repeated an outrageous insult upon the British government.

On the other hand what rights of our citizens has the government vindicated against any aggressions? Mr. Morton says our commerce is *less interrupted*, and says it at the very moment when foreign armed ships, both English and French, have violated our own territorial rights, and taken men from our merchant vessels, men within our own harbors. Never since the United States have been an independent nation, never have they been so grossly insulted; and what satisfaction has our government obtained? What satisfaction could they ask? When every article of complaint they could advance might be retorted with tenfold recrimination upon themselves.

We have waded through the sickening detail of Mr. Morton's praises, and shall have but little to remark when he comes to generalize. It is so easy to say that the objects and pursuits of the government have been *one continued effort* to promote the faith, justice and honor of the nation; and the peace, security and happiness of all its citizens. It is so easy to say all this without conveying or even forming any fixed or determinate idea, that we may consider the object of those words to be rather to round a period, than to have any meaning. To all general encomium on this administration, the destruction of the judiciary, and the system of political *removals* from office, must forever remain insuperable objections. The first has overthrown all confidence in the stability of justice, and the second has given the pernicious example of setting up the government as the prize and the instrument of faction. These two corrupted streams, issuing from the same fountain, will spread their pestilence over this Union, beyond the lapse of ages to purify. They have entailed a curse upon our posterity, which the blessings of a thousand Louisianas will never compensate.

Such then being the materials of which Mr. Morton's motion consisted, it is not at all surprising that when its accuracy was once becoming a subject of discussion, he should have shrunk from the test and withdrawn it from the scrutiny of his opponents. But it still remains for him to account for having produced a rhapsody so grossly variant from the truth, and so abhorrent to the sentiments of the legislature and people of Massachusetts. It appears that he withdrew the motion on consultation with some members of his own party. This is thus far honorable to them; since it shows that they were not prepared to go with him into the rapturous regions of romance, for the purpose of daubing Mr. Jefferson with unmerited flattery; but why did he produce it? Was it to operate as a letter of recommendation for himself; as a passport to office from which some honest man must be turned out? Or was it to propitiate the evil genius of Mr. John Randolph to the Yazoo claimant of Georgia lands? If the former was his motive, he may perhaps have reason for his hopes. We have seen services of a similar character very lately rewarded by the office of Commissioner of Loans; and there are still a few federalists of unimpeachable worth, who may be thrown breadless upon the world to accommodate candidates of such exemplary fervor. But as to the Yazoo purchasers, they may rest assured that ferocity will give as little, or less aid to their cause than its justice. Mr. John Randolph's opposition is not thus to be appeased or overpowered, and the next winter as the last, their agents will have the most indisputable proofs of Mr. Jefferson's favoring their claims; but it will so happen that they will again be set aside. Desirous as Mr. Jefferson may be to have justice done, severe as his *one* continued effort may be for their relief, it can only be obtained by the vote of both houses of Congress, and the world knows how little influence he has over them. Mr. John Randolph knows very well when to oppose a motion "from whatever quarter of the House it may come," and if on any improper occasion Mr. Jefferson's influence should be in hazard of weighing too much in the House, his own sons-in-law will take care to restore the balance. The sins of a first purchaser will be visited upon all the subsequent assignees, and the corruptions of a Georgia legislature will be punished by the spoils of New-England claimants. Grant, however, that the issue should be more favorable to their claim, grant that the services of so zealous a partisan should find favor in the sight of the national rulers, it is obvious that the motives which led to such flaming panegyrics as those of Mr. Morton's motion are partial, are private, are personal, that they relate only to particular interests, and are in unequivocal hostility to the interests of the people.

JOHN QUINCY ADAMS (WASHINGTON, DC) TO JOSEPH HALL, DECEMBER 11, 1807

With implementation of the Non-Importation Act against Britain looming in a few days, John Quincy repeated his long-standing doubts of its success. As with all attempts at economic coercion, it was much more likely to distress the American people than affect British policy.

And it appeared to him that the crisis over the Chesapeake Affair was on the verge of resolution. "But so long as the executive, the responsible department, believes that this measure will help and not hinder them in negotiation, I think its repeal ought not to be pressed by its opponents in Congress."

The ground taken by our government on the subject of the attack upon the *Chesapeake* has been sanctioned even by the British ministry, who in the most unqualified manner have disavowed the orders of Admiral Berkeley, have disclaimed in the most pointed terms every pretension to search a national ship for deserters; and have declared themselves willing to make proper reparation for the aggression. You know that I was as averse to the encouragement or enlistment of deserters, as the warmest friend to the British navy could possibly be; and that I thought our government ought to *keep this identical outrage entirely separate from every other topic of controversy*. This opinion I still retain; and if the extraordinary mission from England should be accomplished on principles avowed by Mr. Canning, I have no doubt *that war between the two nations may yet be avoided*. To this end I would contribute every possible aid to soften points of controversy which can be left open, to retreat from extremities which can be shunned, and to preserve peace where I can have no hope left that the parties can ever meet upon terms of amity.

With respect to the non-importation act, I wish you to understand that it is no *favorite* of mine. I have to some urged its immediate repeal; not with a view to any effect which it can produce upon Great Britain; but with reference to its probable effect among ourselves. It had my approbation two years ago, because the merchants throughout the Union called upon Congress for some measure to aid negotiation with England; and because the administration, and a great portion of our people, had a confidence in its efficacy, which could only *be tested by experience*. The experiment has been made. Whatever good effect it could produce it seems to me is past. It is too much, or too little, for the present state of things; and its effects will distress our own people, without producing the purpose for which it was intended beyond the Atlantic. I believe the administration, for their own sakes, ought to give it up. But so long as the executive, the responsible department, believes that this measure will help and not hinder them in negotiation, I think its repeal ought not to be pressed by its opponents in Congress. Your petition, as I presume it will be, if couched in respectful terms, without tincture of party spirit, I have no doubt will be treated with due consideration; and may perhaps be acceptable to the government, as furnishing an apology for abandoning what I believe they do not rely upon with much confidence. There is a bill now before the House to modify the act, and I suppose any modification for which you ask, may be introduced into it, if they should be thought just....

DRAFT OF SENATE COMMITTEE RESPONSE TO A PETITION BY THE MERCHANTS OF PHILADELPHIA AND BOSTON, ANTE-NOVEMBER 14, 1807

These petitions called for the modification, suspension, or repeal of the Non-Importation Act. John Quincy, on behalf of the Senate committee to which the petitions were referred, drafted a response that declined to pursue such a course. But what particularly drew his ire was the argument that Congress should "interpose" itself on matters of foreign policy that, in his view, clearly belonged to the executive.

The Committee to whom on the 14th inst: were referr'd this Petition of the merchants and others of the town of Boston praying for the modification, suspension, or repeal, of the act entitled an Act to prohibit the importation of certain goods wares and merchanize, passed the 18th day of April 1806 – And also, the Memorial of the merchants and others, of the City of Philadelphia, presented on the 27th of November last, suggesting their wish for the repeal of the same Act, submit this following Report.

The *Petition* from Boston, and the *Memorial* from Philadelphia, though agreeing in one particular request, are so different both in form and substance from each other, that your Committee have thought it their duty to consider and report upon them distinctly; and as the *suggestion* in the Philadelphia Memorial, for the repeal of the Act to which both the addresses refer, would, if complied with, have rendered unnecessary any further consideration of the Petition, your Committee directed their first attention to that advice, and after a full and deliberate discussion, are (*unanimously*) of opinion that the Act in question *ought not to be repealed.*

Had the Memorialists of Philadelphia contented themselves with representing the disastrous operation which they apprehended from that act upon their *wealth*, and the alarm which they felt at its possible effects, up their *extensive property*, your Committee believe that they would have done no more, than exert the unquestioned right of petition, and that their representations would have received all that attention which is due from a Government whose feelings and whose interests are identified with those of its Citizens – But the Memorial is not thus confined – Its subscribers have undertaken to "connect *the national honor and interest* with their individual claims and privileges" and under colour of this connection to obtrude their advices upon the National Legislative and Executive Authorities, upon subjects of the deepest concernment to the whole Nation, and upon points on which the acknowledge themselves utterly destitute of all official or authentic information – Could your Committee have concurred in the opinion that this advice, thus urged by persons totally uninformed, upon those who must be the best informed, by persons totally irresponsible, upon those who are under the highest responsibility, was however in itself favourable to the national honor and interest, they would still have deemed it the duty of the Senate to receive it without disapprobation, however they might have believed it unnecessary – But the advice itself is not the patriotic effusion of well-meaning, over-officious tool – Your Committee are of opinion that it is not less injudicious in substance that exceptionable in form.

On the mere foundation of public reports, the memorialists insinuate that the Executive of the United States, in the exercise of his functions of negotiations with foreign powers, has made demands calculated to commit the commercial interests of the United States, and has endangered their peace, by an improper assertion of *doubtful and unsettled principles* – And they invoke the wisdom and patriotism of the *National Legislature*, to interpose their authority for the purposes of preventing an unyielding adherence to those principles, and for the reference of the matters of *seeming* interest to a more propitious and less hazardous moment for adjustment.

By the Constitution of the United States, the People have entrusted the powers of negotiation with foreign States, to the Executive Department of the Government – The power of declaring War is vested by the same instrument in Congress; but untill such Declaration of War, has become a subject of their deliberations, your Committee are of opinion that any interference on the part of the National Legislature, to controul or to dictate the course of negotiation pursued by the Executive, would be a violation of the Constitution in some of its most important principles – If upon any occasion when controversies arise between the United States, and a foreign Nation, Congress were to assume the right of prescribing to the Executive the nature and extent of the demands he should make, of declaring the principles which he had asserted, doubtful and unfettered, of pronouncing interests which he has deemed essential to the welfare of the Nation, mere *forming* interests, the result of such intestine war between the highest departments of the administration, could be no other than the prostration of the Nation itself and of all its rights at the feet of a foreign Enemy.

The memorialists therefore have called upon Congress to assume a power not delegated to them by the Constitution. To transcend the authority Committed to them by the People – and for what purpose is this encroachment recommended? – For the purpose of compelling the Executive to surrender the rights of the Nation, to the domineering arrogance, and insolent injustice, of a Government, with whom by admission of the memorialists themselves we are contending for other essential rights to which as an independent nation we are indisputably entitled, and which ought to be maintained to the last extremity –

The memorialists have not thought proper to specify, what are in their own opinion those essential rights to be maintained at every hazard, and what those forming interests, which may be referred to a more propitious moment – Were the interference of Congress, to counteract the President in the discharge of his duties as clearly within their legitimate powers, as in the opinion of your Committee it would unquestionably exceed them, they would still be without the means of complying with the requests of this Memorial – They have been furnished with no precise test of the national rights, by which they could estimate the pretensions to be maintained, and the pretensions to be relinquished – In this weighing and gauging of national interests and principles the memorialists have not transmitted their own standard weights and measures. – Their censures on the conduct of the Executive are express'd in terms as loose and indefinite as the rumours upon which they are professedly founded – in those vague generalities, so well calculated to scatter jealousies, while they shrink from ??, to disseminate distrust and at the same time elude the grasp of detection.

Your Committee believe that these inputations upon the honour of the Executive are as groundless, as they are invidious – They are acquainted with no *seeming* interests, upon which any serious controversy with the British Government has ever occurr'd – If a scale of comparative magnitude were drawn between the several important principles, for which the Government of the Union, has long been insisting, those which in the judgement of your Committee, and they believe in that of the whole Nation, would be deemed less momentous that the rest, are those which relate to the colonial trade. Of *these* principles, the opinions entertained by the merchants and traders of Philadelphia, may be found in their Memorial of Congress presented on the 15th of January 1806. – "In those principles (said the memorialists of that day) they feel all the confidence of justice, and all the tenacity of truth. To surrender them, they conceive, would derogate from the national character and independence of the United States. From the justice of Government they hope for their avowal; from the Spirit of government, they hope for their defence; and from the blessing of heaven, they hope for their establishment."

Your Committee forbear to comment upon that Spirit, which after first stimulating the Government of this Union, to the defence of these principles, as undissolubly connected with the national independence, can now attempt to stigmatize the Executive for asserting them, or others of equal magnitude, as contending for doubtful or unfettered principles, and urging with frivolous obstinacy matters of more seeming interest – Perhaps indeed the present memorialists may say that in these general expressions, they did not mean to include the question relating to the Colonial trade – What then did they mean? – Was it the earnestness with which the Executive has endeavoured to protect our Seamen from *impressment*? – Your Committee are unwilling to believe that it was? – They would reluctantly admit the supposition, that the merchants of Philadelphia, should have deliberately subscribed a paper, which would sacrifice as an object of no real interest, the dearest *personal* rights of their fellow citizens, for the avowed purpose of saving their own *wealth*, from some possible diminution – They hope the Memorialists would disclaim this intention as sincerely and as forcibly as that of renouncing the colonial trade; nor would the Committee have imagined they could mean either, if they could have recollected any other subject of contest with Great Britain, to which the harsh imputations of the Memorial could be conjectured to apply –

Your Committee take no pleasure in passing these strictures on the Memorial from Philadelphia – They are aware that it is signed by many persons, whose individual characters are highly respectable – that very circumstance in their opinion renders these animadversions the more indispensable – At a moment when the nation is in the most imminent danger of inevitable War, when its only security from the maintenance of its most sacred rights, is in the vigour of its principles, and the union of its energies, if the men who by their wealth and their station in Society have a natural influence over the minds of others, are the first to desert the Standard of their Country, to propose pusillanimous Councils – to side by their advice with the common Enemy, and to invoke the surrender of every claim in which their individual interest is not implicated, what can be expected from those classes of their fellow Citizens from whom their Country cannot claim so much support – Your Committee have an undoubting Confidence in the Spirit of the Nation – They believe nothing can be more remote from its temper at this time, than confusion or surrender – And when they consider the moderation and equity of the principles for which we are contending, the long and more than patient forbearances, with which we have endured injury and outrage, and that regular gradation of aggressions, which has now arrived at the pitch of denying us the most unquestionable rights of all Independent Nations, they believe the great mass of the People will reject with scorn the dastardly Councils of Submission – That instead of disavowing the assertion of their rights, the will mark with severe displeasure any of their public servants who would renounce them, and will brand with pointed indignation that policy which would make internal discord the instrument of external cowardice –

Your Committee wish not to impute such designs to those Memorialists – They believe that most of the subscribers, signed their names, merely as to a request for the repeal of the Law, without perceiving the drift of its reasoning, or the purpose of its composition – They know that signatures are often obtained to petitions, and memorials, on the credit of their ostensible request, when the signers themselves would be the first to resist their collateral object – And they trust that the patriotism of the Philadelphia merchants is of too pure a character, for them ever to harbour the design of stirring up dissension between the Legislative and Executive authorities to promote the purposes of a foreign antagonist against the rights and liberties of their Country.

The Petition from Boston is properly restricted to remonstrances against the operation of the Laws, apprehended by the petitioners as it may affect their own interests – And although the Committee do not with the petitioners deem the repeal of the Laws expedient, they think it reasonable that it should be so modified, as to avoid the oppressive effects, dreaded by the petitioners – Those modifications may properly come before the Senate, together with those which have been suggested by a document from the department of the Treasury – and your Committee ask leave of the Senate to report a Bill for that purpose.

JOHN QUINCY ADAMS (WASHINGTON, DC) TO JOHN ADAMS, DECEMBER 27, 1807

John Quincy seeks his father's counsel on the critical issues of the day. He is especially anxious to solicit John Adams's views on the proper position that the United States ought to take on impressment. "Is not the impressment of a native born American citizen from an American vessel in point of principle precisely the same thing, as if a British recruiting officer from Canada should come within our lines and forcibly take away a man to make him a British soldier? And is not this forcible levying of recruits by the officer of one nation within the jurisdiction of another the offence against the laws of nations known by the name of plagiat or man-stealing? And is not that offence by the universal usage of civilized nations punished with death?"

MY DEAR SIR:

Your favor of the 14th instant came to my hands just at a moment to renew and to strengthen impressions which had been weighing heavily upon my mind for near a month. The general questions relating to the powers and processes of expulsion under our Constitution had been forced upon me by the situation in which I was placed as chairman of the committee on the present inquiry. My own inclinations would have led me to investigations of a different kind, for which indeed I was making preparations and collecting materials. This subject however came on quite unexpectedly, and still more unexpectedly was it made my duty to take the principal labor of its management upon myself. The committee have been in session almost every day, Saturday and Christmas day not excepted, since their appointment. Their report is now ready and will be presented in the course of a very few days. It is long, and has been agreed to by the committee almost to a line as drafted by myself. It will probably form a subject of animated discussion on the question of acceptance and, if printed, I shall immediately send you a copy. If its *principles* should not meet your approbation, it will be a subject of the deepest regret to me. But even then, I think you will find in it internal evidence that its errors, if such you should deem them, have not arisen from carelessness or inattention. That they should have proceeded from any less excusable origin I am sure you will not suspect.

I perceive, by the newspapers and by letters from more than one of my friends, that the bill which has here commonly been termed the aggression bill, and which was also reported by me as chairman of the committee, has excited surmises and occasioned imputations among my federal friends not very auspicious to their good opinion of me. I think that when I inclosed you a copy of the bill I informed you that scarcely any of its provisions were mine, although I gave the bill as it passed the Senate my vote and my support. I know not anything that has given me so much pleasure as to have learnt by a letter from Dr. Waterhouse that you approved its *principles*. I have, however, inferred from your silence respecting it and from some other circumstances, that you supposed it a measure too high-toned for our situation and perhaps hazardous to our peace. That may possibly be. It passed by a vote almost unanimous in Senate, but has not finally been acted upon in the House of Representatives. It may, therefore, be considered as indicative of the tone of sentiment in the Senate particularly with regard to the affair of the *Chesapeake*, and to the support of our own authority within our own jurisdiction. That I have contributed to the best of my abilities, and as far as my very slender influence in that body extended, to pledge them by this bill to the assertion and support of its principles, I can never deny. But I had evidence too clearly irrefragable of the temper prevailing through both branches of Congress to fear, that any measure which might unnecessarily endanger the peace of the nation would be over hastily adopted.

Our prospects have indeed been growing more gloomy from day to day. And we have now, at the express call of the President, an unlimited embargo. To this measure, also, as merely precautionary and defensive, I gave my assent and vote. It was in Senate carried through in one day, but was contested with much more violence in the other House. Under the decrees of France and Great Britain dooming to capture and confiscation all our ships and cargoes trading with either of those powers, we had no other alternative left but this, or taking our side at once in the war. I do not believe indeed that the embargo can long be continued; but if we let our ships go out without arming them and authorizing them to resist the decrees, they must go merely to swell the plunder of the contending parties.

The British proclamation, expressly commanding impressment from our merchant vessels and assuming in fact a right of annulling our laws of naturalization, has given again a new and darker complexion to our old controversies on that subject. We ought not I think to suffer this new encroachment, and yet I know not how we can take a stand against it without coming to immediate war. Mr. Canning in his correspondence with Mr. Monroe has insisted very strenuously upon keeping the case of the *Chesapeake* distinct from all other subjects of negotiation between us; and yet the proclamation itself improperly connects them, by taking occasion with the disclaimer of the right of search in national ships to place upon new ground and under the formal tenor of a *proclamation* the pretension to impress from merchant vessels.

There are some important lights in which this question of impressment has not yet been presented to the people of this country. You have seen the resolution which I offered in Senate some weeks since, to request from the President information as to the impressments within the two last years. The returns have not yet been made.

If it would not be too troublesome to you I would intreat you to send me an account, as minute and particular as your recollection will admit, of the case of the man whom you defended for killing Lieutenant Panton. If you have any minutes of the trial, or any means of reference to your argument, the authorities you adduced, and the opinion of the court, they might be of service to me. I think I have heard you say that in that case it was admitted by that decision, that the practice of impressment was even then held to be inadmissible in the colonies.

I would also thank you for your opinion on the following points. Is not the impressment of a native born American citizen from an American vessel in point of principle precisely the same thing, as if a British recruiting officer from Canada should come within our lines and forcibly take away a man to make him a British soldier? And is not this forcible levying of recruits by the officer of one nation within the jurisdiction of another the offence against the laws of nations known by the name of *plagiat* or *man-stealing*? And is not that offence by the universal usage of civilized nations punished with death?

Is there any law or usage of nations which forbids an American merchant or master of a vessel from engaging by *contract* a foreign seaman to serve him as a sailor upon a lawful voyage?

Is not every seaman thus engaged by signing a shipping paper according to law? And is not the *personal service* of a seaman thus engaged a *debt*?

I put the case of deserting from ships of war, or any other vessel, out of the question; but setting that aside, if the personal service of a British seaman has become by contract a *debt* to an American merchant, and if a British officer is warranted and *ordered* by his government forcibly to take the seaman away from the service to which he is bound, is it not *in principle* an undertaking by the British government to cancel a *debt* due by the individual of one nation to the individual of the other, and as such in substance a direct violation of the tenth article of Mr. Jay's treaty?

Perhaps these last questions may at first blush carry an appearance of refinement in their train of reasoning more than they really deserve. I will thank you to weigh deliberately the nature of the contract between seamen and their owners, and the moral reason professedly assigned in the tenth article of the treaty for placing contracts between individuals even beyond the reach of war, and say whether the forcible dissolution of contract, which must be involved in every case of impressment, does not violate the substance if not the form of that article?

These are not the only subjects of public concern upon which I feel the want of your judgment and advice. My situation here at this moment is singular and critical. My views of present policy, and my sense of the course enjoined upon me by public duty, are so different from those of the federalists that I find myself in constant opposition to them. Yet I have no communication with the administration but that which my place in the Senate of course implies. The friends of the Executive in Senate repose little confidence in me, and discover occasionally unequivocal marks of their distrust and suspicion. Even when concurring in my opinions, some of them betray an involuntary anxiety lest their popularity should be affected by having their names go out as supporters of measures linked with mine. This temper does, indeed, appear in some small degree to be wearing off, but any trifle light as air would restore it in all its vigor. Yet since the commencement of the present session I have been placed upon every committee of national importance, and made the reporter of several. Without having the weight of a single vote besides my own in point of personal influence, I find myself charged with the duty of originating and conducting measures of the highest interest. I am made a leader without followers. Until the present session I have always had two friends (Tracy and Plumer) with whom I could consult in the most intimate and confidential manner and on whose friendship I could always rely, almost always upon their concurrence. But death has removed one of them, and changes of political party the other. I am compelled, therefore, to lean upon my own judgment more than it will always bear. My only consolation is in the consciousness of good intentions and unwearied attention to my duty. Man can give no more, the rest must be left to a higher power.

Mr. Monroe is here and has been received with great demonstrations of respect and affection by his own state. There is said to be some electioneering on foot, of which he is one of the objects. Electioneering, indeed, is reported to be very active, but I know nothing of its course of proceedings.

P. S. I hear there is a private correspondence now passing between General Wilkinson and J. Randolph, which is expected to terminate in a meeting of honor.

JOHN QUINCY ADAMS (WASHINGTON, DC) TO GOVERNOR JAMES SULLIVAN, JANUARY 10, 1808

In the face of Federalist calls for Massachusetts to join with other commercial states to resist the embargo, John Quincy defends his support for the policy in an open letter to Republican Governor James Sullivan: "On the whole I considered it as a measure eminently calculated for the preservation of peace, as it would at once diminish the temptations and opportunities of the enemy to commence war against us, and as it would prepare our own people for an acquiescence in terms on our part, which, without sacrificing any of our rights, might still go further to conciliation than the temper of the people would have brooked without it." He acknowledged that he hesitated because of the public distress it would cause, but he concurred on the "decisive recommendation of the President."

SIR:

I lose not a moment in answering your Excellency's inquiries with regard to the causes of the embargo so far as they were understood by me.

1. It was explicitly recommended by the President in a message communicating a decision by order of the French Emperor, that the decree of 21 November, 1806, should be strictly executed against the Americans, as well as all others; and also the British proclamation commanding their naval officers to impress British subjects from our vessels.

2. The answer of Mr. Rose, transferring the negotiations between Great Britain and this country from London to this place, was considered as an extraordinary and suspicious circumstance. There were reasons for supposing that the tone of Mr. Rose's instructions would be so arrogant and overbearing that they would be deemed inadmissible here, and the negotiation arrested at the threshold. It was thought probable that the British squadron on our coast would have instructions to commence hostilities immediately on the rupture of the negotiation, and prudence

seemed to call for a measure which would avoid exposing to capture any of our vessels which might be *issuing from* our ports. The occurrences since Mr. Rose's arrival have tended very much to confirm these expectations. He has raised a punctilio without landing concerning the treatment not of himself, but of the ship in which he came; and the British ship Triumph has been into Lynn Haven Bay, and received dispatches from the station.

3. There was all but official intelligence that the British king had issued a retaliating proclamation to counteract that of France, and of equal extent. It was obvious that between the two, every American vessel that should be permitted to sail would go to almost certain capture and condemnation. A temporary suspension of their departure was thought therefore necessary.

4. It was probable that the embargo, by throwing out of employment the British sailors in this country, would induce them to return of their own accord to the ships of their own sovereign. *To me* this was a very desirable circumstance, for I believed it would take away the only pretext the British have to offer for engaging in a quarrel with us.

5. It was an experiment to see how far the Government might calculate upon the support of the people for the maintenance of their own rights. It was useful and might be of importance to the country, to commence this experiment and observe its effects before the negotiation with Mr. Rose should commence. On the whole I considered it as a measure eminently calculated for the preservation of peace, as it would at once diminish the temptations and opportunities of the enemy to commence war against us, and as it would prepare our own people for an acquiescence in terms on our part, which, without sacrificing any of our rights, might still go further to conciliation than the temper of the people would have brooked without it. Yet it was a measure so necessarily distressing to ourselves, that I should have hesitated upon it, but for the decisive recommendation of the President.

The letters of Messrs. Armstrong and Champagny about which so much has been said, related solely to the decree of 21 November,

1806. Nothing more was communicated to Congress. It was, however, in my mind a measure merely precautionary and which I had and have no idea will be of long continuance. General embargoes of six or twelve months, of which some gentlemen talk so lightly, never entered my brain as practicable things in a great commercial country. I question whether an example of the kind can be found in history.

I am, etc.

LETTER TO HARRISON GRAY OTIS, MARCH 31, 1808 (PUBLISHED AS A PAMPHLET)

In this public letter to Federalist leader Harrison Gray Otis, John Quincy offered a detailed history of the embargo and an extended defense of his position. He had no sympathy for Napoleon's Berlin or Milan decrees but was convinced that British maritime regulations, based on the infamous Rule of 1756, were aimed at the destruction of neutral commerce and thus were at the root of the crisis. "They strike at the root of our independence. They assume the principle that we shall have no commerce in time of war, but with her dominions, and as tributaries to her. The exclusive confinement of commerce to the mother country, is the great principle of the modern colonial system; and should we by dereliction of our rights at this momentous stride of encroachment surrender our commercial freedom without a struggle, Britain has but a single step to take, and she brings us back to the stamp act and the tea tax."

DEAR SIR:

I have received from one of my friends in Boston a copy of a printed pamphlet, containing a letter from Mr. Pickering to the Governor of the Commonwealth, intended for communication to the legislature of the State, during their session, recently concluded. But this object not having been accomplished, it appears to have been published by some friend of the writer, whose inducement is stated, no doubt truly, to have been the importance of the matter discussed in it, and the high respectability of the author.

The subjects of this letter are the embargo, and the differences in controversy between our country and Great Britain – subjects upon which it is my misfortune, in the discharge of my duties as a Senator of the United States, to differ from the opinions of my Colleague. The place where the question upon the first of them, in common with others of great national concern, was between him and me, in our official capacities a proper object of discussion, was the Senate of the Union. There it was discussed, and, as far as the constitutional authority of that body extended, there it was decided. Having obtained alike the concurrence of the other branch of the national legislature, and the approbation of the President, it became the law of the land, and as such I have considered it entitled to the respect and obedience of every virtuous citizen.

From these decisions, however, the letter in question is to be considered in the nature of an appeal; in the first instance, to our common constituents, the legislature of the State; and in the second, by the publication, to the people. To both these tribunals I shall always hold myself accountable for every act of my public life. Yet, were my own political character alone implicated in the course which has in this instance been pursued, I should have forborne all notice of the proceeding, and have left my conduct in this, as in other cases, to the candor and discretion of my Country.

But to this species of appeal, thus conducted, there are some objects on constitutional grounds, which I deem it my duty to mention for the consideration of the public. On a statement of circumstances attending a very important act of national legislation, a statement which the writer undoubtedly believed to be true, but which comes only from one side of the question and which, I expect to prove in the most essential points erroneous, the writer with the most animated tone of energy calls for the *interposition* of the commercial States, and asserts that "nothing but their sense, clearly and emphatically expressed, will save them from ruin." This solemn and alarming invocation is addressed to the legislature of Massachusetts, at so late a period of their session, that had it been received by them, they must have been compelled either to act upon the views of this representation, without hearing the counter statement of the other side, or seemingly to disregard the pressing interest of their constituents, by neglecting an admonition of the most serious complexion. Considering the application as a precedent, its tendency is dangerous to the public. For on the first supposition, that the legislature had been precipitated to act on the spur of such an instigation, they must have acted on imperfect information, and under an excitement, not remarkably adapted to the composure of safe deliberation. On the second they would have been exposed to unjust imputations, which at the eve of an election might have operated in the most inequitable manner upon the characters of individual members.

The interposition of one or more State legislatures, to control the exercise of the powers vested by the general Constitution in the Congress of the United States, is at least of questionable policy. The views of a State legislature are naturally and properly limited in a considerable degree to the particular interests of the State. The very object and formation of the *national* deliberative assemblies was for the compromise and conciliation of the interests of all – of the whole nation. If the appeal from the regular, legitimate measures of the body where the whole nation is represented, be proper to one State legislature, it must be so to another. If the commercial States are called to interpose on one hand, will not the agricultural States be with equal propriety summoned to interpose on the other? If the East is stimulated against the West, and the Northern and Southern Sections are urged into collision with each other, by appeals from the acts of Congress to the respective States – *in what are these appeals to end?*

It is undoubtedly the right, and may often become the duty of a State legislature, to address that of the nation, with the expression of its wishes, in regard to interests peculiarly concerning the State itself. Nor shall I question the right of every member of the great federative compact to declare its own sense of measures interesting to the nation at large. But whenever the case occurs that this sense should be "clearly and emphatically" expressed, it ought surely to be predicated upon a full and impartial consideration of the whole subject – not under the stimulus of a one-sided representation – far less upon the impulse of conjectures and suspicions. It is not through the medium of personal sensibility, nor of party bias, nor of professional occupation, nor of geographical position, that the whole truth can be discerned, of questions involving the rights and interests of this extensive Union. When their discussion is urged upon a State legislature, the first call upon its members should be to cast all their feelings and interests as the citizens of a single State into the common stock of the national concern.

Should the occurrence upon which an appeal is made from the councils of the nation, to those of a single State be one, upon which the representation of the State had been divided, and the member who found himself in the minority, felt impelled by a sense of duty to invoke the interposition of his constituents, it would seem that both in justice to them, and in candor to his colleague, some notice of such intention should be given to him, that he too might be prepared to exhibit his views of the subject upon which the difference of opinion had taken place; or, at least that the resort should be had, at such a period of time as would leave it within the reach of possibility for his representations to be received, by their common constituents, before they would be compelled to decide on the merits of the case.

The fairness and propriety of this course of proceeding must be so obvious, that it is difficult to conceive of the propriety of any other. Yet it presents another inconvenience which must necessarily result from this practice of appellate legislation. When one of the senators from a State proclaims to his constituents that a particular measure, or system of measures which has received the vote and support of his colleague, are pernicious and destructive to those interests which both are bound by the most sacred of ties, with zeal and fidelity to promote, the denunciation of the measures amounts to little less than a denunciation of the man. The advocate of a policy thus reprobated must feel himself summoned by every motive of self-defence to vindicate his conduct: and if his general sense of his official duties would bind him to the industrious devotion of his whole time to the public business of the session, the hours which he might be forced to employ for his own justification, would of course be deducted from the discharge of his more regular and appropriate functions. Should these occasions frequently recur, they could not fail to interfere with the due performance of the public business. Nor can I forbear to remark the tendency of such antagonizing appeals to distract the councils of the State in its own legislature, to destroy its influence, and expose it to derision, in the presence of its sister States, and to produce between the colleagues themselves mutual asperities and rancors, until the great concerns of the nation would degenerate into the puny controversies of personal altercation.

It is therefore with extreme reluctance that I enter upon this discussion. In developing my own views and the principles which have governed my conduct in relation to our foreign affairs, and particularly to the embargo, some very material differences in point of fact as well as of opinion, will be found between my statements, and those of the letter, which alone can apologize for this. They will not, I trust, be deemed in any degree disrespectful to the writer. Far more pleasing would it have been to me, could that honest and anxious pursuit of the policy best calculated to promote the honor and welfare of our country, which, I trust, is felt with equal ardor by us both, have resulted in the same opinions, and have given them the vigor of united exertion. There is a candor and liberality of conduct and of sentiment due from associates in the same public charge, towards each other, necessary to their individual reputation, to their common influence, and to their public usefulness. In our republican government, where the power of the nation consists alone in the sympathies of opinion, this reciprocal deference, this open hearted imputation of honest intentions, is the only adamant at once attractive and impenetrable, that can bear, unshattered, all the thunder of foreign hostility. Ever since I have had the honor of a seat in the national councils, I have extended it to every department of the government. However differing in my conclusions, upon questions of the highest moment, from any other man, of whatever party, I have never, upon suspicion, imputed his conduct to corruption. If this confidence argues ignorance of public men and public affairs, to that ignorance I must plead guilty. I know, indeed, enough of human nature to be sensible that vigilant observation is at all times, and that suspicion may occasionally become necessary, upon the conduct of men in power. But I know as well that confidence is the only cement of an elective government. Election is the very test of confidence, and its periodical return is the constitutional check upon its abuse; of which the electors must of course be the sole judges. For the exercise of power, where man is free, confidence is indispensable; and when it once totally fails, when the men to whom the people have committed the application of their force, for their benefit, are to be presumed of the vilest of mankind, the very foundation of the social compact must be dissolved. Towards the gentleman whose official station results from the confidence of the same legislature, by whose appointment I have the honor of holding a similar trust, I have thought this confidence peculiarly due from me, nor should I now notice his letter, not withstanding the disapprobation it so obviously implies at the course which I have pursued in relation to the subjects of which it treats, did it not appear to me calculated to produce upon the public mind, impressions unfavorable to the rights and interests of the nation.

Having understood that a motion in the Senate of Massachusetts was made by you, requesting the Governor to transmit Mr.

Pickering's letter to the legislature, together with such communications, relating to public affairs, as he might have received from
me, I avail myself of the circumstance, and of the friendship
which has so long subsisted between us, to take the liberty of
addressing this letter, intended for publication, to you. Very few
of the facts which I shall state will rest upon information peculiar
to myself. Most of them will stand upon the basis of official documents, or of public and undisputed notoriety. For my opinions,
though fully persuaded, that even where differing from your
own, they will meet with a fair and liberal judge in you, yet of the
public I ask neither favor nor indulgence. Pretending to no extraordinary credit from the authority of the writer, I am sensible they
must fall by their own weakness, or stand by their own strength.

The first remark which obtrudes itself upon the mind upon
the perusal of Mr. Pickering's letter is, that in enumerating all the
pretences (for he thinks there are no causes) for the embargo,
and for a war with Great Britain, he has totally omitted the British Orders of Council of November II, 1807, those orders under
which millions of the property of our fellow citizens, are now
detained in British hands, or confiscated to British captors, those
orders, under which tenfold as many millions of the same property would have been at this moment in the same predicament,
had they not been saved from exposure to it by the embargo,
those orders, which if once submitted to and carried to the extent
of their principles, would not have left an inch of American canvas upon the ocean, but under British license and British taxation. An attentive reader of the letter, without other information,
would not even suspect their existence. They are indeed in one or
two passages, faintly, and darkly alluded to under the justifying
description of "the orders of the British government, *retaliating*
the French imperial decree:" but as causes for the embargo, or as
possible causes or even *pretences* of war with Great Britain, they
are not only unnoticed, but their very existence is by direct implication denied.

It is indeed true, that these orders were not officially communicated with the President's message recommending the embargo. They had not been officially received. But they were announced in several paragraphs from London and Liverpool newspapers of the 10th, 11th and 12th of November, which appeared in the *National Intelligencer* of 18th December, the day upon which the embargo message was sent to Congress. The British government had taken care that they should not be authentically known before their time – for the very same newspapers which gave this inofficial notice of these orders, announced also the departure of Mr. Rose, upon a special mission to the United States. And we know that of these all-devouring instruments of rapine Mr. Rose was not even informed. His mission was professedly a mission of conciliation and reparation for a flagrant, enormous, acknowledged outrage. But he was not sent with these Orders of Council in his hands. His text was the disavowal of Admiral Berkeley's conduct. The commentary was to be discovered on another page of the British ministerial policy. On the face of Mr. Rose's instructions, these Orders of Council were as invisible, as they are on that of Mr. Pickering's letter.

They were not merely without official authenticity. Rumors had for several weeks been in circulation derived from English prints, and from private correspondences, that such orders were to issue; and no inconsiderable pains were taken here to discredit the fact. Assurances were given that there was reason to believe no such orders to be contemplated. Suspicion was lulled by declarations equivalent nearly to a positive denial: and these opiates were continued for weeks after the embargo was laid, until Mr. Erskine received instructions to make the official communication of the orders themselves, in their proper shape, to our government.

Yet, although thus unauthenticated, and even although thus in some sort denied, the probability of the circumstances under which they were announced, and the sweeping tendency of their effects, formed to my understanding a powerful motive, and together with the papers sent by the President, and his express recommendation, a decisive one, for assenting to the embargo. As a precautionary measure, I believed it would rescue an immense property from depredation, if the orders should prove authentic. If the alarm was groundless, it must very soon be disproved, and the embargo might be removed with the danger.

The omission of all notice of these facts in the pressing enquiries "why the Embargo was laid?" is the more surprising, because they are of all the facts, the most material, upon a fair and impartial examination of the expediency of that Act, when it passed. And because these orders, together with the subsequent "retaliating decrees" of France and Spain, have furnished the only reasons upon which I have acquiesced in its continuance to this day. If duly weighed, they will save us the trouble of resorting to jealousies of secret corruption, and the imaginary terrors of Napoleon for the real cause of the embargo. These are fictions of foreign invention. The French Emperor had *not* declared that he would have no neutrals. He had *not* required that our ports should be shut against British commerce – but the Orders of Council if submitted to would have degraded us to the condition of colonies. If resisted would have fattened the wolves of plunder with our spoils. The embargo was the only shelter from the Tempest – the last refuge of our violated peace.

I have indeed been myself of opinion that the embargo, must in its nature be a temporary expedient, and that preparations manifesting a determination of resistance against these outrageous violations of our neutral rights ought at least to have been made a subject of serious deliberation in Congress. I have believed and do still believe that our internal resources are competent to the establishment and maintenance of a naval force, public and private, if not fully adequate to the protection and defence of our commerce, at least sufficient to induce a retreat from these hostilities and to deter from a renewal of them, by either of the warring parties; and that a system to that effect might be formed, ultimately far more economical, and certainly more energetic than a three years embargo. Very soon after the closure of our ports, I did submit to the consideration of the Senate, a proposition for the appointment of a committee to institute an enquiry to this end. But my resolution met no encouragement. Attempts of a similar nature have been made in the House of Representatives, but have been equally discountenanced, and from these determinations by decided majorities of both houses, I am not sufficiently confident in the superiority of my own wisdom to appeal, by a topical application to the congenial feelings of any one – not even of my own native section of the Union.

The embargo, however, is a restriction always under our own control. It was a measure altogether of defence and of experiment. If it was injudiciously or over-hastily laid, it has been every day since its adoption open to a repeal: if it should prove ineffectual for the purposes which it was meant to secure, a single day will suffice to unbar the doors. Still believing it a measure justified by the circumstances of the time, I am ready to admit that those who thought otherwise may have had a wiser foresight of events, and a sounder judgment of the then existing state of things than the majority of the national legislature, and the President. It has been approved by several of the State legislatures, and among the rest by our own. Yet of all its effects we are still unable to judge with certainty. It must still abide the test of futurity. I shall add that there were other motives which had their operation in contributing to the passage of the act, unnoticed by Mr. Pickering, and which having now ceased will also be left unnoticed by me. The Orders of Council of 11th November still subsist in all their force; and are now confirmed, with the addition of *taxation*, by act of Parliament.

As they stand in front of the real causes for the embargo, so they are entitled to the same pre-eminence in enumerating the causes of hostility, which the British ministers are accumulating upon our forbearance. They strike at the root of our independence. They assume the principle that we shall have no commerce in time of war, but with her dominions, and as tributaries to her. The exclusive confinement of commerce to the mother country, is the great principle of the modern colonial system; and should we by a dereliction of our rights at this momentous stride of encroachment surrender our commercial freedom without a struggle, Britain has but a single step more to take, and she brings us back to the stamp act and the tea tax.

Yet these orders – thus fatal to the liberties for which the sages and heroes of our revolution toiled and bled – thus studiously concealed until the moment when they burst upon our heads – thus issued at the very instant when a mission of atonement was professedly sent – in these orders we are to see nothing but a "retaliating order upon France" – in these orders, we must not find so much as a cause – nay not so much as a pretence, for complaint against Britain.

To my mind, sir, in comparison with those orders, the three causes to which Mr. Pickering explicitly limits our grounds for a rupture with England, might indeed be justly denominated *pretences*; in comparison with them, former aggressions sink into insignificance. To argue upon the subject of our disputes with Britain, or upon the motives for the embargo, and keep them out of sight, is like laying your finger over the *unit* before a series of noughts, and then arithmetically proving that they all amount to nothing.

It is not however in a mere omission, nor yet in the history of the embargo, that the inaccuracies of the statement I am examining have given me the most serious concern – it is in the view taken of the questions in controversy between us and Britain. The wisdom of the embargo is a question of great, but transient magnitude, and omission sacrifices no national right. Mr. Pickering's object was to dissuade the nation from a war with England, into which he suspected the administration was plunging us, under French compulsion. But the tendency of his pamphlet is to reconcile the nation, or at least the commercial states, to the servitude of British protection, and war with all the rest of Europe. Hence England is represented as contending for the common liberties of mankind, and our only safe-guard against the ambition and injustice of France. Hence all our sensibilities are invoked in her favor, and all our antipathies against her antagonist. Hence, too, all the subjects of difference between us and Britain are alleged to be on our part mere *pretences*, of which the *right* is unequivocally pronounced to be *on her side*. Proceeding from a Senator of the United States, specially charged as a member of the executive with the maintenance of the nation's rights, against foreign powers, and at a moment extremely critical of pending negotiation upon all the points thus delineated, this formal *abandonment* of the American cause, this summons of unconditional surrender to the pretensions of our antagonist, is in my mind highly alarming. It becomes therefore a duty to which every other consideration must yield to point out the errors of this representation. Before we strike the standard of the nation, let us at least examine the purport of the summons.

And first, with respect to the impressment of our seamen. We are told that "the taking of British seamen found on board our merchant vessels, by British ships of war, is agreeably to a *right*, claimed and exercised for ages." It is obvious that this claim and exercise of ages, could not apply to us, as an independent people. If the right was claimed and exercised while our vessels were navigating under the British flag, it could not authorize the same claim when their owners have become the citizens of a sovereign state. As a relict of colonial servitude, whatever may be the claim of Great Britain, it surely can be no ground for contending that it is entitled to our submission.

If it be meant that the right has been claimed and exercised for ages over the merchant vessels of other nations, I apprehend it is a mistake. The case never occurred with sufficient frequency to constitute even a practice, much less a right. If it had been either, it would have been noticed by some of the writers on the laws of nations. The truth is, the question arose out of American independence – from the severance of one nation into two. It was never made a question between any other nations. There is therefore no right of prescription.

But, it seems, it has also been *claimed* and *exercised*, during the whole of the three administrations of our national government. And is it meant to be asserted that this claim and exercise constitute a right? If it is, I appeal to the uniform, unceasing and urgent remonstrances of the three administrations – I appeal not only to the warm feelings, but cool justice of the American people – nay, I appeal to the sound sense and honorable sentiment of the British nation itself, which, however, it may have submitted at home to this practice, never would tolerate its sanction by law, against the assertion. If it is not, how can it be affirmed that it is on our part a mere pretence?

But the first merchant of the United States, in answer to Mr. Pickering's late enquiries has informed him that since the affair of the *Chesapeake* there has been no cause of complaint – that he could not find a single instance where they had taken one man out of a merchant vessel. Who it is, that enjoys the dignity of first merchant of the United States we are not informed. But if he had applied to many merchants in Boston as respectable as any in the United States, they could have told him of a valuable vessel and cargo, totally lost upon the coast of England, last in August last, and solely in consequence of having had two of her men, native Americans taken from her by impressment, two months after the affair of the *Chesapeake*.

On the 15th of October, the king of England issued his proclamation, commanding his naval officers, to impress his subjects from neutral vessels. This proclamation is represented as merely "requiring the return of his subjects, the seamen especially, from foreign countries," and then "it is an acknowledged principle that every nation has a right to the service of its subjects in time of war." Is this, sir, a correct statement either of the proclamation, or of the question it involves in which our right is concerned? The king of England's right to the service of his subjects in time of war is nothing to us. The question is, whether he has a right to seize them forcibly on board of our vessels while under contract of service to our citizens, within our jurisdiction upon the high seas?

And whether he has a right expressly to command his naval officers so to seize them. Is this an acknowledged principle? Certainly not. Why then is this proclamation described as founded
upon uncontested principle? and why is the command, so justly
offensive to us, and so mischievous as it might then have been
made in execution, altogether omitted?

But it is not the taking of British subjects from our vessels, it is
the taking under color of that pretence of our own, native American citizens, which constitutes the most galling aggravation of
this merciless practice. Yet even this, we are told is but a pretence –
for three reasons.

1. Because the number of citizens thus taken is small.

2. Because it arises only from the impossibility of distinguish-
    ing Englishmen from Americans.

3. Because, such impressed American citizens are delivered
    up, on duly authenticated proof.

1. Small and great in point of numbers are relative terms. To suppose that the native Americans form a small proportion of the
whole number impressed is a mistake. The reverse is the fact.
Examine the official returns from the Department of State. They
give the names of between four and five thousand men impressed
since the commencement of the present war. Of which number,
not one-fifth part were British subjects. The number of naturalized Americans could not amount to one-tenth. I hazard little in
saying that more than three-fourths were native Americans. If it
be said that some of these men, though appearing on the face of
the returns American citizens, were really British subjects, and
had fraudulently procured their protections; I reply that this
number must be far exceeded by the cases of citizens impressed,
which never reach the Department of State. The American consul
in London estimates the number of impressments during the war
at nearly three times the amount of the names returned. If the

nature of the offence be considered in its true colors, to a people having a just sense of personal liberty and security, it is in every single instance, of a malignity not inferior to that of murder. The very same act, when committed by the recruiting officer of one nation within the territories of another, is by the universal law and usage of nations punished with death. Suppose the crime had in every instance, as by its consequences it has been in many, deliberate murder. Would it answer or silence the voice of our complaints to be told that the number was small?

2. The impossibility of distinguishing English from American seamen is not the only, nor even the most frequent occasion of impressment. Look again into the returns from the Department of State – you will see that the officers take our men without pretending to enquire where they were born; sometimes merely to show their animosity, or their contempt for our country; sometimes from the wantonness of power. When they manifest the most tender regard for the neutral rights of America, they lament that they want the men. They regret the necessity, but they *must* have their complement. When we complain of these enormities, we are answered that the acts of such officers were unauthorized; that the commanders of men-of-war are an unruly set of men, for whose violence their own government cannot always be answerable, that enquiry shall be made. A court martial is sometimes mentioned. And the issue of Whitby's court martial has taught us what relief is to be expected from that. There are even examples I am told, when such officers have been put upon the yellow list. But this is a rare exception. The ordinary issue when the act is disavowed, is the promotion of the actor.

3. The impressed native American citizens however, upon *duly authenticated proof* are delivered up. Indeed! how unreasonable then were complaint! How effectual a remedy for the wrong! an American vessel, bound to a European port, has two, three or four native Americans, impressed by a British man-of-war, bound

to the East or West Indies. When the American captain arrives at his port of destination he makes his protest, and sends it to the nearest American minister or consul. When he returns home, he transmits the duplicate of his protest to the Secretary of State. In process of time, the names of the impressed men, and of the ship into which they have been impressed, are received by the agent in London. He makes his demand that the men may be delivered up. The Lords of the Admiralty, after a reasonable time for enquiry and advisement, return for answer, that the ship is on a foreign station, and their Lordships can therefore take no further steps in the matter. Or, that the ship has been taken, and that the men have been received in exchange for French prisoners. Or, that the men had no protections (the impressing officers often having taken them from the men). Or, that the men were *probably* British subjects. Or that they have entered, and taken the bounty; (to which the officers know how to reduce them). Or, that they have been married, or settled in England. In all these cases, without further ceremony, their discharge is refused. Sometimes, their Lordships, in a vein of humor, inform the agent that the man has been discharged as *unserviceable*. Sometimes, in a sterner tone they say he was *an impostor*. Or perhaps by way of consolation to his relatives and friends, they report that he has fallen in battle, against nations in amity with his country. Sometimes they coolly return that there is *no such man on board the ship*; and what has become of him, the agonies of a wife and children in his native land may be left to conjecture. When all these and many other such apologies for refusal fail, the native American seaman is discharged – and when by the charitable aid of his government he has found his way home, he comes to be informed, that all is as it should be – that the number of his fellow-sufferers is *small* – that it was impossible to distinguish him from an Englishman – and that he was delivered up, on *duly authenticated proof*.

Enough, of this disgusting subject. I cannot stop to calculate how many of these wretched victims are natives of Massachusetts, and how many natives of Virginia. I cannot stop to solve that knotty question of national jurisprudence whether some of them might not possibly be slaves, and therefore not citizens of the United States. I cannot stay to account for the wonder, why, poor, and ignorant and friendless as most of them are, the voice of their complaints is so seldom *heard* in the great navigating states. I admit that we have endured this cruel indignity, through all the administrations of the General Government. I acknowledge that Britain claims the right of seizing her subjects in our merchant vessels, and that even if we could acknowledge it, the line of discrimination would be difficult to draw. We are not in a condition to maintain this right, by war; and as the British government have been more than once on the point of giving it up of their own accord, I would still hope for the day when returning justice shall induce them to abandon it, without compulsion. Her subjects we do not want. The degree of protection which we are bound to extend to them, cannot equal the claim of our own citizens. I would subscribe to any compromise of this contest, consistent with the rights of sovereignty, the duties of humanity, and the principles of reciprocity: but to the right of forcing even her own subjects out of our merchant vessels on the high seas I never can assent.

The second point upon which Mr. Pickering defends the pretensions of Great Britain, is her denial to neutral nations of the right of prosecuting with her enemies and their colonies, any commerce from which they are excluded in time of peace. His statement of this case adopts the British doctrine, as sound. The *right*, as on the question of impressment, so on this, it surrenders at discretion – and it is equally defective in point of fact.

In the first place, the claim of Great Britain, is not to "a right of imposing on this neutral commerce some *limits and restraints*" but of interdicting it altogether, at her pleasure; of interdicting it without a moment's notice to neutrals, after solemn decisions of her courts of admiralty, and formal acknowledgments of her ministers, that it is a lawful trade. And, on such a sudden, unnotified interdiction, of pouncing upon all neutral commerce navigating upon the faith of her decisions and acknowledgments, and of gorging with confiscation the greediness of her cruisers. This is the right claimed by Britain. This is the power she has exercised. What Mr. Pickering calls "limits and restraints," she calls relaxations of her right.

It is but little more than two years, since this question was agitated both in England and America, with as much zeal, energy and ability, as ever was displayed upon any question of national law. The British side was supported by Sir William Scott, Mr. Ward, and the author of *War in Disguise*. But even in Britain their doctrine was refuted to demonstration by the Edinburg reviewers. In America, the rights of our country were maintained by numerous writers profoundly skilled in the science of national and maritime law. The *Answer to War in Disguise* was ascribed to a gentleman whose talents are universally acknowledged, and who by his official situations had been required thoroughly to investigate every question of conflict between neutral and belligerent rights which has occurred in the history of modern war. Mr. Gore and Mr. Pinkney, our two commissioners at London, under Mr. Jay's treaty, the former, in a train of cool and conclusive argument addressed to Mr. Madison, the latter in a memorial of splendid eloquence from the merchants of Baltimore, supported the same cause; memorials, drawn by lawyers of distinguished eminence, by merchants of the highest character, and by statesmen of long experience in our national councils from Salem, from Boston, from New Haven, from New York, and from Philadelphia, together with remonstrances to the same effect from Newburyport, Newport, Norfolk and Charleston. This accumulated mass of legal learning, of commercial information and of national sentiment from almost every inhabited spot upon our shores, and from one extremity of the Union to the other, confirmed by the unanswered and unanswerable memorial of Mr. Monroe to the British minister, and by the elaborate research and irresistible reasoning of the *examination* of the British doctrine, was also made a subject of full, and deliberate discussion in the Senate of the United States. A committee of seven members of that body, after three weeks of arduous investigation, reported three resolutions, the first of which was in these words: "*Resolved*, that the capture and condemnation, under the orders of the British government, and adjudications of their courts of admiralty of American vessels and their cargoes, on the pretext of their being employed in a trade with the enemies of Great Britain, prohibited in time of peace, is an unprovoked aggression upon the property of the citizens of these United States, a violation of their neutral *rights, and an encroachment upon their national independence.*"

On the 13th of February, 1806, the question upon the adoption of this resolution, was taken in the Senate. The yeas and nays were required; but not a solitary *nay* was heard in answer. It was adopted by the unanimous voice of all the senators present. They were twenty-eight in number, and among them stands recorded the name of Mr. Pickering.

Let us remember that this was a question most peculiarly and immediately of commercial, and not agricultural interest; that it arose from a call, loud, energetic and unanimous from all the merchants of the United States upon Congress, for the national interposition; that many of the memorials invoked all the energy of the legislature, and pledged the lives and properties of the memorialists in support of any measures which Congress might deem necessary to vindicate those rights. Negotiation was particularly recommended from Boston, and elsewhere – negotiation was adopted – negotiation has failed – and now Mr. Pickering tells us that Great Britain has claimed and maintained her *right*! He argues that her claim is just – and is not sparing of censure upon those who still consider it as a serious cause of complaint. But there was one point of view in which the British doctrine on this question was then only considered incidentally in the United States – because it was not deemed material for the discussion of our rights. We examined it chiefly as affecting the principles as between a belligerent and a neutral power. But in fact it was an infringement of the rights of war, as well as of the rights of peace.

It was an unjustifiable enlargement of the sphere of hostile operations. The *enemies* of Great Britain had by the universal law of nations a right to the benefits of neutral commerce within their dominions (subject to the exceptions of *actual* blockade and contraband) as well as neutral nations had a right to trade with them. The exclusion from that commerce by this new principle of warfare which Britain, in defiance of all immemorial national usages, undertook by her single authority to establish, but too naturally led her enemies to resort to new and extraordinary principles, by which in their turn they might retaliate this injury upon her. The pretence upon which Britain in the first instance had attempted to color her injustice, was a miserable *fiction*. It was an argument against fact. Her reasoning was, that a neutral vessel by mere admission in time of war, into ports from which it would have been excluded in time of peace, became thereby deprived of its national character, and *ipso facto* was transformed into enemy's property.

Such was the basis upon which arose the far famed rule of the war of 1756. Such was the foundation upon which Britain *claimed* and *maintained* this supposed right of adding that new instrument of desolation to the horrors of war. It was distressing to her enemy. Yes! Had she adopted the practice of dealing with them in poison; had Mr. Fox accepted the services of the man who offered to rid him of the French Emperor by assassination, and had the attempt succeeded, it would have been less distressing to France than this rule of the war of 1756; and not more unjustifiable. Mr. Fox had too fair a mind for either, but his comprehensive and liberal spirit was discarded, with the cabinet which he had formed.

It has been the struggle of reason and humanity, and above all the Christianity for two thousand years to mitigate the rigors of that scourge of humankind, war. It is now the struggle of Britain to aggravate them. Her rule of the war of 1756, in itself and in its effects, was one of the deadliest poisons, in which it was possible for her to tinge the weapons of her hostility.

In itself and in its effects, I say. For the French decrees of Berlin and of Milan, the Spanish and Dutch decrees of the same or the like tenor, and her own orders of January and November – these alternations of licensed pillage, this eager competition between her and her enemies for the honor of giving the last stroke to the vitals of maritime neutrality, all are justly attributable to her assumption and exercise of this single principle. The rule of war of 1756 was the root, from which all the rest but suckers, still at every shoot growing ranker in luxuriance.

In the last decrees of France and Spain, her own ingenious fiction is adopted; and under them, every neutral vessel that submits to English search, has been carried into an English port, or paid a tax to the English government, is declared *denationalized*, that is to have lost her national character, and to have become English property. This is cruel in execution; absurd in argument. To refute it were folly, for to the understanding of a child it refutes itself. But it is the reasoning of British jurists. It is the simple application to the circumstances and powers of France, of the rule of the war of 1756.

I am not the apologist of France and Spain; I have no national partialities; no national attachments but to my own country. I shall never undertake to justify or to palliate the insults or injuries of any foreign power to that country which is dearer to me than life. If the voice of reason and of justice could be heard by France and Spain, they would say, you have done wrong to make the injustice of your enemy towards neutrals the measure of your own. If she chastises with whips do not you chastise with scorpions. Whether France would listen to this language, I know not. The most enormous infractions of our rights hitherto committed by her, have been more in menace than in accomplishment. The alarm has been justly great; the anticipation threatening; but the amount of actual injury small. But to Britain, what can we say? If we attempt to raise our voices, her minister has declared to Mr. Pinkney that she will not hear. The only reason she assigns for her recent Orders of Council is, that France proceeds on the same principles. It is not by the light of blazing temples, and amid the groans of women and children perishing in the ruins of the sanctuaries of domestic habitation at Copenhagen, that we can expect our remonstrances against this course of proceeding will be heard.

Let us come to the third and last of the causes of complaint, which are represented as so frivolous and so unfounded – "the unfortunate affair of the *Chesapeake*." The orders of Admiral Berkeley, under which this outrage was committed, have been disavowed by his government. General professions of a willingness to make reparation for it, have been lavished in profusion; and we are now instructed to take these professions for *endeavors*; to believe them sincere, because his Britannic Majesty sent us a special envoy; and to cast the odium of defeating these endeavors upon our own government.

I have already told you, that I am not one of those who deem suspicion and distrust, in the highest order of political virtues. Baseless suspicion is, in my estimation, a vice, as pernicious in the management of public affairs, as it is fatal to the happiness of domestic life. When, therefore, the British ministers have declared their disposition to make ample reparation for an injury of a most atrocious character, committed by an officer of high rank, and, as they say, utterly without authority, I should most readily believe them, were their professions not positively contradicted by facts of more powerful eloquence than words.

Have such facts occurred? I will not again allude to the circumstances of Mr. Rose's departure upon his mission at such a precise point of time, that his commission and the Orders of Council of 11th November, might have been signed with the same penful of ink. The subjects were not immediately connected with each other, and his Majesty did not chuse to associate distinct topics of negotiation. The attack upon the *Chesapeake* was disavowed; and ample reparation was withheld only, because with the demand for satisfaction upon that injury, the American government had coupled a demand for the cessation of others; alike in kind, but of minor aggravation. But had reparation really been intended, would it not have been offered, not in vague and general terms, but in precise and specific proposals? Were any such

made? None. But it is said Mr. Monroe was restricted from negotiating upon this subject apart; and therefore Mr. Rose was to be
sent to Washington; charged with this single object; and without
authority to treat upon or even to discuss any other. Mr. Rose
arrives. The American government readily determine to treat
upon the *Chesapeake affair*, separately from all others; but before
Mr. Rose sets his foot on shore, in pursuance of a pretension made
before by Mr. Canning, he connects with the negotiation, a subject far more distinct from the butchery of the *Chesapeake*, than
the general impressment of our seamen, I mean the proclamation,
interdicting to British ships of war, the entrance of our harbors.

The great obstacle which has always interfered in the adjustment of our differences with Britain, has been that she would not
acquiesce in the only principle upon which fair negotiation
between independent nations can be conducted, the principle of
reciprocity, that she refuses the application to us of the claim
which she asserts for herself. The forcible taking of men from an
American vessel, was an essential part of the outrage upon the
Chesapeake. It was the ostensible purpose for which that act of
war unproclaimed, was committed. The President's proclamation
was a subsequent act, and was avowedly founded upon many
similar aggressions, of which that was only the most aggravated.

If then Britain could with any color of reason claim that the
general question of impressment should be laid out of the case
altogether, she ought upon the principle of reciprocity to have
laid equally out of the case, the proclamation, a measure so easily
separable from it, and in its nature merely defensive. When
therefore she made the repeal of the proclamation an indispensable preliminary to all discussion upon the nature and extent of
that reparation which she had offered, she refused to treat with
us upon the footing of an independent power. She insisted upon
an act of self-degradation on our part, before she would even tell
us, what redress she would condescend to grant for a great and
acknowledged wrong. This was a condition which she could not
but know to be inadmissible, and is of itself proof nearly conclu-

sive that her cabinet never intended to make for that wrong any reparation at all.

But this is not all. It cannot be forgotten that when that atrocious deed was committed, amidst the general burst of indignation which resounded from every part of this Union, there were among us a small number of persons, who upon the opinion that Berkeley's orders were authorized by his government, undertook to justify them in their fullest extent. These ideas probably first propagated by British official characters, in this country, were persisted in until the disavowal of the British government took away the necessity for persevering in them, and gave notice where the next position was to be taken. This patriotic reasoning however had been so satisfactory at Halifax, that complimentary letters were received from Admiral Berkeley himself highly approving the spirit in which they were inculcated, and remarking how easily *peace*, between the United States and Britain might be preserved, if *that* measure of our national rights could be made the prevailing standard of the country.

When the news arrived in England, although the general sentiment of the nation was not prepared for the formal avowal and justification of this unparalleled aggression, yet there were not wanting persons there, ready to *claim and maintain* the right of searching national ships for deserters. It was said at the time, but for this we must of course rest upon the credit of inofficial authority, to have been made a serious question in the Cabinet Council; nor was its determination there ascribed to the eloquence of the gentleman who became the official organ of its communication. Add to this a circumstance, which without claiming irrefragable credence of a diplomatic note, has yet its weight upon the common sense of mankind; that in all the daily newspapers known to be in the ministerial interest, Berkeley was justified and applauded in every variety of form that publication could assume, excepting only that of official proclamation. The only part of his orders there disapproved was the reciprocal offer which he made of submitting his own ships to be searched in return – that was very unequivocally disclaimed. The ruffian right of superior force, was the solid base upon which the claim was asserted, and so familiar was this argument grown to the casuists of British national jurisprudence, that the right of a British man-of-war to search an American frigate, was to them a self-evident proof against the right of the American frigate to search the British man-of-war. The same tone has been constantly kept up, until our accounts of latest date; and have been recently further invigorated by a very explicit call for war with the United States, which they contend could be of no possible injury to Britain, and which they urge upon the ministry as affording them an excellent opportunity to accomplish a *dismemberment of this Union*. These sentiments have even been avowed in Parliament, where the nobleman who moved the address of the house of Lords in answer to the king's speech, declared that the right of searching national ships, ought to be maintained against the Americans, and disclaimed only with respect to European sovereigns.

In the meantime Admiral Berkeley, by a court martial of his own subordinate officers, hung one of the men taken from the *Chesapeake*, and called his name Jenkin Ratford. There was, according to the answer so frequently given by the Lords of the Admiralty, upon applications for the discharge of impressed Americans, *no such man on board the ship*. The man thus executed had been taken from the *Chesapeake* by the name of Wilson. It is said that on his trial he was identified by one or two witnesses who knew him, and that before he was turned off he confessed his name to be Ratford and that he was born in England. But it has also been said that Ratford is now living in Pennsylvania; and after the character which the disavowal of Admiral Berkeley's own government has given to his conduct, what confidence can be claimed or due to the proceedings of a court martial of his associates held to sanction his proceedings. The three other men had not even been demanded in his orders. They were taken by the sole authority of the British searching lieutenant, after the surrender of the *Chesapeake*. There was not the shadow of a pretence before the court martial that they were British subjects, or born in any of the British dominions. Yet by this court martial they were sentenced to *suffer death*. They were reprieved from execution, only upon condition of renouncing their rights as Americans by voluntary service in the king's ships. They have never been restored. To complete the catastrophe with which this bloody tragedy was concluded, Admiral Berkeley himself in sanctioning the doom of these men, thus obtained, thus tried, and thus sentenced, read them a grave moral lecture on the enormity of their crime, in its tendency to provoke a war between the United States and Great Britain.

Yet amidst all this parade of disavowal by his government – amidst all these professions of readiness to make reparation, not a single mark of the slightest disapprobation appears ever to have been manifested to that officer. His instructions were executed upon the *Chesapeake* in June. Rumors of his recall have been circulated here. But on leaving the station at Halifax in December, he received a complimentary address from the colonial assembly, and assured them in answer, that he had no official information of his recall. From thence he went to the West Indies; and on leaving Bermuda for England in February was addressed again by that colonial government, in terms of high panegyric upon his energy, with manifest allusion to his achievement upon the *Chesapeake*.

Under all these circumstances, without applying any of the maxims of a suspicious policy to the British professions, I may still be permitted to believe that their ministry never seriously intended to make us honorable reparation, or indeed any reparation at all for that "unfortunate affair."

It is impossible for any man to form an accurate idea of the British policy towards the United States, without taking into consideration the state of parties in that government, and the views, characters and opinions of the individuals at their helm of state. A liberal and a hostile policy towards America, are among the strongest marks of distinction between the political systems of the rival statesmen of that kingdom. The liberal party are reconciled to our independence; and though extremely tenacious of every right of their own country, are systematically disposed to preserve *peace* with the United States. Their opponents harbor sentiments of a very different description. Their system is coercion. Their object the recovery of their lost dominion in North America. This party now stands high in power. Although Admiral Berkeley may never have received written orders from them for his enterprise upon the *Chesapeake*, yet in giving his instructions to the squadron at Norfolk, he knew full well under what administration he was acting. Every measure of that administration towards us since that time has been directed to the same purpose – to break down the spirit of our national independence. Their purpose, as far as it can be collected from their acts, is to force us into war with them or with their enemies; to leave us only, the bitter alternative of their vengeance or their protection.

Both these parties are no doubt willing, that we should join them in the war of their nation against France and her allies. The late administration would have drawn us into it by treaty, the present are attempting it by compulsion. The former would have admitted us as allies, the latter will have us no otherwise than as colonists. On the late debates in Parliament, the Lord Chancellor freely avowed that the Orders of Council of 11th November were intended to make America *at last* sensible of the policy of joining England against France.

This too, sir, is the substantial argument of Mr. Pickering's letter. The suspicions of a *design* in our own administration to plunge us into a war with Britain, I never have shared. Our administration have every interest and every motive that can influence the conduct of man to deter them from any such purpose. Nor have I seen anything in their measures bearing the slightest indication of it. But between a design of war with England, and a surrender of our national freedom for the sake of war with the rest of Europe, there is a material difference. This is the policy now in substance recommended to us, and for which the interposition of the commercial States is called. For this, not only are all the outrages of Britain to be forgotten, but the very assertion of our rights is to be branded with odium. *Impressment. Neutral trade. British taxation.* Everything that can distinguish a state of national freedom from a state of national vassalage, is to be *surrendered at discretion*. In the face of every fact we are told to believe every profession. In the midst of every *indignity*, we are pointed to British protection as our only shield against the universal conqueror. Every phantom of jealousy and fear is evoked. The image of France with a scourge in her hand is impressed into the service, to lash us into the refuge of obedience to Britain. Insinuations are even made that if Britain "with her thousand ships of war," has not destroyed our commerce, it has been owing to her indulgence, and we are almost threatened in her name with the "destruction of our fairest cities."

Not one act of hostility to Britain has been committed by us, she has not a pretence of that kind to allege. But if she will wage war upon us, are we to do nothing in our own defence? If she issues orders of universal plunder upon our commerce, are we not to withhold it from her grasp? Is American pillage one of those rights which she has claimed and exercised until we are foreclosed from any attempt to obstruct its collection? For what purpose are we required to make this sacrifice of everything that can give value to the name of freemen, this abandonment of the very right of self-preservation? Is it to avoid a war? Alas! Sir, it does not offer even this plausible plea for pusillanimity. For, as submission would make us to all substantial purposes British colonies, her enemies would unquestionably treat us as such, and after degrading ourselves into voluntary servitude to escape a war with her, we should incur inevitable war with all her enemies, and be doomed to share the destinies of her conflict with a world in arms.

Between this unqualified submission, and offensive resistance against the war upon maritime neutrality waged by the concurring decrees of all the great belligerent powers, the embargo was adopted, and has been hitherto continued. So far was it from being dictated by France, that it was calculated to withdraw, and has withdrawn from within her reach all the means of compulsion which her subsequent decrees would have put in her possession. It has added to the motives both of France and England, for preserving peace with us, and has diminished their inducements to war. It has lessened their capacities of inflicting injury upon us, and given us some preparation for resistance to them. It has taken from their violence the lure of interest. It has dashed the philter of pillage from the lips of rapine. That it is distressing to ourselves – that it calls for the fortitude of a people, determined to maintain their rights, is not to be denied. But the only alternative was between that and war. Whether it will yet save us from that calamity, cannot be determined, but if not, it will prepare us for the further struggle to which we may be called. Its double tendency of promoting peace and preparing for war, in its operation upon both the belligerent rivals, is the great advantage, which more than outweighs all its evils.

If any statesman can point out another alternative, I am ready to hear him, and for any practicable expedient to lend him every possible assistance. But let not that expedient be, submission to trade under British licenses, and British taxation. We are told that even under these restrictions we may yet trade to the British dominions, to Africa and China, and with the colonies of France, Spain, and Holland. I ask not, how much of this trade would be left, when our intercourse with the whole continent of Europe being cut off would leave us no means of purchase, and no market for sale? I ask not, what trade we could enjoy with the colonies of nations with which we should be at war? I ask not, how long Britain would leave open to us avenues of trade, which even in these very orders of Council, she boasts of leaving open as a special indulgence? If we yield the principle, we abandon all pretence to national sovereignty. To yearn for the fragments of trade which might be left, would be to pine for the crumbs of commercial servitude. The boon, which we should humiliate ourselves to accept from British bounty, would soon be withdrawn. Submission never yet set boundaries to encroachment. From pleading for half the empire, we should sink into supplicants for life. We should supplicate in vain. If we must fall, let us fall, freemen. If we must perish, let it be in defence of our RIGHTS.

To conclude, sir, I am not sensible of any necessity for the extraordinary interference of the commercial States, to control the general councils of the nation. If any interference could at this critical extremity of our affairs have a kindly effect upon our common welfare, it would be an interference to promote union and not a division – to urge mutual confidence, and not universal distrust – to strengthen the arm and not to relax the sinews of the nation. Our suffering and our dangers, though differing perhaps in degree, are universal in extent. As their causes are justly chargeable, so their removal is dependent not upon ourselves, but upon others. But while the spirit of *independence* shall continue to beat in unison with the pulses of the nation, no danger will be truly formidable. Our duties are, to prepare with concerted energy, for those which threaten us, to meet them without dismay, and to rely for their issue upon heaven.

I am, etc.

JOHN QUINCY ADAMS (BOSTON) TO EZEKIEL BACON, NOVEMBER 17, 1808

One year into the embargo, it was clear to John Quincy that it had failed in its purpose to coerce the British and that it had brought commercial New England close to rebellion. He himself had favored its application for only a few months but feared that the administration seemed determined to continue on its present course. In this letter to Republican congressman Ezekiel Bacon, who had solicited his advice, John Quincy considered and dismissed two alternatives: war with either Britain or France (unwise); and arming neutral shipping (too late). Simply repealing the embargo would be an act of submission and an abandonment of American rights. He strongly recommended substituting for the embargo a policy of non-intercourse with Britain and France. This would be more acceptable to the public and take some of the air out of the New England Federalist leaders' efforts to bring about civil war and disunion.

MY DEAR SIR:

Your obliging letter of the 8th instant, with a copy of the President's message at the commencement of the session, has come to hand. I see with much concern, though without surprise, that the prospect of obtaining anything like justice from the great belligerent powers of Europe, is no better than it was at the close of the last session. The alternatives mentioned in your letter embrace all the varieties of policy, between which a choice can be made. Among these that of declaring war I presume will have the fewest advocates. The wrongs we are suffering from both the scourges of mankind are so similar, that we would scarcely assume a foundation for the declaration against one, which would not equally require it against the other, and a declaration against either would place the country in a more dangerous situation, and the administration in a deeper perplexity to get along, than can arise from the present state of things. A war with England would probably soon if not immediately be complicated with a civil war, and with a desperate effort to break up the Union, the project for which has been several years preparing in this quarter, and which waits only for a possible chance of popular support to explode. A war with France would be extremely unpopular in every part of the Union, for it would be odious to all the friends of the administration, as directly contrary to the permanent interests and policy of the Union; and although it would exactly meet the wishes of the *tories*, yet it would not be with the view to support the administration in carrying on the war, but as a ground for pursuing further measures of attack against the administration itself. Nor is there any prospect that we should at the issue of a war with either power obtain any security for any rights, which we may not at least as reasonably expect by further perseverance in the pacific policy. *War*, therefore, I presume we shall not immediately have. Under the present state of affairs, to open our commerce with permission to *arm* in defence of the exercise of *neutral* trade, would be *war* in the result, though it would be upon a principle more exclusively *defensive*, than would be implied in a declaration. *Arming*, both public and private, was the system which in my particular opinion ought to have been adopted last winter, immediately after the embargo was first laid; but at that time I found very few of any party who thought with me, and now the season for it is past, even if it was then expedient.

The circumstances, too, of the present time render it much more questionable to my mind than it was then. The British Orders of Council were then not sanctioned by Parliament. The Milan decree, and I know not how many others equally savage, had not issued. The very determination of resistance then manifested might have deterred from these extremities of outrage.

The British government had not been stimulated to perseverance, either by the Spanish and Portuguese diversion in their favor, or by the open and shameless support which they have found from faction in this country.

Arming now would be less efficacious as a measure for preserving peace, would lead more inevitably to war, and would have less support from the approbation of the people. The real choice, then, seems to be, between a continuance of the embargo, and its removal, with a substitution of total nonintercourse with France and England in its stead. For as to *submission*, I will not disgrace the Congress of this Union so much as to suppose, that this project will receive any countenance from either branch of the legislative authority.

Between the embargo and the non-intercourse system, under my present state of information I should strongly incline to the last. It would, indeed, incur a new hazard of eventual war abroad, but I think it would remove the risk of war at home for the present. I believe the embargo cannot possibly be continued much longer, without meeting direct and forcible resistance in this part of the country. The people have been so long stimulated to this forcible resistance, and they have been so unequivocally led to expect support from the State authorities in such resistance, that I do not think the temptation will be much longer withstood. If the law should be openly set at defiance, and broken by direct violence under support from the State authorities, it is to be considered how the general government will be able to carry it through. No doubt by military execution. But that will make civil war, the very point at which the tories are driving, and in the event of which it may at least be conjectured that they have already secured British and assistance. For it is precisely in this form, an organized insurrection against the national government by State authority, that the project of disunion can alone be accomplished, and that this project has been in serious contemplation of those, whom you describe as being called in England Colonel P's party, for several years, I know by the most unequivocal evidence, though it be not provable in a court of law. To this project as matured, a very small party of the *federal* party is privy. The great proportion of them do not even believe its existence. They are not *prepared* for supporting this system, and the object of the leaders is, to take advantage of every circumstance which can enable them to work upon the popular mind to support the scheme of division by the necessary force. Now the embargo is, unfortunately, one of those measures, upon which the two public authorities may be brought in collision with each other, and that the *party* has been laboring with unwearied industry to produce that effect, the proceedings of our legislature, the instigations to resistance against the embargo laws on the pretence of their unconstitutionality, the countenance given to this paltry pretence by a STATE JUDGE, and the connection between his extra-judicial opinions and the attempts at forcible resistance, which have already been made, and with the experiment upon the District Court at Salem, afford the evidence, which the most purblind observer cannot but observe. A non-intercourse, it seems to me, would not be so liable to this species of opposition as an embargo. Another reason for preferring it is, that in the spirit of party, the faction is afraid of it. For among themselves, I know that they chuckle and exult as much at the operation of the embargo, as in public they whine and rave against it. They now feel perfectly confident that the embargo will not answer its purpose as a compulsory measure, and they hope to see the government so pledged to it, as not to be able consistently to depart from it. The non-intercourse would take away from them a great part of the two *impostures* by which they have been playing upon the jealousies of the people, that the administration act under the dictates of France, and that they intend the total annihilation of commerce.

I do not mean that it would entirely remove these despicable calumnies, for popular jealousy, like individual jealousy, will feed and thrive upon trifles lighter than air; but the machine would not work so well under the non-intercourse system, as they will under the continuance of the embargo.

I am aware that in reply to these observations there are many forcible reasons which may be alleged for *persevering*, precisely in the stand which we have taken. We are sure that will not produce war, for both France and England have avowed that they do not consider it as a cause of war. It would have the appearance of a more steady and determinate purpose, and it would not expose to foreign depredation that property, and to impressment and captivity those seamen, which have hitherto been preserved. Legislative deliberation, and mutual communication of ideas and information between those members of the executive and legislature, who concur in the pursuit of the same end, will doubtless shed on the whole subject a light, by which you will at last most safely proceed. That it may ultimately secure our peace, independence and union, I confidently hope and fervently pray.

The proceedings of our legislature, relative to the choice of presidential electors, will come before you at the proper time.

They are unprecedented, and the precedent they exhibit is a very bad one. A suspicious temper would conclude that this mode of proceeding was adopted for the express purpose of producing a new collision between the State and the Union. This purpose, however, will I hope be frustrated. There may be a great constitutional question, how far the authority of Congress extends with regard to the rejection of votes returned from the States for the presidential election; and although I have no doubt that the State legislature on these proceedings have violated our own constitution, yet I should wish if possible to avoid stirring the other question upon these returns. The most prudent course in my mind will be to receive the votes, and count them, leaving it to the people of this Commonwealth, if they think proper, to vindicate their own constitution from the outrages of their own representatives. Of this, however, you, who will be on the spot and acting under the responsibility of your public trust, will decide with full consideration.

I have, my dear sir, according to your desire given you my opinions in the fullest confidence and sincerity. It will give me pleasure to hear from you as often as your leisure will permit, and with unabated ardor for the cause of our country, I remain, &c.

P. S. In using the term *tories* in this letter I mean to designate the partisans for a French war and for submission to Great Britain. They do not include the whole federal party, but they now *preside* over its policy. They are the political descendants in direct line from the tories of our Revolutionary war, and hold most of their speculative opinions.

CHAPTER FIVE

MINISTER TO RUSSIA, 1809–1814

INTRODUCTION

WITH THE ELECTION of James Madison to the presidency, it was widely rumored that John Quincy Adams would be offered a post in the new administration. Indeed, he was offered such a post, but to an unexpected destination. With Britain at war against Russia after Emperor Alexander had signed the Treaty of Tilsit with Napoleon in 1807, Jefferson had seen Russian and American interests on maritime rights potentially coinciding, at least as far as opposition to Britain's treatment of neutrals was concerned. He was certainly not prepared to enter into an alliance with Russia (or France) and thus entangle America in a European war, but he would encourage the two emperors in any future peace settlement to include liberal maritime rights along the lines always supported by the United States. To that end, Jefferson had nominated William Short to serve as the first American ambassador to St. Petersburg. The Senate, however, had refused to confirm the appointment. When Madison became president, he nominated John Quincy as the first American minister to Russia. Despite strong resistance form the family, John Quincy accepted the position. He was politically ambitious, and this position offered a way back into public service.

The passage to St. Petersburg through the Baltic was harrowing. In addition to the horrible weather, John Quincy observed firsthand the effects of the conflicting economic systems of France and Britain. He found dozens of American ships trapped in port and waiting for disposition under Napoleon's Continental System. In the meantime, British warships constantly challenged American bona fides. John Quincy's ship was subject to search and seizure and one of the sailors on board narrowly avoided impressment, saved perhaps only by the presence of an American diplomat.

Immediately after arriving in St. Petersburg, John Quincy met with the Russian chancellor, Count Rumyantsev.[1] The count was friendly but, when John Quincy inquired whether Russia could aid in supporting the release of American ships wrongly detained by French clients in the Baltic, the response was not encouraging. He was also granted an audience with Emperor Alexander in the imperial palace. While the emperor was speaking, he took John Quincy by the arm and walked him away from the door to a window overlooking the Neva (which John Quincy interpreted as being a move aimed to foil eavesdroppers). Alexander set the substantive tone immediately. He told John Quincy that he was greatly pleased with the opening of full diplomatic relations with the United States. He also defended his current alliance with France and his participation in the Continental System – which, regrettably but necessarily, impinged on American neutral shipping – in order to overcome Britain's intolerable ambitions. He nevertheless made it clear that the end of it all was to establish a just system of maritime rights.

John Quincy responded carefully, deflecting Alexander's praise of French policy and focusing on the common interest both nations had in security for fair commerce in time of war, and on the emperor's general support of liberal maritime principles. At John Quincy's request, the Russian government, under Alexander's direction, intervened with Danish authorities to free American ships that had been held in port, ostensibly in conformity with the Continental System. John Quincy did so, even though he had no official authority to make such a request.

In the spring and summer of 1810, Napoleon upped the ante by annexing or occupying much of the northern continental

European states, and by issuing a new round of French commercial restrictions declaring that vessels flying the American flag that had entered ports under French control subsequent to May 20, 1809, were to be seized and confiscated. Hundreds of US ships were seized, and their crews were imprisoned. The remainder flocked to the Russian ports, including Riga and Archangel in the far north, which remained open to legitimate American shipping. American owners and captains appealed to John Quincy for assistance so they could dispose of their cargoes and depart before the winter.

Success for John Quincy and the American shippers came grudgingly, slowly, and incrementally. But a large measure of success did come, to John Quincy's considerable surprise. In December 1810, Alexander issued an edict that, among other things, permitted American ships to enter all Russian ports legally.

Before John Quincy left for Russia, President Madison had repealed the March 1809 Non-Importation Act as it pertained to Britain, based on misleading information from the new British minister, David Erskine. The British government immediately repudiated the agreement and Madison reimposed the original legislation. Non-importation strained American commerce (although not as severely as the embargo), and it seemed to have little effect on the belligerents. In May 1810, Congress lifted the non-intercourse with Britain and France (known as Macon's Bill No. 2). Trade was now free. The new legislation, however, pledged the United States to close trade with one belligerent if the other ceased to violate American rights, unless the first party also recognized those rights.

The French seemed to take up the American offer to lift non-importation, through the so-called Cadore Letter. On November 2, 1810, President Madison issued a proclamation that treated the Cadore Letter as an authoritative repeal of the Berlin and Milan decrees. Moreover, Madison announced that unless London reciprocated, all trade with Britain would cease as of February 2, 1811. When word of the proclamation reached St. Petersburg in late December, John Quincy did not record any immediate reaction, but he soon concluded that the French were insincere and he tried to communicate that view to his superiors, although the transmission would take months to arrive.

By now, it was clear to John Quincy that Napoleon intended to provoke an Anglo-American war. What should the president and Congress have done, instead of adopting a policy of coercive economic diplomacy that pointed toward war with Britain and de facto cooperation with Napoleon? The answer was to reclaim the high ground of George Washington and John Adams: strict neutrality. If the escalation to war was to be halted, John Quincy believed that another course correction during the ensuing congressional session was necessary. John Quincy's initial inclination had been to return to the grounds of Macon's Bill, with no trade restrictions placed on either Britain or France. But he came to favor another form of strict neutrality, a return to non-importation against both parties.

Back in Russia, John Quincy was sending to Washington detailed reports on the growing crisis in Franco-Russian relations, which he was sure would lead to war between the two emperors. If war broke out or seemed imminent with France, John Quincy explained, Russia would surely come to terms with Britain. British ships would flood Russian markets and crowd out or seek preferential treatment over American merchants. But more importantly, the United States must expect the British line toward the United States to harden as London's confidence in an impending rapprochement with Russia grew, and Britain gained secure access to Russian supplies for critical naval stores and foodstuffs.[2] America's old enemy, Britain, would become Russia's new ally in a much wider war. "The effect of the new Congressional legislation [the act, supplementary to that commonly called the non-intercourse], will I hope be favorable, in regard to our relations with France, as it will probably increase the inveteracy of the present British ministry against us." John Quincy put the issue as carefully as he could to Washington.[3]

Meanwhile, Anglo-American relations deteriorated, and the United States lurched toward war with Britain. Although John Quincy placed the primary blame on the British Orders in Council, he believed that Napoleon's perfidy was the immediate cause. He still saw national salvation in the avoidance of war with Britain, if it could be done with American independence intact. He believed that the pressures of war would soon cause the British to ease their commercial restrictions, if the United States remained patient. As to impressment, it was an attack on American honor, worthy of defense – but not now. In good time, America could insist on its renunciation and achieve it without war.

John Quincy's hopes to avoid war were raised when news reached him that Britain had, as he had predicted, repealed the most obnoxious Orders in Council. On August 5, however, an express arrived in St. Petersburg from Gothenburg that contained a copy of the *New York Commercial Advertiser* of June 22. The newspaper reprinted the American declaration of war against Britain, voted by Congress on June 18 before news of the repeal had arrived.[4] The express included other relevant documents justifying the declaration, including a May 30 letter from the British minister Foster to Secretary of State Monroe that had been issued prior to the decision to repeal. The out-of-date letter reaffirmed the British position that since Napoleon had not repealed his decrees, the Orders in Council remained in effect. Not only that; the British insisted the French decrees must be lifted against British commerce, not just American commerce, with the Continent. The letter also refused compensation for the *Chesapeake* affair.

John Quincy was no war hawk. He had always favored a balanced and patient approach based on sensible military preparations short of outright war that signaled America's determination, leading to a diplomatic settlement or at least a cold peace. But under the circumstances he did not blame Madison or those who voted for war. He undoubtedly would have done so himself, albeit reluctantly, had he been in Congress at the time. As a patriot and public official, he certainly felt he now had no choice other than to support the president and the war. He had no place else to go politically. He could not re-embrace the Federalists, who sought "a separation of the States, and an Alliance with Britain," a course that John Quincy thought not only wrong on its own merits but also deeply unpopular. "This doctrine of truckling to England for the sake of going to war with France never will, never can, obtain an ascendancy over the people of the United States, and it will forever end by tripping up the heels of those who build it upon the narrow scale of a New England or Massachusetts political system," he wrote to John Adams.[5]

From his post in St. Petersburg, a critical question for John Quincy was, would Russia now align itself diplomatically with Britain against the United States, even though the United States was not allied with France? Count Rumyantsev had previously put it this way, when the Treaty of Tilsit still held: Russia was anxious to find a great commercial power that could help it offset Britain's maritime pretensions; the United States was such a power; and since the two nations were so far apart, they did not endanger their respective interests. But would this logic still hold in present circumstances, when British aid to St. Petersburg seemed imperative?

In late September 1812, even as Napoleon had marched deep into Russian territory, the Russian foreign minister, at the initiative of the emperor, suggested that Alexander might serve as a mediator between Britain and America. On the spot, John Quincy gave a carefully worded response. He had no authority on the matter, he said, but he did not see why the United States would decline. Although he had not exactly committed his government, he had gone out on a limb. The easiest course, especially if he thought the Russian gesture was hostile or disingenuous, would have been to tell the foreign minister that he would have to write his government for instructions; or that Russia should use its own diplomatic channels to propose through its minister in Washington. For John Quincy tacitly to encourage the Russian approach meant that his government might be faced with a choice of unwanted mediation or antagonizing Russia. But John Quincy concluded that the Russian offer was a friendly one. The alternatives would take time, and John Quincy suspected – correctly – that the Madison administration wanted a quick diplomatic resolution if possible.

Although this possible path to peace did not directly bear fruit, it opened up diplomatic channels with London with which John Quincy would soon be intimately involved.

DIARY ENTRY (ST PETERSBURG), NOVEMBER 5, 1809

In his first meeting with the Russian emperor, John Quincy listened with interest to Alexander's explanation of his foreign policy, and he endeavored to lay down America's policy. "The political duty of the United States towards the powers of Europe, was to forbear interference in their dissensions, ... That being at once a great commercial and a pacific Nation, they were deeply interested in the establishment of a system which should give security to the fair commerce of Nations in time of War – That the United States, and the world of Mankind, expected that this blessing to humanity would be accomplished by his Imperial Majesty, himself, and that the United States by all the means in their power, consistent with their Peace, and their separation from the political system of Europe would contribute to the support of the liberal principles to which his Majesty had express'd so strong and so just an attachment."[6]

5th. At ten minutes past one, according to the appointment of M. de Maisonneuve, I went to the Imperial Palace, and at about two was conducted by him to the entrance of the Emperor's cabinet, the door of which was opened, and at which he stopped. I entered, and found the Emperor alone.

As I stepped forward, he advanced to me near to the door, and said, in French, "Monsieur, je suis charmé d'avoir le plaisir de vous voir ici."

I then presented to him my credential letter, and, addressing him in French, said that in delivering it, I was charged to add that the President of the United States hoped his Imperial Majesty would consider the mission as a proof of the President's respect for his Majesty's person and character, of his desire to multiply and to strengthen the relations of friendship and commerce between his Majesty's provinces and the United States, and of grateful acknowledgment for the frequent testimonials of good will which his Majesty, on many occasions, had given towards the United States.

He replied by desiring me to assure the President of the United States that this new addition to the relations between the two countries gave him great pleasure; that in everything that depended upon him he should be happy to contribute towards increasing the friendly intercourse between them; that with regard to the political relations of Europe, and those unhappy disturbances which agitated its different states, the system of the United States was wise and just, and they might rely upon it he would do nothing to withdraw them from it; that the Continent of Europe was now in a manner pacified, and that the only obstacle to a general pacification was the obstinate adherence of England to a system of maritime pretensions which was neither liberal nor just; that the only object now to be attained by the war was to bring England to reasonable terms on this subject, and that she could no longer flatter herself with any support for her system upon the Continent; that Austria, after abandoning herself to inconsiderate counsels, and disregarding the advice which *he* had given her (qu'on lui avoit donné), had now been obliged to make peace, and to sacrifice several of her provinces; that Austria was thus not in a condition to renew the contest; that the King of Prussia was in a situation to make peace equally necessary to him; that he himself was convinced that the good of his empire, and of Europe, was best promoted by a state of peace and friendship between Russia and France, whose views, he believed, from the assurance of that Government, were not at all directed to the conquest of England, but merely to make her recognize the only fair and equitable principles of neutral navigation in time of war; that the only danger to England from the establishment of those principles would be that France might be enabled, in consequence of them, to form and maintain again a large navy; but this could be no justification for England's maintaining a system oppressive and destructive to the fair and lawful commerce of other nations; that the establishment of this just system of maritime rights was the purpose of France, "and as for me, I shall adhere invariably to those which I have declared. I am sensible that it subjects us to inconvenience; that the people suffer privations and some distress under the present state of things. But the English maxims are much more intolerable, and, if submitted to, would be permanent."

In expressing his determination to abide by his declared principles, his tone and attitude assumed a firmness and dignity which he had not taken before, and which, immediately after, slided again into that easy and familiar manner with which he had first accosted me.

In the midst of this conversation he had taken me by the arm and walked from near the door to a window opening upon the river – a movement seemingly intended to avoid being overheard. I occasionally answered his remarks, by observing to him that, as the political duty of the United States towards the powers of Europe was to forbear interference in their dissensions, it would be highly grateful to the President to learn that their system in this respect met the approbation of his Imperial Majesty; that being at once a great commercial and a pacific nation, they were greatly interested in the establishment of a system which should give security to the fair commerce of nations in time of war; that the United States, and the world of mankind, expected that this blessing to humanity would be accomplished by his Imperial Majesty himself, and that the United States, by all the means in their power, consistent with their peace and their separation from the political system of Europe, would contribute to the support of the liberal principles to which his Majesty had expressed so strong and so just an attachment.

He said that as between Russia and the United States there could be no interference of interests and no causes for disunion; but that by means of commerce the two states might be greatly useful to each other, and his desire was to give the greatest extension and facility to these means of mutual benefit.

After this he passed from topics of general politics to conversation more particularly concerning myself and my country. He enquired how long we had been upon our voyage, and how we had borne the inconveniences and fatigues of the sea; whether I had ever been in Russia before; what were our principal cities in America – the number of their inhabitants, and the manner in which they were built.

I told him that I had been in Russia formerly, and had passed a winter at St. Petersburg during the reign of the Empress Catherine; that I had then admired the city as the most magnificent I had ever seen, but that I scarcely knew it again now; that the two principal cities in population of my country were New York and Philadelphia, the latter of which had been founded by the celebrated Quaker Penn, of whom his Majesty had certainly heard; that the inhabitants in each of these two cities were now about one hundred thousand; that they were both elegant cities, with handsome buildings, three and four stories high for the most part, and forming handsome and convenient dwelling-houses suitable to the citizens of a republic, but which in point of splendor and magnificence could not vie with the buildings of Petersburg, which to the eye of a stranger appeared like a city of princes.

He said that was nothing – that a republican government whose principles and conduct were just and wise was as respectable as any other.

I said, Assuredly; but in regard to the buildings, no person would know better than his Majesty that Petersburg was the most magnificent city of Europe, or of the world.

He said he had not been at Vienna or at Paris; but he had been at Dresden and at Berlin; that Dresden was small, but Berlin was a beautiful city, as to all the part of it which could be called modern, and to which Frederic the Second had been specially attentive; that the ancient part of Berlin was not so handsome; that Petersburg had the advantage of being a city entirely modern, and built upon a plan.

On which I remarked that this was not its only advantage: that this plan was that of a man such as very seldom appeared on the face of this globe, and that it bore the marks of his sublime genius; that it had the further advantage of all the improvement which a succession of sovereigns could give it, who had entered into the ideas of that great prince, and had taken a pride in contributing to their full execution.

He asked me to which of the United States I belonged, and upon being told Massachusetts, he asked me what was its climate. I told him that it was in the northern part of the Union, and had the climate the most nearly resembling that of this residence of any in the United States. He asked how long our winter commonly was. I said between five and six months. "Then," said he, " we have two months more here. We have eight months of winter – September, October, November, December, January, February, March, and April; and sometimes it lasts till June. But," said he, "you have good sledging in your country?" I said we had; but that the snow seldom lasted long upon the ground at a time. "We cannot complain of that," said he. "When it once comes, it is sure to last long enough." I then said that there was an advantage in that, inasmuch as it facilitated the communications by the roads. It was, he said, a very great advantage, for it made roads in the winter better than any that could be made by human art; that all the gravel stones or iron in the world could not make such a road as a few hours of snow and frost; and that the advantage of this was immense to an empire so extensive as this – so extensive that its size was one of its greatest evils; that it was very difficult to hold together so great a body as this empire.

I was on the point of saying that, great as this evil was, his

Majesty had recently increased it – referring to the Treaty of peace with Sweden, and the acquisition of Finland; but reflecting that the remark might be taken in ill part, or at least thought too familiar and smart for such an occasion, I suppressed it, and made no reply.

After a short pause, the Emperor dismissed me, by renewing the assurance of his pleasure at receiving a Minister from the United States, and with the obliging addition, that he was well pleased that the choice of the American Government had fallen upon me; that he should be happy to promote the relations between the two countries through this medium, and he hoped I should find my residence agreeable here.

Upon which I took my leave in the usual form, and went again with M. de Maisonneuve to the apartment of the Empress. Here he entered with me and stood near the door, while I advanced up to her Imperial Majesty, who was about the middle of the room, standing alone, with a lady, whether of honor or a waiting woman I did not ascertain, standing behind her Majesty, near the stove in the corner of the chamber.

The Empress, who was dressed in a gown of lace, without a hoop, with a necklace of rubies, and a chain of the like precious stones round her head, connecting the utmost simplicity with most costly ornament, addressed me by saying she was happy to see me here, and enquiring how I found the roads. I told her that I had come the whole way by water. Upon which she made enquiries about the length of our voyage, and others of the same kind. From this she passed to remarks upon the climate, the bad weather, the cold season which was approaching, and the city of Petersburg. Upon this my answers and observations were of the commonplace kind.

Her Majesty then said that two or three years since they had had the pleasure of seeing here two of my countrymen, Mr. Smith and Mr. Poinsett, whose manners had been calculated to inspire great esteem personally to themselves and to their country, and asked me whether I had seen them since their return.

I said that I heard that two of my countrymen had been favored with the honor of admission to her Imperial Majesty's presence, and that I knew they recollected with great pleasure the reception they had met here; that I had not the pleasure of being acquainted with Mr. Poinsett, but I had seen Mr. Smith at Washington upon his return from Europe, about two years since, and knew how much he prized the manner of his treatment at this Court.

On taking leave of her Majesty immediately after this conversation, conformably to the established usage, I kissed her hand, a ceremony which M. de Maisonneuve told me many persons forgot to perform, which the Empress herself never took in ill part, being the most amiable princess in the world, but that the Empress Dowager was more apt to be displeased at such an omission.

Having thus finished the ceremonies of presentation to the Emperor and Empress, I went in person to the house of the French Minister, the Duke de Vicence, who not being at home, I left a card there. He had sent two cards yesterday, one for Mrs. Adams and one for me – a circumstance for which I know not how to account.

JOHN QUINCY ADAMS (ST PETERSBURG) TO THOMAS BOYLSTON ADAMS, MAY 1–13, 1811

John Quincy reiterates his view that neutrality, not war, is the best course for the United States. The protection of commerce was the only reason to enter into a war, but commerce would be the immediate casualty of such a war with Britain. "Once involved in the contest it is impossible to foresee how long it would continue, or where it would leave us. In Europe the prospect of peace is more remote than war.... Commerce is everywhere in the deepest distress, and not a symptom on either side denotes a disposition to relax from the oppressive and ruinous measures under which it groans. The war is, therefore, yet likely to be long. So say the ministers of the French Emperor, so says Mr. Perceval, in Parliament, and so proclaims every act of both the governments. Should we join in the conflict, we could scarcely hope for a better fate than to be sacrificed as one of the victims at its close."

There was one of the small English poets, I think it was Dodsley, who on the reformation of the calendar in England published a poem upon the tears of old May day. As this is the only country in Europe where old May day is held in honor, it would not be expected that here, too, is precisely the spot where she sheds the most tears. If she sheds none upon the present visit which she is making us, it will be because they freeze upon her face into snow. At least she advances veiled in no shower of shadowing roses. Winter verily lingers in her lap, and I think I shall excuse myself from attendance at the celebration of her festival in the procession of carriages this afternoon, remembering that in reward for having joined in this act of devotion to her lady ship last year, she gave me one of the severest colds that I have suffered in Russia. The procession of carriages takes place from six to nine o'clock in the evening, just without the city gate, and to a village called Catherineshoff about two miles distant from it. The Emperor and all the Imperial family usually appear in it, and all the splendid equipages and liveries of the court and city exhibit themselves in their proudest magnificence.

Although the day wears so unpromising an aspect, the season has hitherto been uncommonly fine, and is at least three weeks farther advanced than it was at the same time last year. There are clearly symptoms of vegetation upon the fields and upon the trees. It so happens, however, that I feel here more interested in the influence of spring upon the waters, than in her generative progress upon the land. Whether the bud shows its lip or the blossom opens its petals a month sooner or later engages little of my concern. But when the governor of the fortress upon the island opposite the imperial palace shall cross the river in the first boat, to receive from his Majesty's hand a hundred ducats for a glass of Neva water; when the benumbed and torpid members of the river god shall recover warmth and energy enough to pour from his urn the floating crystals of the Ladoga; when Mr. Sparrow, the consular agent at Cronstadt shall in his official bulletin announce that "between here (Cronstadt) and St. Petersburg likewise, as far as the eye can see to the westward, the water is entirely clear of ice " (which notice he sent only three days ago); when lastly, his register of emigrating ice shall be changed for a daily list of vessels arrived and sailed, these are all progressive stages towards the summer solstice, which, if I was a poet, I should be more strongly tempted to sing, than the returning verdure and harmony of the groves, or the reviving genial raptures of the flocks and herds.

And yet when the arrivals come, how often do we find ourselves disappointed in the expectation of letters from our friends. In my last I told you I thought it impossible but that some of you must have written by the *Washington*, Captain Brown. He is not yet here, but he has sent me a letter of about five lines from Lieut. Governor Gray, and I conclude that if he had any other letters he would have sent them at the same time. We must be patient again, and transfer our hopes to the next vessel.

I wrote you in the letter of which a press copy is inclosed, that a war between Russia and France was highly probable, and that it was on the point of breaking out. Since then, however, various incidents have occurred which make it still more improbable that the peace will be some time longer preserved. The serious objects of controversy all remain as unsettled as they were then, but France has yielded upon certain points of form, and has discovered certain procedures, which threatened immediate rupture. Mons. de Champagny has been very suddenly and unexpectedly removed from the office of Minister of Foreign Affairs, and Mr. Maret, Duke of Bassano, appointed in his place. That the war will blaze out yet before the end of the summer is not improbable, but there is now a likelihood that this event will be further postponed.

Count Lauriston, a native of Pondicherri and a lineal descendant from the famous John Law, the prince of paper financiers, arrived here last week, and has presented his credentials as ambassador extraordinary from France, superseding the Duke de Vicence, who has resided here between three and four years in the same capacity, and who has rendered himself so generally agreeable here that his successor will find it difficult to replace him.

In the total dearth of direct intelligence from the United States I am obliged to take such as I find in the Hamburg *Correspondent*, which is extracted usually from the Paris *Moniteur*, where it is introduced by translation from the English newspaper. In passing through all these vehicles it often gets disfigured, besides the risk of falsehood in the original importation from America. It is about three months since we were told through this channel that Judge Livingston was immediately coming out as minister to France, and now the appointment of Mr. Barlow to that office comes through the same source. Neither of these gentlemen had arrived at Paris on the 4th of April, the date of my last advices from Mr. Russell. Mr. Erving continues also to be expected at Copenhagen, where I think his presence at this time would be useful. By the same circuitous route I now learn that Congress before they rose did pass an act supplementary to the non-intercourse, prohibiting all importations from the British dominions subsequent to the second day of February. You will see by my last letter that I expect no benefit from this measure, and that I shall regret that it actually passed. It is not for me to blame the measures of the legislature under which I serve, and at this distance I cannot be qualified to judge with a full knowledge of their motives upon that propriety. I wish the new non-importation may be productive of good, and that it may be more successful than the preceding measures of a similar nature. Spain and Portugal will still need the advantage of a free trade with us, which may withhold the hand of England from proceeding to extremities. To the policy of *neutrality* we have more than ever reason to adhere. The only object for which we could engage in a war would be commerce, and from the moment war would take place our commerce would be annihilated. Once involved in the contest it is impossible to foresee how long it would continue, or where it would leave us. In Europe the prospect of peace is more remote than war. England adheres more and more obstinately to her orders in council, which France counteracts by her decrees and her encroachments upon the continent of Europe. Portugal has a third time been rescued from subjugation. Spain is neither subdued nor liberated. France is preparing for new wars and new conquests, which England cannot prevent. Commerce is everywhere in the deepest distress, and not a symptom on either side denotes a disposition to relax from the oppressive and ruinous measures under which it groans. The war is, therefore, yet likely to be long. So say the ministers of the French Emperor, so says Mr. Perceval, in Parliament, and so proclaims every act of both the governments. Should we join in the conflict, we could scarcely hope for a better fate than to be sacrificed as one of the victims at its close.

I was under apprehensions at the date of my last letter of being dispossessed of the dwelling house where we have resided nearly a year, and of which I have a lease for another year by a sale of the house itself to the Emperor. It is now said, however, that another house has been found more suitable to the purpose for which this was wanted, and that I shall have another chance for the full privilege of my lease. I have, therefore, abandoned the intention of taking a house for the summer in the country, though a summer country seat is as fashionable as it is desirable everywhere.

I received a few days since from my son George a letter dated 24 September last, the same day with the most recent letter that I have from you. George's however did not come with yours. It was sent under cover to Mr. Preble at Paris, and there underwent the learned and profound examination of the police to ascertain what secrets of state it might disclose. I have already answered it, and hope George will prove as punctual a correspondent as his father. He tells me, as you do, that he is afraid of losing his French, to which I could only reply, as I did to you, and as I now repeat, that I rely both upon you and upon him that he will not. His letter is partly written with his own hand, which I was rejoiced to see, though the progress of his improvement in writing is not so rapid as I could wish. This at least it is obvious he is learning *invita natura*. So much the more necessary will it be to conquer her obstacles by assiduity.

I have written to Mr. Copley in London requesting him to deliver the portrait of my father to the order of Mr. Boylston; but I suppose it will be necessary to send him at the same time a supplementary order from my father, directing Mr. Copley to comply with my request, as he will have from me only my assurance that the picture was given to me. But if this non-intercourse or non-importation has been renewed, I suppose it will oblige us to wait again two or three years before the order can be executed. As it is the only full length portrait of the original good for anything that ever was taken, I am most anxious that it may be safely transported and deposited in the Hall where I have consented that it should be placed. I never think of this subject without feeling against Stuart an indignation, which I wish I could change into contempt. If there was another portrait painter in America, I could forgive him. I beg you to try to get the portrait he has of my mother, and to buy of him that of my father for me. If he will finish it, I will gladly give him his full price for pictures of that sort for it. Perhaps you may tempt him by this offer, taking care to withhold the payment until the work is finished.

We are all so well that the ladies intend going this afternoon to the May day parade. Whether May or January, I am always with equal warmth of affection yours.

JOHN QUINCY ADAMS (ST PETERSBURG) TO THOMAS BOYLSTON ADAMS, JULY 31, 1811

Although his fondest hope had been to avoid war with Britain, John Quincy now feared that would not be the case, and he reflected on war's impact on the national character. The time was apparently coming when the temper and character of the American people would be sorely tried, as it was during the revolution: "unfortunately the unparalleled prosperity which for more than a quarter of a Century they have enjoyed, has been constantly unfitting them from year to year for the reverse of Fortune, which they now have to encounter – The school of affliction however is as necessary to form the moral character of Nations as of individuals – I hope that ours will be purified by it." That would depend, in part, on whether the cause was just and conducted with a precise and definitive objective. But in any event, John Quincy thought that changes in popular sentiment and even the Constitution were bound to result.

MY DEAR BROTHER:

A letter of 28 May from my mother would in some sort have tranquillized my mind in respect to you, if it had not at the same time alarmed me by mentioning the severe and dangerous accident which you had met with by a fall from your horse. She says that you intended to write me by the same opportunity, and as I have not received the letter, I am afraid that it was because you found yourself unable to write. But in general she observes that your health had improved by your excursion to the district of Maine, and I rejoice to find in Governor Gerry's speech to the Legislature, that your mission with your colleagues had been satisfactory and successful. By the same gazette, too, which we have received to 4 June, I learn your appointment as a member of the Council, an event upon which I cannot congratulate you as being likely to contribute to your tranquillity. The time is apparently coming when the temper and character of the American people will be tried by a test to which, since the war of our revolution, they have been strangers. And unfortunately, the unparalleled prosperity which for more than a quarter of a century they have enjoyed has been constantly unfitting them from year to year for the reverse of fortune, which they now have to encounter. The school of affliction is, however, as necessary to form the moral character of nations as of individuals. I hope that ours will be purified by it. The prospect of a war with England has been so long approaching us, that we ought to have been better prepared for it than we are. It was to prevent this war, which I believed altogether otherwise unavoidable, that I assented to and voted for the embargo, when a member of the Senate. I hoped it would have saved us from the war. I have ever been convinced, and now believe more firmly than ever, that it did save us from the war for that time, and postponed it for four years. The same causes which would have produced it then are producing it now, and according to all appearance, if anything can possibly save us from it again it will be another embargo.

Whether our government will have the time, or the inclination, or the resolution, to resort to this expedient again, I do not know. From the accounts received here from England, since the news of the rencounter between the *President* frigate and the *Little Belt*, measures appear to have been adopted for the express purpose of "humbling the Yankees," and a squadron of five ships of the line, to be followed it is said by a regiment of troops, has sailed for America with sealed orders to be opened west of Scilly. Their object will doubtless be known to you long before you receive this letter. Whether it be of mere menace or direct hostility, I trust the spirit of my country will prove true to itself. But it opens in either case a prospect before [us], at least as formidable as that of 1775 and 1776 was to our fathers.

You tell me that you sent me a letter, which you had written me, expressing perhaps too freely your opinions of certain late measures of our government. Perhaps I ought to have burnt two letters which I wrote you expressing my opinions with regard to the non-intercourse or non-importation act of the last session of Congress. I do sincerely respect and honor the motives, and I fully approve the spirit of those by whom it was passed. They had given a pledge by the act of the former session, which they thought they were bound to redeem, and they might justly expect that France would carry into effect her engagements on her part, so positively and explicitly stated by the Duke de Cadore. But it was my opinion that France had already violated her own engagements in a manner which absolved us from all obligation contracted by the act of the former session, and I strongly apprehended that the tendency of the new act would be to precipitate a war with England. The new incident which has occurred, and upon which the accounts of the two parties differ so materially with regard to the facts, undoubtedly increases the danger, and seems to render the war unavoidable.

If the war must come I hope that the temper and the energy of the government and people will rise to a dignity and firmness adapted to the emergency. So far as it may be defensive, I can only pray, that as our day is, so our strength may prove. But the first and most important quality for war, in my estimation, is *justice*; and may God Almighty grant that we may be careful to keep that on our side. That we may not undertake it presumptuously, nor impelled by passion, nor without a precise and definite object for which to contend.

At all events there is no doubt but a war will produce great and extraordinary changes of popular sentiments of administrations, and perhaps of constitutions in our country. It is probable the time in which you are coming forward as a public man will be a time of turbulence and of difficulty. This reflection increases my anxiety on account of your health. But on the other hand it will be the time *for the virtues* to be brought into action, and I flatter myself that you will be equal to it.

This state of affairs is also calculated to turn back my reflections upon myself. It has led me to review my own public conduct in past times, and to consider my prospects and my duties for the future. You will already see that I find in it an additional justification to my own mind for the part I took in relation to our foreign affairs, during the last session of Congress in which I held a seat in the Senate. My principle was one which no result of events could possibly shake. But in respect to *policy*, I always considered the embargo as justifiable on no other ground, than that its only alternative was war. This opinion from the necessity of the thing was conjectural. It is even now not demonstrable that war would have followed without it; but if war comes from the same operative causes as I believed would have produced it then, I shall certainly consider my reasoning at that time as more completely sanctioned by the events than I could if it should not ensue.

Since my residence in Russia our relations both with France and England have taken a variety of turns, and new incidents affecting them have occurred, but in which it has not been my duty to take any part. I have of course none of the responsibility connected with them upon me. I have had nothing *English* to guard against but forgery. My most difficult and important labors have been to struggle against another influence. But let me tell you an anecdote. In the month of February last I heard that there was an American vessel, somewhere in the river Elbe going shortly with a special permission from the French government to Boston. Thinking this might be a good opportunity to write a *private* letter or two, (I took special care not to send by that way any public ones,) I wrote you on the 5th of March, No. 12, and inclosed it together with a duplicate of No. 11, under a cover directed to my father, and sent it by post to Mr. Forbes at Hamburg, with a request that he would forward it by the first safe opportunity to the United States.

On the 26th of March Mr. Forbes wrote me that he had received my letters, and should send the inclosures by the ship *Packet*, Captain Hinkley, which was to sail for Boston in a very few days. I congratulated myself on having thus found one more chance of conveyance for my winter letters, and was indulging the hope that my number twelve had reached you at least in June, until about ten days since I received a subsequent letter from Mr. Forbes, informing me that a few days previous to the departure of Captain Hinkley, at 7 o'clock in the morning, his bedchamber was entered by order of the police, and all his letters amounting to seven or eight were taken from him, and that my letter directed to my father was among them. Mr. Forbes made immediately a written application for the restoration of my letter. He was referred from the police to the post office, and from the post office to the police, but never obtained the letter.

You may perhaps have thought me particularly cautious of writing you and my other friends at Quincy upon topics of political interest, and if you receive my letters Nos. 11 and 12, you may wonder what motives there could be, not for breaking them open, but for eluding the return of them. And I trust you will perceive that I have had sufficient reason for great reserve in writing politics, and that you will find some excuse for letters on subjects which might be thought too trifling for a man of my years and gravity. To resume the thread of my reflections, if we have a war with England I may perhaps find it difficult to get home, but I suppose a passport for myself and family would be obtainable. I am now on a new account glad that I had a substantial reason for declining the seat on the bench. It is now (setting aside all my old objections) one of the last places that I could be willing to hold. I need not enlarge. For myself, for my family, the private station to which I expect to return has, besides all its other advantages, an attraction of safety from the storm, to which I look with comfort and hope. Do not understand me, however, as intending to shrink from any station which my country through her constitutional organs may assign to me. I owe her too much to decline any post of danger to which she may ever think fit to call me. Hitherto I thank her equally for what she has given, for what she has offered, and for what she has overlooked. I shall be equally grateful, if she over looks me again....

JOHN QUINCY ADAMS TO JOHN ADAMS, OCTOBER 14, 1811

Heretofore, John Quincy, in line with his father, had been a staunch supporter of a navy as a necessary complement to a foreign policy of independence. But exactly what kind, and how large, and for what purpose? Here, perhaps to encourage a response from John Adams, John Quincy seriously considers the argument against a naval buildup, because of its cost and the fact that it might provoke rather than deter or coerce the British. Ironically, an extended period of peace with Britain would be the best opportunity – and justification – for a navy. As to its value in protecting American commerce, John Quincy goes so far as to question the value of commerce itself, if the commercial and naval interests were to conjoin and threaten to overwhelm the whole of the nation.

DEAR SIR:

I endeavor as much as possible to be your disciple in the opinion that a navy would remedy many of our evils. But there are two sides to that question, and I have not definitely settled in my mind whether the evil or the remedy is the worst. If a navy, a respectable navy, could be formed, and at the same time a steady peace with England could be preserved, it would certainly tend to raise our national character in the estimation of the rest of the world. But if, even in our present state of impotence upon the ocean, the commercial rivalry, jealousy and fears of England are pushing her into a war with us for the sole purpose on her part of arresting and reducing our prosperity, how much more inevitable would it be if her rancorous feelings were envenomed by the sight of an American navy, which she could take or destroy. It would be a perpetual stimulus to England for making war against us, stronger than all those by which she is now instigated put together. Nor would it be possible, for us, even with the most liberal appropriations for a navy, to create one in half a century of uninterrupted and unremitting effort, capable of coping with hers. If she could not endure the thought of our commercial profits, all of which ultimately flow into her own lap, how much more eagerly would she seize every occasion to annihilate any naval force which should be rising to an aspect which could give her a moment of alarm. The only possible chance we could have for growing into strength at sea would be a time when we should be upon good terms with her, and when we might seem to be building for a contest against her enemies. The affair of the *Chesapeake* and that of the *Little Belt* have shown us samples of the questions that are apt to arise between armed ships, and of a very compendious manner of settling such questions to which, in certain tempers of mind, they are no less prone. Multiply tenfold or fifty the number of our frigates and send them out to meet British men of war on the high seas, and you will have ten or fifty such questions to one that occurs now. Convoy questions, salute questions, first hailing and first answering questions, with a burning match at the touch hole of every gun in both ships, and then solemn official reports on each side charging the other with having fired the first gun. I cannot disguise to myself the tendency of a navy to embroil us with Great Britain, arising from the very nature of the thing. Nor can I contemplate without anxious concern any instrument so powerful, the character of which must be to produce and multiply such collisions.

As to our internal policy, the argument for a navy is liable to much controversy too. Its expense must be an important object. The annual cost of the British navy now exceeds twenty millions sterling. A tenth part of that sum equals the whole expenditure of our national government. Ten millions of dollars a year would give us just such a navy as I think the English would for its own sake choose to destroy. With ten millions of dollars a year we should have about half the force which the same sum pays for in England. There is no department of the English government in which the nation is so outrageously plundered as in the navy. Our nation would be plundered about twice as much as the English, for in the first place we must double pay both officers and men. The officers, because we must take them from occupations of which profit is the soul, and must indemnify them for the advantages they give up for the service. The men, because we have no power of impressment, because their engagements must be voluntary, and because the public to obtain them must *outbid* the wages of the merchant service. Then the navy contracts, and the navy agents and the pursers, the multitude of electioneering canvassers to be provided for in the seaports, the riggers and caulkers, and ship carpenters and mastmakers, and victuallers and poulterers, and all the little world who have something to do in fitting out a ship, and who have also something to do upon all our election days, will too easily discover the art of swelling their bills for work done or articles furnished, with an invisible item for their services in the *political* department. And when money comes to be wanted by the public to pay for all these expenses, the bank directors and stockholders who can alone command it will find out and prove that eight per cent, or perhaps ten, is the most moderate interest for which it can possibly be obtained. Something too much of this we have seen in our small experience. If my friend Quincy had an oration to make upon the subject, it would afford an ample field for his eloquence and his wit.

But all this is political heresy. That without a navy we shall never have any security for our commerce, and shall be contiuually injured and insulted by foreign nations, is beyond all question. Now comes a new point to be mooted. Is our commerce worth the cost and sacrifices which must be made to protect it? To commerce, considered as *trade*, as an honest calling affording employment, subsistence, and fortune to a portion of the community, favor and even protection are due to a certain extent. To commerce considered as the *broker* and *carrier* of agriculture (for Mr. Jefferson's epithet of *handmaid* I do not approve) still higher importance and more extensive protection is due. To commerce as the purveyor of most of the comforts and enjoyments of our physical existence, as holding the great link of human association between the remotest regions of the earth, as furnishing the great vehicle of civilization and science, the most distinguished favor and most liberal protection ought to be given. But from all that I have seen and all that I have heard and read of commerce, in this or in former ages, in our own or in any other quarter of the globe, commerce is the very last constituent interest in the nation upon which I would bestow power. Mercury made a very good messenger, but he would have been a detestable master. It is very obvious however that a large navy would not only increase the relative weight and influence of the commercial interest in our country, but would arm it with a power which would be extremely formidable to the whole. I will not, however, turn my letter into a dissertation. I will only add the hope that we shall not suffer ourselves to be entrapped into a war while we have no navy. Congress I learn are soon to meet. They must take care to steer clear of war. Your friend Timothy has been sweating to prove that the war is already, begun. How Commodore Rodger's story will turn out upon his Court of Inquiry remains to be seen. But the British government is not so ready for a war with the United States as Timothy calculated.

Mr. Barlow has arrived in France, but brought us no letters. I have seen however Boston newspapers to the tenth of August. Mr. R. Smith's vindication of his resignation looks as if it would turn out not much better than that of a predecessor in his office. If he made his explosion with the view to take a higher station in the third party, which we hear is putting in a claim to the next Presidency, he was not well advised. I fancy by this time he wishes he had taken the *Siberian exile*. For my own part I am not displeased that he chose to stay at home, for I should have been in rather a ridiculous situation spending the winter here as a private gentleman which I must have done, and with a successor seated in my place. But I would rather have submitted to that than that he should expose himself and his country as he has done by his pamphlet.

All the accounts which we get from America lead me to be more and more contented with that dispensation of Providence which prevented our return to the United States the present year. I should probably have mingled, whether willingly or not, in some electioneering projects from which it is my wish to be entirely disconnected. They will have blown over by the next summer, and on my return I shall have the prospect of at least some little quiet. We have resided during the summer months in the country.

Last week we returned to the city where we are settled until next June. What is then to be our destination still depends upon the pleasure of the President of the United States.

The political state of affairs on the European continent is equivocal and threatening. But on this head I can say little. I mentioned to my brother not long since a proof of curiosity in the French police department to read my letters. I have just had another. Mr. J. S. Smith wrote me a few lines from London in disgust, and addressed to me a small packet of English newspapers. The person who had charge of them happened to land in France. These letters for me were taken from him by the police at Havre and sent to Paris. Mr. Russell on hearing of it wrote to the Duke de Bassano, claiming my letters. The Duke de Bassano sent him two, assuring him that the Duke de Rovigo (Minister of the Police) had found no more *for me*. Mr. Russell has sent them to me. They were sealed but had apparently been opened. What became of the third letter or what it contained I am not informed. I suppose it is in the paradise of fools. Perhaps the foolish forgery just at that time published in the English papers, and in which my name was used, sharpened the Duke of Rovigo's optics. At any rate I have mementos enough for discretion, and so I bid you adieu.

JOHN QUINCY ADAMS (ST PETERSBURG) TO JOHN ADAMS, OCTOBER 31, 1811

The imperative of Union continued to dominate John Quincy's thinking as reports of New England's disaffection with the Republican administration continued to circulate. In addition to his fears that civil war would result in the creation of perpetually warring mini-states, there was also the possibility that "a Jeroboam, a Julius Caesar, a Cromwell or some such ferocious animal,... might or might not unite the Country again under one Government – If he did it must be military, and arbitrary – ." This led him to a noteworthy assessment: "In short Union is to me what the Balance is to you; and as without this there can be no good Government among mankind in any state, so without that, there can be no good Government among the People of North-America in the state in which God has been pleased to place them."

DEAR SIR:

In the month of June last Mr. Myers Fisher, Junior, of Philadelphia, who is established here as a partner of a commercial house, called upon me with a gentleman who had just arrived with a vessel and cargo of which he was the owner, and whom he introduced to me by the name of Mr. David, of Philadelphia. I thought this gentleman a total stranger to me, and was a little surprised when he said to me, "Sir, you and I are very old acquaintances with each other. Do you not recollect a boy by the name of David who was one of your school fellows at Mr. Le Coeur's, at Passy, in 1778?" "I recollect two boys of that name who were brothers, born in London of French parents, and who had been sent over to France for their education." "Well, sir, I am the younger of those two brothers;" and then he told me several anecdotes of occurrences at the school which had as completely escaped my memory until he reminded me of them as his own person. I excused myself as well as I could for not having had a memory so retentive as his, but the passage from twelve to forty-five years of age accomplishes a metamorphosis in one's looks, which it requires something more than memory to trace back. It was remarkable that this was the second since I have been here in which I have been recognized by schoolmates of Le Coeur's pension. The other was a Mr. Rudolphe, an engineer, whom I had more irretrievably forgotten than Mr. David. For even now, after he brought circumstances to my mind which I do remember, I can recall no trace either of his person or his name. I have not been well pleased with myself to find that my schoolmates of that period have so much better memories than mine, and I have set all the usual casuistry of self-love in motion to account for it in a manner which may spare me all the mortification of the discovery.

But the occasion upon which I mention Mr. David to you is, that after having passed the summer here, he is now going to Gothenburg, intending to return hence either directly or through England to Philadelphia, and it is by him that I shall take the opportunity of forwarding this letter. It is already the third that has occurred since the navigation directly from Cronstadt has been closed, and I hope to have several others in November and perhaps December. There is, however, a very troublesome, and at this season a very dangerous, water passage over the gulf of Bothnia between this place and Gothenburg, and the winter has already declared itself here with such severity that the River Neva is completely frozen over.

Since I wrote you last we have had no further news from America, and expect none of any material importance until the session of Congress. We hear of nothing but the violence of political parties concentrated in the state of Massachusetts and especially in the town of Boston. Old Hillhouse used to say seven years ago, that there was no remedy for our evils but "*a little surgical operation;*" and it was he, and a number of heads in Connecticut and Boston about as wise and comprehensive as his, who then seriously formed the project for dividing the Union, of which at the last session of Congress Mr. Quincy condescended to become the herald. It was on the very same Lilliputian scale of policy too, because Louisiana and the western states would soon be able to out vote New England in Congress. I had settled it in my mind long before that time, that this project would never be carried into execution, but by *treason* and *rebellion*, and that those were the greatest of two evils, in comparison with the chance of New England's being occasionally out voted in Congress. To my mind, therefore, the bare intimation of what Mr. Quincy seriously avowed in Congress, and what Hillhouse hinted by the jocose figure of an amputation, contained these two crimes, *treason* and *rebellion*, as completely as in the physical world the grub obscene contains the wriggling worm. I do not imagine that either Hillhouse or Quincy ever pursued their own reflections so far as to be brought to this conclusion, though Quincy by his "violently if they must" has admitted that the division may cost a *civil war*, the chances of which I suppose he will not deny might, if unsuccessful, finish by giving it the name of rebellion. Such however was my conclusion, that individual *treason* and collective *rebellion* were necessarily implied in the execution of the scheme for dividing the Union; and the system of conduct uniformly pursued by the party which first conceived that design has uniformly confirmed me in the opinion which / had formed upon a consideration of it *a priori* as a mere theoretical speculation.

It seems to me that there were *littleness* and contraction stamped upon the very conception that the American Union must be dissolved, because the New England interest might be outvoted in Congress. There was, indeed, no New England interest clear or strong enough to unite its own representatives in their votes. But admitting that there had been, or that in future there might be, I saw no indication that it would be without its proper and reasonable influence in the national councils, nor could I possibly discover any interest which would not suffer more by the natural and inevitable collisions of independent and disconnected bordering nations, having no common deliberative principle of association, than it could while they were united under one and the same system of legislation.

As the conception of dividing the Union appeared to me little and narrow, I could not avoid assuming it as a measure of the minds by which it was entertained; and as I thought the execution of the project would on the contrary require minds of a very enlarged and capacious character, I did not think the persons so ready to undertake this mighty work exactly calculated to carry it through. I therefore believed that it would ultimately prove unsuccessful, though probably not until after the experiment of a civil war. What and whom a *civil war* might in its progress bring forth, I could not foresee; but judging from past and present experience I supposed a Jeroboam, a Julius Caesar, a Cromwell, or some such ferocious animal, who might or might not unite the country again under one government. If he did, it must be *military* and *arbitrary*. If he did not, it would be because another tyrant like himself would head another state of a similar description, to feed between them a perpetual state of future war between the different sections that now compose the Union. It was possible that instead of two such wild beasts, the nation when once split up might produce an indefinite number of them, and monarchies, and oligarchies, and democracies, might arise as among the states of ancient Greece, and the more they multiplied the more materials would they furnish for future war. Now in all these prospects of future times, grounded on the assumed principle of dividing the Union, I did see chances of splendid fortunes for individual avarice and ambition, which our present simple republican and federative government does not and cannot hold out, but at the expense of blood and treasure, and freedom and happiness to the great mass of the nation in all its parts, from which the hand of a parricide would shrink with compunction.

From the frequency with which I return to this subject in my letter to you and to others of my friends which will be seen by you, may be judged how much it occupies my thoughts, and how deeply it affects my feelings. It enters into most of my meditations upon history, upon government, and even upon the poetry that I read. Marmion, and the Minstrel, and the Lady of the Lake, have no moral to me but to show the consequences of dividing states which nature admits of being united. The picture of border wars is a memento to me of what awaits us, if we ever yield to that senseless and stupid call for division, which I have so long heard muttered in my own neighborhood, and which Quincy has now taken trumpet to sound forth in the very sanctuary of legislation. In that *Union* is to me what the *balance* is to you, and as without this there can be no good government among mankind in any state, so without that there can be no good government among the people of North America in the state in which God has been pleased to place them.

Of ourselves we have little else to say than that we are all well.

I have got into such a regular and quiet course of life, and have now so little troublesome public business to do, that my time passes smoothly away, and it would pass as happily as the condition of human nature admits but for the irresistible calls which I hear from my parents and my children. As respects myself, the interests of my family, and the service of my country, I know not which would be most desirable, for me to remain here or to return home; but the sense of duty prescribing my return is so strong that I shall feel myself uneasy until I comply with its commands. Hitherto I have felt it altogether at the pleasure of the President, after declining the appointment to the bench. I have had motives which it is unnecessary for me to explain to you, for avoiding hitherto an explicit request to be recalled. It still remains, therefore, at the President's option. If he recalls me without such a request, I shall however be perfectly satisfied with his determination. If he authorizes me to remain here longer, I shall soon make the request which I have hitherto delayed. At all events I do hope to see you in the course of the ensuing year, and to take upon me that imperious duty of superintending the education of my sons.

I pray you to assure them of my constant affection, and my mother of my unalterable duty, with my kind remembrance to all the branches of the family, and particularly to my sister.

JOHN QUINCY ADAMS (ST PETERSBURG) TO THOMAS BOYLSTON ADAMS, NOVEMBER 6, 1811

Napoleon's supposed removal of the Berlin and Milan decrees was essentially a fraud, in John Quincy's view. French policy all along had been designed to bring the United States into war with Britain. The proper course for the United States was to restore non-importation against both belligerents – strict neutrality. John Quincy had come around to the view that "our non-importation act, is of all the measures hitherto taken, most seriously and severely felt by England – The

*course of Exchange is a proof, and an unanswerable proof of its great
efficacy – It occasions no doubt many partial inconveniencies in our
own Country, but as a defensive weapon it works so well that I should
incline strongly to its continuance."*

Congress are already in session and probably before you receive
this letter will have taken some decisive step to fix the state of our
relations with Europe. But I trust that step will not have been
taken without a knowledge of the manner in which France is
treating us, nor without a cool and deliberate consideration of
the effect which this treatment ought to have upon our course of
policy. You know my sentiments with respect to the non-importation act of the last session. It passed upon the conviction that
the Berlin and Milan decrees had been effectually and bona fide
repealed. In all the proceedings of France on that subject I had
seen a character which was far from deserving the discrimination
which was then made on our part between her and her enemy,
but I did and do still respect most highly the motive upon which
the act was adopted – the sacred fulfillment of an honorable
promise. At this time I think little doubt can remain upon any mind
concerning the real intentions of France. The dispute whether
the Berlin and Milan decrees have or have not been repealed is
degenerating into a cavil upon words. Yes! as to us they have been
repealed. At least I know not of any official act of the French government contrary to their declarations to that effect. But as prohibitory duties are in common sense and common reason always
equivalent to prohibition, the tariff issued cotemporaneously with
the declaration that the two decrees were revoked was substantially a non-importation act, pointed directly against us. In form
it certainly did not violate our neutral rights but in substance was
the same thing. By internal regulation it made the exercise of our
neutral rights impracticable with regard to the most profitable
part of our commerce. It satisfied the letter but not the spirit of
our prior law. If however all this be admitted it is clear that our
pledge has been completely redeemed. If we promised to our loss

we have made our promise good. We have now a new score of injury and outrages to take up. The depredations of the present year are not committed by virtue of the decrees of Berlin and Milan, but upon simple orders of the Emperor Napoleon that all colonial merchandises coming from whence and belonging to whom they may are to be considered as English, and coming from England, therefore to be confiscated. Surely after this it is perfectly useless to inquire whether the Berlin and Milan decrees are or are not repealed. At the same time it becomes constantly more and more evident that Napoleon is ardently desirous of a war between the United States and England, a war which would be highly propitious to his purposes which would hasten undoubtedly the ruin of England but which would either rivet upon us the fetters of France, or make them so intolerably galling that the feeling of our country would cast them off for the still more cruel and insufferable manacles of England. Now if there were not other reasons in abundance to deter us from a war with England, one reason equivalent to ten thousand is that he desires we should have it. For the very reason that our neutrality is the state the most unfavorable to his views I hope we shall adhere inflexibly to it. At present we may with great safety set in substance his enmity defiance. And the most effectual way of doing it will be by placing him and his adversary again precisely upon the same footing.

Our non-importation act is of all the measures hitherto taken most seriously and severely felt by England. The course of exchange is a proof, and an unanswerable proof, of its great efficacy. It occasions no doubt many partial inconveniences in our own country, but as a defensive weapon it works so well that I should incline strongly to continuance. But I would apply it as an equivalent measure without hesitation and without delay to France. And I would assume a tone in negotiation with her which should leave no room for anybody to talk of our partiality in her favor. Armstrong's letter of the 10 of March and its effects sufficiently showed the true tone that ought to be taken with her. When I say incline to the continuance of the non-importation,

I speak of course without a full knowledge of its operation at home. If that should make a repeal expedient, I think it will be difficult to substitute any measure of equal power in its stead. England besides her pauperism and her paper money is getting upon very bad terms with her allies in Sicily, in Spain and even in Portugal. She is in a great dilemma between the Cortes of Cadiz and the South American patriots of independence. This claim becomes as from day to day more entangled and she will never be able to control it. It will I flatter myself be our policy to keep ourselves cool and calm and to do nothing to involve us in the catastrophe which cannot be very remote.

JOHN QUINCY ADAMS (ST PETERSBURG) TO ABIGAIL ADAMS, JANUARY 1, 1812

At the start of this fateful year for America and the world, John Quincy considered the case for and against war with either Britain or France. Neither would be a suitable ally, even if America were willing to become embroiled in Europe's wars. The causes of both belligerents were unjust, and America lacked the military power to enforce its will independently. Instead, let the wheel of history turn in favor of peace. "France and England are now obviously fighting for objects which neither will ultimately obtain – Both in spite of themselves are compelled to admit our participation in Commerce to a certain extent – Both, if we have Patience, and preserve ourselves from War, will be compelled to admit us still further – Their necessities will do more for the restoration of our rights, than we could do by any exertion of our own forces."

I hope and trust that Congress will have the wisdom still to preserve our country from war in which we could gain nothing and could not fail to lose something of what is worth more than all other possessions to a nation, our independence. If between the two belligerent powers, France and England, It were possible to discern a just or honorable cause; if in their treatment of us it were possible to discern anything but jealousy, hatred, and eagerness to despoil us of all the advantages which they saw us enjoy, we have ample cause to appeal to the last resort of nations against either. Were it possible by any rational calculation to foresee that by joining either of them against the other we should be able to obtain justice for ourselves, and look back at the close of the war with satisfaction as having contended successfully for a suitable object, I should wish for war. If a profound and indignant feeling of the wrongs which both are committing against us, and the most cordial wish to see them redressed, were it at the sacrifice of more than my life, would avail instead of line of battleships and battalions, my voice should be for war, and I would strike as soon as preparation could make it prudent at the party which is most vulnerable to us, a point by no means difficult to ascertain. But "what king," says our Saviour, "going to make war against another king, sitteth not down first and consulteth whether he be able with ten thousand to meet him that cometh against him with twenty thousand. " The proportion of the numbers about which we are to consult are much more unfavorable to us than those of ten and twenty thousand. They are in point of naval force scarcely ten to five hundred, and our principal object to contend for is unfortunately on the sea. Our consultation need not therefore be long. The position which is not pleasing to acknowledge, but which it behoves us well to know and to consider, is that we have not the means to protect our commerce upon the ocean against the violent injustice of England. Still less have we the means of forcing our commerce upon the continent of Europe, which with some inconsiderable exception excludes it by prohibitions or prohibitory duties. In the present condition of the world, and it is much to be doubted whether it will ever be otherwise, that right is not worth a straw which a nation has without force to defend it. We have not force to defend our rights upon the sea, or exercise our rights upon it at the pleasure of others. So it would still be if we were at war. There is, however, a consideration in our favor which ought not to escape us. Both England and France have mounted their policy upon systems as impracticable for them to carry through as would be an attempt by us to maintain our maritime rights by force. England abuses her naval dominion by attempting to engross to herself exclusively the commerce of the world. This she never can accomplish. France heaps conquest upon conquest until she is unable to govern what she has conquered, and loses from one hand while she is grasping with another. France and England are now obviously fighting for objects which neither will ultimately obtain. Both in spite of themselves are compelled to admit our participation in commerce to a certain extent. Both, if we have patience and preserve ourselves from war, will be compelled to admit us still further. Their necessities will do more for the restoration of our rights than we could do by any exertion of our own forces.

JOHN QUINCY ADAMS (ST PETERSBURG) TO ABIGAIL ADAMS, APRIL 30, 1812

In the spring of 1812, information from London suggested to John Quincy that Britain had determined on war with the United States. He thought the British might still desist, but only if France did not invade Russia, which he fully expected would happen that summer. He had hoped fervently for peace, but he was resigned to the situation if Britain initiated the conflict. "To forego the right of navigating the Ocean, would be a pusillanimity which of itself would degrade us from the rank and the rights of an Independent Nation – Yet it has been too clearly demonstrated that nothing but force can now maintain it…. But as it is the nature of the serpent to sting, it is the duty of man to bruise his head for self-protection – On the high seas, we have no resource and can have no efficacious defence against her. But she has vulnerable parts; and I pray to God, that those who have the Administration of our public affairs may have studied and discovered where they are situated, and prepared to touch them till she shall feel."

The inclosed is a copy of a letter which was written near a month before an opportunity occurred of sending it on its way to you. I am afraid that the delay will entirely defeat its object, and that it will be found impracticable to send out my two sons to me the next summer. The river Neva is now again open, and I trust that in about six weeks or two months opportunities for writing to you again will present themselves. To you, my dear Mother and to you alone, I am indebted for information concerning my family and friends in your quarter of the world. From June last until the commencement of the present year I have received from you several letters in the course of the winter, and have never suffered a month to pass by without writing to you. Since I wrote you last we have received your letter to my wife of 25 November which she has answered. I sent last week this answer, with another letter from her, and my own of 30 March to Mr. Russell at London, with a request to him to forward them. I suppose he will have no difficulty to do this; for although Mr. Foster did threaten that if our non-importation should not be repealed his government would retaliate; and although I trust it has not been repealed, yet a non-importation from America may not be so convenient in England just now, with the quartern loaf at eighteen or nineteen pence, and all the importation of grain and flour from France, of which they boasted so much last year, prohibited not only by law but by scarcity.

The effects of our non-importation are doubtless felt and pretty strongly felt in England, nor is there any doubt of her disposition to retaliate whenever retaliation shall not consist in self starvation. There was no inconsiderable pains taken last summer to demonstrate in Parliament and to the public that England was quite independent of America for supplies of *bread*, and official statements were published to show that in the course of the preceding year more than double the quantity of the staff of life had been imported from France to that which had come from the United States. The strength of this argument rested on the position that France was an infallible source of subsistence for

England, and that it was better to depend upon France for subsistence than upon America. Therefore England might boldly threaten America with non-importation, and even proceed to war with perfect indifference as to the consequences. This calculation has been for the present disconcerted by a scanty harvest in France. The Emperor Napoleon says that nine years of abundance in France have been succeeded by one year of *mediocrity*. That is to say a year when famine has driven the people to such riotous extremities that in one city he has been shooting a number of men and women to preserve peace. He has also been obliged to provide two millions of Rumford soups a day, from April to September, to be distributed throughout the Empire. A good harvest in France the present year will doubtless supply the deficiencies of the last, but will not produce grain sufficient for her own consumption, and although she may this year have markets open to her which for some years past have been closed, yet for her own wants, as well as for those of her armies in Spain and Portugal, she must depend upon importation from America. Her threats of retaliation upon non-importation are therefore not very formidable, and whether she perseveres in her present system of war with the language of peace, or proceeds to that of open and avowed war, I am persuaded the event will prove to all who have eyes to see or ears to hear that her dependence upon commercial intercourse with us is more essential to her than ours upon her is to us. Her government, however, has not yet acquired this conviction nor is it probable they will until the evidence of it shall be more clear and unequivocal than five years of experience has yet proved it....

JOHN QUINCY ADAMS (ST PETERSBURG) TO ABIGAIL ADAMS, AUGUST 10, 1812

When news arrived in Russia that Britain had repealed its most obnoxious Orders in Council, John Quincy was delighted – his strategy of patience and the application of strict neutrality seemed vindi-

cated. Unfortunately, he soon learned that the Madison administration and Congress, unaware of the favorable change of British policy, had reacted to an earlier threats from the British minister, Thomas Foster: "I cannot indeed perceive any other course which was left to the American Government, without self-degradation to pursue, than that which they did adopt," John Quincy noted sadly. "I cannot be surprized that they should have considered all pacific and conciliatory means of obtaining justice as exhausted, and no alternative left but War, or the abandonment of our rights as an Independent Nation." Still, he hoped that the misunderstanding would be corrected, and that peace would soon be restored. And in the background was Napoleon's invasion of Russia, which was now at peace with Britain – an invasion that John Quincy believed would likely end in failure for France.

I then flattered myself that the revocation of the British Orders in Council, of which I had just been informed, would be known in the United States in season to prevent the war which I knew would otherwise be unavoidable. In this hope I have been disappointed. After reading Mr. Foster's letter to Mr. Monroe of 30 May I cannot indeed perceive any other course which was left to the American government without self degradation to pursue than that which they did adopt; but when I remark that within fifteen days after that letter of Mr. Foster was written, the very same British ministers by whose instructions he sent it had determined totally to repeal the whole system which was kindling the war, which they had always pretended was necessary to the national existence of England, and which they now ordered Mr. Foster to say was more necessary than ever, I see no room left for calculation beforehand upon anything. I lament the declaration of war as an event which in the actual state of things when it passed was altogether unnecessary, the greatest and only insuperable causes for it having been removed; but as it was not and could not be known to Congress I cannot be surprised that they should have considered all pacific and conciliatory means of obtaining justice as exhausted, and no alternative left but war or the abandonment of our right as an independent nation.

The declaration, however, so essentially alters the aspect of affairs between the two countries and their governments that I now consider everything again thrown upon the chances of events. That the British ministers are now desirous of peace with us is obvious from the steps they have taken. How far the policy of our government will be affected by the revocation of the Orders in Council when they learn that it preceded the declaration of war, I can hardly foresee. My own most fervent wishes and prayers are that peace may be restored before any further irritating and aggravating hostilities shall have been committed on either side.

JOHN QUINCY ADAMS (ST PETERSBURG) TO SECRETARY OF STATE JAMES MONROE, SEPTEMBER 30, 1812

On September 20, even as Napoleon still occupied Moscow, Count Rumyantsev asked John Quincy if the United States would consider Russian mediation in its conflict with Britain. At the first opportunity, John Quincy sent a summary of his conversation to Washington, DC. He had not and could not commit his government, but he indicated to the president and the secretary of state that he personally favored exploring this route. He told the Russian foreign minister: "I well knew it was with extreme reluctance they [the United States] had engaged in the war; that I was very sure that whatever determination they might form upon the proposal of the Emperor's mediation, they would receive and consider it as a new evidence of his Majesty's regard and friendship for the United States; and that I was not aware of any obstacle or difficulty which could occasion them to decline accepting it."[7]

SIR:

I have the honor to enclose copies of a note which I received from the Chancellor, Count Romanzoff, communicating two printed copies of the treaty of peace late concluded with the Ottoman Porte, and of my answer. One of the copies of the treaty is likewise enclosed.

On the 20th instant I received a note from the Chancellor requesting me to call upon him the next evening which I accordingly did. He told me that he had asked to see me by the Emperor's command; that having made peace and established the relations of amity and commerce with Great Britain, the Emperor was much concerned and disappointed to find the whole benefit which he expected his subjects would derive commercially from that event defeated and lost by the new war which had arisen between the United States and England; that he had thought he perceived various indications that there was on both sides a reluctance at engaging in and prosecuting this war, and it had occurred to the Emperor that perhaps an amicable arrangement of the differences between the parties might be accommodated more easily and speedily by indirect than by a direct negotiation; that his Majesty had directed him to see me and to enquire if I was aware of any difficulty or obstacle on the part of the government of the United States, if he should offer his mediation for the purpose of effecting a pacification. I answered that it was obviously impossible for me to speak on this subject any otherwise than from the general knowledge which I had of the sentiments of my government; that I was so far from knowing what their ideas were with regard to the continuance of the war, that I had not to that day received any official communication of its declaration, but that I well knew it was with reluctance they had engaged in the war; that I was very sure whatever determination they might form upon the proposal of the Emperor's mediation, they would receive and consider it as a new evidence of his Majesty's regard and friendship for the United States, and that I was not aware of any obstacle or difficulty which could occasion them to decline accepting it. For myself I deeply lamented the very existence of the war; that I should welcome any facility for bringing it to a just and honorable termination. I lamented it, because I thought that the only cause which had made it absolutely unavoidable was actually removed at the moment when the declaration was made. If the course which had been adopted by my government had been such as I could not in my own mind approve, it would still not become me to censure it, but it was not so. The declaration of the English Regent in April, and the letter Mr. Foster had written to the American Secretary of State in communicating it, had as it appeared to me left the American government no alternative but an immediate appeal to arms, or a dishonorable abandonment of all the unquestionable rights for which they had contended, and even the essential characteristics of an independent nation. The blame of the war was therefore entirely on the English side, but the war was not the less disagreeable to me. I lamented it particularly as occurring at a period when, for my good wishes for Russia and the Russian cause, I should have rejoiced to see friendship and harmony taking place between American and England, rather than discord and hostility. I knew the war would affect unfavorably the interests of Russia. I knew it must be highly injurious both to the United States and England. I could see no good result as likely to arise from it to anyone. The Count replied that he had considered it altogether in the same light, and so had the Emperor who was sincerely concerned at it, and who had himself conceived this idea of authorising his mediation. He thought one indirect negotiation conducted here, aided by the conciliatory wishes of a friend of both parties, might smooth down difficulties which in direct discussion between the principals might be found insuperable. To a mutual friend each party might exhibit all its claims and all its complaints, without danger of exciting irritations or raising impediments. The part of Russia would only be to hear both sides, and to use her best endeavors to conciliate them. I observed that there was a third party to be consulted as to the proposal – the British government. The count answered that it had already been suggested by him to the British ambassador, Lord Cathcart, who had the day before dispatched it by a messenger to his court. Some question occurred concerning the mode of enabling me to transmit this communication to the United States, upon which the Count promised to see me again in the course of a few days. He said that he should write to Mr. Daschkoff and instruct him to make the proposition to the government of the United States.

I am with great respect, etc.

JOHN QUINCY ADAMS (ST PETERSBURG) TO JOHN ADAMS, NOVEMBER 5, 1812

The defeat of General William Hull and the surrender of Detroit to a numerically inferior British-Indian force at the outset of the War of 1812 was a matter of considerable shame for John Quincy, and it caused him to reflect on the character of the martial spirit. He feared that Americans might have too little after years of peace, whereas "Russia has not only discovered a vigour and energy of defence beyond the expectations of both her friends and foes; but she has perhaps discovered to herself a secret of her own strength, of which she was not aware." Perhaps the war with Britain was necessary after all. Europe burned with the martial spirit and the United States could not hope to escape war forever. Still, "My daily and hourly prayer is never the less for Peace."

DEAR SIR:

Having not received directly from you, or from any of my friends at Quincy, a line later than the 10th: of April, it was with no small pleasure, that a few days since, I met in an English Newspaper, an extract of a letter from you to Mr E. Watson, dated the 6th: of July – It relates to the War, and expenses your opinion that this was both just and necessary – Although I am unable to maintain by any rational argument a different sentiment – Although with regard to the Justice of the War, I cannot perceive the shadow of a doubt, if War in *any* case can be just, and although with regard to its necessity, as the state of affairs *appeared* in America to stand, when the War was declared and when you wrote; I cannot question it, yet I must lament, deeply lament, that the change of system which at the same time had taken place in England, couldbeknowntoproduceitseffectuponthedeliberationsofCongress–

As it is, we seem to have been involved in the War by a *fatality* – For although after the Revocation of the Orders in Council, the War was still perfectly *just*, to abolish the British practice of Impressment, yet to my mind its *necessity* no longer existed – and most especially do I deem the *time* inauspicious for commencing it – But it is of no avail to regret, the chain of Events which have been ordered by a wise disposer – We have long, very long enjoyed; we have not a little abused the blessings of Peace – and now we must even learn again what it is to be deprived of them – what it is to exchange them for the calamities of War.

Among these, the surrender of Genl: Hull and his army, to a force about one half of his own in number, with the loss of Fort Detroit, has already reached my ears – More distressing Events might doubtless have occurred; but one more humiliating to the honest feelings of an American, who would fain see his Country respected by other Nations, was scarcely within the compass of possible things – Was it cowardice? I cannot imagine cowardice sufficiently base, for such a transaction – Was it Treachery? – I should be more reluctant at this conclusion even that at the other – One of them it must have been – Imagination cannot conceive a third alternative.

To escape as much as possible from the ineffable mortification of this burlesque upon War, I endeavour to persuade myself that it is a new proof that War was necessary to us – We are indeed coping with an Enemy whose naval and military force is so disproportional to ours, that nothing but the consideration of the other Enemies, with whom he must at the same time contend, could save us from the sentence of gross and glaring folly for engaging him at all – But in addition to all his other advantages at the outset of this contest, he has that of beginning, with the skill and experience of twenty years previous War, with the greatest and most formidable Powers, while all our martial metal has been gathering the rust of the same twenty years – With troops and Generals so perfectly raw, as those with which from the nature of things we must enter the field, awkward, unskilful and unsuccessful operations were naturally to be expected – I was prepared to hear of them; though for such *grinning infamy* as this I confess I had not looked forward – If then our military faculty has already degenerated to such excessive debasement, it seems high-time for us to have the experiment whether it is yet capable of being retrieved – The Courage of Soldier, Gibbon says, is the cheapest quality of human nature; but it will often fail, and at the most critical and fatal moment, without the aid of use, discipline, and example. – If it had been possible for us to avoid a War at this time and even to have enjoyed many more years of Peace, War must after all have come at last, and if we are so disqualified for it now, is it not probable that in the progress of enervation and languor which another long period of inaction would have produced, the very Spirit of Independence itself might have been extinguished, and we should have been really, what Fisher Ames, said we were ten years ago, "of all men on Earth, the fittest to be Slaves"?

We live indeed in an age, when it is not lawful for any civilized Nation to be unprepared for or incapable of War. – Never, with an aching Heart I say it, never did the warlike spirit burn with so intense a flame throughout the civilized World as at this moment – Never was the prospect of its continuing to burn and becoming still fiercer, so terrible as now – It would perhaps not be difficult to shew that the State of War has become indispensable to the existence both of the French and British *Governments* – That in Peace they would both find their destruction – That they both must force outwards those deadly humours of National Corruption, which if allowed to be thrown back upon their own vitals would produce speedy and inevitable death. – Add to this, that War has become not only in France but even in England, and Spain, and Portugal, and now in Russia, the great, if not the only

Career of Wealth, Honour and Renown – That while the glory of Principalities, Kingdoms and Empires, as Rewards of martial atchievement, is blazing in the bosoms of men in the higher Classes of Society, the misery and famine which War itself has brought upon numberless multitudes of the lower Classes, is forcing them into the ranks, and filling every vacant spot as fast as the sword can make it – The fruits of Victory by land are no longer exclusively reserved for France – England has at length brought forth a General, who bids fair to redeem the military Fame of his Country, and to take his stand in History, if not with the Edwards and the Henry's of former ages, at least with the Wolf and the Marlborough of the last. A more extraordinary phenomenon is here unfolding itself before my eyes – With a standing army at least five hundred thousand men, the Emperor of Russia, by a simple summons to his people has called forth in less than three months three hundred thousand more; who with the Caftan, and the Beard, and the hatchet, are mingled in among the regiments of smooth-faced, uniformed veterans, and already rivalize with them in martial exploit – Napoleon has taken Moscow, but it is doubtful whether he or his army will ever get back from it – In his attempts upon St: Petersburg and Riga, he has been foiled, and his troops and his marshals have been repeatedly and effectually beaten. Russia has not only discovered a vigour and energy of defence beyond the expectations of both her friends and foes; but she has perhaps discovered to herself a secret of her own strength, of which she was not aware – It is not for Riga, Moscow or St: Petersburg that France and Russia are now contending, it is for the dominion of the European Continent – In this Campaign, and while I write Napoleon has exposed and is exposing, many believe to certain destruction, absurdly to the most imminent danger, not only himself and his army, but the whole mass of French Power, accumulated in twenty years of Revolution – But if Europe changes its master, the armies still covering its surface will still find occupation, the victorious generals will still thirst for the field of glory, and still drench it in blood – While Europe is so warlike, we cannot, must not hope, to recline unmolested on the pillow of peace, and enjoy, without being called to defend, anything that the European Warrior can take from us – War then we must have; and if it be only foreign War, I hope it will eventually produce to us fruits of national honour and advantage, compensating for the evils it has brought with it, and even atoning for this worse than shameful beginning. – If this reasoning is fallacious, I can imagine no other more satisfactory – My daily and hourly prayer is never the less for Peace.

Peace or War, I am ever dutifully your's

JOHN QUINCY ADAMS (ST PETERSBURG) TO THOMAS BOYLSTON ADAMS, NOVEMBER 24, 1812

For the war with Britain to prove truly successful – in the sense of helping to improve the character of the American people, as well of defending their independence – John Quincy believed the war must be just and have precise and well-defined objectives. Taking Canada militarily in order to conquer it, in his opinion, was not one of them. "Great Britain is yet too powerful and values her remaining possessions too highly to make it possible for us to retain them at the Peace, if we should conquer them by the War – The time is not come – But the power of Great Britain must soon decline – She is now straining it so excessively beyond its natural extent that it must before long sink under the violence of its own exertions. It is in the stage of weakness, which must inevitably follow that of overplied and exhausted strength, that Canada and all her other possessions, would have fallen into our hands without the need of any effort on our part, and in a manner more congenial to our principles, and to Justice, than by Conquest."

SIR:

You know how deeply I was disappointed at the breaking out of our war, precisely at the moment when I entertained the most ardent and sanguine hopes that war had become unnecessary. Its events have hitherto been far from favorable to our cause, but they have rather contributed to convince me of its necessity upon principles distinct from the consideration of its causes. The termination of General Hull's campaign in upper Canada is known to us, as far as the English government have seen fit to make it known, by the dispatches from the Governor General and General Brock, and by the capitulation. We are informed also of an armistice agreed to by General Dearborn, which the President refused to ratify, and from these two portents I have come to the conclusion, which indeed it was not very difficult to anticipate before, that our projected invasion of Canada will end this year in total and most disgraceful defeat.

This misfortune, considered by itself, is not a very heavy one to the nation. But it is a deep mortgage of reputation to redeem. Its effects upon the spirits and dispositions of the people present the most important light in which it is to be viewed, and these to my mind are problematical. If the effect upon the national sentiment should be similar to that of the *Chesapeake* affair, we shall not have ultimately much reason to regret the disasters of Hull's army, or the failure of our first military expeditions. Our means of taking the British possessions upon our continent are so ample and unquestionable that, if we do not take them, it must be owing to the worst of qualities, without which there is no independent nation, and which we must acquire at any hazard and any cost.

The acquisition of Canada, however, was not and could not be the object of this war. I do not suppose it is expected that we should keep it, if we were now to take it. Great Britain is yet too powerful, and values her remaining possessions too highly, to make it possible for us to retain them at the peace, if we should conquer them by the war. The time is not come. But the power of Great Britain must soon decline. She is now straining it so excessively beyond its natural extent, that it must before long sink under the violence of its own exertions. Her paper credit is already rapidly declining, and she is daily becoming most extravagant in the abuse of it. I believe that her government could not exist three years at peace without a national convulsion, and I doubt whether she can carry on three years longer the war in which she is now engaged without such failure of her finances as she can never recover. It is in the stage of weakness which must inevitably follow that of overplied and exhausted strength that Canada and all her other possessions would have fallen into our hands, without the need of any effort on our part, and in a manner more congenial to our principles and to justice than by conquest.

The great events daily occurring in the country whence I now write you are strong and continual additional warnings to us, not to involve ourselves in the inextricable labyrinth of European politics and revolutions. The final issue of the campaign in the north of Europe is not yet completely as certained, but there is no longer a doubt but that it must be disastrous in the highest degree to France, and no less glorious to Russia. It may not improbably end in the utter annihilation of the invading army, three fourths of which have already been destroyed. Whether the Emperor Napoleon will personally escape the fate which has befallen so many of his followers is yet doubtful, but it may be taken for granted that he will never be able again to assemble against Russia a force which can be formidable to the security or integrity of her empire. The politicians who have been dreading so long the phantom of universal monarchy may possess their souls in quietness. Never having been infected with the terror of it I shall desire no new source of tranquillity from these occurrences, but I cannot say that my foresight was clear enough to expect that the Colossus of French power would in so short a period be staggering upon its foundations so manifestly as it is. It is impossible not to consider the internal state of France as greatly depending upon the course of these external events. The empire of Napoleon was built upon victory alone. Defeat takes away its foundations, and with such defeat as he is now suffering it would be nothing surprising to see the whole fabric crumble into ruins. France, indeed, still remains a formidable mass of power, but into what condition she may be plunged by the overthrow of his government I am scarcely able to conjecture. The day of trial to Russia has been severe, but it has been short, and her deportment under it will raise her high in the estimation of mankind. Her plan of defence has the most decisive demonstration in its favor – success – and success under numerous incidental circumstances disadvantageous to her. Not only her armies, but her peasantry, armed and sent into the field as if by enchantment, have fought with the most invincible courage, though not always with favorable fortune. The chances of war have been sometimes with and sometimes against them, but they have arrested the career of the conqueror of the age, and drawn him on to ruin, even when they have yielded him the victory.

JOHN QUINCY ADAMS (ST PETERSBURG) TO WILLIAM PLUMER, AUGUST 13, 1813

John Quincy lays out his strongest case against impressment – that it was a direct threat to American independence because, if the principle were acceded to, it would breach the social compact that protected every citizen. Americans had once fought to assert their right not to be taxed without representation, even though the actual tax was small. "The principle for which we are now struggling is of a higher and more sacred nature than any question about mere taxation can involve. It is the principle of personal liberty and of every social right. The question is not how many of our children we shall sacrifice without resistance to the Minotaur of the ocean, but whether our children shall have any security to protect them from being devoured by him."

DEAR SIR:

A year, a most eventful year in both hemispheres, is on the point of expiring since the date of your favor of 19 August, 1812, which was delivered to me very recently by our old brother Senator, Mr. Bayard, who has now become one of my colleagues in a mission extraordinary to Russia.

The object of this mission was the restoration of peace between the United States and Britain. In the month of September last, the Emperor of Russia, moved by his friendship for both those powers, and by the interest of his own nation which were suffering in consequence of the war that had arisen between them, conceived the idea of offering his mediation between them. I have every reason for supposing that this idea was the suggestion of his own mind and originated entirely with himself. I state this to you, because I have seen intimations in English newspapers that the government of the United States had solicited the Emperor of Russia's mediation, which party spirit in our country believes or pretends to believe that our government is systematically bent upon the war, and has no desire whatever for the restoration of peace. Party spirit I know is very capable of contending for both these pretences at once. I have seen it most eloquently demonstrated in the same papers, that eternal inextinguishable war with Britain is the master passion, the very Aaron's serpent of Mr. Madison's breast, and also that he is heartily tired and sick of the war, and ready to catch at any straw to get out of it. Certain it is that he did not ask for the mediation of Russia, but that it was offered spontaneously by the Emperor of Russia himself. He was then and still is engaged in a war with France, in which he is the ally of England. The United States, as being at war with England, have a common cause with France. Yet the government of the United States immediately accepted the mediation of Russia, while the ally of Russia shows the utmost reluctance to accept, if not a positive determination to reject it.

The attachments of the American people to peace are so strong that I believe it would be impossible for them to be unanimous in a war for any cause whatever. The present is essentially a war for the independence of the nation. For no nation can be independent which suffers her citizens to be stolen from her at the discretion of the naval or military officers of another. I have seen that the legislature of Massachusetts had been making inquiries *how many* citizens of the United States had been impressed by the British. I should be glad to know *how many* of their native fellow citizens the legislature of Massachusetts would think it reasonable annually to abandon to a slavery, more degrading and more cruel than that of Algiers or of the West Indies, before they should consider the duty of protection to commerce. I read in the Constitution of Massachusetts that "the body politic is a social compact by which the *whole people* covenants with *each citizen* and *each citizen* with the *whole people*." Governor Strong and the majority of the Massachusetts legislature allow great weight to the British king's argument, that he has a right to impress his subjects, because he has a right to their allegiance. But what other foundation has the right of a sovereign to allegiance than the duty of protection? The right and the duty are reciprocal, and the state is under a perfect obligation to protect every one of its citizens, as much as it has a right to claim their allegiance. The state by the social compact is bound to *protect* every one of its citizens, and the inquiry how many of them a foreign nation may be allowed to rob with impunity is itself a humiliation to which I blush to see that the legislature of my native state could descend. I remember that during the war of our Revolution it was a fashionable argument on the British side to say, that the Yankees were in rebellion to save three pence a pound in the cost of their tea. But the legislatures of Massachusetts of that day never instituted an inquiry *how much* the people of America would have to pay by submitting to the tax. It was "for a principle," as one of our poets said at that time, that "the Nation bled." It was a high minded war of a nation contending for its rights, and not basely casting up the farthings and pence which they might have to pay of impost upon glass and oil and painters' colors. The principle for which we are now struggling is of a higher and more sacred nature than any question about mere taxation can involve. It is the principle of personal liberty and of every social right. The question is not *how many* of our children we shall sacrifice without resistance to the Minotaur of the ocean, but whether our children shall have any security to protect them from being devoured by him. If in such a war we have not been able to unite, it is evident that nothing can unite us for the purpose of war. As to the project of separating the states, I apprehend it less than I have done heretofore, though the preservation of the Union may eventually cost us a civil war.

What the issue of that with which we are now afflicted will be is in the hand of providence. A career of success has attended the British government from the time when the war began, which could not have been expected by anyone, and which they were far from expecting themselves. How long it is to continue, and how far it is to extend, is not at this moment easy to foresee. The exertions however which they are now making are too violent to be capable of lasting long. Their expenditures for the present year amount to little less than 130 millions sterling. Their paper progresses in depreciation, gold is at £5.8 sterling an ounce (its standard value is £3.17.10½), and dollars pass for 6 shillings and 10 pence each. This is a depreciation of 50 per cent and at the same time they have enacted by law that there is no depreciation at all.

The war upon the continent of Europe has subsided for a few weeks by an armistice, but it is only to break out with new and more aggravated fury. In less than a week the hostilities are to recommence, and the fate of Europe is again to be committed to the wager of battle. It is said there are nearly a million of men arrayed in arms against one another in Germany. Half the number will suffice to fatten the region kites before the close of the year. The negotiations now broken off may possibly be resumed during the winter; but even then, unless something should occur to make the balance preponderate on one side or the other more than it now does, the furies will not yet be satiated with blood. I believe we must not expect a peace for ourselves until the general peace shall be made in Europe.

I am, etc.

CHAPTER SIX

PEACE COMMISSIONER, 1813–1815

INTRODUCTION

In March 1813, the Russian envoy to the United States formally presented the offer to mediate. John Quincy's report of Rumyantsev's inquiry the previous September arrived in Washington at the same time. President Madison jumped at the opportunity. Despite a few spectacular successes at sea, the war was going badly. The campaign against Canada had failed miserably; Fort Detroit had been surrendered without a fight; federal finances were in disarray; and New England seemed on the verge of revolt. Without waiting to hear confirmation of Britain's acceptance, he dispatched Secretary of the Treasury Albert Gallatin and Federalist Senator James Bayard to join John Quincy in St. Petersburg to negotiate peace. The duo arrived in July 1813.

Monroe's original instructions to the commission called for British recognition of neutral rights, eschewing the use of illegal blockades especially, and compensating for the losses of American merchants when the British had violated American rights. Monroe later suggested that Britain might consider ceding all or part of Canada. Only one of the American demands, however, was to be considered a sine qua non – a commitment to end impressment. If the British refused to take up that point, the commission was to break off the negotiations and, in the case of Gallatin and Bayard, return home.

As it turned out, the British declined to accept Russian mediation, suspecting that Alexander would lean to the American side, especially on maritime issues. But the British did want talks. Having raised the possibility through various unofficial channels, Lord Castlereagh, the British foreign secretary, dispatched a message to Secretary Monroe in November 1813 stating that his government was prepared to negotiate either in London or at a neutral site – in Gothenburg, Sweden. Madison accepted both the negotiations and the neutral site, and appointed two more commissioners, Kentucky Congressman Henry Clay (former Speaker of the House of Representatives) and Jonathan Russell, who had held several overseas posts. John Quincy was named first in the joint commission and was thus technically the head of the delegation.

After his arrival in Gothenburg, John Quincy learned that the negotiations had been shifted to Ghent, in Flanders (Belgium), an arrangement agreed to by Gallatin and Bayard in London. John Quincy disapproved of the shift but at that distance he was not in a position to object. He was convinced that ever since Alexander had made his mediation proposal, Britain had adopted a diplomatic strategy of stalling, with no intention of negotiating seriously. The shift to Ghent was merely another ploy. Left to his own devices, John Quincy would have turned back to St. Petersburg and considered the negotiations aborted. But for now there was nothing to do but travel on through lands that John Quincy had known so well as a teenager and novice diplomat.

The American commission assembled in July. The British arrived six weeks later, evidently in no hurry, with leverage over the Americans. With Napoleon defeated, the full might of the Royal Navy – and now the British Army – could be unleashed. The American coastline was already blockaded. It was rumored that the Duke of Wellington himself would lead an expeditionary force, perhaps in an invasion from Canada or perhaps against New Orleans, to conquer Louisiana. This while the navy was in a position to torch American cities. There were some bright spots for the Americans, particularly Oliver Hazard Perry's victory on

Lake Erie. But these barely held the line. Meanwhile, the New England financial community had largely shut down its support for the Federal Treasury. Federalist leaders planned to convene in Hartford, Connecticut, to insist on amendments to the Constitution, perhaps as a prelude to disunion. The American delegation could only hope that the British were so war weary and deep in debt – and focused on the still-unsettled situation in Europe – that they might agree to a marginally acceptable settlement.

The American commissioners initially assumed the negotiations would turn on the single issue of impressment. Most of them felt that it was unrealistic to think that the British would formally concede the point, but that it would be unwise to break off the talks. To their relief, just as the conference began, they received a dispatch from the secretary of state authorizing a settlement that did not address impressment, as long as the Americans pushed as hard as they could, and they put on the record that their silence did not mean abandonment of the principled stance against the practice. John Quincy had hitherto assumed that the public would rebel against such a treaty – and excoriate those who negotiated it. Now, at least, he and his colleagues had political cover.

But impressment proved to be a somewhat secondary concern. London was prepared to discuss impressment, although its delegates gave no indication they would bend on the subject. But ominously, as a sine qua non, they demanded that the Indian tribes must be included in the settlement and a boundary be established between them and the United States (which turned out to encompass much of the Northwest Territory). The boundary between Canada and the United States, parts of which had never been authoritatively resolved, would also be adjusted, presumably to British advantage. The continued liberty of Americans to have access to the fisheries within British colonial (Canadian) waters, as set out in the Treaty of Paris, would depend on some equivalent concession by the United States.

John Quincy responded that the American commissioners

had no instructions on the Indian matter or the fisheries. The British delegation pressed back and proposed that the Americans agree to a provisional treaty that conceded the principle of an Indian boundary, subject to the final ratification of the US government. John Quincy and his colleagues said that was completely unacceptable. The British then suspended further talks, pending instructions from London.

John Quincy and his fellow commissioners now considered whether to break off talks in the face of what they considered outrageous demands, which went well beyond impressment. If London was serious, no settlement was possible, and the war must continue. But even if that was the case, the Americans were mindful of the potential political consequences of simply picking up and going home. London could win the propaganda battle with the British public, its allies, and its sympathizers in the United States, by portraying the Americans as the intransigent party. Better, then, to stay put and force Britain to initiate the break. The American commission initially assumed that the British would do so immediately, after hearing from London.

The American delegates were determined to present a united front to their British counterparts, but they had numerous internal squabbles, especially between the Bible-reading, Northeastern John Quincy and the card-playing, Western Clay. These disputes were in large part over tone and diplomatic style. When the two delegations began negotiating through an exchange of memoranda, John Quincy thought that the British notes deserved bold and spirited responses. But his colleagues found his drafts excessively argumentative and long. The assignment was gradually assumed by the more concise and diplomatic Gallatin, much to John Quincy's chagrin. Indeed, over time, Gallatin became the central figure in the delegation, mediating the internal disagreements.

As it turned out, London did not break off the talks, but insisted on the establishment of an Indian barrier state. The British claimed that the Americans initiated the war from a spirit of aggrandizement, particularly the desire to annex Canada – an accusation that the American commissioners piously denied. To protect Canada in the future, Britain now demanded boundary concessions to Canada, especially in Maine, as well as a commitment by the United States to forego construction and maintenance of armed ships on the Great Lakes and their adjoining rivers, and to stop building forts on their shores. This, while the British were permitted to maintain their own inland fleet there.

Again, such terms were unacceptable. Week by week, the Americans chipped away at the British position. And there was some movement, whether made seriously or as another stalling tactic. John Quincy suspected the latter, as part of a long-standing British strategy of delay. London, he believed, assumed that continuing victories in America would strengthen their position even further. On October 1, the commissioners received word that the British had entered Washington and burned the Capitol and other public buildings. This only steeled John Quincy's resolve. "We must say as Kutuzoff wrote to the Emperor Alexander, when he lost Moscow, Washington is not America."[1]

The next major moves occurred later that month. The British abandoned the Indian barrier state idea as a sine qua non for a settlement, and offered one based on the principle of *uti possidetis*, which meant that each side would retain whatever territory it held at the war's end. Their hope was to retain northern Maine (for the overland route between Quebec and Halifax) and certain key forts.

John Quincy and the commission found this offer to be as unacceptable as the previous one. They would not surrender any sovereign American territory. The British delegation responded by asking the Americans to make a counterproposal. John Quincy and his colleagues produced the project of a treaty, dated November 10, based on their original instructions, which included the abolition of impressment, British recognition of neutral rights, mutual agreement not to use Indians in warfare, and a boundary settlement favorable to the United States. But at John Quincy's insistence, it also expressed a willingness to settle on the basis of *status quo ante bellum*, not just on territorial issues but across the board – to return to the state of things before the war. Clay thought that the proposal was likely to be rebuffed, and noted the commission had no instructions authorizing such a proposal. John Quincy contended that they should exercise their discretion. The commissioners agreed to include that in the treaty project.

One issue dogged the American commission to the very end. The British claimed that the American liberty to fish in Canadian waters and to dry fish on Canadian shores, granted in the Treaty of Paris in 1783, had been abrogated by the American declaration of war. The Americans offered as a quid pro quo to restore the British right to navigate the Mississippi, which, too, had been part of the Treaty of Paris. More broadly, the Americans argued that the treaty and its provisions remained in effect. But what if the British insisted otherwise? Would the United States be willing to forego peace on that point? John Quincy was adamant that it should – the fisheries were too important to New England's economy. Gallatin proposed that liberty and rights be mutually recognized. Clay objected. He was opposed to the continued recognition of British rights on the Mississippi if that was the price to be paid for the fisheries. John Quincy's rejoinder was that the British right was practically meaningless – they had no land access to the river – whereas the fisheries were a major national asset. Clay said he would never sign such a treaty. The American proposal was silent on the subject, with a covering note that the Americans did not agree that fishing liberties had been abrogated.

On November 26, John Quincy and the commissioners were surprised when the British delegation accepted the status quo ante bellum solution (while, as expected, rejecting the American provisions on impressment, neutral rights, and the like). However, on the topic of fisheries and the Mississippi, Britain's proposal was to allow the British subjects to cross American territory and inland waters to reach the Mississippi, with full rights of navigation. It said nothing about the fisheries. Gallatin went back to the idea of a quid pro quo arrangement. The American commission split, with Clay and Russell vehemently dissenting. The American counteroffer set geographical restrictions on overland passage to the river and required the payment of customs fees. Clay eventually signed off.

Their work was finally completed on December 24, 1814. The Treaty of Ghent addressed none of the maritime issues that had caused the war. It was essentially a simple cessation of hostilities on the basis of the *status quo ante bellum*. It provided for the mutual restoration of all territory, places, and possessions that had been taken during the war or after signing the treaty – the restoration of prisoners of war. In addition, mixed commissions were established to deal with border and territorial issues. Nothing was said in the final treaty about either fishing liberties or navigation rights on the Mississippi.

When the agreement was signed, John Quincy said to the British delegation that he "hoped it would be the last Treaty of Peace between Great-Britain and the United States." He wrote to his wife to say that, though he still had doubts about the document, "I consider the day on which I signed it the happiest of my life; because it was the day on which I had my share in restoring the peace of the world."[2]

JOHN QUINCY ADAMS (ST PETERSBURG) TO SECRETARY OF STATE JAMES MONROE, DECEMBER 11, 1812

Based on a dispatch from Monroe, Adams assured Count Rumyantsev that the United States had not reached a separate alliance or understanding with France, which was now the enemy of Russia, and Russia's recent ally, Britain. Rumyantsev asked John Quincy whether he objected to him passing this information on to the British government. The obvious response was to object, on the grounds that this information would prematurely show the Americans' diplomatic hand and encourage the British to continue the war. John Quincy

thought otherwise – it might "have a tendency to remove the preju-
dice of the British cabinet, and I would hope produce on their part a
disposition more inclining to conciliation." He indicated his assent –
without authorization – and the count did so, through his ambassa-
dor in London.

SIR:

On the 4th instant I received the duplicate of your favor of 1st
July last, announcing the declaration by the Congress of the
United States of war against Great Britain, and enclosing printed
copies of the President's proclamation founded upon it, of his
previous message recommending it, Df the report of the Committee of Foreign Relations proposing it, and of the National
Intelligencer of the 20th June. The original of your letter, with
these documents, not having yet come to hand, these gave me the
first official communication of the war.

I had on the 7th instant an interview with the Chancellor,
Count Romanzoff, in which I communicated to him the substance of those parts of your dispatch which relate to Russia, and
those which concern the state of our relations with France. In the
present state of the war between this country and France I was
convinced that the view of the American government's intentions
with regard to that power, so explicitly and so strongly manifested in your letter, would not only be gratifying to the Chancellor, but that it would be satisfactory to the Emperor, and would
powerfully counteract any impressions unfavorable to the United
States which the English interest here is endeavoring to excite. I
therefore told the Count that, although I had not been instructed
to make to him any official communication of the declaration of
war, the dispositions of the American Government towards other
powers, and particularly towards Russia on this occasion, had
been distinctly suggested to me in a manner which I felt it my
duty to make known to him. That the United States, compelled by
unavoidable necessity to vindicate their violated rights against
Great Britain by war, were desirous that it might be confined

exclusively to them and their enemy, and that no other power might be involved in it. That 'it was particularly and earnestly their wish to propose and maintain in their fullest extent their commercial and friendly relations with Russia. That the war on which the Emperor is now engaged against France, although it could not be known by the President to have been actually commenced at the time when your dispatch was written, was, however, contemplated as more than probable, and the necessity which obliged the Emperor to take a part in it was mentioned to me as a cause of regret to the American government. But it was hoped it would not in the slightest degree affect the friendly dispositions between Russia and the United States. That I was informed by you that the principal subjects of discussion which had long been subsisting between us and France remained unsettled; that there was no immediate prospect that there would be a satisfactory settlement of them; but that whatever the event in this respect might be, it was not the intention of the government of the United States to enter into any more intimate connections with France. This disposition I added was expressed in terms as strong and clear as I thought language could afford. It was even observed that the government of the United States did not anticipate any event whatever that could produce that effect, and I was the more happy to find myself authorized by my government to avow this intention, as different representations of their views had been widely circulated as well in Europe as in America.

The Count received this communication with assurances of his own high satisfaction at its purport, and of his persuasion that it could prove equally satisfactory to the Emperor, before whom he should lay it without delay. He said that with regard to the friendly and commercial relations with the United States *it was the Emperor's fixed determination to maintain them so far as depended upon him in their fullest extent. Even if he should enter into engagements more intimate than he was at present inclined to contract with any power whatsoever, he would assent to nothing which could interrupt or impair his relations of friendship with the*

United States; and it was the wish that they not might not be liable to the interruption which they would be expected to suffer by the English, that had been his principal inducement to offer his mediation to effect a reconcilement. He asked me if I had any objection to his communicating to the British government itself that part of my information to him which related to France? I said that on the contrary, as the British government had in the course of our discussions with them frequently intimated the belief that the American government was partial to France, and even actuated by French influence, I supposed that the knowledge of this frank and explicit statement, with a due consideration of the time and occasion upon which it was made, must have a tendency to remove the prejudice of the British cabinet, and I would hope produce on their part a disposition more inclining to conciliation.

Yesterday the Count sent me a note requesting me to call upon him again, which I accordingly did. He showed me the draught of a despatch to Count Lieven, the Russian ambassador in England, which he had prepared to lay before the Emperor for his approbation, and which related the substance of my conversation with him, particularly in regard to the intentions of the American government with reference to France, instructing Count Lieven to make it known to Lord Castlereagh, and to use it for the purpose of convincing the British government of their error in suspecting that of the United States of any subserviency to France; in the expectation that it would promote in the British ministry the disposition to peace with the United States which he (Count Lieven) knew his Imperial Majesty had much at heart, believing it equally for the interest of both powers and also for that of his own empire. The Chancellor said that as this dispatch would refer to what I had verbally stated to him in our preceding conversation, he wished before submitting it to the Emperor that I should peruse it, to satisfy himself that he had correctly represented the purport of my communication to him, and he desired me, if I should find any inaccuracy or variance from what I had said to him, to point it out to him that he might make the dispatch perfectly correspond with what I had said. I did accordingly notice several particulars in which the exact purport of what I had said might be expressed with more precision. He immediately struck out the passages which I noticed in this manner from the draught, and altered them to an exact conformity with the ideas I had intended to convey. The changes were inconsiderable, and were no otherwise material than as I was desirous of the utmost accuracy in the relation of what I had said under the authority of your dispatch.

Although this communication of the settled determination of the American government, not to contract any more intimate engagements with France, will thus be made to the British ministry with my full consent, the Chancellor's dispatch does not say that he was authorized by me to make it. It merely relates the substance of that part of my conversation with him, and directs Count Lieven to use it with a view to promote the purpose of pacification. The Chancellor understands that my consent was merely my own act without authority from you, and my motive in giving it was the same with that of his instruction to Count Lieven, because I believed its tendency would be to promote the spirit of pacification in the British cabinet. I told the Chancellor that I was aware that its effect might be different. That the very certainty that we should not seek or even accept a community of cause with their most dreaded enemy might make them more indifferent to a peace with us. But in calculating the operation of a generous purpose even upon the mind of an inveterate enemy, I feel an irresistible impulse to the conclusion that it will be generous like itself.

I asked the Chancellor whether he had received an answer from England upon the proposal of the Emperor's mediation. He said that without accepting or rejecting it they had intimated the belief that it would not be acceptable in America. He added that they rested their expectations of peace with America upon the result of the American election.

I am with great respect, sir, your humble and obedient servant,

JOHN QUINCY ADAMS (ST PETERSBURG) TO JOHN ADAMS, SEPTEMBER 3, 1813

John Quincy considers why Britain should reject Russian mediation to help end the war – thereby failing to recognize the consequences of its insistence on antagonizing the United States. "The fear of complicating the maritime question between Britain and America, with the general Politicks of Europe, is just and rational on the part of England. But it ought to operate upon her as a warning to her to settle her differences with America, upon liberal principles. The dread of French intrigue, by the Mediation of a Prince at deadly War with France can have no foundation. No Nation ever more steadily and more earnestly pursued any one course of policy, than America has sought to avoid all entanglement with European Politicks; but if England will persist in having a War with America, she must not expect that America will always be willing to fight her single-handed. She will eventually find it for her interest to make a common cause with the Enemies of England wherever they are to be found, ..."

DEAR SIR:

This day thirty years ago you signed a definitive treaty of peace between the United States of America and Great Britain, and here am I authorized together with two others of our fellow citizens to perform the same service, but with little prospect of a like successful issue. The British government shows great disinclination to treat with the United States under a mediation. They have not yet formally rejected that of the Emperor of Russia, and since the arrival of our two envoys this government has renewed the proposal, to which an evasive answer had been in the first instance returned. Mr. Gallatin and Mr. Bayard are waiting for the ultimate answer from England; they will probably be under the necessity of passing from London before the 1st of November, and by that time the waters will be locked up until June.

Inofficial and indirect hints have been communicated to us that the British government are willing to treat with us directly, and without the intervention of a mediator. But for this we must be invested with new powers; for our government had so little expectation that England would spurn the good offices of her close ally that no provision was made for the contingency. The English ministerial gazettes have avowed as one objection to the Russian mediation, that Russia must be supposed to be partial in favor of the principles of the armed neutrality. But a peace between America and Britain may be made without reference to any of the principles of the armed neutrality. Another and more decisive objection they allege is, that England ought never to submit the discussion of her maritime rights to *any* mediation.

The reasoning has from other sources been presented to us in a different form. We have been told that as the only point between the two nations upon which the war now hinges is impressment, it is a question concerning the relative rights and duties of sovereign and subject. That it is a question which never can arise between any two nations besides England and America. That it is a sort of family quarrel with which other nations can have no concern, and in which their interference can be productive of no good result. That the tendency of a mediation would be to complicate the controversy, to entangle it in the snarl of general European politics, and to make it an engine for French intrigue to work upon, to scatter abroad still more abundantly than ever the seeds of discord and confusion.

The controversy as between the two nations does not involve any question of the relative rights and duties of sovereign and subject. Admitting the British king's right to impress his subjects in all the extent he can claim, the question remains whether he can exercise the right out of his own jurisdiction. This question does not touch the right either of sovereign or subject, and this is precisely the question between Britain and America. It is a question, therefore, which in point of *principle* concerns all other nations as much as it does the two belligerents. It is whether the British king can inforce the municipal law of England on board of the ships of all other nations in the jurisdiction which is common to them all. That it is exclusively a contest between the United States and England is directly at variance with the pretence so often and so loudly urged, that impressment from foreign ships on the high seas has been practised by immemorial usage. It is indeed true that no such immemorial usage ever existed, and that as American ships were the only foreign vessels on board of which the British officers did impress, it is not likely ever to be a specific cause of war between any other two nations. But the correct inference from this would be, that it is a subject peculiarly suitable for a mediation, the mediator having no interest of his own to bias him on either side, and both parties being therefore more sure of his impartiality. Even if it were true that the rights of sovereign and subject were implicated in the contest, how would they be implicated? Britain fights for the right of the sovereign, and America for the duty of the sovereign. Britain fights for the claim to the service of the subject, and America for the claim of the subject to protection. In referring the question to the mediation of the Emperor of Russia, were it possible to suppose him susceptible of a bias which way would it be? Could the most absolute sovereign in Europe be supposed to favor any claim of the subject to exemption from the duty of service? If we disputed the British king's right to the service of his subjects, *we* might now naturally object to the mediation of any sovereign, because it would be a question upon which the partialities of all sovereigns must be against us; and least of all could we have reason to expect favor from the autocrat of Russia, within whose dominions Magna Carta and the Habeas Corpus act have no force. But England could have no occasion for distributing a mediation, of which she must know that the whole interest of the mediator would be on her side.

The fear of complicating the maritime question between Britain and America with the general politics of Europe is just and rational on the part of England. But it ought to operate upon her as a warning to her to settle her differences with America upon liberal principles. The dread of French intrigue by the mediation of a prince at deadly war with France can have no foundation. No nation ever more steadily and more earnestly pursued any one course of policy than America has sought to avoid all entanglement with European politics; but if England will persist in having a war with America, she must not expect that America will always be willing to fight her single handed. She will eventually find it for her interest to make a common cause with the enemies of England wherever they are to be found, and how far that may make her subservient to the views of France, she will consider for herself without asking the advice of England.

There are probably other motives besides those that are acknowledged which indispose the British government to the mediation, and which must protract the war, if they do not ultimately defeat the negotiation for peace. The war on the European continent has again broken out, and the coalition against France is more formidable than it ever has been since the year 1793. On the south she is already contending for her own frontiers. In the north Russia, Austria, Sweden, Prussia, and a great part of Germany are combined against her. Two of her most famous generals are in the field under the banners of her enemies, and a third at the moment when hostilities were renewed deserted to them. There is no doubt but at this moment a battle has already been fought upon which the issue of the campaign will depend, and in that the destinies of the European world are involved. The symptoms of weakness and of rottenness in the French force are so great and so numerous, that according to every rational anticipation she must sink in the struggle. The coalesced powers have not yet declared their views on the terms upon which they would agree to a peace.

I am, etc.

JOHN QUINCY ADAMS (ST PETERSBURG) TO JOHN ADAMS, FEBRUARY 17, 1814

With the defeat of France and a general European peace in the offing, John Quincy was convinced that an end to the war with Britain could easily be achieved – except for the issue of impressment. In his view, London would not concede the principle – and neither should the United States. "I would sooner look forward to the chance of ten successive Wars, to be carried on ten times more weakly than we have the present one, then concede one particle of our principle, by a Treaty Stipulation – The only way of coming to terms of Peace with England therefore at this time, which I suppose practicable and in any degree admissable is to leave the question just where it was; saying nothing about it – But I know such a Peace would not satisfy the People of America, and I have no desire to be instrumental in concluding it."

MY DEAR SIR:

There are still here a small number of Americans who came to this country upon commercial pursuits and who after bringing their affairs to a conclusion successively take their departure to return home, and thereby afford us opportunities of writing to our friends. One of them is Mr. Hurd of Boston, who goes to Gothenburg there to embark directly for the United States, and by whom I propose to send this letter.

I wrote to you by Mr. Gallatin and Mr. Bayard, who left this city the 25th of last month, and to my dear mother by Mr. Harris, who followed them on the 9th instant. As they intended to travel not very rapidly Mr. Harris expected to overtake them by the time they reach Berlin. Their object is to go to Amsterdam and thence to England, where they expect to receive a new commission and powers to treat of peace with the British government directly. Since their departure I have additional reason for expecting that such new powers will be transmitted to them, knowing that Lord Castlereagh has written to the American Secretary of State making the formal proposition of such a negotiation.

Whether I shall be associated in this new commission or not is to me extremely doubtful. I have a multitude of very substantial reasons for wishing I may not be, and only one for an inclination to the contrary. My negative reasons are not of a nature to be committed to paper. My positive reason is, because the voyage to England would be just so much performed of my voyage to the United States, and because it would make my return home as certain, as direct and as early as I could desire. From your letters which were brought me by Mr. Gallatin I perceived you had been informed of a subsequent destination which was intended for me had the mediation terminated in a peace. As however it has scarcely resulted even in a negotiation, other circumstances will naturally lead to other views. That in the present situation of Europe, or rather in that which must infallibly and very shortly be the situation of Europe, a peace between the United States and Great Britain may be concluded, I have little doubt. A general peace, at least something which will pass under that name, is highly probable in the course of a few months. According to all present appearances the catastrophe of the French Revolution is at hand. The Bourbons will at last be restored, not as the Stuarts were in England by the spontaneous and irresistible voice of the nation, but by the dictates of a foreign coalition. But the allied powers in conferring this blessing upon France will claim the reward of their generosity, and be specially careful to reduce her within dimensions which will carry with them what they may consider as a guaranty of future tranquillity, and in their solicitude to effect this as well as in the distribution of the spoils of conquest the seeds of further wars will in every probability be thickly disseminated. That a peace, however, of some kind will very soon take place is not to be doubted, from the total inability now manifested by France to resist the invasion of the allied armies. The allies proclaim to the world that they are waging war not against France but against Napoleon Bonaparte, and the French people are as willing to believe them as the other nations of Europe were to believe the Jacobins when they promised liberty, equality and fraternity to every people, and declared war against individual kings and princes. The throne of Napoleon was built upon his fields of battle. Its only solid basis was victory. So long as he was victorious the French nation was submissive, but with his fortune all his ties upon them have dissolved. If it were possible for any conqueror to possess a hold upon the *affections* of mankind, it would be an exception to a general rule, and of all conquerors he is the last who would be entitled to it. In the real moment of distress it was not to be expected that the French people would make any effort or sacrifice for his sake. That they will make none is perfectly ascertained, and the wisdom of a woman may perhaps not be necessary to persuade them to deal with him as the Israelites of Abel dealt with Sheba the son of Bichri, and to propitiate their invaders by throwing over to them his head. At the dissolution of his government France will be in the hands of the allies, and their intention is undoubtedly to restore the Bourbons, who must of course subscribe to any terms which may be required of them. Peace therefore cannot be remote, and a peace in Europe will leave the war between us and England without any object but an abstract principle to contend for. Neither of the parties will be disposed to continue the war upon such a point, and the predisposition to peace which will really influence both I hope and believe will make the peace not very difficult to be accomplished. The object for which the war was declared was removed at the very time when the declaration was made. I do not believe it possible now to make a peace which shall settle the point upon which the war has been continued. It seems to me, and I indulge the idea with pleasure, that the new and unexpected prospect opening to Europe will take away great part of the *interest* which Great Britain has in the question. She will neither have the need of such a navy, nor the means of maintaining it, as will constantly supply the temptation to recruit for it by such an odious practice as that of impressment upon the seamen of a foreign power. But I see no probability that she will yield the principle, and as to the modifications to render it palatable to us, if the government of the United States are of my opinion, they will not suffer their negotiators to listen for a moment to any modification whatsoever; because any modification, be it what it will, must involve a concession of the principle on our part. I would sooner look forward to the chance of ten successive wars, to be carried on ten times more weakly than we have the present one, than concede one particle of our principle by a treaty stipulation. The only way of coming to terms of peace with England therefore at this time, which I suppose practicable and in any degree admissible, is to leave the question just where it was, saying nothing about it. But I know such a peace would not satisfy the people of America, and I have no desire to be instrumental in concluding it. If our land warriors had displayed a career of glory, equal to that of our naval heroes, we should be warranted in demanding more even after all the changes that have happened in Europe. If we can obtain more by continuing the war, we are in duty bound to continue it. At this distance, and with the communications interrupted as they are, I am incompetent to decide this question. It must be settled at home, and may the spirit of wisdom inspire the determination!...

THE AMERICAN COMMISSION TO SECRETARY OF STATE JAMES MONROE, DRAFT PREPARED BY JOHN QUINCY ADAMS, AUGUST 11, 1814

On August 9, the American delegation assigned John Quincy the responsibility of preparing the draft of a dispatch to the secretary of state on the two opening conferences with the British plenipotentiaries. This was found to be unsatisfactory. Bayard prepared a new draft, but it too was deemed unsuitable. Gallatin drew up another paper, which was finally accepted with some amendments, dated August 12. All the documents reflected the Americans' determination to resist what they regarded as outrageous British demands.

SIR:

The British Commissioners arrived in this city on Saturday evening the 6th inst. They are Admiral Lord Gambier, Henry Goulburn, Esq., and Dr. William Adams. The day after their arrival Mr. Baker, the secretary to their commission called upon one of us (Mr. Bayard) and notified to us that event, with the proposal from them to meet us the day succeeding at one o'clock afternoon, at their lodgings. We were of opinion that unless they should think fit to hold the first conference at our dwelling house, it would be more expedient to hold it at a third place. The option of either was offered them, and they assented to the proposal of meeting at a third place. We met accordingly at one o'clock on Monday the 8th inst. and on the proposal of the British commissioners agreed to hold the future conferences at each other's houses alternately, and until they shall have taken a house, entirely at ours.

We have the honor to enclose herewith copies of the full powers produced by them at the first conference, and of the protocol of the first and second conferences as ultimately agreed to by mutual consent. They opened the subject of our meetings by assurance that the British government had a sincere and earnest desire that the negotiation might terminate in the conclusion of a solid and honorable peace; and particularly that no events which had occurred since the first proposal for this negotiation had produced the slightest alteration either in the pacific dispositions of Great Britain, or in the terms upon which she would be willing to concur in restoring to both countries the blessings of peace.

These professions were answered by us, for our government and ourselves, with expressions of reciprocal earnestness and sincerity in the desire of accomplishing a peace, and of the satisfaction with which we received those they had addressed to us. With regard to the first point stated by them as a proper subject for discussion, that of impressment and allegiance, they intimated that the British government did not propose this, as one which they were desirous of discussing; but that in adverting to the origin of the war, it was one which they could not overlook, among those which they supposed likely to arise.

The principal stress of their instructions appeared to have been concentrated upon the second point – the Indian pacification and boundary. Their statement of it in the first instance was in terms not conveying altogether the full import of its meaning. The motive which they appeared to impress upon our minds as that of the British government in this proposal, was fidelity to the interests of their Indian allies; a generous reluctance at concluding a peace with the United States, leaving their auxiliaries unprotected from the resentments of a more powerful enemy, and a desire by the establishment of a definite boundary for the Indians to lay the foundation of a permanent peace, not only to the Indians, but between the United States and Great Britain.

They expressly disclaimed any intention of Great Britain to demand an acquisition of territory for herself. But upon being questioned, whether it was understood as an effect of the proposed Indian boundary that the United States and the Indians would be precluded from the right they have hitherto exercised of making amicable treaties between them, without the consent of Great Britain; whether for example the United States would be restricted from purchasing and they from selling their lands; it was first answered by one of the commissioners that the Indians would not be restricted from selling their lands, but the United States would be restricted from purchasing them; and on reflection another of the commissioners observed that it was intended that the Indian territories should be a barrier between the British possessions and those of the United States; that both Great Britain and the United States should be restricted from purchasing their land, but that the Indians would not be restricted from selling them to a third party.

On the point respecting the fisheries they stated that this was regarded by their government as an object of minor importance. That it was not intended to deny the right of the Americans to the fisheries generally; but with regard to the right of fishing within the limits of their jurisdiction, and of landing and drying fish upon their territories, which had been conceded by the treaties of peace heretofore, those privileges would not be renewed without an equivalent.

They manifested some desire to be informed even at the first meeting whether the American commissioners were instructed to treat with them upon these several points, and they requested us to present to them such further points as we might be instructed by our government to offer for discussion. They assented however to the desire expressed on our part to consult together among ourselves, previous to answering them in relation to the points presented by them, or to stating those which we should offer on our part. This was done at the second conference, and in the interval between the two we received the originals of your letters of 25 and 27 June, the duplicates of which have since then also come to our hands.

At the second meeting after answering that with regard to the two points of the Indian pacification and boundary, and the fisheries, we were not instructed to discuss them, we observed that as they had not been objects of controversy between the two governments heretofore, but were points entirely new, to which no allusion had even been made by Lord Castlereagh in his letter to you proposing this negotiation, it could not be expected that they should have been anticipated by the government of the United States. That it was a matter of course that our instructions should be confined to the subjects of difference in which the war originated, and to the topics of discussion known by our government to exist. That as to peace with the Indians, we considered that as an inevitable consequence of peace with Great Britain; that the United States would have neither interest nor motive for continuing the war against the Indians separately. That commissioners had already been appointed by the American government to treat of peace with them, and that *very* possibly it might before this have been *concluded*. That the policy of the United States towards the Indians was the most liberal of that pursued by any nation. That our laws interdicted the purchase of lands from them by any individual, and that every precaution was taken to prevent the frauds upon them which had heretofore been practised by others. *We remarked* that this proposition to give them a distinct boundary different from the boundary already existing, a boundary to be defined by a treaty between the United States and Great Britain, was not only new, it was unexampled. No such treaty had been made by Great Britain, either before or since the American Revolution. No such treaty had to our knowledge ever been made by any other European power.

In reply to the remark that no allusion had been made to these new and extraordinary points in Lord Castlereagh's letter to you, it was said that it could not be supposed that Lord Castlereagh, in a letter merely proposing a negotiation, should have enumerated the topics which might be proper for discussion in the course, since those would naturally be determined by the events which had subsequently occurred. And this remark was made by the same gentleman, who had the day before assured us, *with sufficient solemnity of manner*, that no events which had taken place since the proposal of the negotiation had in *the slightest* degree altered the pacific dispositions of the British government, or the terms upon which she would be willing to conclude the peace.

Upon the observation from us that the proposition for an Indian boundary was unexampled in the practice of civilized nations, it was answered, that the Indians must in some sort be considered as *sovereigns*, since treaties were concluded with them both by Great Britain and the United States. To which we replied by marking the obvious distinction between *making treaties* WITH *them*, and a treaty between two civilized nations defining a boundary FOR *them*.

We informed the British commissioners, that we wished to receive from them a statement of the views and objects of Great Britain upon all the points, and expressed our readiness to discuss *them all*. They inquired, whether, if they should enter further upon discussion, and particularly on the point respecting the Indian boundary, we could expect that it would terminate by some provisional arrangement which we could conclude subject to the ratification of our government.

We said that as any arrangement to which we could agree upon the subject must be without specific authority from our government, it was not possible for us previous to discussion to decide whether an article on the subject could be formed which would be mutually satisfactory, and to which we should think ourselves, under our discretionary powers, justified in acceding. [The difficulty that we felt we stated in its full force *from a principle* of perfect candour. They would perceive that nothing could be easier for us than to admit that an article might be formed which we would provisionally sign, and yet to break off upon the details of any article which we *might discuss*.] That our motive in asking the discussion was, that even if no arrangement could be agreed to upon this point which was prescribed to them as the sine qua non of a treaty, the government of the United States might be possessed of the entire and precise intentions of that of Great Britain upon it; and the British government be fully apprised of all the objections on the part of the United States to any such arrangement. That if unfortunately the present negotiation must be broken off upon this preliminary, the two governments might be aware of each other's views, and enabled to judge of the expediency of a renewal of the negotiation.

The British commissioners objected that it would be wasting time upon an unprofitable discussion, unless we could give them the expectation that we should ultimately agree to an article on this subject. They proposed an adjournment of an hour that we might have an opportunity of consulting between ourselves, whether we could give them this pledge of a possible assent on our part to their proposal. We needed no time for such consultation, as there was no hesitation upon the mind of any one of us with regard to it, and we declined the adjournment. They then proposed to suspend the conferences until they could consult their own government on the state of things. They sent off a special messenger the same evening, and we are now waiting for the result.

It was agreed upon their proposition that a report should be drawn up of the proceedings at these two meetings, by each party, and that we should meet the next day to compare and collate them together, and from the two form a final protocol agreed to on both sides. The paper marked (C) is a copy of the report thus drawn up on our part. We inclose it to make known to you the passages, to the introduction of which the British commissioners at this third meeting objected. Their objections to some of the passages were that they appeared rather to be argumentative, and that the object of the protocol was to contain a mere statement of facts. *But* they also objected to the insertion of the fact, that they had declared the conferences suspended, until they could obtain further instructions from their government. Such was nevertheless the fact, and the return of their messenger may perhaps disclose the motive of their reluctance to its appearing on the record.

We have the honor, etc.

THE AMERICAN COMMISSION, ANSWER TO BRITISH COMMISSIONERS, DRAFT PREPARED BY JOHN QUINCY ADAMS, AUGUST 24, 1814

In responding to the British clarification of their demands for a peace treaty, John Quincy offers a vigorous rejection of London's Indian barrier state demand. He bases his argument on his long-standing belief that it was the moral and religious duty of a people to settle, cultivate, and improve their territory – a principle recognized by the laws of nations – which the Indian tribes, small in number and needing vast lands in order to hunt, could not do. The expanding American empire was therefore justified in extinguishing the rights of the tribes, by fair and amicable means. Britain had no right to interfere with this process in sovereign American territory.

The undersigned Ministers plenipotentiary and extraordinary from the United States of America have given to the official note which they have had the honor of receiving from His Britannic Majesty's Commissioners, the deliberate attention which the importance of the contents required, and have now that of transmitting to them their answer on the several points to which it refers.

They would present to the consideration of the British Commissioners that in Lord Castlereagh's letter to the American Secretary of State, dated on the 4th of November last, and proposing the present negotiation, his Lordship pledges the faith of the British government, that they were "willing to enter into discussion with the government of America, for the conciliatory adjustment of the differences subsisting between the States, with an earnest desire on their part to bring them to a favorable issue, upon principles of *perfect reciprocity* not inconsistent with the established maxims of public law, and with the maritime rights of the British empire."

It will doubtless be within the recollection of His Britannic Majesty's Commissioners, that at the first conference which the undersigned had the honor of holding with them they gave on the part of their government to the undersigned the most explicit assurances that no events which have occurred since the first proposal for this negotiation, had in any manner varied either the disposition and desire of the British government that it might terminate in a peace honorable to both parties, or the terms upon which they would be willing to conclude it.

These remarks the undersigned trust will suffice to relieve the British government from the surprise which their Commissioners have been instructed to express that the American government had not provided the undersigned with instructions, authorizing them to treat with British commissioners for the interests or pretensions of Indians situated within the boundaries of the United States.

The undersigned might justly ask in what established maxim of public law the British government have found the right of one civilized nation to interfere with the concerns of the Indians included within the territories of another? If Great Britain considers the Indians as her subjects, what established maxim of public law will warrant her in extending her claim to their allegiance to tribes inhabiting the territory of the United States? If she considers them as independent nations, where is her authority to treat for them, or to bind them by her engagements? The Commissioners of His Britannic Majesty have produced to the undersigned their full powers to treat on the part of Great Britain. But they have not yet done them the honor to communicate to them their Indian full powers.

The undersigned are persuaded that they will not be contradicted in the assertion that no maxim of public law has hitherto been more universally established among the powers of Europe, possessing territories in America; and particularly none to which Great Britain has more uniformly and inflexibly adhered, than that of suffering no interposition of a foreign power, in the relations between the sovereign of the territory and the Indians situated upon it. The proposition to constitute the Indian tribes into neutral and independent nations to serve as a barrier between the dominions of two European powers is not indeed without example. It was proposed by France in the abortive negotiation which preceded the peace of 1763, and rejected by an administration to which the British nation is accustomed to look back with pride and veneration.

The undersigned deem it proper further to observe that independent of the insuperable objections which may render such a proposition inadmissible on the part of the United States, they could not assent to it without injustice toward the Indians themselves. In precluding perpetually the Indians from the right of selling their lands, they would deprive them of a privilege of the highest importance and advantage to them. It cannot be unknown to the British government that the principal if not the only value of lands to the Indian state of society is their property as hunting grounds. That in the unavoidable, and surely not to be regretted, progress of a population increasing with unexampled rapidity, and of the civilized settlements consequent upon it, the mere approximation of cultivated fields, of villages and of cities, necessarily diminishes and by degrees annihilates the only quality of the adjoining deserts, which makes them subject of Indian occupancy. The unequivocal interest of the Indians there is to cede, for a valuable consideration the remnant of that right, which from the nature of things he must shortly cease to enjoy; to retire from the forest which has already been deserted by his prey, [into remote recesses of the wilderness where] and to yield for a liberal compensation to the hand of tillage the soil which can no longer yield to him, either the pleasures, the profits, or the substance of the chase. Such a liberal compensation is provided for them by the system of legislation adopted by the United States in their relations with all the Indian tribes within their territories. Under this system, the undersigned have already had the honor of informing the British Commissioners, that an uninterrupted peace had subsisted between the people of the United States and all the Indian tribes within their limits, for a longer period of time than ever had been known since the first settlement of North America. Nor would that peace have been interrupted to this day, had not the British government drawn some of the Indians, and compelled others, to take their side in the war. With those Indians the United States, as the undersigned have already declared, have neither interest nor inclination to continue the war. They have nothing to ask of them but peace. Commissioners on the part of the United States have been appointed to conclude it with them, and the pacification may before this have been accomplished. To a provisional article, similar to what has been stipulated in former treaties, engaging that the Indians within the territories of either party shall be restrained from committing hostilities against the citizens, subjects, dominions, or Indians of the other, the undersigned might assent, subject to the ratification of their government, as proposed by the British Commissioners, but under the color of giving to perhaps 20,000 Indians, and the tribes for which this provision is proposed to be made cannot much exceed that number, the rights of sovereignty, attributable only to civilized nations, and a boundary not asked or consented to by themselves, to surrender both the rights of sovereignty and of soil, over nearly one-third of the territorial dominions of the United States, the undersigned are so far from being instructed or authorized by their government, that they assure the British Commissioners it will never be conceded by the United States, so long as they are in a condition to contest the last badge of submission to a conqueror.

The undersigned may be permitted further to suggest in reference to the motive assigned by the British government for this proposal of a permanent Indian boundary, that nothing could be so ill-adapted to the purpose which it would be intended to accomplish. To place a number of wandering Indian hunters, comparatively so small and insignificant, in a state of nominal independence, on the borders of a free and civilized nation, chiefly of British descent, whose settlements *must* correspond with their increasing numbers, and whose numbers must increase in proportions unknown before in human annals, would be not only to expose both the parties to those incessant and fatal collisions, to which the unsettled relations between men in the civilized and the savage state must always be liable, but it must ultimately be to produce the total destruction of that party which such a project professes to protect. Were it possible for Great Britain at this moment to extort from the United States a concession so pernicious and so degrading, can she imagine that the growing multitudes of the American people would long endure the shackles which the humiliating condition would impose upon them? Can she believe that the swarming myriads of her own children, in the process of converting the western wilderness to a powerful empire, could long be cramped or arrested by a treaty stipulation confining whole regions of territory to a few scattered hordes of savages, whose numbers to the end of ages would not amount to the population of one considerable city? Were the boundary to remain even inviolable on the part of the United States, it is neither in the right nor in the power of Great Britain to secure it from transgression by the Indians themselves. Incessant wars between the Indians and the borderers would be the inevitable result, and of these wars all former experience and all rational forecast concur to prove that cruel and inhuman as their operations would be to the American settlers, they could only terminate in the total destruction of their savage foes.

As little are the undersigned instructed or empowered to accede to the propositions of the British government in relation to the military command of the western lakes. If they have found the proposal of an Indian boundary wholly incompatible with every established maxim of public law, they are no less at a loss to discover by what rule of perfect reciprocity the United States can be required to renounce their equal right of maintaining a naval force upon those lakes, and of fortifying their own shores, while Great Britain reserves exclusively the corresponding rights to herself. That in point of military preparation, the British possessions in North America ever have been, or in any time of peace are ever likely to be in a condition to be termed with propriety the weaker power in comparison with the United States, the undersigned believe to be incorrect in point of fact. In regard to the fortification of the shore, and to the forces actually kept on foot upon those frontiers, they believe the superiority to have always been, and on the return of peace again likely to be on the side of Great Britain. If the relative strength of the parties were a substantial ground for requiring that the strongest should dismantle the forts upon her shores, strike forever her military flag upon the lakes, and lay her whole frontier bare and defenceless in the presence of her armed and fortified neighbor, that proposal should have come in due consistency with the fact, not from Great Britain to the United States, but from the United States to Great Britain. The undersigned may safely appeal to the bosoms of His Britannic Majesty's Commissioners for the feelings with which not only in regard to the interests, but to the honor of their nation, they would have received such a proposal.

The undersigned further perceive that under the alleged purpose of opening a direct communication between two of the British provinces in America, the British government require a cession of territory forming a part of one of the states of the American union, and that without purpose specifically alleged, they propose to draw the future boundary line westward, not like the present boundary from the Lake of the Woods, but from Lake Superior. It must be perfectly immaterial to the United States whether the object of the British government in demanding the dismemberment of the United States is to acquire territory as such, or for purposes less liable in the eyes of the world to be ascribed to the rapacity of ambition. Whatever the motive may be, and with whatever consistency views of conquest may be disclaimed, while demanding a cession of territory more extensive than the whole island of Great Britain, the duty marked out for the under-signed is the same. They have no authority to cede one inch of the territory of the United States, and to no stipulation to that effect will they subscribe.

The undersigned deem it proper here to notice an intimation apparently held out towards the close of the note of the British Commissioners as an amicable warning to themselves. They are informed that unless they will, without even referring to their government, sign a provisional article on a point concerning which they had expressly declared they were not instructed, and to which they trust they have proved it was impossible they should be impowered to accede, the British government "cannot be pre-cluded by anything that has passed from varying the terms at present proposed, in such a manner as the state of the war at the time of resuming the conferences may in their judgment render advisable." The undersigned are well aware that the British government cannot be precluded from varying the terms proposed by themselves, whenever they think proper; but they remind the British Commissioners that at the very second day of their meetings with the undersigned, they themselves found it advisable not to proceed in the conferences, until they should have recurred for fresh instructions to their own government. That a reference of plenipotentiaries to their government upon points which could not have been foreseen, and in all respects of the most extraordinary complexion, will justly warrant the other party in varying the terms proposed by herself, the undersigned can by no means admit. They believe it to be as contrary to the usage of pacific negotiation as it is to the spirit and purpose of peace. If by this admonition the British government intended to disclose the suspicion that the undersigned were seeking pretexts for delay, they trust that the explicit nature of the present communication will remove every such impression. If the object was to operate upon the fears of the undersigned, to induce them by a menace to sign in violation of their instructions the provisional disgrace of their country, they flatter themselves the British government will not be surprised to find them unprepared to purchase even the present moderation of Great Britain by treachery to their liberty and their country.

It is well known to Great Britain and to the world that the present war owed neither its origin nor its continuance to any desire of conquest on the part of the United States; that on the contrary its causes were, etc.

JOHN QUINCY ADAMS (GHENT) TO SECRETARY OF STATE JAMES MONROE, SEPTEMBER 5, 1814

For the record, John Quincy recounts his private September 1 meeting with the British delegate Henry Golbourn. Incidental to a discussion of the stalemate over the Indian barrier state, John Quincy brings up British Admiral Alexander Cochrane's April 1814 proclamation that the Americans understood to promise freedom to slaves, and to encourage a slave revolt. John Quincy accuses British naval officers of selling the supposedly emancipated blacks for profit to slaveholders in Jamaica and elsewhere in the West Indies. He did not comment on the justice of slavery itself, but a letter from his wife had expressed alarm over the safety of her relatives in Maryland and Washington, DC, as a result of the proclamation.

SIR:

On the 25th ultimo we sent in to the British plenipotentiaries an answer to their note, and have every reason to expect that before this day the negotiation would have been terminated. Two days afterwards Mr. Bayard was explicitly told in a conservation with Mr. Goulburn that their reply would be sent to us without delay, and that they should have no occasion previous to sending it for any further reference to their government. On Wednesday, the 31st, Mr. Baker called upon Mr. Gallatin with an apology for a delay of a very few days, the British Plenipotentiaries having concluded, in consideration of the great importance of the thing, to send their note to England for the approbation of their government before they transmitted it to us. The next morning I had a conversation with Mr. Goulburn which convinced me that the sole object of this reference was to give a greater appearance of deliberation and solemnity to the rupture.

Some of the particulars of this conversation render it in my mind sufficiently interesting for the substance of it to be reported to you. I began it by expressing some satisfaction at having learnt their reference to their government, as it tended to encourage the hope that they would *reconsider* some part of their proposals to theUnited States. He did not think it probable, and in the whole tenor of his discourse I perceived a spirit of inflexible adherence to the terms which we have rejected; but, under the cover of a personal deportment sufficiently courteous, a rancorous animosity against America which disclosed there was nothing like peace at the heart. The great argument to which he continually recurred in support of the Indian boundary and the exclusive military possession of the Lakes by the British, was the necessity of them for the security of Canada. The American government, he said, had manifested the intention and the determination of conquering Canada.

And *excepting you* (said he) I believe it was the astonishment of the whole world that Canada had not been conquered at the very outset of the war. Nothing could have saved it but the excellent dispositions and military arrangements of the Governor who commanded there. We were then not prepared for an attack upon that province with such an overwhelming force. But now we have had time to send reinforcements, and I do not think you will conquer it. In order, however, to guard against the same thing in future it is necessary to make a barrier against the American settlements, upon which neither party shall be permitted to encroach. The Indians are but a secondary object. As the allies of Great Britain she must include them in the peace, as in making peace with other powers she included Portugal as her ally. But when the boundary is once denned it is immaterial whether the Indians are upon it or not. Let it be a desert. But we shall know that you cannot come upon us to attack us, without crossing it. The stipulation to maintain no armed force on the Lakes is for the same purpose – the security of Canada. I can see nothing dishonorable or humiliating in it. The United States can never be in any danger of invasion from Canada. The disproportion of force is too great. But Canada must always be in the most imminent danger of invasion from the United States, unless guarded by some such stipulations as are now demanded. It can be nothing to the United States to agree not to arm upon the Lakes, since they never had actually done it before the present war. Why should they object to disarming there where they had never before had a gun floating.

I answered that the conquest of Canada had never been an object of the war on the part of the United States. It has been invaded by us in consequence of the war, as they themselves had invaded many parts of the United States. It was an effect and not a cause of the war. I thought with him that we should not *now* conquer it. But I had no doubt we should, and that at no very distant period, if any such terms as they now required should ever be submitted to by us. The American government, I said, never had declared the intention of conquering Canada. He referred to General Hull's proclamation. I answered that the American government was not responsible for that. It was no uncommon thing for commanding officers to issue proclamations which were disavowed by their government, of which a very recent example had occurred in a proclamation of Admiral Cochrane. He said that the American government had not disavowed Hull's proclamation, and that the British government had not disavowed any proclamation of Admiral Cochrane's. I replied that the American government had never been called upon either to avow or disavow Hull's proclamation, but I had seen in a printed statement of the debates in the House of Commons that Lord Castlereagh had been called upon to say whether Admiral Cochrane's proclamation had been authorized or not, and had answered that it was not. He said that Lord Castlereagh had been asked whether a proclamation of Admiral Cochrane's, *encouraging the negroes to revolt*, had been authorized by the government, and had answered in the negative; that is, that no proclamation encouraging the negroes to revolt had been authorized. But the proclamation of Admiral Cochrane referred to gave no such encouragement, there was not a word about negroes in it. It merely offered employment or a settlement in the British colonies to such persons as might be disposed to leave the United States. I asked

him what was the import of the term *free* used in the proclamation in connection with the offer of settlements ? He answered
the question with some hesitation, but admitted that it might
be understood as having reference to slaves. I admitted on my
part that the word "negroes" was not in the proclamation, but
remarked that he must be as sensible as I was that it could have
reference only to them. That certainly no person in America could
mistake its meaning. It was unquestionably intended for the
negroes, and corresponded sufficiently with the practice of others
of their naval officers. It was known that some of them, under
similar inducements, had taken away blacks who had afterwards
been sold in the West India islands. Upon this Mr. Goulburn, with
an evident struggle to suppress a feeling of strong irritation, said,
"*that* he could undertake to deny in the most unqualified terms;
the character of British naval officers was universally known,
their generosity and humanity could never be contested; and
besides that since the act of Parliament of 1811, the act of selling
any man for a slave, unless real slaves, from one British island to
another, was felony without benefit of clergy. I replied that without contesting the character of any class of people generally, it
was certain there would be in all classes individuals capable of
committing actions of which others would be ashamed. That at a
great distance from the eye and control of the government, acts
were often done with impunity, which would be severely punished nearer home. That the facts I had stated to him were among
the objects which we were instructed to present for consideration, if the negotiation should proceed, and he might in that
case find it more susceptible of proof than he was aware. He
thought it impossible, but that it was one of those charges against
their officers, of which there were many, originating only in the
spirit of hostility and totally destitute of foundation.

With respect to the Indian allies, I remarked that there was no
analogy between them and the case of Portugal. The peace would
of itself include all the Indians included within the British limits;
but the stipulation which might be necessary for the protection

of Indians situated within the boundaries of the United States who had taken the British side in the war, was rather in the nature of an amnesty than of a provision for allies. It resembled more the case of subjects who in cases of invasion took part with the invader, as had sometimes happened to Great Britain in Ireland. He insisted that the Indians must be considered as independent nations, for that we ourselves made treaties with them and acknowledged boundaries of their territories. I said that wherever they *would* form settlements and cultivate lands, their possessions were undoubtedly to be respected, and always were respected by the United States. That some of them had become civilized in a considerable degree; the Cherokees, for example, who had permanent habitations and a state of property like our own. But the greater part of the Indians never could be prevailed upon to adopt this mode of life. Their habits, and attachments, and prejudices were so averse to any settlement that they could not reconcile themselves to any other condition than that of wandering hunters. It was impossible for such people ever to be said to have possessions. Their only right upon land was a right to use it as hunting grounds; and when those lands where they hunted became necessary or convenient for the purposes of settlement, the system adopted by the United States was by amicable arrangement with them to compensate them for renouncing the right of hunting upon them, and for removing to remoter regions better suited to their purposes and mode of life. This system of the United States was an improvement upon the former practice of all European nations, including the British. The original settlers of New England had set the first example of this liberality towards the Indians, which was afterwards followed by the founder of Pennsylvania. Between it and taking the lands for nothing, or exterminating the Indians who had used them, there was no alternative. To condemn vast regions of territory to perpetual barrenness and solitude, that a few hundred savages might find wild beasts to hunt upon it, was a species of game law that a nation descended from Britons would never endure. It was as incompatible with the moral as with the physical nature of things. If Great Britain meant to preclude forever the people of the United States from settling and cultivating those territories, she must not think of doing it by a treaty. She must formally undertake and accomplish their utter extermination. If the government of the United States should ever submit to such a stipulation, which I hoped they would not, all its force, and all that of Britain combined with it, would not suffice to carry it long into execution. It was opposing a feather to a torrent. The population of the United States in 1810 passed seven millions. At this hour it undoubtedly passed eight. As it continued to increase in such proportions, was it in human experience or in human power to check its progress by a bond of paper, purporting to exclude posterity from the natural means of subsistence which they would derive from the cultivation of the soil? Such a treaty, instead of closing the old sources of dissension, would only open new ones. A war thus finished would immediately be followed by another, and Great Britain would ultimately find that she must substitute the project of exterminating the whole American people, to that of opposing against them her barrier of savages. The proposal of dooming a large extent of lands, naturally fertile, to be forever desert by compact, would be a violation of the laws of nature and of nations, as recognized by the most distinguished writers on public law. It would be an outrage upon Providence, which gave the earth to man for cultivation, and made the tillage of the ground the condition of his nature and the law of his existence. "What (said Mr. Goulburn), is it then in the inevitable nature of things that the United States must conquer Canada?" "No." "But what security then can Great Britain have for her possession of it?" "If Great Britain does not think a liberal and amicable course of policy towards America would be the best security, as it certainly would, she must rely upon her general strength, upon the superiority of her power in other parts of her relations with America, upon the power which she has upon another element to indemnify herself by sudden impression upon American interests, more defenceless against her superiority than Canada against ours, and in their amount far more valuable than Canada ever was or ever will be." He said that Great Britain had no intention to carry on a war either of extermination or of conquest, but recurred again to our superior force, and to the necessity of providing against it. He added that in Canada they never took any of the Indian lands, and even the government (meaning the provincial government) was prohibited from granting them. That there were among the Indians very civilized people; there was particularly one man whom he knew, Norton, who commanded some of the Indians engaged on the British side in the war, and who was a very intelligent and well informed man. But the removing the Indians from their lands to others was one of the very things of which Great Britain complained. That it drove them over into their provinces, and made them annoy and encroach upon the Indians within their limits. This was a new idea to me. I told him I had never heard any complaint of that kind before, and I supposed that a remedy for it would very easily be found. He made no reply, and seemed as if in the pressure for an argument he had advanced more than he was inclined to maintain. It was the same with regard to the proposal that we should keep no armed force on or near the lakes of Canada. He did not admit that there was anything humiliating to the United States or unusual in it, but he evaded repeatedly answering the question how he or the English nation would feel if the proposition were made to them of binding themselves by such a stipulation. I finally said that if he did not feel that there was anything dishonorable to the party submitting to such terms, it was not a subject susceptible of argument. I could assure him that we and our nation would feel it to be such. That such stipulations were indeed often extorted from the weakness of a vanquished enemy; but they were always felt to be dishonorable and had certainly occasioned more wars than they had ever prevented. It was true, as he had said, the United States had never prior to the war had an armed naval force upon the Lakes. I thought it infinitely probable that if Great Britain had said nothing upon the subject in the negotiation, the United States would not have retained a naval force there after the restoration of the peace. It was more than I could say that this anxiety manifested by Great Britain to disarm them would not operate as a warning to them to keep a competent portion of the force now created, even during peace, and whether his government, by advancing the proposal to dismantle, will not eventually fix the purpose of the United States to remain always armed even upon the lakes.

The whole of this conversation was on both sides perfectly cool and temperate in the manner, though sometimes very earnest on mine, and sometimes with a hurry of reply and an embarrassment of expression on his, indicating an effort to control the disclosure of feelings under strong excitement. The most remarkable instance of this was upon the intimation from me, that some of their naval officers had enticed away numbers of our black people, who had afterwards been sold in the West India islands. I stated the fact on the authority of your instructions to the present joint mission of 28 January last, and persisted in asserting it, on the assurance that there is proof of it in possession of the Department of State. In the present state of public opinion in England respecting the traffic of slaves, I was well aware of the impression which the mere statement would make upon Mr. Goulburn. The rupture of this negotiation will render it unnecessary for us to possess the proof which it was your intention at the date of your instructions of 28th January to furnish us, but at any future attempt to treat for peace it will be important to produce it, and I would even suggest the expediency of giving as much publicity as possible to it in Europe, while the war continues.

The avowal of Admiral Cochrane's proclamation, and the explanation of Lord Castlereagh's disavowal of it in the House of Commons, were remarkable as examples of the kind of reasoning to which the British government is willing to resort. Whether the distinction taken in this case really belonged to Lord Castlereagh, or whether erroneously asscribed to him by Mr. Goulburn, I cannot say; but Mr. Goulburn was present in the House of Commons when the debate referred to took place.

The strangest feature in the general complexion of his discourse was the inflexible adherence to the proposed Indian boundary line. But the pretext upon which this proposition had in the first instance been placed, the pacification with the Indians and their future security, was almost abandoned – avowed to be a secondary and very subordinate object. The security of Canada was now substituted as the prominent motive. But the great and real one, though not of a nature ever to be acknowledged, was occasionally discernible through all its veils. This was no other than a profound and rankling jealousy at the rapid increase of population and of settlements in the United States, an impotent longing to thwart their progress and to stunt their growth. With this temper prevailing in the British councils, it is not in the hour of their success that we can expect to obtain a peace upon terms of equal justice or of reciprocity.

I am, etc.

THE AMERICAN COMMISSION, ANSWER TO THE BRITISH COMMISSIONERS, DRAFT PREPARED BY JOHN QUINCY ADAMS, SEPTEMBER 9, 1814

Building on his political and legal case to reject London's demands for an Indian barrier state and the prohibition of American armaments on the Great Lakes, John Quincy refutes the British argument that these are necessary measures to protect Canada from sudden invasion. There was a balance of military power that would preclude that. "But no sudden invasion of Canada by the United States could be made without leaving on their Atlantic shores and on the ocean, exposed to the great superiority of British force, a mass of American property tenfold more valuable than Canada ever was or ever can be.

In her relative superior force over all the rest of the globe to that of the United States, Great Britain may find a pledge infinitely more efficacious for the safety of a single vulnerable point, than in stipulations, ruinous to the interests and degrading to the honor of America."

The undersigned Ministers plenipotentiary and extraordinary from the United States of America have had the honor of receiving the note of his Britannic Majesty's plenipotentiaries of the 4th inst.

If in the tone or the substance of the former note of the undersigned the British Commissioners have perceived no disposition on the part of the American government for a discussion of some of the propositions advanced in the first note which the undersigned had the honor of receiving from them, they will please to ascribe it to the nature of the propositions themselves; to their incompatibility with the assurances in Lord Castlereagh's letter to the American Secretary of State, proposing their negotiation, and with the solemn assurances of the British plenipotentiaries themselves to the undersigned, at their first conference with them.

Of the frankness with which the British plenipotentiaries now represent themselves to have disclosed all the objects of their government while those of the American government are stated to have been withheld, a sufficient elucidation may be formed in the facts, that the British plenipotentiaries have hitherto declined all discussion even of the points proposed by themselves, unless the undersigned would be prepared to sign a provisional article upon a subject concerning which they had from the first declared themselves to be without instructions and upon a basis unexampled in the negotiations of civilized states, and which they have shown to be inadmissible. That one of the most objectionable demands of the British government was never disclosed until the third conference, after the points suggested for discussion on both sides had been reciprocally submitted for consideration. That upon the inquiry whether this new proposition was considered also as a *sine qua non* of a treaty, the undersigned were answered that one *sine qua non* at a time was enough, and when they had disposed of that already given them, it would be time enough to talk of another.

If the undersigned had proposed to the British plenipotentiaries, as an indispensable preliminary to all discussion, the admission of a principle contrary to the most established maxims of public law, and with which the United States under the pretence of including Indian allies in the peace, would have annexed entire provinces to their dominions, the reproach of being actuated by a spirit of aggrandizement might justly have been advanced against them; to the assertion that the declared policy of the American government has been to make the war a part of a system of conquest and aggrandizement the undersigned oppose the most pointed denial of its truth; and they are willing to leave it to the judgment of an impartial world to decide with what propriety the charge proceeds from a state demanding an extensive cession of territory, to a state making no such demand.

The undersigned repeat what they have already had the honor explicitly to declare to the British plenipotentiaries; that they have no authority to treat with them for the interests of Indians inhabiting within the boundaries of the United States. That the question of their boundary is a question exclusively between the United States and themselves, with which Great Britain has no concern. That the undersigned will therefore subscribe to no provisional article upon the subject. That they will not refer it to the consideration of their government; first, because the British Commissioners have warned them that if they do, the British government will not hold itself bound to abide by the terms which they now offer, but will vary them at their pleasure; and secondly because they know that their government would instantaneously reject the proposal. That they will subscribe to no article renouncing the right of the United States to maintain fortifications on their own shores, or that of maintaining a naval force on those lakes, where such a force has been during the war so efficaciously felt. And finally that they have no authority to cede any part of the territory of the United States.

If the Governor General of Canada has made to the Indians under the protection of the United States, to seduce them to betray the duties of their obligations, and to violate their treaties, any promises of British protection, it is for his government to fulfil those promises at their own expense, and not at that of the United States. But the employment of savages, whose known rule of warfare is the indiscriminate torture and butchery of women, children, and prisoners, is itself a departure from the principles of humanity observed between all civilized and Christian nations even in war. [Great Britain herself employs them only in her wars against the United States and] the United States have constantly protested and still protest against it as an unjustifiable aggravation of the barbarities and horrors of war. Of the peculiar atrocities of the Indian warfare, the allies of Great Britain in whose behalf she now demands sacrifices from the United States have during the present war shown many deplorable examples; among them, the massacre of wounded prisoners in cold blood, and the refusal of the rites of burial to the dead, under the eyes of British officers, who could only plead their inability to control those savage auxiliaries, have been repeated and are notorious to the world. The United States have with extreme reluctance been compelled to resort on their part to the same mode of warfare thus practiced against them. The United States might at all times have employed the same kind of force against Great Britain, and to a greater extent than it was in her power to employ it against them; but from their reluctance to resort to means so abhorrent to the natural feelings of humanity, they abstained from the use of them, until compelled to the alternative of employing themselves Indians who would otherwise have been drawn into the ranks of their enemies. But the undersigned, in suggesting to the British Commissioners the propriety of an article by which Great Britain and the United States should reciprocally stipulate, never hereafter, if they should again be at war, to employ savages in it believe [that it would readily meet the approbation and ratification of their government, and] that it would be infinitely more honorable to the humanity and Christian temper of both parties, more advantageous to the Indians themselves, and more adapted to secure the permanent peace, tranquillity, and progress of civilization, than the boundary proposed by the British Commissioners.

If the United States had now asserted that the Indians within their boundaries who have acknowledged the United States as their only protectors, were their subjects, living only at sufferance on their lands, far from being the first in making that assertion they would only have followed the example of the principles, uniformly and invariably asserted in substance, and frequently avowed in express terms by the British government itself. What was the meaning of all the colonial charters granted by the British monarchs from that of Virginia by Elizabeth to that of Georgia by the immediate predecessor of the present king, if the Indians were the sovereigns and possessors of the lands bestowed by those charters? What was the meaning of that article in the treaty of Utrecht, by which the Five Nations were described in terms, as subject to the dominion of Great Britain? Or of that treaty with the Cherokees, by which it was declared that the king of Great Britain granted them the privilege to live where they pleased, if those subjects were independent sovereigns, and these tenants at the license of the British King were the rightful lords of the lands where he granted them permission to live? What was the meaning of that proclamation of his present Britannic Majesty, issued in 1763, declaring all purchases of lands from Indians null and void unless made by treaties held under the sanction of his Majesty's government, if the Indians had the right to sell their lands to whom they pleased? In formally protesting against this system, it is not against a novel pretension of the American government, it is against the most solemn acts of their own sovereigns, against the royal proclamations, charters and treaties of Great Britain for more than two centuries, from the first settlement of North America to the present day, that the British plenipotentiaries protest. What is the meaning of the boundary lines of American territory in all the treaties of Great Britain with other European powers having American possessions, in her treaty of peace with the United States of 1785: nay, what is the meaning of the north-western boundary line now proposed by the British Commis-sioners themselves, if it is the rightful possession and sovereignty of independent Indians, of which those boundaries dispose?

From the rigor of this system, however, as practised by Great Britain and all the other European powers in America, the humane and liberal policy of the United States has voluntarily relaxed. A celebrated writer on the laws of nations, to whose authority British jurists have taken particular satisfaction in appealing, after stating in the most explicit manner the legitimacy of colo-nial settlements in America, to the exclusion of all rights of uncivilized Indian tribes, has taken occasion to praise the moder-ation of the first settlers of New England, and of the founder of Pennsylvania, in having purchased of the Indians the lands they resolved to cultivate, notwithstanding their being furnished with a charter from their sovereign. It is this example which the United States, since they became by their independence the sovereigns of the territory, have adopted and organized into a political sys-tem. Under that system the Indians residing within the United States are so far independent that they live under their own cus-toms and not under the laws of the United States; that their rights upon the lands where they inhabit or hunt, are secured to them by boundaries defined in amicable treaties between the United States and themselves, and that whenever those boundaries are varied it is also by amicable treaties, by which they receive from the United States ample compensation for every right they have to the lands ceded by them. They are so far dependent as not to have the right to dispose of their lands to any private persons, nor to any power other than the United States, and to be under their protection alone, and not under that of any other power. Whether called subjects, or by whatever name designated, such is the rela-tion between them and the United States. [These principles have been uniformly recognized by the Indians themselves, not only by the treaty of Greenville, but by all the other treaties between the United States and the Indian tribes.] Is it indeed necessary, etc.

These stipulations by the Indians to sell their lands only to the United States do not prove that without them they would have the right to sell them to others. The utmost that they can contend to show would be a claim by them to such a right, never acknowledged by the United States. It is indeed a novel process of reasoning to consider [the renunciation of a claim as a proof of a right] a disclaimer as the proof of a right.

An Indian boundary and the exclusive military possession of the lakes could after all prove but futile and ineffectual securities to Great Britain for the permanent defense of Canada against the great and growing preponderancy of the United States, on that particular point of her possessions. But no sudden invasion of Canada by the United States could be made without leaving on their Atlantic shores and on the ocean, exposed to the great superiority of British force, a mass of American property tenfold more valuable than Canada [ever was or ever can be.] In her relative superior force [over all the rest of the globe] to that of the United States, Great Britain may find a pledge infinitely more efficacious for the safety of a single vulnerable point, than in stipulations, ruinous to the interests and degrading to the honor of America.

DIARY ENTRY (GHENT), NOVEMBER 10, 1814

John Quincy argues that the American commissioners should express in their projet of a treaty, a willingness to make peace on the principle of status quo ante bellum. *To be sure, it was a departure from their original instructions. But John Quincy pointed out that the government had already granted the commission the authority to take impressment off the table if necessary, something they were originally told to insist on. "I felt so sure that they would now gladly take the state before the war as the general basis of the peace, that I was prepared to take on me the responsibility of trespassing upon their instructions thus far. Not only so, but I would at this moment cheerfully give my life for a peace on this basis. If peace was possible, it would be on no other. I had, indeed, no hope that the proposal would be accepted. But on the rupture, it would make the strongest case possible in our favor, for the world both in Europe and America. It would put the continuance of the war entirely at the door of England, and force out her objects in continuing it."*

10th. VI. 30. A second day belated. On examining the drafts for the note with the amendments of Messrs. Clay, Bayard, and Russell, I found more than three-fourths of what I had written erased. There was only one paragraph to which I attached importance, but that was struck out with the rest. It was the proposal to conclude the peace on the footing of the state before the war, applied to all the subjects of dispute between the two countries, leaving all the rest for future and pacific negotiation. I abandoned everything else that was objected to in my draft, but wrote over that paragraph again, to propose its insertion in the note. I had gone through my examination of the papers at breakfast-time, and Mr. Gallatin took them. At eleven o'clock we had the meeting of the mission. Everything in the note, as amended, was agreed to without difficulty, excepting my proposed paragraph. Mr. Clay objected strongly against it, because we are forbidden by our instructions from renewing the article of the Treaty of 1794, allowing the British to trade with our Indians. Mr. Gallatin, who strenuously supported my proposition, thought it did not necessarily include the renewal of that article of the Treaty of 1794, because it only offers the state before the war with regard to the objects in dispute. The Indian trade never had been in dispute. He admitted, however, that if the British Government should accept the principle and propose the renewal of the treaties, we could not after this offer refuse it.

I stated in candor that I considered my proposal as going that full length; that I was aware it would be a departure from our instructions as prepared in April, 181 3. But the Government, for the purpose of obtaining peace, had revoked our instructions of that date upon a point much more important in its estimation, the very object of the war; and I have no doubt would have revoked them on the other point, had it occurred to them that they would prove an obstacle to the conclusion of peace. I felt so sure that they would now gladly take the state before the war as the general basis of the peace, that I was prepared to take on me the responsibility of trespassing upon their instructions thus far. Not only so, but I would at this moment cheerfully give my life for a peace on this basis. If peace was possible, it would be on no other. I had, indeed, no hope that the proposal would be accepted. But on the rupture, it would make the strongest case possible in our favor, for the world both in Europe and America. It would put the continuance of the war entirely at the door of England, and force out her objects in continuing it.

Mr. Clay then said, if the proposal was to be made at all, now was not the time for making it. If our projet should be rejected, and we should hereafter find peace unattainable upon other terms, we might offer it as a last resource; but that it was not proper at present. As to the Indians, he had gone as far in concession upon that subject as was possible; he would concede no more; and if we wanted peace, Great Britain wanted it quite as much. He saw no reason to believe that she would continue the war merely for the Indian trade.

I said it was for the British Government, not for me, to consider how far peace might be necessary for them. I believed they were not sufficiently convinced of its necessity. If my proposal was to be made at all, now was precisely the best time for making it, because it would take off whatever there might appear to be of exorbitancy in our demands, and would not, as it might hereafter, have the appearance of shrinking from our own grounds. Mr. Gallatin dwelt upon the same argument, and urged that several of our articles very much needed some such softener.

Mr. Bayard thought now the most favorable time for making the proposal, as the state of the war is now much more favorable to us than we have reason to expect it will be in one or two months.

Mr. Russell wavered; he asked how the proposal offered more than the projet itself.

I told him that the projet offered all the knots of the negotiation for solution now; and the proposal was to make peace first, and leave them to be solved hereafter.

Mr. Clay finally said that he would agree to the insertion of my proposal in the note, but reserving to himself the right of refusing to sign the treaty if the offer should be accepted and the principle extended beyond his approbation.

The draft was then taken by Mr. Hughes to be copied out fair, and Mr. Gallatin, Mr. Russell, and myself remained to compare the residue of the articles as they were prepared. A concluding article, providing for the ratifications and their exchange, was prepared by Mr. Gallatin and me; after which I went out and walked about an hour. Mr. Hughes was prepared with the note at his rooms, at the back of our house. I took the projet to him, and he copied on it the concluding article. They were then brought back to our dining-room, and we signed the note – Mr. Clay still manifesting signs of reluctance. He objected to the formal concluding article, and thought it ridiculous, and he recurred again to the paragraph proposing the state before the war as the general basis of the treaty. He said the British Plenipotentiaries would laugh at us for it. They would say, Ay, ay! pretty fellows you, to think of getting out of the war as well as you got into it!

I think it very probable this commentary will be made on our proposal; but what would be the commentary on our refusing peace on those terms? Mr. Russell dined with us about five o'clock, and immediately after dinner Mr. Hughes took our note and projet to the British Plenipotentiaries.

JOHN QUINCY ADAMS (GHENT) TO
WILLIAM CRAWFORD, NOVEMBER 17, 1814

John Quincy explains to Crawford his idea of a peace settlement based on the status quo ante bellum. *"I was earnestly desirous that this offer should be made, not from a hope that it would be accepted, for I entertained none; but with the hope that it would take from them the advantage of cavilling at any of our proposed articles, as manifesting no disposition for peace, and compel them to avow for what object they intend to continue the war." In terms of the European balance of power, he was encouraged by France's revival: "It appears that the principles asserted by the French plenipotentiaries at Vienna have made a profound impression, that they have already disconcerted some of the projects of Lord Castlereagh, and that without offering any pretext for hostility from any quarter, they have laid the foundation for the restoration to France of that influence in the affairs of Europe without which this continent would be little more than a British colony."*

DEAR SIR:

I received yesterday your favor of the 10th instant, which was brought by Mr. Storrow. My expectations with regard to the issue of the campaign in America are colored perhaps more by general reasoning than by reference to the particular state of facts. I cannot suppose it possible that Izard's object was an attack upon Kingston. I take it for granted it was to relieve and reinforce our army at Fort Erie, which by our most recent accounts was in a situation more critical than that of Drummond, and still beseiged by him. Among the last rumors from Halifax is that of a successful *sortie* from Fort Erie, and if that report was well founded we might rely more upon the issue of Izard's expedition. My distrust of it arises from the necessity of exact correspondence in the execution of combined operations, and a want of confidence in our military manoeuvres upon the land. We have not yet learnt to play the game.

The debates in Parliament upon the Regent's speech have disclosed the system pursued by his government in the negotiation at this place. Lord Liverpool avows without scruple that their demands and propositions are to be regulated by circumstances, and of course while that policy prevails nothing can be concluded. Even when all the preparations are made, and all the funds provided for another campaign, it is not clear that they will find it expedient to break off this negotiation, and it is certain that we shall not break it off without orders from our government. We sent on the 10th instant the projet of a treaty, assuming the basis of *status ante bellum* with regard to the territory, and have offered in the note sent with it to extend the same principle to all other objects in dispute between the two countries. We have presented articles on the subjects of impressment, blockades, indemnities, exclusion of savage cooperation in future wars, and amnesty. But we have declared ourselves willing to sign a peace placing the two nations precisely as they were at the commencement of the war, and leaving all controversial matter for future and pacific negotiation. I was earnestly desirous that this offer should be made, not from a hope that it would be accepted, for I entertained none; but with the hope that it would take from them the advantage of cavilling at any of our proposed articles, as manifesting no disposition for peace, and compel them to avow for what object they intend to continue the war. We have offered no equivalent for the fisheries. We have considered the rights and liberties connected with them as having formed essential parts of the acknowledgement of our independence. They need no additional stipulation to secure us in the enjoyment of them, and that our government upon these principles had instructed us not to bring them into discussion. This was originally my view of the subject, and the principle on which I thought the rights to the fisheries must be defended, from the moment when we were informed in the first conference they would be contested. The offer of an equivalent was afterwards suggested from a doubt whether the ground I had proposed to take was tenable, and with the intention of relieving it from all contention. I was prepared for either alternative, but I held the one or the other to be indispensable. We finally assumed the principle on which I had originally rested the cause. It is urged, that the principle, if correct, includes the equivalent which it had been contemplated to offer, and I admit that it may. The general basis of the state before the war includes in substance both, to my mind beyond all doubt. And although I have no hope that this offer will be now accepted, yet if it should, I am not only ready to adhere to it and abide by it in all its consequences, but to sign the treaty with a degree of pleasure which has not yet fallen to my lot in this life. I am very certain that after seven years of war we shall not obtain more, and what heart would continue the war another day, finally to obtain less?

You will have observed that the atrocious manner in which the British are carrying on the war in our country has been a subject of animadversion in Parliament. The ministers placed it on the footing of retaliation. Lord Grenville and Mr. Whitbread censure in the style which Burke described as "above all things afraid of being too much in the right". They are evidently not in possession of the facts which shed the foulest infamy upon the British name in these transactions. We have seen several interesting speculations in the Paris papers on the same subject. Would it not be possible through the same channel to show the falsehood of the pretext of retaliation, or to make the principle recoil upon themselves? You have no doubt the report of the committee made 31 July, 18 13, on the spirit and manner in which the war had been waged against us even then. It has occurred to me that a short abstract from that might be presented to the public in Europe, with a reference to dates, which would point the argument of retaliation, such as it is, directly against the enemy. In general, the British have had ever since the commencement of the war such entire possession of all the printing presses in Europe, that its public opinion has been almost exclusively under their guidance.

From the access which truth and humanity have obtained in several of the public journals in France in relation to our affairs, it may be inferred that no control unfavorable to them will be exercised, however unwelcome the real exposition of facts may be across the channel.

It appears that the principles asserted by the French plenipotentiaries at Vienna have made a profound impression, that they have already disconcerted some of the projects of Lord Castlereagh, and that without offering any pretext for hostility from any quarter, they have laid the foundation for the restoration to France of that influence in the affairs of Europe without which this continent would be little more than a British colony. The issue of the Congress at Vienna will undoubtedly be pacific; but if France has taken the attitude ascribed to her by the rumored contents of Talleyrand's memorial, her rival will not long enjoy the dream of dictating her laws to the civilized world. France had lost her place in the family of nations. It was at Vienna that it became her to resume it. We have reason to hope that she did resume it exactly where she ought, and as the place she took was marked at once with dignity and moderation, it is to be presumed it will be maintained with firmness.

I am, etc.

DIARY ENTRIES (GHENT), NOVEMBER 27, 28, AND 29, 1814

The American commissioners received word that the British delegation had rejected their proposed articles on impressment, blockade and the like – but otherwise agreed to a settlement on the principle of status quo ante bellum. John Quincy wrote: "All the difficulties to the conclusion of a Peace appear to be now so nearly removed, that my Colleagues all considered it as certain – I think it myself probable – But unless we take it precisely as it is now offered, to which I strongly *incline, I distrust so much the intentions of the British Government, that I still consider the conclusion as doubtful and precarious." There were still a few barriers to reaching a settlement, especially in the matters of the fisheries and the navigation of the Mississippi, which set off a major row between John Quincy and Clay.*

27th. About eleven in the morning, Mr. Gallatin came into my chamber, with a note received from the British Plenipotentiaries. They have sent us back with this note the projet of a treaty which we had sent them, with marginal notes and alterations proposed by them. They have rejected all the articles we had proposed on impressment, blockade, indemnities, amnesty, and Indians. They have definitively abandoned the Indian boundary, the exclusive military possession of the Lakes, and the uti possidetis; but with a protestation that they will not be bound to adhere to these terms hereafter, if the peace should not be made now. Within an hour after receiving these papers we had a meeting of the mission at my chamber, when the note and the alterations to our projet proposed by the British Plenipotentiaries were read, and we had some desultory conversation upon the subject. All the difficulties to the conclusion of a peace appear to be now so nearly removed, that my colleagues all considered it as certain. I think it myself probable. But unless we take it precisely as it is now offered, to which I strongly incline, I distrust so much the intentions of the British Government, that I still consider the conclusion as doubtful and precarious.

It was agreed that we should meet at eleven o'clock to-morrow morning, and in the meantime that the note and projet should be taken successively by each of us, to make minutes for the reply to it. Mr. Gallatin suggested the propriety of asking a conference, to which I expressed some objection, but without insisting upon it. Mr. Bayard and Mr. Clay took the note and projet, and returned it to me with their minutes just before dinner. Mr. Gallatin took it this evening, with the promise to send it to me at six o'clock to-morrow morning.

28th. Mr. Gallatin's servant, Peter, brought me this morning, as the clock struck six, the British note and projet, with Mr. Gallatin's minutes upon them. I kept them until nine, made my own minutes upon them, and then sent all the papers, excepting my own minutes, which were of no importance, to Mr. Russell. As Mr. Gallatin understands the British projet, there are still some things in it so objectionable that they ought on no consideration to be admitted. At eleven o'clock we met, and continued in session until past four, when we adjourned to meet again at eleven to-morrow morning. Our principali discussion was on an article proposed by the British Government as a substitute for the eighth of our projet. And they have added a clause securing to them the navigation of the Mississippi, and access to it with their goods and merchandise through our territories.

To this part of the article Mr. Clay positively objected. Mr. Gallatin proposed to agree to it, proposing an article to secure our right of fishing and curing fish within the British jurisdiction. Mr. Clay lost his temper, as he generally does whenever this right of the British to navigate the Mississippi is discussed. He was utterly averse to admitting it as an equivalent for a stipulation securing the contested part of the fisheries. He said the more he heard of this the more convinced he was that it was of little or no value. He should be glad to get it if he could, but he was sure the British would not ultimately grant it. That the navigation of the Mississippi, on the other hand, was an object of immense importance, and he could see no sort of reason for granting it as an equivalent for the fisheries. Mr. Gallatin said that the fisheries were of great importance in the sentiment of the eastern section of the Union; that if we should sign a peace without securing them to the full extent in which they were enjoyed before the war, and especially if we should abandon any part of the territory, it would give a handle to the party there, now pushing for a separation from the Union and for a New England Confederacy, to say that the interests of New England were sacrificed, and to pretend that by a separate confederacy they could obtain what is refused to us.

Mr. Clay said that there was no use in attempting to conciliate people who never would be conciliated; that it was too much the practice of our Government to sacrifice the interests of its best friends for those of its bitterest enemies; that there might be a party for separation at some future day in the Western States, too.

I observed to him that he was now speaking under the impulse of passion, and that on such occasions I would wish not to answer anything; that assuredly the Government would be reproached, and the greatest advantage would be taken by the party opposed to it, if any of the rights of the Eastern States should be sacrificed by the peace; that the loss of any part of the fisheries would be a subject of triumph and exultation, both to the enemy and to those among us who had been opposed to the war; that if I should consent to give up even Moose Island, where there was a town which had been for many years regularly represented in the Legislature of the State of Massachusetts, I should be ashamed to show my face among my countrymen; that as to the British right of navigating the Mississippi, I considered it as nothing, considered as a grant from us. It was secured to them by the Peace of 1783, they had enjoyed it at the commencement of the war, it had never been injurious in the slightest degree to our own people, and it appeared to me that the British claim to it was just and equitable. The boundary fixed by the Peace of 1783 was a line due west from the Lake of the Woods to the Mississippi, and the navigation of the river was stipulated for both nations. It has been since that time discovered that a line due west from the Lake of the Woods will not touch the Mississippi, but goes north of it. The boundary, therefore, is annulled by the fact. Two things were contemplated by both parties in that compact – one, that the line should run west from the Lake of the Woods; the other, that it should touch the Mississippi. In attempting now to supply the defect, we ask for the line due west, and the British ask for the shortest line to the Mississippi. Both demands stand upon the same grounds – the intention of both parties at the Peace of 1783. If we grant the British demand, they touch the river and have a clear right to its navigation. If they grant our demand, they do not touch the river; but in conceding the territory they have a fair and substantial motive for reserving the right of navigating the river. I was not aware of any solid answer to this argument. I believed the right to this navigation to be a very useless thing to the British, especially after they have abandoned all pretence to any territorial possessions upon the river. But the national pride and honor were interested in it. The Government could not make a peace which would abandon it. They had the same reasons for insisting upon it that we had for insisting on the fisheries and the entire restoration of territory.

Mr. Clay said that by the British article now proposed they demanded not only the navigation of the river, but access to it through our territories generally, from any part of their dominions and by any road, and without any guard, even for the collection of our duties; that this might be an advantage to the people of Kentucky, for it was the shortest way to them for all imported merchandise. Goods could in that manner be sent by the St. Lawrence River from Europe to his house with a land carriage of not more than fourteen miles. But it would give the British access to our country in a dangerous and pernicious manner. It would give them the trade with the Indians in its full extent, and enable them to use all the influence over those savages which had already done us so much harm.

I observed that with regard to the trade with the Indians, I had no doubt the British Government meant and understood that to be already conceded in the article to which we had agreed; that I understood it so myself; that by restoring to the Indians all the rights they had in 1811, we had restored to them the right of trading with the British, and of having the British traders go among them for the purposes of trade; that if there could at any time have been a doubt that such would be its operation, the explanatory article after Mr. Jay's treaty and the Greenville Indian Treaty would remove it. How could we possibly be said to restore to the Indians the right of trade, if we debarred those who carried it on from trading with them? As to the duties, undoubtedly provision must be. Made for collecting them, and no doubt that would be agreed to.

Mr. Gallatin declared himself of the same opinion with me, as to the grant of the mere right of the navigation of the Mississippi; but he asked me why I had then hesitated so much about offering it as an equivalent for the fisheries.

Mr. Clay, on the other hand, thought there would be a gross inconsistency in asking a specific stipulation for the fisheries, after the ground we had taken, that no article was necessary to secure us in the enjoyment of them.

I said that my reluctance at granting the navigation of the Mississippi arose merely from the extreme interest that Mr. Clay and the Western people attached to it; that as to the ground we had taken upon the fisheries, I believed it firm and solid. I had put my name to it, and considered myself as responsible for it. But when some of my colleagues, who had also put their names to it, told me, in this chamber, among ourselves, that they thought the ground untenable, and that there was nothing in our principle, I found it necessary to mistrust my own judgment, particularly after the enemy had given us notice that they meant to deprive us of the fisheries in part, unless a new stipulation should secure them. If our principle was good for the fisheries on our part, it was good to the British for the navigation of the Mississippi. The Plenipotentiaries had made no reply to our remarks concerning the fisheries. That silence might be taken for acquiescence, and if there was nothing more I would rest it upon that. But they asked for a new stipulation of their right to navigate the Mississippi. This implied their opinion that they had lost the right as agreed to in the Treaty of 1783. It became necessary, therefore, for us to ask a similar stipulation for the fisheries within their jurisdiction; but I would not accept it even for the rights of fishing on the banks. I would not sign a treaty containing such a stipulation; for it would be a sort of admission that the right would be liable to forfeiture by every war we might have with Great

Britain. I would not take, therefore, a stipulation for anything recognized in the Treaty of Peace as a right.

No more (said Mr. Gallatin) than an article acknowledging again our independence.

I said, Certainly.

Mr. Bayard thought there was a material difference between the rights secured by the Peace of 1783 to us, and the British right of navigating the Mississippi, in the same treaty. The rights recognized as belonging to us were certainly permanent, and not to be forfeited by a subsequent war. But we had nothing to grant. We recognized no new rights to the British. The Mississippi was not then ours to grant; it was held by Spain, and the aspect of the subject was entirely changed by our subsequent acquisition of Louisiana. Our argument for the fisheries might therefore be sound, and yet not apply to the British for the navigation of the Mississippi.

It became necessary to determine by a vote whether Mr. Gallatin's proposal to offer an article making the navigation an equivalent for the fisheries should be adopted, and it was determined that it should. At the meeting to-morrow he is to produce it, and the draft of a note to the British Plenipotentiaries.

29th. I had barely time to finish my letter to my wife, to go by this day's post, when the meeting of the mission began. Mr. Gallatin had prepared his draft of a note to the British Plenipotentiaries, closing with the request for a conference, and his proposed article offering the navigation of the Mississippi as an equivalent for the fisheries within the British jurisdiction. This renewed our discussion of the whole subject, but it was now on all sides good-humored. I had some doubt whether it would be perfectly safe to ask a conference, while we were so far from being agreed among ourselves. Mr. Clay said he could put the subject of the Mississippi navigation upon principles to which it was impossible we should not all agree. I said that nothing like that had been apparent from our discussion hitherto; that he certainly would not be willing that I should be the spokesman of his sentiments, and I did not think it likely that he would very accurately express mine.

He said he did not think there was so irreconcilable a difference in the structure of our minds; and that it was remarkable there was so exact a coincidence of views on this point between persons at a great distance from each other as there was between Mr. Crawford and him. Mr. Russell had received a letter from Mr. Crawford, in which he had urged in very strong terms objections against granting the navigation of the Mississippi as an equivalent for the fisheries, and had used the same arguments against it as those he had adduced.

Mr. Gallatin brought us all to unison again by a joke. He said he perceived that Mr. Adams cared nothing at all about the navigation of the Mississippi, and thought of nothing but the fisheries. Mr. Clay cared nothing at all about the fisheries, and thought of nothing but the Mississippi. The East was perfectly willing to sacrifice the West, and the West was equally ready to sacrifice the East. Now, he was a Western man, and would give the navigation of the river for the fisheries. Mr. Russell was an Eastern man, and was ready to do the same.

I then told Mr. Clay that I would make a coalition with him of the East and West. If the British would not give us the fisheries, I would join him in refusing to grant them the navigation of the river.

He said that the consequence of our making the offer would be that we should lose both.

Upon the rest of Mr. Gallatin's draft there was no difference of opinion, and little discussion. It was admitted that if the navigation of the river was granted, and access to it through our territories, provision must be made for collecting the duties, and their access must be limited to particular points of departure and a mere road. Or if general access, like that which they demand, should be granted, they ought to grant in return to our people access through their territories to the St. Lawrence, and the navigation of that river. I then suggested that I wished to make an addition of one or two paragraphs to Mr. Gallatin's draft of a note, the object of which would be to show our sense of the importance of the concessions we had made, and intimating our determination to make no cession of territory, and to sacrifice none of the rights or liberties which we enjoyed at the commencement of the war. There was an adjournment from two to three o'clock, for me to make the draft of the additional paragraphs that I proposed. I had them ready at the adjourned meeting. They were read arid discussed until past four, our dinner-time. It was finally concluded to meet again to-morrow morning, at eleven, and in the meantime that all my colleagues should successively revise my draft.

JOHN QUINCY ADAMS (GHENT) TO LOUISA CATHERINE ADAMS, JANUARY 3, 1815

The peace negotiations behind him, John Quincy offered his considered judgment on the outcome: "We obtained nothing but peace, and we have made great sacrifices to obtain it. But our honor remains unsullied; our territory remains entire. The peace in word and indeed has been made upon terms of perfect reciprocity, and we have surrendered no one right or pretension of our country. This is the fair side of the treaty. Its darkest shade is that it has settled no one subject of dispute between the two nations. It has left open, not only all the controversies which had produced the war; but others not less important which have arisen from the war itself. The treaty would more properly be called an unlimited armistice than a peace ..."

You perceive that I dwell with delight upon the contemplation of the peace; not that the treaty has been satisfactory to me, or that I flatter myself it will be satisfactory to my country. For the justification of the American negotiators, the present relative situation of the two parties to the war, and the state in which the European pacification had left the world, must be duly weighed. We have obtained nothing but peace, and we have made great sacrifices to obtain it. But our honor remains unsullied; our territory remains entire. The peace in word and in deed has been made upon terms of *perfect reciprocity*, and we have surrendered no one right or pretension of our country. This is the fair side of the treaty. Its darkest shade is that it has settled no one subject of dispute between the two nations. It has left open, not only all the controversies which had produced the war; but others not less important which have arisen from the war itself. The treaty would more properly be called an unlimited armistice than a peace, and the day we agreed to sign it, I told my colleagues that it would immortalize the negotiators on both sides, as a masterpiece of diplomacy, by the address with which it avoided the adjustment of any one dispute that had ever existed between the parties. Certain it is, that no other than such a peace could have been made.

We have felt some curiosity to know how the peace would be received in England. Mr. Baker arrived, as we had expected, on Monday the 26th, about two in the afternoon, at London. But owing to the accident which had happened to him on the way between this place and Ostend, he was not the first to announce the news. The stock jobbers (and probably Bentzon) were before him. There had been a report on Saturday that the peace was signed; but on Monday about noon it was circulated as a certainty. The *Courier* of that day in one paragraph mentioned it, and adds that the business done upon the Stock Exchange was immense. The funds rose nearly one per cent. But the government had no information of the event. Then in a second edition, dated 4 o'clock, is another paragraph stating by authority from government that the peace had been signed on Saturday the 24th. We have not yet seen any *Courier* or *Chronicle* of a later date, but Mr. Goulburn was kind enough to bring me yesterday the *Times* down to Friday last, the 30th. It has abated none of its virulence against America. In announcing on the 27th the "fatal intelligence" of the treaty, it calls upon the nation to rise unanimously and address the Regent against its ratification. It continues every day to Friday pouring forth its lamentations and its execrations;

and when despairing of the perfidy that it had recommended, of a refusal to ratify, still resting upon a savage hope that before the ratification can take place in America, the British will take care to inflict some signal stroke of vengeance to redeem their reputation. It states that after the first day of the peace's being known, there was a depression instead of a rise of the funds; and attributes it to an universal belief that the state of affairs at Vienna rendered the prospect of a new European war inevitable, as nothing else could possibly have induced the cabinet to conclude such a peace. This reasoning is probably not altogether unfounded....

We broke up our establishment at the Hotel Lovendeghem, Rue des Champs, last Friday.... Yesterday Lord Gambier and Dr. Adams left the city for London. We dined with General Alten and a large party of English and Hanoverian officers. In the evening we went to the concert and redoute parée. It was excessively crowded and the music of the concert was adapted to the celebration of the peace. At one end of the hall there was a transparent inscription: HARMONIE / entre ALBION et COLUMBIA / PAIX de GAND / conclue XXIV Decembre. God save the King and Hail Columbia were part of the performances. The hall was extremely crowded with company, and the notes of peace gave a double delight to the pleasures of the song and the dance....

The anecdote about Decatur is excellent; but I am not sure that it was not too severe upon Carden. But the trick the English actors played upon us, and that I told you of, was a match for it – taking our money, asking our *patronage*, and then singing,

> O Lord our God arise
> Scatter his enemies
> before our faces....

I presume you will be presented to the Empress mother (and to the Empress if she returns), but let it only be for an *absence* to join me – not a final leave, because I am not yet recalled. If you have an opportunity at the audience, tell their Majesties that I expect to be recalled, and if I should be, how infinitely I shall regret not having it in my power to take leave of them in person, and how ineffaceable the remembrance I shall ever retain of their gracious condescension to us, while at their court.

JOHN QUINCY ADAMS (PARIS) TO PETER PAUL FRANCIS DE GRAND, APRIL 28, 1815

Prior to the signing of the Treaty of Ghent, John Quincy had feared that peace without honor would severely damage the national character and lead to future war. But in light of "the most glorious triumphs" of the past year – notably, the Battle of Plattsburgh and the defense of Baltimore – he thought that character vindicated. "Our naval heroes from the commencement of the war had maintained and increased the honor of the nation, but the campaign of 1814 was necessary to restore the credit of our reputation for the conduct of war upon the land. The effect of the war had been to raise our national character in the opinion of Europe, and I hope it will have the consequence of raising us in the British nation and government; that it will convince them that we are not to be trampled upon with impunity; that, dearly as we love peace, the experiment of kicking us into war is not a safe one; and that it is a far wiser policy in them not to drive us to extremities which may be essential, but which cannot fail to bring forth energies which they might flatter themselves we did not possess so long as they should suffer them to lie dormant."

DEAR SIR:

I received at Ghent on the 24 November last your favor of 16 October preceding. I was on the 27th writing an answer to it and, as there was until then no prospect that the negotiation upon which we were engaged would terminate in the conclusion of a peace, I was descanting upon the manner in which the British were waging war in America, and upon the course which their government were pursuing in their transaction with us, in a temper which the topics touched upon in your letter and the excitement of the outrage at Washington, as well as of the treatment we had ourselves experienced, had not been calculated to render very amicable. While I was writing, and before I had finished my letter, a communication was brought to me from the British plenipotentiaries. It was their note of 26 November, which I presume has been published among the documents of the negotiation in America. It was the first opening to the expectation that the British government would eventually accede to our terms – the first dawn of peace that had arisen to our hopes. It produced so immediate an effect upon my disposition that I could not finish my letter to you in the spirit with which it had been commenced. I laid it aside, and as my confidence in the new pacific appearances was not very strong, reserved it for conclusion in case it should ultimately prove to be desirable. The state of uncertainty between hope and distrust continued until the 23rd of December, and on the 24th we signed the treaty. My fragment of a letter to you became then altogether unseasonable. An immediate pressure of official duty then succeeded which left us not a moment for that of our private correspondence. I remained at Ghent for a month subsequent to the conclusion of the treaty, and then came to this city where I am waiting for orders from the government of the United States. Here I received a few days since your favors of 5 and 6 of March, with a duplicate of that of 16 October. They were brought by Mr. Copeland. During the continuance of the war the predominating sentiment of my mind was of regret that it existed. The situation in which we were left by the sudden and wonderful turn of affairs in Europe was so full of danger, and the support given to our enemy by the disaffection of so large a portion of our own countrymen was so disheartening, that, highly as I always estimated the general character of the nation, there were moments when I almost despaired of our issuing honorably from the war. When by the most extraordinary concurrence of circumstances Britain became the mistress of Europe, and, at peace with all the rest of the world, pointed the whole force of her empire against us, the most sanguine temper could not have anticipated that precisely then would be the period of our most glorious triumphs. Our naval heroes from the commencement of the war had maintained and increased the honor of the nation, but the campaign of 1814 was necessary to restore the credit of our reputation for the conduct of war upon the land. The effect of the war had been to raise our national character in the opinion of Europe, and I hope it will have the consequence of raising us in the British nation and government; that it will convince them that we are not to be trampled upon with impunity; that, dearly as we love peace, the experiment of *kicking* us into war is not a safe one; and that it is a far wiser policy in them not to drive us to extremities which may be essential, but which cannot fail to bring forth energies which they might flatter themselves we did not possess so long as they should suffer them to lie dormant. Most seriously do I wish that the result of the war may also be instructive to ourselves; that the confidence in our own vigor and resources which its issue is calculated to inspire may be tempered by the full and serious consideration of the deficiencies that it has disclosed; that it will teach us to cherish the defensive strength of a respectable navy, to persevere in the encouragement of our domestic manufactures; that it will lead us to a more vigorous and independent system of finance; and, above all, that it will teach those among us who in the time of the distresses of their country have taken a pride in hanging as a dead weight upon its councils, who have refused their aid to its exertions and have denied even their gratitude and applause to the valiant achievement of its defenders, that they have equally mistaken the true path of honor and patriotism. They have now full leisure to reflect that without their assistance, without even the trifling boon of their applause, in spite of all their opposition, in spite of their utmost ill-will, and in spite almost of their treason, the nation has issued in face of the whole world in face of its enemy and with its own conscious satisfaction honorably from the war. Their prejudices are indeed so inveterate, their self-conceit is so arrogant, and their views of public affairs are so contracted, that I have little expectation of ever seeing them converted from the error of their ways. I trust, however, that they will find it more difficult than ever to convince the country that all the talents or all the integrity of the nation are in their hands. I perceive in the newspaper brought by Mr. Copeland that some feeble efforts were making by their wise and virtuous party to damp the general joy at the ratification of the treaty, by representing it as a disadvantageous one to us. These efforts are however much more insignificant than I had expected they would be. It is so unusual to find either candor, consistency, or even decency, in the spirit of party, that I fully reckoned upon seeing the same persons, who had been loading the federal presses with groans and execrations at our rejecting the terms first proposed by the British commissioners, turn against the peace itself the moment after it should be published, and proclaim it the disgrace of the nation. I was even far from hoping that the treaty would be unanimously ratified by the Senate. The federal members of that body have done honor to themselves by rising on that occasion above the suggestions of party feelings, and have left them to rankle only in the state legislature of Massachusetts and the gazettes. The Hartford Convention probably did not realize the hopes or expectations of those by whom it was convoked. From the apologetic manner in which its proceedings are defended by one of its members upon his return, it would seem not to have given satisfaction to its own partisans. The commission afterwards sent by the Massachusetts legislature to propose that the resources of the general government should be placed at the disposal of that of the state was unlucky in arriving at Washington just in time to meet the ratification of the peace. But the precedent may be laid up for a more propitious time. The peace of Ghent, it is to be hoped, will be longer lived than that of Europe, settled by the treaty of Paris on the 30th May, 1814, and which the Congress of Vienna has been dancing all the last winter to consolidate as the basis of the permanent tranquillity of Europe. They had previously by a solemn treaty constituted Napoleon Buonaparte Emperor of the island of Elba. On the first of March last, Louis le Desiré was quietly seated upon his throne in the 20th year of his reign by divine right, and in the first year by the bayonets of the allied armies. The Emperor of Elba lands in France with eleven hundred men and four pieces of cannon. On the twentieth day after his landing he takes possession of the palace of the Tuileries, after a triumphant and unresisted march of two hundred leagues. Louis le Desiré, who had proclaimed the Emperor of Elba a traitor and rebel, and commanded him to be shot without a trial by any court martial that should catch him, escapes only by a rapid flight beyond the French territory from being his prisoner. The Duke of Bourbon capitulates for permission to escape from the Vendeé, the Duchess of Angoulême from Bordeaux, and the Duke of Angouleme, after attempting resistance a few days, becomes actually the Emperor of Elba's prisoner, and obtains only from his clemency the permission to quit the country. In the meantime the high allies at Vienna solemnly declared that the Emperor of Elba, constituted by themselves, had no longer any legal right to existence, because he had broken the treaty; that there could be neither peace nor truce with him, and that he had delivered himself up to the public vengeance. They have since bound themselves to wage a new joint war, professedly for the sole purpose of accomplishing his destruction; they have refused to listen to his entreaties for peace, and have solemnly stipulated never to treat with him or with any person in his name. This war is now on the eve of blazing. I cannot undertake to foretell its result....

CHAPTER SEVEN

MINISTER TO ENGLAND, 1815–1817

INTRODUCTION

Wɪᴛʜ ᴛʜᴇ ᴘᴇᴀᴄᴇ ɴᴇɢᴏᴛɪᴀᴛɪᴏɴꜱ at Ghent completed, John Quincy traveled to Paris to await further orders from Washington – presumably to assume the post of minister to England, although that appointment might depend on the treaty's fate in the US Senate and with the public. There need have been no concern on that score. Andrew Jackson's victory in the Battle of New Orleans in January 1815, before the news of the agreement arrived in America, stirred the national spirit. The Hartford Convention, called by Federalist leaders to encourage the dissolution of the Union (at least so John Quincy feared), faded into insignificance. The Senate unanimously offered its consent to the Treaty of Ghent. John Quincy received his new commission on May 7, 1815.

It was now up to the new minister to England to untangle the matters left unsettled by the Treaty of Ghent. These included the following: negotiating a new treaty of commerce, ideally covering neutral and belligerent rights and impressment; the possible regulation of naval forces on the Great Lakes; the resolution of border and territorial issues; the status of the fisheries; compensation for slaves who escaped to, or were taken by, British forces during the war; and abolition of the slave trade.

John Quincy's basic goal during his ministry was to bring about a degree of reconciliation between the two English-speaking peoples, one that would be at least sufficient to avoid another unnecessary war. He thought that most of the British aristocratic class was still unreconciled to American independence, and that the political system remained corrupt, despite the theoretical beauty of the English constitution. But intelligent men in government, like Lord Castlereagh, the foreign secretary, might be persuaded that reconciliation was in Britain's interest, given all the uncertainties on the continent.

In 1816, John Quincy received instructions from Washington to attempt to negotiate a comprehensive treaty of commerce that would address the outstanding issues between the two countries. The treaty would allow reciprocal trade rights between the United States and the British West Indies and British North America, without discrimination, set out an agreement on the impressment issue, define neutral and belligerent rights, and provide for arbitration by a friendly sovereign of compensation for slaves taken by British forces after the ratification of the Treaty of Ghent. John Quincy recommended to Washington against trying to address the issues piecemeal, as he felt that the British would merely put him off.

Additionally, there were a number of loose ends to be tied up related to the cessation of hostilities and the implementation of the Treaty of Ghent. On instructions from Monroe, John Quincy proposed an agreement to mutually reduce armaments on the Great Lakes, preferably to zero, except for vessels necessary to enforce revenue laws. A freshwater arms race, John Quincy argued, suited neither side's interest. Castlereagh responded that his government would take the proposal under advisement but he personally doubted its efficacy. When it came to the security of Canada, he told John Quincy, the United States possessed all the advantages of geography – which, in his opinion, would have been fairly balanced by the creation of an Indian barrier state, as the British had proposed at Ghent. In the end, Castlereagh requested that such negotiations be transferred to Washington. The surprising result was the Rush-Bagot Agreement of 1817, which essentially accepted the American proposal.

Regarding fisheries, John Quincy insisted that the right and the liberty to fish were parts of the division of British North America codified (so to speak) in the Treaty of Paris, and were integral to American independence. The British dropped their position on the American right to fish in international waters off the Canadian coast, and they indicated a willingness to negotiate a modified renewal of the liberties. Castlereagh again preferred that the talks be held in Washington. Meanwhile, London indicated it would grant access on a year-to-year basis. John Quincy's task was to hold the British at least to that standard.

The first article of the Treaty of Ghent required both sides to restore all captured territory, places, and possessions, including "Slaves or other private property." The British took the position that this applied only to slaves in British garrisons after the end of the war, not to those aboard British ships (or, the Americans claimed, to those who had been sold by Royal Navy officers to slave masters in the British West Indies). John Quincy, under instructions from Washington, insisted on the return of, or compensation for, all slaves, especially those taken or held by the British in violation of the Treaty of Ghent. After much back and forth, the two sides agreed to have the matter arbitrated by a third party (who turned out to be Emperor Alexander I of Russia). After probing by the prime minister, Lord Liverpool, John Quincy acknowledged the difference between an inanimate object and a human being, but he contended that the treaty for this purpose had treated them both as property, and that the British delegates at Ghent had accepted this.

The matter of slavery came up again when, in August 1816, Castlereagh told John Quincy that in light of provocations by the dey of Algiers, he had ordered the fleet under Lord Exmouth to insist on a treaty with the dey that would free Christian slaves and stop the practice of enslaving Europeans. John Quincy enthusiastically supported such actions, as well as those designed to stop piracy and the practice of paying tribute (although he had to deal with the potential diplomatic tangles of conflicts between British and American treaties with the Barbary regencies). His own nation was technically at war with Algeria – the dey had rejected a treaty of peace with the United States negotiated the previous July. Castlereagh added that he thought there should be international cooperation to enforce standards of civilization on the Barbary regencies. John Quincy expressed his opinion that the United States would readily participate in such actions, although he privately wished America would do so on its own, to its greater glory.

Castlereagh made no proposal for the United States to participate in such an international coalition against the slave trade, and John Quincy did not suggest that the United States would do so. The matter took on a different light for John Quincy during a discussion with William Wilberforce, an influential member of parliament and an advocate for the abolition of slavery in Britain's overseas possessions. Wilberforce proposed that the United States and other maritime nations agree to allow the Royal Navy to stop and search ships suspected of engaging in the slave traffic. John Quincy raised a number of practical objections – but above all, it struck him as a backdoor way to get the United States to accept the right of the British to visit and search American vessels, and thus an acceptance of impressment.

Throughout his tenure, John Quincy continued to send intelligence assessments to Washington about developments in Europe that would affect his country. For now, the partial revival of France had stabilized a balance on the continent. He reported that Castlereagh had offered assurances that Britain had not acquired Florida from Spain, contrary to rumors, and that it did not intend to acquire new territory in the Americas – unless, for defensive purposes, it had to resist American aggrandizement. John Quincy was deeply alarmed by reports that some Americans were urging intervention on behalf of the Spanish American insurgencies against Spanish rule. He wrote to his government and colleagues to warn that war with Spain would mean another war with Britain, to be avoided at all costs save that of the national honor – which was not then at stake.

In April 1817, John Quincy received notice from Washington of his recall – and his appointment as secretary of state by the new president, James Monroe. He took the oath of office as secretary of state on September 22, 1817. His selection by President Monroe reflected in part a recognition of John Quincy's unquestioned qualifications as a diplomat. His overseas career culminated with the leading position on the American commission that negotiated the treaty ending the War of 1812, and his subsequent service as minister to Britain. But, as always, politics played a role in such matters. Given the jealousies raised by the domination of Virginians in the presidency, Monroe explained to Thomas Jefferson, "I have thought it advisable to select a person from the eastern states, in consequence of which my attention has been turned to Mr. Adams, who by his age, long experience in our foreign affairs, and adoption into the republican party, seems to have superior pretensions to any there."[1]

JOHN QUINCY ADAMS (LONDON) TO SECRETARY OF STATE JAMES MONROE, JUNE 23, 1815

John Quincy summarizes the first meeting between two of the titans of nineteenth-century diplomacy. He offered assurances to Castlereagh that the United States was committed to peaceful relations and to meeting all its obligations under the Treaty of Ghent. He reviewed the status of several outstanding issues (although not the fisheries), especially impressment. The United States would not go to war over an abstract principle, as long as the principle was not abandoned and practical accommodations could be reached.

SIR:

I gave immediate notice of my appointment and of my arrival to Lord Castlereagh, the principal Secretary of State for the Department of Foreign Affairs, and requested an interview with him, for which he appointed Monday the 29th ultimo. I then delivered to him a copy of the credential letter to the Prince Regent, who afterwards appointed the 8th of this month, a levee day, to receive it. Lord Castlereagh had intimated to me that if I desired it, a private audience at an earlier day would be granted to me by the Prince to receive the letter of credence, but I did not consider it to be necessary. On the day of the levee Mr. Chester, the assistant Master of the Ceremonies, enquired of me whether I had a letter for the Queen. I informed him that I had not.

He said that such a letter was usual though not indispensable; that it was generally given by courts where there were family connections with this court, and had always been sent by the Republic of Holland. That an audience however would be granted to me by the Queen when she could come to town.

At the meeting with Lord Castlereagh I had some loose conversation with him on the subjects mentioned in your instructions of 13 March, and on some others which had arisen from certain occurrences here.

I stated to him that the first object to which my attention was directed in the instructions which I had received from the American government, was the means of preserving the peace which had been so happily restored; that I was authorized to give the most positive assurances that the United States would perform with strict fidelity the engagements contracted on their part, and I presented as tokens of a disposition to proceed still further in the adoption of measures of a conciliatory nature towards Great Britain, the act of Congress for the repeal of the discriminating duties, and the message of the President recommending to Congress the adoption of measures for confining to American seamen the navigation of American vessels; and that although Congress, owing to the shortness of time, had not acted upon that message, its principles would probably be hereafter adopted. I promised to furnish him copies of these papers which I accordingly sent him the next morning.

He said that what had been done by the government of the United States with regard to seamen had given the greater satisfaction here, as an opinion, probably erroneous, had heretofore prevailed that the American government encouraged and invited the service of foreign seamen. That as to the principle he was afraid that there was little prospect of a possibility of coming to an agreement, as we adhered to the right of naturalization for which we contended, and as no government here could possibly abandon the right to the allegiance of British subjects.

I answered that I saw no better prospect than he did of an agreement upon the principle. But it was not the disposition of the American government or nation to apply the force of arms to the maintenance of any mere abstract principle. The number of British seamen naturalized in America was so small that it would be no object of concern to this government. If British subjects were excluded for the future, there could be no motive for taking men from American vessels. If the practice totally ceased, we should never call upon the British government for any sacrifice of their principle. When the evil ceased to be felt, we should readily deem it to have ceased to exist. He said that there would be every disposition in this government to guard against the possibility of abuse, and that the Admiralty was now occupied in prescribing regulations for the naval officers, which he hoped would prevent all cause of complaint on the part of the United States. He then mentioned the late unfortunate occurrence at Dartmoor prison, and the measures which had been taken by agreement between him and Messrs. Clay and Gallatin on that occasion. I said I had received a copy of the report made by Mr. King and Mr. Larpent after their examination into the transaction, and of the written depositions which had been taken as well on that examination as previously at the Coroner's inquest.

That after what had been done I considered the procedure as so far terminated that I was not aware of any further step to be taken by me until I should receive the instructions of my government on the case. From the general impression on my mind by the evidence that I had perused, I regretted that a regular trial of Captain Shortland had not been ordered, and I thought it probable that such would be the opinion of my government. He said that undoubtedly there were cases in which a trial was the best remedy to be resorted to, but there were others in which it was the worst; that a trial, the result of which should be an acquittal, would place the whole affair in a more unpleasant situation than it would be without it; that the evidence was extremely contradictory; that it had been found impossible to trace to any individual the most unjustifiable part of the firing, and that Captain Shortland denied having given the order to fire. I admitted that the evidence was contradictory, but said that from the impression of the whole mass of it upon me, I could not doubt, either that Captain Shortland gave the order to fire, or that under the circumstances of the case it was unnecessary. It was true the result of a trial might be an acquittal, but as it was the regular remedy for a case of this description, the substitution of any other was susceptible of strong objections, and left the officer apparently justified, where I could not but consider his conduct as altogether unjustifiable.

I mentioned the earnest desire of the American government for the full execution of the stipulations in the treaty of Ghent, and that my instructions had expressed the hope of an appointment as soon as possible of the commissioners on the part of this country for proceeding to the settlement of the boundaries. He asked what would be the most convenient season of the year for transacting this business. I said I believed it might be done at any season, but, as the line would be in a high northern latitude, the summer season would probably be most for the personal convenience of the commissioners. He said the appointments would be made with reference to that consideration. I further observed that the British Admiral stationed in the Chesapeake had declined restoring slaves that he had taken, under a construction of the first article of the treaty which the government of the United States considered erroneous, and which I presumed this government would likewise so consider; that a reference to the original draft of the British projet, and to an alteration proposed by us and assented to by the British plenipotentiaries, would immediately show the incorrectness of this construction.

He said he thought it would be best to refer this matter to the gentlemen who were authorized to confer with us on the subject of a treaty of commerce.

He asked me if Mr. Clay and Mr. Gallatin had communicated to me what had passed between them and this government on that head. I said they had. After inquiring whether I was joined in that commission, he said that the same person had been appointed to treat with us who had concluded with us the treaty of Ghent, and that Mr. Robinson, the Vice President of the Board of Trade, had been added to them. They had already had some conferences with Messrs. Clay and Gallatin, and their powers were now made out and ready for them to proceed in the negotiation.

On the 6th instant I received from Lord Castlereagh a note, informing me that the Prince Regent had appointed the Hon. Charles Bagot his Envoy Extraordinary and Minister Plenipotentiary to the United States. He was presented to the Prince upon his appointment at the levee on the same day that I had presented my credentials – a circumstance which was remarked by the Prince himself, doubtless with the intention that it should be understood as an evidence of the promptitude with which the British government was disposed to meet the friendly advances of our own. In delivering my credential letter to the Prince at the private audience previous to the levee, I had told him that I fulfilled the commands of my government in expressing the hope that it would be received as a token of the earnest desire of the President not only for the faithful and punctual observance of all our engagements contracted with Great Britain, but for the adoption of every other measure which might tend to consolidate the peace and friendship and to promote the harmony between the two nations.

The Prince answered me by the most explicit assurances of the friendly disposition of this government towards the United States, and of his own determination punctually to carry into execution all the engagements on the part of Great Britain.

I was requested by Morier, one of the Under Secretaries of State in the foreign department, to call at that office the day after the levee. I complied with that request. He inquired whether I thought there would be any objection on your part to the appointment of the same person as the British commissioner on the fourth and fifth articles of the treaty of Ghent. I said I did not anticipate any objection, especially as we should be under no obligation to appoint the same person upon the two commissions on our part. He told me that Colonel Barclay, having already been employed on the commission under the treaty of 1794, would be the commissioner on those two articles and would be attended by the same person who was also on that occasion employed as the surveyor. It was intended that they should go out in the July packet. Another person would be ap pointed the commissioner on the sixth article.

I have, etc.

JOHN QUINCY ADAMS (LONDON) TO SECRETARY OF STATE JAMES MONROE, AUGUST 22, 1815

John Quincy reports on an argument with the British prime minister, Lord Liverpool, over the construction of the Treaty of Ghent concerning the fate of American slaves in British possession at the end of the war. Liverpool argued that slaves, as human beings, should not be equated with private property. John Quincy agreed that that was true in the abstract but that that distinction was not made in the treaty. He tried to capture the moral high ground by accusing Royal Navy officers of selling those slaves to slave masters in the British West Indies.

SIR:

The subjects upon which I was induced to request an interview with the Earl of Liverpool were not confined to those upon which I had been favored with your instructions. I was desirous of ascertaining the intentions of the British government with regard to the period of time when the mutual abolition of the discriminating duties would take place. I had been informed by American merchants here that the extra duty of two pence sterling per pound upon cotton imported in American vessels, mentioned in the joint dispatch to you of 3 July last, had been and continued to be levied, although the act of Parliament by which it was raised as an extra duty had begun to operate only from two days after the signature of the convention. I took with me and left with Lord Liverpool copies of the act of Congress of 3 March last, concerning the repeal of the discriminating duties, and of the fifth article of the commercial convention. It was my opinion, and I told him I had so given it to the merchants who had asked me when the convention would take effect, that when ratified by both parties and the ratifications exchanged, its operation would be from the date of the signature, and that the government would be bound to refund any extra duties collected in the interval. He said that was unusual, which I admitted, observing that it was the unequivocal import of the words in which the article was drawn up. They deviated from the usual form of such articles, and the deviation was made at the proposal of the British plenipotentiaries, our projet having proposed that the convention should take effect as usual from the exchange of the ratifications. They had chosen to say that though binding only when the ratifications should be exchanged, yet it should then be binding for four years *from the date of the signature*. We had agreed to this alteration, and when the convention should be once ratified in the United States, any individual affected by it would be entitled to the benefit of a construction of its purport by the judicial authorities. He said it was the same here, and asked me if I had spoken on the subject to Mr. Robinson, the Vice President of the Board of Trade. I answered that I had, some weeks since, but Mr. Robinson had not then formed a decisive opinion upon the purport of the article. I added that when the convention was signed, we had understood from the British plenipotentiaries, and particularly from Mr. Robinson, that this extra duty upon cotton imported in our vessels would not be permitted to commence; that it would have been immediately removed by an Order in Council, which until the exchange of ratifications would stand instead of the convention. At all events, however, it was material to know what the construction of the article by this government would be as the operation in either case must be reciprocal. If it was understood here that the revocation of the discriminating duties would commence only from the exchange of the ratifications, the same principle must be observed in the United States, with which he fully agreed. He said they had taken an act of Parliament to enable the king in Council to regulate the trade with America, as had been done for some years after the peace of 1783. An Order of Council was to have been made out in consequence of the treaty. It had been for some time accidentally delayed, but might perhaps be ready to be signed at the Council to be held the next day. It was the disposition here to put all the amicable and conciliatory arrangements into operation as soon as possible, and the discriminating duties might be immediately removed, in the confidence that the same measures would be adopted on the part of the United States. I told him that Great Britain had already a pledge of that reciprocity by the act of Congress of the last session, so that the revocation might be accomplished at the pleasure of this government, even independent of the stipulation in the treaty.

Before we passed to another subject Lord Liverpool said that he thought it proper to mention to me that a note would be sent to Mr. Baker previous to the ratification of the convention respecting the island of St. Helena. That by a general agreement among the allies Bonaparte was to be transferred to be kept under custody in that island, and by a general regulation the ships of all nations, excepting those of their own East India Company, would be excluded from it. The circumstance which had led to the necessity of this measure had not been in contemplation when the convention was signed, and the measure itself would not be extended beyond the necessity by which it was occasioned. That it was authorized by the precedent of the convention which had been signed by Mr. King and himself in 1803, and which the American government had proposed to modify on the consideration that a subsequent treaty, containing the cession of Louisiana to the United States, had altered the situation of the parties, although unknown both to Mr. King and to him when they signed the convention. And that as the Cape of Good Hope would still be left for American vessels to touch at, he presumed the island of St. Helena would not be necessary to them for that purpose. I said I did not know that the stipulation with regard to the island of St. Helena was in itself of very material importance, but the American government might consider the principle as important. The stipulation was in express and positive terms and the island of St. Helena was identically named. The case referred to by him did not appear to me to apply as a precedent for two reasons. One was that the Louisiana convention had been signed before, and not as he thought after that signed by him and Mr. King, though it was true that neither he nor Mr. King knew that it has been signed. The other was that Great Britian had declined ratifying that convention upon the ground of the modification to it proposed by the American government in consequence of the change produced by the Louisiana convention. He said that at all events Mr. Baker would be instructed to present such a note, previous to the ratification by the American government. He had thought best to give me notice of it.

Referring then to the contents of my letter of the 9th instant to Lord Castlereagh which he had seen, I told him that having expected Mr. Bagot was on the eve of his departure, I had been anxious that he might go provided with instructions which might give satisfaction to the government of the United States with regard to the execution of two very important stipulations in the treaty of Ghent. He said that as to the surrender of Michillimackinac there could be no sort of difficulty. The orders for its evacuation had been long since given. It was merely the want of barracks for their troops that had occasioned a momentary delay, and he had no doubt the fort had been before this delivered up. There never had been for a moment the intention on the part of the British government to retain any place which they had stipulated to restore. But with respect to the slaves they certainly construed very differently from the American government the stipulation relating to them. They thought that applied only to the slaves in the forts and places, which having been taken during the war were to be restored at the peace. I said that independent of the construction of the sentence which so strongly marked the distinction between the artillery and public property, and slaves and private property, the process by which the article had been [framed] demonstrated beyond all question that a distinction between them was intended and understood by both parties. The first projet of the treaty had been presented by us. This had been required and even insisted upon by the British plenipotentiaries. The article was therefore drawn up by us, and our intention certainly was to secure the restoration both of the public and private property, including slaves which had been in any manner captured on shore during the war. The projet was returned to us with a limitation upon the restoration of property, whether public or private, to such as had been in the places when captured, and should remain there at the time of the evacuation. We assented to this so far as artillery and public property, which by the usages of war is liable to be taken and removed, but not with regard to private property and slaves, which we thought should at all events be restored because they ought never to be taken. We therefore proposed the transposition of the words as stated in my letter to Lord Castlereagh. The construction upon which the British commanders have carried away the slaves would annul the whole effect of the transposition of the words. Artillery and public property had of course been found, and could therefore be restored almost or quite exclusively in the *forts* or places occupied by troops. But there was not perhaps a slave to carry away in all those which were occupied by the British when the treaty was concluded, and to confine the stipulation relating to slaves within the same limits as those agreed to with regard to public property would reduce them to a dead letter. He said that perhaps the British plenipotentiaries had agreed to the transposition of the words there at Ghent without referring to the government here, and that although the intentions of the parties might be developed by reference to the course of the negotiations, yet the ultimate construction must be upon the words of the treaty as they stood. He would see Mr. Goulburn and inquire of him how they understood this transposition; but certainly for himself, and he could speak for the whole government here, he had considered them as only promising not to carry slaves from the places which were occupied by their forces and which they were to evacuate. There were perhaps few or no slaves in the places then occupied by them, but there was a probability at the time when the treaty was signed that New Orleans and other parts of the Southern States might be in their possession at the time of the exchange of the ratifications. If they had understood the words to imply that persons who from whatever motive had taken refuge under the protection of the British forces should be delivered up to those who, to say the least, must feel unkindly towards them and might treat them harshly, they should have objected to it. Something also, he could not say what, would have been proposed. I said I had referred to the progress of the negotiation and the protocol of conferences only as confirming what I thought the evident purport of the words of the treaty. To speak in perfect candor I would not undertake to say that the British plenipotentiaries had taken a view of the subject different from that of their government. But certainly we had drawn up the article without any anticipation that New Orleans, or southern ports not then in their possession, would at the ratification of the treaty be occupied by them. Our intentions were to provide that no slaves should be carried away. We had no thought of disguising or concealing those intentions. Had the British plenipotentiaries asked of us an explanation of our proposal to transpose the words, we should instantly have given it. We evidently had an object in making the proposal, and we thought the words themselves fully disclosed it. Our object was the restoration of all property, including slaves, which by the usages of war among civilized nations ought not to have been taken. All private property on shore was of that description. It was entitled by the laws of war to exemption from capture. Slaves were private property. Lord Liverpool said that he thought they could not be considered precisely under the general denomination of private property. A table or chair for instance might be taken and restored without changing its condition; but a living and a human being was entitled to other considerations. I replied that the treaty had marked no such distinction. The words implicitly recognized slaves as private property – in the article alluded to, "slaves or *other* private property." Not that I meant to deny the principle assumed by him. Most certainly a living sentient being, and still more a human being, was to be regarded in a different light from the inanimate matter of which other private property might consist, and if on the ground of that difference the British plenipotentiaries had objected to restore the one while consenting to restore the other, we should readily have discussed the subject. We might have accepted or objected to the proposal they would have made. But what could that proposal have been? Upon what ground could Great Britain have refused to restore them? Was it because they had been seduced away from their masters by the promises of British officers? But had they taken New Orleans, or any other Southern city, would not all the slaves in it have had as much claim to the benefit of such promises, as the fugitives from their masters elsewhere? How then could the place, if it had been taken, have been evacuated according to the treaty, without carrying away any slaves, if the pledge of such promises was to protect them from being restored to their owners? It was true, proclamations inviting slaves to desert from their masters had been issued by British officers. We considered them as deviations from the usage of war. We believed that the British government itself would, when the hostile passions arising from the state of war should subside, consider them in the same light; that Great Britain would then be willing to restore the property, or to indemnify the sufferers by its loss. If she felt bound to make good the promises of her officers to the slaves, she might still be willing to do an act of justice by compensating the owners of the slaves for the property which had been irregularly taken from them. Without entering into a discussion which might have been at once unprofitable and irritating, she might consider this engagement only as a promise to pay to the owners of the slaves the value of those of them which might be carried away. Lord Liverpool manifested no dissatisfaction at these remarks, nor did he attempt to justify the proclamation to which I particularly alluded. I added that there was a branch of the same subject upon which I had not written to Lord Castlereagh, because involving considerations of a very delicate nature. I had thought it might be treated more confidentially by verbal conferences than by written communications which would be liable to publication. During the war it had been stated in a letter of instructions from the American Secretary of State to the negotiators of the Ghent treaty, that some of the slaves enticed from their masters by promises of freedom from British officers had afterwards been sold in the West Indies. This letter of instructions had afterwards been published. "Yes," said Lord Liverpool, and I believe some explanation of it has been asked." I said there had; first by the British plenipotentiaries at Ghent, and afterwards by Admiral Cochrane of the American Secretary of State. He had answered this last application by a letter to Mr. Baker, which His Lordship had doubtless seen. But I had been authorized to say that in making this charge in the midst of the war, the American government had not expected, and was not desirous, that it should lead to discussions to be protracted to a time and in a state of peace. They believed that evidence to substantiate in some degree the charge was obtainable, but would prefer if the British government wished to obtain it, they should seek it from other sources, many of which were more accessible to them than to the government of the United States. The sales, if made, had been in British possessions and from British ships. These were of course entirely open to the investigation of inquiries under British authority. The proclamations had promised employment in the military service of Great Britain (which could apply only to men), or *free* settlement in the West Indies. But in fact numbers of women and children had been received and carried away as well as of men. The numbers of them, and in a very great degree the identical individuals that had been taken, might easily be ascertained in the United States, and I expected to be enabled to furnish accurate lists of them. If not sold, some provision must have been made for them at the charge of the British government itself. It could not be at a loss to know those whom it had to maintain. And as the whole subject had a tendency rather to irritation than to the conciliatory spirit which it was the wish of the American government to cultivate exclusively, they would prefer superseding the search and exhibition of evidence through them, and dropping any further communications as between the governments relating to it. I concluded, however, by observing that with this explanation I was directed to say that if the British government still desired evidence from that of the United States, they would furnish such as they could collect. He said that was certainly all that could be asked. The British officers had universally and very strenuously denied the charge, which, if true, deserved severe animadversion and punishment. The British government had believed, and still believed, the charge to have been without foundation, and in the deficiency of evidence could come to no other conclusion....

There is little prospect, as it would seem, of our obtaining any satisfaction with regard to the carrying away of the slaves. Lord Liverpool did not indeed attempt to support the construction upon which the naval commanders had acted in removing those that were on board their ships, but he insisted that they had never intended to stipulate for the restoration of those who had sought refuge under their protection. I therefore thought it indispensable to recur to the unjustifiable nature of the invitations by which the slaves had been induced to seek that refuge, and to infer from it the obligation of Great Britain to restore them or to indemnify their owners; to show that she was bound to know the extent of the stipulation to which she had agreed, and that she could not have proposed an exception founded upon any promises of her officers to the slaves, when those very promises were violations of the laws of war. I also took the opportunity to propose that with regard to the sale of some of those people by British officers in the West Indies, no further discussion might be had as between the governments. This proposal will, I am convinced, be accepted, if the evidence mentioned in your dispatch as to be hereafter transmitted should be conclusive to ascertain the fact. But the charge has been repeatedly made a subject of Parliamentary inquiry. It has touched a sinew in which the nation is peculiarly sensitive at this time. You will observe that Lord Liverpool strongly expressed the disbelief of the fact of this government, and that disbelief will continue until the existence of evidence possessed by us to prove it shall be known. I think it will not then be called for.

I am, etc.

JOHN QUINCY ADAMS (LONDON) TO JOSEPH HALL, SEPTEMBER 9, 1815

John Quincy reflects on the lessons of the war, and on the type of national security structure needed in the future to preserve the peace and, if necessary, defend the nation. "Let us inquire how much we suffered by want of adequate preparation for war before it was undertaken; how much for the want of a more efficient naval force; how much by the miserable composition of our army; how much by an unreasonable reliance upon militia soldiers and militia officers; how much by an undigested and unsuitable system of finances; and, above all, how much by disaffection, by disunion, by an inveterate and unprincipled spirit of faction."

DEAR SIR:

Our old friend Dr. Eustis upon his arrival at the Hague forwarded to me your favor of 8th June last, which I received with great satisfaction. You have estimated too favorably the services of the American negotiators of the treaty of Ghent: and if the party to which you refer had not ruined its own credit by snapping like gulls at the British *sine qua non*: could they have seen, to use a vulgar expression, far enough before their noses to perceive that they would soon have to thrust their stings, not against the war but against the peace, they would have been adversaries far more formidable than they have proved themselves. After abusing us for not accepting the *sine qua non*, they to be sure had left themselves nothing to say when the peace came, and accordingly their arguments against the peace have proved nothing but their own inconsistency. It is something too despicable for ridicule itself to pretend, like Governor Strong, that because we have failed in one struggle to shake off forever the galling yoke of the press-gang, we are therefore precluded from ever struggling to shake it off again. But true, and lamentably true, it is that in the late war our struggle to shake it off did fail. True it is that the peace of Ghent was in its nature and character a truce rather than a peace. Neither party gave up anything; all the points of collision between them which had subsisted before the war were left open. New ones opened by the war itself were left to close again after the peace. Nothing was adjusted, nothing was settled – nothing in substance but an indefinite suspension of hostilities was agreed to. For my own part, far from claiming any credit for the conclusion of the peace, my own deliberate opinion was, and is, that the American plenipotentiaries needed all candor and all the indulgence of their country for having put their signatures to such a treaty. That the very peculiar circumstances of the times, the commanding attitude which Great Britain had acquired in Europe, the removal of the principal cause of war by the general European pacification, the disordered and almost desperate situation of our finances, and, above all, our intestine divisions imminently threatening the complication of a civil with the foreign war, with a formal and avowed confederacy of five states to dissolve the union; that all this was in candor to be taken into consideration when the conduct was to be estimated of the American negotiators in signing the treaty. I believed that with all these things duly weighed, they would stand acquitted in the face of their country and of the world. And when all the particulars of the negotiation should be known I believed they would deserve the credit of having faithfully done their duty. When the wise men of the east were loading the Boston newspapers with dissertations to prove that the *sine qua non* was a fair and honorable and acceptable proposition, and with insults upon the ex-professor for rejecting it with disdain, they little thought that they were laboring with the most painful and ignominious industry to give to the ex-professor and his associates more credit than they deserved. It was lucky for us that the wise men in their simplicity so conspicuously divulged what they were willing to take for a fair and honorable peace. The misery of the wise men is that there is yet too much colonial blood flowing in their veins. The late Chief Justice, the progenitor of the Boston rebel, and even our magnanimous governor, you know were late and lukewarm *converts* in the first and great war for our national independence. They were willing enough to fall into "pursue the triumph and partake the gale;" but if such men had been the favorites and leaders of our country at the trying period of our Revolution, the studies of our children at the university might have terminated in loyal epithalamiums upon the marriage of the Princess Charlotte of Wales. When the

American plenipotentiaries at Ghent rejected the *sine qua non*, there was not one of them who thought himself entitled to any credit for it as for an act of individual firmness; all knew that we could not accept it. We all knew that if we should accept it, we should only cover ourselves with infamy, and that the treaty would be rejected by our own government. The path was too plain to be mistaken. Not one of us hesitated an instant, nor would it have been possible for any other men representing the United States in the same situation to have done otherwise. The Boston rebel in our situation would have done as we did. And as to any advantage in argument which we may have had over the British plenipotentiaries in that negotiation, we could in truth as little pretend to merit in that as for spurning at the *sine qua non*. They were men of sound understanding, but they were little more than a medium of communication between us and the British Privy Council. Now that body, like all the other governments of Europe, is accustomed to reason so little and so much to force, that a victory over them of mere logic is as easy as it is insignificant. The weakness of the intellectual weapons with which American public ministers have to contend is almost as mortifying as the utter inefficacy of the most irrefragable arguments advanced by them. The statesmen of Europe seldom take the trouble to use reasoning, and when they do the success of their cause may be generally considered as desperate. If the notes of the British plenipotentiaries at Ghent were scarcely worthy of refutation, it was because reason had been sacrificed for a supposed expediency at the laying of the basis of the negotiation. That basis was laid not upon reason or argument, but upon the expeditions to Plattsburg and New Orleans. It was not to Lord Gambier, H. Goulburn and Dr. Adams that they looked for success, but to Sir George Prevost, and Sir James Yeo, and Ross, and Cockburn, to Cochrane and Pakenham.

The result of the late war has been to raise the American character in the estimation of Europe. But let us not be elated by it; let us look back to it, not with an eye of vain and idle exultation at the successes with which it was checked, but with a regard anxiously provident of the future. Let us inquire how much we suffered by want of adequate preparation for war before it was undertaken; how much for the want of a more efficient naval force; how much by the miserable composition of our army; how much by an unreasonable reliance upon militia soldiers and militia officers; how much by an undigested and unsuitable system of finances; and, above all, how much by disaffection, by disunion, by an inveterate and unprincipled spirit of faction. Let us not be afraid or ashamed to look at our disasters – at sea we had our full share of misfortunes, but I think not a single instance of disgrace. Our triumphs there were the more precious, because they were all hardly and dearly bought. But on the land, if we might boast of some glorious, and be grateful for some fortunate achievements, for how many defects should we be called to confess, and for how many disgraces should we blush? It is true that our enemies were teaching us the practical art of which they themselves had learnt from the French. They found our countrymen apt scholars, and in two or more campaigns I have no doubt we should have swept them off from the continent of North America. But at the period when the war closed our improvement had manifested itself only in defensive warfare; and without detracting from the merit of our officers or men, we must attribute much of our success at Plattsburg to the victory on the lake, and something of that at New Orleans to good fortune – to the errors of the enemy, and to the casualty of their general's being killed. If the war had done us no other good than to disclose the talents and energy of such men as Jackson, Brown, Scott, Macomb and Gaines, it would still have been great. It was winnowing the grain from the chaff; but should we ever again be involved in war I hope the appointments will be made with the solemn consideration that for the field of blood important military command is not to be committed to superannuated, shallow, intemperate and worthless characters with impunity. A more cheering if not more confident hope is that we shall yet enjoy many years of peace. But the general peace about to be restored in Europe may increase the difficulty of preserving ours. The state of Europe is indeed yet, and for some time will remain unsettled. France is to experience the fate of Poland, and thus terminates the revolution which began with liberty, equality, and fraternity, and which for a long time scared the nations of Europe and the children of America with the bugbear of universal monarchy.

The disciples of the Socrates, of whom Fisher Ames was the Plato, may go to bed and sleep in quiet. Their children will not be taken for the St. Domingo conscription. Let them not believe, however, that the revolutionary flame is extinct. Europe still consists only of victors and vanquished, between whom no permanent state of social repose can exist. May we persevere in the system of keeping aloof from all their broils, and in that of consolidating and perpetuating our own Union.

I am, etc.

DIARY, JOHN QUINCY ADAMS (LONDON), SEPTEMBER 14, 1815

John Adams had previously written to urge his son not to concede an inch on the right and liberty of Americans to fish in Canadian and international waters. John Quincy needed no encouragement. In a meeting with Lord Bathurst, he made in detail the case that the right and liberty were coterminous with American independence, and that it was actually in Britain's interest. Bathurst argued to the contrary, but offered assurances that the matter would not be pressed at the moment.

I went into London, and, as I had anticipated, found a note from Lord Bathurst appointing two o'clock this day to see me at Downing Street. It was then just two, and I went immediately to his office, and had an interview with him of about an hour.

I said that, having lately received dispatches from the American Secretary of State respecting several objects of some importance to the relations between the two countries, my first object in asking to see him had been to enquire whether he had received from Mr. Baker a communication of the correspondence between Mr. Monroe and him, relative to the surrender of Michilimakinac, to the proceedings of Colonel Nicolls in the southern part of the United States, and to the warning given by the captain of a British armed vessel to certain American fishing vessels to withdraw from the fishing grounds to the distance of twenty leagues from the coast.

He said that he had received all these papers from Mr. Baker about four days ago; that an answer with regard to the warning of the fishing vessels had immediately been sent; but on the other subjects there had not been time to examine the papers and prepare the answers.

I asked him if he could, without inconvenience, state the substance of the answer that had been sent. He said, certainly. It had been that as, on the one hand, Great Britain could not permit the vessels of the United States to fish within the creeks and close upon the shores of the British Territories, so, on the other hand, it was by no means her intention to interrupt them in fishing anywhere in the open sea or without the territorial jurisdiction – a marine league from the shore; and therefore that the warning given in the place stated in the case referred to was unauthorized.

I said that, the particular act being disavowed, I trusted the British Government, before adopting any final determination upon the subject, would estimate in candor, and in the spirit of amity which my own Government was anxious to have prevailing in our relations with this country, the considerations which I was instructed to present in support of the right of the people of the United States to fish on the whole coast of North America, which they have uniformly enjoyed from the first settlement of the country; that I should in the course of a few days address a letter to him on the subject.

He said that they would give due attention to the letter that I should send him, but that Great Britain had explicitly manifested her intention upon the subject; that there was a great deal of feeling on it in this country, as I doubtless knew, and their own fishermen considered it as an excessive hardship to be supplanted by American fishermen even upon the very shores of the British dominions.

I said that those whose sensibilities had been thus excited had probably not considered the question of right in the point of view in which it had been regarded by us; that the question of right had not been discussed at the negotiation of Ghent; that the British Plenipotentiaries had given a notice that the British Government would not hereafter allow the people of the United States to fish and cure and dry fish within the exclusive British territorial jurisdiction in America without an equivalent; that the American Plenipotentiaries had given notice in return that the American Government considered all the rights to the fisheries on the whole coast of North America as sufficiently secured by their enjoyment of them from the settlement of the country by them, and by the recognition of it in the Treaty of Peace of 1783; that they did not think any new stipulation necessary for a further confirmation of the right, no part of which did they consider as having been forfeited by the war. It was perfectly obvious that the Treaty of Peace of 1783 was not one of those ordinary treaties which by the usages of nations were considered as annulled by a subsequent war between the same parties. It was a treaty of partition between two parts of one nation, agreeing thenceforth to be separated into two distinct sovereignties. The conditions upon which this was done constituted essentially the independence of the United States, and the preservation of all the fishing rights which they had always enjoyed over the whole coast of North America was among the most important of them. This was no concession, no grant, on the part of Great Britain which would be annulled by war. There had been in the same Treaty of 1783 a right recognized in British subjects to navigate the Mississippi. This right the British

Plenipotentiaries at Ghent had considered a just claim of Great Britain, notwithstanding the war that had intervened. The American Plenipotentiaries, to remove all future discussion on both points, had offered to agree to an article expressly confirming both the rights. In declining this, an offer had been made on the part of Great Britain stipulating to negotiate in future for the renewal of both rights *for an equivalent*. This was declined by the American Plenipotentiaries, because its only effect would have been an implied admission that both the rights were annulled. There was therefore no article concerning them in the treaty, and the question as to the right was not discussed. I now stated the ground upon which the Government of the United States considered the right as subsisting and unimpaired. It would be for the British Government ultimately to determine how far this reasoning was to be admitted as correct. There were also considerations of policy and expediency, to which I hoped the British Government would give suitable attention before they came to a final decision on this point. I thought it my duty to suggest them, that they might not be overlooked. The subject was viewed by my countrymen as highly important, and I was profoundly anxious to omit nothing which might possibly have an influence to promote friendly sentiments between the two nations or to guard against the excitement of others. These fisheries afforded the means of subsistence to multitudes of people who were destitute of any other. They also afforded the means of remittance to Great Britain in payment for articles of her manufacture exported to America. It was well understood to be the policy of Great Britain that no unnecessary encouragement or stimulus should be given to manufactures in the United States which would diminish the importations from those of Great Britain. But by depriving the fishermen of the United States of this source of subsistence, the result must be to throw them back upon the country and drive them to the resort of manufacturing for themselves, while, on the other hand, it would cut off the means of making remittances in payment for the manufactures of Great Britain. I might add that the people in America whose interests would be immediately and severely affected by this exclusion were in the part of the country which had always manifested of late years the most friendly dispositions towards Great Britain. This might perhaps be less proper for me to suggest than for a British Cabinet to consider. To me the interests of all my countrymen in every part of the United States were the same: I could know no distinction between them. But upon a point where I was contending for what we conceived a strict right, I thought it best to urge every consideration which might influence the other party to avoid a collision upon it. I would even urge considerations of humanity. I would say that fisheries, the nature of which was to multiply the means of subsistence to mankind, were usually considered by civilized nations as under a sort of special sanction. It was a common practice to leave them uninterrupted even in time of war. He knew, for instance, that the Dutch had been for centuries in the practice of fishing upon the coasts of this island, and that they were not interrupted in this occupation even in ordinary times of war. It was to be inferred from this that to interrupt a fishery which had been enjoyed for ages was itself an indication of more than ordinary animosity.

He said that no such disposition was entertained by the British Government; that, to show the liberality which they had determined to exercise in this case, he would assure me that the instructions which he had given to the officers on that station had been not even to interrupt the American fishermen who might have proceeded to those coasts within the British jurisdiction for the present year; to allow them to complete their fares, but to give them notice that this privilege could be no longer allowed by Great Britain, and that they must not return the next year. It was not so much the fishing as the drying and curing on the shores that had been followed with bad consequences. It happened that our fishermen, by their proximity, could get to the fishing stations sooner in the season than the British, who were obliged to go from Europe, and who, upon arriving there, found all the fishing places and drying and curing places preoccupied. This had often given rise to disputes and quarrels between them, which in some instances had proceeded even to blows. It had even disturbed the peace among the inhabitants on the shores, and for several years before the war the complaints to this Government had been so great and so frequent that it had been impossible not to pay regard to them.

I said that I had not heard of any such complaints before; but that as to the disputes arising from the competition of the fishermen, they could surely be easily made a subject of regulation by the Government; and as to the peace of the inhabitants, there could be no difficulty in securing that, as the liberty enjoyed by the American fishermen was in all settled and inhabited places expressly subjected to the consent of the inhabitants and by agreement with them.

I then adverted to other topics – Michilimakinac, Bois Blanc, and Colonel Nicolls. I asked him if he had any account of the delivery of the post.

He said he had no doubt whatever but that it had been long since delivered up. But he had no late dispatches from the Canadian Government. Some delay had occurred by the change of the Governor-General, by Sir George Prevost's leaving Quebec to come to Europe, and consequently by General Drummond's coming from Upper Canada to Quebec. As to the indisposition manifested by the Indians to accept the peace offered by the United States, he regretted it very much. It had been the sincere wish and intention of the British Government that the peace with the Indians should immediately follow that agreed to by this country; the British officers there had been formally instructed to make known to them the peace which had been concluded, and to advise them to take the benefit of it.

As to Colonel Nicolls, I said that the American Government had been peculiarly concerned at the proceedings of that officer, because they appeared marked with unequivocal characters of hostility.

"Why," said Lord Bathurst, "to tell you the truth, Colonel Nicolls is, I believe, a man of activity and spirit, but a very wild fellow. He did make, and send over to me, a treaty offensive and defensive with the Indians, and he is now come over here, and has brought over some of those Indians. I sent for answer that he had no authority whatever to make a treaty offensive and defensive with the Indians, and that the Government would make no such treaty. I have sent him word that I could not see him upon any such project. The Indians are here in great distress, indeed, but we shall only furnish them with the means of returning home, and advise them to make their terms with the United States as well as they can." Perceiving that I had noticed his declaration that he had declined seeing Colonel Nicolls, he said that perhaps he should see him upon the general subject of his transactions, but that he had declined seeing him in regard to his treaty with the Indians.

I then observed that Mr. Monroe had also sent me his letter to Mr. Baker concerning the island of Bois Blanc. He said it seemed merely a question of fact whether the island had been in the possession of the British at the commencement of the late war or not. He did not know how that was, but he thought it could not be difficult to ascertain, and it was altogether of very little importance.

JOHN QUINCY ADAMS (LONDON) TO JOHN ADAMS, OCTOBER 9, 1815

Although he stresses the need to avoid another war with Britain for as long as possible, John Quincy wants his countrymen to understand that it might not be their choice. The causes of the past conflict had gone away but different ones had taken their place: "the Canadian Boundary – the fur trade – the fisheries – The commercial intercourse with the East and West Indies – The Floridas; and a general commercial competition all over the world, are already producing collisions, which in the temper of the two Nations, towards each other, it is not to be expected will leave them long at Peace." But if war it must be, the federal government had to be assured of the support of the North and East, for whom those issues were of the greatest importance.

MY DEAR SIR:

Your favors of 27, 28, and 30 August, were all received together. They as well as your preceding letters express so much uneasiness for me, and on my account, that I wish it were in my power to tranquillize your feelings. Aware as I am of the heavy responsibility of my present situation, and diffident as I ought to be of my own fitness for it, I have certainly seen times and gone through emergencies, more painful and more distressing than any of those which now embarrass and perplex me. Now, indeed, *incedo per ignes suppositos cineri doloso.* I am well aware that the most formidable dangers are those that I cannot see. But my vigilance is not asleep, neither has that portion of industry to which I have been long habituated deserted me. That there is nothing to be obtained here, I am fully convinced. That they now strongly grudge what they have conceded, is likewise evident. The commercial convention as you remark was a "temporary expedient to keep the world along;" and I fear the sentence is too prophetical, that "this tranquillity will be of short duration." I must be content to say, like Hezekiah, "Is it not good, if peace be in my days"? Our country now enjoys the blessing of peace, and although the period may be not far distant when she will again be called to defend her rights by force of arms, there is yet reason to hope that she will enter upon the field under more favorable auspices than she was compelled to do in the late war. So far as human foresight can anticipate, there is no danger of a new war from the causes which produced the last. With a navy reduced to the peace establishment, and with a hundred thousand sailors upon her hands more than she can employ, Britain is not likely to have any occasion very soon for the services of a press-gang for a European war. As little will she need Orders in Council and paper blockades to destroy neutral commerce. But the Canadian boundary, the fur trade, the fisheries, the commercial intercourse with the East and West Indies, the Floridas, and a general commercial competition all over the world, are already producing collisions, which in the temper of the two nations towards each other, it is not to be expected will leave them long at peace. But as the interests for which it will be necessary for us to contend will be almost exclusively those of the northern and eastern sections of the Union, I hope and trust that the government of the United States will take special care, not to get involved in a new war, without being certain of the support and cooperation of those for whom it must be waged. Upon the question concerning the right to the coast fisheries, the two governments are already at issue. You know that our fishermen have been excluded the present season, and the British government has formally notified to ours their determination to exclude us from them in future. I have, under instructions from the Secretary of State, addressed a letter on the subject to Lord Bathurst, asserting our right and supporting it to the utmost of my power. As yet I have received no answer to it; but from the conversation which I previously had with Lord Bathurst I know that the determination here upon that point is irrevocable. Nothing therefore will remain for us, but to maintain the right as it is contested – by force; but I have purposely written the letter in such a manner as to leave the American government and nation the choice of the time when they may deem it expedient to apply force to the support of their right. The commercial convention contains only two articles of any importance; one mutually abolishing what were called the discriminating duties; and the other stipulating the admission of American commercial vessels at the four principal British settlements in the East Indies. The duration of the convention is to be only four years from the time of the signature; but at this very moment an attempt is making to excite a clamor against the ministers for having assented even to those two articles. You will not be surprised that this attempt proceeds from the opposition, and that the *Morning Chronicle* is the vehicle by which it is made. The loss by the British of the privilege of trading with the Indians within our jurisdiction, and the loss of the fur trade which they foresee as the consequence that must result from it, is another source of heartburning and of discontent which will breed much ill blood here. It has already been the cause of the Indian war which we are now obliged to sustain, and which I hope our government will see the necessity of terminating in the most effectual manner.

On the subject of our intercourse with the West Indies the British plenipotentiaries, with whom we negotiated the commercial convention, would not even listen to us. From the first moment they declined all discussion about it. The system of universal exclusion was already established, and not one particle from it would they swerve. They extended it likewise in all its rigor to their provinces in North America, and refused to allow us even the privilege of carrying in boats down to the St. Lawrence and to Montreal our own produce, for exportation thence in their ships to Europe. One consequence of this rigor you will find in the newspaper inclosed. The council and assembly of the island of Antigua are deliberating upon the distressed state of the colony, and their joint committee report that it is all owing to this total exclusion of American vessels from the island. Other colonies will undoubtedly suffer in like manner from the same cause. But the sufferings of the colonies are the gain of the West India merchants, whose influence with the government will always overpower that of the planters, and the more certainly, because combining with the jealousies and fears and prejudices always operating against the United States.

Nothing can however be more clear in my mind than our interest and policy to avoid as long as possible a new war with England. How long it will be possible I know not; for the problem is now to be decided whether this country can exist in peace, and if, as is very possible, their government should find that it cannot, the danger is that they will plunge the nation headlong into a war with us, because it is against us only that they will be able to stimulate the national passions to the tone of war. It is a singular symptom that the state of peace has brought a very oppressive burden upon the farmers and landholders of the country. The price of wheat, and consequently of bread, has fallen within these two years more than one-third. The value of land has fallen at least in the same proportion. Rents are coming down in the same manner, but the taxes are not reduced. The farmers, however, become more and more unable to pay them, and unless something should occur to restore the prices to the level of the former years, the landed and the funded interests of the kingdom will be brought into such a state of opposition against each other, as to threaten the tranquillity of the nation.

On the side of France they have henceforth forward nothing to fear. The elements of civil society in that country are dissolved. For the price of two or three provinces, and of all her important fortresses, the Bourbons are to be saddled upon the remnant of that wretched people, and to be maintained by an army of two or three hundred thousand foreign soldiers, fed upon their vitals. Partial insurrections must inevitably be the consequence of this state of things; but the internal war of interests and passions will render any general and united effort impossible. Every struggle for deliverance will be smothered in blood, and be made the pretext for new spoliations and partitions. France is irretrievably lost, unless she can produce another Joan of Arc. You will have more reason than ever to say that the wars of the Reformation still continue, when you learn the late massacres of the Protestants, under the auspices of the Duke and Duchess of Angouleme. You will have many of the miserable fugitives from that persecution in America, and may they find there a country where St. Bartholomew butcheries are not in honor and in fashion.

Let me hope that in our country religious controversy will not extend beyond the consumption of paper. I think the first time I ever saw Dr. Morse was in a pulpit at an ordination, addressing a prayer to the *triune God*. It seems he is steady to the faith. As he and the Boston rebel are both members of the corporation, I wish they would agree to hold a forensic dissertation on a commencement day, upon the question which of the two, Athanasius or Socinus, was the greater man. I wrote you some time ago how my belief inclined upon this question. But I have no desire to make converts, because I believe that a sincere Socinian may be saved, and that a very honest and intelligent man may be a Socinian. There is something of this dispute rumbling also here; but the Unitarians are losing ground. They will never, probably, become the prevailing sect of Christians, for the plain reason that when you are going down a steep hill, the nearer you are to the bottom the harder it is to stop.

I will send you Tucker's *Light of Nature* by the first opportunity, but they ask *nine guineas* for the six volumes of Brucker. If you wish to have it at that price, be kind enough to let me know. I have hesitation, because I was not certain that you meant to order it.

I am, etc.

JOHN QUINCY ADAMS (LONDON) TO SECRETARY OF STATE JAMES MONROE, FEBRUARY 8, 1816

John Quincy reviews a recent meeting with Castlereagh on various points of possible contention between the two countries, including the disposition of slaves under the terms of the Treaty of Ghent, British policy toward the revolutions in Spanish America (and American-Spanish border issues), and the security of the Canadian-American frontier. On that point, he makes his best case for disarmament of the Great Lakes. The two sides were on the verge of a freshwater arms struggle triggered by the increase of the British armaments there since the peace. "Both governments would thus be subjected to heavy, and in time of peace useless expenses, and every additional armament would create new and very dangerous incitements to mutual irrita-

tion and acts of hostility.... The extent of this reduction the President left at the pleasure of Great Britain, observing that the greater it would be the more it would conform to his preference, and that it would best of all suit the United States if the armaments should be confined to what is necessary for the protection of the revenue."

SIR:

By way of introduction to the proposals which I was instructed to make to this government, in relation to the naval armaments on the Canadian lakes, I observed to Lord Castlereagh at the conference with him on the 25th ultimo, that next to the subject of seamen and impressment the most dangerous source of disagreement between the two countries arose in Canada. It had occasioned much mutual ill will heretofore and might give rise to great and frequent animosities hereafter, unless guarded against by the vigilance, firmness and decidedly pacific dispositions of the two governments. That there were continual tendencies to bad neighborhood and even to acts of hostility in that quarter proceeding from three distinct causes: the Indians, the temper of the British local authorities, and the British armaments on the lakes. The post of Michillimackinac had been surrendered not immediately after the ratification of the peace, nor until late in the last summer, and some of the British officers in Upper Canada had been so far from entering into the spirit of their government, which had so anxiously provided for securing a peace for the Indians, that they took no small pains to instigate the Indians to a continuance of hostilities against the United States. The detention of the post had also contributed to lead the Indians to expect further aid from Great Britain in the prosecution of war, and the consequences had been that it remained long very doubtful, whether the Indians in that quarter would accept the peace, the option of which had been secured to them. You had represented these circumstances in a letter to Mr. Baker. I had under your instructions repeated these representations to Lord Liverpool and Lord Bathurst, both of whom had given the strongest assurances that the intentions of this government were sincerely pacific, and that its earnest wish had been that the Indians should agree to the peace. That no detention of Michillimackinac had been authorized by its orders, and no instigation of the Indians against the United States had been warranted by it. The fort was surrendered in July, and as soon as the Indians found they would not be supported by Great Britain in the war they had manifested a readiness for peace, which I believe had been concluded with all or most of the tribes in that direction. Other and more recent incidents had however occurred of an unpleasant nature. A British officer had pursued into the territory of the United States a deserter, had taken him there, and carried him away. The officer himself had afterwards been arrested within the American jurisdiction, tried and, owing to the absence of a principal witness, convicted only of a riot, and moderately fined. An Indian with a party, trespassing on the property of an American citizen at Gross Isle, had been killed in a boat while in the act of levelling his musket at the American, and although this had happened on the American territory the British Commandant at Maiden had offered a reward of four hundred dollars for the apprehension of the person who had killed the Indian. An American vessel upon Lake Erie had also been fired upon by a British armed vessel. But the most important circumstance was the increase of the British armaments upon the Canadian lakes since the peace. Such armaments on one side rendered similar and counter armaments on the other indispensable. Both governments would thus be subjected to heavy, and in time of peace useless expenses, and every additional armament would create new and very dangerous incitements to mutual irritation and acts of hostility. That the American government, anxious above all for the preservation of peace, had authorized me to propose a reduction of the armaments upon the lakes upon both sides. The extent of this reduction the President left at the pleasure of Great Britain, observing that the greater it would be the more it would conform to his preference, and that it would best of all suit the United States if the armaments should be confined to what is necessary for the protection of the revenue. Lord Castlereagh admitted that the proposal was perfectly fair, and assured me that so far as it manifested pacific and amicable dispositions it would meet with the sincerest reciprocal dispositions on the part of this government. He inquired if it was meant to include in this proposition the destruction of the armed vessels already existing there? I answered that it was not so expressed in my instructions. I did not understand them to include that, but if the principle should be acceptable to Great Britain there would be ample time to consult the American government with regard to the details. The immediate agreement which I was directed to propose was that there should be no new armament on either side. He replied that as to keeping a number of armed vessels parading about upon the lakes in time of peace, it would be ridiculous and absurd. There could be no motive for it, and everything beyond what should be necessary to guard against smuggling would be calculated only to produce mischief. That he would submit the proposal to the consideration of His Majesty's government, but we were aware that Great Britain was on that point the weaker party. And therefore it was that she had proposed at the negotiation of Ghent that the whole of the lakes including the shores should belong to one party. In that case there would have been a large and wide natural separation between the two territories, and there would have been no necessity for armaments. He expressed a strong predilection in favor of such broad natural boundaries, and appeared to consider the necessity for Great Britain to keep up considerable naval force on her side of the lakes as resulting from the objections made on the part of the United States to the expedient for preserving the future peace between the two countries by Great Britain upon that occasion. He said that just before the conclusion of the peace Great Britain had been under the necessity of making extraordinary exertions, and to build a number of new vessels upon the lakes to enable her to maintain her footing there. And when I remarked that this was not what had drawn the animadversion of the American government but the new armaments, vessels of war begun and built since the peace, he replied that we had so much the advantage over them there by our position that a mutual stipulation against arming during the peace would be unequal and disadvantageous in its operation to Great Britain. For as the hands of both parties would by such an engagement be tied until war should have commenced, the Americans by their proximity would be able to prepare armaments for attack much sooner than those of the British could be prepared for defence. I urged that, as at all events the state of the armaments during peace on one side must be the measure of those on the other, this advantage of proximity must be nearly the same, whether they are great or small; that the agreements to forbear arming in time of peace would rather diminish than add to it; and that a war could not break out on the part of the United States suddenly, or without such a previous state of the relations between the two nations as would give the British government warning to be prepared for the event, to take such measures as might enable them to arm on the lakes when the war commenced, quite as rapidly and effectually as the United States could do on their side. But although Lord Castlereagh promised to submit the proposal to the Cabinet, his own disinclination to accede to it was so strongly marked that I cannot flatter myself it will be accepted. The utmost that he may be induced to consent to may be an arrangement to limit the force which either party shall keep in actual service upon the lakes. I next observed that at the other extremity of the United States the Indians again appeared in the shape of disturbers of the peace between our countries. I recapitulated your remonstrances to Mr. Baker and mine by your order to Lord Bathurst against the conduct of Colonel Nicholls; that officer's pretended treaties of alliance, offensive and defensive, and of commerce and navigation, with certain runaway Indians whom he had seen fit to style the Creek nation; and the very exceptionable manner in which he had notified his transactions to the agent of the United States with the Creeks, with an intimation that we were to hear more about these treaties when they should be ratified in England. I mentioned that Lord Bathurst had in the most candid and explicit manner verbally disavowed to me those proceedings of Colonel Nicholls; had told me that the pretended treaty of alliance, offensive and defensive, had been indeed transmitted by the Colonel for ratification, but this government had refused to ratify it, and informed Colonel Nicholls that they would agree to no such treaty; that the Colonel had even brought over some of his Indians here, who would be sent back with advice to make their terms with the United States as they could. These *verbal* assurances I had reported to my government and presumed they had been received with much satisfaction. Whether they had been repeated in a more formal manner and in any written communication I had not been informed. I had noticed the conduct of Colonel Nicholls in one of my notes to Lord Bathurst, and to that part of the note had received no answer. As the complaint had also been made through Mr. Baker, a written answer might perhaps have been returned through that channel. My motive for referring to the subject now was that by the President's message to Congress at the opening of the session I perceived that the conduct of the Indians in that part of the United States still threatened hostilities, and because there, as in the more northern parts, the Indians would certainly be disposed to tranquillity and peace with the United States, unless they should have encouragement to rely upon the support of Great Britain. Lord Castlereagh said with a smile that he had a good many treaties to lay before Parliament, but none such as those I described were among them. I observed that this affair had given more concern to the government of the United States, because they had received from various quarters strong and confident intimations that there had been a cession of Florida by Spain to Great Britain. "As to that (said Lord Castlereagh with a little apparent emotion) I can set you at ease at once. There is not and never has been the slightest foundation for it whatever. It never has been mentioned. " I replied that he must be aware that such rumors had long been in circulation, and that the fact had been positively and most circumstantially asserted in their own public journals. "Yes (said he) but our journals are so addicted to lying! No! If it is supposed that we have any little trickish policy of thrusting ourselves in there between you and Spain, we are very much misunderstood indeed. You shall find nothing little or shabby in our policy. We have no desire to add an inch of ground to our territories in any part of the world. We have as much as we want or wish to manage. There is not a spot of ground on the globe that I would annex to our territories, if it were offered to us tomorrow." I remarked that the United States, without inquiring what might in that respect be the views of Great Britain generally, did think that with dominions so extensive and various as hers, she could not wish for such an acquisition as Florida, unless for purposes unfriendly to the United States, and hence it was that these rumors had given concern to the American government, who I was sure would receive with pleasure the assurance given by him that no such cession had been made. "None whatever (I quote his words as accurately as I can recollect them). It has never been mentioned, and if it had, it would have been decisively declined by us. Military positions may have been taken by us during the war of places which you had previously taken from Spain, but we never intended to keep them. Do you only observe the same moderation. If we shall find you hereafter pursuing a system of encroachment upon your neighbors, what we might do *defensively* is another consideration."

The tone of struggling irritation and complacency with which this was said induced me to observe, that I did not precisely understand what he intended by this advice of moderation. That the United States had no design of encroachment upon their neighbors, or of exercising any injustice towards Spain. Instead of an explanation he replied only by recurring to the British policy with regard to Spain. "You may be sure (said he) that Great Britain has no design of acquiring any addition to her possessions there. Great Britain has done everything for Spain. We have saved, we have delivered her. We have restored her government to her, and we had hoped that the result would have proved more advantageous to herself as well as more useful to the world than it has been. We are sorry that the event has not altogether answered our expectations. We lament the unfortunate situation of her internal circumstances, owing to which we are afraid that she can neither exercise her own faculties for the comfort and happiness of the nation, nor avail herself of her resources for the effectual exertion of her power. We regret this, but we have no disposition to take advantage of this state of things to obtain from it any exclusive privilege for ourselves. In the unfortunate troubles of her colonies in South America we have not only avoided to seek, but we have declined even exclusive indulgence or privilege to ourselves. We went even so far as to offer to take upon us that most unpleasant and thankless of all offices, that of mediating between the parties to those differences. We appointed a formal mission for that purpose, who proceeded to Madrid, but there the Court of Spain declined accepting our offer, and we have had the usual fortune of impartiality, we have displeased both parties – the Spanish government for not taking part with them against their colonies, and the South Americans for not countenancing their resistance." I told him that the policy of the American government towards Spain had in this particular been the same. They had not, indeed, made any offer of their mediation. The state of their relations with the Spanish government would neither have warranted nor admitted of such an offer. But they have observed the same system of impartial neutrality between the parties. They have sought no peculiar or exclusive advantage for the United States, and I was happy to hear from him that such was the policy of Great Britain for it might have an influence upon the views of my own government to cooperate with it. "I have always (resumed he) avowed it to be our policy in Parliament. We have never acknowledged the governments put up by the South Americans, because that would not have comported with our views of neutrality. But we have not consented to prohibit the commerce of our people with them, because that was what Spain had no right to require of us. Our plan in offering the mediation which Spain rejected was, that the South Americans should submit themselves to the government of Spain as colonies, because we thought she had the right to authority over them as the mother country, but that she should allow them commerce with other nations. Nothing exclusive to us. We neither asked, nor would have accepted, any exclusive privileges for ourselves. We have no little or contracted policy. But we propose that Spain should allow a *liberal* commercial intercourse between her colonies and other nations, similar to that which we allow in our possessions in India." I then asked him what he thought would be the ultimate issue of this struggle in South America? Whether Spain would subdue them, or that they would maintain their independence? He answered that everything was so fluctuating in the councils of Spain, and generally everything was so dependent upon events not to be calculated, that it was not possible to say what the result might be. The actual state of things was the only safe foundation for present policy which must be shaped to events as they may happen. In closing this part of our conversation Lord Castlereagh desired me to consider all that he had said with regard to Spain, the situation of her internal affairs, and the conduct of her government as *confidential*, it having been spoken with the most perfect freedom and openness, and that if I should report it to my government I would so state it. I have therefore to request that it may be so received.

In adverting to the subject of the slaves I reminded him that there were three distinct points relating to them which had been under discussion between the two governments. The first, regarding the slaves carried away by the British commanders from the United States contrary, as the American government holds, to the express stipulation of the treaty of Ghent. After referring to the correspondence which has taken place on this topic at Washington and here, I observe that the last note concerning it which I had received from Lord Bathurst seemed to intimate that this government had taken its final determination on the matter. That

I hoped it was not so. I hoped they would give it further consideration. It had been the cause of so much anxiety to my government; it was urged so constantly and so earnestly in my instructions; the language of the treaty appeared to us so clear and unequivocal, the violation of it in carrying away the slaves so manifest, and the losses of property occasioned by it to our citizens were so considerable and so serious, that I could not abandon the hope that further consideration would be given to it here, and ultimately that satisfaction would be made to the United States on this cause of complaint. Lord Castlereagh said that he had not seen the correspondence to which I referred, but that he would have it looked up and examine it. There was I told him a special representation concerning eleven slaves taken from Mr. Downman by the violation of a flag of truce sent ashore by Captain Barrie. I also had received from Lord Bathurst an answer relative to this complaint, stating that it had been referred to Captain Barrie for a report and giving the substance of that which he had made. It did not disprove any of the facts alleged by Mr. Downman. But I must remark that Captain Barrie was himself the officer who had sent the flag of truce, and who was responsible for the In adverting to the subject of the slaves I reminded him that there were three distinct points relating to them which had been under discussion between the two governments. The first, regarding the slaves carried away by the British commanders from the United States contrary, as the American government holds, to the express stipulation of the treaty of Ghent. After referring to the correspondence which has taken place on this topic at Washington and here, I observe that the last note concerning it which I had received from Lord Bathurst seemed to intimate that this government had taken its final determination on the matter. That I hoped it was not so. I hoped they would give it further consideration. It had been the cause of so much anxiety to my government; it was urged so constantly and so earnestly in my instructions; the language of the treaty appeared to us so clear and unequivocal, the violation of it in carrying away the slaves so manifest, and the losses of property occasioned by it to our citizens were so considerable and so serious, that I could not abandon the hope that further consideration would be given to it here, and ultimately that satisfaction would be made to the United States on this cause of complaint. Lord Castlereagh said that he had not seen the correspondence to which I referred, but that he would have it looked up and examine it. There was I told him a special representation concerning eleven slaves taken from Mr. Downman by the violation of a flag of truce sent ashore by Captain Barrie. I also had received from Lord Bathurst an answer relative to this complaint, stating that it had been referred to Captain Barrie for a report and giving the substance of that which he had made. It did not disprove any of the facts alleged by Mr. Downman. But I must remark that Captain Barrie was himself the officer who had sent the flag of truce, and who was responsible for the of either alternative to the Earl of Liverpool last summer, and he had appeared to prefer that the evidence should be produced. I had now received a considerable mass of it, and although preferring to repeat the proposal of dropping the subject altogether, I would, if he should desire it, furnish him with copies of it all. He said that so far as it might contain matter of irritation, they had no wish to pursue the inquiry any further. If the American government, in the heat of war and under the feelings of that state, had advanced against the British officers a charge beyond what the proof of facts would bear out, there was no wish here to carry the discussion of it into the state of peace, and in that point of view it would be readily dismissed. But with regard to the fact they were obliged to ask for the evidence, because, if established, it affected the character of their officers and the observance of their laws. In that case the officers who have been guilty should be punished and, if otherwise, it should be known for the vindication of the character of individuals. I remarked that in the charge as originally made no individual had been named, but that in the documents that I had secured there were several and that from one of the papers it appeared that slaves taken as prize were actually sold. He said that by the last act of Parliament those that were taken, for example, on the vessels which carry on the slave trade by contraband, were committed to the care of certain conservators appointed by royal authority, but they were not slaves. I suggested that the documents in my possession would probably induce this government to pursue the investigation further. That the proof which the American government could obtain in the places where the sales were alleged to have been made must be imperfect. It had no control over the local authorities, but for a full and satisfactory investigation the cooperation of both governments would be necessary. The mode suggested to me, and which had already been proposed by you to Mr. Baker, was that the American government would furnish lists of the slaves taken during the war, and in most instances the names of the vessels into which they had been taken, and that the British government should show what disposal had been made of them. Lord Castlereagh expressed his approbation of this course of proceeding and thought it would have the assent of this government. In relation to the fisheries little was said. He told me that he had the evening before read my note to him concerning them. That the British government would adhere to their principle respecting the treaty and to the exclusive rights of their territorial jurisdiction. But that they had no wish to prevent us from fishing, and would readily enter into a negotiation for an arrangement on this subject. Copies have been transmitted to you of the note I have addressed to Lord Castlereagh, concerning a discrimination made in the ports of Ireland between British and American vessels in regard to the number of passengers which they are allowed to take in proportion to their tonnage upon voyages to the United States, of his answer and of my reply. As no answer to this had been returned, and no determination of the government upon my application had been known to me, I spoke of these papers, but he avoided any explicit assurance concerning it. He said that the regulation had perhaps been made before the convention had been concluded. "But (said he) we might question the application of it to the case, as the convention was not intended to interfere in any restrictions under which we may think proper to prevent emigration from Ireland." I assured him that my intention had not been to object to the regulation as a restriction upon emigration; *that*, I was aware, must be exclusively the consideration of this government. We had nothing to say about it. It was the discrimination between the shipping of the two countries of which I had complained. I presumed that an order to the port office would remove the distinction. He said he did not know that. It might be by act of Parliament, and they might question our right to consider passengers as articles of merchandize. They might regard the discrimination itself as a mode of restriction upon emigration. "You do not want our people" (said he), to which I readily assented, observing that our increase of native population was sufficiently rapid so far as mere public policy was concerned. We invited no foreigners. We left all to individual option. "No (he repeated), our people and our seamen – you really do not want them." I observed that if that were the case, this country should rather be under obligation to us for relieving it of such unprofitable subjects. He did not assent to this conclusion, and left me uncertain whether the regulation in question would be removed or retained. The great length into which this report has already run precludes any comment of mine upon the substance of this conference, in which Lord Castlereagh's manner was uniformly courteous, and his assurances of the friendly disposition of this government towards the United States were earnest and repeated.

I am, etc.

JOHN QUINCY ADAMS (LONDON) TO ALEXANDER HILL EVERETT, MARCH 16, 1816

John Quincy provides more reflections on the impact and lessons of the war, positive and negative. "Every mind not besotted by the spirit of faction may draw two conclusions: one of caution against commencing war without a fair prospect of attaining its objects, as well as a good cause; the other, that the object of the last war must perhaps, and not improbably, be fought for again." He offers recommendations for the behavior of one who is willing to accept the call of public service, at home or abroad: "I will give you one word which you may lay down as the foundation of the whole political system to which you may boldly and safely devote from this moment all the energies of your character, all your talents, and all your genius – that word is Union. Let that be the center from which all your future exertions emanate, and to which all your motives tend. Let your conduct be at once bold, resolute, and wary; preserve inflexibly your personal independence, even while acting in concurrence with any party ..."

DEAR SIR:

Your letter of 11th March, 1815, principally relates to two subjects, now obsolete enough; but one of which, the victory at New Orleans, will always be in season to the memory of Americans; and the other, the peace of Ghent, will I hope prove to be likewise composed of durable materials. Judging as the character of all political measures should be judged from the existing circumstances of the time, the peace was undoubtedly seasonable and was probably as good a one as could have been obtained; but all who, like you, have devoted their lives to the honor and welfare of their country, will remember that the peace did not obtain the objects for which the war was waged. From which every mind not besotted by the spirit of faction may draw two conclusions: one of caution against commencing war without a fair prospect of attaining its objects, as well as a good cause; the other, that the object of the last war must perhaps, and not improbably, be fought for again. In an enlarged point of view the war was much more beneficial than injurious to our country. It has raised our national character in the eyes of all Europe. It has demonstrated that the United States are both a military and a naval power, with capacities which may hereafter place them in both these respects on the first line among the nations of the earth. It has given us generals, and admirals, and subordinate officers, by land and sea, to whom we may hereafter look with confidence for the support of our national rights and interests in war, if the necessity should recur. It has partly removed the prejudice against that best and safest of national defences, an efficient navy. And it has shown us many secrets of our own strength and weakness, until then not sufficiently known to ourselves, and to which it is to be hoped we shall not hereafter wilfully shut our eyes. But some of the worst features in our composition that it has disclosed are deformities which, if not inherent in the very nature of our constitution, will require great, anxious and unremitting care to enable us to outgrow them. The most disgusting of them all is the rancorous spirit of faction which drove one part of the country headlong towards the dissolution of the union, and towards a treacherous and servile adherence to the enemies of the country. This desertion from the standard of the nation weakened all its exertions to such a degree that it required little less than a special interposition of Providence to save us from utter disgrace and dismemberment; and although the projects of severing the Union were signally disconcerted by the unexpected conclusion of the peace, they were too deeply seated in the political systems, as well as in the views of personal ambition of the most leading men in our native state, to be yet abandoned. They will require to be watched, exposed, and inflexibly resisted, probably for many years.

You have doubtless been informed that a few days after I last wrote you, Mr. J. A. Smith arrived here as secretary of legation to this court, and since the meeting of Congress his appointment has been confirmed by the Senate. Whether the government inferred from his personal relation to me this appointment would of course be agreeable to me, or whether it was made upon distinct considerations, and without reference to my wishes at all, I think it necessary, from what had previously passed between you and me, to state that your name is the only one that I ever recommended to the government for the office, and that although I knew he had been recommended for it by others, his appointment to it was altogether unexpected by me, until I was informed it had actually taken place.

It is natural that you should entertain some solicitude with regard to your future prospects, and your idea is just that the situation of secretary to an American legation in Europe is no permanent prospect for a condition in life. The government of the United States have no system of diplomatic gradation, and the instances of persons who have commenced as secretaries of legation and afterwards received higher appointments have been very few. But the reason of this has been, because most of the secretaries have been young men, who obtained their appointments by the influence and solicitations of their friends, and who after obtaining it think more of their own pleasure than of the public service. They come to Europe not to toil, but to enjoy; to dangle about courts and solace themselves for the rest of their lives, with the delightful reflection that kings or princes have looked at them, to see sights, to frequent theatres, balls, masquerades, and fashionable society. I speak not of those who have sunk into baser and more vicious pursuits; nor of those who come to make themselves scientific, or virtuosi. Scarcely one in fifty ever came to his duty, and nothing but his duty, or to devote his leisure to the acquisition of the proper diplomatic knowledge. The habits of life into which they fall relax their industry into indolence, and turn their activity to dissipation. They go home with heads as empty, and with hearts fuller of vanity, than they came; generally with a hankering to return to Europe, and almost always with a distaste to the manners and institutions of their own country, disdaining or disqualified to take a part in its public affairs, and incapable of making themselves necessary, either to the general government, or to any of the political parties in the country.

Nothing of all this applies to you. Had your station been assigned to the mission here, you would have found that the mere drudgery of the office would have absorbed all, and more than all your time. At The Hague you have much leisure, and I am quite sure you are making good use of it. You will never for an instant forget that you are responsible to your country for the employment of every hour; that every moment not devoted to the discharge of present duty must be given to the acquisition of future capability. You will never adopt the fancy of the school boy, who left school and went home because he had *learnt out*. But as you have asked my advice, I cannot in candor recommend it to you to remain long in your present station under the idea that it will lead to something better. After a suitable period, properly employed, I should say return home, and resume your station at the Bar. Take an interest and exercise an influence in the public affairs. You must steel your heart and prepare your mind to encounter multitudes of political enemies, and to endure all the bufferings without which there is no rising to distinction in the American world. When the knaves and fools open upon you in full pack, take little or no notice of them, and be careful not to lose your temper. Preserve your private character and reputation unsullied, and confine your speculations upon public concerns to objects of high and national importance. You will certainly be favored with no patronage, political or professional, by the prevailing party at Boston; but you must make your way in opposition to and in defiance of them. Their system is rotten to the core, and you may render essential service to the nation by persevering exertions against it. I will give you one word which you may lay down as the foundation of the whole political system to which you may boldly and safely devote from this moment all the energies of your character, all your talents, and all your genius – that word is *Union*. Let that be the center from which all your future exertions emanate, and to which all your motives tend. Let your conduct be at once bold, resolute, and wary; preserve inflexibly your personal independence, even while acting in concurrence with any party, and take my word for it, you will not need to go in search for public office, at home or abroad. For public office, at home or abroad, at your option will soon come in search of you.

Be good enough to present my best remembrance to Mr. Eustis, to whom I am yet indebted for a letter, and propose shortly to write. Apthorp did not bring Turreau's book upon America. That illustrious Vendean general told me last spring that he intended to publish a book against us. I did not think the worse of him or ourselves for that. *Laudari a laudato* has a counterpart which will easily reconcile me to his vituperation.

Our accounts from the United States do not appear propitious to your projects of perpetual peace. Once the Spaniard, they say, has sprung a mine at Washington and gone off. But I have not room to expatiate, and must remain ever faithfully yours.

JOHN QUINCY ADAMS (LONDON) TO GEORGE W ERVING, JUNE 10, 1816

John Quincy Adams professed himself to be a man of peace, but there were exceptions, including a defense of civilized norms against the uncivilized, where national honor and interest were at stake. "Pacific as I am, I hope we shall never again, after beating Algiers, truckle to her in substance, and then swagger as if we had obtained a triumph. A real and a glorious triumph awaits us there, if we will but undertake to win it. But we must have fighting as gallant and skilful as heretofore, and no trifling negotiations, no gratuitous restitutions, no consular presents, no bullying articles against tribute, and tacit ticklings of the pirates' palm. This war, if we have it, will be quite as much as we can manage well, and will not necessarily, nor even probably, lead us into any other. Its tendency would on the contrary be to cement our peace with the rest of the world, by increasing at once our moral strength in the respect of mankind, and our physical power of defense in the naval bulwark. War! say I, with Algiers, and peace with the universe beside."

DEAR SIR:

Your favors of 28th ultimo and 2nd instant came to hand only the day before yesterday. I accept your amendment to turn away the esquires as well as the excellencies from our tête-a-tête with-inside our letters. But for the superscriptions going by post, the simple name might excite a suspicion of Jacobinism which might tempt the legitimate to inspect their contents.

I thought you had stouter nerves than to admit the conjuring up of devils of any color by my croaking spells. If you think that in my two last letters my discretion got the better of my valor, I can only say that much of my alarm came from home. There seemed to me too much of the warlike humor in the debates of Congress – propositions even to take up the cause of the South Americans; predictions of wars with this country to the end of time, as cool and as causeless, as if they were talking of the expense of build-ing a light house, or of adding five cents to the salary of the Sec-retary of State, which you see they have had the magnanimity to refuse. I say nothing of the foreign missions, only to congratulate you upon the failure of the discriminating plan. But a quarrel with Spain for any cause can scarcely fail of breeding a quarrel with Great Britain – for the cause of the South Americans it would be infallible.

You know the purport of Lord Exmouth's treaties at Algiers, and you will soon hear of his second visit there, to protest against the application in any case to Great Britain of the eighteenth article of our last Algerine treaty. Pacific as I am, I hope we shall never again, after beating Algiers, truckle to her in substance, and then swagger as if we had obtained a triumph. A real and a glori-ous triumph awaits us there, if we will but undertake to win it. But we must have fighting as gallant and skilful as heretofore, and no trifling negotiations, no gratuitous restitutions, no consular presents, no bullying articles against tribute, and tacit ticklings of the pirates' palm. This war, if we have it, will be quite as much as we can manage well, and will not necessarily, nor even prob-ably, lead us into any other. Its tendency would on the contrary be to cement our peace with the rest of the world, by increasing at once our moral strength in the respect of mankind, and our physical power of defense in the naval bulwark. War! say I, with Algiers, and peace with the universe beside.

You will continue to hear much talk about the distresses of this country, and to see highly colored pictures of petty riots among workmen to raise their wages, or to reduce the price of bread. Notwithstanding which I remain fixed in the opinion that never in our time was there so little prevailing distress, and never so little discontent throughout the island as at this time. You have seen the most confident and formidable predictions that there would be a falling off of thirty or forty per cent in the revenue; and if a hundredth part of the clamor about distress had been founded, that effect would have been inevitable. The revenue in all its branches is increasing instead of diminishing, and although fifteen or sixteen millions of annual taxes have been abolished, the stocks are constantly rising. The whole amount of loans for the present year will not equal the sum discharged by the sinking fund, the exchanges with all the world are largely in favor of this country, and yet the Bank makes paper money *ad libitum*. The government will this year face an expenditure of thirty millions, besides the interest of the debt. Parliament have been trifling with economy, retrenchment, agricultural distresses, tithes, poor laws, and all the standing themes of declamation; but trifling is all they have done. If there was more than usual distress, Parliament could not get rid of the subject by speeches and abstract resolutions. If there was real distress among the classes above pauperism, the assessed taxes upon luxuries and the excise upon luxurious consumption would and must fall off. If there was extraordinary distress among the poor, how could there be a complaint of excessive plenty? I will not say what the state of things may come to, but I rely upon it that if real distress ever comes, it will be in a very different shape from that in which it has yet appeared.

I had lately a letter from Mr. McCall, consul at Barcelona, who wishes much for your arrival in Spain. He complains much of the arrest of Mr. Andrew Thorndike and of irregular proceedings against him. He adds that we are much out of favor with the Spaniards.

I shall hope to hear from you at Madrid and remain, etc.

JOHN QUINCY ADAMS (LONDON) TO JOHN ADAMS, AUGUST 1, 1816

After reviewing the growing hostility of Europe to the United States, and reaffirming his attachment to the Union, John Quincy turns to a recent toast given by Commodore Stephen Decatur – "Our country! In her intercourse with foreign nations may she always be in the right; but our country, right or wrong!" John Quincy's rejoinder: "I cannot ask of Heaven success, even for my Country, in a Cause where she should be in the wrong. Fiat Justitia, pereat Coelum. My toast would be, may our Country be always successful – but whether successful or otherwise, always right. I disclaim as unsound all patriotism incompatible with the principles of eternal Justice. But the truth is that the American Union, while united may be certain of success in every rightful cause, and may if it pleases never have any but a rightful cause to maintain. They are at this moment the strongest Nation upon the globe, for every purpose of Justice. May they be just to secure the favour of Heaven; and wise, to make a proper application of their strength. May they be armed in thunder for the defence of Right, and self-shackled in eternal impotence for the support of Wrong."

MY DEAR SIR:

The multiplicity of business, and of things that consume more time than business, have in spite of all my efforts broken down to such a degree the regularity of my private correspondence that I am now to acknowledge the receipt of your favors of 20 and 28 March, of 10 and 20 May, and of 16 and 25 June, every one of which contains matter upon which, if I had the time and the talents, I could write you a volume in return.

You are alarmed at the restoration of the Jesuits; but whether it is that I was fascinated by my good old friend, the Father General at St. Petersburg, or that I have a firmer reliance upon the impossibility of reviving exanimated impostures, I have not been able to work myself up into anything like fear of evil consequences at this event. I had a diplomatic colleague in Russia, a man of excellent heart, of amiable temper, of amusing and sportive wit, a profound classical and mathematical scholar, an honest moralist and a conscientious Roman Catholic Christian, who used to maintain to me with the most diverting seriousness and from the deepest conviction of his soul that Father Malebranche was the only metaphysician, and that Locke was the veriest pestilence of modern times. Locke was the father of the Encyclopaedists; Locke was the founder of the French Revolution and of all its horrors. I understand that there is a learned Theban laying it down to the people of France in the *Moniteur*, that all the miseries of mankind in the present age are imputable to the pretended reformation of Luther; and at Madrid a professor of mathematics has commenced a course of lectures by announcing to his pupils that he shall omit all the higher branches of the science, because it has been proved by experience that they lead to Atheism. But if Julian, the genius, the conqueror, the philosopher, the master of the world, did but kick against the pricks when he undertook to restore the magnificent mythology of the Greeks, is it conceivable that the driveling dotards of this age can bring back the monkeries and mummeries of the twelfth century? Oh! No! Europe is tyrannized not by priests but by soldiers. It is overshadowed by a military despotism. Let the bayonets be taken away, and there will be no danger of the Jesuits.

A friend of mine has sent me a large parcel of Boston newspapers, mostly of the last days of June. By them and by other accounts I learn that Governor Brooks' speech has not given satisfaction to those who patronized his election. It is, however, such as I should have expected from the man before he was their candidate. His total silence upon the merits of his predecessor is eloquence of the best kind. I always entertained a very respectful opinion of the character of General Brooks; but when I found him selected as the candidate of the Junto men, I could not avoid the suspicion that he had condescended, or would condescend, to some compromise of principle which could not fail to sink him in my estimation. He has steered clear of this rock in his speech. But he has a year of painful probation to go through, and with a prospect almost certain of being deserted by his supporters if he maintains his own independence. Since the peace it has evidently been the great struggle of the faction still calling themselves federalists, not as during the war to grasp or destroy the national government, but merely to maintain their own ascendency in the states where they had obtained it. They have, however, failed even of that in Vermont, New Hampshire, and New York. In Massachusetts, Connecticut, and Maryland, their majorities have dwindled almost into nothing. Should no national misfortune befall us I anticipate their complete overthrow in another year. It is hinted to me that the separation of the District of Maine will prolong their dominion perhaps a year or two more in the remnant of old Massachusetts; but as the new state will immediately be redeemed from their misgovernment, it will weaken them in the national councils and scatter their ranks nearly as much as if they were reduced to a minority in the whole Commonwealth.

If I were merely a man of Massachusetts I should deeply lament this dismemberment of my native state. But the longer I live the stronger I find my national feelings grow upon me, and the less of my affections are compassed by partial localities. My system of politics more and more inclines to strengthen the union and its government. It is directly the reverse of that professed by Mr. John Randolph, of relying principally upon the state governments. The effort of every one of the state governments would be to sway the whole union for its own local advantage. The doctrine is therefore politic enough for a citizen of the most powerful state in the union, but it is good for nothing for the weaker states, and pernicious for the whole. But it is the contemplation of our external relations that makes me specially anxious to strengthen our national government. The conduct and issue of the late war has undoubtedly raised our national character in the consideration of the world; but we ought also to be aware that it has multiplied and embittered our enemies. This nation is far more inveterate against us than it ever was before. All the restored governments of Europe are deeply hostile to us. The Royalists everywhere detest and despise us as Republicans. All the victims and final vanquishers of the French Revolution abhor us as aiders and abettors of the French during their career of triumph. Wherever British influence extends it is busy to blacken us in every possible manner. In Spain the popular feeling is almost as keen against us as in England. Emperors, kings, princes, priests, all the privileged orders, all the establishments, all the votaries of legitimacy, eye us with the most rancorous hatred. Among the crowned heads the only friend we had was the Emperor Alexander, and his friendship has, I am afraid, been more than cooled. How long it will be possible for us to preserve peace with all Europe it is impossible to foresee. Of this I am sure, that we cannot be too well or too quickly prepared for a new conflict to support our rights and our interests. The tranquillity of Europe is precarious, it is liable to many sudden changes and great convulsions; but there is none in probable prospect which would give us more security than we now enjoy against the bursting of another storm upon ourselves. I can never join with my voice in the toast which I see in the papers attributed to one of our gallant naval commanders. I cannot ask of heaven success, even for my country, in a cause where she should be in the wrong. *Fiat justitia, pareat caelum.* My toast would be, may our country be always successful, but whether successful or otherwise always right. I disclaim as unsound all patriotism incompatible with the principles of eternal justice. But the truth is that the American union, while united, *may* be certain of success in every rightful cause, and may if it pleases never have any but a rightful cause to maintain. They are at this moment the strongest nation upon the globe for every purpose of justice. May they be just to secure the favor of heaven, and wise to make a proper application of their strength. May they be armed in thunder for the defense of right, and self-shackled in eternal impotence for the support of wrong.

We have been much affected by the intelligence of the decease of Colonel Smith, following in such quick succession upon that of his two brothers. It has severely distressed his son, in whom I have an industrious, attentive and faithful assistant. He had been in some measure prepared for the event by the accounts he had previously received. The news of Mr. Dexter's death came upon us sudden and unexpected. We first heard of it on the 5th of June. I had written him a long letter on the 14th of April, in answer to one that I had received from him by Captain Stuart. It must have arrived in America after his departure and I hope will not fall into improper hands.

I shall write as soon as possible to my dear mother. We are all in good health, only as I have been troubled with six weeks of holidays, my three boys are now beginning to complain of a relapse into the school headache. They write by this opportunity for themselves.

I remain, etc.

JOHN QUINCY ADAMS TO CHRISTOPHER HUGHES, DECEMBER 25, 1816

How should an aspiring diplomat prepare himself to carry out his duties? John Quincy outlines a two-year course of study of classic texts of history and international law, not all of which would be easy to work through. But above all, "I would suggest to you the utility of preparing your mind for application when you return home to the history, the internal interests, and the external relations of our own country." Know thyself.

DEAR SIR:

The enclosed list will more than suffice for eighteen months or two years, reading. Many of them will prove by no means attractive. To Smith, Montesquieu, Grotius and Ward, I would recommend your particular attention for the development of the *principles* which are generally recognized in the intercourse of nations. Vattel is the author most commonly resorted to in practical diplomacy, and his work being written in a popular and easy style is among those that you will find the least tedious in reading. If your object were to form a diplomatic library, the list should be much larger, and would include many books in other languages than the English; several voluminous collections of treaties, particular as well as general histories of the European nations, and numerous dissertations and treatises upon special questions of national law. The enclosed list contains only books of a general nature and all published in Europe which I thought most conforming to your request. They will sufficiently absorb your time for two years. But as you have a *career* before you, and do me the favor to consult my opinion, I would suggest to you the utility of preparing your mind for application when you return home to the *history*, the internal *interests*, and the external *relations* of our own country. In the history of the several colonial establishments united together by the war of our independence, you will find the source of the various and in some respects conflicting interests which it is the first duty of an American statesman to conciliate and unite. In the collections of American state papers and the Journals of Congress under the confederation you will find the best key to the interests and rights of our country in her internal administration and in her intercourse with foreign powers. But all the books upon these subjects are to be procured in America, and many of them are not to be found elsewhere.

Wishing you success in your studies and in your negotiations, I remain with great esteem, etc.

List of authors in general, modern history, national law and diplomatic intercourse.

> Robertson's History of Charles the fifth
> History of America
> Watson's History of Phillip the second
> Phillip the third and
> Roscoe's Life of Lorenzo de Medici
> Leo the tenth
> Coxe's History of the House of Austria
> Russell's Letters on Ancient and Modern History
> Raynal's History of the East and West Indies
> Edward's History of the West Indies
> Brougham's Colonial Policy
> Annual Register from 1758 to 1815
> Jenkinson's or Chalmer's collection of Treaties
> Smith's Wealth of Nations
> Montesquieu's Spirit of Laws
> Grotius' Rights of War and Peace with Barbeyrac's
>   Commentary
> Puffendorf, Law of Nature and Nations with do
> Vattel's Law of Nations
> Marten's Summary of the Modern Law of Nations
> Burlamaqui, Law of Nature and Nations
> Ward's History of the Law of Nations.

JOHN QUINCY ADAMS TO WILLIAM PLUMER, JANUARY 17, 1817

John Quincy paints a bleak picture of international relations. The American performance during the war had raised its public character in Europe – but it had also crested fears and jealousies. "We are considered not merely as an active and enterprising, but as a grasping and ambitious people." Britain, if anything, was even more hostile

than before, having been embarrassed at sea. Throughout the Conti-
nent Americans were despised as republicans, "and the primary causes
of the propagation of those political principles, which still make the
throne of every European monarch rock under him as with the throes
of an earthquake." Conflict with Spain seemed on the horizon; France
would welcome another Anglo-American war; the Barbary regencies
seethed with resentment; and even Emperor Alexander had grown
cold. "The conclusion from all which that we must draw is, to do jus-
tice invariably to every nation, and at the same time to fix our mili-
tary naval and fiscal establishment upon a foundation adequate to
our defense and enabling us to obtain justice from them."

MY DEAR SIR:

I am yet to acknowledge the receipt of your two obliging
favors of 6 March and 30 July last, the latter enclosing a copy of
your speech to the legislature. During the whole time that I have
enjoyed the happiness of an acquaintance and friendship with
you, there has been so general a coincidence of sentiment between
us upon all the objects of concernment to our country, which
have successively arisen, that I can ascribe it to no other cause
than to the similitude, or rather the identity, of our political and
moral principles. It was therefore not possible for me to read your
excellent speech without great pleasure, and I was much gratified
to see that its merits did not escape public notice even in this
country. It was republished entire in one of the newspapers of
most extensive circulation, not as during our late war some of our
governor's speeches were republished, to show the subserviency
of the speakers to the bulwark of our holy religion and to the press
gang, but professedly for the pure and patriotic and genuine
republican sentiments with which it abounded. It has been a truly
cheering contemplation to me to see that the people of New Hampshire have recovered from the delusions of that unprincipled faction, which under the name of Federalism were driving to the
dissolution of the Union, and under the name of Washington to
British reconciliation; to see them returning to the counsels of

sober and moderate men, who are biassed by no feelings but those of public spirit, and by no interests but those of their country. Such a person I well knew they had found in you, and such I hope you will find in your present and future coadjutors. Although the progress of reformation has not been so rapid and effectual in our native state as it has been with you, yet the tendency of the public opinion has been steadily since the peace in that direction, as it has been throughout the Union; and as that faction cannot fail to sink in proportion ai the country prospers, I do not despair of seeing the day when the policy of all the state governments will be in union with that of the nation.

We have lately received what may be termed President Madison's valedictory message to Congress, and grateful indeed must it be to his feelings to compare the condition of the country at the close of his administration, with the turbulent and perilous state in which it was at the period of his first election. It will be the great duty of his successor, and of the Congress with which he is to cooperate, to use diligently the days of peace to prepare the nation for other trials which are probably not far distant, and which sooner or later cannot fail to arise. Your speech most justly remarks that the late war raised our public character in the estimation of other nations; but we cannot be too profoundly impressed with the sentiment that it has by no means added to the number of our friends. In this country more particularly, it is impossible for me to disguise to myself that the national feeling of animosity and rancor against America and the Americans is more universal and more bitter than it was before the war. A considerable part of the British nation then despised us, and contempt is a feeling far less active in spurring to acts of hostility, than hatred and fear which have taken its place. No Briton of any party ever imagined that we should be able to sustain a contest against them upon the ocean. Very few among ourselves expected it. Our victories both by sea and land, though intermingled with defeats and disasters which we ought to remember more studiously than our triumphs, have placed our character as a martial nation upon a level with the most respectable nations of Europe; but the effect here has been to unite all parties in the conviction that we are destined to be the most formidable of the enemies and rivals of their naval power. Now the navy is so universally the idol of this nation that there is not a statesman of any description or party who dares befriend anything opposed to it, or look with other than hostile eyes to anything that threatens its glory or portends its downfall. The opposition party and its leaders before the war were much more liberally disposed towards America than the ministerialists; but after the war commenced they joined the ministers in full pack, and since the peace their party tactics have constantly been to cavil against any liberality or concession of the ministers to America. The issue of the late European wars has been to give for the moment (though it will not last long) to the British government an ascendency of influence over the whole continent of Europe which they will naturally use to inspire prejudices and jealousies against us. There is already in all the governments of Europe a strong prejudice against us as Republicans, and as the primary causes of the propagation of those political principles, which still make the throne of every European monarch rock under him as with the throes of an earthquake. With Spain we are and have been on the verge of war. Nothing but the impotence of the Spanish government has hitherto prevented the explosion, and we have so many collisions of interest as well as of principles with Spain, that it is not only the Court but the nation which hates and fears us. In France the government, besides being in tutelage under Britain, have feelings against America more venomous even than the British. The mass of the French nation have no such feelings; but they have no attachment to us, or friendship for us. Their own condition absorbs all their feelings, and they would delight in seeing us at war with Great Britain, because they flatter themselves that would operate as a diversion in their favor, and perhaps enable them to break the yoke under which they are groaning. We have claims for indemnification against the governments of France, Spain, the Netherlands, Naples, and Denmark, the justice of which they do not admit, and which nothing but necessity will ever bring them to acknowledge. The very pursuit of those claims has a tendency to embroil us with those nations, as has been fully exemplified in the result of Mr. Pinkney's late mission to Naples; and yet as the claims are just they ought not to be abandoned. The states of Barbary owe us a heavy grudge for the chastisements we have inflicted upon all of them, and for the example first set by us to the European nations, of giving them battle instead of tribute, and of breaking up their system of piracy. We have therefore enemies in almost every part of the world, and few or no friends anywhere. If there be an exception it is in Russia; but even there the shameful misconduct of the Russian Consul General at Philadelphia, and the infamous manner in which he has been abetted by the Minister Daschkoff, have produced a coldness on the part of the Emperor which endangered at least the harmony of the relations between the two countries. Add to all this, that there is a vague and general sentiment of speculative and fomenting jealousy against us prevailing all over Europe. We are considered not merely as an active and enterprising, but as a grasping and ambitious people. We are supposed to have inherited all the bad qualities of the British character, without some of those of which other nations in their dealings with the British have made their advantage. They ascribe to us all the British rapacity, without allowing us the credit of the British profusion. The universal feeling of Europe in witnessing the gigantic growth of our population and power is that we shall, if united, become a very dangerous member of the society of nations. They therefore hope what they confidently expect, that we shall not long remain united. That before we shall have attained the strength of national manhood our Union will be dissolved, and that we shall break up into two or more nations in opposition against one another. The conclusion from all which that we must draw is, to do justice invariably to every nation, and at the same time to fix our military naval and fiscal establishment upon a foundation adequate to our defense and enabling us to obtain justice from them.

I have not yet been able to procure for you Adair's *History of the Indians*, but I have found at a very moderate price a complete set of the *Remembrancer*, including the *Prior Documents*, all in eleven volumes, which I purpose to send you by the *Galen*, to sail about the first of March.

I remain, etc.

DIARY ENTRY (LONDON), JUNE 6, 1817

The famous British abolitionist, William Wilberforce, proposed that the United States and other maritime nations agree to allow the Royal Navy to stop and search their ships suspected of engaging in the slave traffic. John Quincy had previously heard Lord Castlereagh make similar suggestions, but he feared that this was a way to get the United States to accept the right of the British to visit and search American vessels, thereby legitimizing impressment. The source of the proposal was also suspicious – Wilberforce was the brother-in-law of James Stephens, the author of a prewar pamphlet that defended the most extreme British maritime practices against neutral maritime commerce.

Mr. Wilberforce had called at Craven Street the day before yesterday while I was out, and left a note requesting to see me. I answered him yesterday morning, that I would call at two this day at his lodgings, 8 Downing Street. I went at the time, but he had missed of receiving my note, and was not at home. Lord Castlereagh had also, by a note, requested me, instead of calling at his house yesterday morning, as we had agreed, to come this afternoon at four o'clock to the Foreign Office; but when I went at the time, he was not there. I went twice to the House of Commons to see if I could find either of them there. Lord Castlereagh came at last, and, with an apology for missing his appointment, asked me to call at his house to-morrow morning. Mr. Goulburn and Mr. Sharp came under the gallery, and took leave of me. Sir John Cox Hippisley, whom I met in the lobby, did the same, and charged me with a message of his kind remembrance to his old friend H. Cruger at New York.

I finally found Mr. Wilberforce at his lodgings, with his friend Mr. Babbington, also a member of the House of Commons. The suppression of the slave-trade was the subject of Mr. Wilberforce's wish to see me, and we had an hour's conversation relating to it. His object is to obtain the consent of the United States, and of all other maritime powers, that ships under their flags may be searched and captured by the British cruisers against the slave-trade – a concession which I thought would be liable to objections. There had been published in the London papers of 4th June a resolution of the Congress of the United States, passed at their last session, requesting the President to enter into negotiation with Great Britain and other European powers for completing, if possible, the suppression of the slave-trade, and for sending certain free people of color from the United States to Sierra Leone, or some such settlement on the coast of Africa. Wilberforce intimated to me, but did not expressly assert, that he had not seen this resolution till after he had written me the note in Craven Street requesting to see me, and he said he had been gratified at the coincidence. But the great object of his wish to see me was evidently to start the proposition that the British cruisers against the slave-trade should be authorized to overhaul and search, and even capture, American vessels suspected to be engaged in that trade.

Probably this project originated in the brain of Master Stephen, the author of "War in Disguise," and brother-in-law to Wilberforce, one of the party called in derision the Saints, and who under sanctified visors pursue worldly objects with the ardor and perseverance of saints. Wilberforce is at the head of these Saints in Parliament, and is said to possess more personal influence in the House of Commons than any other individual. Lord Castlereagh has more than once thrown out this idea of a mutual stipulation that the cruisers of every nation which has passed laws for abolishing the slave-trade should be authorized to search and capture the slave-trading vessels of the other nations by whose laws the trade is prohibited. In substance, it is a barefaced and impudent attempt of the British to obtain in time of peace that right of searching and seizing the ships of other nations which they have so outrageously abused during war. I never discussed the subject with Castlereagh, because he never brought the point to an explicit proposal, and it was not necessary to sift the proposition to the bottom; but Wilberforce, after much lamentation at the inefficacy of the existing laws and measures for suppressing the trade, and asserting that it was now carried on with as much activity and inhumanity as ever, professed to be unable to devise anything that should effectually suppress it. And yet, he said, there was one thing that would accomplish the end if the nations would agree to it, and then came out with the proposal, and enquired whether the United States would agree to it : that all vessels, whatever nation's flag they should bear, but which might be suspected of being engaged in the slave-trade, should be liable to search and capture by the cruisers of any other nation.

I told him I thought there would be some objection to this. In the first place, no American vessel engaged in the slave trade could use the American flag, for the trade was prohibited by law, and a vessel which should be captured while engaged in it could not obtain any interference of the American Government to rescue her. The flag could be no protection to her. The commander of the capturing vessel would only act at his peril, and if he seized a vessel not really concerned in the trade he must be responsible to indemnify the sufferer. Again, a stipulation of this nature, though nominally reciprocal, would be really one-sided. Cruisers against the slave-trade are in fact kept only by Great Britain. British vessels, therefore, would be liable to no search or capture but by officers under the authority of their own Government, while the vessels of other nations would be subject to seizure by foreigners not amenable or accountable to their own sovereigns. Some degree of prejudice must also be supposed to exist against the naval power of Great Britain, and particularly some jealousy of the exercise of an arbitrary power by her naval officers.

Mr. Babbington appeared to admit there was more foundation in these objections than Wilberforce was ready to allow. He suggested that in each cruiser there should be an officer of each power agreeing to the principle, and that he should be present at every search, and no capture be made without his consent. I objected to this, that it would lead to conflicts of opinion, and perhaps even of authority, between the officers of the different Governments; and Wilberforce did not like this expedient any better than I did. I also alluded to the misconduct of many naval British officers, to the manner in which they had taken slaves from the United States and had probably sold many of them, and I explained the manner in which the Judge of the Vice-Admiralty Court had evaded the British Statute and Order in Council by which captured slaves were to be liberated, or rather made the King's slaves for life.

Wilberforce was much struck by this information, of which I authorized him to make such use as he thought proper. He somewhat equivocally expressed his disapprobation of Admiral Cochrane's proclamation inviting the slaves to run away from their masters and join him, and said he knew too much of what had been the lot of those slaves. He added that there were very few of them in Halifax. I believe that Wilberforce was, on the whole, disappointed in the result of this interview; though we parted in perfect good humor and civility.

Mr. West, with Zerah Colburn and his father, spent the evening with us. Mr. West then told me that he had in the year 1783 made a sketch for a picture of the peace which terminated the war of the American Revolution, which he would send me to look at the next morning, as he accordingly did. I then recollected having seen it before, at the time when my father was sitting to him for his likeness in it. The most striking likeness in the picture is that of Mr. Jay. Those of Dr. Franklin, and his grandson, W. T., who was Secretary to the American Commission, are also excellent. Mr. Laurens and my father, though less perfect resemblances, are yet very good. Mr. Oswald, the British Plenipotentiary, was an ugly-looking man, blind of one eye, and he died without leaving any picture of him extant. This Mr. West alleged as the cause which prevented him from finishing the picture many years ago. Caleb Whitefoord, the Secretary of the British Commission, is also dead, but his portrait exists, from which a likeness may be taken. As I very strongly expressed my regret that this picture should be left unfinished, Mr. West said he thought he could finish it, and I must not be surprised if some day or other it should be received at Washington. I understand his intention to be to make a present of it to Congress.

Zerah Colburn's father urged me to let him communicate to me the secret of his instinctive arithmetic. I consented, and he made the attempt, but without success. I might perhaps have understood him but for the continual interposition of the father himself, who, without understanding it, by his frequent explanatory interruptions disconcerted both Zerah and me. I was, however, satisfied that the secret is only a rapidity of intellect with which the boy performs the processes of multiplication and division, and that it is communicable only to minds equally quick in their operations.

CHAPTER EIGHT

SECRETARY OF STATE, 1817–1821

INTRODUCTION

ALTHOUGH THE DUTIES of the secretary of state extended to domestic affairs, John Quincy Adams stayed away from commenting on hot-button political topics outside foreign affairs. Throughout his tenure he would keep his official focus on strengthening the strategic position of the United States in a transatlantic world still reeling from two decades of global war. Europe had settled into an uneasy strategic equilibrium maintained by a concert of the victorious powers and supported by the restored monarchy in France. John Quincy concluded that the major Continental states, and Britain, were sincerely anxious to preserve a period of interstate peace.

Three matters principally consumed his time in office: First, normalizing relations with Britain such that the two nations would never again go to war unnecessarily, as had been the case in 1812; second, dealing with the impending breakup of the Spanish Empire in the New World, which created both opportunities and dangers for the United States. Both these issues involved questions of boundary. John Quincy, the expansionist, naturally wanted those that would favor the United States, not only because of the addition of territory and resources, but as a means to increase American security by reducing potential threats coming from other powers in the Western Hemisphere.

Third, John Quincy faced the challenge to republican government, and to the United States, posed by the reactionary regimes of Europe. These regimes, under the nominal rubric of Emperor Alexander's Holy Alliance, sought to suppress any political change on the Continent. John Quincy did not believe that the United States had an immediate or vital interest in the social or political struggles of Europe, despite America's natural sympathy for the cause of liberty. But there was the possibility that the European despotisms might not confine their reactionary policies to the Continent and instead seek to spread them militarily to the New World – first to the rebellious colonies of Spain, and then to the seedbed of republicanism, the United States.

Under instructions from Monroe and John Quincy, Richard Rush, minister to Great Britain, together with Albert Gallatin, the minister to France, negotiated the Treaty (or Convention) of 1818, which sidestepped the wartime issues and extended the commercial terms of the Convention of 1815 for ten years. Monroe had originally sought a more comprehensive agreement, although John Quincy doubted that there was much hope of progress on key issues, including impressment. The British had proved willing to make some concessions on trade with the West Indies but, in the opinion of Monroe and John Quincy, they were cosmetic only. The British foreign minister, Lord Castereagh, seemed surprisingly open to conceding on impressment, but only for a fixed period and with certain caveats. John Quincy was strongly opposed to an agreement that would allow the British to impress seamen at any time, and under any circumstances. Although Monroe was willing to accept, the negotiators in London could not work out certain technical arrangements, and the matter was left unresolved.

On the matter of the fisheries, John Quincy also preferred to take a hard line, defending the position his father had taken in negotiating the Peace of Paris – that the term "liberty" to fish in North American waters under British jurisdiction, equated to a "right" in perpetuity. Here he was overruled by Monroe, and in London the two sides compromised. In the Treaty, the United States was granted the liberty "for ever" to fish in certain specified areas, and to dry and cure the fish only on uninhabited shores. This was a substantive victory for the United States, but John Quincy always hated giving up a principle, even if only partly, when he thought America was in the right. As to compensation for slaves escaped to or captured by British forces during the war, the Treaty referred the matter to "some Friendly Sovereign or State to be named for that purpose," who turned out to be Alexander of Russia. In 1822, the Russian government ruled that the United States was entitled to indemnity. After further diplomatic wrangling, the British in 1826 agreed to pay compensation of $1.2 million.

With respect to the disputed northern boundary with Canada, the two sides again compromised. According to the Treaty, the boundary would be set at the forty-ninth parallel, up to the Rocky Mountains, which placed the Mississippi River entirely within the United States. The territory west of the mountains and north of Spanish Alta California, whose exact boundary was undefined (known to the Americans as the Oregon Country) was left open to the people and vessels of both nations for a renewable period of ten years, with no prejudice to the claims of sovereignty by either party. In discussions with the British minister in Washington, John Quincy did his best to protect American claims to private property at the mouth of the Columbia River, giving the United States a toehold on the Pacific coast.

The Treaty of 1818, limited as it was, meant that there were no immediate issues that would bring on a direct conflict with Britain. With that, John Quincy felt he had running room to seek resolution of several outstanding issues with Spain, whose unstable colonial borderlands abutted the United States. Florida was of immediate concern. For Southerners and Westerners, possession of Florida by a major foreign power (Britain or France) would be a grave threat to the Mississippi Valley and the American South (where it would serve as a magnet for escaped slaves). Both Jefferson and Madison had sought by overt and covert means to acquire east and west Florida but to no avail. Since Spanish authority there had largely collapsed in the wake of the Napoleonic wars, the void had been filled by adventurers, former slaves, and Indians, who sometimes raided across the border.

In addition, Spain had never accepted the validity of the Louisiana Purchase, whose boundary was in any case in dispute. Madrid took the position that the United States had no valid claim west of the Mississippi. To complicate matters further, rebels from Spanish colonies throughout the hemisphere declared their independence, seeking aid and diplomatic recognition from the United States. Ordinary Americans were naturally sympathetic to the independence movements and some of them offered their services to the insurgents. American merchants supplied the revolutionaries with arms and supplies. Spain demanded that the United States stay out of the matter and strictly enforce its laws to stop Americans from aiding the rebels. Madrid, playing on long-standing Anglo-American antagonisms, counted on British support in the diplomatic conflict, and in any war with the United States.[1]

It was up to John Quincy, under Monroe's direction, to untangle this mess. He believed that if the United States played its diplomatic, economic, and military cards correctly, it could legitimately expand its territory in the Floridas, enhance its security, and all without going to war. First, the United States must isolate Spain from any European, and especially British, support. Second, America would make clear that it would use force to ensure the safety of the borderlands (with the implicit threat that it would occupy Florida if necessary). Third, it would insist on an agreement with Madrid that recognized American sovereignty over much of the territory west of the Mississippi, as well as Florida. In exchange, the United States would pay for claims of American citizens against Spain; and it would not actively support or recognize the South American revolutionaries. The latter concession, however, was not to be made explicitly, and it was contingent on events.

The playing out of John Quincy's script was indeed contingent on events. Amelia Island was a speck of Spanish-owned land off the Georgia-Florida coast. It had been seized by a group claiming to be South American revolutionaries who used it as a base to launch privateering missions against Spanish shipping (and, occasionally, American flagged ships). Many Americans regarded them as patriots. John Quincy did not; piracy was piracy, no matter the cause. He advised the president to evict the "marauding parties" immediately. Monroe agreed and dispatched a land and naval force that occupied the island in December 1817.

Spain expected the United States to turn over Amelia once the pirates – or revolutionaries – had been removed. That was the initial inclination of Monroe and a majority of the cabinet as well. Spain could regard continued American occupation as a casus belli. But John Quincy convinced the president to retain the island. It served as a lesson about the administration's determination to enforce regional security, if Spain could not.

This lesson was repeated when General Andrew Jackson invaded Florida to suppress raids into Georgia by Seminole Indians. That action had been authorized by Washington if deemed necessary – but Jackson also captured and held two Spanish forts and summarily executed two British citizens, Alexander Arbuthnot and Robert Ambrister, who Jackson claimed had supported the Indians. Jackson's actions created a domestic furor. At first blush, it seemed likely to provoke a war with Britain, or at the very least to derail the negotiations with Spain.

The cabinet almost unanimously recommended that Jackson be disavowed and censured. Prominent congressmen, above all Henry Clay, demanded it. John Quincy, who was certainly not party to any secret understanding, was the lone holdout in the administration. He helped persuade the president that Jackson should not be disavowed. The forts would be returned, but only when Spain could adequately garrison them to control the Indians.

To influence congressional and public opinion in the United States and abroad, especially in Britain, John Quincy released to the press a note to the Spanish minister to the United States, Luis de Onis, with supporting documents, vigorously defending Jackson's actions and the American position on Florida. John Quincy argued that the blame lay with incendiaries like Arbuthnot and Ambrister, as well as with Spain, for failing to do anything about it. If Spain could not govern Florida properly, it must cede the province to a nation that could – the United States.

John Quincy rightly calculated that Britain would not fight over the treatment of Arbuthnot and Ambrister. He was now strengthened in his belief that he had succeeded in isolating Spain diplomatically and politically. He was confident that Congress would take no action against Jackson, and, if requested, would pass a resolution authorizing the administration to take possession of Florida by force, along with claiming Texas as indemnity for the expense of doing so, if the Spanish did not come to terms.[2]

As to the matter of the quid pro quo, the Monroe administration held back from recognition of the South American revolutionaries, although John Quincy refused to make an explicit commitment to Onis on this point. South American representatives and their US supporters, particularly Henry Clay, vehemently resented John Quincy's apparent indifference toward the cause. John Quincy thought Clay had seized on the South American issue as an expedient device to rally opposition against the Monroe administration in general, and John Quincy in particular.

It was not that John Quincy opposed South American independence. He had long believed it to be inevitable and desirable. Under the right circumstances, he was prepared to recognize at least Buenos Aires despite the sensitive negotiations with Onis over Florida. But he believed that quiet diplomacy behind the scenes was the best aid that the United States could give. As he wrote to an American diplomat, "You understand that the policy of the government of the United States is to favor by all suitable means compatible with a fair neutrality the total independence of the South American provinces."[3] He encouraged the major

European powers, particularly Britain, to persuade Spain that its cause was hopeless and that it should cut its losses (and thereby preserve its most valuable possession, Cuba). He insisted that America would not participate in any mediation of the conflict by Britain, and certainly not by the Holy Alliance, which was found to favor Spain; to do so might lead to armed intervention.

If left to his own devices, John Quincy's diplomacy probably would have been even more cautious with respect to the South American cause, in order first to secure a treaty with Spain. Recognition, he told Monroe, depended on the facts on the ground. Merely because a people had the right to independence did not mean it was actually independent. It was unclear to him what type of governments would emerge once they achieved independence; based on some reports, it seemed they might become monarchies, quite possibly attached to European dynasties. He had long expressed doubts whether the political culture of the South Americans would admit of stable, republican government. The new states might grant Spain special commercial privileges, which would make their independence qualified. Whatever the outcome, neutrality between the parties was the correct course, to be fulfilled according to the law of nations and congressional legislation.

Through 1821, the President's Annual Message (the foreign policy sections of which were substantially drafted by John Quincy) held out only words of sympathy to the South Americans, with no promise of material support and no acknowledgement of their independent status. In the opinion of impatient Americans like Clay, John Quincy had supinely ceded control of US foreign policy on South American liberty to the reactionary Holy Alliance. For John Quincy, it was a question of one step at a time.

The next step was to secure westward expansion. In January 1818, Onis offered for the first time to cede Florida and consider a boundary west of the Mississippi. This would take place if the Americans agreed to suppress effectively the South American privateers operating out of American ports and explicitly commit to a policy of non-recognition. These concessions occurred even before Jackson's invasion. With Florida seemingly in their pocket, Monroe and John Quincy considered what else they wanted. Monroe seemed to prefer a straight-up deal, gaining Florida in exchange for American claims, stemming from the Louisiana Purchase, on Spanish Texas. If Onis would not agree, the president was inclined to let matters rest, as time favored the Americans.

For his part, Onis sought to keep the United States as far to the east and north as possible; John Quincy sought the opposite. The American position included a demand for all or part of Texas, and for extending the boundary all the way to the South Sea (Pacific) coast. He was consistently more aggressive in his territorial ambitions than Monroe and the rest of the cabinet, although he of course deferred to the president when a decision was made. Onis, for his part, wanted Texas, if possible, to be kept out of the deal. Retention of that province would serve as a buffer between the United States and the rich silver mines of Mexico.

That left it for John Quincy and Onis to hammer out the details. John Quincy was of the view that he could have had both the Pacific and Texas, up to the Colorado River if not the Rio Grande, if he had been allowed to press hard enough. The documentary records support him on this, but Monroe, in his own mind, regarded it as a matter of trading Texas for Florida (rather than trading Texas for Oregon, as John Quincy was later accused of doing). Jackson, when consulted, supported the proposed arrangement, and John Quincy accepted it without major objection.

Onis finally agreed to a line beginning at the Sabine River (the current Louisiana-Texas border), working to the northwest, by way of the Red River, the Arkansas River, and the Continental Divide, to the forty-second parallel (the present northern border of California). John Quincy was insistent on protecting American claims to the Columbia River basin. He also insisted that the border lie on the south and west banks of the rivers, not in the center, as was customary. The Transcontinental Treaty ceded Florida to the United States, and the American government assumed the responsibility to pay up to $5 million to settle the spoliation claims against Spain. At John Quincy's request, it was signed on Washington's Birthday, February 22, 1819. Despite some grumbling that Texas was not included in the deal, the Senate unanimously consented to the treaty.

Less than two weeks later, John Quincy learned that the treaty was flawed. Henry Clay, of all people, informed the president that enormous land grants in Florida had been made to a few Spanish noblemen, dated before such grants were prohibited by the treaty. John Quincy was thoroughly embarrassed when he discovered that the American minister to Spain, George Erving, had warned him about this several months earlier. The normally meticulous John Quincy had filed and forgotten Erving's dispatch. The Spanish government, meanwhile, wanted a better deal and delayed ratification. It took two more years of stubborn diplomacy on his part, and a change in government in Madrid, to straighten things out. John Quincy, through various diplomatic means, made it clear to the Spanish that the United States would otherwise occupy Florida, insist on indemnities, and demand Texas in any new settlement. The final document was ratified – again, on Washington's Birthday, February 22, 1821.

One reason that Monroe had decided not to press for Texas was his fear that its acquisition would stir up the lingering issue of slavery and its expansion. That same year, the emerging crisis over the admission of Missouri as a slave state, had already brought to the surface the latent problem of slavery and sectionalism. The compromises that settled the crisis were fresh and of uncertain duration.

John Quincy stayed out of the political fray over Missouri but it caused him, perhaps for the first time, to reflect deeply on the dire threat that slavery posed to the Union. He was personally opposed to the institution. In his letters and diary entries, he had previously made snide references to Southern slaveholders. He had written an anonymous article during the campaign of 1804 laying out the objections to slavery. Having lived in the District of Columbia, he had first-hand experience of the practice.

But in his diplomatic career, John Quincy had staunchly carried out his instructions to defend the rights of American slaveholders. He had rejected London's proposal for an international convention that would allow the navies of the contracting parties to stop vessels under foreign flags suspected of engaging in the trade. To his mind, Britain was actually seeking to vindicate the right of impressment. The British minister, Stratford Canning, repeatedly pressed him on the subject. "He asked if I could conceive of a greater and more atrocious evil than this slave-trade. I said, 'Yes: admitting the right of search by foreign officers of our vessels upon the seas in time of peace; for that would be making slaves of ourselves.'" John Quincy's counter proposal, therefore, was as follows: "If the British government will begin by stipulating never from this day forth to the end of time to take by force a white man from an American merchant vessel on the high seas (unless as a prisoner of war), we will listen to proposals to let them search American vessels for black men in time of peace."[4]

One possible solution to the slavery issue would be to send emancipated slaves out of the country and to sponsor their colonization in Africa or elsewhere (the American Colonization Society, supported by prominent political figures such as Henry Clay). John Quincy had sympathy for the intent. But he thought the project doomed to failure. It had inherent in it such inconsistencies, contradictions, and impracticalities that to hope for its success seemed delusional. And even if it were successful in establishing a territory in Africa to which free blacks would migrate, the new "nation" would be so dependent on the United States that it would be in effect a colony of the sort that many of the European powers possessed in Africa, Asia, South America, and the West Indies. It would be the first step in transforming the American republic into an American empire. It would be a betrayal of the ideology of the revolution and the principles of the Declaration, the unintended but perverse consequence of good intentions.

The following year, 1822, the new nations of Chile, Peru, Colombia, Mexico, and the United Provinces of the Rio de la Plata (Argentina) had, in John Quincy's mind, established their independence beyond doubt. With the Transcontinental Treaty now secure, they were duly recognized by President Monroe. The United States, as before, would remain neutral in any residual conflicts between them and Spain. The Spanish minister in Washington protested, but to no avail. As to John Quincy's own views of the new regimes and their peoples, he wished them well, "but I had seen and yet see no prospect that they would establish free or liberal institutions of government.... Arbitrary power, military and ecclesiastical, was stamped upon their education, upon their habits, and upon all their institutions. War and mutual destruction was in every member of their organization, moral, political, and physical. I had little expectation of any beneficial result to this country from any future connection with them, political or commercial. The United States would have little to gain from any connection with them."[5]

JOHN QUINCY ADAMS (WASHINGTON, DC) TO ALEXANDER HILL EVERETT, DECEMBER 29, 1817

Although John Quincy believed that the rebellions against Spanish colonial rule in the New World were destined to succeed, and that they merited success as a matter of simple justice, he insisted on making a distinction between the American Revolution and those now taking place in South America – just as he insisted on distinguishing between the American and French revolutions. "In our Revolution there were two distinct stages, in the first of which we contended for our civil rights, and in the second for our political independence. The second, as we solemnly declared to the world, was imposed upon us as a necessity after every practicable effort had been made in vain to secure the first. In South America civil rights, if not entirely out of the question, appear to have been equally disregarded and trampled upon by all parties." Unfortunately, Americans of the current generation were only exacerbating the problems of the new revolutionaries by not appreciating this distinction.

DEAR SIR:

Your letter of the 16 has been a full week unanswered upon file, and I am obliged now to answer it very imperfectly. The newspapers mention that Mr. Eustis has gone to pass the winter at Paris, and has left Mr. Appleton chargé d'affaires at The Hague. I suppose this is true, though we have no notice of it. My last letter from Mr. Eustis is of 4th October, from The Hague, and its symptoms instead of indicating an intention of speedy departure rather disclose a willingness to be detained even beyond the period of the ensuing spring. No necessity for any such detention is supposed here to be likely to arise; but if circumstances should occur to render the homeward voyage inconvenient next spring, it may perhaps be postponed for another year. I have no particular reason for this surmise other than that gentlemen abroad who have projects of returning home do not like to be hurried.

I have not seen the article upon Peace Societies in the *North American Review*, nor the review itself; but if our Peace Societies should fall into the fashion of corresponding upon the objects of their institutions with foreign Emperors and Kings, they may at some future day find themselves under the necessity of corresponding with attorney generals and petit juries at home. Philip of Macedon was in very active correspondence with a Peace Society at Athens, and with their cooperation baffled and overpowered all the eloquence of Demosthenes. Alexander of the Neva is not so near nor so dangerous a neighbor to us as Philip was to the Athenians, but I am afraid his love of peace is of the same character as was that of Philip of Macedon. Absolute princes who can dispose of large masses of human force must naturally in applying them be aided by all the pacific dispositions that they can find or make among those whom they visit with the exercise of their power. In the intercourse between *power* and *weakness*, peace in the language of the former means the submission of the latter to its will. While Alexander and his Minister of Religious Worship, Prince Galitzin, are corresponding with the Rev. Noah Worcester upon the blessedness of peace, the venerable founder of the Holy League is sending five or six ships of the line, and several thousand promoters of peace armed with bayonets to Cadiz, and thence to propagate good will to man elsewhere. Whether at Algiers, at Constantinople, or at Buenos Ayres, we shall be informed hereafter.

The mention of Buenos Ayres brings to my mind an article that I have lately seen in the *Boston Patriot* and which I concluded was from your pen. Its tendency was to show the inexpediency and injustice there would be in our taking sides with the South Americans in their present struggle against Spain. It was an excellent article, and I should be glad to see the same train of thought further pursued. As for example by a discussion of the question in politica [*blank*] by what *right* we could take sides? and who in this case of civil war has constituted us *the judges* which of the parties has the righteous cause? Then by an inquiry what the cause of the South Americans is, and whether it really be, as their partisans here allege, the same as our own cause in the war of our Revolution? Whether for instance, if Buenos Ayres has formally offered to accept the Infant Don Carlos as their absolute monarch, upon condition of being politically independent of Spain, their cause is the same as ours was? Whether if Bolivar, being at the head of the republic of Venezuela, has solemnly proclaimed the absolute and total emancipation of the slaves, the cause of Venezuela is precisely the same as ours was? Whether in short, there is any other feature of identity between their cause and ours, than that they are, as we were, colonies fighting for independence? In our Revolution there were two distinct stages, in the first of which we contended for our civil rights, and in the second for our *political independence*. The second, as we solemnly declared to the world, was imposed upon us as a necessity after every practicable effort had been made in vain to secure the first.

In South America civil rights, if not entirely out of the question, appear to have been equally disregarded and trampled upon by all parties. Buenos Ayres has no constitution, and its present ruling powers are establishing [themselves] only by the arbitrary banishment of their predecessors. Venezuela, though it has emancipated all its slaves, has been constantly alternating between an absolute military government, a capitulation to Spanish authority, and guerillas black and white, of which every petty chief has acted for purposes of war and rapine as an independent sovereign. There is finally in South America, neither unity of cause nor unity of effort, as there was in our Revolution. Neither was our Revolution disgraced by that buccaneering and piratical spirit which has lately appeared among the South Americans, not of their own growth, but I am sorry to say chiefly from the continuation of their intercourse with us. Their privateers have been for the most part fitted out and officered in our ports, and manned from the sweeping of our streets. It was more effectually to organize and promote their patriotic system that the expeditions to Galveston and Amelia Island were carried into effect, and that the successive gangs of desperadoes, Scotch, French, Creole, and North Americans, that no public exertions have been constituting the republic of the Florida. Yet such is the propensity of our people to sympathize with the South Americans, that no feeble exertion is now making to rouse a party in this country against the government of the Union, and against the President, for having issued orders to put down this host of freebooters at our doors.

Your preparations for the next spring elections in Massachusetts appear to be judicious, and I hope they will be successful. I neither see nor hear anything more of Brighter Views nor of Old North than what you tell me, and there is at present not much to be apprehended from the authors of either of them.

We have the prospect of a troublesome Indian war in the

South, and its bearings upon our political affairs may be more extensive and important than is expected.

I am, etc.

DIARY ENTRIES (WASHINGTON, DC), JANUARY 27 AND 31, 1818

An agreement to allow a third party or third parties to mediate disputes between nations was a common diplomatic tool in the eighteenth and nineteenth centuries, one that John Quincy did not necessarily eschew, despite his fierce insistence on American independence. When Spain approached Britain to suggest that London mediate disputes between the United States and Spain, however, John Quincy demurred when the matter was put to him by the British minister, Charles Bagot. He felt that the British were hardly a disinterested party. That said, he was also anxious to improve Anglo-American relations where possible, and therefore the way in which the United States declined should not give unnecessary offense to London. His solution, based on discussions in the cabinet, was highly unusual for him: rather than aggressively challenge Britain's motives, he would cite American public opinion as being so hostile to Spain that any such arrangement with Britain would have the unfortunate effect of exacerbating tensions between the two English-speaking nations.

27th. Mr. Bagot came to my office according to appointment, at one o'clock, and, by order of his Government, made an offer of their mediation to settle the differences between the United States and Spain. This offer was accompanied with many professions of a friendly disposition towards the United States, and many intimations of no good harmony subsisting between Great Britain and Spain. He read to me an extract from a dispatch from Lord Castlereagh to him referring to his conferences with me before I left England; to his belief that he had convinced me of the frankness and candor with which he had disclosed to me the whole policy of the British Government at this time, and that it was bent upon nothing so earnestly as upon the preservation of universal peace; that he had derived great satisfaction from the assurances given him by me of the same disposition on the part of the American Government, and on my own part personally; with many flattering compliments to me, which Bagot, after reading to me, said he believed he ought not to have done. He also read to me in confidence a copy of a dispatch from Lord Castlereagh to Sir Henry Wellesley, the British Ambassador from Madrid, dated 27th August last, and being an answer to a dispatch from him, with which a note from Pizarro, the Spanish Minister for Foreign Affairs, asking for this mediation of Great Britain, had been forwarded – and Pizarro had made an extended statement of the subjects of dispute between Spain and the United States. Castlereagh answers, that before the Prince Regent could definitively answer this proposal he must know much more of the subject than he could from Pizarro's statement, however extended, and also that the mediation was desired by both parties. At the same time he complains in very angry terms of certain restrictions upon the British commerce in Spain, and hints that unless they are removed England will not act as a mediator between Spain and the United States. This letter Mr. Bagot allowed me in confidence to take and show to the President, on condition that it should not be otherwise used.

At the same time he read me another part of his dispatch, relating to South America, explicitly declaring that if Great Britain alone, or the allied powers jointly, should interpose between Spain and the South American Provinces, the system recommended and urged by Great Britain would be one of perfect liberality to the Provinces – a system which would open their ports and their commerce to all nations, including the United States, and in which Great Britain would neither ask nor accept any exclusive privilege for herself – and adding that this subject was now in negotiation among the allied powers.

I told Mr. Bagot that I must, of course, refer the subject to the consideration of the President, who I was sure would receive the communication as a proof of a friendly disposition in Great Britain. I desired him to thank Lord Castlereagh for the kindness and confidence in me expressed in his dispatch, and with the full promise of my hearty concurrence in the good work of preserving universal peace. As to the mediation, the only objection I could anticipate to it was, that Great Britain had heretofore taken some part with Spain on the very points now in controversy.

He said that whatever may have been the feelings or policy of the British Government under different circumstances and at another period, if she should now assume the character of a mediator, it would be with perfect impartiality, and solely with a view to conciliate the parties to each other. Abstractly speaking, it might be more agreeable to Great Britain to have a weak neighbor than a strong one, but she must accommodate her policy to the nature of things, and she was sincerely desirous of maintaining the best understanding with this country. He had told Onis, the Spanish Minister, yesterday, that if the interposition of Great Britain should be desired by this country, he must not expect that she would support Spain in any extravagant pretensions. He also told him that he should make this communication to me this day. Bagot also told me that McGregor had, when he was here, called upon him, and told him that Dr. Thornton had sent him. He told him that he was going to take Florida, and asked him what the opinion of the British Government upon it would be. Bagot told him he could give him no answer to that question, and could say nothing about it. Bagot afterwards asked Thornton if he really had sent McGregor to him, and he admitted that he had.

31st. There was a full Cabinet meeting at the President's on the question what answers shall be given to Mr. Bagot's proposal and to Mr. Onis's last note, in connection with which were considered the question of South American independence and the transactions at Amelia Island. The sentiment against accepting the mediation was unanimous, but more earnest in all the others than in me. I had doubts whether we should ultimately be able to avoid European interference in this affair, and therefore whether we ought now absolutely to decline that of Great Britain. The determination, however, was positive to decline, and the only question was upon what grounds we should decline. The President and Mr. Crawford suggested the ground that our differences with Spain were not such as to threaten a war – they were of little comparative consequence, and we had no intention to push them to a war. But Mr. Calhoun remarked that if we should take this ground, and Spain should be very urgent for the mediation, it would be a temptation to her to commit some act of hostility to make the mediation necessary. The President and Mr. Crawford also inclined, while rejecting the mediation, to make a statement to the British Government of the merits of our case, in answer to that sent them by Pizarro. I objected that if we gave any statement of the merits, it would give a plausible pretext to the British to reply, and go deeper into the case. I suggested the idea of answering, with thanks for the friendly manifestations of Great Britain, and the strongest assurances of their being reciprocated, that we were obliged to accommodate our measures to the public feelings of the country; that our controversies with Spain, though not of the first rank in importance, had a strong hold upon the popular sentiments; that to refer them to any interposition of a third party would certainly be disapproved by all parties in this country, and have the tendency to create ill will between this country and England, which we were very desirous of avoiding.

This was agreed upon as the principle to be assumed for declining, and the President desired me to make a minute in writing, to be shown him on Monday, of the substance of what should be said to Mr. Bagot. It was also agreed that the next reply to Mr. Onis must be longer, and more particular, than the last. It was four when the meeting broke up.

SECRETARY OF STATE JOHN QUINCY ADAMS (DEPARTMENT OF STATE) TO ALBERT GALLATIN, MAY 19, 1818

Proposals for mediation between Spain and its rebellious colonies were being floated by the European powers jointly to interpose themselves in the conflict. Here, too, John Quincy would have none of it: "If the object of this mediation be any other than to promote the total independence, political and commercial, of South America, we are neither desirous of being invited to take a part in it, nor disposed to accept the invitation if given. Our policy in the contest between Spain and her colonies has been impartial neutrality. The policy of all the European states has been hitherto the same." He had little doubt that mediation would be a pretext for the abandonment of neutrality and the restoration of Spanish sovereignty, which was neither just nor in America's interest.

SIR:

Your dispatches to number 65, inclusive, have been received, with the packets of newspapers and books, occasionally transmitted with them. During the session of Congress, which closed on the 20th ulto. it was found impossible to pay that immediate attention to your communications as from time to time they were received, which their importance demanded. In reviewing them at this time that which appears to require the most immediate and particular notice is your letter of 17 January, No. 59.

By the newspapers and public documents transmitted to you, the extraordinary interest which has been felt in the contest between Spain and the South American provinces will be disclosed, in the various forms under which it has occupied the deliberations of Congress. You will see how it has been complicated with our own Spanish relations, by the transactions relating to Amelia Island, by the negotiation which Spain has thought fit to have the appearance of keeping alive, and by the question incidental to our neutrality in that warfare, which the course of events has frequently produced.

The correspondence between Mr. Onis and this government has been little more than a repetition on both sides, of that which had taken place at Aranjuez, at the period of the extraordinary mission to Spain in 1805, and it has terminated in a note from Mr. Onis stating that he is under the necessity of sending again a messenger to Spain for new instructions, and a further enlargement of his powers; on the strange allegation that his government had always supposed that the United States, in proposing to agree to the river Colorado, as the western boundary of Louisiana, had reference to the Red River of Natchitoches and not to the Colorado which falls into the Gulph of Mexico. Mr. Onis's messenger is gone, and Mr. Onis expects his return in August next, till when nothing further will be done in the negotiation, nor does the nature of this proceeding afford any encouragement to suppose that after his return its progress will be more satisfactory.

Mr. Onis thought proper to address several notes of protestation against the occupation of the United States of Amelia Island. At the time when that measure was taken, instructions were forwarded to Mr. Erving, to give such explanations to the Spanish government relating to it, as it was concluded could not but be satisfactory. The documents on that subject communicated to Congress at two different periods of the session have shown the necessity and the urgency by which the step was dictated and justified. Mr. Onis's remonstrances have excited very little attention; but some dissatisfaction at the measure has been manifested by the more ardent friends of the South American revolutionists. The disclosure of the transactions, in which McGregor's expedition originated, of the manner and materials of its execution, and of the pernicious influence which it had and portended to important interests of our own country, have conciliated to the proceedings of this government the general acquiescence and assent of the public opinion of the country.

A motion was made in the House of Representatives, while the general appropriation bill was under consideration, to introduce the appropriation of an outfit and a year's salary for a minister to be sent to the provinces of La Plata, if the President should think proper to make such an appointment. The object of this motion was to obtain the sanction of a legislative opinion, in favor of the immediate acknowledgment of the government of Buenos Ayres; but it was rejected by a majority of 115 to 45. Independently of the objection to it that it had the appearance of dictating to the executive with regard to the execution of its own duties, and of manifesting a distrust of its favorable disposition to the independence of the colonies for which there was no cause, it was thought not advisable to adopt any measure of importance upon the imperfect information then possessed, and the motive for declining to act was the stronger, from the circumstance that three commissioners had been sent to visit several parts of the South American continent, chiefly for the purpose of obtaining more precise and accurate information.

Dispatches have been received from them, dated 4 March, immediately after their arrival at Buenos Ayres. They had touched on their way, for a few days, at Rio de Janeiro; where the Spanish Minister, Count Casa Flores, appears to have been so much alarmed by the suspicion that the object of this mission was the formal acknowledgment of the government of La Plata, that he thought it his duty to make to Mr. Sumter an official communication that he had received an official despatch from the Duke of San Carlos, the Spanish Ambassador at London, dated the 7th of November last, informing him *that the British government had acceded to the proposition made by the Spanish government of a general mediation of the powers to obtain the pacification of Spanish America, the negotiation of which it was upon the point of being decided whether it should be at London or at Madrid.*

This agitation of a Spanish Minister, at the bare surmize, of what might be the object of the visit of our commissioners to Buenos Ayres, affords some comment upon the reserve which *all* the European powers have hitherto observed in relation to this affair, towards the United States. No official communication of this projected general mediation has been made to the government of the United States, by any one of the powers, who are to participate in it; and although the Duke de Richelieu and the Russian Ambassador both, in conversation with you, admit the importance of the United States to the subject, and of the subject to the United States, yet the former abstains from all official communication to you of what the allies are doing in it, and the latter apologizes for the silence of his government to us, concerning it, on the plea that, being upon punctilious terms with England, they can show no mark of confidence to us but by concert with her.

On the 27th of January last, Mr. Bagot, at the same time when he informed us of the proposal of Spain to Great Britain to mediate between the United States and Spain, did also by instruction from Lord Castlereagh state that the European allies were about to interpose in the quarrel between Spain and her revolted colonies; and that very shortly a further and full communication should be made to us of what was proposed to be done – with the assurance that Great Britain would not propose or agree to any arrangement in which the interests of all parties concerned, including those of the United States, should not be placed on the same foundation. Nearly four months have since elapsed; and the promised communication has not been made; but we have a copy of the Russian *answer*, dated in November at Moscow, to the first proposals made by Great Britain to the European allies, and we know the course which will be pursued by Portugal in regard to this mediation. If the object of this mediation be any other than to promote the total independence, political and commercial, of South America, we are neither desirous of being invited to take a part in it, nor disposed to accept the invitation if given. Our policy in the contest between Spain and her colonies has been impartial neutrality. The policy of all the European states has been hitherto the same. Is the proposed general mediation to be a departure from that line of neutrality? If it is, which side of the contest are the allies to take? The side of Spain? On what principle, and by what right? As contending parties in a civil war, the South Americans have rights, which other powers are bound to respect as much as the rights of Spain; and after having by an avowed neutrality admitted the existence of those rights, upon what principle of justice can the allies consider them as forfeited, or themselves as justifiable in taking side with Spain against them?

There is no discernible motive of justice or of interest, which can induce the allied sovereigns to interpose for the restoration of the Spanish colonial dominion in South America. There is none even of policy; for if all the organized power of Europe is combined to maintain the authority of each sovereign over his own people, it is hardly supposable that the sober senses of the allied cabinets will permit them to extend the application of this principle of union to the maintenance of colonial dominion beyond the Atlantic and the Equator.

By the usual principles of international law, the state of *neutrality* recognizes the cause of both parties to the contest *as just* – that is, it avoids all consideration of the merits of the contest. But when abandoning that neutrality, a nation takes one side in a war of other parties, the first question to be settled is the *justice* of the cause to be assumed. If the European allies are to take side with Spain, to reduce her South American colonies to submission, we trust they will make some previous inquiry into the justice of the cause they are to undertake. As neutrals we are not required to decide the question of justice. We are sure we should not find it on the side of Spain.

We incline to the belief that on a full examination of the subject, the allies will not deem it advisable to interpose in this contest, by any application of force. If they advise the South Americans to place themselves again under the Spanish government, it is not probable their advice will be followed. What motives can be adduced to make the Spanish government acceptable to them? Wherever Spain can maintain her own authority she will not need the cooperation of the allies. Where she cannot exact obedience, what value can be set upon her protection?

The situation of these countries has thrown them open to commercial intercourse with other nations, and among the rest with these United States. This state of things has existed several years, and cannot now be changed without materially affecting our interests. You will take occasion not by formal official communication, but verbally as the opportunity may present itself, to let the Duke de Richelieu understand that we think the European allies would act but a just and friendly part towards the United States by a free and unreserved communication to us of what they do, or intend to do in the affair of Spain and South America. That it is our earnest desire to pursue a line of policy at once just to both parties in that contest, and harmonious with that of the European allies. That we must know their system, in order to shape our own measures accordingly; but that we do not wish to join them in any plan of interference between the parties, and above all that we can neither accede to nor approve of any interference to restore any part of the Spanish supremacy in any of the South American provinces.

I have the honor to be, etc.

JOHN QUINCY ADAMS (WASHINGTON, DC) TO PRESIDENT MONROE, AUGUST 24, 1818

The decision whether and when to recognize the independence of states that emerged from the rebellion against Spanish colonial rule in the Western Hemisphere was a critical question for John Quincy as he sought leverage over Madrid in his negotiations concerning boundaries. In addition to thinking about the practicalities of the matter, he felt it necessary to establish a general framework, based on the law of nations, regarding a neutral party's obligations in such circumstances.

Specifically, independence may (not must) be recognized when the neutral party judges that independence has been achieved beyond reasonable doubt, and that the particular claim to independence is just. But prudence must be applied because recognition might lead to war – if, that is, the colonial power should use recognition as a pretext for war with the power claiming to be neutral. The justice of the cause alone was insufficient reason to abandon neutrality.

SIR:

Since I had the honor of writing you yesterday, I have received several dispatches from Mr. Gallatin, none of them relating to objects of general importance, except that which with its enclosure is now transmitted to you, together with the dispatches from Mr. Rush yesterday noticed. Mr. del Real, the deputy from New Granada, the author of the protest, was well known to me during my residence in England, and was a very respectable and rational man. His paper, as well as that of Mr. Rivadavia, prove at how much greater distance the British government have even to this time kept the South American agents than we have.

In the draft of a letter to Mr. Aguirre which was to have been forwarded to you yesterday, but which by the course of the mail I find cannot go till this day, I have stated to him the grounds upon which the government of the United States have been deterred from acknowledgment of that of Buenos Ayres, as including the dominion of the whole vice royalty of La Plata. The result of the late campaign in Venezuela, by comparing the royal and the republican bulletins, has been so far disadvantageous to the latter that they have totally failed in obtaining possession of any part of the coast. They have therefore at least one more campaign of contest to go through, for which they will need several months of preparation. Bolivar appears to have resigned the chief military command to Paez, and the army is to be reorganized. But the royalists do not appear to have gained any ground, and are evidently too much weakened by their losses to act upon the offensive. In this state the independence of Venezuela can scarcely be considered in a condition to claim the recognition of neutral powers. But there is a stage in such contests when the party struggling for independence have, as I conceive, a right to demand its acknowledgment by neutral parties, and when the acknowledgment may be granted without departure from the obligations of neutrality. It is the stage when the independence is established as a matter of fact, so as to leave the chance of the opposite party to recover their dominion utterly desperate. The neutral nation must, of course, judge for itself when this period has arrived, and as the belligerent nation has the same right to judge for itself, it is very likely to judge differently from the neutral and to make it a cause or a pretext for war, as Great Britain did expressly against France in our Revolution, and substantially against Holland. If war thus results in point of fact from the measure of recognizing a contested independence, the moral right or wrong of the war depends upon the justice, and sincerity, and prudence with which the recognizing nation took the step. I am satisfied that the cause of the South Americans, so far as it consists in the assertion of independence against Spain is *just*. But the justice of a cause, however it may enlist individual feelings in its favor, is not sufficient to justify third parties in siding with it. The fact and the right combined can alone authorize a neutral to acknowledge a new and disputed sovereignty. The neutral may indeed infer the right from the fact, but not the fact from the right. If Buenos Ayres confined its demand of recognition to the provinces of which it is in actual possession, and if it would assert its entire independence by agreeing to place the United States upon the footing of the most favored nation (which you recollect Pueyrredon declined in his pseudo treaty with Worthington, upon the avowed intention of reserving some special favors to Spain as compensation for his abandonment of her claims of sovereignty), I should think the time now arrived when its government might be recognized without a breach of neutrality. I did not think it necessary or proper to say this in the letter to Mr. Aguirre, but I submit the observations to your consideration.

From the proposals made to Mr. Rush by Lord Castlereagh in relation to the measures to be agreed upon for the abolition of the slave trade, I presume they will be repeated in case of the negotiation of a new commercial convention or treaty. I therefore send you all the treaties communicated by Lord Castlereagh, and request your directions whether any, and if any, what instructions shall be given to Mr. Gallatin and Mr. Rush on the subject.

You will see that the British government have shown some dissatisfaction at an observation made in a printed report of the Committee of Foreign Relations on the projected four articles to be added to the commercial convention of 1815. Mr. Bagot has also been instructed on this affair, and a copy of Lord Castlereagh's note to Mr. Rush was some time since received by him.

I am, etc.

JOHN QUINCY ADAMS (DEPARTMENT OF STATE) TO GEORGE WILLIAM ERVING, NOVEMBER 28, 1818

In this dispatch to the American minister in Madrid, John Quincy provides the administration's lengthy defense of its policy toward Florida. "The President will neither inflict punishment, nor pass a censure upon General Jackson, for that conduct, the motives for which were founded in the purest patriotism; of the necessity for which he had the most immediate and effectual means of forming a judgment; and the vindication of which is written in every page of the law of nations, as well as in the first law of nature self-defense.... Spain must immediately make her election, either to place a force in Florida adequate at once to the protection of her territory, and to the fulfilment of her engagements, or cede to the United States a province, of which she retains nothing but the nominal possession, but which is, in fact, a derelict, open to the occupancy of every enemy, civilized or savage,

of the United States, and serving no other earthly purpose than as a
post of annoyance to them."

SIR:

Your dispatches to No. 92, inclusive, with their enclosures, have been received at this Department. Among these enclosures are the several notes addressed to you by Mr. Pizarro in relation to the transactions during the campaign of General Jackson against the Seminole Indians, and the banditti of negroes combined with them, and particularly to his procedings in Florida without the boundaries of the United States.

In the fourth and last of those notes of Mr. Pizarro, he has given formal notice that the king, his master, has issued orders for the suspension of the negotiation between the United States and Spain until satisfaction shall have been made by the American government to him for these proceedings of General Jackson, which he considers as acts of unequivocal hostility against him, and as outrages upon his honor and dignity; the only acceptable atonement for which is stated to consist in a disavowal of the acts of the American general thus complained of, the infliction upon him of a suitable punishment for his supposed misconduct, and the restitution of the posts and territories taken by him from the Spanish authorities, with indemnity for all the property taken, and all damages and injuries, public or private, sustained in consequence of it.

Within a very few days after this notification, Mr. Pizarro must have received, with copies of the correspondence between Mr. Onis and this Department, the determination which had been taken by the President to restore the places of Pensacola, with the fort of Barrancas, to any person properly authorized on the part of Spain to receive them, and the fort of St. Marks, to any Spanish force adequate to its protection against the Indians, by whom its forcible occupation had been threatened for purposes of hostility against the United States. The officer commanding at the post has been directed to consider two hundred and fifty men as such adequate force, and in case of their appearance with proper authority, to deliver it to their commander accordingly.

From the last-mentioned correspondence, the Spanish government must likewise have been satisfied that the occupation of these places in Spanish Florida by the commander of the American forces was not by virtue of any orders received by him from this government to that effect, nor with any view of wresting the province from the possession of Spain, nor in any spirit of hostility to the Spanish government; that it arose from incidents which occurred in the prosecution of the war against the Indians, from the imminent danger in which the fort of St. Marks was of being seized by the Indians themselves, and from the manifestations of hostility to the United States by the commandant of St. Marks and the governor of Pensacola, the proofs of which were made known to General Jackson, and impelled him, from the necessities of self-defence, to the steps of which the Spanish government complains.

It might be sufficient to leave the vindication of these measures upon those grounds, and to furnish, in the enclosed copies of General Jackson's letters, and the vouchers by which they are supported, the evidence of that hostile spirit on the part of the Spanish commanders, but for the terms in which Mr. Pizarro speaks of the execution of two British subjects taken, one at the fort of St. Marks, and the other at Suwanee, and the intimation that these transactions may lead to a change in the relations between the two nations, which is doubtless intended to be understood as a menace of war.

It may be, therefore, proper to remind the government of his Catholic Majesty of the incidents in which this Seminole war originated, as well as of the circumstances connected with it in the relations between Spain and her ally, whom she supposes to have been injured by the proceedings of General Jackson; and to give to the Spanish Cabinet some precise information of the nature of the business, peculiarly interesting to Spain, in which these subjects of her allies, in whose favor she takes this interest, were engaged, when their projects of every kind were terminated in consequence of their falling into the hands of General Jackson.

In the month of August, 1814, while a war existed between the United States and Great Britain, to which Spain had formally declared herself neutral, a British force, not in the fresh pursuit of a defeated and flying enemy, not overstepping an imaginary and equivocal boundary between their own territories and those belonging, in some sort, as much to their enemy as to Spain, but approaching by sea, and by a broad and open invasion of the Spanish province, at a thousand miles or an ocean's distance from any British territory, landed in Florida, took possession of Pensacola and the Fort of Barrancas, and invited by public proclamations, all the runaway negroes, all the savage Indians, all the pirates and all the traitors to their country, whom they knew or imagined to exist within reach of their summons, to join their standard, and wage an exterminating war against the portion of the United States immediately bordering upon this neutral and thus violated territory of Spain. The land commander of this British force was a certain Colonel Nicholls, who, driven from Pensacola by the approach of General Jackson, actually left to be blown up the Spanish fort of Barrancas when he found it could not afford him protection; and, evacuating that part of the province, landed at another, established himself on the Appalachicola river, and there erected a fort from which to sally forth with his motley tribe of black, white, and red combatants against the defenceless borders of the United States in that vicinity. A part of this force consisted of a corps of colonial marines, levied in the British colonies, in which George Woodbine was a captain, and Robert Christie Ambrister was a lieutenant.

As between the United States and Great Britain, we should be willing to bury this transaction in the same grave of oblivion with other transactions of that war, had the hostilities of Colonel Nicholls terminated with the war; but he did not consider the peace which ensued between the United States and Great Britain as having put an end, either to his military occupations, or to his negotiations with the Indians against the United States. Several months after the ratification of the treaty of Ghent, he retained his post, and his parti-colored forces in military array. By the ninth article of that treaty the United States had stipulated to put an end, immediately after its ratification, to hostilities with all the tribes or nations of Indians with whom they might be at war at the time of the ratification, and to restore to them all the possessions which they had enjoyed in the year 1811. This article had no application to the Creek nation, with whom the United States had already made peace, by a treaty concluded on the ninth day of August, 1814, more than four months before the treaty of Ghent was signed. Yet Colonel Nicholls not only affected to consider it as applying to the Seminoles of Florida, and the outlawed Red Sticks, whom he had induced to join him there, but actually persuaded them that *they* were entitled, by virtue of the treaty of Ghent, to all the lands which had belonged to the *Creek* nation within the United States in the year 1811, and that the government of Great Britain would support them in that pretension. He asserted also this doctrine in a correspondence with Colonel Hawkins, then the agent of the United States with the Creeks, and gave him notice in their name, with a mockery of solemnity, that they had concluded a treaty of alliance, offensive and defensive, and a treaty of navigation and commerce, with Great Britain, of which more was to be heard after it should be ratified in England. Colonel Nicholls then evacuated his fort, which, in some of the enclosed papers, is called the fort at Prospect Bluff, but which he had denominated the British post on the Appalachicola; took with him the white portion of his force, and embarked for England with several of the wretched savages whom he was thus deluding to their fate, among whom was the prophet Francis or Hillis Hadjo, and left the fort, amply supplied with military stores and ammunitions, to the negro department of his allies. It afterwards was known by the name of the Negro fort.

Colonel Hawkins immediately communicated to this government the correspondence between him and Nicholls, here referred to, (copies of which marked Nos. 1 to 5 are herewith enclosed,) upon which, Mr. Munroe, then Secretary of State, addressed a letter to Mr. Baker, the British chargé d'affaires at Washington, complaining of Nicholls' conduct, and showing that his pretence that the ninth article of the treaty of Ghent could have any application to his Indians was utterly destitute of foundation. Copies of the same correspondence were transmitted to the minister of the United States, then in England, with instructions to remonstrate with the British government against these proceedings of Nicholls, and to show how incompatible they were with the peace which had been concluded between the two nations. These remonstrances were accordingly made, first in personal interview with Earl Bathurst and Lord Castlereagh, and afterwards in written notes addressed successively to them, (copies of which, together with extracts from the dispatches of the American minister to the Secretary of State, reporting what passed at those interviews, are enclosed). Lord Bathurst, in the most unequivocal manner, confirmed the facts, and disavowed the misconduct of Nicholls; declared his disapprobation of the pretended treaty of alliance, offensive and defensive, which he had made; assured the American minister that the British government had refused to ratify that treaty, and would send back the Indians whom Nicholls had brought with him, with advice to make their peace on such terms as they could obtain. Lord Castlereagh confirmed the assurance that the treaty would not be ratified; and if, at the same time that these assurances were given, certain distinctions of public notoriety were shown to the prophet Hillis Hadjo, and he was actually honored with a commission as a British officer, it is to be presumed that these favors were granted him as rewards of past services, and not as encouragement to expect support from Great Britain in a continuance of savage hostilities against the United States; all intention of giving any such support having been repeatedly and earnestly disavowed.

The Negro fort, however, abandoned by Colonel Nicholls,

remained on the Spanish territory, occupied by the banditti to whom he had left it, and held by them as a post from whence to commit depredations, outrages, and murders, and as a receptacle for fugitive slaves and malefactors, to the great annoyance both of the United States and of Spanish Florida. In April, 1816, General Jackson wrote a letter to the Governor of Pensacola, calling upon him to put down this common nuisance to the peaceable inhabitants of both countries. That letter, together with the answer of the Governor of Pensacola, has already been communicated to the Spanish Minister here, and by him doubtless to his government. Copies of them are, nevertheless, now again enclosed; particularly as the letter from the Governor explicitly admits that this fort, constructed by Nicholls in violation both of the territory and neutrality of Spain, was still no less obnoxious to his government than to the United States; but that he had neither sufficient force nor authority, without orders from the Governor General of the Havana, to destroy it. It was afterwards, on the 27th of July, 1816, destroyed by a cannon shot from a gun vessel of the United States, which, in its passage up the river was fired upon from it. It was blown up with an English flag still flying as its standard, and immediately after the barbarous murder of a boat's crew belonging to the navy of the United States, by the banditti left in it by Nicholls.

In the year 1817, Alexander Arbuthnot, of the island of New Providence, a British subject, first appeared as an Indian trader in Spanish Florida, and as the successor of Colonel Nicholls in the employment of instigating the Seminole and outlawed Red Stick Indians to hostilities against the United States, by reviving the pretence that they were entitled to all the lands which had been ceded by the Creek nation to the United States in August, 1814. As a mere Indian trader, the intrusion of this man into a Spanish province was contrary to the policy observed by all the European powers in this hemisphere, and by none more rigorously than by Spain, of excluding all foreigners from intercourse with the Indians within their territories. It must be known to the Spanish government whether Arbuthot had a Spanish license for trading with the Indians in Spanish Florida, or not; but they also know that Spain was bound by treaty to restrain by force all hostilities on the part of those Indians against the citizens of the United States; and it is for them to explain how, consistently with those engagements, Spain could, contrary to all the maxims of her ordinary policy, grant such a license to a foreign incendiary, whose principal if not his only object appears to have been to stimulate those hostilities which Spain had expressly stipulated by force to restrain. In his infernal instigations he was but too successful. No sooner did he make his appearance among the Indians, accompanied by the prophet Hillis Hadjo, returned from his expedition to England, than the peaceful inhabitants on the borders of the United States were visited with all the horrors of savage war – the robbery of their property, and the barbarous and indiscriminate murder of women, infancy, and age.

After the repeated expostulations, warnings, and offers of peace, through the summer and autumn of 1817, on the part of the United States, had been answered only by renewed outrages, and after a detachment of forty men, under Lieutenant Scott, accompanied by seven women, had been waylaid and murdered by the Indians, orders were given to General Jackson, and an adequate force was placed at his disposal to terminate the war. It was ascertained that the Spanish force in Florida was inadequate for the protection even of the Spanish territory itself against this mingled horde of lawless Indians and negroes; and, although their devastations were committed within the limits of the United States, they immediately sought refuge within the Florida line, and there only were to be overtaken. The necessity of crossing the line was indispensable; for it was from beyond the line that the Indians made their murderous incursions within that of the United States. It was there that they had their abode; and the territory belonged, in fact, to them, although within the borders of the Spanish jurisdiction. There it was that the American commander met the principal resistance from them; there it was that were found the still bleeding scalps of our citizens, freshly butchered by them; there it was that he released the only *woman* who had been suffered to survive the massacre of the party under Lieutenant Scott. But it was not anticipated by this government that the commanding officers of Spain in Florida, whose especial duty it was in conformity to the solemn engagements contracted by their nation, to restrain by force those Indians from hostilities against the United States, would be found encouraging, aiding, and abetting them, and furnishing them supplies for carrying on such hostilities. The officer in command immediately before General Jackson was, therefore, specially instructed to respect, as far as possible, the Spanish authority, wherever it was maintained; and copies of those orders were also furnished to General Jackson, upon his taking the command.

In the course of his pursuit, as he approached St. Marks, he was informed direct from the governor of Pensacola that a party of the hostile Indians had threatened to seize that fort, and that he apprehended the Spanish garrison there was not in strength sufficient to defend it against them. This information was confirmed from other sources, and by the evidence produced upon the trial of Ambrister, is proved to have been exactly true. By all the laws of neutrality and of war, as well as of prudence and of humanity, he was warranted in anticipating his enemy by the amicable, and, that being refused, by the forcible occupation of the fort. There will need no citations from printed treatises on international law to prove the correctness of this principle. It is engraved in adamant on the common sense of mankind. No writer upon the laws of nations ever pretended to contradict it. None, of any reputation or authority, ever omitted to assert it.

At the Fort St. Marks, Alexander Arbuthnot, the British Indian trader from beyond the seas, the firebrand by whose touch this negro-Indian war against our borders had been re-kindled, was found an inmate of the commandant's family; and it was also found that, by the commandant himself, councils of war had been permitted to be held within it by the savage chiefs and warriors; that the Spanish storehouses had been appropriated to their use; that it was an open market for cattle known to have been robbed by them from citizens of the United States, and which had been contracted for and purchased by the officers of the garrison; that information had been afforded from this fort by Arbuthnot to the enemy of the strength and movements of the American army; that the date of departure of express had been noted by the Spanish commissary; and ammunition, munitions of war, and all necessary supplies furnished to the Indians.

The conduct of the Governor of Pensacola was not less marked by a disposition of enmity to the United States, and by an utter disregard to the obligations of the treaty, by which he was bound to restrain, by force, the Indians from hostilities against them. When called upon to vindicate the territorial rights and authority of Spain, by the destruction of the Negro fort, his predecessor had declared it to be not less annoying and pernicious to the Spanish subjects in Florida than to the United States, but had pleaded his inability to subdue it. He himself had expressed his apprehensions that Fort St. Marks would be forcibly taken by the savages from its Spanish garrison; yet, at the same time, he had refused the passage up the Escambia River, unless upon the payment of excessive duties, to provisions destined as supplies for the American army, which, by the detention of them, was subjected to the most distressing privations. He had permitted free ingress and egress at Pensacola to the avowed savage enemies of the United States. Supplies of ammunition, munitions of war, and provisions had been received by them from thence. They had been received and sheltered there from the pursuit of the American forces, and suffered again to sally thence, to enter upon the American territory, and commit new murders. Finally, on the approach of General Jackson to Pensacola, the Governor sent him a letter denouncing his entry upon the territory of Florida as a violent outrage upon the rights of Spain, commanding him to depart and withdraw from the same, and threatening, in case of his non-compliance, to employ force to expel him.

It became, therefore, in the opinion of General Jackson indispensably necessary to take from the Governor of Pensacola the means of carrying his threat into execution. Before the forces under his command, the savage enemies of his country had disappeared. But he knew that the moment those forces should be disbanded, if sheltered by Spanish fortresses, if furnished with ammunition and supplies by Spanish officers, and if aided and supported by the instigation of Spanish encouragement, as he had every reason to expect they would be, they would reappear, and, fired, in addition to their ordinary ferociousness, with revenge for the chastisement they had so recently received, would again rush with the war-hatchet and the scalping-knife into the borders of the United States, and mark every footstep with the blood of their defenseless citizens. So far as all the native resources of the savage extended, the war was at an end; and General Jackson was about to restore to their families and their homes the brave volunteers who had followed his standard, and who had constituted the principal part of his force. This could be done with safety, leaving the regular portion of his troops to garrison his line of forts, and two small detachments of volunteer cavalry to scour the country round Pensacola, and sweep off the lurking remnant of savages who had been scattered and dispersed before him. This was sufficient to keep in check the remnant of the banditti against whom he had marched, so long as they should be destitute of other aid and support. It was, in his judgment, not sufficient, if they should be suffered to rally their numbers under the protection of Spanish forts, and to derive new strength from the impotence or the ill-will against the United States of the Spanish authorities.

He took possession, therefore, of Pensacola and of the fort of Barrancas, as he had done of St. Marks, not in a spirit of hostility to Spain, but as a necessary measure of self-defense; giving notice that they should be restored whenever Spain should place commanders and a force there able and willing to fulfil the engagements of Spain towards the United States, or of restraining by force the Florida Indians from hostilities against their citizens. The President of the United States, to give a signal manifestation of his confidence in the disposition of the king of Spain to perform with good faith this indispensable engagement, and to demonstrate to the world that neither the desire of conquest, nor hostility to Spain, had any influence in the councils of the United States, has directed the unconditional restoration, to any Spanish officer duly authorized to receive them, of Pensacola and the Barrancas, and that of St. Marks, to any Spanish force adequate to its defense against the attack of the savages. But the President will neither inflict punishment, nor pass a censure upon General Jackson, for that conduct, the motives for which were founded in the purest patriotism; of the necessity for which he had the most immediate and effectual means of forming a judgment; and the vindication of which is written in every page of the law of nations, as well as in the first law of nature – self-defense. He thinks it, on the contrary, due to the justice which the United States have a right to claim from Spain, and you are accordingly instructed to demand of the Spanish government that inquiry shall be instituted into the conduct of Don Jose Mazot, Governor of Pensacola, and of Don Francisco C. Luengo, Commandant of St. Marks, and a suitable punishment inflicted upon them, for having, in defiance and violation of the engagements of Spain with the United States, aided and assisted these hordes of savages in those very hostilities against the United States which it was their official duty to restrain. This inquiry is due to the character of those officers themselves, and to the honor of the Spanish government. The obligation of Spain to restrain, by force, the Indians of Florida from hostilities against the United States and their citizens, is explicit, is positive, is unqualified. The fact that, for a series of years, they have received shelter, assistance, supplies, and protection, in the practice of such hostilities, from the Spanish commanders in Florida, is clear and unequivocal. If, as the commanders both at Pensacola and St. Marks have alleged, this has been the result of their weakness rather than of their will; if they have assisted the Indians against the United States to avert their hostilities from the province which they had not sufficient force to defend against them, it may serve in some measure to exculpate, individually, those officers; but it must carry demonstration irresistible to the Spanish government, that the right of the United States can as little compound with impotence as with perfidy, and that Spain must immediately make her election, either to place a force in Florida adequate at once to the protection of her territory, and to the fulfilment of her engagements, or cede to the United States a province, of which she retains nothing but the nominal possession, but which is, in fact, a derelict, open to the occupancy of every enemy, civilized or savage, of the United States, and serving no other earthly purpose than as a post of annoyance to them.

That the purposes, as well of the negro-Indian banditti, with whom we have been contending, as of the British invaders of Florida, who first assembled and employed them, and of the British intruding and pretended traders, since the peace, who have instigated and betrayed them to destruction, have been not less hostile to Spain than to the United States, the proofs contained in the documents here with enclosed are conclusive. Mr. Pizarro's note of 29th August speaks of his Catholic Majesty's profound indignation at the "sanguinary executions on the Spanish soil of the subjects of powers in amity with the king" – meaning Arbuthnot and Ambrister. Let Mr. Pizarro's successor take the trouble of reading the enclosed documents, and he will discover who Arbuthnot and Ambrister were, and what were their purposes; that Arbuthnot was only the successor of Nicholls, and Ambrister the agent of Woodbine, and the subaltern of McGregor. Mr. Pizarro qualifies General Jackson's necessary pursuit of a defeated savage enemy beyond the Spanish Florida line as a *shameful invasion of his Majesty's territory*. Yet that territory was the territory also of the savage enemy, and Spain was bound to restrain them by force from hostilities against the United States; and it was the failure of Spain to fulfil this engagement which had made it necessary for General Jackson to pursue the savage across the line. What, then, was the character of Nicholls's invasion of his Majesty's territory? and where was his Majesty's profound indignation at that? Mr. Pizarro says, his Majesty's forts and places have been violently seized on by General Jackson. Had they not been seized on, nay, had not the principal of his forts been blown up by Nicholls, and a British fort on the same Spanish territory been erected during the war, and left standing as a negro fort, in defiance of Spanish authority, after the peace? Where was his Majesty's profound indignation at that? Has his Majesty suspended formally all negotiation with the sovereign of Colonel Nicholls for this shameful invasion of his territory, without color of provocation, without pretence of necessity, without shadow or even avowal of a pretext? Has his Majesty given solemn warning to the British government that those were incidents "of transcendent moment, capable of producing an essential and thorough change in the political relations of the two countries?" Nicholls and Woodbine, in their invitations and promises to the slaves to run away from their masters and join them, did not confine themselves to the slaves of the United States. They received with as hearty a welcome, and employed with equal readiness, the fugitives from their masters in Florida as those from Georgia. Against this special injury the governor of Pensacola did earnestly remonstrate with the British admiral, Cockburn. But against the *shameful invasion* of the territory; against the blowing up of the Barrancas, and the erection and maintenance, under British banners, of the negro fort on Spanish soil; against the negotiation by a British officer, in the midst of peace, of pretended treaties, offensive and defensive, and of navigation and commerce upon Spanish territory, between Great Britain and Spanish Indians, whom Spain was bound to control and restrain – if a whisper of expostulation was ever wafted from Madrid to London, it was not loud enough to be heard across the Atlantic, nor energetic enough to tran spire beyond the walls of the palaces from which it issued, and to which it was borne.

The connection between Arbuthnot and Nicholls, and between Ambrister, Woodbine, and McGregor, is established beyond all question, by the evidence produced at the trials before the court-martial. I have already remarked to you on the very extraordinary circumstance that a British trader from beyond the sea should be permitted by the Spanish authorities to trade with the Indians of Florida. From his letter to Hambly, dated 3d May, 1817, it appears that his trading was but a pretence, and that his principal purpose was to act as the agent of the Indians of Florida, and outlaws from the Creeks, to obtain the aid of the British government in their hostilities against the United States. He expressly tells Hambly there that the chief of these outlaws was the principal cause of his (Arbuthnot's) being in the country, and that he had come with an answer from Earl Bathurst, delivered to him by Governor Cameron, of New Providence, to certain Indian talks, in which this aid of the British government had been solicited.

Hambly himself had been left by Nicholls as the agent between the Indians and the British government; but having found that Nicholls had failed in his attempt to prevail upon the British government to pursue this clandestine war in the midst of peace, and that they were not prepared to support his pretence that half a dozen outlawed fugitives from the Creeks were the Creek nation, when Arbuthnot, the incendiary, came, and was instigating them, by promises of support from Great Britain, to commence their murderous incursions into the United States, Hambly, at the request of the chiefs of the Creeks themselves, wrote to him, warning him to withdraw from among that band of outlaws, and giving him a solemn foreboding of the doom that awaited him from the hand of justice if he persevered in the course that he pursued. Arbuthnot nevertheless persisted, and while he was deluding the wretched Indians with the promise of support from England, he was writing letters for them to the British minister in the United States, to Governor Cameron, of New Providence, to Colonel Nicholls, to be laid before the British government, and even to the Spanish governor of St. Augustine, and the Governor

General of the Havana, soliciting, in all quarters, aid and support, arms and ammunition, for the Indians against the United States, bewailing the destruction of the negro fort, and charging the British government with having drawn the Indians into war with the United States, and deserting them after the peace.

You will remark among the papers produced on his trial, a power of attorney, dated June 17, 1817, given him by twelve Indians, partly of Florida, and partly of the fugitive outlaws from the United States. He states that this power and his instructions were to memorialize the British government and the Governor General of the Havana. These papers are not only substantially proved as of his handwriting on the trial, but, in the daily newspapers of London of 24th and 25th. of August last, his letter to Nicholls is published, (somewhat curiously garbled,) with a copy of Hambly's above-mentioned letter to him, and a reference to this power of attorney to him, *approved by the commandant of St. Marks, F. C. Luengo*. Another of the papers is a letter written in the name of the same chiefs, by Arbuthnot, to the Governor General of the Havana, asking of him permission by Arbuthnot to establish a warehouse on the Apalachicola, bitterly and falsely complaining that the Americans had made settlements on their lands within the Spanish lines, and calling upon the Governor General to give orders to displace them, and send them back to their own country. In this letter they assign as a reason for asking the license for Arbuthnot, their want of a person to put in writing for them their talks of grievances against the Americans, and they add: "The commander of the fort of St. Marks has heard all of our talks and complaints. He approves of what we have done and what we are doing, and it is by his recommendation we have thus presumed to address your excellency." You will find those papers in the printed newspapers enclosed, and in the proceedings of the court-martial, and will point them out to the Spanish government, not only as decisive proofs of the unexampled compliances of the Spanish officers in Florida to foreign intrusive agents and instigators of Indian hostilities against the United States, but as placing beyond

a doubt that participation of this hostile spirit in the commandant of St. Marks which General Jackson so justly complains of,
and of which we have so well-founded a right to demand the punishment. Here is the commandant of a Spanish fort, bound by the
sacred engagement of a treaty to restrain by force the Indians
within his command from committing hostilities against the
United States, conspiring with those same Indians, and deliberately giving his written approbation to their appointment of a
foreigner, a British subject, as their agent to solicit assistance and
supplies from the Governor General of the Havana, and from the
British government, for carrying on these same hostilities.

Let us come to the case of Ambrister. He was taken in arms,
leading and commanding the Indians in the war against the
American troops; and to that charge, upon his trial, pleaded
guilty. But the primary object of his coming there was still more
hostile to Spain than to the United States. You find that he told
three of the witnesses who testified at his trial that he had come
to this country *upon Mr. Woodbine's business at Tampa Bay*, to
see the negroes righted; and one of them, that *he had a commission in the patriot army under McGregor*, and that he expected a
captaincy. And what was the intended business of McGregor and
Woodbine at Tampa Bay? It was the conquest of Florida from
Spain, by the use of those very Indians and negroes whom the
commandant of St. Marks was so ready to aid and support in war
against the United States. The chain of proof that establishes this
fact is contained in the documents communicated by the President to Congress at their last session, relating to the occupation
of Amelia Island by McGregor. From these documents you will
find that while McGregor was there, Woodbine went from New
Providence in a schooner of his own to join him, that he arrived
at Amelia Island just as McGregor, abandoning the companions
of his achievement there, was leaving it; that McGregor, quitting
the vessel in which he had embarked at Amelia, went on board
that of Woodbine, and returned with him to New Providence;
that Woodbine had persuaded him they could yet accomplish the

conquest of Florida with soldiers to be recruited at Nassau from the corps of colonial marines which had served under Nicholls during the late war with the United States, which corps had been lately disbanded, and with negroes to be found at Tampa Bay, and 1,500 Indians already then engaged to Woodbine, who pretended that they had made a grant of all their lands there to him. Among the papers, the originals of which are in our possession, are in McGregor's own handwriting instructions for sailing into Tampa Bay, with the assertion that he calculated to be there by the last of April or first of May of the present year; a letter dated 27th December last, to one of his acquaintances in this country, disclosing the same intention; and the extract of a proclamation which was to have been issued at Tampa Bay, to the inhabitants of Florida, by the person charged with making the settlement there before his arrival, announcing his approach for the purpose of liberating them from the despotism of Spain, and of enabling them to form a government for themselves. He had persuaded those who would listen to him here that his ultimate object was to sell the Floridas to the United States. There is some reason to suppose that he had made indirect overtures of a similar nature to the British government. This was Ambrister's business in Florida. He arrived there in March, the precursor of McGregor and Woodbine; and immediately upon his arrival he is found seizing upon Arbuthnot's goods, and distributing them among the negroes and Indians; seizing upon his vessel, and compelling its master to pilot him, with a body of armed negroes, towards the fort of St. Marks, with the declared purpose of taking it by surprise in the night; writing letters to Governor Cameron, of New Providence, urgently calling for supplies of war and of cannon for the war against the Americans, and letters to Colonel Nicholls, renewing the same demands of supplies, informing him that he is with 300 negroes, "a few of our Bluff people," who had *stuck to the cause*, and were relying on the faith of Nicholls's promises. "Our Bluff people" were the people of the negro fort, collected by Nicholls and Woodbine's proclamations during the American and English war; and *"the cause"* to which they stuck was the savage, servile, exterminating war against the United States.

Among the agents and actors of such virtuous enterprises as we have unveiled, it was hardly to be expected that there would be found remarkable evidences of their respect, confidence, and good faith towards one another. Accordingly, besides the violent seizure and distribution by Ambrister of Arbuthnot's property, his letters to Cameron and to Nicholls are filled with the distrust and suspicions of the Indians that they were deceived and betrayed by Arbuthnot; while, in Arbuthnot's letters to the same Nicholls he accuses Woodbine of having taken charge of poor Francis the prophet, or Hillis Hadjo, upon his return from England to New Providence, and, under pretence of taking care of him and his affairs, of having defrauded him of a large portion of the presents which had been delivered out from the King's stores to him for Francis's use. This is one of the passages of Arbuthnot's letter to Nicholls, *omitted* in the publication of it last August in the London newspapers.

Is this narrative of dark and complicated depravity; this creeping and insidious war, both against Spain and the United States; this mockery of patriotism; these political filters to fugitive slaves and Indian outlaws; these perfidies and treacheries of villains incapable of keeping their faith even to each other; all in the name of South American liberty, of the rights of runaway negroes, and the wrongs of savage murderers – all combined and projected to plunder Spain of her province, and to spread massacre and devastation along the borders of the United States – is all this sufficient to cool the sympathies of his Catholic Majesty's government, excited by the execution of these two "subjects of a Power in amity with the King?" The Spanish government is not at this day to be informed that, cruel as war in its mildest forms must be, it is, and necessarily must be, doubly cruel when waged with savages; that savages make no prisoners, but to torture them; that they give no quarter; that they put to death, without discrimination of age or sex. That these ordinary characteristics of Indian warfare have been applicable, in their most heart-sickening horrors, to that war left us by Nicholls as his legacy, reinstigated by Woodbine, Arbuthnot, and Ambrister, and stimulated by the approbation, encouragement, and aid of the Spanish commandant at St. Marks, is proof required? Entreat the Spanish minister of state for a moment to overcome the feelings which details like these must excite; and to reflect, if possible, with composure, upon the facts stated in the following extracts from the documents enclosed:

LETTER FROM SAILING MASTER JAIRUS LOOMIS TO COMMODORE DANIEL T PATTERSON, 13TH AUGUST, 1816, REPORTING THE DESTRUCTION OF THE NEGRO FORT:

On examining the prisoners, they stated that Edward Daniels, ordinary seaman, who was made prisoner in the boat on the 17th July, was *tarred and burnt alive.*

LETTER FROM ARCHIBALD CLARKE TO GENERAL GAINES, 26TH FEBRUARY, 1817:

On the 24th instant the house of Mr. Garret, residing in the upper part of this county, near the boundary of Wayne County (Georgia), was attacked, during his absence, near the middle of the day, by this party (of Indians), consisting of about fifteen, who shot Mrs. Garret in two places, and then dispatched her by stabbing and scalping. Her two children, one about three years, the other two months, were also murdered, and the eldest scalped; the house was then plundered of every article of value, and set on fire.

LETTER FROM PETER B COOK (ARBUTHNOT'S CLERK) TO ELIZ A CARNEY, AT NASSAU, DATED SEWANEE, 19TH JANUARY, 1818, GIVING AN ACCOUNT OF THEIR OPERATIONS WITH THE INDIANS AGAINST THE AMERICANS, AND THEIR MASSACRE OF LIEUTENANT SCOTT AND HIS PARTY:

There was a boat that was taken by the Indians, that had in it thirty men, seven women, and four small children. There were six of the men got clear, and one woman saved, and all the rest of them got killed. The children were taken by the leg, and their brains dashed out against the boat. If the bare recital of scenes like these cannot be perused without shuddering, what must be the agonized feelings of those whose wives and children are from day to day, and from night to night, exposed to be the victims of the same barbarity? Has mercy a voice to plead for the perpetrators and instigators of deeds like these? Should inquiry hereafter be made why, within three months after this event, the savage Hamathli-Meico, upon being taken by the American troops, was by order of their commander immediately hung, let it be told that that savage was the commander of the party by whom those women were butchered, and those helpless infants were thus dashed against the boat. Contending with such enemies, although humanity revolts at entire retaliation upon them, and spares the lives of their feeble and defenseless women and children, yet mercy herself surrenders to retributive justice the lives of their leading warriors taken in arms, and, still more, the lives of the foreign white incendiaries, who, disowned by their own governments, and disowning their own natures, degrade themselves beneath the savage character by voluntarily descending to its level, is not this the dictate of common sense? Is it not the usage of legitimate warfare? Is it not consonant to the soundest authorities of national law? "When at war (says Vattel) with a ferocious nation which observes no rules, and grants no quarter, they may be chastised in the persons of those of them who may be taken; they are of the number of the guilty; and by this rigor the attempt may be made of bringing them to a sense of the laws of humanity." And again: "As a general has the right of sacrificing the lives of his enemies to his own safety, or that of his people, if he has to contend with an inhuman enemy, often guilty of such excesses, he may take the lives of some of his prisoners, and treat them as his own people have been treated." The justification of these principles is found in their salutary efficacy for terror and for example.

It is thus only that the barbarities of the Indians can be successfully encountered. It is thus only that the worse than Indian barbarities of European impostors, pretending authority from their governments, but always disavowed, can be punished and arrested. Great Britain yet engages the alliance and cooperation of savages in war; but her government has invariably disclaimed all countenance or authorization to her subjects to instigate them against us in time of peace. Yet, it so happened, that, from the period of our established independence to this day, all the Indian wars with which we have been afflicted have been distinctly traceable to the instigation of English traders or agents. Always disavowed, yet always felt; more than once detected, but never before punished; two of them, offenders of the deepest dye, after solemn warning to their government, and individually to one of them, have fallen, *flagrante delicto*, into the hands of an American general; and the punishment inflicted upon them has fixed them on high, as an example awful in its exhibition, but, we trust, auspicious in its results, of that which awaits unauthorized pretenders of European agency to stimulate and interpose in wars between the United States and the Indians within their control.

This exposition of the origin, the causes, and the character of the war with the Seminole Indians and part of the Creeks, combined with McGregor's mock patriots and Nicholls's negroes, which necessarily led our troops into Florida, and gave rise to all those incidents of which Mr. Pizarro so vehemently complains, will, it is hoped, enable you to present other and sounder views of the subject to his Catholic Majesty's government.

It will enable you to show that the cola and St. Marks was occasioned neither by a spirit of hostility to Spain, nor with a view to extort prematurely the province from her possession; that it was rendered necessary by the neglect of Spain to perform her engagements of restraining the Indians from hostilities against the United States, and by the culpable countenance, encouragement and assistance given to those Indians, in their hostilities, by the Spanish governor and commandant at those places, that the United States have a right to demand, as the President does demand, of Spain the punishment of those officers for this misconduct; and he further demands of Spain a just and reasonable indemnity to the United States for the heavy and necessary expenses which they have been compelled to incur by the failure of Spain to perform her engagements to restrain the Indians, aggravated by this demonstrated complicity of her commanding officers with them in their hostilities against the United States; that the two Englishmen executed by order of General Jackson were not only identified with the savages, with whom they were carrying on the war against the United States, but that one of them was the mover and fomenter of the war, which, without his interference, and false promises to the Indians of support from the British government, never would have happened; that the other was the instrument of war against Spain as well as the United States, commissioned by McGregor, and expedited by Woodbine, upon their project of conquering Florida with these Indians and negroes; that as accomplices of the savages, and, sinning against their better knowledge, worse than savages, General Jackson, possessed of their persons and of the proofs of their guilt, might, by the lawful and ordinary usages of war, have hung them both without the formality of a trial; that, to allow them every possible opportunity of refuting the proofs, or of showing any circumstance in extenuation of their crimes, he gave them the benefit of trial by a court-martial of highly respectable officers; that the defense of one consisted solely and exclusively of technical cavils at the nature of part of the evidence against him, and the other confessed his guilt; finally, that, in restoring Pensacola and St. Marks to Spain, the President gives the most signal proof of his confidence that, hereafter, her engagement to restrain by force the Indians of Florida from all hostilities against the United States will be effectually fulfilled; that there will be no more murders, no more robberies, within our borders, by savages prowling along the Spanish line, and seeking shelter within it, to display in their villages the scalps of our women and children, their victims, and to sell, with shameless effrontery, the plunder from our citizens in Spanish forts and cities; that we shall hear no more apologies from Spanish governors and commandants of their inability to perform the duties of their office and the solemn contracts of their country – no more excuses for compliances to the savage enemies of the United States, from the dread of their attacks upon themselves – no more harboring of foreign impostors upon compulsion; that a strength sufficient will be kept in the province to restrain the Indians by force, and officers empowered and instructed to employ it effectually to maintain the good faith of the nation by the effective fulfilment of the treaty. The duty of this government to protect the persons and property of our fellow-citizens on the borders of the United States is imperative – it must be discharged. And if, after all the warnings that Spain has had; if, after the prostration of all her territorial rights and neutral obligations by Nicholls and his banditti during war, and of all her treaty stipulations by Arbuthnot and Ambrister, abetted by her own commanding officers, during peace, to the cruel annoyance of the United States; if the necessities of self-defense should again compel the United States to take pos session of the Spanish forts and places in Florida, declare, with the frankness and candor that become us, that another unconditional restoration of them must not be expected; that even the President's confidence in the good faith and ultimate justice of the Spanish government will yield to the painful experience of continual disappointment; and, that, after unwearied and almost unnumbered appeals to them for the performance of their stipulated duties in vain, the United States will be reluctantly compelled to rely for the protection of their borders upon themselves alone. You are authorized to communicate the whole of this letter, and the accompanying documents, to the Spanish government. I have the honor, etc.

DIARY ENTRY (WASHINGTON, DC), MARCH 12, 1819

One of the most prominent proposed solutions to the crisis of slavery was to establish a colony, or colonies, of freed blacks in Africa or elsewhere, which would encourage emancipation. John Quincy thought that the idea was bad on the merits, but it also set the United States on the road from a republic to an empire. This was expansion of the wrong sort. "The acquisition of Louisiana, and the establishment at the mouth of Columbia river, being in territory contiguous to and continuous with our own, could by no means warrant the purchase of Countries beyond the Seas, or the establishment of a Colonial system of Government subordinate to and dependent upon that of the United States."

12th. At the President's this morning he mentioned that he wished shortly to have a meeting of the members of the Administration to consider the effect of the Acts passed at the late session of Congress against piracy and the slave-trade, and he intimated that the Committee of the Colonization Society had applied to him to purchase a territory on the coast of Africa to which the slaves who may be taken under the late Act may be sent. The President said there had been only an appropriation of one hundred thousand dollars, which could not be sufficient for purchasing a territory, but perhaps Congress would appropriate more hereafter.

I told him I thought it impossible that Congress should have had any purchase of territory in contemplation of that Act, and that I had no opinion of the practicability or of the usefulness of the object proposed by the Colonization Society, which object professes to be to establish a colony in Africa, where all the free blacks and people of color of the United States may be sent and settled. This project is professed to be formed: 1, without intending to use any compulsion upon the free people of color to make them go; 2, to encourage the emancipation of slaves by their masters; 3, to promote the entire abolition of slavery; and yet, 4, without in the slightest degree affecting what they call a certain species of property – that is, the property of slaves. There are men of all sorts and descriptions concerned in this Colonization Society: some exceedingly humane, weak-minded men, who have really no other than the professed objects in view, and who honestly believe them both useful and attainable; some, speculators in official profits and honors, which a colonial establishment would of course produce; some, speculators in political popularity, who think to please the abolitionists by their zeal for emancipation, and the slaveholders by the flattering hope of ridding them of the free colored people at the public expense; lastly, some cunning slave-holders, who see that the plan may be carried far enough to produce the effect of raising the market price of their slaves. But although the plan obviously, imports the engrafting of a colonial establishment upon the Constitution of the United States, and thereby an accession of power to the National Government transcending all its other powers, and although this tremendous machinery would be introduced under an ostensible purpose comparatively so trivial, and in a captivating form which might bring it in unperceived, I do not believe that is the actuating motive of any one member of the Society. For it would only be the motive of a man whose magnificence of design and depravity of principle would both go beyond my opinions of any man belonging to the Institution. The President said this subject had been recommended by a resolution of the Virginia Legislature. And then he enlarged upon the great earnestness there was in Virginia for the gradual abolition of slavery, and upon the excellent and happy condition of the slaves in that State – upon the kindness with which they were treated, and the mutual attachment subsisting between them and their masters. He said that the feeling against slavery was so strong that shortly after the close of our Revolution many persons had voluntarily emancipated their slaves, but this had introduced a class of very dangerous people, the free blacks, who lived by pilfering, and corrupted the slaves, and produced such pernicious consequences that the Legislature were obliged to prohibit further emancipation by law. The important object now was to remove these free blacks, and provide a place to which the emancipated slaves might go: the legal obstacles to emancipation might then be withdrawn, and the black population in time be drawn off entirely from Virginia.

At the office, the Committee from the Society, General John Mason, Walter Jones, and Francis S. Key, came and renewed the subject. Jones argued that the late Slave-Trade Act contained a clear authority to settle a colony in Africa, and that the purchase of Louisiana, and the settlement at the mouth of Columbia River, placed beyond all question the right of acquiring territory as existing in the Government of the United States.

I treated these gentlemen with all possible civility, but gave them distinctly to understand that the late Slave-Trade Act had no reference to the settlement of a colony, and that the acquisition of Louisiana, and the establishment at the mouth of Columbia River, being in territory contiguous to and continuous with our own, could by no means warrant the purchase of countries beyond the seas, or the establishment of a colonial system of government subordinate to and dependent upon that of the United States. To derive powers competent to this from the Slave-Trade Act was an Indian cosmogony: it was mounting the world upon an elephant, and the elephant on a tortoise, with nothing for the tortoise to stand upon.

They took leave of me with good humor, but satisfied, I believe, that they will have no aid from me. A politician would have flattered them. As I was returning home to dinner, I met Mr. Edwards, the Senator from Illinois. I had seen by the newspapers that he had been re-elected by the Legislature of the State, which I mentioned, and told him I now hoped he would come. He said, Yes. He had hoped his friends would have been able to agree upon some other person to take his place, but they could not. Now, however, he should not be obliged to return home after every session of Congress, and travel twice a year eleven hundred miles to take his seat.

I told him General Parker had said to me the other evening at Dr. Thornton's that he was afraid General Jackson had gone from this city to Virginia with the determination to challenge J. W. Eppes. I hoped it was not so. He said, No; that he had intended it; that some intimation of this intention had been given to the President, and J. J. Monroe had come with two earnest messages to him to interfere and restrain Jackson from this design. He had called upon him, and met Eaton, of Tennessee, coming from him. Eaton had been endeavoring to appease him, without success. When he (Edwards) went in, he found Jackson exasperated beyond anything that he ever witnessed in man. But Jackson was always willing to listen to the advice of those Whom he knew to be his friends, and to give it all due weight. So he sat down with him and argued the case till two or three o'clock in the morning, and then left him perfectly calm and good-humored, and rescued from his project of fighting Eppes. But when he had first represented to Jackson that it would have the appearance of an attempt to overawe members of the Legislature in the exercise of their functions, his answer was, "But, by – , sir, the 4th of March is past. Any man may approve or disapprove my actions at his pleasure. But my motives – no man shall impeach my motives with impunity." However, Edwards pressed upon him that his friends, by the earnestness with which they had defended him, had made his cause their own, and that any indiscretion or intemperate violence on his part would affect them in the public opinion almost as much as himself – a consideration to which he finally yielded, and he went off quite cool and composed. Of all this I had no knowledge at the time.

DIARY ENTRY (WASHINGTON, DC), NOVEMBER 16, 1819

John Quincy reflected before the cabinet his belief that the United States would eventually establish dominion over the North American continent. "From the time when we became an independent people, it was as much a Law of Nature that this should become our pretension as that the Mississippi should flow to the sea. – Spain had possessions upon our Southern and Great Britain upon our Northern border – It was impossible that centuries should elapse without finding them annexed to the United States." American expansion was not a matter of excessive ambition, but "because it is a physical, moral and political absurdity that such fragments of territory, with Sovereigns at fifteen hundred miles beyond sea, worthless and burdensome to their owners should exist permanently contiguous to a great, powerful, enterprizing and rapidly growing Nation." However moderately the United States might pursue this goal, it made no sense to deny it publicly as a matter of policy. European opinion must become accustomed to accepting the geopolitical facts of life.

16th. At noon, after a mere call at the office, I attended at the President's, where Mr. Crawford and Mr. Wirt soon afterwards came. The President read to us the portion of his message that he has prepared, and which was very little more than what he read to me last week. It must in all probability undergo an entirely new modification on its principal topic, our relations with Spain, upon the arrival of the Hornet, which I still hope will be before the meeting of Congress. The recommendation of the President is to consider the treaty as if it was ratified, and to carry it into execution in the same manner. He had drawn two concluding paragraphs, referring to the contingency that Spain should assume a hostile attitude, one of which was in general terms, and the other more explicit, glancing at the propriety of occupying the territory between the Sabine and the Rio Bravo.

Crawford preferred the general expressions, and told a story about old Governor Telfair, of Georgia, who, having got into a sharp correspondence with some officer, and looking over a draft of a letter which his Secretary had prepared for him, to the officer, pointed to a paragraph which struck him as too high-toned, and told his Secretary he would thank him to make that passage *"a little more mysterious."*

We all laughed very heartily at the joke – which so pleased Crawford that he told the story over again in detail; but it was good upon repetition. He said he had been conversing with Mr. Lowndes, who told him that, both in England and France, everybody with whom he had conversed appeared to be profoundly impressed with the idea that we were an ambitious and encroaching people, and he thought we ought to be very guarded and moderate in our policy, to remove this impression.

I said I doubted whether we ought to give ourselves any concern about it. Great Britain, after vilifying us twenty years as a mean, low-minded, peddling nation, having no generous ambitions and no God but gold, had now changed her tone, and was endeavoring to alarm the world at the gigantic grasp of our ambition. Spain was doing the same; and Europe, who, even since the commencement of our Government under the present Constitution, had seen those nations intriguing with the Indians and negotiating to bound us by the Ohio, had first been startled by our acquisition of Louisiana, and now by our pretension to extend to the South Sea, and readily gave credit to the envious and jealous clamor of Spain and England against our ambition. Nothing that we could say or do would remove this impression until the world shall be familiarized with the idea of considering our proper dominion to be the continent of North America. From the time when we became an independent people it was as much a law of nature that this should become our pretension as that the

Mississippi should flow to the sea. Spain had possessions upon our southern and Great Britain upon our northern border. It was impossible that centuries should elapse without finding them annexed to the United States; not that any spirit of encroachment or ambition on our part renders it necessary, but because it is a physical, moral, and political absurdity that such fragments of territory, with sovereigns at fifteen hundred miles beyond sea, worthless and burdensome to their owners, should exist permanently contiguous to a great, powerful, enterprising, and rapidly-growing nation. Most of the Spanish territory which had been in our neighborhood had already become our own by the most unexceptionable of all acquisitions – fair purchase for a valuable consideration. This rendered it still more unavoidable that the remainder of the continent should ultimately be ours. But it is very lately that we have distinctly seen this ourselves; very lately that we have avowed the pretension of extending to the South Sea; and until Europe shall find it a settled geographical element that the United States and North America are identical, any effort on our part to reason the world out of a belief that we are ambitious will have no other effect than to convince them that we add to our ambition hypocrisy.

Crawford spoke of an article in the last Edinburgh Review defending us against this charge of ambition; but if the world do not hold us for Romans they will take us for Jews, and of the two vices I had rather be charged with that which has greatness mingled in its composition.

On the part of the message relating to the South Americans there was little said. Crawford said he had met Torres last evening at General Mason's, and he had told him that the change in Venezuela, by which Arismendi had been placed at the head of the civil government, would be for the better, and give them new energy. The message makes an advance towards a recognition of Buenos Ayres, Chili, and Venezuela, but not more than is warranted by circumstances. There were two or three short paragraphs in the draft relating to the late prevalence of the yellow fever, to the drought, and the pecuniary embarrassments of the country. They closed with consolatory assurances that these evils had, in a great measure, ceased. Crawford and Wirt both objected that this would be thought, as regarded the money concerns, a flattering representation; and the President said he would substitute "in part removed" instead of "a great measure." This introduced a desultory conversation upon various topics, and particularly upon the report which Crawford is to make to Congress upon the currency. He said that scarcely any of the State banks, to whom he had applied for returns of the state of their affairs, had made them, and he must wait to receive copies of those which they were obliged to make to the respective State Legislatures.

DIARY ENTRIES (WASHINGTON, DC), FEBRUARY 24, MARCH 18, MARCH 31, APRIL 13, 1820

John Quincy's faith in the primacy of the Union and in territorial expansion, as essential pillars of national independence, was put to a severe test in the political crisis over the admission of Missouri as a state. He attempted to sort out his own views in his diary. He had been startled by the frank pro-slavery arguments made privately to him by the cabinet member to whom he had felt the closest, Secretary of War John C. Calhoun. Calhoun had added another disquieting note that went to the heart of John Quincy's foreign policy: "He said he did not think it would produce a dissolution of the Union, but, if it should, the South would be from necessity compelled to form an alliance, offensive and defensive, with Great Britain. I said that would be returning to the colonial state. He said, yes, pretty much, but it would be forced upon them." John Quincy would not forego future expansion but saw that much of it was now driven by the South's hunger to acquire territories suitable for slavery. "I thought the greatest danger of this Union, was in the overgrown extent of its territory, combining with the Slavery question – ." He wrote that, had he been in Congress, he would have taken the position that Florida (*or Texas*) *should not be acquired without a prohibition against slavery.*

February 24th. I had some conversation with Calhoun on the slave question pending in Congress. He said he did not think it would produce a dissolution of the Union, but, if it should, the South would be from necessity compelled to form an alliance, offensive and defensive, with Great Britain.

I said that would be returning to the colonial state.

He said, yes, pretty much, but it would be forced upon them. I asked him whether he thought, if by the effect of this alliance, offensive and defensive, the population of the North should be cut off from its natural outlet upon the ocean, it would fall back upon its rocks bound hand and foot, to starve, or whether it would not retain its powers of locomotion to move southward by land. Then, he said, they would find it necessary to make their communities all military. I pressed the conversation no further; but if the dissolution of the Union should result from the slave question, it is as obvious as anything that can be foreseen of futurity, that it must shortly afterwards be followed by the universal emancipation of the slaves. A more remote but perhaps not less certain consequence would be the extirpation of the African race on this continent, by the gradually bleaching process of intermixture, where the white portion is already so predominant, and by the destructive progress of emancipation, which, like all great religious and political reformations, is terrible in its means, though happy and glorious in its end. Slavery is the great and foul stain upon the North American Union, and it is a contemplation worthy of the most exalted soul whether its total abolition is or is not practicable: if practicable, by what means it may be effected, and if a choice of means be within the scope of the object, what means would accomplish it at the smallest cost of human sufferance. A dissolution, at least temporary, of the Union, as now constituted, would be certainly necessary, and the dissolution must be upon a point involving the question of slavery, and no other.

The Union might then be reorganized on the fundamental principle of emancipation. This object is vast in its compass, awful in its prospects, sublime and beautiful in its issue. A life devoted to it would be nobly spent or sacrificed. This conversation with Calhoun led me into a momentous train of reflection. It also engaged me so much that I detained him at his office, insensibly to myself, till near five o'clock, an hour at least later than his dining-time.

March

18th. G. A. Otis was at the office. He is proceeding with his translation of Botta's History of the American Revolution, and borrows my French translation of it to take with him to Philadelphia. But his main object was to renew and urge his solicitation for a Consular appointment abroad, and particularly for that of Liverpool, from which he wished that Mr. Maury should be removed; not that he (Otis) would wish to supplant any man, but because Maury is an old man, and that the business of his office is, and for some time has been, transacted by his clerk, who is an Englishman.

There is something so gross and so repugnant to my feelings in this cormorant appetite for office, this barefaced and repeated effort to get an old and meritorious public servant turned out of place by a bankrupt to get into it, that it needed all my sense of the allowances to be made for sharp want and of the tender ness due to misfortune to suppress my indignation. He asked me if I would advise him to press these considerations personally upon the President; to which I barely answered no. He said he had asked Mr. Jonathan Russell his opinion whether it would be indelicate to suggest them, and Russell had told him they were facts which there could be no impropriety in stating. This is not the first sample I have had of Russell's morals connected with the pursuit of office. Otis is an office-hunter equally ravenous, and, like some other ravenous animals, has the gifts of fawning and of tears. But even with such persons no passionate manifestation of sentiment should be indulged; and this is the only way that I can understand as consistent the scriptural injunction, "Be ye angry and sin not!"

I this day received from J. Forsyth a dispatch of 3d January, with a postscript of the 10th. The Russian Chargé d'Affaires had interposed to prevail upon Forsyth not to leave Madrid, as he had threatened. A few days since, I received a dispatch from G. W. Campbell, reporting an interview with Count Nesselrode, the Russian Minister of Foreign Affairs, in which the Emperor's solicitude for the amicable arrangement of our differences with Spain was manifested, and Poletica has shown and read to me extracts of a dispatch from Nesselrode, and of private letters from Capo d'Istrias and Pozzo di Borgo to him, expressing the same sentiments, and earnestly dissuading us from taking measures of self-satisfaction. Gallatin's dispatches indicate the same wishes and advice from the French Government.

I took Forsyth's dispatch to the President, and suggested to him the question whether it would not be advisable to send a message to Congress communicating these facts and documents, and recommending to them to postpone acting upon the Florida questions till the next session. The motives for this measure are various, and among the rest is that of changing the position of the Executive in reference to the Legislature. It has become very awkward. Before the Florida Treaty was signed, Clay's tactics were to push the Executive, if possible, into a quarrel with Spain. As he did not play his game very skilfully, his impetuosity contributed to promote the conclusion of the treaty. Without involving the Executive as he intended, it alarmed Spain, and gave us argument to bring her to reasonable terms. When the treaty was signed, it was so generally considered as highly advantageous to the United States that it was considered very creditable to the Administration, and Clay, though he betrayed his ill will to it, yet dared not make any opposition against it. As soon as the question about the grants arose, Clay seized upon it as a means of defeating the treaty. Spain, by withholding the ratification beyond the stipulated period, has thrown away the bargain, and the United States are no longer bound to abide by it. In the course of the discussion with Spain it became necessary to show that Onis's instructions authorized him to have conceded more than he did. Upon which Clay immediately argues that more was conceded than Onis asked. At the commencement of the session the President proposed that a discretionary power should be given to the Executive to take possession of Florida and to indemnify the claimants upon Spain, as if the treaty had been ratified, from the Florida lands. The House manifested no disposition to comply with this proposal, and the Committee of Foreign Relations brought in a report requiring positively that Florida should be taken, and leaving the claims totally unprovided for. Clay's professed project was to set the treaty aside, to take the province of Texas, and recognize the South Americans; his real object was merely to defeat the treaty and do nothing. It has long been obvious that Congress would do nothing, and the danger to the Executive is, that by that termination of doing nothing the appearance to the world will be of dissension between the executive and the Legislature, the worst of all possible positions for negotiating with the Spaniard when he comes. In the meantime, the Missouri question and its compromise have sharpened the greediness of the Southern interest for more Southern Territories to make more slave States, and given the Northern and Eastern interest a distaste even for Florida, because that would become another slave State. The new disturbances in Spain also threaten a revolution of the Government there, and put an end to all question as to the issue of the revolution in South America. The only powerful interest, therefore, that Spain had for settling her differences with us is disappearing. There is no prospect of the ratification of the treaty, and there is at this moment scarcely any great interest in this country that desires the ratification. Forsyth in his dispatch says that probably the Spanish Government wishes that we may take possession of Florida for the sake of having stronger ground for insisting on the confirmation of the grants, and the proposal of the Committee of Foreign Relations falls into this view as completely as if it had been drawn up by the Duke of Alagon himself.

I suggested most of these considerations to the President as motives for a message to Congress proposing to postpone measures of reprisal for the present. As this will unquestionably be the result, it will show the Executive and Legislature as at least not in direct opposition to each other. It will be an example of moderation and magnanimity to Spain in the time of her distress; of deference and regard to the wishes and advice of Russia and France; and of sound policy as relates to the internal state of our affairs. The President appeared to concur in these opinions generally, and asked me to put in writing such of them as I might think of particular moment, and to see him again on the subject next Monday.

31st. Mr. Ninian Edwards, a Senator from the State of Illinois, came to me this morning upon business which had been also yesterday mentioned by Cook – the nomination of Marshal for that district, in the room of R. Lemen, resigned. He had a recommendation from Judge Pope of a Mr. Conar, who is also supported by him and by Cook. He also talked much about Clay's two resolutions offered to the House of Representatives last Tuesday, the day after the message from the President on Spain and Florida was sent in. Clay's affairs, private and public, have been growing desperate ever since the commencement of Mr. Monroe's Administration. He then refused the War Department and the mission to London; nothing would satisfy him but the Department of State; and, failing to obtain that, he projected a new opposition, of which he should be the head, and which should in the course of two Presidential terms run down Monroe, so that he might come in as the opposition successor. His engines the first session were South America and internal improvement. Both then failed. The next session he took up the Seminole War, but of that mighty controversy he was no longer the primary leader. He had ranged himself under the Crawford banners. That struggle was more stubborn, but also failed. The great majority of the people took the other side. The Missouri question then arose, and disconcerted Clay's projects by presenting party combinations and divisions very unsuitable to them. It looked to a dissolution of the Union upon principles which could not serve his purposes. But, that question having been for the present compromised, he recurs to South American and Spanish affairs for his main engine of opposition. The Florida Treaty, when concluded last winter, was universally considered as obtaining so much more for us than had ever been expected, that not a voice could be raised against it in either House of Congress. Now the public feeling is different. For, while the King of Spain refuses to ratify because, he says, his Minister conceded too much, the people of our Western country have been instigated against the treaty as not having obtained enough. The Missouri question, too, has operated to indispose every part of the Union against the treaty: the North and East, because they do not wish even to have Florida as another slave State; and the South and West, because they wish to have all the territory to the Rio del Norte for more slave States. Clay seizes upon this state of things, and has brought forward these resolutions, which are to operate in every possible contingency against the Administration. By raising a party against the treaty it may prevent its ratification, in which case all our differences with Spain recur to clog the course of the Administration; if not, and the ratification should be obtained, the treaty itself will be rendered obnoxious, and the Administration odious for accepting it – and most especially the Secretary of State who negotiated it. Clay's resolutions are: 1. That Congress alone have power to cede territory, and that no treaty can cede it without their sanction; and, 2. That the Florida Treaty ceded territory without an adequate equivalent, and ought not to be renewed. Edwards says he had at first been told that these resolutions would not have much support, but afterwards that they would, and perhaps might be carried in the House; that all the Western members would vote for them, and that the treaty had been rendered unpopular in the Western country. He also said a member had told him that the President's last message would be the most unpopular act that he ever did, because it recommended to postpone acting at the interposition of Russia and France, after having refused to accept the mediation of Great Britain and to abide by the decision of the allied powers.

I told Edwards that I had very little attachment to the treaty. I believed it now, as when it was signed, an acceptable bargain; but I had been the last man in the Administration to agree to accept the Sabine for the western boundary, and shall now be very ready to abandon the treaty if the opinion of an adequate portion of either House of Congress should be adverse to it; that, as a servant of the whole Union, the interests of every part of the Union were equally dear to me – there was neither East, West, North, or South to my duty or my feelings; but, as an Eastern man, I should be disinclined to have either Texas or Florida without a restriction excluding slavery from them, and if I were now a member of either House of Congress I would offer resolutions that the treaty ought not now to be accepted without an article prohibiting and excluding slavery from the territory to be acquired. I had been continually expecting that such resolutions would be offered by some one of the Northern or Eastern members. As to the President's message, there were other reasons for sending it in besides those apparent upon the face of it – reasons of transcendent influence, but not proper to be publicly assigned. One was, to prevent a long, angry, dangerous, and unprofitable debate, which would certainly have arisen from the report of the Committee of Foreign Relations. A second was, to avoid the certain issue of that debate, which would have exhibited to the nation and the world a disagreement of the worst kind between the Executive and the Legislature. In all probability, the issue would have been the indefinite postponement of the subject, with nothing done, and with great mutual irritation and excitement. A third was, that even if the law for occupying Florida could have passed, we had reason to believe it was precisely what Spain desired, for the purpose of having ground to insist upon the confirmation of the contested grants. And the report of the committee gave anticipated countenance to that pretension. The message puts an end to all this, and now Clay may offer his resolutions and make his speeches. We know that the vote of the House will concur with the recommendation of the message. Why the reference to the interposition of France and Russia should make the President unpopular I could not easily see. The Committee of Foreign Relations had written to me through their Chairman, especially enquiring what information the Executive had of the views of the European powers in relation to our affairs with Spain, and what part they would probably take in the event of a war between the United States and her. The question before the House upon the report and bill of the committee was a question of peace and war. What would have been said of the President if he had withheld from the House the fact of the interposition of France and Russia? That interposition has been altogether friendly, with an unequivocal expression of opinion in our favor on the points of difference with Spain. It was not of a character offensive in the slightest degree to our independence, and it was in a concern upon which they had a right to interpose. They had important interests of their own involved in the issue – the interest of general peace, which was threatened with imminent danger, in the event of a war between us and Spain. It would be a perversion of sound principle to pernicious prejudice to spurn at such interposition. The President therefore deliberately determined to send the message, well aware of the gloss that would be put upon it, but knowing also that whatever opposition it might encounter here would produce a favorable reaction in Europe; and believing that the whole result would be advantageous not only to the country but to the Administration.

Edwards assented to all this, and agreed that the message was a judicious measure. He intimated a wish that there might be some means of explaining the subject by writing for publication in the Western country newspapers; but for this I have neither time nor means. I took the recommendations of Conar for the appointment of Marshal in Illinois to the President, who determined to send immediately the nomination to the Senate. The President also concluded upon the case of the pirates under conviction, of whom there are seven at Baltimore, at Richmond, Virginia, four at Charleston, S.C., four at Savannah, and eighteen at New Orleans. Two are to be executed at each place, and the rest reprieved for two months, excepting one at New Orleans, who is to be immediately pardoned. The warrants and necessary letters to the Marshals of the Districts are to be made out immediately.

April

13th. Mr. Ruggles, a Senator from the State of Ohio, called upon me this morning with a written recommendation, signed by five or six members of the House of Representatives from that State, of a person for the appointment of a Judge in the Territory of Arkansas. I had some conversation with Mr. Ruggles with regard to the opinions of the people in the Western country concerning the Florida Treaty and Mr. Clay's project of setting it aside and taking possession of the province of Texas. Ruggles said that this project was adverse to the interests of the State of Ohio, who would be well satisfied with the ratification of the treaty. Mr. David Trimble, a member of the House from Kentucky, called at the office to enquire what would probably be the result of the negotiation with General Vives. His ostensible, motive was to make up his opinion on the report to be made by the Committee of Ways and Means, of which he is a member. But he came with along argument to convince me that the only way for me to make myself popular in the Western country was to set the treaty aside and urge the recognition of the South American revolutionists, and insist upon the Rio del Norte as the western boundary.

I told him that I understood the map of the country rather too well to suppose it would ever be possible for me to do anything that could make me popular in the Western country; that as to the treaty, I had never set the value upon it that was supposed, and of all the members of the Administration, I was the last who had consented to take the Sabine for our western boundary. I had no doubt that if the treaty should be set aside we should ultimately obtain more territory than it would secure to us, but we should get the same territory with the treaty sooner than we should want it; and even now I thought the greatest danger of this Union was in the overgrown extent of its territory, combining with the slavery question. I added as my belief, that there would be a majority of the House of Representatives now who would not accept of the province of Texas as a gift unless slavery should be excluded from it. Since the Missouri debate, I considered the continuance of the Union for any length of time as very precarious, and entertained serious doubts whether Louisiana and slavery would not ultimately break us up.

He said he himself considered the slavery question as the greatest that can agitate this Union, but that Kentucky would get rid of her slaves and would finally not be in the slaveholding interest – they did not want slaves for the articles of their cultivation; but if the Union should break up there would be three Confederacies – Eastern, Southern, and Western.

I said, so I had heard Clay say – that within five years we should have three Confederacies; but why there should be precisely three I could not see. The slave question might split us in two; because this question, besides involving the strongest oppositions of interest, involved also the principle of all others the most deeply planted in the hearts of this people. There was no existing opposition of mere interest between any two parts of this country, which could possibly produce a dissolution of the Union.

He said he agreed with me in that. But if the Union should break, the country between the Sabine and the Rio del Norte would become indispensably necessary for the Western Confederacy. It would be an excellent country for the cultivation of coffee, and there was an admirable sea-port there which would be necessary to the command of the Gulf of Mexico.

I told him that I did not believe we should ever find either a good sea-port or grounds for cultivating coffee in Texas, nor did I believe there was any article of cultivation that needed slaves. The want of slaves was not in the lands, but in their inhabitants. Slavery had become in the South and Southwestern country a condition of existence. They could not live without them. As to the treaty, we could now very easily disengage ourselves from that. The difficulty would not be in setting it aside, but in obtaining it. He and Mr. Clay were excellent negotiators in theory. They were for obtaining all and granting nothing. They played a game between their own right and left hands, and could allot with admirable management the whole stake to one hand and total discomfiture to the other. In the negotiation with Spain we had a just claim to the Mississippi and its waters, and our citizens had a fair though very precarious claim to indemnities. We had a mere color of claim to the Rio del Norte, no claim to a line beyond the Rocky Mountains, and none to Florida, which we very much wanted. The treaty gives us the Mississippi and all its waters – gives us Florida – gives us an acknowledged line to the South Sea, and seventeen degrees of latitude upon its shores – gives our citizens five millions of dollars of indemnity – and barely gives up to Spain the colorable claim from the Sabine to the Rio del Norte. Now, negotiation implies some concession upon both sides. If after obtaining every object of your pursuit but one, and that one weak in principle and of no present value, what would you have offered to Spain to yield that also?

Trimble had no answer to this question, but he said he believed Onis had deceived me about the grants. He had no doubt Onis knew the grants were dated before the 24th of January, and assumed that date with the intention that it should confirm them. This was no disparagement to me; any honorable man might be thus deceived; but that, he believed, was the fact. I told him that Onis might very possibly have had such an intention, but the fact was, we had never relied upon the date; that the grants were annulled by the terms of the article, independent of the date, and that we have not only the demonstration that such was the professed intention of the parties on both sides, but that the article could, without a violent perversion of language, bear no other construction. To this Trimble agreed.

Trimble is a bustling, talkative, pushing man, professing to be independent of all parties, but in reality a satellite of Clay's. He made a speech in the House the other day upon Clay's resolutions against the treaty, in which he said all that he this morning repeated to me, and much more. He is one of the members who make it a point to keep upon good and friendly terms with me personally, and always to side against me upon public questions involving my opinions, reputation, or character.

JOHN QUINCY ADAMS (DEPARTMENT OF STATE) TO HENRY MIDDLETON, JULY 5, 1820

To the American minister to Russia, John Quincy offers an acute assessment of the European diplomatic scene and the policy of Emperor Alexander. Alexander had been urging the United States to associate itself with the principles of the Holy Alliance, and even to join it. Middleton is instructed to sidestep the offer, if made to him, although not to refuse explicitly. The reason for declining – the principle set out in Washington's Farewell Address – which John Quincy had long held, was as follows: "The political system of the United States is also essentially extra-European. To stand in firm and cautious independence of all entanglement in the European system, has been a cardinal point of their policy under every administration of their government from the peace of 1783 to this day.... it may be observed that for the repose of Europe as well as of America, the European and American political systems should be kept as separate and distinct from each other as possible."

The relations of the United States with the Russian empire and its government, and which in their several bearings will require your constant and earnest attention are: 1, political; 2, commercial; 3, special, resulting from the reference by the United States and Great Britain to the Emperor Alexander, of the question between them upon the construction of the first article of the treaty of Ghent.

1. Political. The present political system of Europe is founded upon the overthrow of that which had grown out of the French Revolution, and has assumed its shape from the body of treaties concluded at Vienna in 18 14 and '15, at Paris, towards the close of the same year 1815, and at Aix la Chapelle in the autumn of 1818. Its general character is that of a compact between the five principal European powers, Austria, France, Great Britain, Prussia, and Russia, for the preservation of universal peace. These powers having then just emerged victorious from a long, portentous and sanguinary struggle against the oppressive predominancy of one of them, under revolutionary sway, appear to have bent all their faculties to the substitution of a system which should preserve them from that evil; the preponderancy of one power by the subjugation, virtual if not nominal, of the rest. Whether they perceived in its full extent, considered in its true colors, or provided by judicious arrangements for the revolutionary temper of the weapons by which they had so long been assailed, and from which they had so severely suffered, is a question now in a course of solution. Their great anxiety appears to have been to guard themselves each against the other.

The League of Peace, so far as it was a covenant of organized governments, has proved effectual to its purposes by an experience of five years. Its only interruption has been in this hemisphere, though between nations strictly European, by the invasion of the Portuguese on the territory claimed by Spain, but already lost to her, on the eastern shore of the Rio de la Plata. This aggression too the European alliance have undertaken to control, and in connection with it they have formed projects, hitherto abortive, of interposing in the revolutionary struggle between Spain and her South American colonies.

As a compact between governments it is not improbable that the European alliance will last as long as some of the states who are parties to it. The warlike passions and propensities of the present age find their principal aliment, not in the enmities between nation and nation, but in the internal dissensions between the component parts of all. The war is between nations and their rulers.

The Emperor may be considered as the principal patron and founder of the league of peace. His interest is the most unequivocal in support of it. His empire is the only party to the compact free from that internal fermentation which threatens the existence of all the rest. His territories are the most extensive, his military establishment the most stupendous, his country the most improvable and thriving of them all. He is, therefore, naturally the most obnoxious to the jealousy and fears of his associates, and his circumstances point his policy to a faithful adhesion to the general system, with a strong reprobation of those who would resort to special and partial alliances, from which any one member of the league should be excluded. This general tendency of his policy is corroborated by the mild and religious turn of his individual character. He finds a happy coincidence between the dictates of his conscience and the interest of his empire. And as from the very circumstance of his preponderancy partial alliances might be most easily contracted by him, from the natural resort of the weak for the succor to the strong, by discountenancing all such partial combinations, he has the appearance of discarding advantages entirely within his command, and reaps the glory of disinterestedness, while most efficaciously providing for his own security.

Such is accordingly the constant indication of the Russian policy since the peace of Paris in 1815. The neighbors of Russia, which have the most to dread from her overshadowing and encroaching powers are Persia, Turkey, Austria, and Prussia, the two latter of which are members of the European and even of the Holy Alliance, while the two former are not only extra-European in their general policy, but of religions, which excluded them from ever becoming parties, if not from ever deriving benefit from that singular compact.

The political system of the United States is also essentially extra-European. To stand in firm and cautious independence of all entanglement in the European system, has been a cardinal point of their policy under every administration of their government from the peace of 1783 to this day. If at the original adoption of their system there could have been any doubt of its justice or its wisdom, there can be none at this time. Every year's experience rivets it more deeply in the principles and opinions of the nation. Yet in proportion as the importance of the United States as one of the members of the general society of civilized nations increases in the eyes of the others, the difficulties of maintaining this system, and the temptations to depart from it increase and multiply with it. The Russian government has not only manifested an inclination that the United States should concur in the general principles of the European league, but a direct though inofficial application has been made by the present Russian minister here, that the United States should become formal parties to the Holy Alliance. It has been suggested as inducement to obtain their compliance, that this compact bound the parties to no specific engagement of anything; that it was a pledge of mere principles; that its real as well as its professed purpose was merely the general preservation of peace, and it was intimated that if any question should arise between the United States and other governments of Europe, the Emperor Alexander, desirous of using his influence in their favor, would have a substantial motive and justification for interposing, if he could regard them as *his allies*, which as parties to the Holy Alliance he would be.

It is possible that overtures of a similar character may be made to you; but whether they should be or not it is proper to apprize you of the light in which they have been viewed by the President. No direct refusal has been notified to Mr. Poletica. It is presumed that none will be necessary. His instructions are not to make the proposal in form, unless with a prospect that it will be successful. It might perhaps be sufficient to answer that the organization of our government is such as not to admit of our acceding formally to that compact. But it may be added that the President approving the general principles, and thoroughly convinced of the benevolent and virtuous motives which led to the conception and presided at the formation of this system by the Emperor Alexander, believes that the United States will more effectually contribute to the great and sublime objects for which it was concluded, by abstaining from a formal participation in it, than they could as stipulated members of it. As a general declaration of principles, disclaiming the impulses of vulgar ambition and unprincipled aggrandizement, and openly proclaiming the peculiarly christian maxims of mutual benevolence and brotherly love, to be binding upon the intercourse between nations no less than upon those of individuals, the United States, not only give their hearty assent to the articles of the Holy Alliance, but will be among the most earnest and conscientious in observing them. But independent of the prejudices which have been excited against this instrument in the public opinion, which time and an experience of its good effects will gradually wear away, it may be observed that for the repose of Europe as well as of America, the European and American political systems should be kept as separate and distinct from each other as possible. If the United States as members of the Holy Alliance could acquire a right to ask the influence of its most powerful members in their controversies with other states, the other members must be entitled in return to ask the influence of the United States for themselves or against their opponents. In the deliberations of the league they would be entitled to a voice, and in exercising their right must occasionally appeal to principles, which might not harmonize with those of any European member of the bond. This consideration alone would be decisive for declining a participation in that league, which is the President's absolute and irrevocable determination, although he trusts that no occasion will present itself rendering it necessary to make that determination known by an explicit refusal.

2. *Commercial*. The aversion of the Emperor Alexander to the negotiation of any commercial treaties has probably undergone no change since the instructions to Mr. Campbell were prepared. We have no motive for desiring that it should. You will however pay suitable attention to the actual state of our commerce with Russia, and particularly to the condition and prospects of the Russian establishments on the Black Sea. Voyages of circumnavigation and of discovery have been since the late general peace in Europe fitted out partly on account of the government, and partly under the direction and at the expense of Count Nicholas Romanzoff, late Chancellor of the empire. Of the objects of those voyages, and of the information obtained from them so far as it is of a public nature we shall be gratified in receiving any communication which you may think proper to transmit.... The movements of the Russian *American* Company may, perhaps, occasionally deserve your attention, as they are connected with the Russian establishments on the northwest coast of this continent; but they will probably be found less important than they have been imagined. A translation of the *whole ukase* by which that company was constituted, if you can obtain and forward it to this department, would be acceptable....

JOHN QUINCY ADAMS (DEPARTMENT OF STATE) TO STRATFORD CANNING, DECEMBER 30, 1820

After extensive discussion in the Cabinet – and some editing – John Quincy sent this missive to the British minister, Stratford Canning, setting out the administration's objections to joining a convention with Britain to repress the slave trade. The United States supported cooperative actions to deal with the trade, but the British proposal as offered was unacceptable. John Quincy cited a want of constitutional authority to establish mixed courts to try those suspected of such trading, as well as a disapproval of the principle of allowing the search, in time of peace, of American merchant vessels by the armed cruisers of another nation. The latter opened up all the ugly issues of impressment.

SIR:

I have had the honor of receiving your note of the 20th instant, in reply to which I am directed by the President of the United States to inform you that, conformably to the assurances given you in the conversation to which you refer, the proposals made by your government to the United States, inviting their accession to the arrangements contained in certain treaties with Spain, Portugal and the Netherlands, to which Great Britain is the reciprocal contracting party, have again been taken into the most serious deliberation of the President, with an anxious desire of contributing to the utmost extent of the powers within the competency of this government, and by means compatible with its duties to the rights of its own citizens, and with the principles of its national independence to the effectual and final suppression of the African slave-trade.

At an earlier period of the communications between the two governments upon this subject, the President, in manifesting his sensibility to the amicable spirit of confidence with which the measures concerted between Great Britain and some of her European allies had been made known to the United States, and to the free and candid offer of admitting the United States to a participation in those measures, had instructed the minister of the United States residing near your government, to represent the difficulties resulting as well from certain principles of international law, of the deepest and most painful interest to these United States, as from limitations of authority prescribed by the people of the United States to the legislative and executive depositaries of the national power, which placed him under the necessity of declining the proposal. It had been stated that a compact giving the power to the naval officers of one nation to search the merchant vessels of another, for offenders and offence against the laws of the latter, backed by a further power, to seize and carry into a foreign port, and there subject to the decision of a tribunal composed of at least one-half foreigners, irresponsible to the supreme corrective tribunal of this Union, and not amenable to the control of impeachment for official misdemeanor, was an investment of power over the persons, property, and reputation of the citizens of this country, not only unwarranted by any delegation of sovereign power to the national government, but so adverse to the elementary principles and indispensable securities of individual rights interwoven in all the political institutions of this country, that not even the most unqualified approbation of the ends, to which this organization of authority was adopted, nor the most sincere and earnest wish to concur in every suitable expedient for their accomplishment, could reconcile it to the sentiments or the principles of which in the estimation of the people and government of the United States no consideration whatsoever could justify the transgression.

In the several conferences which since your arrival here I have had the honor of holding with you, and in which this subject has been fully and freely discussed between us, the incompetency of the power of this government to become a party to the institution of tribunals organized like those stipulated in the conventions above noticed, and the incompatibility of such tribunals with the essential character of the constitutional rights guaranteed to every citizen of the Union, have been shown by direct references to the fundamental principles of our government; in which the supreme, unlimited, sovereign power is considered as inherent in the whole body of its people, while its delegations are limited and restricted by the terms of the instruments sanctioned by them, under which the powers of legislation, judgment and execution are administered; and by special indications of the articles in the constitution of the United States which expressly prohibit their constituted authorities from erecting any judicial courts by the form of process belonging to which American citizens should be called to answer for any penal offence without the intervention of a grand jury to accuse, and of a jury of trial to decide upon the charge. [It has been shown that the trial of an American citizen for offences against the laws of his country, not by a jury of his peers and neighbors, but in a foreign land, by judges and arbitrators strangers both to him and his country, would be a subversion of these liberties to which in our estimation life itself is an object of secondary consideration; and that to be made amenable to tribunals thus constituted would be as repugnant to the general feelings and principles of this nation as to the express letter of several articles of their constitution.]

But while regretting that the character of the organized means of cooperation for the suppression of the African slave-trade, proposed by Great Britain, did not admit of our concurrence in the adoption of them, the President has been far from the disposition to reject or discountenance the general proposition of concerted cooperation with Great Britain to the accomplishment of the common end, the suppression of the trade. For this purpose armed cruisers of the United States have been for some time kept stationed on the coast which is the scene of this odious traffic, a measure which it is in the contemplation of this government to continue without intermission. As there are armed British vessels charged with the same duty constantly kept cruising on the same coast, I am directed by the President to propose that instructions, to be concerted between the two governments with a view to mutual assistance, should be given to the commanders of the vessels respectively assigned to that service. That they may be ordered, whenever the occasion may render it convenient, to cruise in company together, to communicate mutually to each other all information obtained by the one, and which may be useful to the execution of the duties of the other; and to give each other every assistance which may be compatible with the performance of their own service, and adapted to the end which is the common aim of both parties. [It is hoped that by these means the flag of the United States may be effectually shielded from the disgrace of screening the slave trader from punishment without *subjecting the standard of this nation to the humiliation of witnessing the search by a foreign officer of an American vessel, for transgressors of American laws; to be tried and doomed by the decision of foreign arbitrators and judges.*

The President is further disposed, should it be satisfactory to your government, to stipulate by a convention the number of cruisers to be kept stationed on the African coast by both parties, and the time during which and latitudes within which they shall cruise, with a view to the end to be accomplished by these concurrent operations.]

These measures congenial to the spirit which has so long and so steadily marked the policy of the United States in the vindication of the rights of humanity will, it is hoped, prove effectual to the purposes for which this cooperation is desired by your government, and to which this Union will continue to direct its most strenuous and persevering exertions.

I pray you, etc.

DIARY ENTRY (WASHINGTON, DC), JANUARY 27, 1821

In this famous exchange with Stratford Canning, John Quincy frankly set out America's territorial ambitions and a baseline for future amicable relations. The two men had gotten into a row the day before, over Canning's argument that congressionally proposed American plans to establish a new settlement on the mouth of the Columbia River, along the Pacific Ocean, would violate the Convention of 1818. John Quincy responded that the convention certainly did not restrict such American claims on the Pacific. "'And in this,' said he, 'you include our Northern Provinces [Canada] on this Continent?' 'No,' said I; 'there the boundary is marked, and we have no disposition to encroach upon it – Keep what is yours, but leave the rest of this Continent to us.'"

27th. The messenger of the Department announced Mr. Canning. I told the messenger to say to Mr. Canning that I would receive him in a few minutes. Mr. Eddy remained with me not more than five minutes longer; and Mr. Canning when he came in, as he sat down, took out his watch, and observed that it was forty minutes faster than the clock here. While he was speaking, the clock in the office struck one. I made no answer to his remark, which might be considered either as a complaint that he had been made to wait, or as an apology for having come before the time appointed. He proceeded to say that, conformably to the desire expressed by me yesterday, he had now come to have some further conversation upon the subject of our interview then.

There was in his manner an apparent effort of coolness, but no appearance of cheerfulness or good humor. I saw there was no relaxation from the tone he had yesterday assumed, and felt that none would on my part be suitable. I said he would recollect that our conference of this day was not at my desire. I had yesterday repeatedly expressed to him the opinion that if this discussion was to be further pursued it should be in writing. He had with some earnestness urged another conference, and when he requested me to fix the time I had told him that I was ready and willing to hear then anything that he had to say on the subject; that perhaps, under the excitement which he was then manifesting, he might himself prefer to resume the conversation some other day, and, if so, I would see him whenever it should be most agreeable to himself; he had then asked me to name a time, and I appointed this day at one o'clock.

He said, "Well, then, be it so." He then took from his pocket the National Intelligencer of yesterday, folded down to the column in which the proceedings of the House of Representatives were reported, and, referring to the statement that Mr. Floyd had reported a bill for the occupation of the Columbia River, said that was an indication of intentions in this Government which he presumed would leave no question of the propriety of his application to me.

I told him it was precisely that in which its greatest impropriety consisted. But I could only repeat what I had said to him yesterday, that I saw no use in continuing a discussion upon the propriety of his conduct or of mine.

He said he would most cheerfully consent to be the sacrifice, if that only was necessary to the harmony of the two countries; but that nothing could exceed his astonishment at the manner in which I had received his application of yesterday. He could assure me with the utmost sincerity that since the existence of this country as a nation there never had been a time when the British Government had been so anxiously desirous of preserving and cherishing the most perfect good understanding and harmony with this; but that at the same time they would not, on that account, yield one particle of their rights.

I told him I had no doubt of the correctness of his statement in both its parts, and I was happy to give him the same assurance on the part of this Government. It was the earnest wish of the President to preserve the most friendly relations with Great Britain; but he would maintain all the rights of the United States. And I would add, as my individual opinion, that any chicaning of our right to the mouth of Columbia River would assuredly not tend to promote that harmony between the two countries.

Mr. Canning again repeated his surprise at the tone and temper with which his application yesterday had been received. He said he had examined and re-examined himself, and had in vain enquired what could have been the cause of the asperity with which he had been treated by me.

"Sir," said I, "suppose Mr. Rush should be present at a debate in the House of Commons, and should hear a member in the course of a speech say something about the expediency of sending a regiment of troops to the Shetland Islands, or a new colony to New South Wales; suppose another member of Parliament should publish in a newspaper a letter recommending the same project; and suppose Mr. Rush should then go to Lord Castlereagh and formally allege those two facts as his motives for demanding whether the British Government had any such intentions; and, if answered that very probably they might, he should assume an imperious and tragical tone of surprise and talk about a violation of treaties: how do you think it would be received?"

He said that now he fully understood me, and could account for what had passed; this answer was perfectly explicit. But did I consider the cases as parallel?

"So far as any question of right is concerned," said I, "perfectly parallel."

"Have you," said Mr. Canning, "any claim to the Shetland Islands or New South Wales?"

"Have you any *claim*" said I, "to the mouth of Columbia River?"

"Why, do you not *know*" replied he, "that we have a claim?"

"I do not *know*" said I, "what you claim nor what you do not claim. You claim India; you claim Africa; you claim – "

"Perhaps," said he, "a piece of the moon."

"No," said I; "I have not heard that you claim exclusively any part of the moon; but there is not a spot on this habitable globe that I could affirm you do not claim; and there is none which you may not claim with as much color of right as you can have to Columbia River or its mouth."

"And how far would you consider," said he, "this exclusion of right to extend?"

"To all the shores of the South Sea," said I. "We know of no right that you have there."

"Suppose," said he, "Great Britain should undertake to make a settlement there, would you object to it?"

"I have no doubt we should," said I.

"But, surely," said Mr. Canning, "proof was made at the negotiation of the Convention of October, 1818, of the claims of Great Britain, and their existence is recognized in it."

"There was no proof," I said, "made of any claim, nor, to my knowledge, any discussion of claim. The boundary to the Stony Mountains was defined; westward of them Great Britain had no settlement whatever. We had one at the mouth of the Columbia, which, having been broken up during the war, was solemnly restored to us by the British Government, in fulfilment of a stipulation in the treaty of peace. We stipulated in the Convention that the ports and places on the Pacific Ocean should be open to both parties for ten years, and, taking all these transactions together, we certainly did suppose that the British Government had come to the conclusion that there would be neither policy nor profit in cavilling with us about territory on this North American continent."

"And in this," said he, "you include our northern provinces on this continent?"

"No," said I; "there the boundary is marked, and we have no disposition to encroach upon it. Keep what is yours, but leave the rest of this continent to us."

"But," said he, "this affects the rights of Russia and of Spain."

"Russia and Spain," I replied, "are the guardians of their own rights. Have you, Mr. Canning, any right to speak in their name?"

"Why, sir," said he, "I can assure you that Great Britain is in very close alliance with them."

"Yes, sir, Great Britain has strong allies; we know that very well," said I; "but they have not authorized you to speak for them."

"And do you wish me," said he, in a tone highly incensed, "to report to my Government what you have now said to me?"

"Sir," said I, "you may report to your Government just what you please. Report to them, if you think proper, every word that I have said to you, not only now, but at any time, or that I ever shall say, provided you report nothing but the truth, as I have no doubt you will."

He said he thanked me for the addition of that opinion.

I said that I had no doubt he would report nothing but the truth, and should not, by anticipation, admit any suspicion to the contrary. "But," added I, "if you do report our conversation to your Government, I request you to state explicitly that I took strong exception both to the form and to the substance of your application to me on this occasion. To the form, because you came to put questions to me of an irritating nature upon the foundation of the speeches and reports of individual members of Congress; and to the substance, because the questions were of a nature which we do not admit your right to ask. I did, in the first instance, answer an improper question; not in the name of the Government, but merely by giving you an opinion of my own. Upon which the tone and manner assumed by you in reply convinced me that nothing useful to either party could result from any further verbal conference between us. If you meant to make a Falkland Island or Nootka Sound affair of it, I thought it best the discussion should be in writing, which would not be liable to misapprehension."

"I don't know that," said Mr. Canning, interrupting me.

"At least," I resumed, "such misapprehensions would be more easily rectified, and would have over them a guard of public opinion. The objection to the form of your address was the more serious, because you were the representative of a nation having itself a legislature, consisting of deliberative assemblies, tenacious of the perfect freedom of speech of their members, and the Government of which would certainly permit no foreign Minister to interrogate them upon the mere foundation of speeches made by members of Parliament in their places, or of publications made by them through the press."

Mr. Canning then again denied that he had made the application upon the sole ground of Mr. Nelson's speech, and reminded me that he had expressly told me that he should not have noticed it had it stood as a solitary fact.

I replied that he had no right to mention it to me at all as the foundation of debatable questions, but that my objection had reference not alone to his notice of Mr. Nelson's speech. It was equally applicable to his mention of the publication of Mr. Eaton, and to his production this morning of a newspaper to point at a report of a committee of the House of Representatives to that body. He had alleged no ground to me for his application on this subject other than acts of individual members of Congress on measures pending in the legislature. What would be thought of an American Minister in England who should presume to call upon the Secretary of State for Foreign Affairs to account for speeches or writings of members and committees of Parliament?

He said he was much mistaken if, in the lately published correspondence respecting the slave-trade, there had not been references by Mr. Rush to speeches and proceedings in Parliament.

"Undoubtedly," said I, "in Mr. Rush's dispatches to his own Government; and we make no question of your right to report to your Government anything said or done in Congress by any of its members."

He said he believed, but would not positively assert, that there had been in the conferences or correspondence between Lord Castlereagh and Mr. Rush some reference to speeches in Parliament.

I said, "Certainly none having the slightest analogy to that which I considered as exceptionable. Mr. Rush may have alluded to something said in Parliament by Lord Castlereagh himself – but not directly, nor to question him concerning it. With regard to the substance of your application, I have seen the President since our yesterday's interview, and now say that, not admitting your right to enquire into the intentions of this Government with regard to an increase of our settlement at the mouth of Columbia River, I shall decline giving any answer to the enquiry; to which I add the renewed request that if you propose to pursue the discussion you would for the future address me concerning it in writing."

Mr. Canning then said he thought it hard to be denied an answer, and hoped, if this was the determination of the American Government, instructions would be sent to Mr. Rush to give explanations on the subject to Lord Castlereagh.

This intimation appeared to me to be improper; but, unwilling to multiply points of contention and to prolong an irksome conversation, I made no reply to it.

He then pressed, indirectly, questions as to the extent of our claims on the shores of the South Sea, till I said to him, "Mr. Canning, I have said and repeated to you more than once that I am not authorized to answer the enquiries which you thought proper to make yesterday, and I have given you the reasons why these answers were declined. After this, I do not expect to be plied with captious questions to obtain indirectly that which has been directly denied."

Mr. Canning, at these words, again became exceedingly irritated, complaining with great warmth of the term " captious" as applied to his questions. He said that whatever answer I might think proper to give to his questions, he thought I had no right to *qualify* them with epithets of censure.

I recurred to expressions of his own, used in the course of these conversations; and particularly yesterday. He said he had used them *defensively*; to which I replied that the only cause I was conscious of having given him for the excitement which he had manifested had been the request that he would address me on the subject in writing; my motive for which had been, that all further conversation between us concerning it must tend to mutual irritation, and could not lead to a satisfactory settlement.

He said it was not so much the matter as the manner in which I had spoken, which had hurt him.

I said that he must consider both the matter and the manner as defensive on *my* part; and then again reminded him of the exceptionable character which, in my situation, must attach to *any* questioning by a foreign Minister founded upon the speeches of members of Congress in their places, or upon proceedings pending in that body; and of my duty to repel at the first instant, and in the most decisive manner, any such enquiry. I had, therefore, not only thought proper to demand written communications on this subject, but to show by the manner of the demand that I had not been pleased by his reference to any words spoken, or measures under discussion, in Congress. My opinions and feelings on this incident remained unaltered; but I had no wish to extend the asperity of this difference beyond its immediate occasion. He had until now had the freest access to me at all times. I had always been ready either to converse with him in the unrestrained freedom of private life, or to confer with him as a public Minister, or to receive from him any written communication that he might have occasion to address to me. I wished, notwithstanding what had now happened, to continue with him in other respects on the same terms; and that on all other subjects he would consider himself on the same footing with me as if this had never occurred.

He asked, with a warmth which surprised me, how it was *possible* that he should feel himself on the same terms with me as heretofore? He had immediately after his arrival here assured me that his own inclinations, concurring with his instructions from his Government, were to cultivate the most cordial harmony between our respective nations. He had told me that, on all occasions not involving the rights of his country and the public duties of his station, he should ever wish to show me the deference due to more advanced years; that a few days since he had called at the Department, and had said that he came to have, in familiar language, a gossiping conversation with me; that when he called yesterday, he had said, with allusion to that former conversation, that he came as the British Minister, and it was with the intention of giving me notice that his call then was upon business; nothing could exceed his astonishment at the manner in which his application had been received yesterday. And how was it possible, he repeated, that he should consider himself on the same terms with me as heretofore?

I here interrupted him, and said, "Mr. Canning, I was observing that I wished you, on all other subjects than this, to consider yourself upon the same terms with me as heretofore; and I now repeat to you the same overture, which was made by me in the spirit of conciliation. If you think it impossible – " He again stopped me, and said that he would accept the proposal; upon which I told him I was well pleased that he should, as it relieved me from the necessity of replying to his remarks on my first making the proposal. They had been of a nature which I could not otherwise have forborne to notice.

Mr. Canning seemed apprehensive that I was about, nevertheless, to tell him what my reply would have been, and entreated me to withhold it, which I accordingly did. I then repeated that, after what had passed between us, I was confirmed in the opinion that it would be best to discuss hereafter this subject, if it was to be discussed at all, in writing.

He said, hesitatingly, that he did not know that he should have any objection to write me a note on the subject.

I replied that I had yesterday felt myself the more called upon to insist on this, because he had advanced a pretension in which we never could acquiesce, and because it was not the first time it had been raised by a British Minister here.

He asked, with great apparent emotion, who that Minister was. I answered, "Mr. Jackson." "And you got rid of him!" said Mr. Canning, in a tone of violent passion – "and you got rid of him! – and you got rid of him!" This repetition of the same words, always in the same tone, was with pauses of a few seconds between each of them, as if for a reply.

I said, "Sir, my reference to the pretension of Mr. Jackson was not – " Here Mr. Canning interrupted me, by saying, "If you think that by reference to Mr. Jackson I am to be intimidated from the performance of my duty, you will find yourself greatly mistaken."

"I had not, sir," said I, "the most distant intention of intimidating you from the performance of your duty; nor was it with the intention of alluding to any subsequent occurrences of his mission; but – " Mr. Canning interrupted me again, by saying, still in the tone of high exasperation –

"Let me tell you, sir, that your reference to the case of Mr. Jackson is *exceedingly offensive!*'

"I do not know," said I, " whether I shall be able to finish what I intended to say, under such continual interruptions."

He intimated by a bow that he would hear me.

"I was observing," said I, "that in referring to the pretension of Mr. Jackson to take offence at a proposal to continue in writing a discussion commenced by oral conference, I had no intention of alluding to any subsequent transactions of Mr. Jackson or to their consequences. My allusion to it was solely because it was identically the same pretension advanced yesterday by you; and I now assigned it as the reason which had made it necessary for me to repel the demand in a manner more than usually pointed. Of the right of every Government to require from foreign Ministers communications in writing upon any subject of discussion with them we cannot entertain a moment's doubt, and it was but a few days since that, after a verbal conference between us on another subject, I had requested you to write me a note concerning it, which you did. In this case, the very grounds upon which you avowed that you came to interrogate me concerning the intentions of this Government – speeches and newspaper publications of individual members of Congress – the subject itself, upon which I could not admit your right to interrogate me at all – and the tragical tone with which you charged us with intending a violation of a treaty, convinced me that the tendency of further conversation between us on this topic would only be to high irritation, and not to harmonious adjustment. I am still of the same opinion."

Mr. Canning then recapitulated the assurances which he had on his first arrival here given me, and which he had since then more than once reiterated, of the friendly dispositions of his Government towards that of the United States; of his own earnest desire to cultivate the harmony, and to smooth down all remnants of asperity, between the two countries; of the respect which on all occasions, not involving a dereliction of his official duties, he should always wish to show *personally* to me; and of the deference which he should at all times pay to my *age*. He concluded by adding –

"But I *now* only have to say to you, sir, that henceforth, whatever may happen, I shall never forget the respect due from me *to the American Government*."

I made no reply, but bowed, to signify that I considered the conversation as closed, and he withdrew.

CHAPTER NINE

SECRETARY OF STATE, 1821–1825

INTRODUCTION

On July 4, 1821, John Quincy Adams stood before an audience in the chamber of the US House of Representatives to deliver an oration on the Declaration of Independence. He had initially declined the invitation owing to his position. Any honest discussion of the context and the content of the Declaration of Independence from an American secretary of state was bound to sit poorly with the diplomatic representatives of other nations, and with one nation (Britain) in particular.

His mind changed when he saw that an English writer, George Robert Gleig, had argued that England should pursue terroristic tactics, such as the burning of cities, in a future war with the United States. Gleig, according to John Quincy, insisted that such tactics were justified in conflicts with republics, although not in wars between monarchs. "I had just seen the extract from the work containing this sample of British humanity published in twenty of our newspapers, without a single word of comment upon it," John Quincy fumed, "and I thought it high time that we should be asking ourselves, where we were in our relations with that country." From John Quincy's perspective, Gleig's argument was only the latest in a long line of British attacks and slights against the United States, her principles, and her special place in the world. This anti-American attitude was shared, in different forms, by the Continental European despots and their apologists.

As a concession to form, John Quincy delivered his remarks

wearing an academic robe – befitting a former professor of rhetoric and oratory at Harvard University – to indicate that his remarks were to be understood as those of a private citizen. He did not consult President Monroe or any of his colleagues in the cabinet. John Quincy had little or no expectation that the relatively brief ending of his oration would become one of the most famous statements of American foreign policy.

John Quincy later explained to an influential journalist that he had meant to argue, first and foremost, against European-style colonialism. Second, he had meant to combat what he termed the "doctrine of Lexington" (Henry Clay's call for an American hemispheric alliance against the Holy Alliance of despots) and the "doctrine of Edinburgh" (the British Whigs' call for Anglo-American cooperation on behalf of political reform and revolution in Europe). Third, he had meant to answer the condescension of the British elites – what has America done for the world? – and to do so, he had responded by holding up the original copy of the Declaration of Independence. America gave to the world a statement of the true principle of government – the consent of the governed.

More broadly, the oration was an index to John Quincy's entire political thought, including the US role (if any) in promoting foreign regime change and democratization (or, in John Quincy's way of thinking, republicanization). The oration clearly warned America against going abroad in search of monstrous regimes to destroy but John Quincy also did not assume that monsters should be given an entirely free hand or that America must sit passively by. As he explained to other correspondents, he thought he had demonstrated that the South American rebellions against Spanish rule were justified, though whether the new nations would be able to establish republican governments remained unclear and perhaps unlikely.

John Quincy Adams's oration, as he predicted beforehand, received a good deal of public attention and criticism. The British minister, Stratford Canning, naturally stayed away from a Fourth of July celebration, as did the Russian minister, Pierre do Poletica. But Poletica heard all about it, along with the toasts made against the Holy Alliance in the banquet that followed the oration. He sent a copy of John Quincy's oration to St. Petersburg, with disparaging comments in the margins about the boasts of a government based on consent and the rights of mankind. "How about your two million black slaves who cultivate a great expanse of your territory, for your particular and exclusive advantage? You forget the poor Indians whom you have not ceased to despoil. You forget your conduct towards Spain."[1]

During Monroe's first term, relations with Britain and Spain (and the revolutionaries) had been John Quincy's main diplomatic focus. France, however, was not far out of the picture. The French minister, Hyde de Neuville, had been an essential if informal go-between in the negotiations for the Transcontinental Treaty. But all was not smooth sailing. American citizens still had spoliation claims against the French stemming from the Napoleonic Wars. France, meanwhile, had objected strenuously against American seizures of French-flagged vessels, allegedly for smuggling and participating in the slave trade (notably the cases of the *Appolon*, *Neptune*, and *Jeune Eugenie*). In a conversation with John Quincy, Neuville said these seizures were an affront to French honor, perhaps worthy of war.

Relations with France and the other European powers took on a potentially ominous cast in 1823. Members of the Holy Alliance had actively attempted to suppress liberal and revolutionary movements on the Continent. France invaded Spain to overthrow a constitutional government in Madrid. Rumors abounded that the French also might assist Spain in winning back its former American colonies, or that Spain might transfer its colonial possessions to France. With the Transcontinental Treaty finally ratified, the United States had recognized the major South American states in 1822, and had begun to exchange representatives. Britain had not yet done so, but London had broken with the continental powers, not so much out of sympathy for liberal movements as a concern that these actions threatened the balance of power. The new foreign secretary, George Canning, also wanted to protect Britain's commercial markets in South America.

John Quincy thought the coming together of Anglo-American interests might create a new opportunity to settle their old differences over neutral and belligerent rights, as well as commerce with the British colonies. In the summer of 1823, he sounded out Canning. "This coincidence of principle, connected with the great changes in the affairs of the world, passing before us, seemed to me a suitable occasion for the United States and Great Britain to compare their ideas and purposes together, with a view to the accommodation of great interests upon which they had heretofore differed."[2] He sent detailed instructions to Rush in London to see what progress could be made, although he emphasized to Stratford Canning that he was not proposing a formal Anglo-American alliance.

George Canning had a somewhat different idea of Anglo-American concord. He proposed a joint declaration of policy against the recovery of Spain's former colonies in America. That would not involve "any concert of action" – the use of force – Canning explained, because the moral effect of the declaration would be sufficient to deter any French action, given the enormous maritime power with which they would be confronted. His proposal included a commitment by both nations not to acquire colonial territory formerly held by Spain. Rush said that he could not respond authoritatively to such a proposal, which he would refer to Washington. But he saw one possible obstacle: Britain, unlike the United States, had not yet recognized the independence of the new nations. Would Britain now do so? Canning indicated that such recognition was undoubtedly forthcoming, but not yet. He later went so far as to draw up a joint statement of policy. Rush indicated that he might sign such a statement, at the risk of being disavowed by his government – but only if Britain would offer recognition. Canning, or at least his government, was unprepared to do this.

When Monroe received Rush's first dispatches about Canning's proposal in mid-October 1823, he was immediately inclined to accept it. With Britain and its navy on America's side, European intervention in the Western Hemisphere, much less an attack on the United States, would be deterred. On the other hand, would this not violate Washington's warning not to become involved in European affairs? By letter, Monroe sought the opinion of his predecessors, Jefferson and Madison, who both enthusiastically endorsed the idea of a formal Anglo-American entente in the Western Hemisphere.

Things were further complicated because of difficulties with Russia in the Pacific Northwest. Russia had been extending its claims downward from Russian America (Alaska). In 1821, Emperor Alexander had issued an imperial ukase warning foreign ships not to come within a hundred miles of the coast north of the fifty-first parallel of latitude. This edict implied that Russia was preparing to assert its sovereignty over much of the Oregon Country itself, cutting off the lucrative fur trade and fishing there from the United States (and Britain). The two sides had been sparring over this issue for the past two years, and in July 1823 John Quincy had delivered a warning against any further colonization in Oregon.

Later, the Russian minister, Baron de Tuyll, presented John Quincy with a note from Alexander stating that the members of the Holy Alliance would not recognize the independence of the South American colonies and demanding that the United States maintain its neutrality. Tuyll subsequently gave John Quincy a copy of a circular from the Russian foreign minister, Count Nesselrode, which expressed a determination to enforce tranquility in the states of the civilized world. John Quincy asked Tuyll if this included restoring the former Spanish colonies. Tuyll said that it did.[3]

This tense situation took up most of the cabinet's time in November. John Quincy thought that the British wanted a joint agreement not in order to deter the Holy Alliance, but actually to secure commercial advantages for themselves and to prevent the United States from acquiring any more of the former Spanish possessions. He held his ground and substantially had his way in the formulation of an American response.

First, unlike Calhoun, John Quincy did not believe the military effort to suppress the South Americans would actually materialize – and that even if it did, it could not long succeed – so there was no need to panic. Second, in the absence of a real emergency, there was no reason for the United States to agree to Canning's proposal, and thereby appear to the world as a junior partner to Britain. Third, the United States should not agree to a self-denying ordinance concerning the future acquisition of territory. "We have no intention of seizing either Texas or Cuba," he told the cabinet. "But the inhabitants of either or both may exercise their primitive fights, and solicit a union with us. They will certainly do no such thing to Great Britain.... Without entering now into the enquiry of the expediency of our annexing Texas or Cuba to our Union, we should at least keep ourselves free to act as emergencies may arise, and not tie ourselves down to any principle which might immediately afterwards be brought to bear against ourselves."[4]

Fourth, he successfully argued against any attempt to link America's diplomatic position on the independence of the South American nations with explicit support for revolutionary and independence movements in Europe, specifically in Greece. To do so would undermine the case for keeping the Europeans away from the Western Hemisphere. Finally, he wished to offer a ringing defense of republican government in response to Tuyll, along with disclaiming any intent to enforce those principles elsewhere through the use of arms and while demanding that the European despotisms refrain from doing the same in the New World. This note, and the accompanying instructions to American ministers in London, Paris, and St. Petersburg, would be made public, if necessary.[5] Monroe decided to tie all these threads together in his Annual Message to Congress, delivered in writing on December 2, 1823.

What later became known as the Monroe Doctrine addressed the administration's concerns with Latin America, the Pacific Northwest, and Anglo-American relations. It was to become a fundamental statement of American foreign policy. First, the United States proclaimed that the continents of North and South America "are henceforth not to be considered as subjects for future colonization by any European power." The United States, however, would not interfere with existing colonies or dependencies. Second, the United States declared it would regard any European political intervention in the Western Hemisphere as "dangerous to our peace and safety." Third, in a reciprocal gesture, the United States would not intervene in European wars or "internal concerns."[6]

Was Monroe prepared to use force in defense of the newly independent countries if the Holy Alliance actually carried out the threat? Attorney General William Wirt had raised that question in the prior cabinet discussions. If not, was it wise to issue such a categorical statement against European intervention, and potentially to provoke the monarchs by issuing a ringing defense of republican principles? Monroe expressed his fear that Britain might reverse its position and leave the United States in the lurch.

As John Quincy saw things, the executive had gone as far as he could. The next logical step would have been to ask for a joint resolution of Congress that supported Monroe's policy – but that would have required the disclosure of sensitive diplomatic correspondence, which might unnecessarily inflame the situation. In any event, John Quincy remained confident that British interests in the matter were so compelling that London would not change course, and that the Royal Navy was the ultimate and compelling deterrent. For now, the country's options remained open and could be adjusted according to future events, also leaving open the matter of what areas in the Western Hemisphere the United

States was prepared to defend. There was no discussion in the cabinet of whether the representatives of the South American states should be consulted in the matter, or whether they should be brought into any defensive alliance.

Before the address was published, John Quincy read Tuyll a note that set out the American position. He also sent instructions to Rush in London, informing George Canning that the United States would act "in concert" with Britain only if it first recognized the independence of the South American states. Instructions followed to Henry Middleton in St. Petersburg, dealing with the boundary issue in the Pacific Northwest. Meanwhile, unknown to John Quincy, the British foreign secretary had pressured the French to agree not to interfere in the Western Hemisphere, if that was ever their intention (the Polignac Memorandum). In 1824, the United States and Russia agreed to a treaty setting the southern boundary of Russian Alaska at 54° 40″. Britain made a similar treaty in 1825, accepting the same southern limit.

Despite John Quincy's foreign policy, often characterized as realistic and nationalistic, he maintained strong idealistic and sometimes romantic views. As noted above, he was prepared staunchly to defend the principles of the Declaration of Independence and republican government against the rhetorical claims of the Holy Alliance. In 1823, taking advantage of a congressional resolution, he also revisited the matter of an international convention against the slave trade. If those engaging in the trade were treated as pirates – outlaws – then their vessels were subject to search and seizure under the law of nations. He drafted the project of a convention with Britain that would permit both parties to do so, under certain restrictions, subject to prior British legislation that declared slave trading to be piracy. Reluctantly, he did not tie this to any commitment by London on the impressment issue. It took nearly a year for the agreement to be negotiated by Rush and sent back to Washington. The Senate narrowly consented to the convention, but with conditions the British found unacceptable. John Quincy believed the opposition stemmed from Southern slaveholders who feared that this was the precursor of Anglo-American cooperation to abolish slavery itself.

John Quincy also proposed to offer Britain and other maritime powers of Europe a comprehensive convention on neutral and belligerent rights that would abolish "private war" at sea. It would not only outlaw privateering, but also protect private property aboard all ships, enemy and neutral, save for a narrow list of military-related goods. It would reduce wartime destruction and represent a step toward the abolition of war altogether. It would become the template for a multilateral agreement. He instructed the American minister to Russia to broach the idea to Emperor Alexander, the foreign leader most likely to support such an agreement. "My plan involves nothing less than a revolution in the laws of war – a great amelioration in the condition of man. Is it the dream of a visionary, or is it the great and practicable conception of a benefactor of mankind? I believe it the latter; and I believe this to be precisely the time for proposing it to the world. Should it even fail, it will be honorable to have proposed it." The cool and realistic diplomatist admitted to his diary: "When I think, if it possibly could succeed, what a real and solid blessing it would be to the human race, I can scarcely guard myself from a spirit of enthusiasm, which it becomes me to distrust."[7]

Even his congressionally mandated Report on Weights and Measures reflected his idealistic hopes for the future. He concluded that differing monetary and measuring systems contributed to the causes of war. To establish a uniform system throughout the world, he concluded, "would be a blessing of such transcendent magnitude that ... the being who should exercise it would be among the greatest of benefactors of the human race."[8] The French metric system, despite its flaws, was a step in the right direction. But the realistic John Quincy stopped short of recommending its adoption by the United States. At least for now, custom and usage remained on the side of the English system.

John Quincy's final year in office was consumed with presidential electioneering. He was up against stiff competition representing different parts of the country: Andrew Jackson (Tennessee), William Crawford (Georgia), and Henry Clay (Kentucky). John Quincy's preferred result would have been an Adams-Jackson ticket, which likely would have resulted in a comfortable majority of electoral votes, leaving the current cabinet largely intact. But Jackson would have none of that, despite the fact that John Quincy had been his lone supporter during the Florida invasion. Jackson came in first in the electoral college and in the partial popular vote, with John Quincy second, Crawford third, and Clay fourth. But, as no candidate received a majority, the election was decided by the House of Representatives, voting by state, among the three leading candidates. On February 9, 1825, with the aid of Clay's supporters, the House elected John Quincy Adams on the first ballot.

AN ADDRESS, DELIVERED AT THE REQUEST OF THE COMMITTEE OF ARRANGEMENTS FOR CELEBRATING THE ANNIVERSARY OF INDEPENDENCE, AT THE CITY OF WASHINGTON ON THE FOURTH OF JULY 1821 UPON THE OCCASION OF READING THE DECLARATION OF INDEPENDENCE

John Quincy Adams's most famous articulation of the proper orientation and purpose of American foreign policy – "she goes not abroad in search of monsters to destroy. She is the well-wisher to the freedom and independence of all. She is the champion and vindicator only of her own" – came at the end of a lengthy public address that had a number of different political and diplomatic purposes. John Quincy wished to explicate and vindicate the principles of the American Revolution, enshrined in the Declaration of Independence. America gave to the world a statement of the true principle of legitimate government – the consent of the governed. It was a regime based on liberty, not power, and its foreign policy must reflect and defend this foundation.

FELLOW CITIZENS,

UNTIL within a few days before that which we have again assembled to commemorate, our fathers, the people of this Union, had constituted a portion of the British nation; a nation, renowned in arts and arms, who, from a small Island in the Atlantic ocean, had extended their dominion over considerable parts of every quarter of the globe. Governed themselves by a race of kings, whose title to sovereignty had originally been founded on *conquest*, spell-bound, for a succession of ages, under that portentous system of despotism and of superstition which, in the name of the meek and humble Jesus, had been spread over the christian world, the history of this nation had, for a period of seven hundred years, from the days of the conquest till our own, exhibited a conflict almost continued, between the oppressions of power and the claims of right. In the theories of the crown and the mitre, *man* had no rights. Neither the body nor the soul of the individual was his own. From the impenetrable gloom of this intellectual darkness, and the deep degradation of this servitude, the British nation had partially emerged. The martyrs of religious freedom had consumed to ashes at the stake; the champions of temporal liberty had bowed their heads upon the scaffold; and the spirits of many a bloody day had left their earthly vesture upon the field of battle, and soared to plead the cause of liberty before the throne of heaven. Through long ages of civil war the people of Britain had extorted from their tyrants, not *acknowledgments*, but *grants* of right. With this concession they had been content to stop in the progress of human improvement. They received their freedom, as a donation from their sovereigns. They appealed for their privileges to a sign manual and a sea. They held their title to liberty, like their title to lands, from the bounty of a man, and in their moral and political chronology, the great charter of Runnimead was the beginning of the world.

From the earliest ages of their recorded history, the inhabitants of the British islands have been distinguished for their intelligence and their spirit. How much of these two qualities, the fountains of all amelioration in the condition of men, was stifled by these two principles of subserviency to ecclesiastical usurpation, and of holding *rights* as the donations of kings, this is not the occasion to inquire. Of their tendency to, palsy the vigor, and enervate the faculties of man, all philosophical reasoning, and all actual experience concur in testimony. These principles, however, were not peculiar to the people of Britain. They were the delusions of all Europe, still the most enlightened and most improvable portion of the earth. The temporal chain was riveted upon the people of Britain, by the conquest. Their spiritual fetters were forged by subtilty working upon superstition. Baneful as the effect of these principles was, they could not forever extinguish the light of reason in the human mind. The discovery of the mariner's compass was soon followed by an extension of commercial intercourse between nations the most distant, and which, without that light beaming in darkness, to guide the path of man over the boundless waste of waters, could never have been known to each other; the invention of printing, and the composition of gunpowder, which revolutionized at once the art and science of war and the relations of peace; the revelation of India to Vasco de Gama, and the disclosure to Columbus of the American hemisphere; all resulted from the incompressible energies of the human intellect, bound and crippled as it was by the double cords of ecclesiastical imposture and political oppression. To these powerful agents in the progressive improvement of our species, Britain can lay no claim. For them the children of men are indebted to Italy, to Germany, to Portugal, and to Spain. All these improvements, however, consisted in successful researches into the properties and modifications of external nature. The religious reformation was an improvement in the science of mind; an improvement in the intercourse of man with his Creator, and in his acquaintance with himself. It was an advance in the knowledge of his *duties* and his *rights*. It was a step in the progress of man, in comparison with which the magnet and gunpowder, the wonders of either India, nay the printing press itself, were but as the paces of a pigmy to the stride of a giant. If to this step of human advancement Germany likewise lays claim in the person of Martin Luther, or in the earlier, but ineffectual martyrdom of John Huss, England may point to her Wickliffe as a yet more primitive Vindicator of the same righteous cause, and may insist on the glory of having contributed her share to the improvement of the moral condition of man.

The corruptions and usurpations of the church were the immediate objects of these reformers; but at the foundation of all their exertions there was a single plain and almost self-evident principle – that man has a *right* to the exercise of his own reason. It was this principle which the sophistry and rapacity of the church had obscured and obliterated, and which the intestine divisions of that same church itself first restored. The triumph of reason was the result of inquiry and discussion. Centuries of desolating wars have succeeded, and oceans of human blood have flowed, for the final establishment of this principle; but it was from the darkness of the cloister that the first spark was emitted, and from the arches of a university that it first kindled into day. From the discussion of religious rights and duties, the transition to that of the political and civil relations of men with one another was natural and unavoidable; in both, the reformers were met by the weapons of temporal power. At the same glance of reason, the tiara would have fallen from the brow of priesthood, and the despotic sceptre would have departed from the hand of royalty, but for the sword, by which they were protected; that sword which, like the flaming sword of the Cherubims, turned every way to debar access to the tree of life.

The double contest against the oppressors of church and state was too appalling for the vigor, or too comprehensive for the faculties of the reformers of the European continent. In Britain alone was it undertaken, and in Britain but partially succeeded.

It was in the midst of that fermentation of the human intellect, which brought right and power in direct and deadly conflict with each other, that the rival crowns of the two portions of the

British Island were united on the same head. It was then, that, released from the fetters of ecclesiastical domination, the minds of men began to investigate the foundations of civil government. But the mass of the nation surveyed the fabric of their Institutions as it existed in fact. It had been founded in *conquest*; it had been cemented in *servitude*; and so broken and moulded had been the minds of this brave and intelligent people to their actual condition, that instead of solving civil society into its first elements in search of their rights, they looked back only to conquest as the origin of their liberties, and claimed their rights but as donations from their kings. This faltering assertion of freedom is not chargeable indeed upon the whole nation. There were spirits capable of tracing civil government to its first foundation in the moral and physical nature of man: but conquest and servitude were so mingled up in every particle of the social existence of the nation, that they had become vitally necessary to them, as a portion of the fluid, itself destructive of life, is indepensably blended with the atmosphere in which we live.

Fellow citizens, it was in the heat of this war of moral elements, which brought one Stuart to the block, and hurled another from his throne, that our forefathers sought refuge from its fury, in the then Wilderness of this Western World. They were willing exiles from a country dearer to them than life. But they were the exiles of liberty and of conscience: dearer to them even than their country. They came too, with charters from their kings; for even in removing to another hemisphere, they "cast longing, lingering looks behind," and were anxiously desirous of retaining ties of connexion with their country, which, in the solemn compact of a charter, they hoped by the corresponding links of allegiance and protection to preserve. But to their sense of *right*, the charter was only the ligament between them, their country, and their king. Transported to a new world, they had relations with one another, and relations with the aboriginal inhabitants of the country to which they came; for which no royal charter could provide. The first settlers of the Plymouth colony, at the eve of landing from their ship, therefore, bound themselves together by a written covenant; and immediately after landing, purchased from the Indian natives the right of settlement upon the soil.

Thus was a social compact formed upon the elementary principles of civil society, in which conquest and servitude had no part. The slough of brutal force was entirely cast off; all was voluntary; all was unbiassed consent; all was the agreement of soul with soul.

Other colonies were successively founded, and other charters granted, until in the compass of a century and a half, thirteen distinct British provinces peopled the Atlantic shores of the North American continent with two millions of freemen; possessing by their charters the rights of British subjects, and nurtured by their position and education, in the more comprehensive and original doctrines of human rights. From their infancy they had been treated by the parent state with neglect, harshness and injustice. Their charters had often been disregarded and violated; their commerce restricted and shackled; their interest wantonly or spitefully sacrificed; so that the hand of the parent had been scarcely ever felt, but in the alternate application of whips and scorpions.

When in spite of all these persecutions, by the natural vigor of their constitution, they were just attaining the maturity of political manhood, a British parliament, in contempt of the clearest maxims of natural equity, in defiance of the fundamental principle upon which British freedom itself had been cemented with British blood; on the naked, unblushing allegation of absolute and uncontrollable power, undertook by their act to levy, without representation and without consent, *taxes* upon the people of America for the benefit of the people of Britain. This enormous project of public robbery was no sooner made known, than it excited, throughout the colonies, one general burst of indignant resistance. It was abandoned, reasserted and resumed, until fleets and armies were transported, to record in the characters of fire, famine, and desolation, the transatlantic wisdom of British legislation, and the tender mercies of British consanguinity.

Fellow citizens, I am speaking of days long past. Ever faithful to the sentiment proclaimed in the paper, which I am about to present once more to your memory of the past and to your forecast of the future, you will hold the people of Britain as you hold the rest of mankind, – Enemies in war – in peace, Friends. The conflict for independence is now itself but a record of history. The resentments of that age may be buried in oblivion. The stoutest hearts, which then supported the tug of war, are cold under the clod of the valley. My purpose is to rekindle no angry passion from its embers: but this annual solemn perusal of the instrument, which proclaimed to the world the causes of your existence as a nation, is not without its just and useful purpose.

It is not by the yearly reiteration of the wrongs endured by your fathers, to evoke from the sepulchre of time the shades of departed tyranny; it is not to draw from their dread abode the frailties of an unfortunate monarch, who now sleeps with his fathers, and the sufferings of whose latter days may have atoned at the bar of divine mercy, for the sins which the accusing angel will read from *this scroll* to his charge; it is not to exult in the great moral triumph by which the Supreme Governor of the world crowned the cause of your country with success. No; the purpose for which you listen with renewed and never languishing delight to the reading of this paper, is of a purer and more exalted cast. It is sullied with no vindictive recollection. It is degraded by no rankling resentment. It is inflated with no vain and idle exultation of victory. The Declaration of Independence, in its primary purport, was merely an *occasional* state-paper. It was a solemn exposition to the world, of the *causes* which had *compelled* the people of a small portion of the British empire, to cast off the allegiance and renounce the protection of the British king: and to dissolve their social connexion with the British people. In the annals of the human race, the separation of one people into two is an event of no uncommon occurrence. The successful resistance of a people against oppression, to the downfall of the tyrant and of tyranny itself, is the lesson of many an age, and of almost every clime. It lives in the venerable records of Holy Writ. It beams in the brightest pages of profane history. The names of Pharaoh and Moses, of Tarquin and Junius Brutus, of Geisler and Tell, of Christiern and Gustavus Vasa, of Philip of Austria and William of Orange, stand in long array through the vista of time, like the Spirit of Evil and the Spirit of Good, in embattled opposition to each other, from the mouldering ages of antiquity, to the recent memory of our fathers, and from the burning plains of Palestine, to the polar frost of Scandinavia.

For the independence of North America, there were ample and sufficient causes in the laws of moral and physical nature. The tie of colonial subjection is compatible with the essential purposes of civil government, only when the condition of the subordinate state is from its weakness incompetent to its own protection. Is the greatest moral purpose of civil government, the administration of justice? And if justice has been truly defined, the constant and perpetual will of securing to everyone his right, how absurd and impracticable is that form of polity, in which the dispenser of justice is in one quarter of the globe, and he to whom justice is to be dispensed is in another; where "moons revolve and oceans roll between the order and its execution;" where time and space must be annihilated to secure to everyone his right. The tie of colonial subjection may suit the relations between a great naval power, and the settlers of a small and remote Island in the incipient stages of society: but was it possible for British intelligence to imagine, or British sense of justice to desire, that through the boundless ages of time, the swarming myriads of freemen, who were to civilize the wilderness and fill with human life the solitudes of this immense continent, should receive the mandates of their earthly destinies from a council chamber at St. James's, or bow forever in submission to the omnipotence of St. Stephen's Chapel? Are the essential purposes of civil government, to administer to the wants, and to fortify the infirmities of solitary man? To unite the sinews of numberless arms, and combine the councils of multitudes of minds, for the promotion of the well-being of all? The first moral element then of this composition is sympathy between the members of which it consists; the second is sympathy between the giver and the receiver of the law. The sympathies of men begin with the relations of domestic life. They are rooted in the natural relations of husband and wife, of parent and child, of brother and sister; thence they spread through the social and moral propinquites of neighbor and friend, to the broader and more complicated relations of countryman and fellow – citizen; terminating only with the circumference of the globe which we inhabit, in the co-extensive charities incident to the common nature of man. To each of these relations, different degrees of sympathy are allotted by the ordinances of nature. The sympathies of domestic life are not more sacred and obligatory, but closer and more powerful, than those of neighborhood and friendship. The tie which binds us to our country is not more holy in the sight of God, but it is more deeply seated in our nature, more tender and endearing, than that common link which merely connects us with our fellow-mortal, man. It is a common government that constitutes our *country*. But in THAT association, all the sympathies of domestic life and kindred blood, all the moral ligatures of friendship and of neighbourhood, are combined with that instinctive and mysterious connexion between man and physical nature, which binds the first perceptions of childhood in a chain of sympathy with the last gasp of expiring age, to the spot of our nativity, and the natural objects by which it is surrounded. These sympathies belong and are indispensable to the relations ordained by nature between the individual and his country. They dwell in the memory and are indelible in the hearts of the first settlers of a distant colony. These are the feelings under which the children of Israel "sat down by the rivers of Babylon, and wept when they remembered Zion." These are the sympathies under which they "hung their harps upon the willows," and instead of songs of mirth, exclaimed, "If I forget thee, O Jerusalem, let my right hand forget her cunning." But these sympathies can never exist for a country, which we have never seen. They are transferred in the hearts of succeeding generations, from the country of human institution, to the country of their birth; from the land of which they have only heard, to the land where their eyes first opened to the day. The ties of neighbourhood are broken up, those of friendship can never be formed, with an intervening ocean; and the natural ties of domestic life, the all-subduing sympathies of love, the indissoluble bonds of marriage, the heart riveted kindliness of consanguinity, gradually wither and perish in the lapse of a few generations. All the elements, which form the basis of that sympathy between the individual and his country, are dissolved.

Long before the Declaration of Independence, the great mass of the people of America and of the people of Britain had become total strangers to each other. The people of America were known to the people of Britain only by the transactions of trade; by shipments of lumber and flax-seed, indigo and tobacco. They were known to the government only by half a dozen colonial agents, humble, and often spurned suitors at the feet of power, and by royal governors, minions of patronage, sent from the footstool of a throne beyond the seas, to rule a people of whom they knew nothing; as if an inhabitant of the moon should descend to give laws to the dwellers upon earth. Here and there, a man of letters and a statesman, conversant with all history, knew something of the colonies, as he knew something of Cochin China and Japan. Yet even the prime minister of England, urging upon his Omnipotent parliament laws for grinding the colonies to submission, could talk, Without amazing or diverting his hearers, of the island of Virginia: even Edmund Burke, a man of more ethereal mind, *apologizing* to the people of Bristol, for the offence of sympathizing with the distresses of our country, ravaged by the fire and sword of Britons, asked indulgence for his feelings on the score of general humanity, and expressly declared that the Americans were a nation utter strangers to him, and among whom he was not sure of having a single acquaintance. The sympathies therefore most essential to the communion of country were, between the British and American people, extinct. Those most indispensable to the just relation between sovereign and subject, had never existed and could not exist between the British government and the American people. The connexion was unnatural; and it was in the moral order no less than in the positive decrees of Providence, that it should be dissolved.

Yet, fellow-citizens, these are not the causes of the separation assigned in the paper which I am about to read. The connexion between different portions of the same people and between a people and their government, is a connexion of *duties* as well as of *rights*. In the long conflict of twelve years which had preceded and led to the Declaration of Independence, our fathers had been not less faithful to their duties, than tenacious of their rights. Their resistance had not been rebellion. It was not a restive and ungovernable spirit of ambition, bursting from the bonds of colonial subjection; it was the deep and wounded sense of successive wrongs, upon which complaint had been only answered by aggravation, and petition repelled with contumely, which had driven them to their last stand upon the adamantine rock of human rights.

It was then fifteen months after the blood of Lexington and Bunker's hill, after Charlestown and Falmouth, fired by British hands, were but heaps of ashes, after the ear of the adder had been turned to two successive supplications to the throne; after two successive appeals to the people of Britain, as friends, countrymen, and brethren, to which no responsive voice of sympathetic tenderness had been returned,

> "Nought but the noise of drums and timbrels loud,
> Their children's cries unheard that passed through fire
> To the grim idol: –"

Then it was that the thirteen United Colonies of North America, by their delegates in Congress assembled, exercising the first act of sovereignty by a right ever inherent in the people, but never to be resorted to, save at the awful crisis when civil society is solved into its first elements, declared themselves free and independent states; and two days afterwards, in justification of that act, issued this

UNANIMOUS DECLARATION OF THE THIRTEEN UNITED STATES OF AMERICA.

"WHEN, in the course of human events, it becomes necessary for one people to dissolve the political bands which have connected them with another, and to assume among the powers of the earth, the separate and equal station to which the laws of nature and of nature's God entitle them, a decent respect for the opinions of mankind requires, that they should declare the causes which impel them to the separation.

We hold these truths to be self evident – that all men are created equal; that they are endowed by their Creator with certain unalienable rights; that among these are life, liberty, and the pursuit of happiness. That, to secure these rights, governments are instituted among men, deriving their just powers from the consent of the governed; that whenever any form of government becomes destructive of these ends, it is the right of the people to alter or to abolish it, and to institute a new government, laying its foundation on such principles, and organizing its powers in such form, as to them shall seem most likely to effect their safety and happiness. Prudence, indeed, will dictate, that governments long established, should not be changed for light and transient causes; and accordingly all experience hath shown, that mankind are more disposed to suffer, while evils are sufferable, than to right themselves by abolishing the forms to which they are accustomed. But when a long train of abuses and usurpations, pursuing invariably the same object, evinces a design to reduce them under absolute despotism, it is their right, it is their duty to throw off such government, and to provide new guards for their future security. Such has been the patient sufferance of these colonies; and such is now the necessity which constrains them to alter their former systems of government. The history of the present king of Great Britain is a history of repeated injuries and usurpations, all having in direct object the establishment of an absolute tyranny over these states. To prove this, let facts be submitted to a candid world.

He has refused his assent to laws the most wholesome and necessary for the public good.

He has forbidden his governors to pass laws of immediate and pressing importance, unless suspended in their operation, till his assent should be obtained; and, when so suspended, he has utterly neglected to attend to them.

He has refused to pass other laws for the accommodation of large districts of people, unless those people would relinquish the right of representation in the legislature – a right inestimable to them, and formidable to tyrants only.

He has called together legislative bodies, at places unusual, uncomfortable, and distant from the depository of their public records, for the sole purpose of fatiguing them into compliance with his measures.

He has dissolved representatives houses repeatedly, for opposing, with manly firmness, his invasions on the rights of the people.

He has refused for a long time, after such dissolutions, to cause others to be elected; whereby the legislative powers, incapable of annihilation, have returned to the people at large, for their exercise; the state remaining, in the meantime, exposed to all the danger of invasion from without, and convulsions within.

He has endeavoured to prevent the population of these states; for that purpose obstructing the laws for naturalization of foreigners; refusing to pass others, to encourage their migration hither, and raising the conditions of new appropriation of lands.

He has obstructed the administration of justice, by refusing his assent to laws for establishing judiciary powers.

He has made judges dependent on his will alone, for the tenure of their offices, and the amount and payment of their salaries.

He has erected a multitude of new offices, and sent hither swarms of officers to harass our people and eat out their substance.

He has kept among us, in times of peace, standing armies, without the consent of our legislatures.

He has affected to render the military independent of, and superior to, the civil power.

He has combined with others, to subject us to a jurisdiction, foreign to our constitution, and unacknowledged by our laws; giving his assent to their acts of pretended legislation: –

For quartering large bodies of armed troops among us:

For protecting them by a mock trial, from punishment for any murder which they should commit on the inhabitants of these states:

For cutting off our trade with all parts of the world:

For imposing taxes on us, without our consent:

For depriving us, in many cases, of the benefits of trial by jury:

For transporting us beyond seas, to be tried for pretended offences:

For abolishing the free system of English law in a neighbouring province, establishing therein an arbitrary government, and enlarging its boundaries so as to render it at once an example and fit instrument for introducing the same absolute rule into these colonies:

For taking away our charters, abolishing our most valuable laws, and altering fundamentally the forms of our governments:

For suspending our own legislatures, and declaring themselves invested with power, to legislate for us in all cases whatsoever.

He has abdicated government here, by declaring us out of his protection, and waging war against us.

He has plundered our seas, ravaged our coasts, burnt our towns, and destroyed the lives of our people.

He is, at this time, transporting large armies of foreign mercenaries, to complete the works of death, desolation and tyranny, already begun, with circumstances of cruelty and perfidy, scarcely paralleled in the most barbarous ages, and totally unworthy the head of a civilized nation.

He has constrained our fellow citizens, taken captive on the high seas, to bear arms against their country, to become the executioners of their friends and brethren, or to fall themselves by their hands.

He has excited domestic insurrections amongst us, and has endeavoured to bring on the inhabitants of our frontiers, the merciless Indian savages, whose known rule of warfare is an undistinguished destruction of all ages, sexes, and conditions.

In every stage of these oppressions, we have petitioned for redress, in the most humble terms: our petitions have been answered only by repeated injury. A prince whose character is thus marked, by every act which may define a tyrant, is unfit to be the ruler of a free people.

Nor have we been wanting in attention to our British 'brethren. We have warned them, from time to time, of attempts made by their legislature, to extend an unwarrantable jurisdiction over us. We have reminded them of the circumstances of our emigration and settlement here. We have appealed to their native justice and magnanimity, and we have conjured them by the ties of our common kindred, to disavow these usurpations, which would inevitably interrupt our connexions and correspondence. They, too, have been deaf to the voice of justice and consanguinity. We must, therefore, acquiesce in the necessity, which denounces our separation, and hold them, as we hold the rest of mankind – enemies in war; – in peace, friends.

WE, therefore, the representatives of the United States of America, in general congress assembled, appealing to the Supreme Judge of the world, for the rectitude of our intentions, Do, in the name and by the authority of the good people of these colonies, solemnly publish and declare, that these united colonies are, and of right ought to be, free and independent states;

that they are absolved from all allegiance to the British crown, and that all political connexion between them and the state of Great Britain is and ought to be totally dissolved; and that as free and independent states, they have full power to levy war, conclude peace, contract alliances, establish commerce, and to do all other acts and things which independent states may of right do. And for the support of this declaration, with a firm reliance on the protection of Divine Providence, we mutually pledge to each other our lives, our fortunes, and our sacred honour."

It is not, let me repeat, fellow-citizens, it is not the long enumeration of intolerable wrongs concentrated in this declaration; it is not the melancholy catalogue of alternate oppression and intreaty, of reciprocated indignity and remonstrance, upon which, in the celebration of this anniversary, your memory delights to dwell. Nor is it yet that the justice of your cause was vindicated by the God of battles; that in a conflict of seven years, the history of the war by which you maintained that declaration, became the history of the civilized World; that the unanimous voice of enlightened Europe and the verdict of an after age have sanctioned your assumption of sovereign power, and that the name of your Washington is enrolled upon the records of time, first in the glorious line of heroic virtue. It is not that the monarch himself, who had been your oppressor, was compelled to recognise you as a sovereign and independent people, and that the nation, whose feelings of fraternity for you had slumbered in the lap of pride, was awakened in the arms of humiliation to your equal and no longer contested rights. The primary purpose of this declaration, the proclamation to the world of the causes of our revolution, is "with the years beyond the flood." It is of no more interest to us than the chastity of Lucretia, or the apple on the head of the child of Tell. Little less than forty years have revolved since the struggle for independence was closed; another generation has arisen; and in the assembly of nations our republic is already a matron of mature age. The cause of your independence is no longer upon trial. The final sentence upon it has long since been passed upon earth and ratified in heaven.

The interest, which in this paper has survived the occasion upon which it was issued; the interest which is of every age and every clime; the interest which quickens with the lapse of years, spreads as it grows old, and brightens as it recedes, is in the principles which it proclaims. It was the first solemn declaration by a nation of the only *legitimate* foundation of civil government. It was the corner stone of a new fabric, destined to cover the surface of the globe. It demolished at a stroke the lawfulness of all governments founded upon conquest. It swept away all the rubbish of accumulated centuries of servitude. It announced in practical form to the world the transcendent truth of the unalienable sovereignty of the people. It proved that the social compact was no figment of the imagination; but a real, solid, and sacred bond of the social union. From the day of this declaration, the people of North America were no longer the fragment of a distant empire, imploring justice and mercy from an inexorable master in another hemisphere. They were no longer children appealing in vain to the sympathies of a heartless mother; no longer subjects leaning upon the shattered columns of royal promises, and invoking the faith of parchment to secure their rights. They were a *nation*, asserting as of right, and maintaining by War, its own existence. A nation was born in a day.

> "How many ages hence
> Shall this their lofty scene be acted o'er
> In states unborn, and accents yet unknown?"

It will be acted o'er, fellow-citizens, but it can never be repeated. It stands, and must forever stand alone, a beacon on the summit of the mountain, to which all the inhabitants of the earth may turn their eyes for a genial and saving light, till time shall be lost in eternity, and this globe itself dissolve, nor leave a wreck behind. It stands forever, a light of admonition to the rulers of men; a light of salvation and redemption to the oppressed. So long as this planet shall be inhabited by human beings, so long as man shall be of social nature, so long as government shall be necessary to the great moral purposes of society, and so long as it shall be abused to the purposes of oppression, so long shall this declaration hold out to the sovereign and to the subject the extent and the boundaries of their respective rights and duties; founded in the laws of nature and of nature's God. Five and forty years have passed away since this Declaration was issued by our fathers; and here are we, fellow-citizens, assembled in the full enjoyment of its fruits, to bless the Author of our being for the bounties, of his providence, in casting our lot in this favored land; to remember with effusions of gratitude the sages who put forth, and the heroes who bled for the establishment of this Declaration; and, by the communion of soul in the reperusal and hearing of this instrument, to renew the genuine Holy Alliance of its principles, to recognize them as eternal truths, and to pledge ourselves and bind our posterity to a faithful and undeviating adherence to them.

Fellow-citizens, our fathers have been faithful to them before us. When the little band of their Delegates, "with a firm reliance on the protection of Divine Providence, for the support of this declaration, mutually pledged to each other their *lives*, their *fortunes*, and their *sacred honor*," from every dwelling, street, and square of your populous cities, it was re-echoed with shouts of joy and gratulation! and if the silent language of the heart could have been heard, every hill upon the surface of this continent which had been trodden by the foot of civilized man, every valley in which the toil of your fathers had opened a paradise upon the wild, would have rung, with one accordant voice, louder than the thunders, sweeter than the harmonies of the heavens, with the solemn and responsive words, "*We swear.*"

The pledge has been redeemed. Through six years of devastating but heroic war, through nearly forty years of more heroic peace, the principles of this declaration have been supported by the toils, by the vigils, by the blood of your fathers and of yourselves. The conflict of war had begun with fearful odds of apparent human power on the side of the oppressor. He wielded at will the collective force of the mightiest nation in Europe. He with more than poetic truth asserted the dominion of the waves. The power, to whose unjust usurpation your fathers hurled the gauntlet of defiance, baffled and vanquished by them, has even since, stripped of all the energies of this continent, been found adequate to give the law to its own quarter of the globe, and to mould the destinies of the European world. It was with a sling and a stone, that your fathers went forth to encounter the massive vigor of this Goliah. They slung the heaven-directed stone, and

"With heaviest sound, the giant monster fell."

Amid the shouts of victory your cause soon found friends and allies in the rivals of your enemies. France recognized your independence as existing in fact, and made common cause with you for its support. Spain and the Netherlands, without adopting your principles, successively flung their weight into your scale. The Semiramis of the North, no convert to your doctrines, still conjured all the maritime neutrality of Europe in array against the usurpations of your antagonist upon the seas. While some of the fairest of your fields were ravaged, while your towns and villages were consumed with fire, while the harvests of your summers were blasted, while the purity of virgin innocence and the chastity of matronly virtue were violated, while the living remnants of the field of battle were reserved for the gibbet, by the fraternal sympathies of Britons throughout your land, the waters of the Atlantic ocean, and those that wash the shores of either India, were dyed with the mingled blood of combatants in the cause of North American independence.

In the progress of time, that vial of wrath was exhausted. After seven years of exploits and achievements like these, performed under the orders of the British king; to use the language of the Treaty of Peace, "it having pleased the Divine Providence to dispose the hearts of the most serene and most potent prince, George the Third, by the grace of God king of Great Britain, France, and Ireland, defender of the faith, duke of Brunswick and Luneburg, arch treasurer and prince elector of the holy Roman empire, and so forth – and of the United States of America, to" – what? – "to forget all past misunderstandings and differences that have unhappily" – what? – "interrupted the good correspondence and friendship which they mutually wish to restore" – what then? why – "His Britannic majesty ACKNOWLEDGES the said United States, viz. New Hampshire, Massachusetts Bay, 'Rhode Island and Providence Plantations, Connecticut, New York, New Jersey, Pennsylvania, Delaware, Maryland, Virginia, North Carolina, South Carolina, and Georgia, to be *free*, *sovereign*, and *independent* States; that he treats with them as such; and for himself, his heirs and successors, relinquishes all claims to the government, propriety, and territorial rights of the same, and every part thereof."

Fellow-citizens, I am not without apprehension that some parts of this extract, cited to the word and to the letter from the Treaty of Peace of 1783, may have discomposed the *serenity* of your temper. Far be it from me, to *dispose your hearts* to a levity unbecoming the hallowed dignity of this day. But this Treaty of Peace is the *dessert*, appropriate to the sumptuous banquet of the Declaration. It is the epilogue to that unparalleled drama, of which the Declaration is the prologue. Observe, my countrymen and friends, how the rules of unity, prescribed by the great masters of the fictive stage, were preserved in this tragedy of pity and terror in real life. Here was a beginning, a middle, and an end, of one mighty action. The beginning, was the Declaration which we have read: the middle, was that sanguinary, calamitous, but glorious war, which calls for deeper colors and a brighter pencil than mine to pourtray: the end, was the disposal of Divine Providence, that same Divine Providence, upon whose protection your fathers had so solemnly and so effectually declared their firm reliance, of the heart of the most serene and most potent prince, to acknowledge your independence to the precise extent in which it had been declared. Here was no great charter of Runnimead, yielded and accepted as a grant of royal bounty. That which the Declaration had asserted, which seven years of mercy-harrowing war had contested, was here in express and unequivocal terms *acknowledged*. And how? By the mere disposal of the heart of the most serene and most potent prince.

The Declaration of Independence pronounced the irrevocable decree of political separation, between the United States and their people on the one part, and the British king, government, and nation on the other. It proclaimed the first principles on which civil government is founded, and derived from them the justification before earth and heaven of this act of sovereignty. But it left the people of this union, collective and individual, without *organized* government. In contemplating this state of things, one of the profoundest of British statesmen, in an ecstacy of astonishment exclaimed, "Anarchy is found tolerable!" But there was no anarchy. From the day of the Declaration, the people of the North American union, and of its constituent states, were associated bodies of civilized men and christians, in a state of nature, but not of anarchy. They were bound by the laws of God, which they all, and by the laws of the gospel, which they nearly all, acknowledged as the rules of their conduct. They were bound by the principles which they themselves had proclaimed in the declaration. They were bound by all those tender and endearing sympathies, the absence of which, in the British government and nation, towards them, was the primary cause of the distressing conflict in which they had been precipitated by the headlong rashness and unfeeling insolence, of their oppressors. They were bound by all the beneficent laws and institutions, which their forefathers had brought with them from their mother country, not as servitudes but as rights. They were bound by habits of hardy industry, by frugal and hospitable manners, by the general sentiments of social equality, by pure and virtuous morals; and lastly they were bound by the grappling-hooks of common suffering under the scourge of oppression. Where then, among such a people, were the materials for anarchy! Had there been among them no other law, they would have been a law unto themselves.

They had before them in their new position, besides the maintenance of the independence which they had declared, three great objects to attain; the first, to cement and prepare for perpetuity their common union and that of their posterity; the second, to erect and organize civil and municipal governments in their respective states: and the third, to form connexions of friendship and of commerce with foreign nations. For all these objects, the same Congress which issued the Declaration, and at the same time with it, had provided. They recommended to the several states to form civil governments for themselves; with guarded and cautious deliberation they matured a confederation for the whole Union; and they prepared treaties of commerce, to be offered to the principal maritime nations of the world. All these objects were in a great degree accomplished amid the din of arms, and while every quarter of our country was ransacked by the fury of invasion. The states organized their governments, all in republican forms, all on the principles of the Declaration. The confederation was unanimously accepted by the thirteen states: and treaties of commerce were concluded with France and the Netherlands, in which, for the first time, the same just and magnanimous principles, consigned in the Declaration of Independence, were, so far as they could be applicable to the intercourse between nation and nation, solemnly recognized. When experience had proved that the confederation was not adequate to the national purposes of the country, the people of the United States, without tumult, without violence, by their delegates all chosen upon principles of equal right, formed a more perfect union, by the establishment of the federal constitution. This has already passed the ordeal of one human generation. In all the changes of men and of parties through which it has passed, it has been administered on the same fundamental principles. Our manners, our habits, our feelings, are all republican; and if our principles had been, when first proclaimed, doubtful to the ear of reason or the sense of humanity, they would have been reconciled to our understanding and endeared to our hearts by their practical operation. In the progress of forty years since the acknowledgment of our Independence, we have gone through many modifications of internal government, and through all the vicissitudes of peace and war, with other mighty nations. But never, never for a moment have the great principles, consecrated by the Declaration of this day, been renounced or abandoned.

And now, friends and countrymen, if the wise and learned philosophers of the older world, the first observers of nutation and aberration, the discoverers of maddening ether and invisible planets, the inventors of Congreve rockets and shrapnel shells, should find their hearts disposed to inquire, what has America done for the benefit of mankind? Let our answer be this – America, with the same voice which spoke herself into existence as a nation, proclaimed to mankind the inextinguishable rights of human nature, and the only lawful foundations of government. America, in the assembly of nations, since her admission among them, has invariably, though often fruitlessly, held forth to them the hand of honest friendship, of equal freedom, of generous reciprocity. She has uniformly spoken among them, though often to heedless and often to disdainful ears, the language of equal liberty, equal justice, and equal rights. She has, in the lapse of nearly half a century, without a single exception, respected the independence of other nations, while asserting and maintaining her own. She has abstained from interference in the concerns of others, even when the conflict has been for principles to which she clings, as to the last vital drop that visits the heart. She has seen that probably for centuries to come, all the contests of that Aceldama, the European World, will be contests between inveterate power, and emerging right. Wherever the standard of freedom and independence has been or shall be unfurled, there will her heart, her benedictions and her prayers be. But she goes not abroad in search of monsters to destroy. She is the well-wisher to the freedom and independence of all. She is the champion and Vindicator only of her own. She will recommend the general cause, by the countenance of her voice, and the benignant sympathy of her example. She well knows that by once enlisting under other banners than her own, were they even the banners of foreign independence, she would involve herself, beyond the power of extrication, in all the wars of interest and intrigue, of individual avarice, envy, and ambition, which assume the colors and usurp the standard of freedom. The fundamental maxims of her policy would insensibly change from liberty to force. The frontlet upon her brows would no longer beam with the ineffable splendor of freedom and independence; but in its stead would soon be substituted an imperial diadem, flashing in false and tarnished lustre the murky radiance of dominion and power. She might become the dictatress of the world: she would be no longer the ruler of her own spirit.

Stand forth, ye champions of Britannia, ruler of the waves! Stand forth, ye chivalrous knights of chartered liberties and the rotten borough! Enter the lists, ye boasters of *inventive* genius! ye mighty masters of the palette and the brush! ye improvers upon the sculpture of the Elgin marbles! ye spawners of fustian romance and lascivious lyrics! Come, and inquire what has America done for the benefit of mankind! In the half century which has elapsed since the declaration of American independence, what have *you* done for the benefit of mankind? When Themistocles was sarcastically asked by some great musical genius of his age, whether he knew how to play upon the lute, he answered, No! but he knew how to make a great city of a small one. We shall not contend with you for the prize of music, painting, or sculpture. We shall not disturb the extatic trances of your chemists, nor call from the heavens the ardent gaze of your astronomers. We will not ask you who was the last president of your Royal Academy. We will not inquire by whose mechanical combinations it was, that your steam-boats stem the currents of your rivers, and vanquish the opposition of the winds themselves upon your seas. We will not name the inventor of the cotton-gin, for we fear that you would ask us the meaning of the word, and pronounce it a provincial barbarism. We will not name to you him, whose graver defies the imitation of forgery, and saves the labor of your executioner, by taking from your greatest geniuses of robbery the power of committing the crime. He is now among yourselves; and since your philosophers have permitted him to prove to them the compressibility of water, you may perhaps claim him for your own. Would you soar to fame upon a rocket, or burst into glory from a shell? We shall leave you to inquire of your naval heroes their opinion of the steam-battery and the torpedo. It is not by the contrivance of agents of destruction, that America wishes to commend her inventive genius to the admiration or the gratitude of after times; nor is it even by the detection of the secrets or the composition of new modifications of physical nature.

"Excudent alii spirantia mollius aera."

Nor even is her purpose the glory of Roman ambition; nor "tu regere *imperio* populos" her memento to her sons. Her glory is not *dominion*, but *liberty*. Her march is the march of mind. She has a spear and a shield; but the motto upon her shield is *Freedom, Independence, Peace*. This has been her declaration: this has been, as far as her necessary intercourse with the rest of mankind would permit, her practice.

My countrymen, fellow-citizens, and friends; could that Spirit, which dictated the Declaration we have this day read, that Spirit, which "prefers before all temples the upright heart and pure," at this moment descend from his habitation in the skies, and within this hall, in language audible to mortal ears, address each one of us, here assembled, our beloved country, Britannia ruler of the waves, and every individual among the sceptred lords of humankind; his words would be,

"Go thou and do likewise!"

JOHN QUINCY ADAMS (WASHINGTON, DC) TO ROBERT WALSH JR., JULY 10, 1821

John Quincy Adams's July 4 oration stirred up much public discussion and criticism. He felt that his basic argument was being misunderstood or distorted. John Quincy hastened to explain to an influential journalist that he meant, first and foremost, to make the case against European-style colonialism. Second, he meant to combat what he termed the "doctrine of Lexington" (Henry Clay's call for an American hemispheric alliance against the Holy Alliance of despots) and the "doctrine of Edinburgh" (the British Whigs' call for Anglo-American cooperation and intervention on behalf of political reform and revolution in Europe).

MY DEAR SIR:

I inclose you a copy of an address delivered by me to citizens of Washington at their request, on reading to them on the 4th instant the Declaration of Independence.

The task in the first instance allotted to me was merely the reading of the Declaration. Disappointed in their application to an orator equal to the theme of the day, the Committee invited me to accompany the reading with an appropriate address. This is the result of my compliance with their desire.

There may be those among my fellow citizens who will consider that the avowal of some of the sentiments in the address, however suitable to a private citizen of the United States, was in the mouth of a person exercising a peculiarly responsible public office more indicative of sound principle than of *discretion*. I have not been unaware that my accidental and transient connection while it existed with an office, through which the principal political intercourse with foreign countries is held, prescribed a measure of prudence in the public expression of my opinions, even upon occasions altogether extra official. Yet in commenting upon the Declaration of Independence, it was impossible to point out that which distinguishes it from any other public document ever penned by man, and that which alone can justify its annual public reperusal, forty years after the close of the conflict of which it was the manifesto, without touching upon topics of peculiar delicacy at this time, and without coming into collision with principles which the British government itself disclaim, but which Emperors and Kings yet maintain at the point of all their bayonets and at the mouths of all their cannon.

Far from thinking that this was an occasion for flinching from the assertion of our peculiar and imperishable principles, I am free to confess that one of my reasons for assenting to the request that I would deliver an address was to avail myself of the opportunity of asserting them. The sentiments were indeed exclusively my own; neither the chief magistrate nor either of my colleagues was aware of a word that I should say until he heard it spoken. The responsibility of having spoken it rests exclusively upon myself, but I have no reason to believe that either of them would disclaim his concurrence in any one sentiment that I expressed.

Another objection which may be anticipated to the character of the address is perhaps a seeming inconsistency between the disavowal of Revolutionary resentments, and the tone of sentiment preserved in it with regard to the British government and nation. In this case I trust every discerning mind will perceive the difference between the oblivion of past resentments, and the resistance to present hostility. The animosity which we have now to encounter from Britain is purely national. It is rather discountenanced than stimulated by the government, and is inspired by the two deepest and most malignant passions of the human heart – revenge and envy – revenge for the national humiliation of two successive wars, envy at the unparalleled growth and prosperity which associate with all their thoughts of America the torturing terror of a rival growing every day more formidable to them. Can a stronger illustration of this truth be given than in the elaborate dissertation of the British author of the campaigns of Washington and New Orleans, to prove that in the next war with the United States, the only possible chance of successful warfare for Britain will be a systematic destruction of all our populous towns – a system which he admits would be too atrocious for a war with the people of a monarchy, but which he maintains would be perfectly justifiable against Republicans. What a vulture must be pouncing on that heart which could heave up such a sentiment for the execration of mankind! That vulture is pouncing constantly on the heart of the British nation, and it is well that we should be aware of it, that we may be duly prepared to meet that form of British hostility whenever it may be displayed.

It is to cater for that vulture that all the literature of Britain is so generously and so incessantly employed in depreciating the intellectual and vilifying the moral character of the American people. It is for that vulture that their travellers cross the seas, and that their daily, monthly and quarterly journals, Whig and Tory, concoct with emulous industry the aliment. It is the vulture which prompts a distinguished peer of the realm to avouch a despicable radical lampooner of America, for the corruption of our elections, and hence to infer the superior purity of the rotten borough system. With a few, a very few exceptions, it pervades them all.

It is not too much to say that the literature of the public journals in Britain has more influence both upon the nation and upon their neighbors than the government.

It was upon this consideration that I did not think it beneath the dignity of the day, nor incongruous to the station of the speaker, to allude to some of the most venomous effusions of the British periodical press. It will be obvious that in retorting upon their bombastic pretensions to superior inventive genius, I have not intended to discredit their real discoveries and inventions, or to shed ridicule upon their ardent and meritorious pursuits in the fine or mechanical arts, or in the fields of literature and science. Though I think the steamboat an invention of more extensive usefulness to mankind than all their inventions since our Declaration of Independence put together, yet I would to God that there was not an useful invention of which they can boast, but for which we could show them a counterpart of our own.

In this warfare of the mind which we are compelled to maintain, in defence of the character of our country, I hope you will consider me as a follower and fellow labourer of your own. If even the Aristarchs of Edinburgh had taken your castigation kindly, and made a fair and honest apology for the insidious hostility which you had exposed, with due promise of amendment, I would not have disturbed the truce. But the Edinburgh article upon your book is every way exceptionable; it shuffles between candid avowal and ingenuous recantation, without either the spirit to defend or the generosity to atone for its offence.

It inculcates a political doctrine in my estimation of the most pernicious tendency to this country, and the more pernicious, because it flatters our ambition – the doctrine that it is the duty of America to take an active part in the future political reformation of Europe. It is most especially to that doctrine that a passage alludes in the address, which the hearers generally understood as referring only to the South American contest. The principle applies to them both, and my intention in pronouncing it was to reply both to Edinburgh and Lexington.

There are passages in the address to which I cannot expect your assent. Those I mean which have reference to what we call the religious reformation. I know not how far to a philosophical Roman Catholic, which I know you to be, the doctrine of infallibility upon earth is an article of faith, or a mere article of church discipline. But I take it for granted that at this day, the usurpation of the ecclesiastical power during the middle ages may be descanted upon without departing from that liberality which should be observed towards all religious opinions. It was indeed impossible to treat the subject upon which I was called to speak in the manner which I thought most appropriate to it, without connecting the religious revolution of the 16th century with the origin of the doctrines which issued in our Independence. I have only to assure you that nothing could be farther from my intention than to reflect upon articles really essential to the Catholic faith, or to wound the feelings of those who receive the doctrines of the Church even in wider latitude.

I need not say that this letter is entirely private and confidential. I have wished to assure you that I am not insensible either to your good opinion, or to the manifestations of it which you have more than once given to the world. And I know not of a more suitable occasion to give you this assurance than on requesting your acceptance of a copy of this address, of which, although particular passages may differ from your opinions, I flatter myself the general scope and tenor will meet with your approbation.

I am, etc.

JOHN QUINCY ADAMS (WASHINGTON, DC) TO EDWARD EVERETT, JANUARY 31, 1822

In response to a letter from Everett, John Quincy highlighted what he felt most reviewers had missed from his oration of July 4, 1821. He anticipated "a great question in the national policy of this Union which may be nearer at hand than most of our countrymen are aware of: Whether we too shall annex to our federative government a great system of colonial establishments." He argued that "such establishments are incompatible with the essential character of our political institutions," and that "great colonial establishments are but mighty engines of wrong, and that in the progress of social improvement it will be the duty of the human family to abolish them, as they are now endeavoring to abolish the slave-trade." But America must avoid "direct interference in foreign wars, even wars for freedom," which would change the very foundations of our own government from liberty to power.

DEAR SIR:

I have received your letter of the 20th instant and its enclosure and thank you for both. Your brother's letter gave me great pleasure as a token of the warmth of his friendship for me. I believe with you that the motives of the severity with which my address was criticised at Boston lay much nearer the surface than your brother supposes. The motive avowed by the pamphleteer reviewer was a very laudable one – to guard the public taste against the contagion of a bad example. I have no right to believe that this motive was not sincere. And when once the reviewer had made up his mind that the example was bad, it would be too rigorous a rule to hold him to the standard of impartiality, and call upon his acuteness to discover merits where his only purpose was to expose defects.

Fourth of July orations and addresses have seldom been made the subject of elaborate criticism, nor have I reason to believe that my address on the last fourth of July would have shared a different fate, but for the public station accidentally occupied by its author. On another anniversary of the same day twenty-eight years before, I had delivered an oration upon the same subject in Boston. They were both emanations of the same mind and doubtless bear the same characteristic marks of composition. They were both equally well received by their respective auditories, but of the first no watchful guardian of our literary chastity felt himself summoned in the discharge of patriotic duty to detect and expose the deadly danger to the public taste.

That the modern eunuchs of Apollo's harems are more faithful in their vigilance over the purity of the muses under their charge than their predecessors (I had like to have said their forefathers,) twenty-eight years ago, is not impossible; but I rather presume that they measured the malignity of the temptation by the standing of the tempter, and concluded that although the wanton excitement of a county court attorney of twenty-six might be disregarded, it was high time to sound the alarm when the solicitor to sin was a Secretary of State of fifty-four. However this may be, it is well that the morals of these ladies are now under such keen scented custody, as their spotless virtue is of high import to the public weal and it is very desirable that they should be preserved "chaste as an icicle."

You will not understand me as pleading guilty to the charge of attempting to corrupt the public taste. Still less as admitting the justice of any part of the reviewer's censure upon the sentiments of the address. I have cultivated *style* as much, perhaps, as any man in the country whose life has been necessarily so much a life of business as mine. Style and ethics, or rather to arrange them according to my own sense of their relative importance, ethics and style, have been the two branches of human knowledge to which I have most assiduously devoted the leisure of my life, and my reason for studying them in preference to other portions of general science has been, because I have thought them more constantly and more usefully applicable to *all* the business of life than any others. With regard to style I have considered that the first object of a writer for the public was to obtain as many readers as he could, and that something *remarkable* in the style of composition was among the most attractive lures to readers. Sir Joshua Reynolds who was a philosophical painter was in the practice of making frequent experiments in the mixing of his colors for the purpose of trying their effect. It sometimes happened that his experiment failed and he lived to see many of his portraits almost vanish from the canvas on which he had painted them. I have treated style much in the same way as Sir Joshua treated his colors and in some cases with similar success. In popular discourses especially I have written more for *effect* than was perhaps always wise, and in mixing up colors which I knew would at all events be evanescent I have given them a momentary glow beyond the warmth of nature.

In the *address* of the last summer I indulged myself in this experimental mood more than I had ever done before. It was a hasty composition prepared in the midst of a multitude of other avocations, and I had no time for the labor of the file. Its effect upon the crowded auditory who heard me was as great and as favorable as I could have desired – the effect of unremitting rivetted attention, with more than one occasional burst of applause. When it came before the public from the press the effect was different. Criticism fastened at once upon the writer and upon the work. Opinions became various. The address was *read* by friend and foe, and it was judged more by the spirit of feeling than by that of scrutiny, more by what was thought of the author than by what was found in the discourse. The consequence was that neither friend nor foe, so far as I have observed, discovered what was really in the address and what I had thought the most noticeable thing in it. To instance what your brother calls the doctrine of sympathy, upon which he remarks that what the reviewer says is pitiful, but adds no comment of his own; this doctrine of *sympathy* in the address is merely incidental to the demonstration from the moral and physical nature of man that *colonial establishments cannot fulfil the great objects of government in the just purpose of civil society*. Is the demonstration complete and unanswerable? I think it is. Had it ever been exhibited before? Not to my knowledge. Let us assume it as a new but demonstrated axiom and examine its bearing upon the past, present and future history of mankind, upon the system of political morality, and upon the future improvement of the human character.

1. It places on a new and solid ground the *right* of our struggle for independence, considering the intolerable oppression which provoked our fathers to the revolt only as its proximate causes, themselves proof of the viciousness of the system from which they resulted.

2. It settles the justice of the present struggle of South America for independence, and prepares for an acknowledgment upon the principle of public law of that independence, whenever it shall be sufficiently established by the fact.

3. It looks forward prospectively to the downfall of the British Empire in India as an event which must necessarily ensue at no very distant period of time.

4. It anticipates a great question in the national policy of this Union which may be nearer at hand than most of our countrymen are aware of: Whether we too shall annex to our federative government a great system of colonial establishments.

5. It points to a principle proving that such establishments are incompatible with the essential character of our political institutions.

6. It leads to the conclusion that great colonial establishments are but mighty engines of *wrong*, and that in the progress of social improvement it will be the duty of the human family to abolish them, as they are now endeavoring to abolish the slave-trade. Did I deceive myself in imagining that by asserting this principle and supporting it by a demonstration, logical in substance and highly, perhaps too highly, oratorical in form, I was offering to the minds of my countrymen matter for meditation other than the inquiry how many times the word sympathy was repeated in the compass of three pages? The eyes of the Boston reviewer see nothing in it, nothing novel, nothing original, nothing comprehensive, nothing dignified, nothing but shadowy metaphysics about sympathy.

Nor to their idle orbs doth sight appear
Of sun, or moon or star throughout the year.

Let me give one instance more. The Edinburgh reviewer of Mr. Walsh's book, foreseeing times of future turbulence in his own country, and panting for a revolution with English and Scottish Whigs at its head, descanted largely upon the importance of a good understanding between the Americans and that party, and upon the supposed duty of the United States to take an active part in the impending European conflicts between *Power* and *Right*. This doctrine has already twice in the course of our history brought the peace and the permanent welfare of the Union into jeopardy: under Washington's administration at the early stage of the French Revolution; under the present administration in the efforts to entangle us in the South American conflict. The address has presented a principle of *duty* directly the reverse as that which ought forever to govern the councils of the Union, and has assigned as a reason for it the inevitable tendency of a direct interference in foreign wars, even wars for freedom, to change the very foundations of our own government from *liberty* to *power*. Had this view of a question in political morality transcendently important to the future destiny of this country ever been presented before? Certainly not to my knowledge. It may be controverted no doubt, but I believe the principle to be impregnably true, and it was assuredly no commonplace topic of orations upon Independence. The Boston reviewer is unconscious that it exists in the address at all. I will weary you no more with examples. From the high opinion which your brother expresses of my general style of writing, and from the avowal of his judgment that this address has its merits as well as its defects, I conclude that he discerned some of these things which had escaped the optics of the reviewer. I have given you the clue to the true cause of the defects and perhaps the merits of my style, and I will now point you to the source of all the matter of my composition good or bad.

The merits of whatever compositions I have given to the world, either as a literary man or a politician, consist in the application of moral philosophy to business, in the incessant reference direct or indirect of all narrative, argument, and inference, to the standard of *right* and *wrong*. Erroneous moral principle is the most fruitful of all the sources of human calamity and vice. The leaders of nations and parties are generally but accomplished sophists, trained to make the worse appear the better reason. The intercourse of private life is full of sophistical palterings and human law itself, with deference to Hooker be it said, law, itself national, civil and municipal, is too often but a system of formal sophistry substituted for eternal truth and justice. Yet so congenial are truth and justice to the human mind, that it is always vehemently moved by a skilful and forcible appeal to them, and of appeals to them direct or implied, explicit or deductive, the whole substance of my public writings is composed.

You have now the whole secret of the merits, such as they are, and of the defects of my compositions, literary and political. The sources both of their matter and style are before you. I need not add that I am infinitely more solicitous about the substance than about the form. If you have read my lectures on rhetoric you have seen in the 30th, 31st, and 32nd of them my theory of figurative language, and have perceived that it is more indulgent to the excesses of energy and less to the prudery of taste than Dr. Blair, the French critics, or even Quintillian and Horace. In the use of language, as in the conduct of life, I would certainly aim at the precise line between licentiousness and servitude; but so far as mere taste is concerned, if I must err, let it be on the side of liberty.

Your brother has allowed himself a little of this liberty in his description of the estimate which was once made of my talents at composition by those whom he calls your *Eastern politicians*. I think there never was a time when that class of our fellow citizens had much opinion of the merit, or were at all insensible to the defects of my style. On the very first occasion that I ever presented myself as a writer and speaker in the face of my country, which was by the delivery of an oration upon taking my first degree at Harvard University, an elaborate critical review of the performances of the day from the pen of one of these Eastern politicians was published in a Boston newspaper, pronouncing one of my classmates who had also delivered an oration on that day my *indisputable superior* in *style*, *elegance*, and oratory. I could prove to you by a long, but it would be a very tedious, historical detail that from that day to this my credit for talents at writing has been very low with those Eastern politicians, and that even while they numbered me in their political ranks, whatever favor they showed me was a tribute not to me but to a public taste, vitiated as they believed, but stronger than themselves.

I have told you that I have been much in the habit of writing to the public for *effect*. In the year 1802 I delivered an address to the Massachusetts Charitable Fire Society. In that address there was a parallel between *Catanea* with a burning mountain at its gates, and *Boston* with a burning mountain within its walls. You were then a child. Did you ever hear that this address, and especially this parallel, contributed to the effect of casting away clapboards and shingles and of building only with incombustible materials? If you did not, ask our common friend to whom your brother's letter is directed whether he remembers it? He may perhaps not remember that it was proved by a newspaper critic of that day, quite to the satisfaction of your *Eastern politicians*, that there was in this parallel nothing new, nothing original, that it was merely *a quotation from Brydone's Travels*, and that the use of such words as clapboards and shingles in a public oration was much too vulgar for the relish of refined taste.

In the year 1808 I published a letter to Mr. H. G. Otis upon the embargo. It was defensive against a masked battery which had opened upon me by the *Eastern politicians* at a crisis and in a manner so adroitly chosen that it was thought it would demolish me to the foundation. About a hundred thousand copies of my letter were printed, and column was piled upon column in the newspapers, and pamphlet upon pamphlet issued from the press, to prove not only that I was a Judas in politics, but that there was not a sentence of common sense or tolerable English in my letter. This was the sound doctrine of the Eastern politicians, who accordingly dismissed me as insultingly as was in their power from the service of the Commonwealth as a Senator of the United States. In truth the pamphlet review of my last summer's address and the strictures of Mr. Hale's paper were so far from indicating inconsistency with the opinion always entertained of my talents and style by the Eastern politicians, that I have something more than surmise for the belief that they had the same identical origin as the review of my commencement oration upon my taking the bachelor's degree in 1787. Shall I acknowledge to you that I regret nothing of all this? Shall I confess that this unrelenting and almost unrelaxing opposition of your Eastern politicians which I have now breasted these five and thirty years, and against which the cheering voice of my country has hitherto triumphantly supported me instead of casting me down, has been my highest pride? Weak and vain as the confession is I cannot deny it. Were it therefore true that Virginia has been a partial mother to her own sons and a stepmother to those of her sisters, right glad should I be that at least in my person no such dandling spirit should have been manifested by my good mother Massachusetts. The reputation which must be pampered and cosseted has no charms for me. Give me that which is spontaneously bestowed by strangers. Give me that which is reluctantly extorted from rivals. Give me that which the whole nation shall sanction and after ages shall ratify, or give me none.

It is not assuredly for me to complain of the partialities of Virginia. Of the last twenty-eight years of my life twenty have been employed in offices of trust and profit and honor in the service of the Union at the call of Virginian Presidents. I have never courted her favor. I have never ministered to her passions. I have never flattered her prejudices. Yet three of the four eminent citizens born of her who have presided over the Union have successively confided to me several of the highest trusts of the Nation. From the fourth I have received multiplied tokens of esteem, such as the Eastern politicians never thought me to deserve. Under this patronage I have rendered as in duty bound faithful services to the Union. Of their value or importance I am not to judge. Great or small, some of them are now beyond the power of time and out of the reach of fortune. Clouds and darkness rest upon the future; but whatever my fortune may be, whether my reputation as a statesman or a writer is to stand or fall will, I trust, depend as little upon the policy or the good will of the Eastern politicians, as upon the strictures of Mr. Hale's gazette or the pamphlet of the Boston reviewer.

There is much of egotism and so little of discretion in this letter that after having written it thus far, I have long hesitated whether it should be committed to the post office or to the flames. I have at length concluded to forward it to you in strict confidence, with permission to give its perusal only to the friend to whom your brother's letter was addressed. He has been to me for more than thirty years the true and disinterested friend of all hours and under every vicissitude. He knows as well as any living man all the good and all the evil of my character, and though as quick to discern and as judicious to distinguish a blemish or a beauty as the clearest sighted of Eastern politicians, if he should here and there espy some trivial crudity of diction or deportment, will yet not make it his business or his pleasure to blazon it forth to the world.

I regret that it will not be in my power to review the memoir of Mr. Onis. It is indeed of very little consequence in itself and scarcely deserves the notice of your miscellany, unless it were as an occasion for reviewing the political relations of this Union with Spain from their commencement amid the storm of our Revolution until this time. Such a review would make a curious and interesting article for your work, but I could not write it as it ought to be written without walking upon firebrands. "Suppositos cineridoloso."

I send you however as a substitute for my half promised communication, two-thirds of a review of Don Luis's *Memoir* published at Philadelphia, and in which that most excellent Lord is handled more roughly than I should permit myself to treat him, though not more severely than he deserves.

I will thank you to acknowledge the receipt of this letter, and remain with very high regard and esteem, etc.

JOHN QUINCY ADAMS (DEPARTMENT OF STATE) TO HUGH NELSON, APRIL 28, 1823

The island of Cuba, then under the nominal control of Spain, was of immense strategic importance to the United States, as John Quincy set out in great detail in this dispatch to Nelson, the American minister in Madrid. Within a half century, John Quincy believed, it was destined to become a member of the North American Union. But the time was not yet ripe. The present risk was that Spain might cede the island to a serious European power, either Britain or France; or that Britain would seize it in the event of a European war. Nelson was instructed to discourage the present or a future Spanish government from abandoning its sovereignty, benignly administered. But if worse came to worst, "there are laws of political as well as of physical gravitation; and if an apple severed by the tempest from its native tree cannot choose but fall to the ground, Cuba, forcibly disjoined from its own unnatural connection with Spain, and incapable of self-support, can gravitate only towards the North American Union, which by the same law of nature cannot cast her off from its bosom."

SIR:

The period at which you enter upon the mission with which you are charged is of no common interest, and the relations of the United States with the country to which you are destined, at all times important, are now of the deepest moment. The situation of Spain herself, that of France, from whence she has been threatened with invasion, ere this probably commenced, that of the great continental European powers leagued against her, and that of Great Britain, which now for the first time has seceded from the political system of the European alliance, all combine to darken the immediate prospects of the future in the eastern hemisphere, and to summon the attention of this government to the interests of the Union which may be affected by them.

It has been a maxim in the policy of these United States, from the time when their independence was achieved, to keep themselves aloof from the political systems and contentions of Europe. To this principle it is yet the purpose of the President to adhere: and in the war about to commence, the attitude to be assumed and maintained by the United States will be that of neutrality.

But the experience of our national history has already shown that, however sincerely this policy was adopted, and however earnestly and perseveringly it was maintained, it yielded ultimately to a course of events by which the violence and injustice of European powers involved the immediate interests and brought in conflict the essential rights of our own country.

Two of the principal causes of the wars between the nations of Europe since that of our own Revolution, have been, indeed, the same as those in which that originated – civil liberty and national independence. To these principles, and to the cause of those who contend for them, the people of the United States can never be indifferent. A feeling of sympathy and of partiality for every nation struggling to secure or to defend these great interests, has been and will be manifested by this Union; and it is among the most difficult and delicate duties of the general government, in all its branches, to indulge this feeling so far as it may be compatible with the duties of neutrality and to withhold and restrain from encroaching upon them. So far as it is indulged, its tendency is to involve us in foreign wars, while the first and paramount duty of the government is to maintain *peace* amidst all the convulsions of foreign wars, and to enter the lists as parties to no cause, other than our own.

In the *maritime* wars of Europe, we have, indeed, a direct and important interest of our own; as they are waged upon an element which is the common property of all; and as our participation in the possession of that property is perhaps greater than that of any other nation. The existence of maritime war, itself, enlarges and deepens the importance of this interest; and it introduces a state of things in which the conflict of neutral and belligerent rights becomes itself a continual and formidable instigation to war. To all maritime wars Great Britain can scarcely fail of becoming a party; and from that moment arises a collision between her and these states, peculiar to the situation, interests and rights of the two countries, and which can scarcely form a subject of discussion between any other nation and either of them.

This cause then is peculiarly our own: and we have already been once compelled to vindicate our rights implicated in it by war. It has been too among the dispensations of Providence, that the issue of that war should have left that question unsettled for the future; and that the attempts which on the part of the United States have been repeatedly made since the peace for adjusting it by amicable negotiation, have in like manner proved ineffectual. There is therefore great reason to apprehend, that if Great Britain should engage in the war, now just kindled in Europe, the United States will again be called to support by all their energies, not excepting war, the rights of their national independence, enjoyed in the persons of their seamen.

But in the war between France and Spain now commencing, other interests, peculiarly ours, will in all probability be deeply involved. Whatever may be the issue of this war, as between those two European powers, it may be taken for granted that the dominion of Spain upon the American continents, North and South, is irrecoverably gone. But the islands of Cuba and of Porto Rico still remain nominally and so far really dependent upon her, that she yet possesses the power of transferring her own dominion over them, together with the possession of them, to others. These islands, from their local position, are natural appendages to the North American continent; and one of them, Cuba, almost in sight of our shores, from a multitude of considerations has become an object of transcendent importance to the political and commercial interests of our Union. Its commanding position with reference to the Gulf of Mexico and the West India seas; the character of its population; its situation midway between our southern coast and the island of San Domingo; its safe and capacious harbor of the Havana, fronting a long line of our shores destitute of the same advantage; the nature of its productions and of its wants, furnishing the supplies and needing the returns of a commerce immensely profitable and mutually beneficial; give it an importance in the sum of our national interests, with which that of no other foreign territory can be compared, and little inferior to that which binds the different members of this Union together.

Such indeed are, between the interests of that island and of this country, the geographical, commercial, moral, and political relations, formed by nature, gathering in the process of time, and even now verging to maturity, that in looking forward to the probable course of events for the short period of half a century, it is scarcely possible to resist the conviction that the annexation of Cuba to our federal republic will be indispensable to the continuance and integrity of the Union itself. It is obvious however that for this event we are not yet prepared. Numerous and formidable objections to the extension of our territorial dominions beyond the sea present themselves to the first contemplation of the subject. Obstacles to the system of policy by which it alone can be compassed and maintained are to be foreseen and surmounted, both from at home and abroad. But there are laws of political as well as of physical gravitation; and if an apple severed by the tempest from its native tree cannot choose but fall to the ground, Cuba, forcibly disjoined from its own unnatural connection with Spain, and incapable of self-support, can gravitate only towards the North American Union, which by the same law of nature cannot cast her off from its bosom.

In any other state of things than that which springs from this incipient war between France and Spain, these considerations would be premature. They are now merely touched upon, to illustrate the position that, in the war opening upon Europe, the United States have deep and important interests involved, peculiarly their own. The condition of Cuba cannot but depend upon the issue of this war. As an integral part of the Spanish territories, Cuba has been formally and solemnly invested with the liberties of the Spanish constitution. To destroy those liberties, and to restore in the stead of that Constitution the dominion of the Bourbon race, is the avowed object of this new invasion of the Peninsula. There is too much reason to apprehend that in Spain itself this unhallowed purpose will be attended with immediate, or at least with temporary success; the constitution of Spain will be demolished by the armies of the Holy Alliance; and the Spanish nation will again bow the neck to the yoke of bigotry and despotic sway.

Whether the purposes of France, or of her continental allies, extend to the subjugation of the remaining ultra-marine possessions of Spain or not, has not yet been sufficiently disclosed. But to confine ourselves to that which immediately concerns us, the condition of the island of Cuba, we know that the republican spirit of freedom prevails among its inhabitants. The liberties of the constitution are to them rights in possession: nor is it to be presumed that they will be willing to surrender them, because they may be extinguished by foreign violence in the parent country. As Spanish territory the island will be liable to invasion from France during the war: and the only reasons for doubting whether the attempt will be made are the probable incompetency of the French maritime force to effect the conquest, and the probability that its accomplishment would be resisted by Great Britain. In the meantime and at all events, the condition of the island in regard to that of its inhabitants, is a condition of great, imminent, and complicated danger: and without resorting to speculation upon what such a state of things must produce upon a people so situated, we know that its approach has already had a powerful effect upon them, and that the question what they are to do upon contingencies daily pressing upon them and ripening into reality, has for the last twelve months constantly excited their attention and stimulated them to action.

Were the population of the island of one blood and color, there could be no doubt or hesitation with regard to the course which they would pursue, as dictated by their interests and their rights. The invasion of Spain by France would be the signal for *their* Declaration of Independence. That even in their present state it will be imposed upon them as a necessity is not unlikely; but among all their reflecting men it is admitted as a maxim fundamental to all deliberation upon their future condition, that they are not competent to a system of permanent self-dependence. They must rely for the support of protection upon some force from without; and as, in the event of the overthrow of the Spanish constitution, that support can no longer be expected from Spain, their only alternative of dependence must be upon Great Britain, or upon the United States.

Hitherto the wishes of this government have been that the connection between Cuba and Spain should continue, as it has existed for several years. These wishes are known to the principal inhabitants of the island, and instructions, copies of which are now furnished you, were some months since transmitted to Mr. Forsyth, authorizing him in a suitable manner to communicate them to the Spanish government. These wishes still continue, so far as they can be indulged with a rational foresight of events beyond our control, but for which it is our duty to be prepared. If a government is to be imposed by foreign violence upon the Spanish nation, and the liberties which they have assisted by their constitution are to be crushed, it is neither to be expected nor desired that the people of Cuba, far from the reach of the oppressors of Spain, should submit to be governed by them. Should the cause of Spain herself issue more propitiously than from its present prospects can be anticipated, it is obvious that the trial through which she must pass at home, and the final loss of *all* her dominions on the American continents, will leave her unable to extend to the island of Cuba that protection necessary for its internal security and its outward defence.

Great Britain has formally withdrawn from the councils of the European Alliance in regard to Spain. She disapproves the war which they have sanctioned, and which is undertaken by France: and she avows her determination to defend Portugal against the application of the principles, upon which the invasion of Spain raises its only pretence of right. To the war as it commences, she has declared her intention of remaining neutral; but the spirit of the British nation is so strongly and with so much unanimity pronounced against France, their interests are so deeply involved in the issue, their national resentments and jealousies will be so forcibly stimulated by the progress of the war, whatever it may be, that unless the conflict should be as short and the issue as decisive as that of which Italy was recently the scene, it is scarcely possible that the neutrality of Great Britain should be long maintained. The prospect is that she will be soon engaged on the side of Spain; but in making common cause with her, it is not to be supposed that she will yield her assistance upon principles altogether disinterested and gratuitous. As the price of her alliance the two remaining islands of Spain in the West Indies present objects no longer of much possible value or benefit to Spain, but of such importance to Great Britain, that it is impossible to suppose her indifferent to the acquisition of them.

The motives of Great Britain for desiring the possession of Cuba are so obvious, especially since the independence of Mexico, and the annexation of the Floridas to our Union; the internal condition of the island since the recent Spanish revolution, and the possibility of its continued dependence upon Spain, have been so precarious; the want of protection there; the power of affording it possessed by Great Britain, and the necessities of Spain to secure, by some equivalent, the support of Great Britain for herself; have formed a remarkable concurrence of predispositions to the transfer of Cuba; and during the last two years rumors have been multiplied, that it was already consummated. We have been confidentially told by indirect communication from the French government, that more than two years since Great Britain was negotiating with Spain for the cession of Cuba; and so eager in the pursuit as to have offered Gibraltar, and more, for it in exchange. There is reason to believe that, in this respect, the French government was misinformed; but neither is entire reliance to be placed on the declaration lately made by the present

British Secretary for Foreign Affairs to the French government, and which, with precautions indicating distrust, has been also confidentially communicated to us; namely, that Great Britain would hold it disgraceful to avail herself of the distressed situation of Spain, to obtain possession of any portion of her American colonies. The object of this declaration, and of the communication of it here, undoubtedly was to induce the belief that Great Britain entertained no purpose of obtaining the possession of Cuba: but these assurances were given with reference to a state of peace, then still existing, and which it was the intention and the hope of Great Britain to preserve. The condition of all the parties to them has since changed; and however indisposed the British government might be, ungenerously to avail themselves of the distress of Spain, to extort from her any remnant of her former possessions, they did not forbear to take advantage of it, by orders of reprisals given to two successive squadrons, dispatched to the West Indies, and stationed in the immediate proximity to the island of Cuba. By measures thus vigorous and peremptory, they obtained from Spain immediate revocation of the blockade which her generals had proclaimed on the coast of Terra Firma, and pledges of reparation for all the captures of British vessels made under color of that military fiction. They obtained also an acknowledgment of many long standing claims of British subjects upon the Spanish government, and promises of payment of them, as a part of the national debt. The whole amount of them, however, as well as that of the reparation and indemnity promised for the capture of British property under the blockade of General Morales and by the Porto Rico privateers, yet exists in the form of claims; and the whole mass of them now is acknowledged claim, for the satisfaction of which pledges have been given, to be redeemed hereafter; and for which the island of Cuba may be the only indemnity in the power of Spain to grant, as it will undoubtedly be to Great Britain the most satisfactory indemnity which she could receive.

The war between France and Spain changes so totally the

circumstances under which the declaration above mentioned of Mr. Canning was made, that it may, at its very outset, produce events, under which the possession of Cuba may be obtained by Great Britain without even raising a reproach of intended deception against the British government for making it. An alliance between Great Britain and Spain may be one of the first fruits of this war. A guarantee of the island to Spain may be among the stipulations of that alliance; and in the event either of a threatened attack upon the island by France, or of attempts on the part of the islanders to assume their independence, a resort to the temporary occupation of the Havana by British forces may be among the probable expedients, through which it may be obtained, by concert between Britain and Spain herself. It is not necessary to point out the numerous contingencies by which the transition from a temporary and fiduciary occupation to a permanent and proprietary possession may be effected.

The transfer of Cuba to Great Britain would be an event unpropitious to the interests of this Union. This opinion is so generally entertained, that even the groundless rumors that it was about to be accomplished, which have spread abroad and are still teeming, may be traced to the deep and almost universal feeling of aversion to it, and to the alarm which the mere probability of its occurrence has stimulated. The question both of our right and our power to prevent it, if necessary, by force, already obtrudes itself upon our councils, and the administration is called upon, in the performance of its duties to the nation, at least to use all the means within its competency to guard against and forefend it.

It will be among the primary objects requiring your most earnest and unremitting attention, to ascertain and report to us any movement of negotiation between Spain and Great Britain upon this subject. We cannot indeed prescribe any special instructions in relation to it. We scarcely know where you will find the government of Spain upon your arrival in the country; nor can we foresee with certainty by whom it will be administered. Your credentials are addressed to Ferdinand, the king of Spain under the constitution. You may find him under the guardianship of a Cortes, in the custody of an Army of Faith, or under the protection of the invaders of his country. So long as the *constitutional* government may continue to be administered in his name, your official intercourse will be with his ministers; and to them you will repeat what Mr. Forsyth has been instructed to say, that the wishes of your government are, that Cuba and Porto Rico may continue in connection with independent and constitutional Spain. You will add, that no countenance has been given by us to any projected plan of separation from Spain, which may have been formed in the island. This assurance becomes proper, as, by a late despatch received from Mr. Forsyth, he intimates that the Spanish government have been informed, that a revolution in Cuba was secretly preparing, fomented by communications between a society of Free Masons there, and another of the same fraternity in Philadelphia. Of this we have no other knowledge: and the societies of Free Masons in this country are so little in the practice of using agency of a political nature on any occasion, that we think it most probable the information of the Spanish government in that respect is unfounded. It is true that the Free Masons at the Havana have taken part of late in the politics of Cuba; and so far as it is known to us, it has been an earnest and active part in favor of the continuance of their connection with Spain.

While disclaiming all disposition on our part, either to obtain possession of Cuba, or of Porto Rico, ourselves, you will declare that the American government had no knowledge of the lawless expedition undertaken against the latter of those islands last summer. This was one among many subjects upon which the Spanish minister residing here, Anduaga, remonstrated in a style of complaint to which, from respect for Spain, and that alone, no answers were returned to him. Translations of some of the invectives in which he has indulged himself are herewith enclosed. You will distinctly state to the Spanish government the President's expectation that Mr. Anduaga will not return in his official capacity to this country. His character was already so well known before he came to the United States, that Mr. Brent, then at Madrid, did even then formally remonstrate against his appointment, though without success. The President wishes not to dwell upon the character of his communications, in case he should not come back to renew them: but in the case of the expedition against Porto Rico, there is reason to believe that it was known to him before the departure of the vessels concerned in it from New York and Philadelphia, and that he voluntarily forebore to call the attention of this government to it.

You will not conceal from the Spanish government the repugnance of the United States to the transfer of the island of Cuba by Spain to any other power. The deep interest which would to them be involved in the event gives them the right of objecting against it; and as the people of the island itself are known to be averse to it, the right of Spain herself to make the cession, at least upon the principles on which the present Spanish constitution is founded, is more than questionable. Informal and verbal communications on this subject with the Spanish Minister of Foreign Affairs will be most advisable. In casual conversation, and speaking as from your own impressions, you may suggest the hope, that if any question of transferring the island to any other power is, or shall be in agitation, it will not be withheld from your knowledge, or from ours; that the condition of Cuba cannot be changed without affecting in an eminent degree the welfare of this Union, and consequently the good understanding between us and Spain; that we should consider an attempt to transfer the island, against the will of its inhabitants, as subversive of their rights, no less than of our interests; and that, as it would give them the perfect right of resisting such transfer, by declaring their own independence, so if they should, under those circumstances, resort to that measure, the United States will be fully justified in supporting them to carry it into effect.

Should immediate success attend the French invasion of Spain, its probable consequence will be the restoration of Ferdinand, not perhaps to the unlimited exercise of sovereign power, but to a phantom of constitution, which, under the auspices of a Holy League of absolute monarchs, he will graciously give to his people. There will in that event be no disposition, either in Ferdinand or his allies, to transfer the only remaining colonies of Spain to another power; but it may incite the people of Cuba to declare themselves independent, and will certainly give them the right so to do, if the charter of the restored government should import an abridgment of any of the liberties which they now enjoy under the constitution. It is now necessary to look forward to this contingency only to say, that if a counter-revolution should be effected, you will continue accredited to king Ferdinand, and will hold official inter course with whatever administration shall be conducted in his name. But in the event of a revolution by which he should be dethroned, or if he should go out of Spain, you will remain with the government *de facto*, waiting for new credentials which in that case become necessary.

In a late answer to an address from the Cortes he declared his intention, in case the country should be invaded, to put himself at the head of the army for its defence. Other accounts announce the probability that a removal of the seat of government to Corunna, or to Cadiz, was in contemplation. Should the king repair to the army, whether of the constitution or of the Faith, it is not to be expected that *any* foreign minister will be required to attend him: but in the case of the removal of the government from Madrid, you will follow it, or remain there, according as the circumstances, which at this distance of time and place cannot be foreseen, may guide your discretion.

The critical and convulsed condition of Spain may indeed bring forth many incidents now unforeseen, and upon which the President relies upon your own judgment for the course which under them you will find it prudent to pursue. But with regard to the ordinary relations between the two countries, there are various objects upon which I now proceed to request your attention.

The renewal of the war in Venezuela has been signalized, on the part of the Spanish commander, by proclamations of blockade unwarranted by the laws of nations, and by decrees regardless of those of humanity. With no other naval force than a single frigate, a brig, and a schooner, employed in transporting supplies from Curasao to Porto Cabello, they have presumed to declare a blockade of more than 1200 miles of coast. To this outrage upon all the rights of neutrality, they have added the absurd pretension of interdicting the peaceable commerce of other nations with *all* the ports of the Spanish main, upon the pretence that it had heretofore been forbidden by the Spanish colonial laws: and on the strength of these two inadmissible principles, they have issued commissions at Porto Cabello and in the island of Porto Rico, to a swarm of privateers, which have committed extensive and ruinous depredations upon the lawful commerce of the United States, as well as upon that of other nations, and particularly of Great Britain.

It was impossible that neutral nations should submit to such a system; the execution of which has been so strongly marked with violence and cruelty, as was its origin with injustice. Repeated remonstrances against it have been made to the Spanish government, and it became necessary to give the protection of our naval force to the commerce of the United States, exposed to these depredations.

By the act of Congress of 3 March, 1819, "to protect the commerce of the United States, and to punish the crime of piracy," the President was authorized to instruct the commanders of the public armed vessels of the United States, to take any armed vessel "which shall have attempted or committed any piratical aggression, search, restraint, depredation or seizure, upon any vessel of the United States, or of the citizens thereof, *or upon any other vessel*; and also to retake any vessel of the United States, or its citizens, which may have been *unlawfully* captured upon the high seas."

A copy of this act, and of the instructions from the Navy Department to the officers who have been charged with the execution of it, is herewith furnished you. The instructions will enable you to show how cautiously this government, while affording the protection due to the lawful commerce of the nation has guarded against the infringement of the rights of all others.

The privateers from Porto Rico and Porto Cabello have been by their conduct, distinguishable from pirates only by commissions of most equivocal character from Spanish officers, whose authority to issue them has never been shown: and they have committed outrages and depredations, which no commission could divest of the piratical character.

During the same period, swarms of pirates and of piratical vessels, without pretence or color of commission, have issued from the island of Cuba, and the immediate neighborhood of the Havana, differing so little in the composition of their crews and their conduct from the privateers of Porto Cabello and Porto Rico, as to leave little distinction other than that of being *disavowed*, between them. These piracies have now been for years continued, under the immediate observation of the government of the island of Cuba; which, as well as the Spanish government, has been repeatedly and ineffectually required to suppress them. Many of them have been committed by boats, within the very harbors, and close upon the shores, of the island. When pursued by superior force, the pirates have escaped to the shores: and twelve months have elapsed since the late Captain General Mahy refused to Captain Biddle the permission to land even upon the desert and uninhabited parts of the island, where they should seek refuge from his pursuit. Governor Mahy at the same time declared, that *he had* taken the necessary measures to defend his territorial jurisdiction, and for the apprehension of every description of outlaws.

Governor Mahy is since deceased; but neither the measures which he had then taken, nor any since adopted by the government of the island, have proved effectual to suppress, or in any manner even to restrain the pirates. From the most respectable testimony we are informed that these atrocious robberies are committed by persons well known, and that the traffic in their plunder is carried on with the utmost notoriety. They are some-times committed by vessels equipped as merchant vessels, and which clear out as such from the Havana. It has also been remarked, that they cautiously avoid molesting Spanish vessels, but attack without discrimination the defenceless vessels of all other nations. You will see, by a letter from Lieutenant Gregory to the Secretary of the Navy (p. 64 of the printed documents) that a large portion of the crews of the Porto Rico privateers consist of those same pirates from Cuba.

In November last a gallant officer of the navy, Lieutenant Allen, lost his life in a conflict with some of those pirates; and an armament was immediately fitted out, and is now on the spot, under the command of Commodore Porter for the defence and protection of our commerce against them. Notice was despatched of this movement to Mr. Forsyth, by a special messenger in January last; with instructions to him to require of the Spanish government the permission to land in case of necessity, in pursuit of the robbers. Copies of the instructions from the Secretary of the Navy are herewith furnished.

From this statement of facts it is apparent, that the naval officers of the United States who have been instructed to protect our commerce in that quarter, have been brought in conflict with two descriptions of *unlawful* captors of our merchant vessels; the acknowledged and disavowed pirates of Cuba, and the ostensibly commissioned privateers from Porto Rico and Porto Cabello; and that in both cases the actual depredations have been of the same class of Spanish subjects, and often probably the same persons. The consequence has been that several of the commissioned privateers have been taken by our cruisers; and that in one instance a merchant vessel belonging to the Havana, but charged upon oath of two persons as having been the vessel from which a vessel of the United States had been robbed, has been brought into port, and is now at Norfolk, to be tried at the next session of the District Court of the United States. In all these cases the Spanish minister, Anduaga, has addressed to this department complaints and remonstrances, in language so exceptionable, that it precluded the possibility of an amicable discussion of the subject with him. In some of the cases, explanations have been transmitted to Mr. Forsyth, to be given in a spirit of amity and conciliation to the Spanish government. But as your mission affords a favorable opportunity for a full and candid exposition of them all, copies of the correspondence with Mr. Anduaga relating to them are annexed to these instructions; to which I add, upon each case of complaint, the following remarks:

1. The first is the case of a man named Escandell, prize master of a Dutch vessel called the *Neptune*, taken by a privateer, armed in Porto Cabello, called the *Virgen del Carmen*, and retaken by the United States armed brig *Spark*, then commanded by Captain John H. Elton, since deceased. From the report of Captain Elton it appears: 1st. That the Dutch vessel had been taken within the territorial jurisdiction of the Dutch island of Curacao; 2ndly. That he, Captain Elton, delivered her up to the governor of the island of Amaba; 3dly. That he retook her as a vessel piratically captured, the prize master, Escandell, having produced to him no papers whatsoever. He therefore brought him and the prize crew to Charleston, S. C, where they were prosecuted as pirates.

Mr. Anduaga's first letter to me on this case was dated the 24th of July, 1822, enclosing a copy of a letter from Escandell to the Spanish Vice Consul at Charleston, invoking his protection; Escandell being then in prison, and under an indictment for piracy. He solicits the interposition of the Vice Consul, that he may obtain from the Captain General of the Havana, and the commanding officers at Porto Cabello, documents to prove that he was lawfully commissioned: and he alleges, that the captain of the privateer had furnished him with a *document*, to carry the prize into Porto Cabello; that he did deliver this document to Captain Elton, who *concealed* it from the court at Charleston; that Elton and his officers well know that he, Escandell, was commissioned by the King of Spain, and had assisted at the disembarking of General La Torre, with the privateer and the prize; but that Elton had withheld his knowledge of these facts from the grand jury. Mr. Anduaga's letter to me noticed this contradiction between the statement of Captain Elton and the declaration of Escandell; and requested that the trial at Charleston might be postponed, till he could receive answers from the Captain General of the Havana, and the Commandant of Porto Cabello, to whom he had written to obtain the documents necessary to prove the legality of the capture. This was accordingly done.

The letter of Mr. Anduaga was unexceptionable in its purport; but on the 17th of October he addressed me a second enclosing the papers he had received from Porto Cabello, and assuming a style of vituperation, not only against Captain Elton, then very recently dead, but against the navy in general, the government, and even the people of the United States, which required the exertion of some forbearance to avoid sending it back to him, as unsuitable to be received at this Department from a foreign minister.

It was the more unwarrantable, because while assuming as proved against an officer of the United States, no longer living to justify himself, that he had *concealed* documents furnished him by Escandell, he declares it "evident, that, not the public service, but avarice, and the atrocious desire of sacrificing upon a gibbet the lives of some innocent citizens of a friendly power, were the moving principles of this commander's conduct." To those who personally knew Captain Elton, what language could reply in terms of indignation adequate to the unworthiness of this charge? And how shall I now express a suitable sense of it, when I say that it was advanced without a shadow of proof, upon the mere original assertion of Escandell, made in the most suspicious manner, and which the very documents from Porto Cabello tended rather to disprove than to sustain!

It was made I say in the most suspicious manner. For in his affidavit before the clerk of the United States court at Charleston, made on the 8th of June, 1822, where he might have been confronted by Captain Elton and the officers of the *Spark*, Escandell had not even hinted at this concealment of his papers by Captain Elton, or pretended that he had produced any to him. But *after* he had been arraigned upon the indictment, and after the court had, at the motion of his counsel, postponed his trial to the next term, for the express purpose of giving him time to obtain proof that he had been commissioned; in a secret letter to Casteo, the owner of the privateer at Porto Cabello, and in another to the Spanish Vice Consul at Charleston, he makes these scandalous allegations against Captain Elton, at times and places where he could not be present to refute them.

That the documents from Porto Bello, transmitted to Mr. Anduaga, tended rather to disprove than to sustain them, you will perceive by an examination of the translations of them, herewith furnished you. The only documents among them showing the authority under which Escandell, when captured by Captain Elton, had possession of the *Neptune*, is a copy of the commission of the privateer, *Virgen del Carmen*, which had taken the *Neptune*, and a declaration by the Captain of the privateer, *Lorenzo Puyol*, that on capturing the *Neptune*, he had put Escandell as prize master, and six men on board of her, ordering her into the port of Porto Cabello, and furnishing Escandell *with the documents necessary for his voyage*. No copy of these documents is produced; and the declaration of this Captain Puyol, himself, is signed only with a cross, he not knowing how to write his name.

It is conceived that the only admissible evidence of Escandell's regular authority as prize master of a captured vessel, would have been an authenticated copy of the document itself furnished him by Puyol. The extreme ignorance of this man, who appears on the face of his own declaration unable to write his own name, raises more than a presumption that he knew as little what could be a regular document for a prize master; and is by no means calculated to give confidence to his declaration as a substitute for the authentic copy of the document itself. The absurdity of the imputation of avaricious motives to Captain Elton is demonstrated by the fact, that he delivered up the prize, which was a

Dutch vessel, to the governor of Amaba, and to her original captain: and as to that of his having concealed Escandell's papers, to bring him and six innocent seamen to the gibbet, I can even now notice it only to leave to the candor of the Spanish government whether it ought ever to be answered.

Copies are herewith furnished of Captain Elton's report of this transaction to the Secretary of the Navy; of the agreement by which the *Neptune* was by him delivered up to the Dutch commandant at the island of Arnba Thielen; and of the receipt given by her original Captain Reynar Romer, to whom she was restored. In these documents you will see it is expressly stipulated both by the Dutch commandant and by Captain Romer, that the "vessel and cargo, or the value thereof, should be returned to any legal authority of the United States of America, or to the Spanish government, or prize claimants, *in due course of the laws of nations.*" You will find also that in the document signed by Captain Romer, he expressly declares that the persons by whom he had been captured, *purported* to belong to a Spanish felucca privateer; but *not having any credentials or authority* to cruise upon the high seas with them, *he supposes them to have been pirates.*

This declaration of Romer himself is directly contradictory to the assertion which Escandell in his affidavit at Charleston, on the 8th of June, 1822, pretends that Captain Romer made to the boarding officer from the *Spark*, in answer to his inquiries whether Escandell and his men were pirates. Escandell says that Romer answered they were *not*. Romer himself says that he supposed they were.

You will remark that in the copy of Escandell's affidavit, transmitted by Mr. Anduaga to the Department of State, the name of the Dutch captain of the *Neptune* is written Reinas Buman, apparent by a mistake in the copy. The name as signed by himself is Reynar Romer.

On a review of the whole transaction as demonstrated by these documents, it will be seen that the conduct of Captain Elton was fair, honorable, cautiously regardful of the possible rights of the captors and Spanish government, and eminently disinterested. He retook the *Neptune*, a Dutch vessel, at the request of an officer of the Dutch government. He had already known and protected her as a neutral before. He restored her to her captain without claiming salvage, and upon the sole condition that the Dutch governor should restore to their owners, citizens of the United States, the proceeds of a vessel and cargo, also wrongfully captured by a Spanish privateer, and which had been brought within her jurisdiction. And he provided that if the capture of the *Neptune* should eventually prove to have been lawfully made, the Dutch commandant and the captain of the *Neptune* himself should be responsible to the Spanish and American governments and to the captors for the result.

I have entered into this detail of the evidence in this case, not only to give you the means of satisfying the Spanish government that the complaints of Mr. Anduaga against Captain Elton were as groundless in substance as they were unjust to him, and disrespectful to this government and nation in form; but to vindicate from unmerited reproach the memory of a gallant officer, of whose faithful and valuable services his country had been deprived by death, only twenty days before those dishonorable imputations were cast upon him by Mr. Anduaga.

The harshness and precipitation of that minister's judgment in preferring this complaint is the more remarkable, inasmuch as he avows in that very note the opinion that the bare word, without proof, of a *merchant* captain, is not evidence sufficient to furnish even a pretext to the naval officers of the United States to attack the armed vessel, by which he had been plundered. If the word of a captain of a merchant vessel, supported by his oath, were of such trivial account, of what weight in the scale of testimony is the bare word of a captain of a privateer, who cannot write his name, to prove the existence and authority of a written or printed document, pretended to have been given by himself?

If the capture of the *Neptune* by Puyol had been lawful, her owners would at this day possess the means of recovering indemnity for their loss by the recapture, in the written engagements of the Dutch commandant, Thieleman, and of Captain Romer. But it was not lawful. By the documents transmitted by Mr. Anduaga it appears, that a part of the cargo of the Neptune, after her capture by the *Virgen del Carmen*, had been transshipped to another vessel; and that at Porto Cabello it was condemned by Captain Lavorde, commander of the Spanish frigate *Ligera*, who had issued the privateer's commission, and then sat as judge of the Admiralty Court upon the prize. And the sole ground of condemnation assigned is the breach of the pretended blockade by the *Neptune*, and her *trading* with the independent patriots. You will remark the great irregularity and incompatibility with the principles of general justice, as well as of the Spanish constitution, that one and the same person should be acting at once in the capacity of a naval officer, of a magistrate issuing commissions to privateers, and of a judge to decide upon the prizes taken by them. But the whole foundation of his decision is a nullity. The blockade was a public wrong. The interdiction of all trade was an outrage upon the rights of *all* neutral nations. And the resort to the two expedients bears on its face the demonstration, that they who assumed them both had no reliance upon the justice of either: for if the interdiction of all *neutral* trade with the independents were lawful, there could be as little occasion or pretence for the interdiction of the trade. The correctness of this reasoning can no longer be contested by the Spanish government itself. The blockade and interdiction of trade have, from the first notice of them, not only been denounced and protested against by the government and officers of the United States, but by those of Great Britain, even when the ally of Spain, and who has not yet acknowledged the independence of the revolted colonies. The consequences of these pretensions have been still more serious to Spain; since they terminated in a formal notification by the British government, that they had issued orders of reprisal to their squadrons in the West Indies, to capture all Spanish vessels, until satisfaction should be made for the property of all British subjects, taken or detained under color of this preposterous blockade and interdiction. And Spain has formally pledged herself to make this demanded reparation.

2. The second case of complaint by Mr. Anduaga, upon which I have to animadvert, is that of the capture of the Porto Rico privateer *Palmira*, by the United States armed schooner *Grampus*, Lieutenant Gregory commander. With his letter of the nth of October, 1822, Mr. Anduaga transmitted copies of a letter from the captain of the privateer, *Escurra*, to the Spanish consul at Charleston, dated the 16th of September, 1822, and of sundry depositions taken at Porto Rico, from seamen who had belonged to her, relating to the capture. The account of the transaction given by Lieutenant Gregory is among the documents to be transmitted to Congress with the President's message at the commencement of the last session, pp. 62, 63, 64, to which I refer.

The subject is yet before the competent judicial tribunal of this country. The captain and seamen of the *Palmira*, with the exception of those charged with the robbery of the *Coquette*, were discharged by a decree of the District Court of the United States at Charleston, and the vessel was restored to her captain; but the judge (Drayton, since deceased,) in giving this decree declared that Lieutenant Gregory had been fully justified in the capture. By a decree of the Circuit Court of the same district, heavy damages were awarded against Lieutenant Gregory, from which sentence there is an appeal pending before the Supreme Judicial Court of the United States. Whatever their final decision may be, the character of the court is a sure warrant that it will be given with every regard due to the rights and interests of all the parties concerned, and the most perfect reliance may be placed upon its justice, impartiality, and independence.

The decision of the Circuit Court indeed would imply some censure upon the conduct of Lieutenant Gregory, and may be represented as giving support to the complaints of the Spanish minister against him. But it is the opinion of a single judge, indirect opposition to that of his colleague on the same bench, and liable to the revisal and correction of the supreme tribunal. It is marked by two principles, upon which it may be fairly presumed the judgment of the Supreme Court will be more in accord with that of the District. The justification of Lieutenant Gregory, for taking and sending in the *Palmira*, rests upon two important facts; first, the robbery committed by part of her crew, sworn to by Captain Souther of the schooner *Coquette*, and confirmed by the oaths of her mate and two of her seamen; and secondly, that at the time of her capture she had commenced the firing upon the *Grampus*, by a full volley from small arms and cannon. But as the fact of the robbery from the *Coquette* was not in rigorously judicial evidence before the Circuit Court, the judge declared, that although he had no doubt the fact was true, yet in the absence of the evidence to prove it he must *officially* decide that it was false; and as to the circumstance of the first fire, as the Spanish and American testimony were in contradiction to each other, he should set them both aside, and form his decision upon other principles. If indeed Lieutenant Gregory is ultimately to be deprived of the benefit of these two facts, he will be left *judicially* without justification. But considered with reference to the discharge of his duty as an officer of the United States, if the declaration of Captain Souther taken upon oath, confirmed by those of his mate and two of his men, was not competent testimony upon which he was bound to act, upon what evidence could an officer of the navy ever dare to execute his instructions and the law, by rescuing or protecting from the robbers of the sea, the property of his fellow citizens?

The robbery of the *Coquette* by the boats' crew from the *Palmira* is assuredly sufficiently proved for all other than judicial purposes, by the fact which was in evidence before the District Court, that the memorandum book sworn by John Peabody, junior, mate of the *Coquette*, to have been taken from him together with clothing, was actually found in a bag with clothing on board the *Palmira*.

In answering Mr. Anduaga's letter of 11 October, I transmitted to him a copy of the printed decree of Judge Drayton, in which the most material facts relating to the case, and the principles applicable to it upon which his decision was given, are set forth. Some additional facts are disclosed in a statement published by Lieutenant Gregory, highly important to *this* discussion, inasmuch as they identify a portion of the crew of the *Palmira*, with a gang of the Cape Antonio pirates, and with an establishment of the same character which had before been broken up by that officer.

In a long and elaborate reply to my letter dated the 11th of December, 1822, Mr. Anduaga, without contesting the fact that the *Coquette* had been robbed by the boarding crew from the *Palmira*, objects to the decision of Judge Drayton, as if, by detaining for trial the individual seamen belonging to the *Palmira*, charged with the robbery, it assumed a jurisdiction, disclaimed by any acknowledgment that the privateer was lawfully commissioned, and sanctioned the right of search, so long and so strenuously resisted by the American government. In this reply, too, Mr. Anduaga attempts by laborious arguments to maintain to the fullest and most unqualified extent the right of the Spanish privateers to capture, and of the Spanish prize courts to condemn, all vessels of every other nation, trading with any of the ports of the independent patriots of South America, because under the old colonial laws of Spain that trade had been prohibited. And with the consistency of candor at least, he explicitly says that the decrees issued by the Spanish commanders on the main, under the name of blockades, were not properly so called, but were mere enforcements of the antediluvian colonial exclusions, and such were the instructions under which the *Palmira*, and all the other privateers from Porto Rico and Porto Cabello have been cruising. Is it surprising that the final answer of Great Britain to this pretension was an order of *reprisals*? or that under the laws of the United States it has brought their naval officers in conflict of actual hostility with privateers so commissioned and so instructed? The

Spanish government have for many years had notice, both from Great Britain and from the United States, that they considered as rightful the peaceful commerce of their people, with the ports in possession of the independent patriots. Spain herself has opened most of those of which her forces have been able to retain or to recover the possession. The blockades proclaimed by General Morillo in 1815 were coupled with this same absurd pretension: they were formally protested against by the government of the United States; and wherever Morillo obtained possession, he himself immediately opened the port to foreign and neutral commerce.

Mr. Anduaga seems to have had much confidence in the conclusiveness of his reasoning, in this letter of 11 December: for without considering the character of our institutions, which have committed to the executive authority all communications with the ministers of foreign powers, he permitted himself the request that the President would communicate it to Congress; without having the apology for this indiscretion, which on a prior occasion he had alleged for a like request, namely, that it was in answer to letters from this Department which *had* been communicated to the legislature. In the former case he was indulged by compliance with his request. In the latter it was passed over without notice. But Mr. Anduaga was determined that his argument should come before the public, and sent a copy of it to the Havana, where it was published in the newspapers; whence it has been translated and inserted in some of our public journals.

The British order of reprisals; the appropriation by the Cortes of forty millions of reals for reparation to British subjects, of damages sustained by them, in part from capture and condemnation of their property under this absurd pretension; and the formal revocation by the king of Spain of these unlawful blockades, will, it is presumed, supersede the necessity of a serious argument in reply to that of Mr. Anduaga upon this point. It is in vain for Spain to pretend that during the existence of a civil war, in which by the universal law of nations, both parties have equal rights with reference to foreign nations, she can enforce against all neutrals by the seizure and condemnation of their property, the laws of colonial monopoly and prohibition, by which they had been excluded from commercial intercourse with the colonies before the existence of the war, and when her possession and authority were alike undisputed. And if at any stage of the war, this pretension could have been advanced with any color of reason, it was preeminently nugatory on the renewal of the war, after the formal treaty between Morillo and Bolivar, and the express stipulation which it contained, that if the war should be renewed, it should be conducted on the principles applicable to wars between independent nations; and not on the disgusting and sanguinary doctrine of suppressing rebellion.

As little foundation is there for the inference drawn by Mr. Anduaga from the decree of the District judge, admitting the *Palmira* to have been lawfully commissioned as a privateer, but detaining for trial the portion of her crew charged with the robbery from the *Coquette*, that it sanctions the right of search, against which the United States have so long and so constantly protested. For in the first place, the United States have never disputed the belligerent right of search as required and universally practised conformably to the laws of nations. They have disputed the right of belligerents under *color* of the right of search for contraband of war, to seize and carry away *men*, at the discretion of the boarding officer, without trial and without appeal; men, not as contraband of war, or belonging to the enemy, but as subjects, real or pretended, of the belligerent himself, and to be used by him against his enemy. It is the fundamental abuse of the right of search, for purposes never recognized or admitted by the laws of nations, purposes in their practical operation of the greatest oppression and most crying in justice, that the United States have resisted and will resist, and which warns them against assenting to the extension in time of peace of a right which experience has shown to be liable to such gross perversion in time of war. And secondly the *Palmira* was taken for acts of piratical aggression and *depredation* upon a vessel of the United States, and upon the property of their citizens. Acts of *piratical* aggression and depredation may be committed by vessels having lawful commissions as privateers, and many such had been committed by the *Palmira*. The act of robbery from the *Coquette* was in every respect piratical; for it was committed while the privateer was under the Venezuelan flag, and under that flag she had fired upon the *Coquette* and brought her to. It was piratical, therefore, not only as depredation of the property by the boat's crew who took it away, but as aggression under the sanction of the captain of the privateer, who was exercising belligerent rights under false colors. To combat under any other flag than that of the nation by which she is commissioned, by the laws of nations subjects a vessel, though lawfully commissioned, to seizure and condemnation as a pirate; and although the decree of the District judge ordered the restitution of the vessel to her captain, because it held him to have been lawfully commissioned, neither did the law of nations require, nor would the law of the United States permit, that men, brought within the jurisdiction of the court, and charged with piratical depredations upon citizens of the United States, should be discharged and turned over to a foreign tribunal for trial, as was demanded by Mr. Anduaga. They had been brought within the jurisdiction of the court, not by the exercise of any right of search, but as part of the crew of a vessel which had committed piratical depredations and aggressions upon vessels and citizens of the United States. The District Court adjudging the commission of the privateer to have been lawful, and considering the gun fired under the Venezuelan flag to bring the *Coquette* to, though wrongful and unwarrantable, as not amounting rigorously to that *combat*, which would have been complete piracy, discharged the captain and portion of the crew which had not been guilty of the robbery of the *Coquette*, but reserved for trial the individuals charged with that act.

The conduct of the *Palmira*, for months before her capture, had been notoriously and flagrantly piratical. She had in company with another privateer, named the *Boves*, both commanded by the same captain, Pablo Llanger, fired upon the United States schooner *Porpoise*, Captain Ramage, who abstained from returning the fire. For this act of unequivocal hostility, Captain Llanger's only apology to Captain Ramage was that he had taken the *Porpoise* for a patriot cruiser. Numbers of neutral vessels of different nations had been plundered by her; and among the affidavits made to Lieutenant Gregory at St. Thomas, was one of the master and mate of a French schooner, that she had been robbed by a boat's crew from her of a barrel of beef and a barrel of rice. In the letter from Captain Escurra to the Spanish consul at Charleston, he admits the taking of these provisions, alleging that the master of the French vessel gave them to him at his own request. The affidavit of the French master and mate shows what sort of a *gift* it was, and is more coincident with all the other transactions of this privateer.

In the same letter of 11 December, Mr. Anduaga with more ingenuity than candor, attempts at once to raise a wall of separation between the pirates of Cuba, and the privateersmen of Porto Rico and Porto Cabello, and to identify the pirates, not only with all those who at a prior period, had abused the several independent flags of South America, but with the adventurers from the United States who at different times have engaged in the patriot service; and he endeavors to blend them all with the foolish expedition of last summer against Porto Rico. While indulging his propensity to complain, he revives all the long exploded and groundless charges of his predecessors in former years, and does not scruple to insinuate that the Cuba pirates themselves are North Americans from the United States.

It is easy to discern and point out the fallacy of these endeavors to blend together things totally distinct, and to discriminate between things that are identical. It is in proof before our tribunals in the case of the *Palmira* itself that some of the pirates of Cuba and of the Porto Rico privateersmen, are the same. Among the Cuba pirates that have been taken, as well by the vessels of the

United States as by British cruisers, *not one* North American has been found. A number of those pirates have been executed at the Bahama Islands, and ten from one vessel at the island of Jamaica, all Spanish subjects, and from the Spanish islands. Not a shadow of evidence has been seen that among the Cuba pirates a single citizen of the United States was to be found.

As to the complaints of Mr. Anduaga's predecessors, meaning those of Don Luis de Onis, it might have been expected that we should hear no more of them after the ratification of the treaty of 1819. Whatever had been the merits of those complaints, full satisfaction for them all had been made by that treaty to Spain, and was acknowledged by the ratification of the Spanish government in October, 1820. Since that time no complaints had been made by Mr. Anduaga's predecessors. It was reserved for him, as well to call up those phantoms from the dead, as to conjure new ones from the living. That supplies of every kind, including arms, and other implements of war have been in the way of lawful commerce procured within the United States for the account of the South America independents, and at their expense and hazard exported to them is doubtless true. And Spain has enjoyed and availed herself of the same advantages.

The neutrality of the United States has throughout this contest between Spain and South America been cautiously and faithfully observed by their government. But the complaints of Mr. Anduaga, as well as those of his predecessor, Mr. Onis, are founded upon erroneous views and mistaken principles of neutrality. They assume that all *commerce*, even the most peaceful commerce of other nations, with the South Americans is a violation of neutrality; and while they assert this in principle, the Spanish commanders, in the few places where they yet hold authority, attempt to carry it into effect in a spirit worthy of itself. The decree of General Morales of the 15th of September, 1822, is in perfect accord with the argument of Mr. Anduaga, on the 11th of December of the same year. The unconcerted but concurring solemn protests against the former; of the Dutch governor of Curacao,

Cantzlaer; of the British admiral Rowley, and of our own Captain Spencer, was but the chorus of all human feeling revolting at the acts of which Mr. Anduaga's reasoning was the attempted justification.

3. The next case of Complaint by Mr. Anduaga is in a letter of the 23d of February last, against Lieutenant Wilkinson, commander of the United States armed schooner *Spark*, for capturing off the Havana a vessel called the *Ninfa Catalana*, or the *Santissima Trinidad*, Nicholas Garyole master, and sending her into Norfolk. As there are reasons for believing that in this case Lieutenant Wilkinson acted upon erroneous information, a court of inquiry has been ordered upon his conduct, the result of which will be communicated to you.

The *Ninfa Catalana* remains for trial at the District Court to be held in the Eastern District of Virginia in the course of the next month. Immediately after receiving Mr. Anduaga's letter on the subject, I wrote to the attorney of the United States for the District instructing him to obtain, if possible, an extraordinary session of the court, that the cause might be decided without delay; but the judge declined appointing such session, unless all the witnesses summoned to the court upon the case could be notified of it, which not being practicable, the short delay till the meeting of the regular session of the court has been unavoidable. You will assure the Spanish government that the most impartial justice will be rendered to all the parties concerned, as well by the adjudication of the Admiralty Court as by the military enquiry on the conduct of Lieutenant Wilkinson. I ought to add that no evidence hitherto has come to the knowledge of the government which has implicated the correctness of Lieutenant Wilkinson's intentions, or manifested any other motive than that of discharging his duty and protecting the property of his fellow citizens.

4. The capture of the Spanish schooner *Carmen* alias *Gallega the Third* by the United States sloop of war *Peacock*, Captain Cassin, has furnished the fourth occasion for this class of Mr. Anduaga's remonstrances.

There are two declarations or depositions made by the captain and persons who were on board of this vessel at the time of her capture, one at Pensacola and the other at New Orleans. The first before the notary José Ecaro, by Jacinto Correa, Captain of the *Gallega*, the pilot Ramon Echaverria, boatswain Manuel Agacis, three sailors, and Juan Martin Ferreyro, a passenger. All the witnesses after the first only confirm in general and unqualified terms *all* his statements; although many of the circumstances asserted by him as facts could not have been personally known to himself, but by hearing from some of them. The protest for example avers that when first captured by the *Peacock*, Captain Correa, with his steward and cook were taken on board that vessel; and while they were there he represents various disorders to have been committed on board of his own vessel, by the boarding officer from the *Peacock*, though by his own showing he was not present to witness them. His whole narrative is composed of alleged occurrences on board of three vessels, the *Peacock*, the *Louisiana* cutter, and the *Gallega*, and no discrimination is made between those of his own knowledge, and those which he had heard from others. The second declaration was made before Antonio Argote Villalobos, Spanish consul at New Orleans, only by Captain Correa and Echaverria the mate, and gives an account of several other Spanish vessels, captured by the *Peacock*, while they were on board of that vessel as prisoners. A very inadequate reason is assigned by Captain Correa for not having made it at the same time with the first at Pensacola; and the whole purport of it is to represent those *other* vessels which he had seen captured, as inoffensive unarmed vessels, and the capture of them by the *Peacock* as itself piratical.

Copies of the proceedings in the courts at Pensacola and at New Orleans upon these cases are expected at this Department, and the substance of them will be duly communicated to you. In the meantime the reports of Captain Cassin of the *Peacock*, and of Captain Jackson, commander of the revenue cutter *Louisiana* to the Navy Department, will give you a very different, and doubtless more correct account of these transactions.

There is strong reason for believing that the *Gallega* did actually belong to the gang of pirates, of which those pretended inoffensive and unarmed vessels certainly formed a part. That Correa and Echaverria were testifying in behalf of their accomplices; and their warm sympathy with those convicted pirates is much more indicative of their own guilt than of their belief in the innocence of the others.

That the *other* vessels were piratical, is no longer a subject of question or dispute. Two of them were carried by Captain Cassin to the Havana, where one of them, a schooner of nine guns, was claimed by a lady, widow of a merchant in that city, as her property; and at her application, supported by that of the captain, general, was restored to her upon payment of $1000 salvage. The part of the cargo which had been saved was sold in like manner, with the approbation of the Captain General. The vessel had been taken by the pirates but a few days before, and in retaking and restoring her to the owner, Captain Cassin had not only rendered an important service to a Spanish subject, but taken from the pirates the means of committing more extensive and atrocious depredations.

Among the articles found on board of these vessels were some of female apparel, rent and blood-stained; and many other traces to deeds of horror, with which these desperate wretches are known to be familiar. The pirates had, when close pursued abandoned their vessels and escaped to the shore. They were pursued, but not discovered. The coffee was hidden in the woods, and with the vessel brought into New Orleans, had been regularly condemned by the sentence of the court.

And these are the characters, and this the description of people whom Captain Correa and his mate, Echaverria, represent in their declaration before the Spanish consul at New Orleans, as innocent Spanish subjects piratically plundered of their lawful property, by Captain Cassin. And upon such testimony as this has Mr. Anduaga suffered himself to be instigated to a style of invective and reproach not only against that officer, but against the officers of our navy generally, against the government and people of this country, upon which, while pointing it out and marking its contrast with the real facts of the case, I forbear all further comment.

Let it be admitted that the *Catalan Nymph* and the *Gallega* were lawful traders, and that in capturing them as pirates Lieutenant Wilkinson and Captain Cassin have been mistaken. That they had probable cause sufficient for their justification I cannot doubt, and am persuaded will upon a full investigation of the cases be made apparent.

In the impartial consideration of this subject it is necessary to advert to the *character* of these pirates, and to the circumstances which have made it so difficult to distinguish between lawfully commissioned and registered Spanish vessels and the pirates.

The first of these has been the unlawful extent given to the commissions and instructions of the privateers avowed by the Spanish government; an authority to take all commercial vessels bound to any of the ports in possession of the patriots. The very assumption of this principle, and the countenance given to it by the adjudications of the courts was enough to kindle all the passions of lawless rapine in the maritime population of the islands. It was holding out to them the whole commerce of the neutral world as lawful prey.

The next is the impunity with which those robberies have been committed in the very port of the Havana, and under the eye of the local government. It is represented and believed to be true that many inhabitants of the city, merchants in respectable standing of society, are actively concerned in these transactions; that of the village of Regla opposite the city, almost all the inhabitants are with public notoriety concerned in them; that some of the deepest criminals are known and pointed at; while the vigilance or energy of the government is so deficient that there is an open market for the sale of those fruits of robbery; and that threats of vengeance are heard from the most abandoned of the culprits against all who molest them in their nefarious and bloody career.

The third is that many of the piracies have been committed by merchant vessels, laden with cargoes. The Spanish vessels of that description in the islands are all armed, and, when taken by the pirates, are immediately converted to their own purposes. The schooner of nine guns taken by Captain Cassin, and restored to its owner in the Havana, affords one proof of this fact; and one of the most atrocious piracies committed upon citizens of the United States was that upon the *Lady's Delight* by the *Zaragosana*, a vessel regularly cleared at the Havana as a merchant vessel.

There are herewith furnished you copies of the general instructions from the Secretary of the Navy, given to all our naval officers, successively stationed in those seas, for the protection of our commerce and for carrying into effect the laws against piracy and the slave trade, together with printed copies of those laws. They will enable you to present to the Spanish government the most conclusive proof of the friendly sentiments towards Spain, and of the undeviating regard to her rights which have constantly animated this government, and effectually to counteract any representations of a different character which may be made by Mr. Anduaga.

In reflecting upon the conduct of this minister during his residence in the United States, it has been impossible to avoid the suspicion that it has been instigated by a disposition not more friendly to the existing liberal institutions of his own country, than to the harmonious intercourse to which they were so well calculated to contribute between the United States and Spain. From the time of the reestablishment in Spain of a constitutional government, the sympathies of this country have been warm, earnest and unanimous in favor of her freedom and independence. The principles which she asserts and maintains are emphatically ours, and in the conflict with which she is now threatened, for supporting them, a cordial good understanding with us was as obviously the dictate of her policy, as it was the leading principle of ours. This national sentiment has not been silent or unobserved. It was embodied and expressed in the most public and solemn manner in the message to Congress at the commencement of their last session, as will be within your recollection. The conduct of the government has been invariably conformable to it. The recognition of the South American governments, flowing from the same principle which enlisted all our feelings in the cause of Spain, has been in its effects a mere formality; it has in no wise changed our actual relations, either with them or with Spain. All the European powers, even those which have hitherto most strenuously denied the recognition in *form*, have treated and will treat the South Americans as independent in fact. By his protest against the formal acknowledgment Mr. Anduaga had fulfilled his duties to his own government, nor has any one circumstance arisen from that event which could require of him to recur to it as a subject of difference between us and Spain again. We have not been disposed to complain of his protest, nor even of his permanent residence at a distance from the seat of government; but the avidity with which he has seized upon every incident which could cause unpleasant feelings between the two countries, the bitterness with which his continual notes have endeavored to exasperate and envenom, the misrepresentations of others, which he has so precipitously assumed as undeniable facts, and the language in which he has vented his reproaches upon the fair and honorable characters of our naval officers, upon the government, and even the people of this Union, and above all, the artifice by which he suffered the absurd and ridiculous expedition of De Coudray Holstein to obtain some paltry supplies of men and arms in this country, without giving notice of it to this government, when they might have effectually broken it up, leaving it unknown to us till after its inevitable failure, when he could trump it up as a premeditated hostility of ours against Spain, and a profligate project of invasion of her possessions, are indications of a temper which we can trace to no source, either of friendly feeling towards our country, or of patriotic devotion to his own. It has the aspect of a deliberate purpose to stir up and inflame dissensions between the United States and Spain; to produce and cherish every means of alienation and distrust between them, with ultimate views to the counteraction of these differences upon the internal administration and government of his own nation.

It is hoped that he will in no event be permitted to return hither; and in the full and just explanations which you will now be enabled to give upon every complaint exhibited by him while here, the Spanish government will be satisfied with the justice, and convinced of the friendly disposition towards Spain, which have governed all our conduct.

With the same spirit, and the just expectation that it will be met with a reciprocal return, you will represent to them the claim of all the citizens of the United States, whose vessels and other property have been captured by the privateers from Porto Rico and Porto Cabello, and condemned by the courts of those places, for supposed breaches of the pretended blockade, or for *trading* with the South American independents. Restitution or indemnity is due to them all; and is immediately due by the Spanish government, inasmuch as those injuries having been sanctioned by the local authorities, military and civil, the sufferers in most of the cases can have no resort to the individuals by whom the captures were made. A list of all the cases which have come yet to the knowledge of this Department is now enclosed. There are probably many others. An agent will be shortly sent to collect at the respective places the evidence in all the cases not already known, and to obtain as far as may be practicable restitution by the local authorities. Whatever may be restored by them will diminish by so much the amount of claim upon the Spanish government, which will be the more indisputable, as they have already admitted the justice, and made provision for the satisfaction of claims of British subjects, which sprung from the same cause.

Of the formal revocation by the Spanish government of the nominal blockade, the governor of Porto Rico has given express notice to Commodore Porter. As a consequence of this it is hoped that no more commissions for privateers will be issued. The revocation did indeed come at a critical time, for it cannot be too strongly impressed upon the Spanish government, that all the causes of complaint, both by Spanish subjects against the navy officers of the United States, and by the citizens of the United States, with which you are now charged, proceeded directly or as a consequence from those spurious blockades. They were in violation of the laws of nations. They were in conflict with the law of Congress for protecting the commerce of the United States. It was impossible that ships of war of the United States, with commanders instructed to carry that law into execution, and Spanish privateers, commissioned and instructed to carry into effect the atrocious decree of General Morales, should meet and fulfil their respective instructions without hostile collision. The decree of General Morales constituted all these Spanish subjects who acted under it in a state of war *de facto* with all neutral nations; and on the sea it was a war of extermination against all neutral commerce. It is to the responsibility of her own officers, therefore, that Spain must look for indemnity to the wrongs endured by her own subjects, as necessary consequences of their official acts, as well as for the source of her obligation to indemnify all the innocent sufferers under them, who are entitled to the protection of other nations.

You will take an immediate opportunity after your reception to urge upon the Spanish government, the absolute necessity of a more vigorous and energetic exercise of the local authorities in the island of Cuba, for the suppression of the piracies by which it is yet infested. Their professions of coöperation with the naval force of the United States to this object have not been followed up by corresponding action. As long since as last May, Captain Biddle, then commanding the *Macedonian* frigate, represented to the Captain General, Mahy, the necessity that would frequently arise of pursuing them from their boats to the shores on the desert and uninhabited parts of the island, and requested permission to land for such purpose, which was explicitly refused. Mr. Forsyth has been instructed to renew the demand of this permission, to the Spanish government itself, and as there are cases in which the necessity will constitute the right of anticipating that permission, Commodore Porter has been instructed accordingly. From a recent debate in the British Parliament it appears that similar instructions have been given to the commanders of the British squadrons, despatched for the protection of the commerce of that nation, and that when notified to the Spanish government, although at first resisted by them, they finally obtained their acquiescence. These circumstances will serve for answer to one of the most aggravated complaints of Mr. Anduaga against Captain Cassin. That officer did land, and although not successful in overtaking the pirates themselves, he did break up one of the deposits of their lawless plunder, burnt several of their boats, and took from them two of their armed vessels. Mr. Anduaga sees in all this nothing but a *violation of his Catholic Majesty's territory*; a sentiment on such an occasion which would be more suitable for an accessary to the pirates, than for the officer of a government deeply and earnestly intent upon their suppression.

From the highly esteemed and honorable character of General Vivés, who has probably before this arrived at the Havana, as Governor and Captain General of the island, we hope for more effectual cooperation to this most desirable event. There has been according to every account a laxity and remissness on that subject in the executive authority of that port, which we hope will no longer be seen. The boldness and notoriety with which crimes of such desperate die are committed in the very face of authority is of itself irrefragable proof of its own imbecility or weakness. Spain must be sensible that she is answerable to the world for the repression of crimes committed within her jurisdiction, and of which the people of other nations are almost exclusively the victims. The pirates have generally, though not universally, abstained from annoying Spanish subjects, and from the robbery of Spanish property. It is surely within the competency of the government of Cuba to put down that open market of the pirates which has so long been denounced at the Havana. It appears that masters of American vessels which had been robbed have seen their own property openly exposed to sale in that city; but have been dissuaded from reclaiming it by the warning that it would expose them to the danger of assassination. One instance at least has occurred of unpunished murder of a citizen of the United States, for the indiscreet expression of his expectation that the arrival of Commodore Porter's squadron would secure more respect to the persons and property of American citizens; and other cases have happened of outrages upon citizens of the United States, in which the protecting power of the government has been deficient at least in promptitude and vigor.

To the irritation between the people of the two nations, produced by the consequences of the abominable decree of General Morales, must be attributed that base and dastardly spirit of revenge which recently actuated a Spanish subaltern officer at Porto Rico, by which Lieutenant Cocke lost his life. Copies of the correspondence between Commodore Porter and the governor of Porto Rico on that occasion are among the enclosed papers. They will show that the act of firing upon the *Fox* was utterly wanton and inexcusable, and the President desires that you would expressly demand that the officer by whom it was ordered should be brought to trial and punishment for having ordered it.

There are several subjects connected with the execution of the treaty of 22 February, 1819, upon which it may be proper to advert as being likely to claim your attention. On the delivery of the two provinces of the Floridas to the United States, by virtue of stipulations of that treaty, a question arose, whether under the term *fortifications,* which were to be delivered over, with them was included the artillery, without which they could not with propriety bear the name. By another article of the treaty it was agreed that the United States should furnish *transports* for the conveyance of the Spanish officers and troops to the Havana.

Under this engagement the Spanish officers understood it was *implied* that the *provisions* necessary for the passage should also be furnished at the expense of the United States. In this liberal construction of that article this government acquiesced, insisting however that on that same principle provisions for the passage would be understood as implied in an engagement to supply the passage itself, the ordnance which constituted the essential part of the fortifications must be considered as embraced by the word, and that the United States were entitled to claim its delivery with the buildings, which without it would substantially be no fortifications at all. The Spanish officers at Pensacola and St. Augustine objected to this liberal construction of the article which imposed an obligation upon Spain, while they insisted upon it with regard to the article in her favor. It was therefore agreed, both at Pensacola and St. Augustine, that the artillery in the forts should be left there; receipts for it being given by General Jackson and Colonel Butler, leaving the question as to the property in them to the determination of the two governments. A correspondence ensued between this Department and the Spanish legation here, and between the Ministers of Foreign Affairs and our legation at Madrid, the last document of which is a note of 3 September, 1822, from Don Evaristo San Miguel to Mr. Forsyth; from whom, as well as from Mr. Anduaga, separate copies of it have been transmitted to this Department. This note announces his Catholic Majesty's final determination to abide by the *strict* construction of both the articles in question, on the acknowledgment that the value of the cannon is more than the cost of the provisions. It therefore proposes that the cannon should be restored to Spain, and offers to repay the expense incurred by the United States for the provisions; or it offers to receive proposals for the purchase by the United States of the cannon, and, if necessary, to sell them at a fair appraisement by competent persons to be appointed by the two governments; and after deducting the amount paid by the United States for the provisions, to receive the balance.

In the compacts between nations, as in the bargains of individuals, the most essential requisites are candor and fair-dealing. The comparative *value* of the cannon in the forts, and of the provisions for the passage of the Spanish troops, formed no part of the considerations, upon which the artillery was claimed by the United States, together with the walls of which they formed the defence. It was to the *principle* alone that our attention was turned. The officers of Spain, under a stipulation for *passage*, claimed a supply of provisions. Acquiescing in that liberal construction of our engagement which would warrant them in the claim, we thought it in fairness and reciprocity applicable to another article, the benefit of which would enure to the United States. In the course of the discussion no distinction has been shown on the part of Spain that could justify a different rule of construction for the two articles. In both cases the incident was so essential to the main object of the stipulation, as to be inseparable from its existence and accomplishment. The passage without provisions was impracticable. The walls without their artillery were no fortifications. If in one case the implication was just, it was indispensable in the other. But we do not wish to press this controversy further. You are authorized to signify to the Spanish government the acceptance of the proposal contained in Mr. San Miguel's note; and that on the repayment by the Spanish government of the money paid by the United States for provisions for the Spanish officers and troops from the Floridas to the Havana, the ordnance left behind and receipted for by General Jackson and Colonel Butler will be delivered up to the order of the Governor of Cuba, or to any officer duly authorized to receive it.

There is in the note of Mr. San Miguel a complaint somewhat gratuitous, that the American government had not in the first instant adjusted this question with the Spanish minister at Washington, or afterwards prevented the compromise between the commissioners of the two governments at the delivery of the provinces.

The government of the United States was not informed that

the Spanish minister here had any authority to discuss the mode of execution with regard to the delivery of the territory. It was not to him but to the governor and captain general of the island of Cuba that the royal order for the delivery was addressed; nor was it supposed that he had or could have any instructions authorizing him to settle any question of construction which might arise in the details of the execution. That a question might arise, both with regard to the provisions and to the artillery was foreseen; but there was no necessity for anticipating it by a reference to the Spanish minister, when it might not arise at all, and who, if it should, had no power to settle it. The suggestion of it as a question to *him* could in all probability tend only to *delay* the delivery itself of the Floridas. For if his views of the construction of the article concerning the fortifications should differ from those of this government, he could only refer it to his own, and in the meantime the delivery of the country must be postponed, or accepted by the United States, subject to the construction of the Spanish envoy. The American government had no motive for starting questions which might be turned to purposes of delay. It was sufficient for them to proceed upon principles, fair and equitable in themselves, and to foresee questions of instruction only so far as to preclude the admission of one rule when its operation would be against the United States, and of another when its effect would be in their favor. When the question between the commissioners had arisen, it was not more in the power of this government to prevent the compromise upon which they agreed than it was in that of Spain; a reference of it prior to the delivery might have been made to Madrid, in little more time than to Washington; and the intimation of Mr. San Miguel, that the unfortunate disputes in which the ex-governors of St. Augustine and Pensacola were involved, and which issued in occurrences personally unpleasant to them, originated in this compromise concerning the artillery, is founded upon erroneous impressions. Those incidents, much and sincerely lamented by us, arose from the non-delivery, deliberate, concerted and systematic, by the late

Captain General Mahy, and by both the governors of St. Augustine and Pensacola of the *Archives* and *Documents* which they were required by an express stipulation of the treaty and an explicit order of the king of Spain to deliver up. The governor of Cuba, after informing Colonel Forbes, who was commissioned to receive that portion of those Archives and Documents which were at the Havana, that twenty boxes of documents had been sent there from Pensacola relating to West Florida, and that all those relating to East Florida were at St. Augustine, and after detaining Colonel Forbes at the Havana nearly six weeks, in the daily protracted expectation of delivering them, finally obliged him with exhausted patience to depart without the former, and with an explicit assurance that he had instructed the governor of St. Augustine to deliver the latter. Yet the governor of St. Augustine refused to deliver them on the allegation of doubts, whether the engagement of the treaty extended to the delivery of *any* public documents or archives, relating to private property. This extraordinary effort to withhold and to carry away all the records of land titles of both the provinces, has been the fruitful source of all those subsequent misunderstandings and painful occurrences to which Mr. San Miguel's note alludes, and it commenced on the part of the governor of Cuba, long before any question relating to the delivery of the artillery had occurred.

Mr. Thomas Randall is now about to proceed to the Havana, charged with a new commission to demand and receive the archives and documents yet remaining there, and of which, as Mr. Forsyth was informed, a new royal order has been expedited to command the delivery. There are also many at Madrid, in the office of the Ultra-Marine Department, which Mr. Forsyth has taken measures at different times to obtain, hitherto without success. You will learn the state of this concern upon your arrival, and as occasions may present themselves, will give it all the attention it may require.

By the fourth article of the treaty of 22 February, 1819, provision was made for the appointment of commissioners and surveyors to run the boundary line between the United States and the then adjoining Spanish provinces, from the mouth of the Sabine River to the South Sea. They were to meet at Natchitoches within one year from the ratification of the treaty; but the appointment of the Spanish commissioner and surveyor, though repeatedly urged by Mr. Forsyth upon the Spanish government, was not made in seasonable time, and the revolution in Mexico, having soon after demolished the Spanish dominion in that country, it became doubtful whether that article of the treaty could be carried into execution. There was some hesitation in Congress, and different votes between the two Houses with regard to making the appropriation for that purpose. The appropriation was however made, and the appointment of the commissioner and surveyor on the part of the United States was made known to Mr. Anduaga, and also, through Mr. Forsyth, to the Spanish government; with notice that we were ready to proceed in the measures agreed upon for carrying the article into execution. No further notice of the subject has been taken by the Spanish government, nor have we been informed who were the commissioner and surveyor appointed by them. It will not be necessary for you to revive the subject by any communication to that government, unless it should be brought up on their part. The new government of Mexico since the revolution there has made known its assent to the boundary as marked out by the treaty, and it is probable that Spain will henceforth have no interest in the settlement of the line. It may form a subject of further arrangement between us and our immediate neighbors hereafter.

Of the other subjects of discussion with Spain, which may require your official notice, you will be informed by Mr. John James Appleton, remaining there charged with the affairs of the legation after the departure of Mr. Forsyth, and by the archives of the legation, which he will deliver over to you. The laws relating to commerce since the restoration of the Cortes have been rather restrictive than favorable to the relations between the United States and Spain. You will be specially attentive to all negotiations, whether commercial or political, in which Spain may be concerned, during the continuance of your mission; transmit to this Department two copies of every treaty, printed by authority, immediately after its publication, and copies by duplicate of all conventions, treaties, separate articles, or other diplomatic communications, of which you may acquire the knowledge, and which you can obtain without expense or charge.

An object of considerable importance will be to obtain the admission of *consuls* from the United States in the ports of the colonies, specially in the islands of Cuba and of Porto Rico. It was incidental to the old colonial system of Spain, which excluded all commerce of foreign nations with her colonies, to admit in their ports no foreign consuls. The special duties and functions of those officers, consisting in the protection of the commerce, navigation, and seamen of their respective countries in the ports where they reside, it was a natural and necessary consequence of the exclusive colonial principle, that where no commerce was allowed to foreign nations, there could be no duties for a foreign consul to perform, and no occasion for the acknowledgment of such an officer. But when the colonial ports were opened to foreign trade, all the *reasons* which recommend, and all the necessities which urge the appointment and admission of foreign consuls to reside in them, apply as forcibly to those ports as to any others. The commerce between the United States and the Havana is of greater amount and value than with all the Spanish dominions in Europe. The number of American vessels which enter there is annually several hundreds. Their seamen from the unhealthiness of the climate are peculiarly exposed to need there the assistance which it is a primary purpose of the consular office to supply; nor is there any conceivable motive for continuing to maintain the pretension to exclude them, and to refuse the formal acknowledgment of consuls. Informal commercial agents have in many of the ports been allowed to reside, and partially to perform the consular duties; but as they are thus left much dependent on the will of the local government, and subject to control at its pleasure, they have neither the dignity nor authority which properly belongs to the office. There has already been much correspondence between Mr. Forsyth and the Spanish Department of Foreign Affairs on this subject. You will follow it up as there may be opportunity, till a definitive answer shall be obtained....

DIARY ENTRIES (WASHINGTON, DC), NOVEMBER 7, 15, 17–18, 21–22, 25–27, 1823

For most of this month, President Monroe and his cabinet were occupied with the need to respond to the apparent threat of aggression in South America by the Holy Alliance and, with the British proposal, jointly to warn against military action to restore Spain's American colonies. John Quincy did not believe the danger would actually materialize, and he opposed any concert with Britain. It would be imprudent and undignified "to come in as a cock-boat in the wake of the British man-of-war." He did, however, feel the need, through diplomatic channels, to respond to threats with a statement of the basic principles of American foreign policy. "My purpose would be in a moderate and conciliatory manner, but with a firm and determined spirit, to declare our dissent from the principles avowed in those communications; to assert those upon which our own Government is founded, and, while disclaiming all intention of attempting to propagate them by force, and all interference with the political affairs of Europe, to declare our expectation and hope that the European powers will equally abstain from the attempt to spread their principles in the American hemisphere, or to subjugate by force any part of these continents to their will."

Washington, *November* 7th. – Cabinet meeting at the President's from half-past one till four. Mr. Calhoun, Secretary of War, and Mr. Southard, Secretary of the Navy, present. The subject for consideration was, the confidential proposals of the British Secretary of State, George Canning, to R. Rush, and the correspondence between them relating to the projects of the Holy Alliance upon South America. There was much conversation, without coming to any definite point. The object of Canning appears to have been to obtain some public pledge from the Government of the United States, ostensibly against the forcible interference of the Holy Alliance between Spain and South America; but really or especially against the acquisition to the United States themselves of any part of the Spanish- American possessions.

Mr. Calhoun inclined to giving a discretionary power to Mr. Rush to join in a declaration against the interference of the Holy Allies, if necessary, even if it should pledge us not to take Cuba or the province of Texas; because the power of Great Britain being greater than ours to *seize* upon them, we should get the advantage of obtaining from her the same declaration we should make ourselves.

I thought the cases not parallel. We have no intention of seizing either Texas or Cuba. But the inhabitants of either or both may exercise their primitive rights, and solicit a union with us. They will certainly do no such thing to Great Britain. By joining with her, therefore, in her proposed declaration, we give her a substantial and perhaps inconvenient pledge against ourselves, and really obtain nothing in return. Without entering now into the enquiry of the expediency of our annexing Texas or Cuba to our Union, we should at least keep ourselves free to act as emergencies may arise, and not tie ourselves down to any principle which might immediately afterwards be brought to bear against ourselves.

Mr. Southard inclined much to the same opinion.

The President was averse to any course which should have the appearance of taking a position subordinate to that of Great Britain, and suggested the idea of sending a special Minister to *protest* against the interposition of the Holy Alliance.

I observed that it was a question for separate consideration, whether we ought in any event, if invited, to attend at a Congress of the allies on this subject.

Mr. Calhoun thought we ought in no case to attend.

The President, referring to instructions given before the Congress at Aix-la-Chapelle declaring that we would, if invited, attend no meeting relative to South America of which less than its entire independence should be the object, intimated that a similar limitation might be assumed now.

I remarked that we had then not recognized the South American independence ourselves. We would have been willing to recognize it in concert with the European allies, and therefore would have readily attended, if invited, a meeting of which that should have been the object. We could not now have the same motive. We have recognized them. We are very sure there will be now no meeting of the allies with that object. There would, therefore, be no use or propriety in resorting to the same limitation. Our refusal to attend should be less explicit and unqualified.

To this the President readily assented.

I remarked that the communications recently received from the Russian Minister, Baron Tuyl, afforded, as I thought, a very suitable and convenient opportunity for us to take our stand against the Holy Alliance, and at the same time to decline the overture of Great Britain. It would be more candid, as well as more dignified, to avow our principles explicitly to Russia and France, than to come in as a cock-boat in the wake of the British man-of-war.

This idea was acquiesced in on all sides, and my draft for an answer to Baron Tuyl's note announcing the Emperor's determination to refuse receiving any Minister from the South American Governments was read.

Mr. Calhoun objected to two words as sarcastic – the word "*Christian*" annexed to independent nations, and the words "*of peace*" added to the word Minister.

I told him, laughing, that all the point of my note was in those two words, as my object was to put the Emperor in the wrong in the face of the world as much as possible.

The President proposed one or two other alterations, but after examination did not insist upon them. But it was thought the best method of making the profession of our principles would be in answering that part of Baron Tuyl's communication to me which was verbal – the intimation of the Emperor's hope that we should continue to observe neutrality in the contest between Spain and South America. It was proposed that I should in my written answer to the Baron's written note introduce a commentary upon the verbal part of his conferences. The discussion continued till four o'clock, when Mr. Calhoun had an engagement, and the meeting broke up without coming to any conclusion.

I remained with the President, and observed to him that the answer to be given to Baron Tuyl, the instructions to Mr. Rush relative to the proposals of Mr. Canning, those to Mr. Middleton at St. Petersburg, and those to the Minister who must be sent to France, must all be parts of a combined system of policy and adapted to each other; in which he fully concurred. I added that as Baron Tuyl had made one part of his communications written and another verbal, if I should answer the whole in one written note it might place him personally in an awkward predicament. My official intercourse with the Baron had always been of the friendliest character, and I was desirous of observing with him all the forms of courtesy and kindness.

The President then proposed that I should confine my written answer to the purport of the Baron's written note, and see the Baron again upon the verbal part of his communication. This course I shall accordingly take. I told the President I would see the Baron before sending him my written answer. I would then say that, having informed the President of what had passed between us at our recent conferences, he had approved the verbal answer that I had given to the Baron, and had directed me to add that, receiving in friendly part the expression of the Emperor's wish that the United States may continue to observe the neutrality announced on their recognition of the South American Governments, he wished the Baron to state to his Government, in return, the desire of that of the United States that the Emperor, on his part, should continue to observe the same neutrality. The Baron would make this the subject of a dispatch to his Government, which I presume he would, according to his custom, show me before sending it off; and I could commit the substance of all these conferences to writing in the form of a report to the President. Of all this he approved.

The discussion at the Cabinet meeting took a wide range. It was observed that Mr. Canning had not disclosed to Mr. Rush the special facts upon which he expected there would be a Congress to settle the affairs of South America, and Mr. Calhoun expressed some surprise that Mr. Rush did not appear to have made of him any enquiries on that point.

I observed that I was rather glad of the objection of the British Government to the *preliminary* recognition, as I should be sorry that we should be *committed* upon Canning's propositions, even so far as we might have been, by Mr. Rush on his own responsibility.

Calhoun wondered what could be the objection of Great Britain to the recognition.

I said there were two reasons: one, the aversion to fly directly in the face of the Holy Alliance; and, secondly, the engagements of her treaties with Spain, particularly that of 5th July, 1814.

Calhoun and Southard thought that Great Britain would in no event take a stand against the Holy Alliance on South American affairs unless sure of our co-operation. She could not be belligerent leaving us neutral, because it must throw the whole commerce of the adverse party into our hands. It was the opinion of us all that a Minister must immediately be sent to France.

The President read a copy of his letter to A. Gallatin urging him, 15th October, to return, and of Gallatin's answer, saying that he cannot go this winter, but promising to be here about the middle of this month. I left with the President several papers this day received, among which, one from Mr. Constancio, the ex-Consul and Chargé d'Affaires from Portugal, soliciting the pardon of a man named Cartacho, just convicted of piracy at Richmond. So we have now two persons claiming to act as Chargé d'Affaires from Portugal. On returning to the office, I sent to Baron Tuyl requesting him to call at my office tomorrow at one.

15th. I received a note from Mr. D. Brent, saying that the President wished to see me at the office at noon. I went, and found him there. He asked for the correspondence relating to the intercourse with the British American Colonies, with a view to the particular notice which he intends to take of it in the message; which I thought should have been only in general terms. He also showed me two letters which he had received – one from Mr. Jefferson, 23d October, and one from Mr. Madison of 30th October, giving their opinions on the proposals of Mr. Canning. The President had sent them the two dispatches from R. Rush of 23d and 28th August, enclosing the correspondence between Canning and him, and requested their opinions on the proposals. Mr. Jefferson thinks them more important than anything that has happened since our Revolution. He is for acceding to the proposals, with a view to pledging Great Britain against the Holy Allies; though he thinks the island of Cuba would be a valuable and important acquisition to our Union. Mr. Madison's opinions are less decisively pronounced, and he thinks, as I do, that this movement on the part of Great Britain is impelled more by her interest than by a principle of general liberty.

At one I attended the Cabinet meeting at the President's. He read a note from Mr. Crawford saying he was not well enough to attend, but hoped to be out on Monday. Mr. Calhoun and Mr. Southard were there; Mr. Wirt absent at Baltimore. The subject of Mr. Canning's proposals was resumed, and I soon found the source of the President's despondency with regard to South American affairs. Calhoun is perfectly moon-struck by the surrender of Cadiz, and says the Holy Allies, with ten thousand men, will restore all Mexico and all South America to the Spanish dominion.

I did not deny that they might make a temporary impression for three, four, or five years, but I no more believe that the Holy

Allies will restore the Spanish dominion upon the American continent than that the Chimborazo will sink beneath the ocean. But, I added, if the South Americans were really in a state to be so easily subdued, it would be but a more forcible motive for us to beware of involving ourselves in their fate. I set this down as one of Calhoun's extravaganzas. He is for plunging into a war to prevent that which, if his opinion of it is correct, we are utterly unable to prevent. He is for embarking our lives and fortunes in a ship which he declares the very rats have abandoned. Calhoun reverts again to his idea of giving discretionary power to our Minister to accede to all Canning's proposals, if necessary, and not otherwise. After much discussion, I said I thought we should bring the whole answer to Mr. Canning's proposals to a test of right and wrong. Considering the South Americans as independent nations, they themselves, and no other nation, had the right to dispose of their condition. We have no right to dispose of them, either alone or in conjunction with other nations. Neither have any other nations the right of disposing of them without their consent. This principle will give us a clue to answer all Mr. Canning's questions with candor and confidence. And I am to draft a dispatch accordingly.

The President then said that he inclined to appoint Mr. James Brown, of Louisiana, to go as Minister to France, though he had hitherto given hire no intimation to that effect. Mr. Brown's character and qualifications were discussed. Calhoun said he had genius, but was timid. Southard said he was indolent. His rheumatism, his fortune, and his showy wife were not forgotten. The President spoke of sending an Envoy Extraordinary, with no special destination, but with power to act as occasion might require, with reference to these proposals of Mr. Canning, and to any emergency concerning South America. The ostensible motive for the appointment might be as a colleague with R. Rush in the negotiations now committed to him alone. The measure itself was generally approved, but the selection of the person caused much rambling conversation. Calhoun, who in all his movements of every kind has an eye to himself, named Mason, of New Hampshire, De Witt Clinton, Judge Thompson, Mr. Ingham, and Edward Livingston. I mentioned Governor Woodbury and Mr. Forsyth. Mr. Southard spoke of J. Sergeant, Binney, and Hopkinson. The President named Mr. Baldwin. The pro and con for them all was set forth. Federalism was the principal objection to most of them. The President also spoke of Mr. Sanford and Judge Van Ness, of New York, and finally said he wished Mr. Madison would go. From that moment I thought of no other person. I observed the only question was whether it could be proposed to him. And I urged the President seriously to think of it; which he promised he would. I entreated him, above all things, not to appoint an incompetent person. There are objections to Mr. Madison's going, of which he himself and the President are not only the best but the only proper judges. If he would go, there could be no man better suited for the appointment.

17th. I drafted a dispatch to R. Rush in answer to all his dispatches relating to the proposals of G. Canning concerning South America. At the office. The President there. He appears to be still perplexed with the British Colonial Trade question, the arrangements concerning which had entirely escaped his memory. I referred him to my dispatch to R. Rush, No. 64, of which he has a copy, but which he has not read. The President thinks from the tenor of the dispatches received yesterday from R. Rush that Canning had changed his purpose; that he was less alarmed; that probably some inducements had been presented, after the triumph of the French in Spain, to quiet his apprehensions. My own opinion is confirmed that the alarm was affected; that the object was to obtain by a sudden movement a premature commitment of the American Government against any transfer of the island of Cuba to France, or the acquisition of it by ourselves; and, failing in that point, he has returned to the old standard of British belligerent policy. I read to the President and gave him my draft of a dispatch to R. Rush. He desired me to write to Mr. James Brown, of Louisiana, and propose to him the mission to France; and to Mr. Larned, of Rhode Island, for the appointment of Secretary of Legation to Chili.

Mr. Addington called at the office, and mentioned that he had private letters from England confirming the accounts in the newspapers that British Consular Agents had been appointed to the various ports of the South American Governments. I told him I had received further dispatches from Mr. Rush in relation to the negotiation with Mr. Canning concerning South American affairs – that it had rested where it was, Mr. Rush not feeling himself authorized to accede to Mr. Canning's proposals without a preliminary recognition by Great Britain of the independence of the South American States, and the British Government not yet being prepared for that step. I said I could not readily imagine what could withhold Great Britain from the formal recognition, when her measures all implied that it had been given; and I added that, earnestly desirous as we were of co-operating with Great Britain, I saw no other basis for concerted operations than that.

Addington said that he did not know what the motives could be. He thought it very probable that before my instructions could get out to Mr. Rush, Great Britain would have acknowledged some one or other of the South American Governments as independent. Perhaps, as possessing Colonies herself, and especially as some of her Colonies appeared to be in a very bad and turbulent humor, she might be less ready to acknowledge the independence of other Colonies. "Suppose, for instance," said he, "that the island of Cuba should take advantage of the present state of things and declare itself independent. The United States might have no objection to recognizing that in dependence, but with Great Britain, having Colonies of her own, it might be otherwise."

I said that the question as to the independence of Cuba not having yet arisen, I saw no reason for anticipating it for the sake of argument. On the existing state of things the basis for co-operation should be laid, and then, whatever events time might bring forth, it would be easy to accommodate a concerted movement to them. At least I supposed Great Britain must be prepared to say that in no event should Cuba be transferred to France.

"Oh, certainly!" said he.

Baron Tuyl, the Russian Minister, had written me this morning a note requesting an interview, and by appointment now came. I therefore deferred to a future day further conversation with Mr. Addington. The Baron came, and read me a dispatch from Count Nesselrode to him, and extracts from two others, of 29th and 30th August and 2d September last. The dispatch was merely a statement that the Emperor Alexander was just leaving St. Petersburg for a tour of three months for the inspection of his troops. It appears to guard very anxiously against any suspicion that he intended by it any hostile movement. It was doubtless a circular chiefly destined for European Courts, and sent *pro forma* here. The first extract was an acknowledgment of the receipt of the Baron's first dispatches from hence; high expressions of satisfaction at his conduct here; at the reception he had met with; at the consent of this Government to treat of the Northwest Coast question at St. Petersburg; intimations that Sir Charles Bagot had also received powers to treat concerning it on the part of Great Britain, and that Mr. Poletica was authorized to enter upon the negotiation during Count Nesselrode's absence with the Emperor.

The second extract was an exposition of principles relating to the affairs of Spain and Portugal, in a tone of passionate exultation at the counter-revolution in Portugal and the impending success of the French army in Spain; an "Io Triumphe" over the fallen cause of revolution, with sturdy promises of determination to keep it down; disclaimers of all intention of making conquests; bitter complaints of being calumniated, and one paragraph of compunctions, acknowledging that an apology is yet due to mankind for the invasion of Spain, which it is in the power only of Ferdinand to furnish, by making his people happy.

That paragraph is a satire upon all the rest of the paper. The Baron left the two extracts with me to be shown to the President. He assured me that he was perfectly satisfied with my answer to his last note, which he had received this morning; and he spoke with great kindness and good will towards us. I told him I could assure him, from the knowledge I had of the President's sentiments, that they reposed great personal confidence in him. He said he should always endeavor to deserve it.

18th. Mr. G. Hay was here with the letter from the Slave-Indemnity Commissioners, and some questions which I was not able to answer. He spoke also of the dispatches last received from Mr. Rush, and their effect upon the President. He said the President appeared to be much relieved by the view I had taken of them yesterday. I think he is yet alarmed more than will appear to be necessary. I took to the President's the two extracts of dispatches left with me by Baron Tuyl, which I read to him. Mr. Calhoun was there, and Mr. Southard came in shortly afterwards. Mr. Calhoun said he was confirmed in the view he had taken of the designs of the Holy Allies upon South America. I said I was quite confirmed in mine. The President appears yet to be in an extraordinary degree of dejection. There must be something that affects him besides the European news. I read to him two letters from Governor Cass, of the Michigan Territory: one, with a list of legislative Council to be picked; the other, about Drummond's Island. He spoke to me also about General Hull's claim, and asked me to see the Comptroller, Anderson, concerning it. I wrote, by the President's direction, to James Brown, Senator from Louisiana, now at Philadelphia, proposing to him the mission to France; and to Samuel Larned, at Providence, whom he has determined to appoint Secretary to the Legation to Chili.

21st. Mr. Banks called here this morning with Mr. Patterson, of Baltimore. I told him the President thought it most advisable to appoint a native citizen as Consul at Jamaica. He said a native citizen could do no business there, and the Consular fees would not pay for his stationery. I asked him why a citizen of the United States would not be permitted to do business there. He said he would be held a transient person, and they were not allowed to do business. I said it was strange that a Consul acknowledged as such should be held a transient person, and as such forbidden from doing business.

I found in this gentleman the same peremptory tone which is common among Englishmen when discussing political topics with Americans, and I was compelled, most reluctantly, to assume a similar tone myself. He then became more courteous, and promised to send me some papers concerning the trade of Jamaica. He said they imported from the United States a hundred thousand barrels of flour a year, and that they would not suffer the Parliament to make laws for the Colony.

Mr. Gallatin called upon me, just arrived from Pennsylvania. It has been said he was to pass the winter here; but he says he comes only for a few days, to settle his accounts and some private affairs of his own. He said a half outfit having, as he had heard, been allowed to Mr. Clay for his share in the negotiation of the Convention of 3d July, 1815, he thought himself entitled to make the same claim. I told him I would mention it to the President for his consideration. He made enquiries if we had any news from Europe; and I told him what is now passing in our diplomatic relations with Great Britain and Russia. He made some remarks upon them, full of his usual shrewdness and sagacity. I had received a note from the President requesting me to attend a meeting of the members of the Administration at one. The meeting lasted till five. I took with me the draft of my dispatch to R. Rush in answer to Canning's proposals, with the President's projected amendments and my proposal of amendment upon amendment. We had a very long discussion upon one phrase, which seemed to me to require none at all. The sentiment expressed was, that although we should throw no impediment in the way of an arrangement between Spain and her ex-Colonies by *amicable negotiation*, we should claim to be treated by the South Americans upon the footing of equal favor with the most favored nation. The President had proposed a modifying amendment, which seemed to admit that we should not object to an arrangement by which special favors, or even a restoration of authority, might be conceded to Spain. To this I strenuously objected, as did Mr. Calhoun. The President ultimately acceded to the substance of the phrase as I had in the first instance made the draft; but finally required that the phraseology of it should be varied. Almost all the other amendments proposed by the President were opposed principally by Mr. Calhoun, who most explicitly preferred my last substituted paragraph to the President's projected amendment. The President did not insist upon any of his amendments which were not admitted by general consent, and the final paper, though considerably varied from my original draft, will be conformable to my own views. The supplementary instruction I had not finished, but read the part that I had prepared.

I mentioned also my wish to prepare a paper to be delivered confidentially to Baron Tuyl, and the substance of which I would in the first instance express to him in a verbal conference. It would refer to the verbal communications recently made by him, and to the sentiments and dispositions manifested in the extract of a dispatch relating to Spanish affairs which he lately put into my hands. My purpose would be in a moderate and conciliatory manner, but with a firm and determined spirit, to declare our dissent from the principles avowed in those communications; to assert those upon which our own Government is founded, and, while disclaiming all intention of attempting to propagate them by force, and all interference with the political affairs of Europe, to declare our expectation and hope that the European powers will equally abstain from the attempt to spread their principles in the American hemisphere, or to subjugate by force any part of these continents to their will.

The President approved of this idea; and then taking up the sketches that he had prepared for his message, read them to us. Its introduction was in a tone of deep solemnity and of high alarm, intimating that this country is menaced by imminent and formidable dangers, such as would probably soon call for their most vigorous energies and the closest union. It then proceeded to speak of the foreign affairs, chiefly according to the sketch I had given him some days since, but with occasional variations. It then alluded to the recent events in Spain and Portugal, speaking in terms of the most pointed reprobation of the late invasion of Spain by France, and of the principles upon which it was undertaken by the open avowal of the King of France. It also contained a broad acknowledgment of the Greeks as an independent nation, and a recommendation to Congress to make an appropriation for sending a Minister to them.

Of all this Mr. Calhoun declared his approbation. I expressed as freely my wish that the President would reconsider the whole subject before he should determine to take that course. I said the tone of the introduction I apprehended would take the nation by surprise and greatly alarm them. It would come upon them like a clap of thunder. There had never been in the history of this nation a period of so deep calm and tranquillity as we now enjoyed. We never were, upon the whole, in a state of peace so profound and secure with all foreign nations as at this time. This message would be a summons to arms – to arms against all Europe, and for objects of policy exclusively European – Greece and Spain. It would be as new, too, in our policy as it would be surprising. For more than thirty years Europe had been in convulsions; every nation almost of which it is composed alternately invading and invaded. Empires, kingdoms, principalities, had been overthrown, revolutionized, and counter-revolutionized, and we had looked on safe in our distance beyond an intervening ocean, and avowing a total forbearance to interfere in any of the combinations of European politics. This message would at once buckle on the harness and throw down the gauntlet. It would have the air of open defiance to all Europe, and I should not be surprised if the first answer to it from Spain and France, and even Russia, should be to break off their diplomatic intercourse with us. I did not expect that the quiet which we had enjoyed for six or seven years would last much longer. The aspect of things was portentous; but if we must come to an issue with Europe, let us keep it off as long as possible. Let us use all possible means to carry the opinion of the nation with us, and the opinion of the world.

Calhoun said that he thought there was not the tranquillity that I spoke of; that there was great anxiety in the thinking part of the nation; that there was a general expectation that the Holy Alliance would employ force against South America, and that it would be proper that the President should sound the alarm to the nation. A time was approaching when all its energies would be needed, and the public mind ought to be prepared for it.

The President told us confidentially that G. W. Erving had written praying that it might be kept secret, because whatever any person wrote there was reported back against him, but that, whatever might be reported here, we might set it down for certain that France and the allies would support Spain in the attempt to recover her Colonies by force.

I observed to the President that I put very little reliance on anything written by G. W. Erving. It might or might not eventuate as he said; but he knew nothing about the matter more than was known to the world, and had views of his own in whatever he wrote.

Mr. Southard said little, but inclined towards my view of the subject.

The President finally said that he would draw up two sketches for consideration, conformable to the two different aspects of the subject. The President and Mr. Calhoun intimated the idea that there was a material difference in the wars and revolutions which since the year 1789 to this time have been raging in Europe, and this last invasion of Spain by France; that this was a more direct attack upon the popular principle; and that although no former message ever censured those overthrows and conquests before, yet it might be very proper to censure this now. The question, however, is deferred.

22d. I finished the draft of my second dispatch to R. Rush upon Canning's proposals. And there must be yet a third. I also began a written statement of what has passed between Baron de Tuyl and me concerning the intentions of the Russian Cabinet, with a view to transmit copies of it and of the documents to Mr. Middleton and Mr. Rush. Mr. Gallatin was with the President, but withdrew on my going in. I left with the President my draft for a second dispatch to R. Rush on South American affairs. And I spoke to him again urging him to abstain from everything in his message which the Holy Allies could make a pretext for construing into aggression upon them. I said there were considerations of weight which I could not even easily mention at a Cabinet meeting. If he had determined to retire from the public service at the end of his present term, it was now drawing to a close. It was to be considered now as a whole, and a system of administration for a definite term of years. It would hereafter, I believed, be looked back to as the golden age of this republic, and I felt an extreme solicitude that its end might correspond with the character of its progress; that the Administration might be delivered into the hands of the successor, whoever he might be, at peace and in amity with all the world. If this could not be, if the Holy Alliance were determined to make up an issue with us, it was our policy to meet, and not to make it. We should retreat to the wall before taking to arms, and be sure at every step to put them as much as possible in the wrong. I said if the Holy Alliance really intended to restore by force the Colonies of Spain to her dominion, it was questionable to me whether we had not, after all, been over-hasty in acknowledging the South American independence. It had pledged us now to take ground which we had not felt at all bound to take five years ago. At the Congress of Aix-la-Chapelle the allies had discussed what they should do with South America, and we had not even thought of interfering with them. If they intend now to interpose by force, we shall have as much as we can do to prevent them, without going to bid them defiance in the heart of Europe. Something had been said yesterday, that if the President did not recommend the recognition of the independence of the Greeks it would be pressed in the House of Representatives. What would be Mr. Clay's course in this case I could not foresee. But he (the President) well knew that at the time when Mr. Clay so urgently pushed for the South American independence, his main object was popularity for himself and to embarrass the Administration. It did not appear that this object was now so important to him, and, as he had some prospect of coming to the succession himself, I should not suppose he would wish it encumbered with a quarrel with all Europe. But, be that as it may, it was infinitely better that the impulse should come from Congress than that it should go from the Executive. Congress are responsible for their own acts. Foreign powers are apt to take less notice of them than of Executive measures, and if they put us in attitudes of hostility with the allies, be the blame upon them. The ground that I wish to take is that of earnest remonstrance against the interference of the European powers by force with South America, but to disclaim all interference on our part with Europe; to make an American cause, and adhere inflexibly to that.

The President said he had spoken of the Greeks and of the Spaniards in his last year's message. I said I should not object to paragraphs of a like description, in general terms and pledging nothing, but I would be specially careful to avoid anything which may be construed as hostility to the allies. He said he would fully consider what he should say, and when prepared with his draft would call a meeting of the members of the Administration.

25th. I made a draft of observations upon the communications recently received from the Baron de Tuyl, the Russian Minister. Took the paper, together with the statement I had prepared of what has passed between him and me, and all the papers received from him, to the President. I found General Swartwout, of New York, with him, but he immediately withdrew. Mr. Southard just then came in, and the President sent for the other members of the Administration, Mr. Calhoun and Mr. Wirt. Mr. Crawford continues convalescent, but was not well enough to attend. My proposal was that a paper like that which I had prepared, modified as the President should finally direct, be delivered by me to the Baron de Tuyl in the form of an inofficial verbal note; that I should invite him to a conference, then read the paper to him, deliver to him a copy of it, and tell him that I was willing to converse with him concerning it if he thought proper. The paper itself was drawn to correspond exactly with a paragraph of the President's message which he had read me yesterday, and which was entirely conformable to the system of policy which I have earnestly recommended for this emergency. It was also intended as a firm, spirited, and yet conciliatory answer to all the communications lately received from the Russian Government, and at the same time an unequivocal answer to the proposals made by Canning to Mr. Rush. It was meant also to be eventually an exposition of the principles of this Government, and a brief development of its political system as henceforth to be maintained: essentially republican – maintaining its own independence, and respecting that of others; essentially pacific – studiously avoiding all involvement in the combinations of European politics, cultivating peace and friendship with the most absolute monarchies, highly appreciating and anxiously desirous of retaining that of the Emperor Alexander, but declaring that, having recognized the independence of the South American States, we could not see with indifference any attempt by European powers by forcible interposition either to restore the Spanish dominion on the American Continents or to introduce monarchical principles into those countries, or to transfer any portion of the ancient or present American possessions of Spain to any other European power.

This paper was read, and thereupon ensued a desultory discussion till near five o'clock, when the President adjourned the meeting till twelve o'clock to-morrow. Calhoun, with many professions of diffidence and doubt, but only to prompt discussion, questioned whether it would be proper to deliver any such paper to the Russian Minister. The paper contained rather an ostentatious display of republican principles; it was making up an issue, perhaps too soon, with the Holy Alliance. It would perhaps be offensive to the Emperor of Russia, and perhaps even to the British Government, which would by no means relish so much republicanism. He thought it would be sufficient to communicate to Baron Tuyl a copy of the paragraph of the President's message to which my paper was adapted. The message was a mere communication to our own people. Foreign powers might not feel themselves bound to notice what was said in that. It was like a family talking over subjects interesting to them by the fireside among themselves. Many things might be said there without offence, even if a stranger should come among them and overhear the conversation, which would be offensive if they went to his house to say them.

Southard and Wirt both observed that according to that allusion it was Russia, it was the Holy Alliance, who had come to our house to proclaim the virtues and the glories of despotism; and my paper was nothing more than an answer to them.

Calhoun said he thought my paper went rather farther than theirs.

I observed that a copy of that paragraph of the President's message might suffice for an indication of our principles, but I thought it due to the honor and dignity of the nation that an explicit and direct answer should be given to the communications from the Russian Government. After receiving, one upon the back of another, so many broad hints from them, the people of this country, when they come to the knowledge of it, will ask what was said in answer to them. The answer to the written notification of the Emperor's determination not to receive any Minister from South America was the tamest of all State papers. The first draft of it had been softened first at a Cabinet meeting, then by an amended draft of the President, and finally by an amendment of mine upon that of the President. The answers to the notification of the Emperor's hope and wish that the United States would continue their neutrality between Spain and South America were merely verbal. We had no written vouchers of them but in the copies confidentially given by the Baron to me of his dispatches to his Court concerning them. Then came this last extract of 30th August, 1823, bearding us to our faces upon the monarchical principles of the Holy Alliance. It was time to tender them an issue. In the last resort, this was a cause to be pleaded before the world of mankind. Our country, and the world, would require that our ground should be distinctly taken, as well as resolutely maintained. Now, in my belief, was the time for taking it; and as I thought the Holy Alliance would not ultimately invade South America, and firmly believed that the Emperor Alexander did not mean to include us, or any consideration of us, in his invectives against revolution, I wished to give him an opportunity of disclaiming any such intention. I believed the Emperor Alexander was honestly wedded to his system; that he was profoundly penetrated with the conviction that he was laboring for the good of his people and for the welfare of mankind. There was no man living more sensitive to public opinion, as I knew from a multitude of proofs, but which was eminently shown by the importance which the Government itself attached to the editorial article in the National Intelligencer, which, at the instance of the Baron de Tuyl, I had caused to be inserted, concerning the Northwest Coast question. My object in this paper was to appeal much to the personal feelings of the Emperor Alexander: to his love of peace; to his religious impressions; to his sensibility to public opinion; to his old friendly offices and good will towards the United States. I would search all these sources of action, and bring him either to a formal disavowal of any dispositions unfriendly to the United States, or to an express declaration of what his intentions are.

Calhoun's objections were not supported; but Mr. Wirt made a question far more important, and which I had made at a much earlier stage of these deliberations. It was, whether we shall be warranted in taking so broadly the ground of resistance to the interposition of the Holy Alliance by force to restore the Spanish dominion in South America. It is, and has been, to me a fearful question. It was not now discussed; but Mr. Wirt remarked upon the danger of assuming the attitude of menace without meaning to strike, and asked, if the Holy Allies *should* act in direct hostility against South America, whether this country would oppose them by war? My paper and the paragraph would certainly commit us as far as the Executive constitutionally could act on this point; and if we take this course, I should wish that a joint resolution of the two Houses of Congress should be proposed and adopted to the same purport. But this would render it necessary to communicate to them, at least confidentially, the existing state of things. The communications from Mr. Canning were all, at his own request, confidential. Those with Baron de Tuyl were yet so, but *he* was desirous that part of them should be published, and I was yet to settle with him whether they should be communicated to Congress. My wish was to propose to him that they should all be communicated, and also that the substance of them should be communicated to Mr. Greuhm, the Prussian Minister here, for his Court; the King of Prussia being one of the members of the Holy Alliance.

The President did not finally decide upon the point of Mr. Calhoun's objection to the delivery of any paper to Baron Tuyl, but retained my draft and the statement of the transactions between the Baron and me, to resume the consideration of them tomorrow.

Mr. Wirt objected strongly to one paragraph of my draft, which, he said, was a hornet of a paragraph, and, he thought, would be excessively offensive.

I said it was the cream of my paper; but I am sure the President will not suffer it to pass. The President seemed to entertain some apprehension that the republicanism of my paper might indispose the British Government to a cordial concert of operations with us. He said they were in a dilemma between their anti-Jacobin policy, the dread of their internal reformers, which made them sympathize with the Holy Allies, and the necessities of their commerce and revenue, with the pressure of their debts and taxes, which compelled them to side with South American independence for the sake of South American trade. He believed they must ultimately take this side, but if we should shock and alarm them upon the political side of the question, and the Holy Allies could hold out to them anything to appease the craving of their commercial and fiscal interest, they might go back to the allies – as Portugal has gone back – insignificant and despised, but leaving us in the lurch, with all Europe against us.

I replied that, at all events, nothing that we should now do would commit us to absolute war; that Great Britain was already committed more than we; that the interest of no one of the allied powers would be promoted by the restoration of South America to Spain; that the interest of each one of them was against it. and that if they could possibly agree among themselves upon a partition principle, the only possible bait they could offer to Great Britain for acceding to it was Cuba, which neither they nor Spain would consent to give her; that my reliance upon the co-operation of Great Britain rested not upon her principles, but her interest – this I thought was clear; but that my paper came in conflict with no principle which she would dare to maintain. We avowed republicanism, but we disclaimed propagandism; we asserted national independence, to which she was already fully pledged. We disavowed all interference with European affairs, and my whole paper was drawn up to come in conclusion precisely to the identical declaration of Mr. Canning himself, and to express our concurrence with it.

Mr. Southard and Mr. Wirt supported me in these remarks.

26th. Received a note from the President, advising me to detain Mr. H. Allen here a few days, to peruse the late dispatches from R. Rush relating to South America. I sent immediately for Mr. Allen, who called on me and agreed to wait a few days. I desired him to call at the office of the Department and read there Mr. Rush's dispatches.

I attended the adjourned Cabinet meeting at the President's, from half-past twelve – four hours. At the President's request, I read the statement of what has passed between Baron Tuyl and me since the 16th of last month, and then my proposed draft of observations upon the communications recently received from him. The President then read the draft of the corresponding paragraph for his message to Congress, and asked whether it should form part of the message. I took a review of the preceding transactions of the Cabinet meetings; remarking that the present questions had originated in a draft which he had presented merely for consideration, of an introduction to the message, of unusual solemnity, indicating extraordinary concern, and even alarm, at the existing state of things, coupled with two paragraphs, one containing strong and pointed censure upon France and the Holy Allies for the invasion of Spain, and the other recommending an appropriation for a Minister to send to the Greeks, and in substance recognizing them as independent; that the course now proposed is a substitute for that, and that it is founded upon the idea that if an issue must be made up between us and the Holy Alliance it ought to be upon grounds exclusively American; that we should separate it from all European concerns, disclaim all intention of interfering with these, and make the stand altogether for an American cause; that at the same time the answer to be given to the Russian communications should be used as the means of answering also the proposals of Mr. George Canning, and of assuming the attitude to be maintained by the United States with reference to the designs of the Holy Alliance upon South America. This being premised, I observed that the whole of the papers now drawn up were but various parts of one system under consideration, and the only really important question to be determined, as it appeared to me, was that yesterday made by Mr. Wirt, and which had been incidentally discussed before, namely, whether we ought at all to take this attitude as regards South America; whether we get any advantage by committing ourselves to a course of opposition against the Holy Alliance. My own mind, indeed, is made up that we ought thus far to take this stand; but I thought it deserved great deliberation, and ought not to be taken without a full and serious estimate of consequences.

Mr. Wirt then resumed the objection he had taken yesterday, and freely enlarged upon it. He said he did not think this country would support the Government in a war for the independence of South America. There had never been much general excitement in their favor. Some part of the people of the interior had felt warmly for them, but it never had been general, and never had there been a moment when the people thought of supporting them by war. To menace without intending to strike was neither consistent with the honor nor the dignity of the country. It was possible that the proposals of Mr. Canning themselves were traps laid to ensnare us into public declarations against the Holy Allies, without intending even to take part against them; that if we were to be so far committed, all the documents ought to be communicated to Congress, and they ought to manifest their sentiments in the form of resolutions, and that the Executive ought not to pledge the honor of the nation to war without taking the sense of the country with them.

Mr. Calhoun supported the other view of the question. He said the great object of the measure was to detach Great Britain definitively from the Holy Alliance. Great Britain would not, could not, resist them alone, we remaining neutral. She would fall eventually into their views, and the South Americans would be subdued. The next step the allies would then take would be against ourselves – to put down what had been called the first example of successful democratic rebellion. It was probable that by taking the stand now the Holy Alliance would be deterred from any forcible interposition with South America; but if not, we ought to sustain the ground now taken, even to the extent of war. There was danger in both alternatives; but the immediate danger was light, the contingent one to be averted was formidable in the extreme. It was wisdom in this, as in many of the occurrences of life, public and private, to incur the light hazard for the purpose of warding off the great one. And as this was the wise course, he had no doubt it would be sustained by the people of this country, if the exigency should require it. They would always sustain the wisest course when it was properly explained to them. He did believe that the Holy Allies had an ultimate eye to us; that they would, if not resisted, subdue South America. He had no doubt they would retain the country in subjection by military force. Success would give them partisans. Violent parties would arise in this country, one for and one against them, and we should have to fight upon our own shores for our own institutions. He was therefore in favor of the President's message with the proposed paragraph. But he thought a copy of it might be delivered to Baron Tuyl, with notice that it was to be considered as the answer to the communications recently received from him. The paragraph in the message said in substance the same as the draft of the paper; but the message was a talk among ourselves, which foreigners might be told they have no right to take notice of. To say the same thing directly to him might be offensive. There was more development in my draft. There was an ostentatious display of republican *contrasted* with monarchical principles, always showing the superiority of the former. If he consulted his personal inclination, he should be in favor of the draft. He had no doubt that our own people would be delighted with it. but he believed it would be deeply offensive to the Holy Allies, and also to the British Government, who, with regard to monarchical principles, would sympathize entirely with them.

I said, with regard to the objections of Mr. Wirt, that I considered them of the deepest moment. I was glad they had been made, and trusted the President would give them full consideration before coming to his definitive decision. If they prevailed, neither the paragraph in the message nor my draft would be proper. The draft was prepared precisely to correspond with the paragraph in the message. I did believe, however, that both would be proper and necessary. Not that I supposed that the Holy Alliance had any intention of ultimately attacking us, or meant to establish monarchy among us. But if they should really invade South America, and especially Mexico, it was impossible, in the nature of things, that they should do it to restore the old exclusive dominion of Spain. Spain had not, and never could again have, the physical force to maintain that dominion; and if the countries should be kept in subjugation by the armies of the Allies, was it in human absurdity to imagine that they should waste their blood and treasure to prohibit their own subjects upon pain of death to set foot upon those territories? Surely not. If then the Holy Allies should subdue Spanish America, however they might at first set up the standard of Spain, the ultimate result of their undertaking would be to recolonize them, partitioned out among themselves. Russia might take California, Peru, Chili; France, Mexico – where we know she has been intriguing to get a monarchy under a Prince of the House of Bourbon, as well as at Buenos Ayres. And Great Britain, as her last resort. if she could not resist this course of things, would take at least the island of Cuba for her share of the scramble. Then what would be our situation – England holding Cuba, France Mexico? And Mr. Gallatin had told me within these four days that Hyde de Neuville had said to him, in the presence and hearing of ten or twelve persons, that if we did not yield to the claim of France under the eighth article of the Louisiana Convention, she ought to go and take the country, and that she had a strong party there. The danger, therefore, was brought to our own doors, and I thought we could not too soon take our stand to repel it.

There was another point of view, which the President had in part suggested, and which I thought highly important. Suppose the Holy Allies should attack South America, and Great Britain should resist them alone and without our cooperation. I thought this not an improbable contingency, and I believed in such a struggle the allies would be defeated and Great Britain would be victorious, by her command of the sea. But, as the independence of the South Americans would then be only protected by the guarantee of Great Britain, it would throw them completely into her arms, and in the result make them her Colonies instead of those of Spain. My opinion was, therefore, that we must act promptly and decisively. But the act of the Executive could not, after all, commit the nation to a pledge of war. Nor was war contemplated by the proposals of Mr. Canning. He had explicitly stated to Mr. Rush from the beginning that his object was merely a concerted expression of sentiment, which he supposed would avert the necessity of war; and, as Great Britain was not and would not be pledged, by anything Mr. Canning had said or proposed, to war, so would anything now done by the Executive here leave Congress free hereafter to act or not, according as the circumstances of the emergency may require. With regard to the point made by Mr. Calhoun, my opinion was directly opposite to that which he had expressed. The communications from the Russian Minister required a direct and explicit answer. A communication of the paragraph in the President's message would be no answer, and if given *as* an answer would certainly be very inconsistent with the position that foreigners have no right to notice it, because it was all said among ourselves. This would be precisely as if a stranger should come to me with a formal and insulting display of his principles in the management of his family and his conduct towards his neighbors, knowing them to be opposite to mine, and as if I, instead of turning upon him and answering him face to face, should turn to my own family and discourse to them upon my principles and conduct, with sharp innuendoes upon those of the stranger, and then say to him, "There! take that for your answer. And yet you have no right to notice it; for it was only said to my own family, and behind your back." I thought as the Holy Alliance had come to edify and instruct us with their principles, it was due in candor to them, and in justice to ourselves, to return them the compliment. And if the people of our country should hereafter know, as they must, how much good advice the Emperor Alexander has been giving us in private, they would not be satisfied to be told that the only return we had made to him for it was to send him a copy of the President's message to Congress.

I felt the more solicitude that a direct and explicit answer should be given him, because the Baron in one of his dispatches had intimated that I had expressed not only an earnest desire that we might remain on good terms with Russia, but high opinions of the Emperor's moderation. In my report of the conferences, I had stated what was said by me, and from which the Baron had drawn his inference. I had told him that, having, while residing at his Court, witnessed the many acts of friendship for the United States of the Emperor Alexander, I had formed sentiments of high respect for his character, and even of personal attachment to him. This was true. I thought better of him than perhaps any other person at this meeting; and I did not believe there was one word in my draft that would give him offence. The avowal of principles connected with the disclaimer of interference in European affairs, of proselytism, and of hostile purposes, could not offend him. I thought it most essential. I was willing to agree to any modification which might be thought advisable, but the distinct avowal of principle appeared to me to be absolutely required. The paper acknowledged that we were aware the monarchical principle of government was different from ours, but it declared that we saw no reason why they should not be at peace with each other, and that we earnestly desired that peace. The Emperor's reply might be, that he desired equally that peace; that by the invasion of Spain the allies meant to interfere neither with the liberty nor the independence of Spain; that the Spanish nation was with them, and that they had only put down a faction, originating in and supported by military mutiny, which the allies would not recognize.

Mr. Southard and Mr. Wirt both declared that they thought a distinct and direct answer should be given to the Russian communications. But they scrutinized and objected to many of the details of the paper. Wirt, referring again to the paragraph which he had yesterday called a hornet, said it reminded him of a Virginian who declared his principle was that if a man gave him a fillip on the nose he would knock him down with a brickbat.

Southard objected to the admission that we were aware the monarchical principle of government differed from ours, after stating that ours were principles of liberty, independence, and peace. I said that the details of the paper were entirely at the disposal of the President; that in drawing it up my object had been to make it as close, compact, and significant as possible; that every part of it was connected with the whole, and that from the first line to the last I meant all should bear upon the declaration with which it concludes – the answer at once to Russia and Great Britain.

Southard said he had distinctly perceived that was the object of the paper. The President retained the paper, to determine finally upon it to-morrow morning. He approved the draft of the second dispatch, prepared for R. Rush, but enquired what was the particular meaning of one paragraph in the first. I told him that was for me to ask of him, as it was a paragraph in the amendment drawn by himself, and in his own words; at which he heartily laughed. He desired me, however, finally to modify the dispatches to R. Rush, so as not to refuse co-operating with Great Britain even if she should yet demur to the recognition of South American independence. He gave my draft of general instructions to H. Allen to Mr. Southard, to prepare corresponding instructions to Commodore Hull. It was near five when the meeting broke up.

27th. Mr. D. Brent brought me this morning a note from the President, with the draft of my observations on the communications recently received from the Russian Minister; advising the omission of all the paragraphs to which objection had been made at the Cabinet meetings, and requesting me to see the Baron de Tuyl immediately. I directed a copy to be made of the paper, omitting all the passages marked by the President for omission, and desired Mr. Brent to write a note in my name to the Baron, requesting him to call at the office of the Department at three o'clock. In the meantime I went to the President's, and took the draft of my statement of what had passed between me and the Baron since the 16th of October. I told the President that I had directed the copy to be made out, of the observations, conformably to his direction; that I cheerfully gave up all the passages marked for omission excepting one; and that was the second paragraph of the paper, containing the exposition of our principles. That paragraph was, in my own estimation, the heart of the paper. All the rest was only a series of deductions from it. The paper received from Baron Tuyl, and to which the observations were intended for an answer, was professedly an exposition of principles. I had thought it should be met directly by an exposition of ours. This was done in three lines in the paragraph in question. The first paragraph of my paper stated the fact that the Government of the United States was republican; the second, what the fundamental principles of this Government were – referring them all to *Liberty, Independence, Peace*. These were the principles from which all the remainder of the paper was drawn. Without them, the rest was a fabric without a foundation. The positions taken in the paragraph were true. I could not possibly believe they would give offence to anyone. I was sure they would not to the Emperor Alexander, unless he had determined to invade South America; and if he had, this paper, which was to be our protest against it, could not too distinctly set forth the *principles* of our opposition to his design. The object of the paragraph was to set those principles in the broadest and boldest relief; to compress into one sentence the foundation upon which the mind and heart at once could repose for our justification of the stand we are taking against the Holy Alliance, in the face of our country and of mankind. I had much confidence in the effect of that paragraph – first, as persuasion to the Emperor Alexander, and, if that failed, as our manifesto to the world. I added, by way of apology for the solicitude that I felt on this subject, that I considered this as the most important paper that ever went from my hands; that in this, as in everything I wrote in discharge of the office that I held, I was the agent of his Administration, the general responsibility of which rested upon him; but that, having so long served himself in the Department, I need not say to him that besides that general responsibility there was a peculiar one resting upon each head of a Department for the papers issued from his own office, and this was my motive for wishing to retain a paragraph which I considered as containing the soul of the document to which it belonged. I should only say, further, that after making these observations I should cheer fully acquiesce in his decision.

He admitted that there was a peculiar responsibility upon me for the paper, but said he had thought the exposition of principles was sufficiently clear from the part of the paper proposed to be retained; that there had been apprehensions that this paragraph might give offence, appearing as a direct avowal of principles contrary to those acted upon by the Holy Allies, and thus *implying* censure upon them; that the crisis was a great one, and it was all-important that the measures now taken should be adopted with all possible unanimity; that if, however, I would send over to him the original draft of the paper, he would again examine it, and let me know his final opinion with regard to the re-admission of the paragraph.

I returned to the office, and sent him the draft, the copy having been made with the paragraphs omitted.

Baron Tuyl came before I had received my draft back from the President. I told him that according to our agreement I had sent to enquire, with regard to the publication of the two notes which had passed between us, what were his definitive wishes; that the session of Congress was about to commence, and, if he wished it, our two notes would be communicated to them with the President's message; that we should prefer this course, and even that the whole substance of what had passed at our verbal conferences, and the extract which he had communicated to me, dated 30th August, with some observations upon the whole, which I was directed to read and deliver to him now, should be thus made known to Congress and the public. But in this respect we should take the course most agreeable to him.

He said that he did not see any objection to the communication and publication of the two notes, but with regard to the rest perhaps his Government might not wish that it should be made public. The note of 1st September extract might be called even more than confidential, and he would thank me if, after the President shall have done with it, I would return it to him. The extract sent him of 30th August was, in its express terms, to be *confidentially* used; and as the publication would in all probability produce excitement and occasion public obloquy, not only upon his Government but upon the President's Administration itself, he believed it would be on the whole best not to publish them; but he would be glad to take a day or two further to consider of it. As to a publication by him, as I had observed to him, foreign Ministers, by the freedom of the Press, had the power to avail themselves of it, but he should make no use of that expedient.

I said that with regard to the effect of publication to produce animadversions upon his Government, I wished to leave it entirely to his own consideration. I had no doubt it would excite censure upon the Administration; but for that we were prepared. We knew it would come upon anything we should do, and we knew the extent of its power. We wished, therefore, that he should take no account whatever of that, as we should prefer the publication of the whole.

While we were at this stage of the conversation, Mr. Brent called me out and gave me a note from the President, returning my original draft, expressing the apprehension that the paragraph of principles contained a *direct* attack upon the Holy Allies, by a statement of principles which they had violated, but yet consenting that I should re-insert the paragraph, on account of the importance that I attached to it. I returned to the Baron, and read him the copy of my observations as it had been made, omitting the contested paragraph; and I told him that I should furnish him a copy of it in the course of the day. He thanked me for the communication, of which, he said, he should immediately send a copy to his Court. With regard to speculation upon what might be done or intended concerning South American affairs, he could foretell nothing, because he could foresee nothing. His instructions said nothing to him of it. But of the generally friendly dispositions of the Emperor towards the United States he was perfectly sure. The United States were a republic. It was clear that in a republic republican principles must prevail. Between the first principles of republican and of monarchical government it was not necessary, nor could it be useful, to enter upon a discussion. It was one of the most difficult questions of public law, about which it was not probable that the opinions of men would ever be brought to agree; but that difference of principle did not necessarily involve hostile collision between them. The Imperial Government distinguished clearly between a republic like that of the United States and rebellion founded on revolt against legitimate authority. What he complained of was, that in the minds of many persons here, and in the representations of others, this distinction was confounded; that no credit was given to his Government for it, and that a disbelief of its being recognized was inculcated. As to the communication and publication of the papers, he would now say that he wished none of them should be published. I had told him that if the two notes alone should be communicated, and some members of Congress should accidentally hear that anything else had passed, there would probably be a resolution of one or the other House calling for it. And where asking for such a resolution was sufficient to obtain its adoption, and might draw forth all the papers that had passed, he preferred that no part of it should be communicated. It might in some sort personally implicate himself with his own Government. He had, indeed, done nothing that he could not fully justify; but he had not been specially instructed to address an official note to this Government, even upon the resolution of the Emperor not to receive any South American Agents. He had thought it the best mode of making the Emperor's determination known, and with the same view he had informed the other members of the Corps Diplomatique residing here that he had addressed such a note to me. He should deem this a sufficient execution of the instructions to give publicity to the Emperor's decision.

I told him we should in that case consider all that had passed as yet confidential, and he might be assured that his confidence should in no case be abused. It was possible that members of Congress might get some intimation of what had been done, particularly as there had been communications between us and Great Britain also relating to South America. But if such a resolution as I had suggested might pass should be adopted, there was usually reserved an exception of all such information as the President might think it improper to communicate, and nothing would be given which would compromise him.

He said that after receiving the copy of my observations perhaps something would occur to him on which he should be glad to confer with me again, in which case he would ask for another interview. I told him I should always be happy to receive him. Soon after he left me, Mr. Gallatin came in to ask if I had delivered to the President his letter claiming a half outfit upon the negotiation of the Convention of 3d July, 1815, because it had been allowed to Mr. Clay. In the hurry of our late business it had not been taken to the President, and, Mr. Brent having left the office, it could not now be found. Gallatin entered into conversation with me on public affairs, and told me he had been with the President, who had read to him my observations on the late communications from Baron Tuyl. He had seen nothing objectionable in them except one paragraph, which he thought would certainly be offensive to the Emperor, because it contained a direct censure upon what he had done, by an exposition of principles with which he would not agree – liberty being nothing to him; and as to independence, it was his habit to meddle and interfere with everything. Ever since the restoration of the Bourbons, there was nothing, even the smallest details, in which his Ambassadors did not interfere in France. They had destroyed the Duke of Richelieu by making him change the election law against his will; and he had even interfered here, to advise us not to take Florida. The Emperor Alexander had at one time inclined to the liberal opinions; but that was now much changed. In 1814, Canning, answering some smart speech of Madame de Staël's, said to her, "You had that from your Jacobin friend the Emperor of Russia." This was reported within twenty-four hours to the Emperor, to whom some explanatory apology was made. But now the Emperor's prejudices are quite of a different character. The alteration was said to have been effected by the murder of Kotzebue.

I told Mr. Gallatin that I had pleaded hard with the President for the paragraph, which I thought altogether essential to the paper, but that I had read the paper without the paragraph to Baron Tuyl. I went, between five and six, again to the President's, and told him of the interview I had had with the Baron, and that I had read the paper to him, with the omission of the paragraph; and I reported to him the substance of all that had passed between the Baron and me. He desired me to see the Baron again and tell him that if there should be a call of Congress concerning his correspondence and conferences with me, it would be answered by a report from me, which should be shown to him before it is sent in.

OBSERVATIONS ON THE COMMUNICATIONS RECENTLY RECEIVED FROM THE MINISTER OF RUSSIA, DEPARTMENT OF STATE, NOVEMBER 27, 1823

This note, which John Quincy read to Baron de Tuyll, outlined the principles of American foreign policy that President Monroe would soon enunciate in his Annual Message to Congress. John Quincy omitted the following paragraph – which he thought was the cream of the paper – in order to assuage Monroe's concerns that the note was too inflammatory: "The Principles of this form of [Republican] polity are; 1. That the Institution of Government, to be lawful, must be pacific, that is, founded upon the consent, and by the agreement of those who are governed; and 2. that each Nation is exclusively the judge of the Government best suited to itself, and that no other Nation, can justly interfere by force to impose a different form of Government upon it. The first of the principles may be designated, as the principle of Liberty – the second as the principle of National Independence – They are both principles of Peace and of Good Will to Men."

The Government of the United States of America is [essentially] *Republican*. By their Constitution it is provided that "The United States shall guaranty to every State in this Union, a *Republican* form of Government, and shall protect each of them from invasion." [The principles of this form of Polity are; 1 that the Institution of Government, to be lawful, mast be pacific, that is founded upon the consent, and by the agreement of those who are governed; and 2 that each Nation is exclusively the judge of the Government best suited to itself, and that no other Nation, can justly interfere by force to impose a different Government upon it. The first of these principles may be designated, as the principle of Liberty – the second as the principle of National Independence – They are both Principles of Peace and of Good Will to Men.]

[A necessary consequence of the second of these principles is that] The United States recognize in other Nations the right which they claim and exercise for themselves, of establishing and of modifying their own Governments, according to their own judgments, and views of their interests, not encroaching upon the rights of others.

Aware that the Monarchical principle of Government, is different from theirs, the United States have never sought a conflict with it, for interests not their own. Warranted by the principle of National Independence, which forms one of the bases of their political Institutions, they have desired Peace, Commerce and Honest Friendship with all other Nations, and entangling alliances with none.

From all the combinations of European Politics relative to the distribution of Power, or the Administration of Government the United States have studiously kept themselves aloof. They have not sought, by the propagation of their principles to disturb the Peace, or to inter meddle with the policy of any part of Europe. In the Independence of Nations, they have respected the organization of their Governments, however different from their own, and [Republican to the last drop of blood in their veins,] they have thought it no sacrifice of their principles to cultivate with sincerity and assiduity Peace and Friendship even with the most absolute Monarchies and their Sovereigns.

To the Revolution and War which has severed the immense Terri tories, on the american [*Territories*] continents heretofore subject to the dominion of Spain from the yoke of that power, the United States have observed an undeviating neutrality. So long as the remotest prospect existed that Spain by Negotiation or by arms could recover the possession she had once held of those Countries, the United States forbore to enquire by what title she had held them, and how she had fulfilled towards them the duties of all Governments to the People under their charge. When the South-American Nations, after successively declaring their Independence, had maintained it, until no rational doubt could remain, that the dominion of Spain over them was irrecoverably lost, the United States recognized them as Independent Nations, and have entered into those relations with them commercial and political incident to that Condition – Relations the more important to the interests of the United States, as the whole of those emancipated Regions are situated in their own Hemisphere, and as the most extensive, populous and powerful of the new Nations are in their immediate vicinity; and one of them bordering upon the Territories of this Union.

To the contest between Spain and South America all the European Powers have also remained neutral. The maritime Nations have freely entered into commercial intercourse with the South-Americans, which they could not have done, while the Colonial Government of Spain existed. The neutrality of Europe was one of the foundations upon which the United States formed their judgment, in recognizing the South-American Independence; they considered and still consider, that from this neutrality the European Nations cannot rightfully depart.

Among the Powers of Europe, Russia is one with whom the United States have entertained the most friendly and mutually beneficial intercourse. Through all the vicissitudes of War and Revolution, of which the world for the last thirty years has been the theatre, the good understanding between the two Governments has been uninterrupted. The Emperor Alexander in particular has not ceased to manifest sentiments of Friendship and good-will to the United States from the period of his accession to the throne, to this moment, and the United States on their part, have as invariably shown the interest which they take in his Friendship and the solicitude with which they wish to retain it.

In the communications recently received from the Baron de Tuyll, so far as they relate to the immediate objects of intercourse between the two Governments, the President sees with high satisfaction, the avowal of unabated cordiality and kindness towards the United States on the part of the Emperor.

With regard to the communications which relate to the Affairs of Spain and Portugal, and to those of South America, while sensible of the candour and frankness with which they are made, the President indulges the hope, that they are not intended *either* to mark an Æra. either of change, in the friendly dispositions of the Emperor towards the United States or of hostility to the principles upon which their Governments are founded; or of deviation from the system of neutrality hitherto observed by him and his allies, in the contest between Spain and America.

To the Notification that the Emperor, in conformity with the political principles maintained by himself and his Allies, has determined to receive no Agent from any of the Governments de facto, which have been recently formed in the new World it has been thought sufficient to answer that the United States, faithful to their political principles, have recognised and now consider them as the Governments of Independent Nations. To the signification of the Emperor's hope and desire that the United States should continue to observe the neutrality which they have proclaimed between Spain and South-America, the answer has been that the Neutrality of the United States will be maintained, as long as that of Europe, apart from Spain, shall continue and that they hope that of the Imperial Government of Russia will be continued.

[To the confidential communication from the Baron de Tuyll, of the Extract, dated St. Petersburg 30 August 1823. So far as it relates to the affairs of Spain and Portugal, the only remark which it is thought necessary to make, is of the great satisfaction with which the President has noticed that paragraph, which contains the frank and solemn admissions that *"the undertaking of the Allies, yet demands a last Apology to the eyes of Europe."*]

In the general declarations that the allied Monarchs will never compound, and never will even treat with the *Revolution* and that their policy has only for its object by *forcible* interposition to guaranty the tranquility of *all the States of which the civilised world is composed*, the President wishes to perceive sentiments, the application of which is limited, and intended in their results to be limited to the Affairs of Europe.

That the sphere of their operations was not intended to embrace the United States of America, nor any portion of the American Hemisphere.

And finally deeply desirous as the United States are of preserving the general peace of the world, their friendly intercourse with all the European Nations, and especially the most cordial harmony and good will with the Imperial Government of Russia, it is due as well to their own unalterable Sentiments, as to the explicit avowal of them, called for by the communications received from the Baron de Tuyll, to declare that the United States of America, and their Government, could not see with indifference, the forcible interposition of any European Power, other than Spain, either to restore the dominion of Spain over her emancipated Colonies in America, or to establish Monarchical Governments in those Countries, or to transfer any of the possessions heretofore or yet subject to Spain in the American Hemisphere, to any other European Power.

PRESIDENT JAMES MONROE, SEVENTH ANNUAL MESSAGE TO CONGRESS, DECEMBER 2, 1823

With the president and cabinet eventually coming around to accept his views on how to handle the current crisis with the Holy Alliance and Spain's revolted colonies, John Quincy proposed to respond with a series of diplomatic notes setting out the American position. These could be made public if the crisis deepened. But Monroe had different ideas. He wanted to put in a prominent public statement, the opportunity for which was immediately at hand – his Annual Message to Congress. He drew on John Quincy's arguments to the cabinet and in the diplomatic notes to enunciate what later became known as the Monroe Doctrine.

A precise knowledge of our relations with foreign powers, as respects our negotiations and transactions with each, is thought to be particularly necessary. Equally necessary is it that we should form a just estimate of our resources, revenue, and progress in every kind of improvement connected with the national prosperity and public defence. It is by rendering justice to other nations that we may expect it from them. It is by our ability to resent injuries and redress wrongs that we may avoid them.

The Commissioners under the fifth article of the treaty of Ghent, having disagreed in their opinions respecting that portion of the boundary between the Territories of the United States and of Great Britain, the establishment of which had been submitted to them, have made their respective reports, in compliance with that article, that the same might be referred to the decision of a friendly power. It being manifest, however, that it would be difficult, if not impossible, for any power to perform that office without great delay and much inconvenience to itself, a proposal has been made by this Government, and acceded to by that of Great Britain, to endeavor to establish that boundary by amicable negotiation. It appearing, from long experience, that no satisfactory arrangement could be formed of the commercial intercourse between the United States and the British colonies in this hemisphere by legislative acts, while each party pursued its own course without agreement or concert with the other, a proposal has been made to the British Government to regulate this commerce by treaty, as it has been to arrange in like manner the just claim of the citizens of the United States inhabiting the States and Territories bordering on the lakes and rivers which empty into the St. Lawrence to the navigation of that river to the ocean. For these and other objects of high importance to the interests of both parties, a negotiation has been opened with the British Government which, it is hoped, will have a satisfactory result.

The Commissioners under the sixth and seventh articles of the treaty of Ghent, having successfully closed their labors in relation to the sixth, have proceeded to the discharge of those relating to the seventh. Their progress in the extensive survey, required for the performance of their duties, justifies the presumption that it will be completed in the ensuing year.

The negotiation which had been long depending with the French Government on several important subjects, and particularly for a just indemnity for losses sustained in the late wars by the citizens of the United States, under unjustifiable seizures and confiscations of their property, has not as yet had the desired effect. As this claim rests on the same principle with others which have been admitted by the French Government, it is not perceived on what just grounds it can be rejected. A minister will be immediately appointed to proceed to France and resume the negotiation on this and other subjects which may arise between the two nations.

At the proposal of the Russian Imperial Government, made through the minister of the Emperor residing here, a full power and instructions have been transmitted to the minister of the

United States at St. Petersburg, to arrange, by amicable negotiation, the respective rights and interests of the two nations on the northwest coast of this continent. A similar proposal has been made by his Imperial Majesty to the Government of Great Britain, which has likewise been acceded to. The Government of the United States has been desirous, by this friendly proceeding, of manifesting the great value which they have invariably attached to the friendship of the Emperor, and their solicitude to cultivate the best understanding with his Government. In the discussions to which this interest has given rise, and in the arrangements by which they may terminate, the occasion has been judged proper for asserting as a principle in which the rights and interests of the United States are involved, that the American continents, by the free and independent condition which they have assumed and maintain, are henceforth not to be considered as subjects for future colonization by any European powers.

Since the close of the last session of Congress, the Commissioners and arbitrators for ascertaining and determining the amount of indemnification which may be due to citizens of the United States under the decision of his Imperial Majesty the Emperor of Russia, in conformity to the convention concluded at St. Petersburg, on the twelfth of July, one thousand eight hundred and twenty-two, have assembled in this city and organized themselves as a Board for the performance of the duties assigned to them by that treaty. The commission constituted under the eleventh article of the treaty of twenty-second February, one thousand eight hundred and nineteen, between the United States and Spain, is also in session here; and as the term of three years limited by the treaty for the execution of the trust will expire before the period of the next regular meeting of Congress, the attention of the Legislature will be drawn to the measures which may be necessary to accomplish the objects for which the commission was instituted.

In compliance with a resolution of the House of Representatives, adopted at their last session, instructions have been given to all the ministers of the United States accredited to the powers of Europe and America to propose the proscription of the African slave trade by classing it under the denomination, and inflicting on its perpetrators the punishment, of piracy. Should this proposal be acceded to, it is not doubted that this odious and criminal practice will be promptly and entirely suppressed. It is earnestly hoped that it will be acceded to from a firm belief that it is the most effectual expedient that can be adopted for the purpose.

At the commencement of the recent war between France and Spain it was declared by the French Government that it would grant no commissions to privateers, and that neither the commerce of Spain herself nor of neutral nations should be molested by the naval force of France, except in the breach of a lawful blockade. This declaration, which appears to have been faithfully carried into effect, concurring with principles proclaimed and cherished by the United States from the first establishment of their independence, suggested the hope that the time had arrived when the proposal for adopting it as a permanent and invariable rule in all future maritime wars might meet the favorable consideration of the great European powers. Instructions have accordingly been given to our ministers with France, Russia, and Great Britain, to make those proposals to their respective Governments; and when the friends of humanity reflect on the essential amelioration to the condition of the human race which would result from the abolition of private war on the sea, and on the great facility by which it might be accomplished, requiring only the consent of a few sovereigns, an earnest hope is indulged that these overtures will meet with an attention animated by the spirit in which they were made, and that they will ultimately be successful.

The ministers who were appointed to the republics of Colombia and Buenos Ayres during the last session of Congress proceeded, shortly afterwards, to their destinations. Of their arrival there official intelligence has not yet been received. The minister appointed to the republic of Chili will sail in a few days. An early appointment will also be made to Mexico. A minister has been received from Colombia, and the other Governments have been informed that ministers, or diplomatic agents of inferior grade, would be received from each accordingly as they might prefer the one or the other.

The minister appointed to Spain proceeded, soon after his appointment, for Cadiz, the residence of the sovereign to whom he was accredited. In approaching that port, the frigate which conveyed him was warned off by the commander of the French squadron by which it was blockaded, and not permitted to enter, although apprised by the captain of the frigate of the public character of the person whom he had on board, the landing of whom was the sole object of his proposed entry. This act, being considered an infringement of the rights of ambassadors and of nations, will form a just cause of complaint to the Government of France against the officer by whom it was committed ...

CHAPTER TEN

PRESIDENT, 1825–1829

INTRODUCTION

Pʀᴇsɪᴅᴇɴᴛ Jᴏʜɴ Qᴜɪɴᴄʏ Aᴅᴀᴍs took the oath of office on March 4, 1825. Unfortunately for the new president, the viability of his administration was in question from the beginning. He had not even received a plurality of the partial popular and electoral college vote, finishing second to Andrew Jackson in both. His election by the House of Representatives was secured by supporters of Henry Clay, who had been John Quincy's diplomatic and political antagonist for the past decade. President John Quincy Adams then appointed Clay as secretary of state, a position that had become a stepping-stone to the presidency. Howls of "corrupt bargain" from John Quincy's critics were instantly registered.

On the positive side, John Quincy inherited a relatively quiet international situation, with no major threats on the immediate horizon and an economy improving after the depression that followed the Panic of 1819. Despite their past differences on foreign policy, he and Clay had essentially the same view of domestic affairs, at least when it came to those not involving slavery. There were no significant disagreements with the secretary of state in that respect. John Quincy and Clay had essentially come to a meeting of the minds on how to deal with the newly independent South American states. The stage was set for John Quincy to lay out his comprehensive vision of national greatness.

The new president issued his First Annual Message to Congress (State of the Union) in December 1825. In terms of foreign policy, John Quincy proposed to send a delegation to the Inter-American Congress in Panama, which several newly independent South American states were organizing. They planned to discuss, among other things, the question of neutral rights in time of war and the suppression of the international slave trade.

On domestic matters, he asserted his long-standing belief that "the great object of the institution of civil government is the improvement of the condition of those who are parties to the social compact." To this end he proposed a package of measures that included federally funded internal improvements (specifically, road and canal construction), the establishment of a department of the interior, the establishment of a national university, the building of a national astronomical observatory ("lighthouses of the skies"), the financing of scientific expeditions of exploration and research, the creation of a naval academy, the passage of a national bankruptcy law, and the establishment of a uniform system of weights and measures.

Unfortunately for the new president, there was something in the message that aggravated almost everyone. To those holding to the old Jeffersonian creed of strict constitutional construction, the message was portrayed as the discredited doctrine of Hamiltonian federalism – a federal government that would run rampant over the states and the people. John Quincy's seeming praise of European accomplishments revived old accusations that father and son secretly hankered after monarchy.

Even in its boldness, the message did not mention John Quincy's most audacious domestic ambition – the ultimate, although not immediate, end of slavery. At least he did not take it on explicitly. But John Quincy's opponents, especially in the South, thought they well understood the message within the message. "Liberty is power," John Quincy had said. If the federal government were permitted to do all the things he wanted it to do, and in the spirit in which he wanted, it would become so powerful that it could, and undoubtedly would, take every opportunity, constitutional or not, to destroy states' rights and slavery. Its tyrannical impulses certainly would not be "palsied by the will of our constituents."

John Quincy himself did not think of his program in quite this way. He made no references in his diary about his intentions concerning slavery. At the time of the Missouri crisis, he had apocalyptic visions of the breakup of the Union and civil war as being necessary to deal with the peculiar institution. But he undoubtedly hoped for a different, evolutionary path, suggested by the message. His program to strengthen the Union through internal improvements would foster a common sense of national identity and interest. This, coupled with the embrace of a "spirit of improvement," would make clear the anachronism of slavery in a truly "representative democracy." It would wither away, as would another retrograde form of human existence, that of the Indian tribes.

The suspicion about John Quincy's ultimate intentions carried over into foreign policy – specifically, his plans to accept an invitation to attend the Panama Congress, which was announced almost in passing in the message. His thinking about relations with the South American nations had evolved since the United States had recognized them in 1822 and since the scare of European intervention had passed. Although he was certainly not willing to go as far as to form an alliance or collective security arrangement, he saw the conference as an opportunity to promote a hemispheric consensus around a liberalized system of trade. John Quincy also wanted to use the occasion to promote religious freedom. Although he undoubtedly retained his skepticism whether the existing political culture of the South Americans would support republican government, he thought that such a platform would be the best means to influence them in that direction. From a strategic standpoint, it would reinforce the barrier between the Old World and the New.

That was not what his critics thought he was doing. John Quincy's opponents in the Senate insisted that the negotiations in

Panama would create their own momentum and sweep the United States into commitments it would later regret. Southerners warned that the conference might take measures that would affect slavery, such as recognizing the independent regime of Haiti. The Senate eventually approved the nominees, but the anti-Adams elements in the House prevented John Quincy's delegates from attending by delaying appropriations for the mission.

Around such issues John Quincy's opponents coalesced. Their leader was Andrew Jackson, smarting from what he regarded as the stolen election of 1824. The political genius was Martin Van Buren of New York, who set about organizing what became known as the Democratic Party, an alliance between "the planters of the South and the plain republicans of the North." Pro-Adams candidates fared badly in the midterm elections of 1826, leaving both houses of Congress in the hands of adversaries.

After the fight over the Panama Congress, there were also few opportunities for major foreign policy successes. But the administration did negotiate nine commercial treaties and settle a large number of individual claims against foreign powers. John Quincy and Clay took diplomatic steps to discourage the South American states from attacking Cuba and Puerto Rico, the last bastions of Spanish colonial rule in the Western Hemisphere. That might have provoked a larger war and European intervention, or it might have required premature possession of the islands by the United States. John Quincy approved an unsuccessful initiative by Clay to negotiate with the newly independent Mexico an alteration of the southwestern boundary, which had been set at the Sabine River in the Transcontinental Treaty. Essentially, John Quincy and Clay wanted to purchase all or part of Texas. In addition to money, Clay originally planned to offer Mexico ships of war, but this was removed at John Quincy's request.

The most vexing diplomatic issue involved long-standing American efforts to allow trade with the British West Indies on an equal competitive basis with the rest of the Empire. As secretary

of state, John Quincy had persuaded Congress to threaten retalia-
tory duties on certain kinds of British shipping until London
agreed to open the islands. The British retaliated in turn, setting
off a transatlantic row that went unresolved for the rest of his
term in office.

As a diplomat, John Quincy had dealt with matters concerning American Indians in light of their relations with foreign powers – specifically, the imperative to prevent their alliance with
hostile European powers, which would threaten the Union. He
strongly held the view that the Indian hunter-gatherer culture
was retrograde and bound to be overcome by the forces of modern civilization. This process, however, was to be done without
force or fraud. He detected such fraud in a treaty with the Creek
Indians and the state of Georgia, which ceded territorial rights to
the state. John Quincy unfortunately had ratified the treaty without being aware that the Creek negotiators were not representative of the tribe, and that bribery was involved.

Secretary of War James Barbour proposed to halt implementation of the Creek Treaty until it could be renegotiated. John
Quincy and the rest of the cabinet agreed, only to be confronted
with threats by Georgia's Governor Troup that the state would
resist federal intervention. John Quincy was confronted with a
danger to the Union from an unexpected direction. Unfortunately,
he knew that his congressional opposition, under the leadership
of the old Indian fighter Andrew Jackson, would not support the
use of federal coercion. John Quincy went as far as he thought he
could in threatening the use of force. A collision with Georgia was
avoided at the last minute by a face-saving revised treaty, which
ceded all Creek lands and provided for their relocation as a tribe
in the trans-Mississippi West.

The final years of the presidency were a time of despondency
for John Quincy. His program for national greatness had been
foiled, and his defeat in the election of 1828 was virtually certain.
In the summer of 1825, he paid what turned out to be his final

respects to his father. On July 4, 1826, the fiftieth anniversary of the Declaration of Independence, John Adams, along with Thomas Jefferson, passed away.

John Quincy did not attend the inauguration of his successor, Andrew Jackson, just as his father had avoided that of Thomas Jefferson. The younger Adams regarded the outcome as a second national referendum on his family and all it, and the nation, stood for. John Quincy, once the staunch defender of Jackson, now thought him a democratic demagogue of the worst sort. He retired to his gardens and books in Quincy, Massachusetts. Although his great dream of internal physical, moral, and intellectual improvement had failed, he could take satisfaction in his diplomatic record. He had helped transform a new nation into a global power, all while staying united and independent.

INAUGURAL ADDRESS, MARCH 4, 1825

John Quincy attempted to establish a positive and conciliatory tone at the start of his administration, noting that "Less possessed of your confidence in advance than any of my predecessors, I am deeply conscious of the prospect that I shall stand more and oftener in need of your indulgence." He stressed that the union had successfully endured a fiery trial, caused in no small part by the wars of Europe and the political divisions over foreign policy. "Since that period a population of four millions has multiplied to twelve. A territory bounded by the Mississippi has been extended from sea to sea. New States have been admitted to the Union in numbers nearly equal to those of the first Confederation. Treaties of peace, amity, and commerce have been concluded with the principal dominions of the earth. The people of other nations, inhabitants of regions acquired not by conquest, but by compact, have been united with us in the participation of our rights and duties, of our burdens and blessings ... Liberty and law have marched hand in hand."

In compliance with an usage coeval with the existence of our Federal Constitution, and sanctioned by the example of my predecessors in the career upon which I am about to enter, I appear, my fellow-citizens, in your presence and in that of Heaven to bind myself by the solemnities of religious obligation to the faithful performance of the duties allotted to me in the station to which I have been called.

In unfolding to my countrymen the principles by which I shall be governed in the fulfillment of those duties my first resort will be to that Constitution which I shall swear to the best of my ability to preserve, protect, and defend. That revered instrument enumerates the powers and prescribes the duties of the Executive Magistrate, and in its first words declares the purposes to which these and the whole action of the Government instituted by it should be invariably and sacredly devoted – to form a more perfect union, establish justice, insure domestic tranquillity, provide for the common defense, promote the general welfare, and secure the blessings of liberty to the people of this Union in their successive generations. Since the adoption of this social compact one of these generations has passed away. It is the work of our forefathers. Administered by some of the most eminent men who contributed to its formation, through a most eventful period in the annals of the world, and through all the vicissitudes of peace and war incidental to the condition of associated man, it has not disappointed the hopes and aspirations of those illustrious benefactors of their age and nation. It has promoted the lasting welfare of that country so dear to us all; it has to an extent far beyond the ordinary lot of humanity secured the freedom and happiness of this people. We now receive it as a precious inheritance from those to whom we are indebted for its establishment, doubly bound by the examples which they have left us and by the blessings which we have enjoyed as the fruits of their labors to transmit the same unimpaired to the succeeding generation.

In the compass of thirty-six years since this great national covenant was instituted a body of laws enacted under its authority and in conformity with its provisions has unfolded its powers and carried into practical operation its effective energies. Subordinate departments have distributed the executive functions in their various relations to foreign affairs, to the revenue and expenditures, and to the military force of the Union by land and sea. A coordinate department of the judiciary has expounded the Constitution and the laws, settling in harmonious coincidence with the legislative will numerous weighty questions of construction which the imperfection of human language had rendered unavoidable. The year of jubilee since the first formation of our Union has just elapsed that of the declaration of our independence is at hand. The consummation of both was effected by this Constitution.

Since that period a population of four millions has multiplied to twelve. A territory bounded by the Mississippi has been extended from sea to sea. New States have been admitted to the Union in numbers nearly equal to those of the first Confederation. Treaties of peace, amity, and commerce have been concluded with the principal dominions of the earth. The people of other nations, inhabitants of regions acquired not by conquest, but by compact, have been united with us in the participation of our rights and duties, of our burdens and blessings. The forest has fallen by the ax of our woodsmen; the soil has been made to teem by the tillage of our farmers; our commerce has whitened every ocean. The dominion of man over physical nature has been extended by the invention of our artists. Liberty and law have marched hand in hand. All the purposes of human association have been accomplished as effectively as under any other government on the globe, and at a cost little exceeding in a whole generation the expenditure of other nations in a single year.

Such is the unexaggerated picture of our condition under a Constitution founded upon the republican principle of equal rights. To admit that this picture has its shades is but to say that it is still the condition of men upon earth. From evil – physical, moral, and political – it is not our claim to be exempt. We have suffered sometimes by the visitation of Heaven through disease; often by the wrongs and injustice of other nations, even to the extremities of war; and, lastly, by dissensions among ourselves – dissensions perhaps inseparable from the enjoyment of freedom, but which have more than once appeared to threaten the dissolution of the Union, and with it the overthrow of all the enjoyments of our present lot and all our earthly hopes of the future. The causes of these dissensions have been various, founded upon differences of speculation in the theory of republican government; upon conflicting views of policy in our relations with foreign nations; upon jealousies of partial and sectional interests, aggravated by prejudices and prepossessions which strangers to each other are ever apt to entertain.

It is a source of gratification and of encouragement to me to observe that the great result of this experiment upon the theory of human rights has at the close of that generation by which it was formed been crowned with success equal to the most sanguine expectations of its founders. Union, justice, tranquillity, the common defense, the general welfare, and the blessings of liberty – all have been promoted by the Government under which we have lived. Standing at this point of time, looking back to that generation which has gone by and forward to that which is advancing, we may at once indulge in grateful exultation and in cheering hope. From the experience of the past we derive instructive lessons for the future. Of the two great political parties which have divided the opinions and feelings of our country, the candid and the just will now admit that both have contributed splendid talents, spotless integrity, ardent patriotism, and disinterested sacrifices to the formation and administration of this Government, and that both have required a liberal indulgence for a portion of human infirmity and error. The revolutionary wars of Europe, commencing precisely at the moment when the Government of the United States first went into operation under this Constitution, excited a collision of sentiments and of sympathies which kindled all the passions and imbittered the conflict of parties till the nation was involved in war and the Union was shaken to its center. This time of trial embraced a period of five and twenty years, during which the policy of the Union in its relations with Europe constituted the principal basis of our political divisions and the most arduous part of the action of our Federal Government. With the catastrophe in which the wars of the French Revolution terminated, and our own subsequent peace with Great Britain, this baneful weed of party strife was uprooted. From that time no difference of principle, connected either with the theory of government or with our intercourse with foreign nations, has existed or been called forth in force sufficient to sustain a continued combination of parties or to give more than wholesome animation to public sentiment or legislative debate. Our political creed is, without a dissenting voice that can be heard, that the will of the people is the source and the happiness of the people the end of all legitimate government upon earth; that the best security for the beneficence and the best guaranty against the abuse of power consists in the freedom, the purity, and the frequency of popular elections; that the General Government of the Union and the separate governments of the States are all sovereignties of limited powers, fellow-servants of the same masters, uncontrolled within their respective spheres, uncontrollable by encroachments upon each other; that the firmest security of peace is the preparation during peace of the defenses of war; that a rigorous economy and accountability of public expenditures should guard against the aggravation and alleviate when possible the burden of taxation; that the military should be kept in strict subordination to the civil power; that the freedom of the press and of religious opinion should be inviolate; that the policy of our country is peace and the ark of our salvation union are articles of faith upon which we are all now agreed. If there have been those who doubted whether a confederated representative democracy were a government competent to the wise and orderly management of the common concerns of a mighty nation, those doubts have been dispelled; if there have been projects of partial confederacies to be erected upon the ruins of the Union, they have been scattered to the winds; if there have been dangerous attachments to one foreign nation and antipathies against another, they have been extinguished. Ten years of peace, at home and abroad, have assuaged the animosities of political contention and blended into harmony the most discordant elements of public opinion There still remains one effort of magnanimity, one sacrifice of prejudice and passion, to be made by the individuals throughout the nation who have heretofore followed the standards of political party. It is that of discarding every remnant of rancor against each other, of embracing as countrymen and friends, and of yielding to talents and virtue alone that confidence which in times of contention for principle was bestowed only upon those who bore the badge of party communion.

The collisions of party spirit which originate in speculative opinions or in different views of administrative policy are in their nature transitory. Those which are founded on geographical divisions, adverse interests of soil, climate, and modes of domestic life are more permanent, and therefore, perhaps, more dangerous. It is this which gives inestimable value to the character of our Government, at once federal and national. It holds out to us a perpetual admonition to preserve alike and with equal anxiety the rights of each individual State in its own government and the rights of the whole nation in that of the Union. Whatsoever is of domestic concernment, unconnected with the other members of the Union or with foreign lands, belongs exclusively to the administration of the State governments. Whatsoever directly involves the rights and interests of the federative fraternity or of foreign powers is of the resort of this General Government. The duties of both are obvious in the general principle, though sometimes perplexed with difficulties in the detail. To respect the rights of the State governments is the inviolable duty of that of the Union; the government of every State will feel its own obligation to respect and preserve the rights of the whole. The prejudices everywhere too commonly entertained against distant strangers are worn away, and the jealousies of jarring interests are allayed by the composition and functions of the great national councils annually assembled from all quarters of the Union at this place. Here the distinguished men from every section of our country, while meeting to deliberate upon the great interests of those by whom they are deputed, learn to estimate the talents and do justice to the virtues of each other. The harmony of the nation is promoted and the whole Union is knit together by the sentiments of mutual respect, the habits of social intercourse, and the ties of personal friendship formed between the representatives of its several parts in the performance of their service at this metropolis.

Passing from this general review of the purposes and injunctions of the Federal Constitution and their results as indicating the first traces of the path of duty in the discharge of my public trust, I turn to the Administration of my immediate predecessor as the second. It has passed away in a period of profound peace, how much to the satisfaction of our country and to the honor of our country's name is known to you all. The great features of its policy, in general concurrence with the will of the Legislature, have been to cherish peace while preparing for defensive war; to yield exact justice to other nations and maintain the rights of our own; to cherish the principles of freedom and of equal rights wherever they were proclaimed; to discharge with all possible promptitude the national debt; to reduce within the narrowest limits of efficiency the military force; to improve the organization and discipline of the Army; to provide and sustain a school of military science; to extend equal protection to all the great interests of the nation; to promote the civilization of the Indian tribes, and to proceed in the great system of internal improvements within the limits of the constitutional power of the Union. Under the pledge of these promises, made by that eminent citizen at the time of his first induction to this office, in his career of eight years the internal taxes have been repealed; sixty millions of the public debt have been discharged; provision has been made for the comfort and relief of the aged and indigent among the surviving warriors of the Revolution; the regular armed force has been reduced and its constitution revised and perfected; the accountability for the expenditure of public moneys has been made more effective; the Floridas have been peaceably acquired, and our boundary has been extended to the Pacific Ocean; the independence of the southern nations of this hemisphere has been recognized, and recommended by example and by counsel to the potentates of Europe; progress has been made in the defense of the country by fortifications and the increase of the Navy, toward the effectual suppression of the African traffic in slaves; in alluring the aboriginal hunters of our land to the cultivation of the soil and of the mind, in exploring the interior regions of the Union, and in preparing by scientific researches and surveys for the further application of our national resources to the internal improvement of our country.

In this brief outline of the promise and performance of my immediate predecessor the line of duty for his successor is clearly delineated To pursue to their consummation those purposes of improvement in our common condition instituted or recommended by him will embrace the whole sphere of my obligations. To the topic of internal improvement, emphatically urged by him at his inauguration, I recur with peculiar satisfaction. It is that from which I am convinced that the unborn millions of our posterity who are in future ages to people this continent will derive their most fervent gratitude to the founders of the Union; that in which the beneficent action of its Government will be most deeply felt and acknowledged. The magnificence and splendor of their public works are among the imperishable glories of the ancient republics. The roads and aqueducts of Rome have been the admiration of all after ages, and have survived thousands of years after all her conquests have been swallowed up in despotism or become the spoil of barbarians. Some diversity of opinion has prevailed with regard to the powers of Congress for legislation upon objects of this nature. The most respectful deference is due

to doubts originating in pure patriotism and sustained by vener-
ated authority. But nearly twenty years have passed since the construction of the first national road was commenced. The authority
for its construction was then unquestioned. To how many thousands of our countrymen has it proved a benefit? To what single
individual has it ever proved an injury? Repeated, liberal, and
candid discussions in the Legislature have conciliated the sentiments and approximated the opinions of enlightened minds upon
the question of constitutional power. I cannot but hope that by
the same process of friendly, patient, and persevering deliberation all constitutional objections will ultimately be removed. The
extent and limitation of the powers of the General Government in
relation to this transcendently important interest will be settled
and acknowledged to the common satisfaction of all, and every
speculative scruple will be solved by a practical public blessing.

Fellow-citizens, you are acquainted with the peculiar circumstances of the recent election, which have resulted in affording
me the opportunity of addressing you at this time. You have heard
the exposition of the principles which will direct me in the fulfillment of the high and solemn trust imposed upon me in this station. Less possessed of your confidence in advance than any of
my predecessors, I am deeply conscious of the prospect that I
shall stand more and oftener in need of your indulgence. Intentions upright and pure, a heart devoted to the welfare of our
country, and the unceasing application of all the faculties allotted to me to her service are all the pledges that I can give for the
faithful performance of the arduous duties I am to undertake. To
the guidance of the legislative councils, to the assistance of the
executive and subordinate departments, to the friendly cooperation of the respective State governments, to the candid and liberal support of the people so far as it may be deserved by honest
industry and zeal, I shall look for whatever success may attend
my public service; and knowing that "except the Lord keep the
city the watchman waketh but in vain," with fervent supplications for His favor, to His overruling providence I commit with

humble but fearless confidence my own fate and the future destinies of my country.

FIRST ANNUAL MESSAGE TO CONGRESS, DECEMBER 6, 1825

Despite the strenuous objections of the cabinet, John Quincy set out his agenda for national greatness. "The spirit of improvement is upon the earth," he told Congress. "It stimulates the hearts and sharpens the faculties not of our fellow citizens alone, but of the nations of Europe and of their rulers. While dwelling with pleasing satisfaction upon the superior excellence of our political institutions, let us not be unmindful that liberty is power; that the nation blessed with the largest portion of liberty must in proportion to its numbers be the most powerful nation upon earth, and that the tenure of power by man is, in the moral purposes of his Creator, upon condition that it shall be exercised to ends of beneficence, to improve the condition of himself and his fellow men."

Fellow citizens of the Senate and of the House of Representatives:

In taking a general survey of the concerns of our beloved country, with reference to subjects interesting to the common welfare, the first sentiment which impresses itself upon the mind is of gratitude to the Omnipotent Disposer of All Good for the continuance of the signal blessings of His providence, and especially for that health which to an unusual extent has prevailed within our borders, and for that abundance which in the vicissitudes of the seasons has been scattered with profusion over our land. Nor ought we less to ascribe to Him the glory that we are permitted to enjoy the bounties of His hand in peace and tranquillity – in peace with all the other nations of the earth, in tranquillity among ourselves. There has, indeed, rarely been a period in the history of civilized man in which the general condition of the Christian nations has been marked so extensively by peace and prosperity.

Europe, with a few partial and unhappy exceptions, has enjoyed 10 years of peace, during which all her governments, whatever the theory of their constitutions may have been, are successively taught to feel that the end of their institution is the happiness of the people, and that the exercise of power among men can be justified only by the blessings it confers upon those over whom it is extended.

During the same period our intercourse with all those nations has been pacific and friendly; it so continues. Since the close of your last session no material variation has occurred in our relations with any one of them. In the commercial and navigation system of Great Britain important changes of municipal regulation have recently been sanctioned by acts of Parliament, the effect of which upon the interests of other nations, and particularly upon ours, has not yet been fully developed. In the recent renewal of the diplomatic missions on both sides between the two governments assurances have been given and received of the continuance and increase of the mutual confidence and cordiality by which the adjustment of many points of difference had already been effected, and which affords the surest pledge for the ultimate satisfactory adjustment of those which still remain open or may hereafter arise.

The policy of the United States in their commercial intercourse with other nations has always been of the most liberal character. In the mutual exchange of their respective productions they have abstained altogether from prohibitions; they have interdicted themselves the power of laying taxes upon exports, and whenever they have favored their own shipping by special preferences or exclusive privileges in their own ports it has been only with a view to countervail similar favors and exclusions granted by the nations with whom we have been engaged in traffic to their own people or shipping, and to the disadvantage of ours. Immediately after the close of the last war a proposal was fairly made by the act of Congress of 1815-03-03, to all the maritime nations to lay aside the system of retaliating restrictions and exclusions, and to place the shipping of both parties to the common trade on a footing of equality in respect to the duties of tonnage and impost. This offer was partially and successively accepted by Great Britain, Sweden, the Netherlands, the Hanseatic cities, Prussia, Sardinia, the Duke of Oldenburg, and Russia. It was also adopted, under certain modifications, in our late commercial convention with France, and by the act of Congress of 1824-01-08, it has received a new confirmation with all the nations who had acceded to it, and has been offered again to all those who are or may hereafter be willing to abide in reciprocity by it. But all these regulations, whether established by treaty or by municipal enactments, are still subject to one important restriction.

The removal of discriminating duties of tonnage and of impost is limited to articles of the growth, produce, or manufacture of the country to which the vessel belongs or to such articles as are most usually first shipped from her ports. It will deserve the serious consideration of Congress whether even this remnant of restriction may not be safely abandoned, and whether the general tender of equal competition made in the act of 1824-01-08, may not be extended to include all articles of merchandise not prohibited, of what country so ever they may be the produce or manufacture. Propositions of this effect have already been made to us by more than one European government, and it is probable that if once established by legislation or compact with any distinguished maritime state it would recommend itself by the experience of its advantages to the general accession of all.

The convention of commerce and navigation between the United States and France, concluded on 1822-06-24, was, in the understanding and intent of both parties, as appears upon its face, only a temporary arrangement of the points of difference between them of the most immediate and pressing urgency. It was limited in the first instance to two years from 1822-10-01, but with a proviso that it should further continue in force 'til the conclusion of a general and definitive treaty of commerce, unless terminated by a notice, six months in advance, of either of the parties to the other. Its operation so far as it extended has been mutually advantageous, and it still continues in force by common consent. But it left unadjusted several objects of great interest to the citizens and subjects of both countries, and particularly a mass of claims to considerable amount of citizens of the United States upon the government of France of indemnity for property taken or destroyed under circumstances of the most aggravated and outrageous character. In the long period during which continual and earnest appeals have been made to the equity and magnanimity of France in behalf of these claims their justice has not been, as it could not be, denied.

It was hoped that the accession of a new Sovereign to the throne would have afforded a favorable opportunity for presenting them to the consideration of his government. They have been presented and urged hitherto without effect. The repeated and earnest representations of our minister at the Court of France remain as yet even without an answer. Were the demands of nations upon the justice of each other susceptible of adjudication by the sentence of an impartial tribunal, those to which I now refer would long since have been settled and adequate indemnity would have been obtained.

There are large amounts of similar claims upon the Netherlands, Naples, and Denmark. For those upon Spain prior to 1819 indemnity was, after many years of patient forbearance, obtained; and those upon Sweden have been lately compromised by a private settlement, in which the claimants themselves have acquiesced. The governments of Denmark and of Naples have been recently reminded of those yet existing against them, nor will any of them be forgotten while a hope may be indulged of obtaining justice by the means within the constitutional power of the executive, and without resorting to those means of self-redress which, as well as the time, circumstances, and occasion which may require them, are within the exclusive competency of the legislature.

It is with great satisfaction that I am enabled to bear witness to the liberal spirit with which the Republic of Colombia has made satisfaction for well-established claims of a similar character, and among the documents now communicated to Congress will be distinguished a treaty of commerce and navigation with that Republic, the ratifications of which have been exchanged since the last recess of the legislature. The negotiation of similar treaties with all of the independent South American states has been contemplated and may yet be accomplished. The basis of them all, as proposed by the United States, has been laid in two principles – the one of entire and unqualified reciprocity, the other the mutual obligation of the parties to place each other permanently upon the footing of the most favored nation. These principles are, indeed, indispensable to the effectual emancipation of the American hemisphere from the thralldom of colonizing monopolies and exclusions, an event rapidly realizing in the progress of human affairs, and which the resistance still opposed in certain parts of Europe to the acknowledgment of the Southern American republics as independent states will, it is believed, contribute more effectually to accomplish. The time has been, and that not remote, when some of those states might, in their anxious desire to obtain a nominal recognition, have accepted of a nominal independence, clogged with burdensome conditions, and exclusive commercial privileges granted to the nation from which they have separated to the disadvantage of all others. They are all now aware that such concessions to any European nation would be incompatible with that independence which they have declared and maintained.

Among the measures which have been suggested to them by the new relations with one another, resulting from the recent changes in their condition, is that of assembling at the Isthmus of Panama a congress, at which each of them should be represented, to deliberate upon objects important to the welfare of all. The republics of Colombia, of Mexico, and of Central America have already deputed plenipotentiaries to such a meeting, and they have invited the United States to be also represented there by their ministers. The invitation has been accepted, and ministers on the part of the United States will be commissioned to attend at those deliberations, and to take part in them so far as may be compatible with that neutrality from which it is neither our intention nor the desire of the other American states that we should depart.

The commissioners under the seventh article of the Treaty of Ghent have so nearly completed their arduous labors that, by the report recently received from the agent on the part of the United States, there is reason to expect that the commission will be closed at their next session, appointed for May 22 of the ensuing year.

The other commission, appointed to ascertain the indemnities due for slaves carried away from the United States after the close of the late war, have met with some difficulty, which has delayed their progress in the inquiry. A reference has been made to the British government on the subject, which, it may be hoped, will tend to hasten the decision of the commissioners, or serve as a substitute for it.

Among the powers specifically granted to Congress by the Constitution are those of establishing uniform laws on the subject of bankruptcies throughout the United States and of providing for organizing, arming, and disciplining the militia and for governing such part of them as may be employed in the services of the United States. The magnitude and complexity of the interests affected by legislation upon these subjects may account for the fact that, long and often as both of them have occupied the attention and animated the debates of Congress, no systems have yet been devised for fulfilling to the satisfaction of the community the duties prescribed by these grants of power.

To conciliate the claim of the individual citizen to the enjoyment of personal liberty, with the effective obligation of private contracts, is the difficult problem to be solved by a law of bankruptcy. These are objects of the deepest interest to society, affecting all that is precious in the existence of multitudes of persons, many of them in the classes essentially dependent and helpless, of the age requiring nurture, and of the sex entitled to protection from the free agency of the parent and the husband. The organization of the militia is yet more indispensable to the liberties of the country. It is only by an effective militia that we can at once enjoy the repose of peace and bid defiance to foreign aggression; it is by the militia that we are constituted an armed nation, standing in perpetual panoply of defense in the presence of all the other nations of the earth. To this end it would be necessary, if possible, so to shape its organization as to give it a more united and active energy. There are laws establishing an uniform militia throughout the United States and for arming and equipping its whole body. But it is a body of dislocated members, without the vigor of unity and having little of uniformity but the name. To infuse into this most important institution the power of which it is susceptible and to make it available for the defense of the Union at the shortest notice and at the smallest expense possible of time, of life, and of treasure are among the benefits to be expected from the persevering deliberations of Congress.

Among the unequivocal indications of our national prosperity is the flourishing state of our finances. The revenues of the present year, from all their principal sources, will exceed the anticipations of the last. The balance in the Treasury on the first of January last was a little short of $2,000,000, exclusive of $2,500,000, being the moiety of the loan of $5,000,000 authorized by the act of 1824-05-26. The receipts into the Treasury from the 1st of January to the 30th of September, exclusive of the other moiety of the same loan, are estimated at $16,500,000, and it is expected that those of the current quarter will exceed $5,000,000, forming an aggregate of receipts of nearly $22,000,000, independent of the loan. The expenditures of the year will not exceed that sum more than $2,000,000. By those expenditures nearly $8,000,000 of the principal of the public debt that have been discharged.

More than $1,500,000 has been devoted to the debt of gratitude to the warriors of the Revolution; a nearly equal sum to the construction of fortifications and the acquisition of ordnance and other permanent preparations of national defense; $500,000 to the gradual increase of the Navy; an equal sum for purchases of territory from the Indians and payment of annuities to them; and upward of $1,000,000 for objects of internal improvement authorized by special acts of the last Congress. If we add to these $4,000,000 for payment of interest upon the public debt, there remains a sum of $7,000,000, which have defrayed the whole expense of the administration of government in its legislative, executive, and judiciary departments, including the support of the military and naval establishments and all the occasional contingencies of a government coextensive with the Union.

The amount of duties secured on merchandise imported since the commencement of the year is about $25,500,000, and that which will accrue during the current quarter is estimated at $5,500,000; from these $31,000,000, deducting the drawbacks, estimated at less than $7,000,000, a sum exceeding $24,000,000 will constitute the revenue of the year, and will exceed the whole expenditures of the year. The entire amount of the public debt remaining due on the first of January next will be short of $81,000,000.

By an act of Congress of the 3rd of March last a loan of $12,000,000 was authorized at 4.5 percent, or an exchange of stock to that amount of 4.5 percent for a stock of 6 percent, to create a fund for extinguishing an equal amount of the public debt, bearing an interest of 6 percent, redeemable in 1826. An account of the measures taken to give effect to this act will be laid before you by the Secretary of the Treasury. As the object which it had in view has been but partially accomplished, it will be for the consideration of Congress whether the power with which it clothed the executive should not be renewed at an early day of the present session, and under what modifications.

The act of Congress of the 3rd of March last, directing the Secretary of the Treasury to subscribe, in the name and for the use of the United States, for 1,500 shares of the capital stock of

the Chesapeake and Delaware Canal Company, has been executed by the actual subscription for the amount specified; and
such other measures have been adopted by that officer, under the
act, as the fulfillment of its intentions requires. The latest accounts
received of this important undertaking authorize the belief that
it is in successful progress.

The payments into the Treasury from the proceeds of the sales
of the public lands during the present year were estimated at
$1,000,000. The actual receipts of the first two quarters have
fallen very little short of that sum; it is not expected that the second half of the year will be equally productive, but the income of
the year from that source may now be safely estimated at
$1,500,000. The act of Congress of 1824-05-18, to provide for
the extinguishment of the debt due to the United States by the
purchasers of public lands, was limited in its operation of relief
to the purchaser to the 10th of April last. Its effect at the end of
the quarter during which it expired was to reduce that debt from
$10,000,000 to $7,000,000 By the operation of similar prior
laws of relief, from and since that of 1821-03-02, the debt had
been reduced from upward of $22,000,000 to $10,000,000.

It is exceedingly desirable that it should be extinguished altogether; and to facilitate that consummation I recommend to
Congress the revival for one year more of the act of 1824-05-18,
with such provisional modification as may be necessary to guard
the public interests against fraudulent practices in the resale of
the relinquished land.

The purchasers of public lands are among the most useful of
our fellow citizens, and since the system of sales for cash alone
has been introduced great indulgence has been justly extended to
those who had previously purchased upon credit. The debt which
had been contracted under the credit sales had become unwieldy,
and its extinction was alike advantageous to the purchaser and to
the public. Under the system of sales, matured as it has been
by experience, and adapted to the exigencies of the times, the
lands will continue as they have become, an abundant source of

revenue; and when the pledge of them to the public creditor shall have been redeemed by the entire discharge of the national debt, the swelling tide of wealth with which they replenish the common Treasury may be made to reflow in unfailing streams of improvement from the Atlantic to the Pacific Ocean.

The condition of the various branches of the public service resorting from the Department of War, and their administration during the current year, will be exhibited in the report of the Secretary of War and the accompanying documents herewith communicated. The organization and discipline of the Army are effective and satisfactory. To counteract the prevalence of desertion among the troops it has been suggested to withhold from the men a small portion of their monthly pay until the period of their discharge; and some expedient appears to be necessary to preserve and maintain among the officers so much of the art of horsemanship as could scarcely fail to be found wanting on the possible sudden eruption of a war, which should take us unprovided with a single corps of cavalry.

The Military Academy at West Point, under the restrictions of a severe but paternal superintendence, recommends itself more and more to the patronage of the nation, and the numbers of meritorious officers which it forms and introduces to the public service furnishes the means of multiplying the undertakings of the public improvements to which their acquirements at that institution are peculiarly adapted. The school of artillery practice established at Fortress Monroe Hampton, Virginia is well suited to the same purpose, and may need the aid of further legislative provision to the same end. The reports of the various officers at the head of the administrative branches of the military service, connected with the quartering, clothing, subsistence, health, and pay of the Army, exhibit the assiduous vigilance of those officers in the performance of their respective duties, and the faithful accountability which has pervaded every part of the system.

Our relations with the numerous tribes of aboriginal natives of this country, scattered over its extensive surface and so dependent even for their existence upon our power, have been during the present year highly interesting. An act of Congress of 1824-05-25, made an appropriation to defray the expenses of making treaties of trade and friendship with the Indian tribes beyond the Mississippi. An act of 1825-03-03, authorized treaties to be made with the Indians for their consent to the making of a road from the frontier of Missouri to that of New Mexico, and another act of the same date provided for defraying the expenses of holding treaties with the Sioux, Chippeways, Menomenees, Sauks, Foxes, etc., for the purpose of establishing boundaries and promoting peace between said tribes.

The first and last objects of these acts have been accomplished, and the second is yet in a process of execution. The treaties which since the last session of Congress have been concluded with the several tribes will be laid before the Senate for their consideration conformably to the Constitution. They comprise large and valuable acquisitions of territory, and they secure an adjustment of boundaries and give pledges of permanent peace between several tribes which had been long waging bloody wars against each other.

On the 12th of February last a treaty was signed at the Indian Springs between commissioners appointed on the part of the United States and certain chiefs and individuals of the Creek Nation of Indians, which was received at the seat of government only a very few days before the close of the last session of Congress and of the late administration. The advice and consent of the Senate was given to it on the 3rd of March, too late for it to receive the ratification of the then President of the United States; it was ratified on the 7th of March, under the unsuspecting impression that it had been negotiated in good faith and in the confidence inspired by the recommendation of the Senate. The subsequent transactions in relation to this treaty will form the subject of a separate communication.

The appropriations made by Congress for public works, as well in the construction of fortifications as for purposes of internal improvement, so far as they have been expended, have been faithfuly applied. Their progress has been delayed by the want of suitable officers for superintending them. An increase of both the corps of engineers, military and topographical, was recommended by my predecessor at the last session of Congress. The reasons upon which that recommendation was founded subsist in all their force and have acquired additional urgency since that time. The Military Academy at West Point will furnish from the cadets there officers well qualified for carrying this measure into effect.

The Board of Engineers for Internal Improvement, appointed for carrying into execution the act of Congress of 1824-04-30, "to procure the necessary surveys, plans, and estimates on the subject of roads and canals," have been actively engaged in that service from the close of the last session of Congress. They have completed the surveys necessary for ascertaining the practicability of a canal from the Chesapeake Bay to the Ohio River, and are preparing a full report on that subject, which, when completed, will be laid before you. The same observation is to be made with regard to the two other objects of national importance upon which the Board have been occupied, namely, the accomplishment of a national road from this city to New Orleans, and the practicability of uniting the waters of Lake Memphramagog with Connecticut River and the improvement of the navigation of that river. The surveys have been made and are nearly completed. The report may be expected at an early period during the present session of Congress.

The acts of Congress of the last session relative to the surveying, marking, or laying out roads in the Territories of Florida, Arkansas, and Michigan, from Missouri to Mexico, and for the continuation of the Cumberland road, are, some of them, fully executed, and others in the process of execution. Those for completing or commencing fortifications have been delayed only so far as the Corps of Engineers has been inadequate to furnish officers for the necessary superintendence of the works. Under the act confirming the statutes of Virginia and Maryland incorporating the Chesapeake and Ohio Canal Company, three commissioners on the part of the United States have been appointed for opening books and receiving subscriptions, in concert with a like number of commissioners appointed on the part of each of those states. A meeting of the commissioners has been post-poned, to await the definitive report of the board of engineers.

The light-houses and monuments for the safety of our commerce and mariners, the works for the security of Plymouth Beach and for the preservation of the islands in Boston Harbor, have received the attention required by the laws relating to those objects respectively. The continuation of the Cumberland road, the most important of them all, after surmounting no inconsiderable difficulty in fixing upon the direction of the road, has commenced under the most promising of auspices, with the improvements of recent invention in the mode of construction, and with advantage of a great reduction in the comparative cost of the work.

The operation of the laws relating to the Revolutionary pensioners may deserve the renewed consideration of Congress. The act of 1818-03-18, while it made provision for many meritorious and indigent citizens who had served in the War of Independence, opened a door to numerous abuses and impositions. To remedy this the act of 1820-05-01, exacted proofs of absolute indigence, which many really in want were unable and all susceptible of that delicacy which is allied to many virtues must be deeply reluctant to give. The result has been that some among the least deserving have been retained, and some in whom the requisites both of worth and want were combined have been stricken from the list. As the numbers of these venerable relics of an age gone by diminish; as the decays of body, mind, and estate of those that survive must in the common course of nature increase, should not a more liberal portion of indulgence be dealt out to them? May not the want in most instances be inferred from the demand when the service can be proved, and may not the last days of human infirmity be spared the mortification of purchasing a pittance of relief only by the exposure of its own necessities?

I submit to Congress the expediency of providing for individual cases of this description by special enactment, or of revising the act of 1820-05-01, with a view to mitigate the rigor of its exclusions in favor of persons to whom charity now bestowed can scarcely discharge the debt of justice.

The portion of the naval force of the Union in actual service has been chiefly employed on three stations – the Mediterranean, the coasts of South America bordering on the Pacific Ocean, and the West Indies. An occasional cruiser has been sent to range along the African shores most polluted by the traffic of slaves; one armed vessel has been stationed on the coast of our eastern boundary, to cruise along the fishing grounds in Hudsons Bay and on the coast of Labrador, and the first service of a new frigate has been performed in restoring to his native soil and domestic enjoyments the veteran hero whose youthful blood and treasure had freely flowed in the cause of our country's independence, and whose whole life has been a series of services and sacrifices to the improvement of his fellow men.

The visit of General Lafayette, alike honorable to himself and to our country, closed, as it had commenced, with the most affecting testimonials of devoted attachment on his part, and of unbounded gratitude of this people to him in return. It will form here-after a pleasing incident in the annals of our Union, giving to real history the intense interest of romance and signally marking the unpurchasable tribute of a great nation's social affections to the disinterested champion of the liberties of humankind.

The constant maintenance of a small squadron in the Mediterranean is a necessary substitute for the humiliating alternative of paying tribute for the security of our commerce in that sea, and for a precarious peace, at the mercy of every caprice of four Barbary states, by whom it was liable to be violated. An additional motive for keeping a respectable force stationed there at this time is found in the maritime war raging between the Greeks and the Turks, and in which the neutral navigation of this Union is always in danger of outrage and depredation. A few instances have occurred of such depredations upon our merchant vessels by privateers or pirates wearing the Grecian flag, but without real authority from the Greek or any other government. The heroic struggles of the Greeks themselves, in which our warmest sympathies as free men and Christians have been engaged, have continued to be maintained with vicissitudes of success adverse and favorable.

Similar motives have rendered expedient the keeping of a like force on the coasts of Peru and Chile on the Pacific. The irregular and convulsive character of the war upon the shores has been extended to the conflicts upon the ocean. An active warfare has been kept up for years with alternate success, though generally to the advantage of the American patriots. But their naval forces have not always been under the control of their own governments. Blockades, unjustifiable upon any acknowledged principles of international law, have been proclaimed by officers in command, and though disavowed by the supreme authorities, the protection of our own commerce against them has been made cause of complaint and erroneous imputations against some of the most gallant officers of our Navy. Complaints equally groundless have been made by the commanders of the Spanish royal forces in those seas; but the most effective protection to our commerce has been the flag and the firmness of our own commanding officers.

The cessation of the war by the complete triumph of the patriot cause has removed, it is hoped, all cause of dissension with one party and all vestige of force of the other. But an unsettled coast of many degrees of latitude forming a part of our own territory and a flourishing commerce and fishery extending to the islands of the Pacific and to China still require that the protecting power of the Union should be displayed under its flag as well upon the ocean as upon the land.

The objects of the West India Squadron have been to carry into execution the laws for the suppression of the African slave trade; for the protection of our commerce against vessels of piratical character, though bearing commissions from either of the belligerent parties; for its protection against open and unequivocal pirates. These objects during the present year have been accomplished more effectually than at any former period. The African slave trade has long been excluded from the use of our flag, and if some few citizens of our country have continued to set the laws of the Union as well as those of nature and humanity at defiance by persevering in that abominable traffic, it has been only by sheltering themselves under the banners of other nations less earnest for the total extinction of the trade of ours.

The active, persevering, and unremitted energy of Captain Warrington and of the officers and men under his command on that trying and perilous service have been crowned with signal success, and are entitled to the approbation of their country. But experience has shown that not even a temporary suspension or relaxation from assiduity can be indulged on that station without reproducing piracy and murder in all their horrors; nor is it probably that for years to come our immensely valuable commerce in those seas can navigate in security without the steady continuance of an armed force devoted to its protection.

It were, indeed, a vain and dangerous illusion to believe that in the present or probable condition of human society a commerce so extensive and so rich as ours could exist and be pursued in safety without the continual support of a military marine – the only arm by which the power of this Confederacy can be estimated or felt by foreign nations, and the only standing military force which can never be dangerous to our own liberties at home. A permanent naval peace establishment, therefore, adapted to our present condition, and adaptable to that gigantic growth with which the nation is advancing in its career, is among the subjects which have already occupied the foresight of the last Congress, and which will deserve your serious deliberations. Our Navy, commenced at an early period of our present political organization upon a scale commensurate with the incipient energies, the scanty resources, and the comparative indigence of our infancy, was even then found adequate to cope with all the powers of Barbary, save the first, and with one of the principle maritime powers of Europe.

At a period of further advancement, but with little accession of strength, it not only sustained with honor the most unequal of conflicts, but covered itself and our country with unfading glory. But it is only since the close of the late war that by the numbers and force of the ships of which it was composed it could deserve the name of a navy. Yet it retains nearly the same organization as when it consisted only of five frigates. The rules and regulations by which it is governed earnestly call for revision, and the want of a naval school of instruction, corresponding with the Military Academy at West Point, for the formation of scientific and accomplished officers, is felt with daily increasing aggravation.

The act of Congress of 1824-05-26, authorizing an examination and survey of the harbor of Charleston, in South Carolina, of St. Marys, in Georgia, and of the coast of Florida, and for other purposes, has been executed so far as the appropriation would admit. Those of the 3rd of March last, authorizing the establishment of a navy yard and depot on the coast of Florida, in the Gulf of Mexico, and authorizing the building of 10 sloops of war, and for other purposes, are in the course of execution, for the particulars of which and other objects connected with this Department I refer to the report of the Secretary of the Navy, herewith communicated.

A report from the Postmaster General is also submitted, exhibiting the present flourishing condition of that Department. For the first time for many years the receipts for the year ending on the first of July last exceeded the expenditures during the same period to the amount of more than $45,000. Other facts equally creditable to the administration of this Department are that in two years from 1823-07-01, an improvement of more than $185,000 in its pecuniary affairs has been realized; that in the same interval the increase of the transportation of the mail has exceeded 1,500,000 miles annually, and that 1,040 new post offices have been established. It hence appears that under judicious management the income from this establishment may be relied on as fully adequate to defray its expenses, and that by the discontinuance of post roads altogether unproductive, others of more useful character may be opened, 'til the circulation of the mail shall keep pace with the spread of our population, and the comforts of friendly correspondence, the exchanges of internal traffic, and the lights of the periodical press shall be distributed to the remotest corners of the Union, at a charge scarcely perceptible to any individual, and without the cost of a dollar to the public Treasury.

Upon this first occasion of addressing the legislature of the Union, with which I have been honored, in presenting to their view the execution so far as it has been effected of the measures sanctioned by them for promoting the internal improvement of our country, I cannot close the communication without recommending to their calm and persevering consideration the general principle in a more enlarged extent. The great object of the institution of civil government is the improvement of the condition of those who are parties to the social compact, and no government, in whatever form constituted, can accomplish the lawful ends of its institution but in proportion as it improves the condition of those over whom it is established. Roads and canals, by multiplying and facilitating the communications and intercourse between distant regions and multitudes of men, are among the most important means of improvement. But moral, political, intellectual improvement are duties assigned by the Author of Our Existence to social no less than to individual man.

For the fulfillment of those duties governments are invested with power, and to the attainment of the end – the progressive improvement of the condition of the governed – the exercise of delegated powers is a duty as sacred and indispensable as the usurpation of powers not granted is criminal and odious.

Among the first, perhaps the very first, instrument for the improvement of the condition of men is knowledge, and to the acquisition of much of the knowledge adapted to the wants, the comforts, and enjoyments of human life public institutions and seminaries of learning are essential. So convinced of this was the first of my predecessors in this office, now first in the memory, as, living, he was first in the hearts, of our countrymen, that once and again in his addresses to the Congresses with whom he cooperated in the public service he earnestly recommended the establishment of seminaries of learning, to prepare for all the emergencies of peace and war – a national university and a military academy. With respect to the latter, had he lived to the present day, in turning his eyes to the institution at West Point he would have enjoyed the gratification of his most earnest wishes; but in surveying the city which has been honored with his name he would have seen the spot of earth which he had destined and bequeathed to the use and benefit of his country as the site for a university still bare and barren.

In assuming her station among the civilized nations of the earth it would seem that our country had contracted the engagement to contribute her share of mind, of labor, and of expense to the improvement of those parts of knowledge which lie beyond the reach of individual acquisition, and particularly to geographical and astronomical science. Looking back to the history only of the half century since the declaration of our independence, and observing the generous emulation with which the governments of France, Great Britain, and Russia have devoted the genius, the intelligence, the treasures of their respective nations to the common improvement of the species in these branches of science, is it not incumbent upon us to inquire whether we are not bound by obligations of a high and honorable character to contribute our portion of energy and exertion to the common stock? The voyages of discovery prosecuted in the course of that time at the expense of those nations have not only redounded to their glory, but to the improvement of human knowledge.

We have been partakers of that improvement and owe for it a sacred debt, not only of gratitude, but of equal or proportional

exertion in the same common cause. Of the cost of these undertakings, if the mere expenditures of outfit, equipment, and completion of the expeditions were to be considered the only charges,
it would be unworthy of a great and generous nation to take a
second thought. One hundred expeditions of circumnavigation
like those of Cook and La Prouse would not burden the exche-
quer of the nation fitting them out so much as the ways and means
of defraying a single campaign in war. but if we take into account
the lives of those benefactors of man-kind of which their services
in the cause of their species were the purchase, how shall the cost
of those heroic enterprises be estimated, and what compensation
can be made to them or to their countries for them? Is it not by
bearing them in affectionate remembrance? Is it not still more by
imitating their example – by enabling country-men of our own to
pursue the same career and to hazard their lives in the same cause?

In inviting the attention of Congress to the subject of internal
improvements upon a view thus enlarged it is not my desire to
recommend the equipment of an expedition for circumnavigat-
ing the globe for purposes of scientific research and inquiry. We
have objects of useful investigation nearer home, and to which
our cares may be more beneficially applied. The interior of our
own territories has yet been very imperfectly explored. our coasts
along many degrees of latitude upon the shores of the Pacific
Ocean, though much frequented by our spirited commercial
navigators, have been barely visited by our public ships. The
River of the West, first fully discovered and navigated by a countryman of our own, still bears the name of the ship in which he
ascended its waters, and claims the protection of our armed
national flag at its mouth. With the establishment of a military
post there or at some other point of that coast, recommended by
my predecessor and already matured in the deliberations of the
last Congress, I would suggest the expediency of connecting the
equipment of a public ship for the exploration of the whole
north-west coast of this continent.

The establishment of an uniform standard of weights and

measures was one of the specific objects contemplated in the formation of our Constitution, and to fix that standard was one of the powers delegated by express terms in that instrument to Congress. The governments of Great Britain and France have scarcely ceased to be occupied with inquiries and speculations on the same subject since the existence of our Constitution, and with them it has expanded into profound, laborious, and expensive researches into the figure of the earth and the comparative length of the pendulum vibrating seconds in various latitudes from the equator to the pole. These researches have resulted in the composition and publication of several works highly interesting to the cause of science. The experiments are yet in the process of performance. Some of them have recently been made on our own shores, within the walls of one of our own colleges, and partly by one of our own fellow citizens. It would be honorable to our country if the sequel of the same experiments should be countenanced by the patronage of our government, as they have hitherto been by those of France and Britain.

Connected with the establishment of an university, or separate from it, might be undertaken the erection of an astronomical observatory, with provision for the support of an astronomer, to be in constant attendance of observation upon the phenomena of the heavens, and for the periodical publication of his observances. it is with no feeling of pride as an American that the remark may be made that on the comparatively small territorial surface of Europe there are existing upward of 130 of these lighthouses of the skies, while throughout the whole American hemisphere there is not one. If we reflect a moment upon the discoveries which in the last four centuries have been made in the physical constitution of the universe by the means of these buildings and of observers stationed in them, shall we doubt of their usefulness to every nation? And while scarcely a year passes over our heads without bringing some new astronomical discovery to light, which we must fain receive at second hand from Europe, are we not cutting ourselves off from the means of returning light for light while we have neither observatory nor observer upon our half of the globe and the earth revolves in perpetual darkness to our unsearching eyes?

When, on 1791-10-25, the first President of the United States announced to Congress the result of the first enumeration of the inhabitants of this Union, he informed them that the returns gave the pleasing assurance that the population of the United States bordered on 4,000,000 persons. At the distance of 30 years from that time the last enumeration, five years since completed, presented a population bordering on 10,000,000. Perhaps of all the evidence of a prosperous and happy condition of human society the rapidity of the increase of population is the most unequivocal. But the demonstration of our prosperity rests not alone upon this indication.

Our commerce, our wealth, and the extent of our territories have increased in corresponding proportions, and the number of independent communities associated in our federal Union has since that time nearly doubled. The legislative representation of the states and people in the two Houses of Congress has grown with the growth of their constituent bodies. The House, which then consisted of 65 members, now numbers upward of 200. The Senate, which consisted of 26 members, has now 48. But the executive and, still more, the judiciary departments are yet in a great measure confined to their primitive organization, and are now not adequate to the urgent wants of a still growing community.

The naval armaments, which at an early period forced themselves upon the necessities of the Union, soon led to the establishment of a Department of the Navy. But the Departments of Foreign Affairs and of the Interior, which early after the formation of the government had been united in one, continue so united to this time, to the unquestionable detriment of the public service. The multiplication of our relations with the nations and governments of the Old World has kept pace with that of our population and commerce, while within the last 10 years a new family of nations in our own hemisphere has arisen among the inhabitants of the earth, with whom our intercourse, commercial and political, would of itself furnish occupation to an active and industrious department.

The constitution of the judiciary, experimental and imperfect as it was even in the infancy of our existing government, is yet more inadequate to the administration of national justice at our present maturity. Nine years have elapsed since a predecessor in this office, now not the last, the citizen who, perhaps, of all others throughout the Union contributed most to the formation and establishment of our Constitution, in his valedictory address to Congress, immediately preceding his retirement from public life, urgently recommended the revision of the judiciary and the establishment of an additional executive department. The exigencies of the public service and its unavoidable deficiencies, as now in exercise, have added yearly cumulative weight to the considerations presented by him as persuasive to the measure, and in recommending it to your deliberations I am happy to have the influence of this high authority in aid of the undoubting convictions of my own experience.

The laws relating to the administration of the Patent Office are deserving of much consideration and perhaps susceptible of some improvement. The grant of power to regulate the action of Congress upon this subject has specified both the end to be obtained and the means by which it is to be effected, "to promote the progress of science and useful arts by securing for limited times to authors and inventors the exclusive right to their respective writings and discoveries". If an honest pride might be indulged in the reflection that on the records of that office are already found inventions the usefulness of which has scarcely been transcended in the annals of human ingenuity, would not its exultation be allayed by the inquiry whether the laws have effectively insured to the inventors the reward destined to them by the Constitution – even a limited term of exclusive right to their discoveries?

On 1799-12-24, it was resolved by Congress that a marble monument should be erected by the United States in the Capitol at the city of Washington; that the family of General Washington should be requested to permit his body to be deposited under it, and that the monument be so designed as to commemorate the great events of his military and political life. In reminding Congress of this resolution and that the monument contemplated by it remains yet without execution, I shall indulge only the remarks that the works at the Capitol are approaching to completion; that the consent of the family, desired by the resolution, was requested and obtained; that a monument has been recently erected in this city over the remains of another distinguished patriot of the Revolution, and that a spot has been reserved within the walls where you are deliberating for the benefit of this and future ages, in which the mortal remains may be deposited of him whose spirit hovers over you and listens with delight to every act of the representatives of his nation which can tend to exalt and adorn his and their country.

The Constitution under which you are assembled is a charter of limited powers. After full and solemn deliberation upon all or any of the objects which, urged by an irresistible sense of my own duty, I have recommended to your attention should you come to the conclusion that, however desirable in themselves, the enactment of laws for effecting them would transcend the powers committed to you by that venerable instrument which we are all bound to support, let no consideration induce you to assume the exercise of powers not granted to you by the people.

But if the power to exercise exclusive legislation in all cases what so ever over the District of Columbia; if the power to lay and collect taxes, duties, imposts, and excises, to pay the debts and provide for the common defense and general welfare of the United States; if the power to regulate commerce with foreign nations and among the several States and with the Indian tribes, to fix the standard of weights and measures, to establish post offices and post roads, to declare war, to raise and support armies, to provide and maintain a navy, to dispose of and make all needful rules and regulations respecting the territory or other property belonging to the United States, and to make all laws which shall be necessary and proper for carrying these powers into execution – if these powers and others enumerated in the Constitution may be effectually brought into action by laws promoting the improvement of agriculture, commerce, and manufactures, the cultivation and encouragement of the mechanic and of the elegant arts, the advancement of literature, and the progress of the sciences, ornamental and profound, to refrain from exercising them for the benefit of the people themselves would be to hide in the earth the talent committed to our charge – would be treachery to the most sacred of trusts.

The spirit of improvement is abroad upon the earth. It stimulates the hearts and sharpens the faculties not of our fellow citizens alone, but of the nations of Europe and of their rulers. While dwelling with pleasing satisfaction upon the superior excellence of our political institutions, let us not be unmindful that liberty is power; that the nation blessed with the largest portion of liberty must in proportion to its numbers be the most powerful nation upon earth, and that the tenure of power by man is, in the moral purposes of his Creator, upon condition that it shall be exercised to ends of beneficence, to improve the condition of himself and his fellow men.

While foreign nations less blessed with that freedom which is power than ourselves are advancing with gigantic strides in the career of public improvement, were we to slumber in indolence or fold up our arms and proclaim to the world that we are palsied by the will of our constituents, would it not be to cast away the bounties of Providence and doom ourselves to perpetual inferiority? In the course of the year now drawing to its close we have beheld, under the auspices and at the expense of one state of this Union, a new university unfolding its portals to the sons of science and holding up the torch of human improvement to eyes that seek the light. We have seen under the persevering and enlightened enterprise of another state the waters of our Western lakes mingle with those of the ocean. If undertakings like these have been accomplished in the compass of a few years by the authority of single members of our Confederation, can we, the representative authorities of the whole Union, fall behind our fellow servants in the exercise of the trust committed to us for the benefit of our common sovereign by the accomplishment of works important to the whole and to which neither the authority nor the resources of any one state can be adequate?

Finally, fellow citizens, I shall await with cheering hope and faithful cooperation the result of your deliberations, assured that, without encroaching upon the powers reserved to the authorities of the respective states or to the people, you will, with a due sense of your obligations to your country and of the high responsibilities weighing upon yourselves, give efficacy to the means committed to you for the common good. And may He who searches the hearts of the children of men prosper your exertions to secure the blessings of peace and promote the highest welfare of your country.

MESSAGE TO THE SENATE REGARDING THE CONGRESS OF AMERICAN RELATIONS, DECEMBER 6, 1825

Responding to a congressional request for further information on the proposed appropriation for a delegation to attend the Panama Congress, John Quincy argued that the United States' agenda of liberalized trade in peacetime, and freedom of the seas in wartime, could be advanced powerfully through American participation in the congress. As to the argument that attendance would violate George Washington's famous warning about avoiding foreign entanglements, John Quincy contended that it was contingent on a particular set of circumstances. Those circumstances had not changed with respect to America's "distant and detached situation" to the Old World. But the United States had grown much stronger over the past thirty years, in terms of population, wealth, territory, and power. And the American hemisphere as a whole had been transformed. The Spanish colonies had gained their independence, and the United States had important commercial and political relations with them. They were not distant or detached. Their "political principles and systems of government, congenial with our own, must and will have an action and counteraction upon us and ours to which we cannot be indifferent."

To the Senate of the United States:

In the message to both Houses of Congress at the commencement of the session it was mentioned that the Governments of the Republics of Colombia, of Mexico, and of Central America had severally invited the Government of the United States to be represented at the Congress of American nations to be assembled at Panama to deliberate upon objects of peculiar concernment to this hemisphere, and that this invitation had been accepted.

Although this measure was deemed to be within the constitutional competency of the Executive, I have not thought proper to take any step in it before ascertaining that my opinion of its expediency will concur with that of both branches of the Legislature, first, by the decision of the Senate upon the nominations to be laid before them, and, secondly, by the sanction of both Houses to the appropriations, without which it cannot be carried into effect.

A report from the Secretary of State and copies of the correspondence with the South American Governments on this subject since the invitation given by them are herewith transmitted to the Senate. They will disclose the objects of importance which are expected to form a subject of discussion at this meeting, in which interests of high importance to this Union are involved. It will be seen that the United States neither intend nor are expected to take part in any deliberations of a belligerent character; that the motive of their attendance is neither to contract alliances nor to engage in any undertaking or project importing hostility to any other nation.

But the Southern American nations, in the infancy of their independence, often find themselves in positions with reference to other countries with the principles applicable to which, derivable from the state of independence itself, they have not been familiarized by experience. The result of this has been that sometimes in their intercourse with the United States they have manifested dispositions to reserve a right of granting special favors and privileges to the Spanish nation as the price of their recognition. At others they have actually established duties and impositions operating unfavorably to the United States to the advantage of other European powers, and sometimes they have appeared to consider that they might interchange among themselves mutual concessions of exclusive favor, to which neither European powers nor the United States should be admitted. In most of these cases their regulations unfavorable to us have yielded to friendly expostulation and remonstrance. But it is believed to be of infinite moment that the principles of a liberal commercial intercourse should be exhibited to them, and urged with disinterested and friendly persuasion upon them when all assembled for the avowed purpose of consulting together upon the establishment of such principles as may have an important bearing upon their future welfare.

The consentaneous adoption of principles of maritime neutrality, and favorable to the navigation of peace, and commerce in time of war, will also form a subject of consideration to this Congress. The doctrine that free ships make free goods and the restrictions of reason upon the extent of blockades may be established by general agreement with far more ease, and perhaps with less danger, by the general engagement to adhere to them concerted at such a meeting, than by partial treaties or conventions with each of the nations separately. An agreement between all the parties represented at the meeting that each will guard by its own means against the establishment of any future European colony within its borders may be found advisable. This was more than two years since announced by my predecessor to the world as a principle resulting from the emancipation of both the American continents. It may be so developed to the new southern nations that they will all feel it as an essential appendage to their independence.

There is yet another subject upon which, without entering into any treaty, the moral influence of the United States may perhaps be exerted with beneficial consequences at such a meeting – the advancement of religious liberty. Some of the southern nations are even yet so far under the dominion of prejudice that they have incorporated with their political constitutions an exclusive church, without toleration of any other than the dominant sect. The abandonment of this last badge of religious bigotry and oppression may be pressed more effectually by the united exertions of those who concur in the principles of freedom of conscience upon those who are yet to be convinced of their justice and wisdom than by the solitary efforts of a minister to any one of the separate Governments.

The indirect influence which the United States may exercise upon any projects or purposes originating in the war in which the southern Republics are still engaged, which might seriously affect the interests of this Union, and the good offices by which the United States may ultimately contribute to bring that war to a speedier termination, though among the motives which have convinced me of the propriety of complying with this invitation, are so far contingent and eventual that it would be improper to dwell upon them more at large.

In fine, a decisive inducement with me for acceding to the measure is to show by this token of respect to the southern Republics the interest that we take in their welfare and our disposition to comply with their wishes. Having been the first to recognize their independence, and sympathized with them so far as was compatible with our neutral duties in all their struggles and sufferings to acquire it, we have laid the foundation of our future intercourse with them in the broadest principles of reciprocity and the most cordial feelings of fraternal friendship. To extend those principles to all our commercial relations with them and to hand down that friendship to future ages is congenial to the highest policy of the Union, as it will be to that of all those nations and their posterity. In the confidence that these sentiments will meet the approbation of the Senate, I nominate Richard C. Anderson, of Kentucky, and John Sergeant, of Pennsylvania, to be envoys extraordinary and ministers plenipotentiary to the assembly of American nations at Panama, and William B. Rochester, of New York, to be secretary to the mission.

FOURTH ANNUAL MESSAGE TO CONGRESS, DECEMBER 2, 1828

In his final State of the Union report, John Quincy summarized the goals and progress of American commercial relations with the rest of the world: "the mutual abolition of discriminating duties and charges." "There is reason to expect that it will, at no distant period, be adopted by other nations, both of Europe and America, and to hope that, by its universal prevalence, one of the fruitful sources of wars, of commercial competition, will be extinguished."

A treaty of amity, navigation, and commerce, between the United States and His Majesty the Emperor of Austria, King of Hungary and Bohemia, has been prepared for signature by the Secretary of State, and by the Baron de Lederer, instructed with full powers of the Austrian Government. Independently of the new and friendly relations which may be thus commenced with one of the most eminent and powerful nations of the earth, the occasion has been taken in it, as in other recent treaties concluded by the United States, to extend those principles of liberal intercourse and of fair reciprocity which intertwine with the exchange of commerce the principles of justice, and the feelings of mutual benevolence. This system, first proclaimed to the world in the first commercial treaty ever concluded by the United States, that of 6th February, 1778, with France, has been invariably the cherished policy of our Union. It is by treaties of commerce alone that it can be made ultimately to prevail as the established system of all civilized nations. With this principle our fathers extended the hand of friendship to every nation of the globe, and to this policy our country has ever since adhered; whatever of regulation in our laws has ever been adopted unfavorable to the interest of any foreign nation, has been essentially defensive and counteracting to similar regulations of theirs operating against us.

Immediately after the close of the war of independence, commissioners were appointed by the Congress of the Confederation, authorized to conclude treaties with every nation of Europe disposed to adopt them. Before the wars of the French Revolution, such treaties had been consummated with the United Netherlands, Sweden, and Prussia. During those wars, treaties with Great Britain and Spain had been effected, and those with Russia and France renewed. In all these, some concessions to the liberal principles of intercourse proposed by the United States had been obtained; but as, in all the negotiations, they came occasionally in collision with previous internal regulations, or exclusive and excluding compacts of monopoly, with which the other parties had been trammelled, the advances made in them towards the freedom of trade were partial and imperfect. Colonial establishments, chartered companies, and ship building influence, pervaded and encumbered the legislation of all the great commercial States; and the United States, in offering free trade and equal privilege to all, were compelled to acquiesce in many exceptions with each of the parties to their treaties, accommodated to their existing laws and anterior engagements.

The colonial system by which this whole hemisphere was bound has fallen into ruins: totally abolished by revolutions, converting colonies into independent nations, throughout the two American continents, excepting a portion of territory chiefly at the northern extremity of our own, and confined to the remnants of dominion retained by Great Britain over the insular Archipelago, geographically the appendages of our part of the globe. With all the rest we have free trade; even with the insular colonies of all the European nations, except Great Britain. Her Government also had manifested approaches to the adoption of a free and liberal intercourse between her colonies and other nations, though, by a sudden and scarcely explained revulsion, the spirit of exclusion has been revived for operation upon the United States alone.

The conclusion of our last treaty of peace with Great Britain was shortly afterwards followed by a commercial convention, placing the direct intercourse between the two countries upon a footing of more equal reciprocity than had ever before been admitted. The same principle has since been much farther extended, by treaties with France, Sweden, Denmark, the Hanseatic cities, Prussia in Europe, and with the Republics of Colombia and of Central America, in this hemisphere. The mutual abolition of discriminating duties and charges, upon the navigation and commercial intercourse between the parties, is the general maxim which characterizes them all. There is reason to expect that it will, at no distant period, be adopted by other nations, both of Europe and America, and to hope that, by its universal prevalence, one of the fruitful sources of wars, of commercial competition, will be extinguished.

Among the nations upon whose Governments many of our fellow-citizens have had long pending claims of indemnity, for depredations upon their property during a period when the rights of neutral commerce were disregarded, was that of Denmark. They were, soon after the events occurred, the subject of a special mission from the United States, at the close of which the assurance was given, by His Danish Majesty, that, at a period of more tranquillity, and of less distress, they would be considered, examined, and decided upon, in a spirit of determined purpose for the dispensation of justice. I have much pleasure in informing Congress that the fulfilment of this honorable promise is now in progress; that a small portion of the claims has already been settled, to the satisfaction of the claimants; and that we have reason to hope that the remainder will shortly be placed in a train of equitable adjustment. This result has always been confidently expected, from the character of personal integrity and of benevolence which the Sovereign of the Danish dominions has, through every vicissitude of fortune, maintained.

The general aspect of the affairs of our neighboring American nations of the South has been rather of approaching than of settled tranquillity. Internal disturbances have been more frequent among them than their common friends would have desired. Our intercourse with all has continued to be that of friendship, and of mutual good will. Treaties of commerce and of boundaries with the United Mexican States have been negotiated, but, from various successive obstacles, not yet brought to a final conclusion. The civil war which unfortunately still prevails in the republic of Central America has been unpropitious to the cultivation of our commercial relations with them; and the dissensions and revolutionary changes in the republics of Colombia and of Peru, have been seen with cordiat regret by us, who would gladly contribute to the happiness of both. It is with great satisfaction, however, that we have witnessed the recent conclusion of a peace between the Governments of Buenos Ayres and of Brazil; and it is equally gratifying to observe that indemnity has been obtained for some of the injuries which our fellow-citizens had sustained in the latter of those countries. The rest are in a train of negotiation, which we hope may terminate to mutual satisfaction, and that it may be succeeded by a treaty of commerce and navigation upon liberal principles, propitious to a great and growing commerce, already important to the interests of our country....

| DOCUMENT REFERENCES |

CHAPTER ONE

Diary Entry (Astorga, Spain), January 3, 1780.
Diary of John Quincy Adams. Vol. 1.
http://www.masshist.org/publications/adams-papers/index.php/view/
ADMS-03-01-02-0002-0001-0003#sn=7.
John Quincy Adams (St. Petersburg) to John Adams, August 21, 1781 (o.s).
Adams Family Correspondence. Vol. 4.
http://www.masshist.org/publications/adams-papers/index.php/view/
ADMS-04-04-02-0139#AFC04d142n1.
John Quincy Adams (The Hague) to Abigail Adams, July 23, 1783.
Adams Family Correspondence. Vol. 5.
http://www.masshist.org/publications/adams-papers/index.php/view/
ADMS-04-05-02-0120#sn=0.
John Quincy Adams (Paris) to Abigail Adams, September 10, 1783.
Adams Family Correspondence. Vol. 5.
http://www.masshist.org/publications/adams-papers/index.php/view/
ADMS-04-05-02-0136#sn=1.
John Quincy Adams (The Hague) to Elizabeth Cranch, April 18, 1784.
Adams Family Correspondence. Vol. 5.
http://www.masshist.org/publications/adams-papers/index.php/view/
ADMS-04-05-02-0177#sn=0.
Publicola I (*Columbian Centinel*, June 8, 1791).
Writings of John Quincy Adams. Vol. 1, 1779–1796, edited by Worthington
Chauncey Ford, 65–69. New York: Macmillan, 1913.
https://books.google.com/books?hl=en&lr=&id=cU48AAAAIAAJ&oi=
fnd&pg=PA4&dq=related:GSUO4fHAf-QJ:scholar.google.com/&ots
=O5Ep9bkic8&sig=00MwxMm29DDVCycqhNzK7PghFv4#v=onepage&
q=publicola&f=false.
Publicola II (*Columbian Centinel*, June 11, 1791).
Writings of John Quincy Adams. Vol. 1, *1779–1796*, edited by Worthington
Chauncey Ford, 69–73. New York: Macmillan, 1913.
https://books.google.com/books?hl=en&lr=&id=cU48AAAAIAAJ&oi=
fnd&pg=PA4&dq=related:GSUO4fHAf-QJ:scholar.google.com/&ots=
O5Ep9bkic8&sig=00MwxMm29DDVCycqhNzK7PghFv4#v=onepage&
q=publicola&f=false.
Publicola X (*Columbian Centinel*, July 20, 1791).
Writings of John Quincy Adams. Vol. 1, *1779–1796*, edited by Worthington

Chauncey Ford, 103–7. New York: Macmillan, 1913.
https://books.google.com/books?hl=en&lr=&id=cU48AAAIAAJ&oi=
fnd&pg=PA4&dq=related:GSUO4fHAf-QJ:scholar.google.com/&ots=
O5Ep9bkic8&sig=00MwxMm29DDVCycqhNzK7PghFv4#v=onepage&
q=publicola&f=false.

Marcellus I (*Columbian Centinel*, April 24, 1793).
Writings of John Quincy Adams. Vol. 1, *1779–1796*, edited by Worthington
Chauncey Ford, 135–38. New York: Macmillan, 1913.
https://books.google.com/books?hl=en&lr=&id=cU48AAAIAAJ&oi=
fnd&pg=PA4&dq=related:GSUO4fHAf-QJ:scholar.google.com/&ots=
O5Ep9bkic8&sig=00MwxMm29DDVCycqhNzK7PghFv4#v=onepage&
q=publicola&f=false.

Marcellus II (*Columbian Centinel*, May 4, 1793).
Writings of John Quincy Adams. Vol. 1, *1779–1796*, edited by Worthington
Chauncey Ford, 139–42. New York: Macmillan, 1913.
https://books.google.com/books?hl=en&lr=&id=cU48AAAIAAJ&oi=
fnd&pg=PA4&dq=related:GSUO4fHAf-QJ:scholar.google.com/&ots=
O5Ep9bkic8&sig=00MwxMm29DDVCycqhNzK7PghFv4#v=onepage&
q=publicola&f=false.

An Oration, Pronounced July 4, 1793, at the Request of the Inhabitants of the
Town of Boston, in Commemoration of the Anniversary of American
Independence.
*An oration, pronounced July 4th, 1793, at the request of the inhabitants of the
town of Boston, in commemoration of the anniversary of American indepen-
dence*. John Quincy Adams. Boston: Benjamin Edes & Son, 1793.

Columbus II (*Columbian Centinel*, December 24, 1793).
Writings of John Quincy Adams. Vol. 1, *1779–1796*, edited by Worthington
Chauncey Ford, 150–60. New York: Macmillan, 1913.
https://books.google.com/books?hl=en&lr=&id=cU48AAAIAAJ&oi=
fnd&pg=PA4&dq=related:GSUO4fHAf-QJ:scholar.google.com/&ots=
O5Ep9bkic8&sig=00MwxMm29DDVCycqhNzK7PghFv4#v=onepage&
q=publicola&f=false.

CHAPTER TWO

Diary Entry (London), October 22, 1794.
*Memoirs of John Quincy Adams: Comprising Portions of His Diary from 1795
to 1848*. Vol. 1, edited by Charles Francis Adams, 48–51. Philadelphia:
Lippincott, 1874.
https://books.googleusercontent.com/books/content?req=AKW5Qafy
Mqx5MXTTxksbb50-MZujYbsWXSH8PH2wu9O96Y3Pn7edQ9GVqy9h
C3BPGH_O_gKNCke7wVl83mprHRKaiYVUanofo4Zoow_dX3CBFbDZX
egaa_TcRytH3KeSyPy5XDszHucWw-q8oHvJykVnFQvA1AGyxaor_CjlU

PiLvdo-XKIuCMffHwe4HXFNDZVW1xae-ZFLQnok1nUSBQ24Ox6fjzh
HvcCITwlDjo6DMMlDBlOZZFriClvv7H9FMb3fNC6XZ5Xxn_LJb8_Mvk-
BaL-xDpH9L9A.
Checked, with differences noted, against handwritten source: http://www.
masshist.org/jqadiaries/php/doc?id=jqad21_42.

John Quincy Adams (The Hague) to John Adams, May 22, 1795.
Writings of John Quincy Adams. Vol. 1, *1779–1796*, edited by Worthington
Chauncey Ford, 353–63. New York: Macmillan, 1913.
https://books.google.com/books?hl=en&lr=&id=cU48AAAAIAAJ&oi=
fnd&pg=PA4&dq=related:GSUO4fHAf-QJ:scholar.google.com/&ots=
O5Ep9bkic8&sig=ooMwxMm29DDVCycqhNzK7PghFv4#v=onepage&
q=publicola&f=false.

John Quincy Adams to Secretary of State Timothy Pickering, December 22,
1795 (private)
Writings of John Quincy Adams. Vol. 1, *1779–1796*, edited by Worthington
Chauncey Ford, 490–94. New York: Macmillan, 1913.
https://books.google.com/books?hl=en&lr=&id=cU48AAAAIAAJ&oi=
fnd&pg=PA4&dq=related:GSUO4fHAf-QJ:scholar.google.com/&ots=
O5Ep9bkic8&sig=ooMwxMm29DDVCycqhNzK7PghFv4#v=onepage&
q=publicola&f=false.

John Quincy Adams (The Hague) to Joseph Pitcairn, November 13, 1796.
Writings of John Quincy Adams. Vol. 2, *1796–1801*, edited by Worthington
Chauncey Ford, 40–43. New York: Macmillan, 1913.
https://books.google.com/books?hl=en&lr=&id=9Uuoupkev4EC&oi=
fnd&pg=PA1&dq=the+writings+of+john+quincy+adams+vol+2&ots=
jmPtFk48uA&sig=nzSLtZnRhRdtg2G2GYxHmLQclnE#v=onepage&
q=the%20writings%20of%20john%20quincy%20adams%20vol%20
2&f=false.

John Quincy Adams to John Adams, January 14, 1797.
Writings of John Quincy Adams. Vol. 2, *1796–1801*, edited by Worthington
Chauncey Ford, 77–89. New York: Macmillan, 1913.
https://books.google.com/books?hl=en&lr=&id=9Uuoupkev4EC&oi=
fnd&pg=PA1&dq=the+writings+of+john+quincy+adams+vol+2&ots=
jmPtFk48uA&sig=nzSLtZnRhRdtg2G2GYxHmLQclnE#v=onepage&
q=the%20writings%20of%20john%20quincy%20adams%20vol%20
2&f=false.
Checked, with differences noted, against the one available at Founders
Online. https://founders.archives.gov/?q=%20Author%3A%22Adams
%2C%20John%20Quincy%22%20Recipient%3A%22Adams%2C%20
John%22%20Dates-From%3A1797-01-14%20Dates-To%3A1797-
01-15&s=1511311111&r=1.

John Quincy Adams (The Hague) to Joseph Pitcairn, March 9, 1797.
Writings of John Quincy Adams. Vol. 2, *1796–1801*, edited by Worthington

Chauncey Ford, 137–41. New York: Macmillan, 1913.
https://books.google.com/books?hl=en&lr=&id=9Uuoupkev4EC&oi=
fnd&pg=PA1&dq=the+writings+of+john+quincy+adams+vol+2&ots=
jmPtFk48uA&sig=nzSLtZnRhRdtg2G2GYxHmLQclnE#v=onepage&
q=the%20writings%20of%20john%20quincy%20adams%20vol%20
2&f=false.

John Quincy Adams (The Hague) to John Adams, April 3, 1797.
Writings of John Quincy Adams. Vol. 2, *1796–1801*, edited by Worthington
Chauncey Ford, 155–57. New York: Macmillan, 1913.
https://books.google.com/books?hl=en&lr=&id=9Uuoupkev4EC&oi=
fnd&pg=PA1&dq=the+writings+of+john+quincy+adams+vol+2&ots=
jmPtFk48uA&sig=nzSLtZnRhRdtg2G2GYxHmLQclnE#v=onepage&
q=the%20writings%20of%20john%20quincy%20adams%20vol%20
2&f=false.

CHAPTER THREE

John Quincy Adams (Berlin) to John Adams, January 31, 1798.
Writings of John Quincy Adams. Vol. 2, *1796–1801*, edited by Worthington
Chauncey Ford, 247–52. New York: Macmillan, 1913.
https://books.google.com/books?hl=en&lr=&id=9Uuoupkev4EC&oi=
fnd&pg=PA1&dq=the+writings+of+john+quincy+adams+vol+2&ots=
jmPtFk48uA&sig=nzSLtZnRhRdtg2G2GYxHmLQclnE#v=onepage&
q=the%20writings%20of%20john%20quincy%20adams%20vol%20
2&f=false.

John Quincy Adams (Berlin) to William Vans Murray, July 14, 1798.
Writings of John Quincy Adams. Vol. 2, *1796–1801*, edited by Worthington
Chauncey Ford, 336–37. New York: Macmillan, 1913.
https://books.google.com/books?hl=en&lr=&id=9Uuoupkev4EC&oi=
fnd&pg=PA1&dq=the+writings+of+john+quincy+adams+vol+2&ots=
jmPtFk48uA&sig=nzSLtZnRhRdtg2G2GYxHmLQclnE#v=onepage&
q=the%20writings%20of%20john%20quincy%20adams%20vol%20
2&f=false.

John Quincy Adams (Berlin) to William Vans Murray, September 25, 1798.
Microfilms of the Adams Papers. Reel 133, 82–90. Boston: Massachusetts
Historical Society, 1955.

John Quincy Adams (Berlin) to John Adams, September 25, 1798.
Writings of John Quincy Adams. Vol. 2, *1796–1801*, edited by Worthington
Chauncey Ford, 367–69. New York: Macmillan, 1913.
https://books.google.com/books?hl=en&lr=&id=9Uuoupkev4EC&oi=
fnd&pg=PA1&dq=the+writings+of+john+quincy+adams+vol+2&ots=
jmPtFk48uA&sig=nzSLtZnRhRdtg2G2GYxHmLQclnE#v=onepage&

q=the%20writings%20of%20john%20quincy%20adams%20vol%20
2&f=false.
John Quincy Adams (Berlin) to Abigail Adams, May 7, 1799.
Writings of John Quincy Adams. Vol. 2, *1796–1801*, edited by Worthington
Chauncey Ford, 416–19. New York: Macmillan, 1913.
https://books.google.com/books?hl=en&lr=&id=9Uuoupkev4EC&oi=
fnd&pg=PA1&dq=the+writings+of+john+quincy+adams+vol+2&ots=
jmPtFk48uA&sig=nzSLtZnRhRdtg2G2GYxHmLQclnE#v=onepage&
q=the%20writings%20of%20john%20quincy%20adams%20vol%20
2&f=false.
John Quincy Adams (Berlin) to John Adams, November 25, 1800.
Writings of John Quincy Adams. Vol. 2, *1796–1801*, edited by Worthington
Chauncey Ford, 479–84. New York: Macmillan, 1913.
https://books.google.com/books?hl=en&lr=&id=9Uuoupkev4EC&oi=
fnd&pg=PA1&dq=the+writings+of+john+quincy+adams+vol+2&ots=
jmPtFk48uA&sig=nzSLtZnRhRdtg2G2GYxHmLQclnE#v=onepage&
q=the%20writings%20of%20john%20quincy%20adams%20vol%20
2&f=false.
John Quincy Adams (Berlin) to William Vans Murray, January 27, 1801.
Writings of John Quincy Adams. Vol. 2, *1796–1801*, edited by Worthington
Chauncey Ford, 494–98. (New York: Macmillan, 1913)
https://books.google.com/books?hl=en&lr=&id=9Uuoupkev4EC&oi=
fnd&pg=PA1&dq=the+writings+of+john+quincy+adams+vol+2&ots=
jmPtFk48uA&sig=nzSLtZnRhRdtg2G2GYxHmLQclnE#v=onepage&
q=the%20writings%20of%20john%20quincy%20adams%20vol%20
2&f=false.
John Quincy Adams (Berlin) to Thomas Boylston Adams, February 14, 1801.
Writings of John Quincy Adams. Vol. 2, *1796–1801*, edited by Worthington
Chauncey Ford, 499–502. New York: Macmillan, 1913.
https://books.google.com/books?hl=en&lr=&id=9Uuoupkev4EC&oi=
fnd&pg=PA1&dq=the+writings+of+john+quincy+adams+vol+2&ots=
jmPtFk48uA&sig=nzSLtZnRhRdtg2G2GYxHmLQclnE#v=onepage&
q=the%20writings%20of%20john%20quincy%20adams%20vol%20
2&f=false.

CHAPTER FOUR

Notes of a Speech to the US Senate on the Taxation of Louisiana, US Senate,
January 1804.
Writings of John Quincy Adams. Vol. 3, *1801–1810*, edited by Worthington
Chauncey Ford, 26–30. New York: Macmillan, 1914.
https://books.googleusercontent.com/books/content?req=AKW5QacEPru

Itm67medKjOdxiF4SKn88NpDtpF7_q6B8TqHQxDoxPxkCCRmeoty7
rHLxV_NwhpkQntmOmKDC3kZPQP9xDGw7POxyNPEyLbDw6ocp6
XOPDoGojSzpytuWw67qHGKHHcc4C_4zPSdNvhVBxull7FTJ47oR52
Qf3ltGo6RJlITF2CqG9AKhnBqBzQkOKMAO_hRDkK2q6pa8uwRw
W4cW_zD8gfwqckfOJXEYniFHSjx1ReEuMt1NuoTko-cufDGPydA3.
Publius Valerius, No. 3, *The Repertory*, October 30, 1804.
Writings of John Quincy Adams. Vol. 3, *1801–1810*, edited by Worthington Chauncey Ford, 57–62. New York: Macmillan, 1914.
https://books.googleusercontent.com/books/content?req=AKW5QacEPru
Itm67medKjOdxiF4SKn88NpDtpF7_q6B8TqHQxDoxPxkCCRmeoty7
rHLxV_NwhpkQntmOmKDC3kZPQP9xDGw7POxyNPEyLbDw6ocp6
XOPDoGojSzpytuWw67qHGKHHcc4C_4zPSdNvhVBxull7FTJ47oR52
Qf3ltGo6RJlITF2CqG9AKhnBqBzQkOKMAO_hRDkK2q6pa8uwRw
W4cW_zD8gfwqckfOJXEYniFHSjx1ReEuMt1NuoTko-cufDGPydA3.
John Quincy Adams (Washington, DC) to Joseph Hall, December 11, 1807.
Writings of John Quincy Adams. Vol. 3, *1801–1810*, edited by Worthington Chauncey Ford, 164–66. New York: Macmillan, 1914.
https://books.googleusercontent.com/books/content?req=AKW5QacEPru
Itm67medKjOdxiF4SKn88NpDtpF7_q6B8TqHQxDoxPxkCCRmeoty7
rHLxV_NwhpkQntmOmKDC3kZPQP9xDGw7POxyNPEyLbDw6ocp6
XOPDoGojSzpytuWw67qHGKHHcc4C_4zPSdNvhVBxull7FTJ47oR52
Qf3ltGo6RJlITF2CqG9AKhnBqBzQkOKMAO_hRDkK2q6pa8uwRw
W4cW_zD8gfwqckfOJXEYniFHSjx1ReEuMt1NuoTko-cufDGPydA3.
Draft of Senate Committee Response to a Petition by the Merchants of Philadelphia and Boston, ante-November 14, 1807.
Microfilms of the Adams Papers. Reel 405, 13–13A. Boston: Massachusetts Historical Society, 1955.
John Quincy Adams (Washington, DC) to John Adams, December 27, 1807.
Writings of John Quincy Adams. Vol. 3, *1801–1810*, edited by Worthington Chauncey Ford, 166–73. New York: Macmillan, 1914.
https://books.googleusercontent.com/books/content?req=AKW5QacEPru
Itm67medKjOdxiF4SKn88NpDtpF7_q6B8TqHQxDoxPxkCCRmeoty7
rHLxV_NwhpkQntmOmKDC3kZPQP9xDGw7POxyNPEyLbDw6ocp6
XOPDoGojSzpytuWw67qHGKHHcc4C_4zPSdNvhVBxull7FTJ47oR52
Qf3ltGo6RJlITF2CqG9AKhnBqBzQkOKMAO_hRDkK2q6pa8uwRw
W4cW_zD8gfwqckfOJXEYniFHSjx1ReEuMt1NuoTko-cufDGPydA3.
John Quincy Adams (Washington, DC) to Governor James Sullivan, January 10, 1808.
Writings of John Quincy Adams. Vol. 3, *1801–1810*, edited by Worthington Chauncey Ford, 185–87. New York: Macmillan, 1914.
https://books.googleusercontent.com/books/content?req=AKW5QacEPru
Itm67medKjOdxiF4SKn88NpDtpF7_q6B8TqHQxDoxPxkCCRmeoty7
rHLxV_NwhpkQntmOmKDC3kZPQP9xDGw7POxyNPEyLbDw6ocp6

XOPDoGojSzpytuWw67qHGKHHcc4C_4zPSdNvhVBxull7FTJ47oR52
Qf3ltGo6RJlITF2CqG9AKhnBqBzQkOKMAO_hRDkK2q6pa8uwRw
W4cW_zD8gfwqckfOJXEYniFHSjx1ReEuMt1NuoTko-cufDGPydA3.
Letter to Harrison Gray Otis, March 31, 1808, published as a pamphlet.
Writings of John Quincy Adams. Vol. 3, *1801–1810*, edited by Worthington
Chauncey Ford, 189–223. New York: Macmillan, 1914.
https://books.googleusercontent.com/books/content?req=AKW5QacEPru
Itm67medKjOdxiF4SKn88NpDtpF7_q6B8TqHQxDoxPxkCCRmeoty7
rHLxV_NwhpkQntmOmKDC3kZPQP9xDGw7POxyNPEyLbDw6ocp6
XOPDoGojSzpytuWw67qHGKHHcc4C_4zPSdNvhVBxull7FTJ47oR52
Qf3ltGo6RJlITF2CqG9AKhnBqBzQkOKMAO_hRDkK2q6pa8uwRw
W4cW_zD8gfwqckfOJXEYniFHSjx1ReEuMt1NuoTko-cufDGPydA3.
John Quincy Adams (Boston) to Ezekiel Bacon, November 17, 1808.
Writings of John Quincy Adams. Vol. 3, *1801–1810*, edited by Worthington
Chauncey Ford, 248–53. New York: Macmillan, 1914.
https://books.googleusercontent.com/books/content?req=AKW5QacEPru
Itm67medKjOdxiF4SKn88NpDtpF7_q6B8TqHQxDoxPxkCCRmeoty7
rHLxV_NwhpkQntmOmKDC3kZPQP9xDGw7POxyNPEyLbDw6ocp6
XOPDoGojSzpytuWw67qHGKHHcc4C_4zPSdNvhVBxull7FTJ47oR52
Qf3ltGo6RJlITF2CqG9AKhnBqBzQkOKMAO_hRDkK2q6pa8uwRw
W4cW_zD8gfwqckfOJXEYniFHSjx1ReEuMt1NuoTko-cufDGPydA3.

CHAPTER FIVE

Diary Entry (St. Petersburg), November 5, 1809.
*Memoirs of John Quincy Adams: Comprising Portions of His Diary from 1795
to 1848*. Vol. 2, edited by Charles Francis Adams, 50–56. (Philadelphia:
Lippincott, 1874.
https://books.google.com/books?id=A22Bh_xDi7QC&pg=PR1#v=
onepage&q&f=false.
John Quincy Adams to Abigail Adams, September 5/17, 1810.
Founders Online: https://founders.archives.gov/?q=Author%3A%22
Adams%2C%20John%20Quincy%22%20Recipient%3A%22Adams
%2C%20Abigail%20Smith%22%20Period%3A%22Madison%20
Presidency%22&s=1111311111&r=7.
John Quincy Adams to Secretary of State, December 15/27, 1810.
Writings of John Quincy Adams. Vol. 3, *1801–1810*, edited by Worthington
Chauncey Ford, 553–55. New York: Macmillan, 1914.
https://books.google.com/books?id=x1nLbi8qEtgC&printsec=
frontcover&source=gbs_ge_summary_r&cad=0#v=onepage&q&f=false.
John Quincy Adams (St. Petersburg) to Thomas Boylston Adams, May 1–13, 1811.
Writings of John Quincy Adams. Vol. 4, *1811–1813*, edited by Worthington
Chauncey Ford, 65–71. New York: Macmillan, 1914.

https://books.google.com/books?id=wvMsAAAAYAAJ&printsec=
frontcover&source=gbs_ge_summary_r&cad=0#v=onepage&q&f=false.
John Quincy Adams to Abigail Adams, June 30, 1811.
Writings of John Quincy Adams. Vol. 4, *1811–1813*, edited by Worthington
Chauncey Ford, 126–28. New York: Macmillan, 1914.
https://books.google.com/books?id=wvMsAAAAYAAJ&printsec=
frontcover&source=gbs_ge_summary_r&cad=0#v=onepage&q&f=false.
John Quincy Adams to John Adams, July 21–26, 1811.
Writings of John Quincy Adams. Vol. 4, *1811–1813*, edited by Worthington
Chauncey Ford, 142–48. New York: Macmillan, 1914.
https://books.google.com/books?id=wvMsAAAAYAAJ&printsec=
frontcover&source=gbs_ge_summary_r&cad=0#v=onepage&q&f=false.
John Quincy Adams (St. Petersburg) to Thomas Boylston Adams, July 31, 1811.
Writings of John Quincy Adams. Vol. 4, *1811–1813*, edited by Worthington
Chauncey Ford, 160–65. New York: Macmillan, 1914.
https://books.google.com/books?id=wvMsAAAAYAAJ&printsec=
frontcover&source=gbs_ge_summary_r&cad=0#v=onepage&q&f=false.
John Quincy Adams to John Adams, October 14, 1811.
Writings of John Quincy Adams. Vol. 4, *1811–1813*, edited by Worthington
Chauncey Ford, 240–45. New York: Macmillan, 1914.
https://books.google.com/books?id=wvMsAAAAYAAJ&printsec=
frontcover&source=gbs_ge_summary_r&cad=0#v=onepage&q&f=false.
John Quincy Adams to William Eustis, October 26, 1811.
Writings of John Quincy Adams. Vol. 4, *1811–1813*, edited by Worthington
Chauncey Ford, 259–63. (New York: Macmillan, 1914)
https://books.google.com/books?id=wvMsAAAAYAAJ&printsec=
frontcover&source=gbs_ge_summary_r&cad=0#v=onepage&q&f=false.
John Quincy Adams (St. Petersburg) to John Adams, October 31, 1811.
Writings of John Quincy Adams. Vol. 4, *1811–1813*, edited by Worthington
Chauncey Ford, 263–68. New York: Macmillan, 1914.
https://books.google.com/books?id=wvMsAAAAYAAJ&printsec=
frontcover&source=gbs_ge_summary_r&cad=0#v=onepage&q&f=false.
John Quincy Adams (St. Petersburg) to Thomas Boylston Adams,
November 6, 1811.
Writings of John Quincy Adams. Vol. 4, *1811–1813*, edited by Worthington
Chauncey Ford, 272–75. New York: Macmillan, 1914.
https://books.google.com/books?id=wvMsAAAAYAAJ&printsec=
frontcover&source=gbs_ge_summary_r&cad=0#v=onepage&q&f=false.
John Quincy Adams (St. Petersburg) to Abigail Adams, January 1, 1812.
Writings of John Quincy Adams. Vol. 4, *1811–1813*, edited by Worthington
Chauncey Ford, 284–86. New York: Macmillan, 1914.
https://books.google.com/books?id=wvMsAAAAYAAJ&printsec=
frontcover&source=gbs_ge_summary_r&cad=0#v=onepage&q&f=false.

John Quincy Adams (St. Petersburg) to Abigail Adams, April 30, 1812.
Writings of John Quincy Adams. Vol. 4, *1811–1813*, edited by Worthington Chauncey Ford, 318–20. New York: Macmillan, 1914. https://books.google.com/books?id=wvMsAAAAYAAJ&printsec=frontcover&source=gbs_ge_summary_r&cad=0#v=onepage&q&f=false.

John Quincy Adams (St. Petersburg) to Abigail Adams, August 10, 1812.
Writings of John Quincy Adams. Vol. 4, *1811–1813*, edited by Worthington Chauncey Ford, 388–89. New York: Macmillan, 1914. https://books.google.com/books?id=wvMsAAAAYAAJ&printsec=frontcover&source=gbs_ge_summary_r&cad=0#v=onepage&q&f=false.

John Quincy Adams to John Adams, August 16, 1812.
Founders Online: https://founders.archives.gov/?q=%20Author%3A%22Adams%2C%20John%20Quincy%22%20Recipient%3A%22Adams%2C%20John%22%20Dates-From%3A1812-08-01&s=1111311111&r=1.

John Quincy Adams (St. Petersburg) to Secretary of State James Monroe, September 30, 1812.
Writings of John Quincy Adams. Vol. 4, *1811–1813*, edited by Worthington Chauncey Ford, 389–91. New York: Macmillan, 1914) https://books.google.com/books?id=wvMsAAAAYAAJ&printsec=frontcover&source=gbs_ge_summary_r&cad=0#v=onepage&q&f=false.

John Quincy Adams (St. Petersburg) to John Adams, November 5, 1812.
Founders Online. https://founders.archives.gov/?q=Project%3A%22Adams%20Papers%22%20Author%3A%22Adams%2C%20John%20Quincy%22%20Recipient%3A%22Adams%2C%20John%22&s=1511311111&r=188.

John Quincy Adams (St. Petersburg) to Thomas Boylston Adams, November 24, 1812.
Writings of John Quincy Adams. Vol. 4, 1811–1813, edited by Worthington Chauncey Ford, 406–9. New York: Macmillan, 1914. https://books.google.com/books?id=wvMsAAAAYAAJ&printsec=frontcover&source=gbs_ge_summary_r&cad=0#v=onepage&q&f=false.

Diary, November 25, 1812.
Memoirs of John Quincy Adams: Comprising Portions of His Diary from 1795 to 1848. Vol. 2, edited by Charles Francis Adams, 422–23. Philadelphia: Lippincott, 1874. https://books.google.com/books?id=A22Bh_xDi7QC&pg=PR1#v=onepage&q&f=false.

John Quincy Adams to Abigail Adams, February 18, 1813.
Writings of John Quincy Adams. Vol. 4, *1811–1813*, edited by Worthington Chauncey Ford, 433–37. New York: Macmillan, 1914 https://books.google.com/books?id=wvMsAAAAYAAJ&printsec=frontcover&source=gbs_ge_summary_r&cad=0#v=onepage&q&f=false.

John Quincy Adams (St. Petersburg) to William Plumer, August 13, 1813.

Writings of John Quincy Adams. Vol. 4, *1811–1813*, edited by Worthington Chauncey Ford, 504–7. New York: Macmillan, 1914. https://books.google.com/books?id=wvMsAAAAYAAJ&printsec= frontcover&source=gbs_ge_summary_r&cad=0#v=onepage&q&f=false.

CHAPTER SIX

John Quincy Adams (St. Petersburg) to Secretary of State James Monroe, December 11, 1812.
Writings of John Quincy Adams. Vol. 4, *1811–1813*, edited by Worthington Chauncey Ford, 413–17. New York: Macmillan, 1914. https://books.google.com/books?id=wvMsAAAAYAAJ&printsec= frontcover&source=gbs_ge_summary_r&cad=0#v=onepage&q&f=false. Ford omitted the first paragraph. Added from American State Papers: Foreign Relations. 3:626–67. https://0-heinonline-org.library.hillsdale.edu/HOL/Page?collection= congrec&handle=hein.congrec/aspfr0003&id=632&men_tab=srchresults.
John Quincy Adams (St. Petersburg) to John Adams, September 3, 1813.
Writings of John Quincy Adams. Vol. 4, *1811–1813*, edited by Worthington Chauncey Ford, 512–16. New York: Macmillan, 1914. https://books.google.com/books?id=wvMsAAAAYAAJ&printsec= frontcover&source=gbs_ge_summary_r&cad=0#v=onepage&q&f=false.
John Quincy Adams (St. Petersburg) to John Adams, February 17, 1814.
Writings of John Quincy Adams. Vol. 5, *1814–1816*, edited by Worthington Chauncey Ford, 18–22. New York: Macmillan, 1915. https://books.google.com/books?id=MlsSAAAAYAAJ&printsec= frontcover&source=gbs_ge_summary_r&cad=0#v=onepage&q&f=false.
The American Commission to Secretary of State James Monroe, Draft Prepared by John Quincy Adams, August 11, 1814.
Writings of John Quincy Adams. Vol. 5, *1814–1816*, edited by Worthington Chauncey Ford, 75–82. New York: Macmillan, 1915. https://books.google.com/books?id=MlsSAAAAYAAJ&printsec= frontcover&source=gbs_ge_summary_r&cad=0#v=onepage&q&f=false.
The American Commission, Answer to British Commissioners, Draft Prepared by John Quincy Adams, August 24, 1814.
Writings of John Quincy Adams. Vol. 5, *1814–1816*, edited by Worthington Chauncey Ford, 93–101. New York: Macmillan, 1915. https://books.google.com/books?id=MlsSAAAAYAAJ&printsec= frontcover&source=gbs_ge_summary_r&cad=0#v=onepage&q&f=false.
John Quincy Adams (Ghent) to Secretary of State James Monroe, September 5, 1814.
Writings of John Quincy Adams. Vol. 5, *1814–1816*, ed. Worthington Chauncey Ford, 110–20. New York: Macmillan, 1915.

https://books.google.com/books?id=MlsSAAAAYAAJ&printsec=
frontcover&source=gbs_ge_summary_r&cad=0#v=onepage&q&f=false.
The American Commission, Answer to the British Commissioners, Draft
Prepared by John Quincy Adams, September 9, 1814.
Writings of John Quincy Adams. Vol. 5, 1814–1816, edited by Worthington
Chauncey Ford, 122–129. New York: Macmillan, 1915.
https://books.google.com/books?id=MlsSAAAAYAAJ&printsec=
frontcover&source=gbs_ge_summary_r&cad=0#v=onepage&q&f=false.
Diary Entry (Ghent), November 10, 1814.
*Memoirs of John Quincy Adams: Comprising Portions of His Diary from 1795
to 1848*. Vol. 3, edited by Charles Francis Adams, 66–69. Philadelphia: Lip-
pincott, 1874.
https://books.google.com/books?id=mryIYmEIV6EC&printsec=
frontcover&source=gbs_ge_summary_r&cad=0#v=onepage&q&f=false.
John Quincy Adams (Ghent) to William Crawford, November 17, 1814.
Writings of John Quincy Adams. Vol. 5, 1814–1816, edited by Worthington
Chauncey Ford, 192–95. New York: Macmillan, 1915.
https://books.google.com/books?id=MlsSAAAAYAAJ&printsec=
frontcover&source=gbs_ge_summary_r&cad=0#v=onepage&q&f=false.
Diary Entries (Ghent), November 27, 28, and 29, 1814.
*Memoirs of John Quincy Adams: Comprising Portions of His Diary from 1795
to 1848*. Vol. 3, edited by Charles Francis Adams, 70–77. Philadelphia: Lippincott, 1874.
https://books.google.com/books?id=mryIYmEIV6EC&printsec=
frontcover&source=gbs_ge_summary_r&cad=0#v=onepage&q&f=false.
John Quincy Adams (Ghent) to Louisa Catherine Adams, January 3, 1815.
Writings of John Quincy Adams. Vol. 5, 1814–1816, edited by Worthington
Chauncey Ford, 260–63. New York: Macmillan, 1915.
https://books.google.com/books?id=MlsSAAAAYAAJ&printsec=
frontcover&source=gbs_ge_summary_r&cad=0#v=onepage&q&f=false.
John Quincy Adams (Ghent) to Louisa Catherine Adams, January 3, 1815.
Writings of John Quincy Adams. Vol. 5, 1814–1816, edited by Worthington
Chauncey Ford, 312–17. New York: Macmillan, 1915.
https://books.google.com/books?id=MlsSAAAAYAAJ&printsec=
frontcover&source=gbs_ge_summary_r&cad=0#v=onepage&q&f=false.

CHAPTER SEVEN

John Quincy Adams (London) to Secretary of State James Monroe, June 23, 1815.
Writings of John Quincy Adams. Vol. 5, 1814–1816, edited by Worthington
Chauncey Ford, 319–24. New York: Macmillan, 1915.
https://books.google.com/books?id=MlsSAAAAYAAJ&printsec=
frontcover&source=gbs_ge_summary_r&cad=0#v=onepage&q&f=false.

DOCUMENT REFERENCES

John Quincy Adams (London) to Secretary of State James Monroe,
    August 22, 1815.
    Writings of John Quincy Adams. Vol. 5, *1814–1816*, edited by Worthington
    Chauncey Ford, 343–53. New York: Macmillan, 1915.
    https://books.google.com/books?id=MlsSAAAAYAAJ&printsec=
    frontcover&source=gbs_ge_summary_r&cad=0#v=onepage&q&f=false.
John Quincy Adams (London) to Joseph Hall, September 9, 1815.
    Writings of John Quincy Adams. Vol. 5, *1814–1816*, edited by Worthington
    Chauncey Ford, 372–77. New York: Macmillan, 1915.
    https://books.google.com/books?id=MlsSAAAAYAAJ&printsec=
    frontcover&source=gbs_ge_summary_r&cad=0#v=onepage&q&f=false.
Diary, John Quincy Adams (London), September 14, 1815.
    *Memoirs of John Quincy Adams: Comprising Portions of His Diary from 1795
    to 1848.* Vol. 3, edited by Charles Francis Adams, 265–71. Philadelphia:
    Lippincott, 1874.
    https://books.google.com/books?id=mryIYmEIV6EC&printsec=
    frontcover&source=gbs_ge_summary_r&cad=0#v=onepage&q&f=false.
John Quincy Adams (London) to John Adams, October 9, 1815.
    Writings of John Quincy Adams. Vol. 5, *1814–1816*, edited by Worthington
    Chauncey Ford, 407–12. New York: Macmillan, 1915.
    https://books.google.com/books?id=MlsSAAAAYAAJ&printsec=
    frontcover&source=gbs_ge_summary_r&cad=0#v=onepage&q&f=false.
John Quincy Adams (London) to Secretary of State James Monroe,
    February 8, 1816.
    Writings of John Quincy Adams. Vol. 5,*1814–1816*, edited by Worthington
    Chauncey Ford, 497–510. New York: Macmillan, 1915.
    https://books.google.com/books?id=MlsSAAAAYAAJ&printsec=
    frontcover&source=gbs_ge_summary_r&cad=0#v=onepage&q&f=false.
John Quincy Adams (London) to Alexander Hill Everett, March 16, 1816.
    Writings of John Quincy Adams. Vol. 5, *1814–1816*, edited by Worthington
    Chauncey Ford, 537–41. New York: Macmillan, 1915.
    https://books.google.com/books?id=MlsSAAAAYAAJ&printsec=
    frontcover&source=gbs_ge_summary_r&cad=0#v=onepage&q&f=false.
John Quincy Adams (London) to George W. Erving, June 10, 1816.
    Writings of John Quincy Adams. Vol. 6, *1816–1819*, edited by Worthington
    Chauncey Ford, 45–47. New York: Macmillan, 1916.
    https://books.google.com/books?id=71A8AAAAIAAJ&printsec=
    frontcover&source=gbs_ge_summary_r&cad=0#v=onepage&q&f=false.
John Quincy Adams (London) to John Adams, August 1, 1816.
    Writings of John Quincy Adams. Vol. 6, *1816–1819*, edited by Worthington
    Chauncey Ford, 58–62. New York: Macmillan, 1916.
    https://books.google.com/books?id=71A8AAAAIAAJ&printsec=
    frontcover&source=gbs_ge_summary_r&cad=0#v=onepage&q&f=false.

John Quincy Adams to Christopher Hughes, December 25, 1816.
   Writings of John Quincy Adams. Vol. 6, *1816–1819*, edited by Worthington
   Chauncey Ford, 129–30. New York: Macmillan, 1916.
   https://books.google.com/books?id=71A8AAAAIAAJ&printsec=
   frontcover&source=gbs_ge_summary_r&cad=0#v=onepage&q&f=false.
John Quincy Adams to William Plumer, January 17, 1817.
   Writings of John Quincy Adams. Vol. 6, *1816–1819*, edited by Worthington
   Chauncey Ford, 139–44. New York: Macmillan, 1916.
   https://books.google.com/books?id=71A8AAAAIAAJ&printsec=
   frontcover&source=gbs_ge_summary_r&cad=0#v=onepage&q&f=false.
Diary Entry (London), June 6, 1817.
   *Memoirs of John Quincy Adams: Comprising Portions of His Diary from 1795
   to 1848*. Vol. 3, edited by Charles Francis Adams, 556–60. Philadelphia:
   Lippincott, 1874.
   https://books.google.com/books?id=mryIYmEIV6EC&printsec=
   frontcover&source=gbs_ge_summary_r&cad=0#v=onepage&q&f=false.

CHAPTER EIGHT

John Quincy Adams (Washington, DC) to Alexander Hill Everett,
   December 29, 1817.
   Writings of John Quincy Adams. Vol. 6, *1816–1819*, edited by Worthington
   Chauncey Ford, 280–83. New York: Macmillan, 1916.
   https://books.google.com/books?id=71A8AAAAIAAJ&printsec=
   frontcover&source=gbs_ge_summary_r&cad=0#v=onepage&q&f=false.
Diary Entries (Washington, DC), January 27 and 31, 1818.
   *Memoirs of John Quincy Adams: Comprising Portions of His Diary from 1795
   to 1848*. Vol. 4, edited by Charles Francis Adams, 48–50, 51–52. Philadel-
   phia: Lippincott, 1875.
   https://books.google.com/books?id=YLJyeravazEC&printsec=
   frontcover&source=gbs_ge_summary_r&cad=0#v=onepage&q&f=false.
Secretary of State John Quincy Adams (Department of State) to Albert Gallatin,
   May 19, 1818.
   Writings of John Quincy Adams. Vol. 6, *1816–1819*, edited by Worthington
   Chauncey Ford, 312–18. New York: Macmillan, 1916.
   https://books.google.com/books?id=71A8AAAAIAAJ&printsec=
   frontcover&source=gbs_ge_summary_r&cad=0#v=onepage&q&f=false.
John Quincy Adams (Washington, DC) to President Monroe, August 24, 1818.
   Writings of John Quincy Adams. Vol. 6, *1816–1819*, edited by Worthington
   Chauncey Ford, 441–44. New York: Macmillan, 1916.
   https://books.google.com/books?id=71A8AAAAIAAJ&printsec=
   frontcover&source=gbs_ge_summary_r&cad=0#v=onepage&
   q&f=false.

DOCUMENT REFERENCES

John Quincy Adams (Department of State) to George William Erving, November 28, 1818.

Writings of John Quincy Adams. Vol. 6, *1816–1819*, edited by Worthington Chauncey Ford, 474–502. New York: Macmillan, 1916.
https://books.google.com/books?id=71A8AAAAIAAJ&printsec=frontcover&source=gbs_ge_summary_r&cad=0#v=onepage&q&f=false.

Diary Entry (Washington, DC), March 12, 1819.

Memoirs of John Quincy Adams: Comprising Portions of His Diary from 1795 to 1848. Vol. 4, edited by Charles Francis Adams, 292–95. Philadelphia: Lippincott, 1875.
https://books.google.com/books?id=YLJyeravazEC&printsec=frontcover&source=gbs_ge_summary_r&cad=0#v=onepage&q&f=false.

Diary Entry (Washington, DC), November 16, 1819.

Memoirs of John Quincy Adams: Comprising Portions of His Diary from 1795 to 1848. Vol. 4, edited by Charles Francis Adams, 437–40. Philadelphia: Lippincott, 1875.
https://books.google.com/books?id=YLJyeravazEC&printsec=frontcover&source=gbs_ge_summary_r&cad=0#v=onepage&q&f=false.

Diary Entries (Washington, DC), February 24, March 18, March 31, April 13, 1820.

February 24: *Memoirs of John Quincy Adams: Comprising Portions of His Diary from 1795 to 1848*. Vol. 4, edited by Charles Francis Adams, 530–31. Philadelphia: Lippincott, 1875.
https://books.google.com/books?id=YLJyeravazEC&printsec=frontcover&source=gbs_ge_summary_r&cad=0#v=onepage&q&f=false.

March 18, 31; April 13: *Memoirs of John Quincy Adams: Comprising Portions of His Diary from 1795 to 1848*. Vol. 5, edited by Charles Francis Adams, 23–26, 52–56, 67–70. Philadelphia: Lippincott, 1875.
https://books.google.com/books?id=KzCHEqFlwd8C&printsec=frontcover&source=gbs_ge_summary_r&cad=0#v=onepage&q&f=false.

John Quincy Adams (Department of State) to Henry Middleton, July 5, 1820.

Writings of John Quincy Adams. Vol. 7, *1820–1823*, edited by Worthington Chauncey Ford, 46–52. New York: Macmillan, 1917.
https://www.google.com/books/edition/Writings_of_John_Quincy_Adams/Gt12AAAAMAAJ?hl=en&gbpv=1&dq=writings+of+john+quincy+adams+vol.+7&printsec=frontcover.

John Quincy Adams (Department of State) to Stratford Canning, December 30, 1820.

Writings of John Quincy Adams. Vol. 7, *1820–1823*, edited by Worthington Chauncey Ford, 84–88. New York: Macmillan, 1917.
https://www.google.com/books/edition/Writings_of_John_Quincy_Adams/Gt12AAAAMAAJ?hl=en&gbpv=1&dq=writings+of+john+quincy+adams+vol.+7&printsec=frontcover.

Diary Entry (Washington, DC), January 27, 1821.
Memoirs of John Quincy Adams: Comprising Portions of His Diary from 1795 to 1848. Vol. 5, edited by Charles Francis Adams, 249–59. Philadelphia: Lippincott, 1875.
https://books.google.com/books?id=KzCHEqFlwd8C&printsec= frontcover&source=gbs_ge_summary_r&cad=0#v=onepage&q&f=false.

CHAPTER NINE

An Address, Delivered at the Request of the Committee of Arrangements for Celebrating the Anniversary of Independence, at the City of Washington on the Fourth of July 1821 upon the Occasion of Reading the Declaration of Independence.
Cambridge, MA: Harvard University Press, 1821.
https://books.google.com/books?id=QjM5AQAAMAAJ&printsec= frontcover&dq=An+Address,+Delivered+at+the+Request+of+the+ Committee+of+Arrangements+for+Celebrating+the+Anniversary+of+ Independence,+at+the+City+of+Washington+on+the+Fourth+of+ July+1821+upon+the+Occasion+of+Reading+the+Declaration+of+ Independence.&hl=en&sa=X&ved=0ahUKEwiThd_ottrjAhVxAZoJHW nkCzUQ6AEIKjAA#v=onepage&q&f=false.
John Quincy Adams (Washington, DC) to Robert Walsh Jr., July 10, 1821.
Writings of John Quincy Adams. Vol. 7, *1820–1823*, edited by Worthington Chauncey Ford, 113–18. New York: Macmillan, 1917.
https://www.google.com/books/edition/Writings_of_John_Quincy_ Adams/Gt12AAAAMAAJ?hl=en&gbpv=1&dq=writings+of+john+ quincy+adams+vol.+7&printsec=frontcover.
John Quincy Adams (Washington, DC) to Edward Everett, January 31, 1822.
Writings of John Quincy Adams. Vol. 7, *1820–1823*, edited by Worthington Chauncey Ford, 197–207. New York: Macmillan, 1917.
John Quincy Adams (Department of State) to Hugh Nelson, April 28, 1823.
Writings of John Quincy Adams. Vol. 7, *1820–1823*, edited by Worthington Chauncey Ford, 369–421. New York: Macmillan, 1917.
Diary Entries (Washington, DC), November 7, 15, 17–18, 21–22, 25–27, 1823.
Memoirs of John Quincy Adams: Comprising Portions of His Diary from 1795 to 1848. Vol. 6, edited by Charles Francis Adams, 177–81, 185–87, 187–91, 192–98, 199–216. Philadelphia: Lippincott, 1875.
Observations on the Communications Recently Received from the Minister of Russia. Department of State, November 27, 1823.
Worthington C. Ford, ed. "Some Original Documents on the Genesis of the Monroe Doctrine." Massachusetts Historical Society, Proceedings, 2nd ser., 15 (1901–2): 373–436, 405–8.
https://www.google.com/books/edition/Proceedings_of_the_

DOCUMENT REFERENCES

Massachusetts_Histori/o2uXYXE4WDYC?hl=en&gbpv=1&dq=Some+
Original+Documents+on+the+Genesis+of+the+Monroe+Doctrine&
pg=PA373&printsec=frontcover.
President James Monroe. Seventh Annual Message to Congress.
December 2, 1823.
Source: ASPFR, 5:245–50.

CHAPTER TEN

Inaugural Address, March 4, 1825.
https://avalon.law.yale.edu/19th_century/qadams.asp.
First Annual Message to Congress, December 6, 1825.
https://millercenter.org/the-presidency/presidential-speeches/december-6-
1825-first-annual-message.
Message to the Senate Regarding the Congress of American Relations,
December 6, 1825.
https://millercenter.org/the-presidency/presidential-speeches/december-6-
1825-message-regarding-congress-american-nations.
Fourth Annual Message to Congress, December 2, 1828.
Register of Debates, 20th Congress, 2nd session.
https://memory.loc.gov/cgi-bin/ampage?collId=llrd&fileName=007/
llrd007.db&recNum=405.

| NOTES |

1   John Quincy Adams (Boston) to Skelton Jones, April 17, 1809.

CHAPTER ONE

1   In November 1779, John Adams sailed from Massachusetts on his second diplomatic mission to France, accompanied by his sons John Quincy and Charles. They were forced to land in Spain because of the poor condition of their vessel. They decided to travel to Paris overland through the mountains of Spain rather than seek water transportation. This turned out to be a thoroughly miserable trip.

2   John Adams described the conditions at Castellano: "We entered into the Kitchen, where was no floor but the Ground and no Carpet but Straw trodden into mire by Men, Hogs, horses and Mules." See *Diary of John Adams*, vol. 4, http://www.masshist.org/publications/adams-papers/index.php/view/ADMS-01-04-02-0002-0024#sn=4.

3   At his father's request, John Quincy accompanied Francis Dana to St. Petersburg as his secretary, on a diplomatic mission to establish relations with Russia.

4   This was the Prussia of Frederick II (Frederick the Great), who reigned from 1740 to 1786.

5   John Quincy likely refers here to one of history's greatest battles, the November 1700 Battle of Narva, during which Charles XII of Sweden and approximately 10,500 men reinforced the small garrison at Narva against a force of approximately 37,000 Russians. Russia ultimately took Narva in 1704.

6   John Quincy returned alone from his posting in Russia, arriving back in the Netherlands in April 1783.

7   Gustav III (reigned 1771–1792).

8   Frederick VI attained regency in his father's name (Christian VII) one year after John Quincy's visit. He held this position until he was anointed king following his father's death. None of Frederick's sons survived to succeed him.

9   John Adams traveled to The Hague from Paris where, along with Benjamin Franklin and John Jay, he had been negotiating the final treaty of peace with Britain. John Quincy accompanied him back to Paris. The Treaty of Paris was signed in September 1783.

10 William Robertson, Scottish historian, and François-Marie Arouet (Voltaire), French Enlightenment writer. As noted in the Adams Family Papers, John Quincy drew this account largely from published sources, including Christof Hermann von Manstein's *Memoirs of Russia . . . from the year 1727 to 1744* (1770); and Voltaire's *Histoire de l'empire de Russie sous Pierre le grand* (1759–1763).

11 After John Adams took ill in the fall of 1783, following the signing of the Treaty of Paris, he was advised to take a trip to England to improve his health. He took John Quincy on the excursion. The elder Adams, perhaps not surprisingly, found his reception to be cold, even among supposed friends of America, a sign that an early rapprochement with Britain was highly unlikely.

12 John Andre was a British spy who assisted Benedict Arnold's attempt to surrender West Point. He was hanged by the Continental Army.

13 John Quincy was referring to Edmund Burke's *Reflections on the Revolution in France* and Thomas Paine's riposte, *The Rights of Man*.

14 *Common Sense* was the title of Paine's famous January 1776 pamphlet advocating American independence. At the time, John Adams thought that Paine's teachings on government were fundamentally flawed, a view he never changed.

15 Also known as the Glorious Revolution, the Revolution of 1688 deposed James II as king of England after the birth of his son presaged a Catholic dynasty. James was replaced by his Protestant daughter Mary II and her husband William III of Orange (Holland). The revolution produced the English Bill of Rights, which codified the rights of subjects, through Parliament, against the king.

16 John Quincy is referring to the Revolution of 1688, not the American or French revolutions.

17 "It would seem as if Mr. Fenno and Mr. Russell had entered Into a league to insert the detestable heresies of Publicola, without publishing a single essay to counteract their pernicious tendency. But it is to be hoped that the *ex parte* perusal which Publicola obtains in this way will not procure many proselytes either to *monarchy* or *aristocracy*. Publicola seems to have some talents, but perverted as they are, they are worse than thrown away. Like Burke he has attempted to raise a structure upon a rotten foundation; and his tottering edifice, like that of Burke, would soon have fallen into ruins of itself. Its fate, however, has been accelerated by the numerous assailants it has had to encounter. It is a circumstance highly honorable to the political character of our country, that an *host* of enlightened writers have arisen, in every part of the United States, to oppose the abominable heresies of Publicola." See [Brown's] *Federal Gazette*, July, 1791. It was this journal that intimated a communication between John Adams and Burke and asserted that Publicola appeared in consequence of that communication.

See *Writings of John Quincy Adams*, Vol. 1, *1779–1796*, ed. Worthington Chauncey Ford (New York: MacMillan, 1913), 107n1.

18 Letters of marque and reprisal were government sanctions for private persons (privateers) to seize vessels from enemy nations during times of war. Article I, Sec. 8 of the Constitution grants Congress the authority to issue letters of marque and reprisal.

19 The Treaty of Amity and Commerce between Prussia and the United States was cosigned by John Adams in London in 1785. John Quincy would negotiate a successor treaty in 1799.

20 "It is not one of us, to settle such disputes."

21 "We now turn."

22 That is, France.

23 The 1783 Treaty of Paris, which ended the Revolutionary War with Britain. American dissatisfaction centered around British violations of the treaty, including the failure to turn over military posts on American territory in the Northwest. Britain also failed to return or provide restitution for slaves captured during the war. Publius complains of the government's inability, under the Articles of Confederation, to settle these claims and enforce the terms of the treaty in Federalist No. 7. British dissatisfaction included the want of any mechanism to force the return of Loyalist property confiscated by the United States.

CHAPTER TWO

1 John Adams (Philadelphia) to John Quincy Adams, May 26, 1794.

2 John Quincy Adams (The Hague) to John Adams, August 13, 1796.

3 John Adams (Quincy) to John Quincy Adams, August 25, 1795.

4 The Treaty of Paris required the British to return property, including slaves, seized from Americans during the Revolutionary War. This requirement was largely ignored by Britain. Article 7 of Jay's treaty established a commission to hear the grievances of Americans whose property had not been returned and, when deemed appropriate, to provide restitution.

5 The Navigation Acts were laws that regulated foreign trade with Britain and its colonies. The laws attempted to confine all colonial economic activity within the British Empire.

6 Disabilities of alienage are the privileges extended to citizens (or subjects, in the case of England) of a nation that are denied to non-citizens. These privileges may include the ability to own real estate and firearms and to open businesses.

7 Alexander Wedderburn, First Earl of Rosslyn, was lord high chancellor at the time of Jay's treaty negotiations. In 1774, while he was postmaster of the colonies and agent of several colonies, Benjamin Franklin appeared before the Privy Council to entreat the crown to replace Massachusetts

Governor Thomas Hutchinson. Instead, Franklin was subjected to an hour of Wedderburn attacking his character.

8   John Quincy visited England in 1783 and 1785, from his father's postings in Europe, and was introduced to many prominent Englishmen.

9   Charles Cornwallis, a British major-general during the Revolutionary War, had surrendered to George Washington at Yorktown, Virginia in October 1781. He served as governor-general and commander in chief of India from 1786 to 1794, during which time he instituted reforms to the legal system and defeated Tipu Sultan (ruler of Mysore in southeast India) after the Mysorians began attaching British allies in 1790.

10 The famous English writer Samuel Johnson, referring to the poet and satirist Charles Churchill.

11 The Treaty of The Hague, signed in May 1795, established an alliance between the newly founded Batavian Republic and the French Republic. The Batavian Republic received French military support in exchange for several Dutch territories; a large payment reimbursing France for its role in "liberating" the Dutch people from the old federal republic, which had been governed under the executive authority of a Stadholder (William V of Orange-Nassau); and a large loan.

12 "Such aid does not."

13 James Monroe, who was currently serving as US minister to France.

14 Edmond-Charles Genet, often referred to as Citizen Genet, was French minister to the United States from 1793 to 1794. Genet recruited American privateers to assist the French against the British, an action that violated President Washington's Neutrality Proclamation and otherwise challenged Washington's authority. Owing to his continuing defiance, the US government requested that Genet be recalled. The French revolutionary government, however, had changed since Genet's assignment and issued an arrest warrant for him, to be carried out by Jean Antoine Joseph Fauchet, Genet's replacement as minister. Genet, facing execution, was granted asylum in America. Fauchet was replaced in 1795 by Pierre Adet.

15 John Quincy had been ordered to London in October 1795 to exchange ratifications of Jay's treaty. He remained until May 1796 to deal with any remaining problems with treaty implementation, and to gather intelligence about British and French intentions.

16 The British order barred nearly all neutral trade to French colonies in the Caribbean.

17 The twelfth article of Jay's treaty opened to American merchant ships British ports in the West Indies at the same duty rate as British ships, but it limited the cargo to seventy tons. It also barred the trade of certain goods produced in the West Indies or America (sugar, molasses, coffee, cotton, etc.) anywhere else in the world. The Senate advised President Washington

to suspend the article (which he later did); the Senate then approved the treaty in a 20–10 vote. John Quincy later reported that the seventy-ton provision had not appeared in the draft version of the Treaty he had seen in London, and that he would have objected if it had.

18 George Hammond had served as British envoy to the United States from 1791 to 1795. At this time, he was undersecretary in the Foreign Office.

19 Charles Delacroix de Constant was French minister of foreign affairs under the Directory, 1795–1797.

20 The leading candidates in the American presidential election were John Adams and Thomas Jefferson, after President Washington announced that he would not seek a third term. John Quincy was well aware of rumors that the French minister, Pierre Adet, had been interfering on behalf of the Republicans.

21 John Quincy's principal assignment in the Netherlands was to manage American loans held by Amsterdam bankers.

22 Rumors had been circulating that the French were conspiring to establish a friendly republic in the American West.

23 Washington's Farewell Address, published in September 1796.

24 Charles Cotesworth Pinckney, brother of Charles, newly appointed American minister to France, replacing James Monroe.

25 Jean Antoine Joseph Fauchet was French minister to the United States, 1795–1796.

26 Edmond-Charles Genet was French minister to the United States, 1793–1794.

27 Jay's treaty.

28 Jay, then the secretary of foreign affairs under the Articles of Confederation, had negotiated with Spain over navigation rights on the Mississippi River. He agreed to a treaty that would have guaranteed exclusive rights to Spain to navigate the Mississippi for twenty-five years, in exchange for which Spain would grant commercial concessions to the United States. However, the Treaty was opposed by Southerners and Westerners – notably, Virginian James Monroe. Congress voted in favor of the treaty (7–5, voting by state), short of the two-thirds majority required for approval.

29 Charles Gravier de Vergennes was French minister of foreign affairs (1774–1787). John Adams, in his diplomatic postings in France, frequently clashed with Vergennes, attempting to assert an American foreign policy of independence.

30 Presumably Jean-Louis Favier, French diplomat and journalist, and Benjamin Franklin.

31 The late king of Prussia – Frederick II (Frederick the Great).

32 Edmond-Charles Genet was French minister to the United States, 1793–1794.

33 Here John Quincy is referring to the Democratic-Republican Societies that appeared in the United States in the mid-1790s, in imitation, he believed, of the radical Jacobin Club of France.

34 The French minister to the United States, Pierre Adet, had announced that the Directory had suspended diplomatic relations with America and departed to France after the election. Meanwhile, the Directory refused to accept the credentials of the newly appointed American minister, Charles Cotesworth Pinckney.

35 Alexander Hamilton, secretary of the treasury from 1789 to 1795, who had been accused by Jefferson and his Republican associates of being an agent of British influence. A close associate of President Washington, Hamilton had become a political opponent of John Adams within the Federalist Party.

36 "To sow his blazing sparks . . ."

37 Edmond-Charles Genet had served as French minister to the United States in 1793, when the Washington administration asked for his recall for what it regarded as his unacceptable challenges to American neutrality and its form of government. Thomas Paine was the famous author of the pamphlet *Common Sense*, advocate of the French Revolution, and opponent of John Adams. He had lived in Paris since 1792 and had been elected to the French National Convention. He was imprisoned in 1793 by the radical government led by Maximilien Robespierre, and later released – partly because of the intercession of the American minister, James Monroe. He wrote an open letter to George Washington, chastising the president for not doing more on his behalf. Paine did not return to America until 1802. Benjamin F. Bâche was the editor of the staunchly pro-Republican newspaper, the *Aurora*. Pierre Adet, who had been the French minister to the United States since 1795, had openly supported the election of Republicans, including Thomas Jefferson. With the election of John Adams, he suspended diplomatic relations and later returned to France. Madame Roland and her husband were early revolutionary supporters and she became a leading figure within the Girondin political faction. She was arrested and guillotined during the Terror.

CHAPTER THREE

1 John Adams (Washington, DC) to John Marshall, January 31, 1801.

2 Diary Entry (Quincy), January 28, 1802. Cited: MJQA, 1:249.

3 The Congress of Rastatt was convened in late 1797, primarily to negotiate a settlement between France and the Holy Roman Empire (Austria) over the disposition of German lands seized by France during the War of the First Coalition. The congress was interrupted by the start of the War of the Second Coalition.

4 John Quincy served as secretary to Francis Dana in St. Petersburg from 1781 to 1783, during Dana's diplomatic mission to Russia.

5 King Frederick William III of Prussia.

6 The Marquis de Lafayette, while attempting to escape France during the revolutionary turmoil of 1792, was captured by Austrian forces. He was detained for five years, during which time he and his family received financial assistance from various Americans, including John Quincy.

7 Gouvernuer Morris, a friend of George Washington and a major figure in the drafting of the US Constitution, had served from 1792 to -1794 as American minister to France, where he ran afoul of the French revolutionary governments for his association with counterrevolutionary activities and sympathy for the British. At this time he was in Europe on private business, dabbling in diplomatic activities without official sanction by the American government.

8 "To speak to you frankly" (said he) "I believe that he is headstrong in politics, whose ability comes only from himself."

9 In a June 27, 1798 letter to his mother, John Quincy wrote: "A French commissary (*Rapinat by name*) has seized upon the treasures for the benefit of France. The Helvetic executive and legislature interposed and claimed the property; even Mengaud the French agent supports them, but Rapinat proceeds with numerous tokens of insult and mockery, carries off the treasures; the French government openly approve and ratify his conduct, and immediately recall and dismiss Mengaud with public reproaches for his pusillanimity" (Ford, 2:327, or APL). The name, perhaps coincidentally, derives from the French word for "pillage."

10 Thomas Adams, who had served as his brother's secretary in Europe since 1794, left Berlin in September 1798 and arrived in Philadelphia in February 1799. He delivered this letter and other crucial documents to John Adams, as the president deliberated on future policy toward France.

11 The War of the First Coalition against France ended in 1797 with the signature of the Treaty of Campo Formio, leaving Britain to fight alone. Prussia had withdrawn from the coalition in 1795. The Second Coalition was formed in November 1798, with no significant fighting on the continent until 1799. Prussia remained neutral.

12 John Quincy referred to Frederick William I and Frederick II (Frederick the Great) as the strong monarchs, and their successor, Frederick William II, as the weak one. The current king was Frederick William III.

13 Poland and Lithuania were partitioned by Austria, Prussia, and Russia in 1772, 1793, and 1795, with the final partition eliminating the sovereignty of both. This was not restored until the treaty of Versailles in 1919.

14 With an invasion of England ruled out for the moment, in the summer of 1798, Napoleon led a French expedition to conquer Egypt and Syria. He

sought to establish a French presence in the Middle East, block British trade, and lay the groundwork for an eventual invasion of India. The ground campaign was initially successful but a British naval victory in the Battle of the Nile cut off his reinforcements and led Napoleon to return to France in August 1799.

15 In mid-April 1798, a mob insulted the flag of the French embassy in Vienna. The French ambassador, General Bernadotte, threatened to break relations, but war did not result because Napoleon was focused on his impending invasion of Egypt.

16 Francis II, Holy Roman Emperor and archduke of Austria.

17 President John Adams sent Elbridge Gerry, Charles Cotesworth Pinckney, and John Marshall on a diplomatic mission to France in 1797 to resolve outstanding issues between the two countries. The French foreign minister, Talleyrand, rather than dealing openly with the delegation, sent substitutes (known subsequently as W, X, Y, and Z) to demand what amounted to a personal bribe and a national loan from the United States as a precondition for negotiations. When the Americans refused, Pinckney and Marshall returned to America. Gerry remained in an attempt to prevent war. News of the XYZ Affair temporarily inflamed the American public against France.

18 After the failure of the delegation of Gerry, Pinckney, and Marshall even to begin negotiations with the French Directory, Dr. George Logan, a Republican from Pennsylvania, attempted to negotiate with France as a private citizen. In 1799, the Federalist-controlled Congress passed the so-called Logan Act, which criminalized negotiation by unauthorized persons with foreign governments having a dispute with the United States.

19 The Law of 29 Nivôse (French revolutionary calendar for January 1798) allowed privateers to seize British goods from neutral ships.

20 Jonathan Wild was a notorious English underworld figure who operated on both sides of the law in the early eighteenth century.

21 The Congress of Rastatt was convened in late 1797, primarily to negotiate a settlement between France and the Holy Roman Empire (Austria) over the disposition of German lands seized by France during the War of the First Coalition. The congress was interrupted by the start of the War of the Second Coalition.

22 Friedrich Wilhelm von Thulemeyer, Prussian diplomat, with whom John Adams dealt regularly while in Europe.

23 After the XYZ Affair and Logan's intercession, President Adams commissioned William Vans Murray, Oliver Ellsworth, and William Davie to travel to France and negotiate an end to the Quasi-War between that country and the United States. Delayed by political squabbling in America – many Federalists opposed the idea of negotiations with France and favored closer ties or even an alliance with Britain – the delegation arrived in France in

March of 1800, producing the Treaty of Mortefontaine, which ended naval hostilities, on September 30, 1800.

24 In 1799, Revolutionary War veteran John Fries led resistance among farmers in Pennsylvania to tax collectors attempting to enforce the Direct Tax of 1798, which had been passed to fund the government's expenditures in the Quasi-War with France. Federal troops and the local militia put down the rebellion. Fries was sentenced to death for treason, but he was pardoned by President Adams.

25 On February 15, 1798, Federalist congressman Roger Griswold attacked Republican Matthew Lyon with his cane on the floor of the House of Representatives. Lyon attempted to defend himself with a pair of fire tongs. In an earlier argument, the members had insulted each other and Lyon had spit in Griswold's face.

26 William Cobbett, an English journalist and pamphleteer, came to the United States in 1792, where he wrote under the pseudonym "Peter Porcupine." John Quincy is referring to *The Democratic Judge: or The equal Liberty of the press, as exhibited, explained, and exposed, in the prosecution of William Cobbett, for a pretended libel against the King of Spain and his embassador, before Thomas M'Kean, chief justice of the state of Pennsylvania. By Peter Porcupine*. This work was published in 1798.

27 Dietrich Heinrich Freiherr von Bülow, a Prussian soldier and writer, published the work in 1797. John Quincy subsequently translated it.

28 François Alexandre Frédéric de La Rochefoucauld, Duke of La Rochefoucauld, published *Travels Through the United States of North America: The Country of the Iroquis, and Upper Canada, in the Years 1795, 1796, and 1797.*

29 Guy Carleton, First Baron Dorchester, served as general governor of British North America from 1785 to 1795. Lower Canada was a British colony, consisting of parts of present-day Quebec, Newfoundland, and Labrador.

30 During the summer of 1800, John Quincy and his wife toured the lands of Silesia, which Prussia had acquired during the wars of Frederick the Great. He sent a series of letters to his brother Thomas describing his travels, which Thomas had published in the *Port Folio* (Philadelphia) and in a collected volume, *Letters on Silesia*.

31 John Adams blamed his defeat in the election of 1800 to the resistance of the High Federalist faction, notably Alexander Hamilton, to his foreign policy – especially the appointment of a peace delegation to France in 1799.

32 The Convention of 1800, or the Treaty of Mortefontaine, signed in September 1800 and finally ratified by the United States In December 1801, ended the Quasi-War with France.

33 The United States claimed the French owed $20 million to American citizens for shipping losses in violation of the Treaty of 1778; ultimately, the United States agreed to reimburse its citizens as part of the overall settlement.

NOTES

34 The Republican and Federalist parties, respectively.

35 John Quincy is describing the current status of the War of the Second Coalition against France, as it became known, and the fracture of the anti-French alliance. Paul I was the eccentric emperor of Russia.

36 Emperor Paul I of Russia championed an alliance of north European powers to resist British maritime practices that threatened neutral shipping.

37 Napoleon overthrew the five-member Directory and established himself as first consul in 1799, five years before declaring himself emperor.

38 In the run-up to the presidential election of 1800, Alexander Hamilton sent an extended letter to Federalist leaders, which was leaked to the public and published as a pamphlet. Hamilton, who was intriguing to have Thomas Pinckney receive more electoral votes on the Federalist ticket than John Adams, not only criticized Adams's foreign policy and approach to governance but also portrayed him as being mentally deranged.

39 Murray had been part of the three-man commission appointed by President Adams to seek a diplomatic settlement of the Quasi-War with France, against the wishes of most of the Federalist Party leadership. The result was the Convention of 1800 or the Treaty of Mortefontaine.

40 Emperor Paul I of Russia championed an alliance of north European powers to resist British maritime practices that threatened neutral shipping.

41 John Quincy first met Murray during a visit to England from the Netherlands in 1784. Murray was studying law at the Temple in London.

42 John Quincy begins this letter with a continuation of his series of letters to his brother Thomas describing his trip to Silesia during the past year.

43 French mass conscription, requiring every able-bodied man between eighteen and twenty-five years of age to serve in the military.

44 By 1801, the Second Coalition against France (Britain, Austria, Russia, and others) had largely broken apart. France and Austria (the Holy Roman Empire) signed the Treaty of Lunéville in February 1801. France and Britain agreed to the Treaty of Amiens in 1802.

45 During Napoleon's consulship, there were a number of attempts to assassinate him, including what became known as the Dagger Plot and the Plot of the Infernal Machine.

CHAPTER FOUR

1 The French had secretly regained title of the territory from Spain in October 1800, at the same time as they had settled the Quasi-War with America.

2 The bill passed the Senate 21–3, Adams opposing.

3 NEF, 327.

CHAPTER FIVE

1 Spelled "Romanzoff" by John Quincy Adams.
2 John Quincy Adams (St. Petersberg) to the Secretary of State James Monroe, May 26, 1811. Cited in WJQA, 4:88.
3 John Quincy Adams to (St. Petersberg) to the Secretary of State James Monroe, June 2, 1811. Cited in WJQA, 4:91.
4 The Senate, by two votes, barely voted down a simultaneous declaration of war against France.
5 John Quincy Adams (St. Petersberg) to John Adams, July 13, 1812. Cited in WJQA, 4:369–70.
6 John Quincy immediately reported this discussion to Washington. John Quincy Adams (St. Petersberg) to Secretary of State Smith, November 6, 1809.
7 See also MJQA, 2:401–4.

CHAPTER SIX

1 John Quincy Adams (Ghent) to Louisa Catherine Adams, September 30, 1814.
2 John Quincy Adams (Ghent) to Louisa Catherine Adams, December 30, 1814.

CHAPTER SEVEN

1 James Monroe (Washington, DC) to Thomas Jefferson, February 23, 1817.

CHAPTER EIGHT

1 To avoid confusion, we use the term "South America" here, as did John Quincy and his contemporaries, generally speaking, rather than Spanish America or Latin America. South America in this context included Mexico. The status of Portuguese Brazil was treated as a separate diplomatic matter.
2 Jefferson wrote to President Monroe: "I propose then that you select Mr. Adams's four principal letters on the Spanish subject, to wit, that which establishes our right to the Rio Bravo which was laid before the Congress of 1817–18; his letters to Onis of July 23 and November 30, and to Erving of November 28; perhaps also that of December 2. Have them well translated into French, and send English and French copies to all our ministers at foreign courts, and to our consuls. The paper on our right to the Rio Bravo, and the letter to Erving of November 28 are the most important and are among the ablest compositions I have ever seen, both as to logic and style. . . . It is of great consequence to us, and merits every possible

endeavor, to maintain in Europe a correct opinion of our political morality. These papers will place the event with the world in the important cases of our western boundary, of our military entrance into Florida, and of the execution of Arbuthnot and Ambrister." See Jefferson to Monroe, January 18, 1819. *Writings of Jefferson*, 10:122.

3   John Quincy Adams (Washington, DC) to Alexander Hill Everett, August 10, 1818. Cited in WJQA, 6:428.

4   David Waldstreicher and Matthew Mason, eds., *John Quincy Adams and the Politics of Slavery: Selections from the Diary* (Oxford: Oxford University Press, 2017), 103; *The Writings of John Quincy Adams*, ed. Worthington Chauncey Ford, vol. 6, *1816–1819* (New York: Macmillan, 1916), 550.

5   *Memoirs of John Quincy Adams, Comprising Portions of His Diary from 1795 to 1848*, ed. Charles Francis Adams, vol. 5 (Philadelphia: J. B. Lippincott, 1875), 325.

CHAPTER NINE

1   Cited in Bemis, 357.

2   *Memoirs*, 45:152.

3   In that context, over the past year, Russia had warned foreign vessels to stay away from what it claimed to be its territorial waters along the Pacific Northwest coast, extending as far south as fifty-one degrees. All this seemed to indicate an attempt by the Continental despotisms to encircle the United States.

4   Diary Entry (Washington, DC), November 7.

5   John Quincy's note to Tuyll, delivered verbally on November 27, 1823, did not include a paragraph that he had previously drafted, vigorously defending republican government. Monroe had initially removed that paragraph, concerned that it might cause unnecessary offense. John Quincy argued otherwise, and the president relented. In his meeting with Tuyll, however, John Quincy decided on his own accord to omit it.

6   A fourth component, not stated in the address but afterward considered part of the Doctrine, was the non-transfer policy – the United States would oppose the transfer of territories in the Western Hemisphere from one European power to another. It had been foreshadowed by the No Transfer Resolution passed by Congress in 1811.

7   Diary Entry (Washington, DC), July 31, 1823.

8   *Report of the Secretary of State, Upon Weights and Measures* (Washington, DC: Gales & Seaton, 1821), 134.

A NOTE ON THE TYPE

UNITED AND INDEPENDENT has been set in Fernando Mello's Brabo types, which he first developed during a typographic workshop at the Plantin-Moretus Museum in Antwerp and named in honor of Silvius Brabo, the mythic Roman savior of the ancient port city. As legend has it, Brabo defeated the giant Druon Antigoon, who terrorized the city by extorting taxes on shipping and demanding payment to cross the bridge over the river Scheldt, cutting off the hands of those who refused to pay. Brabo defeated the giant and paid him back in kind, tossing his severed hand into the Scheldt, an act that (so the story goes) is commemorated in the the city's name: the Dutch for "hand-throw" is hand werpen, hence, Antwerpen. ✦ A distinctly modern type, Brabo acknowledges the proportions and crisp drawing of sixteenth-century faces like Garamond and Plantin, making it a fine choice for literary texts.

DESIGN & COMPOSITION BY CARL W. SCARBROUGH